AF884999

AutoCAD MEP 2022 for Designers

(6th Edition)

CADCIM Technologies
525 St. Andrews Drive
Schererville, IN 46375, USA
(www.cadcim.com)

Contributing Author
Sham Tickoo
Professor
Department of Mechanical Engineering Technology
Purdue University Northwest
Hammond, Indiana, USA

CADCIM Technologies

AutoCAD MEP 2022 for Designers
Sham Tickoo

CADCIM Technologies
525 St Andrews Drive
Schererville, Indiana 46375, USA
www.cadcim.com

ISBN 978-1-64057-126-6

NOTICE TO THE READER

Publisher does not warrant or guarantee any of the products described in the text or perform any independent analysis in connection with any of the product information contained in the text. Publisher does not assume, and expressly disclaims, any obligation to obtain and include information other than that provided to it by the manufacturer.

The reader is expressly warned to consider and adopt all safety precautions that might be indicated by the activities herein and to avoid all potential hazards. By following the instructions contained herein, the reader willingly assumes all risks in connection with such instructions.

The publisher makes no representation or warranties of any kind, including but not limited to, the warranties of fitness for particular purpose or merchantability, nor are any such representations implied with respect to the material set forth herein, and the publisher takes no responsibility with respect to such material. The publisher shall not be liable for any special, consequential, or exemplary damages resulting, in whole or part, from the reader's use of, or reliance upon this material.

DEDICATION

To teachers, who make it possible to disseminate knowledge
to enlighten the young and curious minds
of our future generations

To students, who are dedicated to learning new technologies
and making the world a better place to live in

SPECIAL RECOGNITION

A special thanks to Mr. Denis Cadu and the ADN team of Autodesk Inc.
for their valuable support and professional guidance to
procure the software for writing this textbook

THANKS

To the faculty and students of the MET department of
Purdue University Northwest for their cooperation

To employees of CADCIM Technologies for their valuable help

Online Training Program Offered by CADCIM Technologies

CADCIM Technologies provides effective and affordable virtual online training on various software packages including Computer Aided Design and Manufacturing and Engineering (CAD/CAM/CAE), computer programming languages, animation, architecture, and GIS. The training is delivered 'live' via Internet at any time, any place, and at any pace to individuals as well as the students of colleges, universities, and CAD/CAM training centers. The main features of this program are:

Training for Students and Companies in a Classroom Setting

Highly experienced instructors and qualified engineers at CADCIM Technologies conduct the classes under the guidance of Prof. Sham Tickoo of Purdue University Northwest, USA. This team has authored several textbooks that are rated "one of the best" in their categories and are used in various colleges, universities, and training centers in North America, Europe, and in other parts of the world.

Training for Individuals

CADCIM Technologies with its cost effective and time saving initiative strives to deliver the training in the comfort of your home or work place, thereby relieving you from the hassles of traveling to training centers.

Training Offered on Software Packages

CADCIM provides basic and advanced training on the following software packages:

***CAD/CAM/CAE**: CATIA, Pro/ENGINEER Wildfire, Creo Parametric, Creo Direct, SOLIDWORKS, Autodesk Inventor, Solid Edge, NX, AutoCAD, AutoCAD LT, AutoCAD Plant 3D, Customizing AutoCAD, AutoCAD MEP, Autodesk Simulation Mechanical, EdgeCAM, and ANSYS*

***Architecture and GIS**: Autodesk Revit Architecture, AutoCAD Civil 3D, Autodesk Revit Structure, AutoCAD Map 3D, Revit MEP, Navisworks, Primavera Project Planner, and Bentley STAAD Pro*

***Animation and Styling**: Autodesk 3ds Max, Autodesk Maya, Autodesk Alias, Foundry NukeX, and MAXON CINEMA 4D*

***Computer Programming**: C++, VB.NET, Oracle, AJAX, and Java*

For more information, please visit the following link: ***https://www.cadcim.com***

Note

If you are a faculty member, you can register by clicking on the following link to access the teaching resources: ***https://www.cadcim.com/Registration.aspx***. The student resources are available at ***https://www.cadcim.com***. We also provide **Live Virtual Online Training** on various software packages. For more information, write us at ***sales@cadcim.com***.

Table of Contents

Chapter 3: Working with Architecture Workspace

Chapter 8: Representation and Schedules

This page is intentionally left blank

Preface

AutoCAD MEP 2022

AutoCAD MEP, also known as AMEP, is based on the AutoCAD Architecture platform. Here, MEP stands for Mechanical, Electrical, and Plumbing. The software has all the required features for creating a Mechanical, Electrical, and Plumbing system. It includes all the features of the AutoCAD platform such as Blocks, Layers, 3D Models, and so on. It also includes architectural features such as walls, doors, windows, and so on.

In AutoCAD MEP, you can add objects with actual parameters to the project. These objects are available in various categories of AutoCAD MEP library and can be customized according to the requirements of the users.

AutoCAD MEP 2022 for Designers textbook is written with the intention of helping the readers effectively use the designing and drafting tools of AutoCAD MEP 2022. This textbook provides a simple and clear explanation of tools that are commonly used in AutoCAD MEP 2022. After reading this textbook, you will be able to design HVAC system, piping system, plumbing system, and electrical layout of a building. The chapter on schematics will enable the users generate the schematic drawings of a system for easy representation. The examples and tutorials used in this textbook ensure that the users can relate the knowledge from this textbook with the actual industry designs.

Since AutoCAD MEP is based on AutoCAD platform, a user must have basic knowledge of AutoCAD. In this textbook, the basic tools of AutoCAD are not explained while explaining the working of MEP tools assuming that the user knows AutoCAD basics.

The main features of this textbook are as follows:

- **Tutorial Approach**
  The author has adopted the tutorial point-of-view and the learn-by-doing approach throughout the textbook. This approach guides the users easily understand the process of designing and drafting with the help of tutorials.

- **Real-World Projects as Tutorials**
  The author has used about real-world mechanical engineering projects as tutorials in this textbook. This enables the readers to relate the tutorials to the engineering industry. In addition, there are exercises that are also based on the real-world engineering projects.

- **Tips and Notes**
  Additional information related to various topics is provided to the users in the form of tips and notes.

- **Heavily Illustrated Text**
  The text in this book is heavily illustrated with about 400 line diagrams and screen capture images.

- **Learning Objectives**
  The first page of every chapter summarizes the topics that are covered in that chapter.

- **Self-Evaluation Test, Review Questions, and Exercises**
  Every chapter ends with Self-Evaluation Test so that the users can assess their knowledge of the chapter. The answers to Self-Evaluation Test are given at the end of the chapter. Also, the Review Questions and Exercises are given at the end of the chapters and they can be used by the Instructors as test questions and exercises.

Symbols Used in the Textbook

Note
The author has provided additional information related to various topics in the form of notes.

Tip
The author has provided a lot of useful information to the users about the topic being discussed in the form of tips.

Formatting Conventions Used in the Textbook

Please refer to the following list for the formatting conventions used in this textbook.

- Names of tools, buttons, options, and palettes are written in boldface. — Example: The **Wall** tool, the **OK** button, the **Left** option, and so on.
- Names of dialog boxes, drop-downs, drop-down lists, list boxes, areas, edit boxes, check boxes, radio buttons, and palettes are written in boldface. — Example: The **Detail Component Manager** dialog box, the **Walls** drop-down, the **Width** edit box in the **PROPERTIES** palette, the **Schematic Curve** check box in the **Drafting Settings** dialog box, the **Keyboard entry** radio button of the **User Preferences** tab in the **Options** dialog box, and so on.
- Values entered in edit boxes are written in boldface. — Example: Enter **5** in the **Radius** edit box.
- Names and paths of the files are written in italics. — Example: *C:\amep\c03*, *c03tut03.dwg*, and so on

Naming Conventions Used in the Textbook

Tool

If you click on an item in a **Ribbon** and a command is invoked to create/edit an object or perform some action, then that item is termed as **tool**.

For example:
To Create: **Line** tool, **Dimension** tool, **Wall** tool
To Modify: **Move** tool, **Explode** tool, **Rotate** tool
Action: **Zoom All** tool, **Pan** tool, **Copy** tool

If you click on an item in the **Ribbon** and a dialog box is invoked wherein you can set the properties to create/edit an object, then that item is also termed as **tool**, refer to Figure 1.

For example:
Air Handler tool, **Pump** tool, **Junction Box** tool

Button

The item in a dialog box that has a 3D shape like a button is termed as **Button**. For example, **OK** button, **Cancel** button, **Apply** button, and so on.

Dialog Box

In this textbook, different terms are used for referring to the components of a dialog box. Refer to Figure 1 for the terminology used.

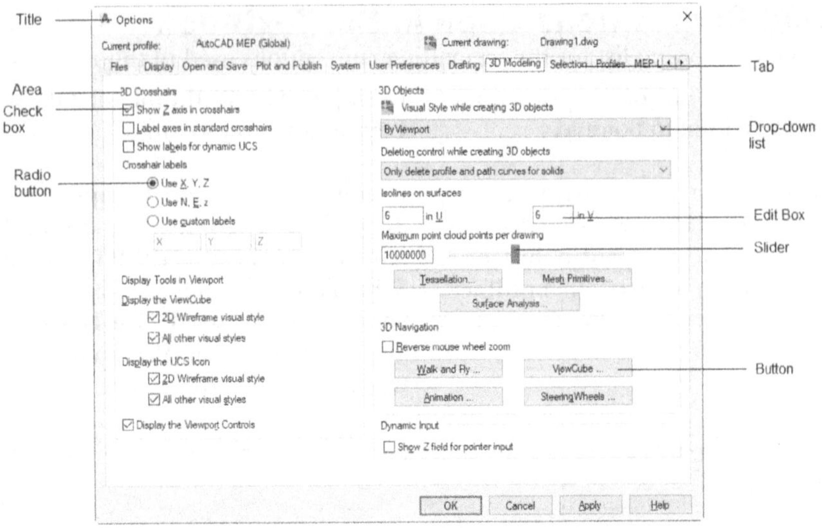

Figure 1 The components of a dialog box

TOOL PALETTE

A TOOL PALETTE is the one in which a set of common tools are grouped together for performing an action. For example, **TOOL PALETTES - PIPING, TOOL PALETTES - ARCHITECTURAL, TOOL PALETTES - HVAC**, and so on, refer to Figure 2.

PROPERTIES Palette

The **PROPERTIES** palette looks similar to the TOOL PALETTE but in this palette, only the properties of the objects are displayed. You can edit these properties as per your requirement. Figure 3 shows the **PROPERTIES** palette displayed after selecting a wall from the drawing area.

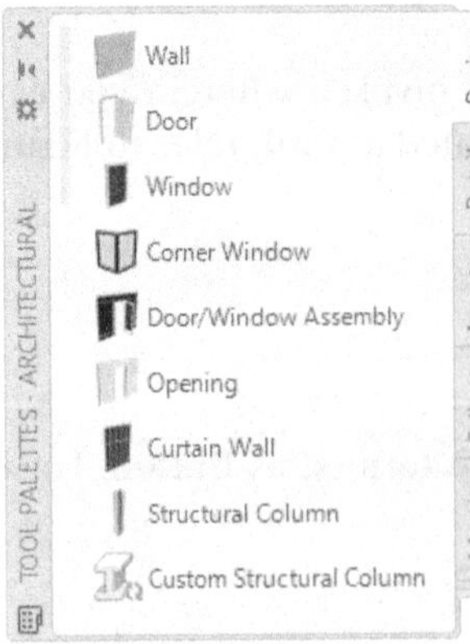

*Figure 2 Tools in the **TOOL PALETTES - ARCHITECTURAL***

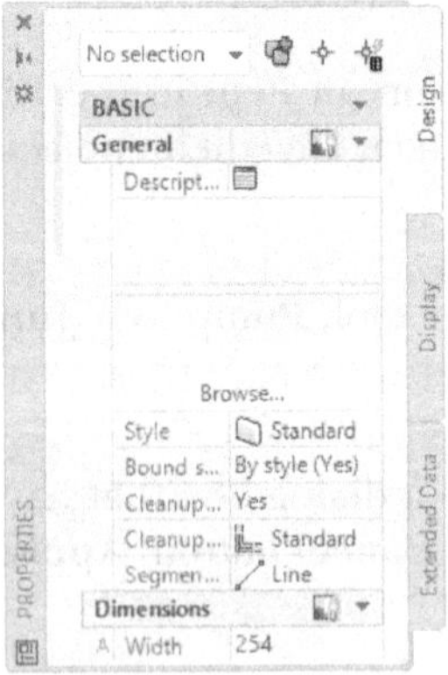

*Figure 3 Properties in the **PROPERTIES** palette*

Free Companion Website

It has been our constant endeavor to provide you the best textbooks and services at affordable price. In this endeavor, we have come out with a Free Companion website that will facilitate the process of teaching and learning of AutoCAD MEP. If you purchase this book, you will get access to the files on the Companion website by visiting *www.cadcim.com*.

The following resources are available for the faculty and students in this website:

Faculty Resources

- **Technical Support**
  You can get online technical support by contacting ***techsupport@cadcim.com***.

- **Instructor Guide**
  Solutions to all review questions and exercises in the textbook are provided in this guide to help the faculty members test the skills of the students.

- **Part Files**
  The part files used in illustrations, tutorials, projects, and exercises are available for free download.

  Note that you can access the faculty resources only if you are registered as faculty at *www.cadcim.com/Registration.aspx*

Student Resources

- **Technical Support**
  You can get online technical support by contacting ***techsupport@cadcim.com***.

- **Part Files**
  The part files used in illustrations, tutorials, and projects are available for free download.

You can access additional learning resources by visiting ***https://allaboutcadcam.blogspot.com***.

If you face any problem in accessing these files, please contact the publisher at ***sales@cadcim.com*** or the author at ***stickoo@pnw.edu*** or ***tickoo525@gmail.com***.

Video Courses

CADCIM offers video courses in CAD, CAE Simulation, BIM, Civil/GIS, and Animation domains on various e-Learning/Video platforms. To enroll for the video courses, please visit the CADCIM website using the link ***https://www.cadcim.com/video-courses***.

Stay Connected

You can now stay connected with us through Facebook and Twitter to get the latest information about our text books, videos, and teaching/learning resources. To stay informed of such updates, follow us on Facebook (***www.facebook.com/cadcim***) and Twitter (***@cadcimtech***). You can also subscribe to our You Tube channel (***www.youtube.com/cadcimtech***) to get the information about our latest video tutorials.

This page is intentionally left blank

Chapter 1

Introduction to AutoCAD MEP

Learning Objectives

After completing this chapter, you will be able to:

- *Start AutoCAD MEP*
- *Use the components of the AutoCAD MEP interface*
- *Invoke AutoCAD MEP commands from the keyboard, menu, toolbar, shortcut menu, TOOL PALETTES, and Ribbon*
- *Use the components of dialog boxes in AutoCAD MEP*
- *Start a new drawing*
- *Save work using various file-saving commands*
- *Close a drawing*
- *Open an existing drawing*
- *Exit AutoCAD MEP*
- *Use various options of AutoCAD MEP help*

INTRODUCTION

AutoCAD MEP is based on the AutoCAD Architecture platform. Since it belongs to the AutoCAD family, it has all the features of AutoCAD such as Blocks, Layers, 3D Models, and so on. Also, the software has all the important architectural features such as walls, doors, windows, and so on. AutoCAD MEP is also referred to as AMEP where MEP stands for Mechanical, Electrical, and Plumbing. Therefore, the software has all the required features for creating a Mechanical, Electrical, and Plumbing system. In this chapter, you will learn to start AutoCAD MEP and use various components displayed in the AutoCAD MEP interface.

GETTING STARTED WITH AutoCAD MEP

When you install AutoCAD MEP 2022 on your system, three shortcuts pointing to the AutoCAD MEP 2022 - English (Global), AutoCAD MEP 2022 - English (US Imperial), and AutoCAD MEP 2022 - English (US Metric) will be created on the desktop. You can start AutoCAD MEP by double-clicking on any of these three icons. In AutoCAD MEP 2022 -English (US Imperial), the units available in drawing will be in Inch, Feet, and Mile. In AutoCAD MEP 2022 - English (US Metric), the units available in the drawing will be in Millimeter, Centimeter, and Meter. In AutoCAD MEP 2022 - English (Global), AutoCAD MEP will start using the global template.

Note

In this textbook, the global unit system is followed, so you need to start AutoCAD MEP 2022 by double-clicking on the AutoCAD MEP 2022 - English (Global) icon on the desktop.

AutoCAD MEP INTERFACE COMPONENTS

When you start AutoCAD MEP 2022 for the first time, you will get the startup interface window, as shown in Figure 1-1.

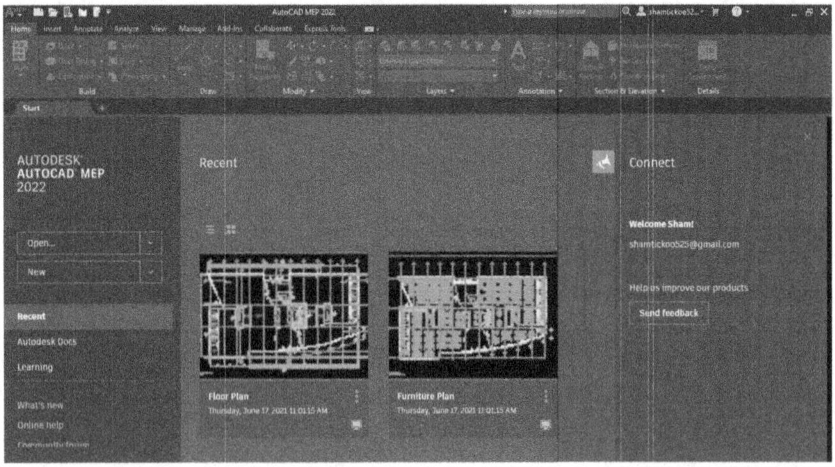

Figure 1-1 The startup interface window of AutoCAD MEP 2022

Start Tab

In AutoCAD MEP 2022, the **Start** tab is displayed with the startup interface window. It provides options for easy access to a variety of initial actions, including access to drawing template files, recently opened drawings and sheet sets, online learning options, and announcements. The options available in the **Start** tab are discussed next.

Open

On choosing this button, the **Select File** dialog box is displayed which allows you to open the existing drawing files. The drop-down list next to the **Open** button has three more options other than the **Open files** options. These options are used to open the existing projects, the sheet sets and explore the sample drawings.

New

On choosing this button, a new drawing file will be created from the default drawing template file. The drop-down list next to the **New** button enables you to view the most recently used templates, view the list of all available drawing template files, helps download additional drawing template files when available, and create sheet sets.

Recent

This page is displayed by default and has the options to view the most recently used documents. You can keep a document listed by pinning it. A pinned document is displayed at the top of the list until you unpin it. You can also choose between the display options for image and text or text only by choosing the two swatch buttons available in the **Recent** area.

Autodesk Docs

This page provides options to open and save files to your connected drives. You will need to have Desktop Connector installed to access the connected drives on Autodesk Docs.

Learning

This page provides options to access the learning resources such as videos, tips, and other relevant online content or services if available. You need to have an active internet connection to access the options available in this page. Under the **Learning** head, links are provided to access other online resources or topics. such as what's new, online help, community forum, customer support, AutoCAD mobile app, and AutoCAD web app. Figure 1-2 shows the **Learning** page.

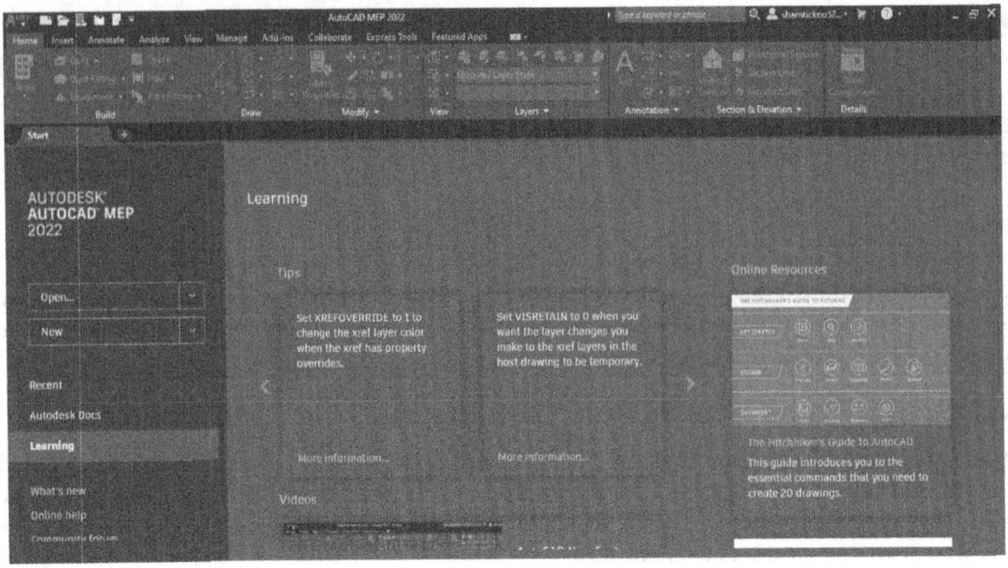

*Figure 1-2 The startup interface window of AutoCAD MEP 2022 with the **Learning** page*

Drawing Area

Choose the **New** button to open the drawing area. The drawing area covers a major portion of the screen. In this area, you can draw objects and use the commands. To draw the objects, you need to define the coordinate points. Position of the pointing device is represented on the screen by the cursor. There is a coordinate system icon at the lower left corner of the drawing area. The drawing area also has the standard windows buttons such as close, minimize, and maximize on the top right corner. These buttons have the same functions as in any other standard window. Figure 1-3 shows the AutoCAD MEP drawing interface components.

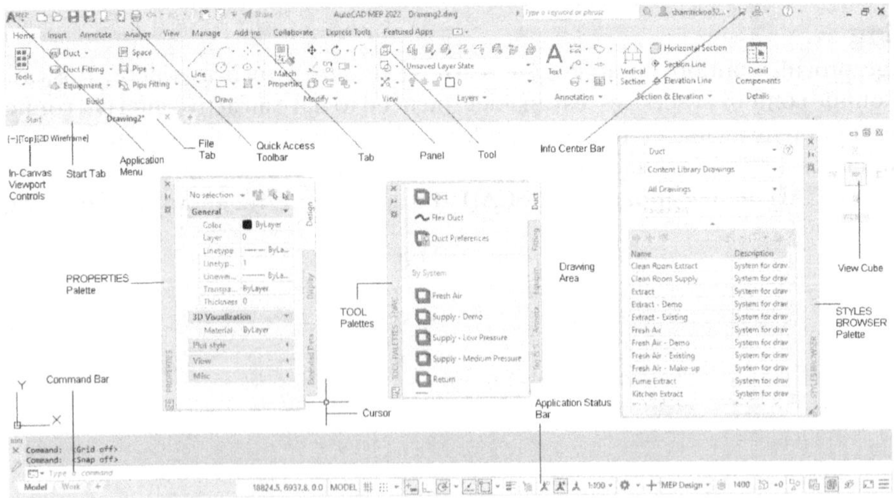

Figure 1-3 AutoCAD MEP drawing interface components

Command Window

The command window available at the bottom of the drawing area has the command prompt where you can enter the commands. It also displays the subsequent prompt sequences and messages. You can change the size of the window by placing the cursor on the top edge (double line bar known as the grab bar) and then dragging it. This way you can increase its size to see all the previous commands you have used. By default, the command window displays only two lines. You can also press the F2 key to display the **AutoCAD Text window**, which displays the previous commands and prompts.

ViewCube

The ViewCube is available at the top right corner of the drawing area and is used to switch between standard and isometric views or roll the current view.

In-Canvas Viewport Controls

In-Canvas Viewport Controls is available at the top left corner of the drawing screen. It enables you to change the drawing view, visual style, and the viewport.

Application Status Bar

The **Application Status Bar** is located at the bottom of the interface. This bar is also referred to as the Status bar. It contains some useful information and buttons, refer to Figure 1-4, that help you in changing the status of some AutoCAD MEP functions. You can toggle between the on and off states of most of these functions by using the corresponding options. You can customize the **Application Status Bar** by using the **Customization** button available on the right on the Status Bar. Some of the options in the **Application Status Bar** are discussed next.

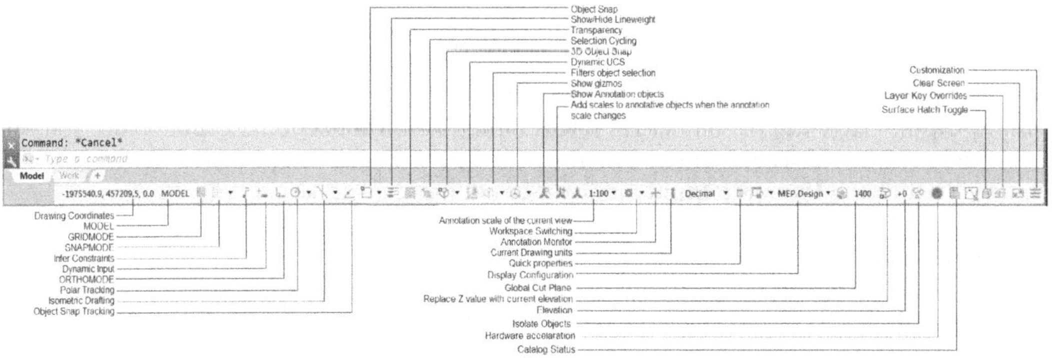

*Figure 1-4 The **Application Status Bar***

Drawing Coordinates

The information about the coordinates is displayed at the lower left corner of the Status bar. The **COORDS** system variable controls the display type of the coordinates. If the value of the **COORDS** variable is set to 0, the coordinate display is static, that is, the coordinate values displayed in the Status bar will change only when you specify a point. If the value of the **COORDS** variable is set to 1 or 2, the coordinate display will be dynamic. When the variable is set to 1, AutoCAD MEP constantly displays the absolute coordinates of the cursor with respect to the UCS origin. The relative polar coordinates (length<angle) are displayed when you are in an AutoCAD MEP command and the **COORDS** variable is set to 2. Click on the **Drawing Coordinates** area to toggle the coordinate status from on to off and vice versa.

Model or Paper space

The **Model or Paper space** button is used to toggle between the model space and the paper space.

GRIDMODE

The **GRIDMODE** button is used to toggle the display of the grid lines on and off on the screen. In AutoCAD MEP, the grid lines are used as reference lines to draw objects. The F7 function key can be used to turn the grid display on or off.

SNAPMODE

On choosing this button, you can move the cursor in fixed increments. The F9 key acts as a toggle key to turn the snap off or on.

Infer Constraints

If this button is chosen, then some of the geometric constraints will be automatically applied to the sketch while it is being drawn.

Dynamic Input

The **Dynamic Input** button is used to turn the **Dynamic Input** mode on or off. Turning it on facilitates the heads-up design approach because all commands, prompts, and dimensional inputs will now be displayed in the drawing area and you do not need to look at the command prompt all the time. This saves the design time and also increases the efficiency of the user. If the **Dynamic Input** mode is turned on, you will be able to enter the commands through the **Pointer Input** boxes, and the numerical values through the **Dimensional Input** boxes. You will also be able to select the command options through the **Dynamic Prompt** options in the graphics window. To turn the **Dynamic Input** mode on or off, use the F12 key.

ORTHOMODE

On choosing the **ORTHOMODE** button, you can draw lines at right angles only. You can use the F8 function key to turn the ortho mode on or off.

Polar Tracking

The **Polar Tracking** button is used to turn the polar tracking on. If you turn the polar tracking on, the movement of the cursor is restricted along a path based on the angle set as the polar angle. You can also use the F10 function key to turn on this option. Note that turning the polar tracking on, automatically turns off the ortho mode.

Isometric Drafting

In AutoCAD MEP 2022, you can create an isometric drafting by using any working plane. To activate a required working plane, choose the **Isometric Drafting** button from the Status Bar;

a flyout will be displayed with the **isoplane Left**, **isoplane Top**, or **isoplane Right** option. You can choose the required option from this flyout to activate the respective work plane.

Object Snap Tracking

This button is used to turn the object snap tracking on or off. On choosing this button, the inferencing lines will be displayed. Inferencing lines are dashed lines displayed automatically when you select a sketching tool and track a particular key point on the screen. You can also choose the F11 function key to turn on or off the object snap tracking.

Object Snap

On choosing the **Object Snap** button, you can use the running object snaps to snap on to a point. You can also use the F3 function key to turn the object snap on or off. The status of **OSNAP** (off or on) does not prevent you from using the immediate mode object snaps.

Show/Hide Lineweight

This button is used to turn on or off the display of line weights in the drawing. If this button is not chosen, the display of lineweight will be turned off.

Transparency

This button is used to turn on or off the transparency set for a drawing. You can set the transparency in the **Properties** panel or in the layer in which the sketch is drawn.

Selection Cycling

On choosing this button, you can cycle through and select the overlapping objects close to the other entities. On selecting an entity when this button is chosen, the **Selection** list box will be displayed with a list of entities.

3D Object Snap

On choosing this button, you can snap the key point on a solid or a surface body. You can also use the F4 function key to turn on or off the 3D object snap.

Dynamic UCS

This button is used to enable or disable the use of dynamic UCS. Allowing the dynamic UCS ensures that the XY plane of the UCS gets dynamically aligned with the selected face of the model. You can also use the F6 function key to turn the **Dynamic UCS** button on or off.

Filters object selection

You can filter objects by using the **Filters object selection** button. If you want to select only vertex, edge, face, solid history, or the drawing view components of a 3D object then you can choose the required option from the flyout which is invoked by clicking on the small arrow located on right of the **Filters object selection** button. You can also select multiple objects using the selection window.

The **Drawing View Components** option is used to select the components of an assembly or the parts in a multi-body. Using this option, you can select components either individually or through window selection. You can also clear the filters by choosing the **Filter object selection** button again.

Show gizmos

You can move, rotate, and scale a 3D object by choosing the **Show gizmos** button from the Status Bar. When you click on the small arrow available next to the **Show gizmos** button, a flyout is displayed with the **Move Gizmo**, **Rotate Gizmo**, and **Scale Gizmo** options.

Show annotation objects

This button is used to control the visibility of the annotative objects that do not support the current annotation scale in the drawing area.

Add scales to annotative objects when the annotation scale changes

If this button is chosen then the annotation scales that are set current to all the annotative objects present in the drawing are applied automatically to the drawing.

Annotation scale of the current view

The annotation scale controls the size and display of the annotative objects in the model space. When you choose this button, a flyout will be displayed showing all the annotation scales available for the current drawing.

Workspace Switching

When you choose this button, a flyout is displayed. You can use the options in this flyout to switch between different workspaces like HVAC, Piping, Electrical, and so on. You can also customize a workspace or create a new workspace by using the options in this flyout.

Annotation Monitor

The **Annotation Monitor** button is used to turn the **Annotation Monitor** on or off. If it is turned on, all the non-associative annotations will get highlighted with a badge placed on them, as shown in Figure 1-5. In this figure, a line leader is not associated with line.

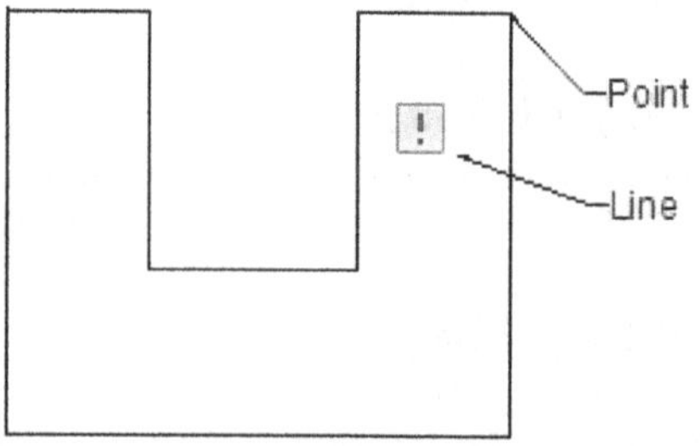

Figure 1-5 The non-associative annotation

Current drawing units

The **Current drawing units** button displays and controls the units of drawing. When you choose this button, a flyout is displayed. This flyout shows all the unit systems available for the drawing.

Quick Properties

On choosing this button, the properties of the selected sketched entity will be displayed in a panel.

Display Configuration

When you choose this button, a flyout will be displayed with **MEP Design** option as the default chosen configuration. Options available in this flyout are used to control the level of details of the objects created in the drawing area. The options in the flyout are arranged according to their area of application. For example, the options related to the **Electrical** workspace are grouped together.

Global Cut Plane

When you click on the **Global Cut Plane** button in the **Application Status Bar**, the **Global Cut Plane** dialog box will be displayed, as shown in Figure 1-6. This dialog box is used to specify the cut plane height and display range for the objects in the drawing area.

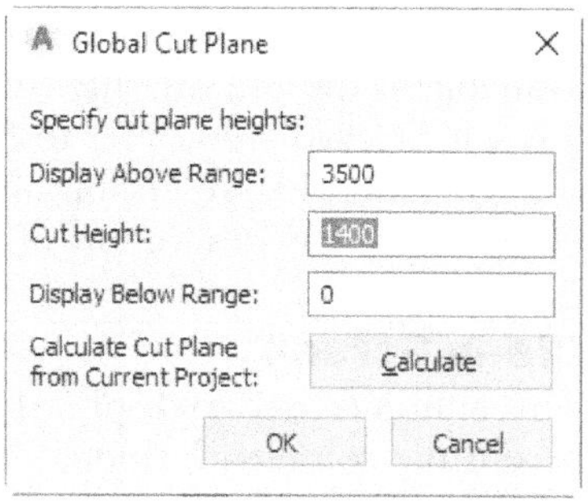

***Figure 1-6** The **Global Cut Plane** dialog box*

Replace Z value with current elevation

This toggle button is used to replace the elevation value with the specified Z value. When this toggle button is chosen, the components are created on the plane having the elevation equal to the Z value entered for the previously created component.

Elevation

The elevation icon displays a value of the current elevation. To specify elevation, click on the elevation value displayed in the **Application Status Bar**; the **Elevation Offset** dialog box will be displayed. You can set the elevation either by specifying the Z offset value or by picking a point from the drawing.

Isolate Objects

When you choose this button, a flyout is displayed. There are two options in this flyout: **Isolate Objects** and **Hide Objects**. Using the **Isolate Objects** option, you can isolate the selected objects so that only the selected objects are displayed in the drawing area. If some objects are already isolated, then the **Isolate Objects** button will be highlighted in blue color in the **Application Status Bar**. To end isolation or display a hidden object, choose this button again; a flyout will be displayed. Now, choose the **End Object Isolation** option from the flyout. To hide objects, choose the **Hide Objects** option from the flyout.

Hardware Acceleration

This button is used to set the performance of the software to the required level. Right-click on this button; a flyout with **Graphic Performance** option will be displayed. Choose this option; the **Graphic Performance** dialog box will be displayed. By using the options in this dialog box, you can control the performance of software.

Catalog Status

This button is used to check the status of equipment in the MEP database. If the database is not updated then you can regenerate the database by using this button. To do so, double-click on the **Catalog Status** button in the **Application Status Bar**; you will be prompted to specify the name of catalog for which you want to regenerate the database. There are five catalogs in AutoCAD MEP: Cabletray, Conduit, Duct, Mvpart, and Pipe. You can update any of the catalogs by specifying its name or you can update all the catalogs by specifying **All** at the command prompt.

Surface Hatch Toggle

Using this button, you can toggle on or off the display of the surface hatch in the drawing area.

Layer Key Overrides

The **Layer Key Overrides** button is used to enable or disable the overrides applied on the layers available in the drawing file. When you choose this button, the **Layer Key Overrides** dialog box will be displayed, refer to Figure 1-7. Using the options available in this dialog box, you can configure the presets for any of the layers available in the drawing. Also, you can enable or disable the overrides for any of the layers available.

Clean Screen

This button is used to display the expanded view of the drawing area by hiding all the toolbars except the command window, Status Bar, and menu bar. The expanded view of the drawing area can also be displayed by using the CTRL+0 keys. Choose the **Clean Screen** button again to restore the previous display state.

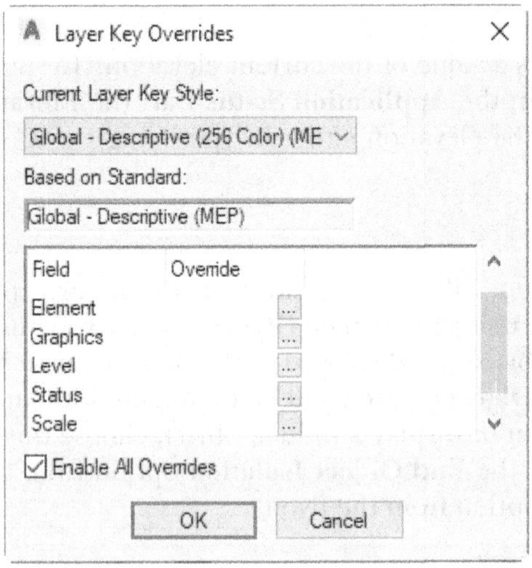

*Figure 1-7 The **Layer Key Overrides** dialog box*

Customization

This button is used to add or remove tools in the **Application Status Bar**.

Plot/Publish Details Report Available

This icon is displayed in the **Application Status Bar** when a plotting or publishing activity is being performed in the background or is completed. When you click on this icon, the **Plot and Publish Details** dialog box, which provides the details about the plotting and publishing activity, will be displayed. You can copy this report to the clipboard by choosing the **Copy to Clipboard** button from the dialog box.

Invoking Commands in AutoCAD MEP

When you are in the drawing area in AutoCAD MEP,\ you need to invoke AutoCAD MEP commands to perform any operation. For example, to draw a pipe line, enter the **PIPEADD** command at the command prompt and then define the start point and the endpoint of the pipe. Similarly, if you want to erase objects, you must invoke the **ERASE** command and then select the objects for erasing. In AutoCAD MEP, you can invoke the commands by using:

Command Prompt	**Ribbon**	**Application Menu**	**TOOL PALETTES**
Menu Bar	**Shortcut Menu**	**Toolbar**	

Command Prompt

You can invoke any AutoCAD MEP command from the command prompt by typing the command name and then pressing ENTER. As you type the first letter of the command, AutoCAD MEP displays all the available commands starting with the letter typed. If the **Dynamic Input** is on and the cursor is in the drawing area, by default the command will be entered through the **Pointer Input** box. The **Pointer Input** box is a small box displayed on the right of the cursor. However, if the cursor is currently placed on any toolbar or menu bar, or if the **Dynamic Input** is turned off, the command will be entered through the Command Prompt. Before you enter a command, the Command Prompt is displayed as the last line in the command window area. If it is not displayed, you must cancel the existing command by pressing the ESC (Escape) key. The following example shows how to invoke the **LINE** command by using the keyboard:

Command: **LINE** or **L** [Enter] (L is command alias)

Ribbon

In AutoCAD MEP, you can also invoke a tool from the **Ribbon**. When you start the AutoCAD MEP session for the first time, by default, the **Ribbon** is displayed below the **Quick Access Toolbar**. The **Ribbon** consists of various tabs. The tabs have different panels which in turn have tools arranged in rows. For example, the tools for creating, modifying, and annotating the objects are available in the **Annotate** tab in panels instead of being spread out in the entire drawing area in different toolbars and menus, refer to Figure 1-8.

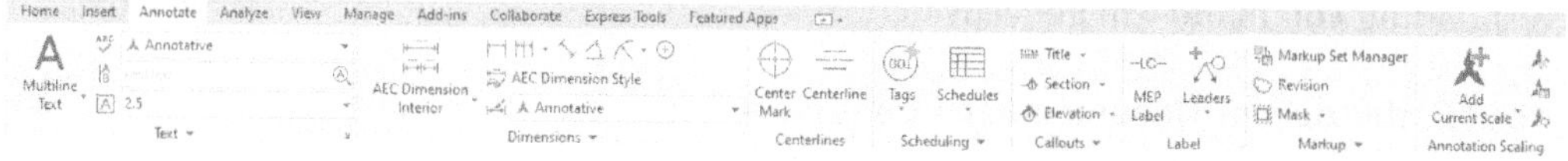

*Figure 1-8 The **Ribbon** with the **Annotate** tab chosen*

Some of the tools have small black down arrows. This indicates that the tools having similar functions are grouped together. To choose a tool, click on the down arrow; a drop-down will be displayed. Choose the required tool from the drop-down displayed. Note that if you choose a tool from the drop-down, the corresponding command will be invoked and the tool that you have chosen will be displayed in the panel. For example, to draw a circle using 2 points, click on the down arrow next to the **Circle, Center, Radius** tool in the **Draw** panel of the **Home** tab; a flyout will be displayed. Choose the **Circle, 2-Point** tool from the flyout and then draw the circle. You will notice that the **Circle, 2-Point** tool is displayed in place of the **Circle, Center, Radius** tool.

You can click on the down arrow to expand the panel. On doing so, you will notice that a push pin is available at the left corner of the panel. Click on the push pin to keep the panel in the expanded state. Also, some of the panels have an inclined arrow at the lower-right corner. When you left click on an inclined arrow, a dialog box is displayed. You can define the setting of the corresponding panel in the dialog box.

You can reorder the panels in the tab. To do so, press and hold the left mouse button on the panel to be moved and drag it to the required position. You can also undock the **Ribbon**. To do so, right-click on the blank space in the **Ribbon** and choose the **Undock** option; the **Ribbon** gets undocked. Now you can move, resize, anchor, and auto-hide the **Ribbon** using the shortcut menu that will be displayed when you right-click on the heading strip. To anchor the floating **Ribbon** to the left or right of the drawing area in the vertical position, right-click on the heading strip of the floating **Ribbon**; a shortcut menu is displayed. Choose the corresponding option from this shortcut menu. The **Auto-hide** option will hide the **Ribbon** into the heading strip and will display it only when you move the cursor over this strip.

You can customize the display of tabs and panels in the **Ribbon**. To customize the **Ribbon**, right-click on any one of the tools in it; a shortcut menu will be displayed. On moving the cursor over one of the options, a flyout will be displayed with a tick mark before all options and the corresponding tab or panel will be displayed in the **Ribbon**. Select/clear appropriate option to display/hide a particular tab or panel.

Application Menu

The **Application Menu** is available at the top-left of the AutoCAD MEP window. It contains some of the tools that are also available in the **Quick Access Toolbar**. Click on the down arrow on the **Application Menu** to display the tools, as shown in Figure 1-9. You can search a command using the search field on the top of the **Application Menu**. To search a tool, enter the complete or partial name of the command in the search field; the relevant tool list will be displayed. If you click on a tool from the list, the corresponding command will get activated.

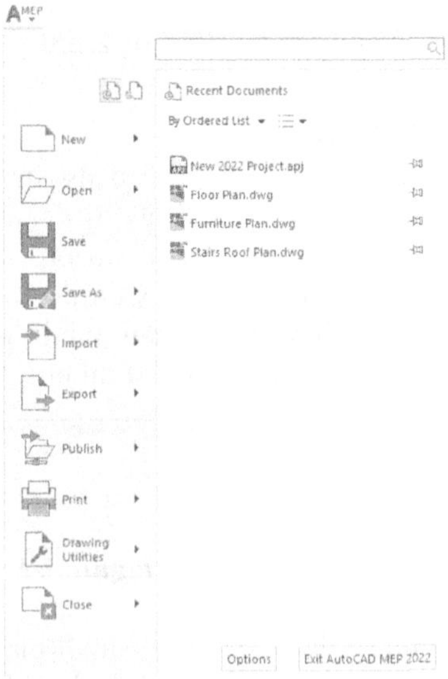

*Figure 1-9 The **Application Menu***

By default, the **Recent Documents** button is chosen in the **Application Menu**. Therefore, the recently opened drawings will be displayed. If you have opened multiple drawing files, choose the **Open Documents** button; the documents that are opened will be listed in the **Application Menu**. To set the preferences of the file, choose the **Options** button available at the bottom of the **Application Menu**. To exit AutoCAD MEP, choose the **Exit AutoCAD MEP 2022** button next to the **Options** button.

TOOL PALETTES

The **TOOL PALETTES** in AutoCAD MEP help you to place and share hatch patterns and blocks in the current drawing in a convenient way. By default, the **TOOL PALETTES** are displayed on the left in the drawing area. If the **TOOL PALETTES** is not displayed then choose **Tools** from the **Tools** drop-down in the **Build** panel of the **Home** tab in the **Ribbon** or choose the CTRL+3 keys to display the **TOOL PALETTES**. You can resize the **TOOL PALETTES** using the resizing cursor that is displayed when you place the cursor on the top or bottom extremity of the **TOOL PALETTES**. The **TOOL PALETTES** will be discussed in detail in later chapters.

Quick Access Toolbar

The **Quick Access Toolbar** is a customizable toolbar located at the top of the application window, just to the right of the **Application Menu**. By default, this toolbar contains a set of frequently used commands for the application. You can add or remove tools as needed. To add the tool to the **Quick Access Toolbar**, locate the tool and then right-click on it; a shortcut menu will be displayed. Next, choose the **Add to Quick Access Toolbar** option; the tool will be added to the **Quick Access Toolbar**. To remove the tool from the **Quick Access Toolbar**, right-click on the tool and then choose the **Remove from Quick Access Toolbar** option.

Share Drawing

This tool is available next to the **Quick Access Toolbar**. It allows you to share a link to a copy of the current drawing to view or edit in the AutoCAD web app. The drawing copy includes all external references and images contained in the current drawing. Anyone having the link can access the drawing in the AutoCAD web app. The link expires seven days after it is created. You can choose between two permission levels for recipients: **View only** and **Edit and save a copy**.

Menu Bar

You can also select commands from the menu bar. Menu bar is not displayed by default. To display the menu bar, choose the down arrow in the **Quick Access Toolbar**; a flyout is displayed. Choose the **Show Menu Bar** option from it; a menu bar will be displayed. You can invoke a command by left-clicking on the menu. In AutoCAD MEP, there are three menus available: **File**, **Window**, and **Help** menus. The **File** menu has the options to manage the drawing file. Using the options available in the **Window** menu, you can close the current session, switch between two sessions, or can display multiple sessions in the display window. The options in the **Help** menu are used to display the help documentation.

Shortcut Menu

AutoCAD MEP has provided shortcut menus as an easy and convenient way of invoking the recently used tools. These shortcut menus are context-sensitive, which means that the tools present in them are dependent on the place/object for which they are displayed. A shortcut menu is invoked by right-clicking and is displayed at the cursor location. You can right-click anywhere in the drawing area to display the general shortcut menu. It generally contains an option to select the previously invoked tool again apart from the common tools, refer to Figure 1-10.

Figure 1-10 *Partial view of shortcut menu with the recently used commands*

If you right-click in the drawing area while a command is active, a shortcut menu with the options related to that particular command will be displayed. Figure 1-11 shows the shortcut menu when the **Duct** tool is active.

If you right-click on the **Start** Tab, a shortcut menu will be displayed that contains the options for creating new drawings, refer to Figure 1-12.

You can also right-click on the command window to display a shortcut menu. This menu displays the six most recently used commands and some of the Windows options like **Copy** and **Paste**, refer to Figure 1-13. The commands and their prompt entries are displayed in the **History** window (previous command lines not visible) and can be selected, copied, and pasted in the command line using the shortcut menu. As you press the up arrow key, the previously entered commands are displayed in the command window. Once the desired command is displayed at the command prompt, you can execute it by simply pressing the ENTER key. You can also copy and edit any previously invoked command by locating it in the **History** window and then selecting the command lines. After selecting the desired command lines from the **History** window, right-click to display a shortcut menu. Choose **Copy** from the menu and then paste the selected lines at the end of the command line.

You can right-click on the coordinate display area of the **Application Status Bar** to display a shortcut menu. This menu contains the options to modify the display of coordinates, as shown in Figure 1-14.

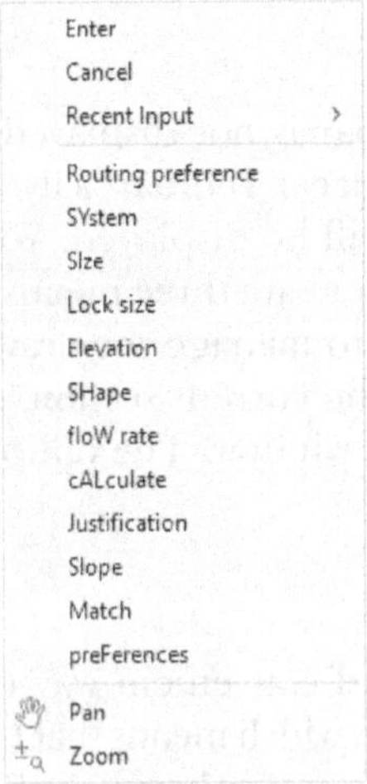

*Figure 1-11 Shortcut menu displayed when the **Duct** tool is active*

*Figure 1-12 Shortcut menu for the **Start** Tab*

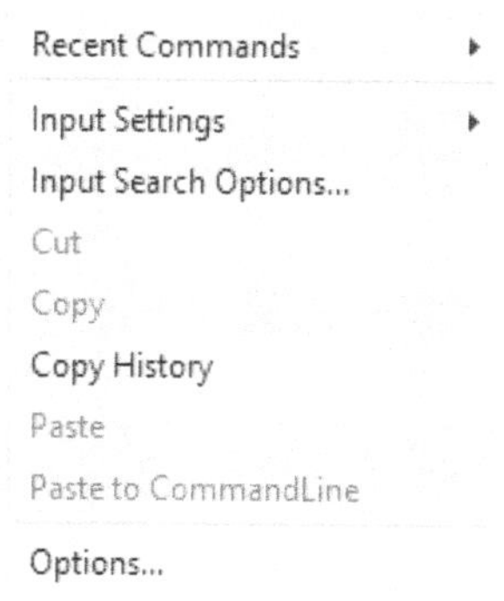

***Figure 1-13** Command line window shortcut menu*

***Figure 1-14** The Coordinate shortcut menu*

AutoCAD MEP DIALOG BOXES

There are certain commands, which when invoked, display a dialog box. When you choose an item from the menu, a dialog box is displayed. For example, when you choose **New** from the **File** menu, the **Select template** dialog box is displayed. In the **Application Menu**, when you choose an item, it may display a dialog box, although there are no ellipses with that item. For example, when you choose **Options** from the **Application Menu**, the **Options** dialog box is displayed. A dialog box contains a number of parts like the dialog label, radio buttons, text or edit boxes, check boxes, slider bars, image boxes, and command buttons. These components are also referred to as tiles. Some of the components of a dialog box are shown in Figure 1-15.

You can select the desired tile using the pointing device, which is represented by an arrow when a dialog box is invoked. The titlebar displays the name of the dialog box. The tabs specify the various sections with a group of related options under them. The check boxes provide toggle options for making a particular option available or unavailable. The drop-down list displays an item and an arrow on the right which when selected displays a list of items to choose from. You can make a selection in the radio buttons. Only one can be selected at a time. The preview displays the preview image of the item selected. The text box is an area where you can enter a text like a file name. It is also called an edit box because you can make any change to the text entered. In some dialog boxes, there is the **[...]** button, which displays another related dialog box. There are certain buttons (**OK**, **Cancel**, **Apply**, and **Help**) at the bottom of the dialog box. The name implies their functions. The button which is highlighted is the default button. The **Help** button in this dialog box is used to display help on various features of the dialog box.

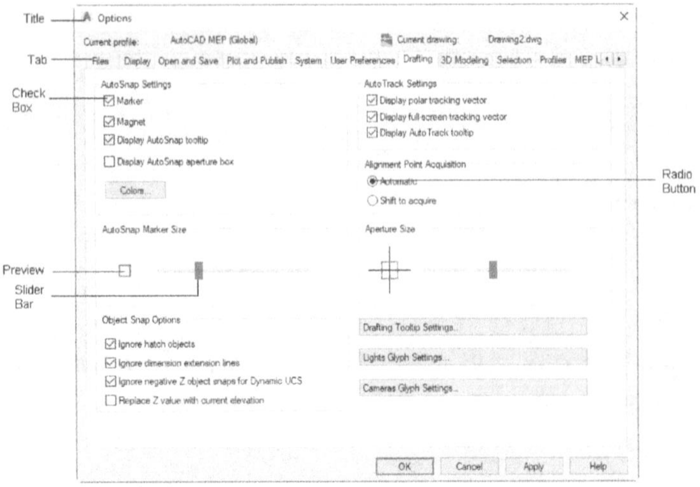

Figure 1-15 Components of a dialog box

STARTING A NEW DRAWING

Application Menu: New > Drawing **Command:** NEW
Quick Access Toolbar: New **Menu Bar:** File > New

You can open a new drawing using the **New** tool in the **File** menu. When you invoke the **New** tool, by default the **Select template** dialog box will be displayed, as shown in Figure 1-16. This dialog box displays a list of default templates available in AutoCAD MEP 2022. The default selected template is ***Aecb Model (Global Ctb).dwt***, which starts the AutoCAD MEP environment with global unit system. You can select any other template to start a new drawing. The drawing will use the settings of the selected template. You can also open any drawing without using any template either in metric or imperial system. To do so, choose the down arrow on the right of the **Open** button from the **Select template** dialog box and select the **Open with no Template-Metric** option or the **Open with no Template-Imperial** option from the flyout.

You can also open a new drawing using the **Use a Wizard** and **Start from Scratch** options from the **Create New Drawing** dialog box. To invoke the **Create New Drawing** dialog box, enter **STARTUP** at the command prompt and then enter **1** as the new value for this system variable. Invoke the **New** tool; the **Create New Drawing** dialog box will be displayed, as shown in Figure 1-17. The options in this dialog box are discussed next.

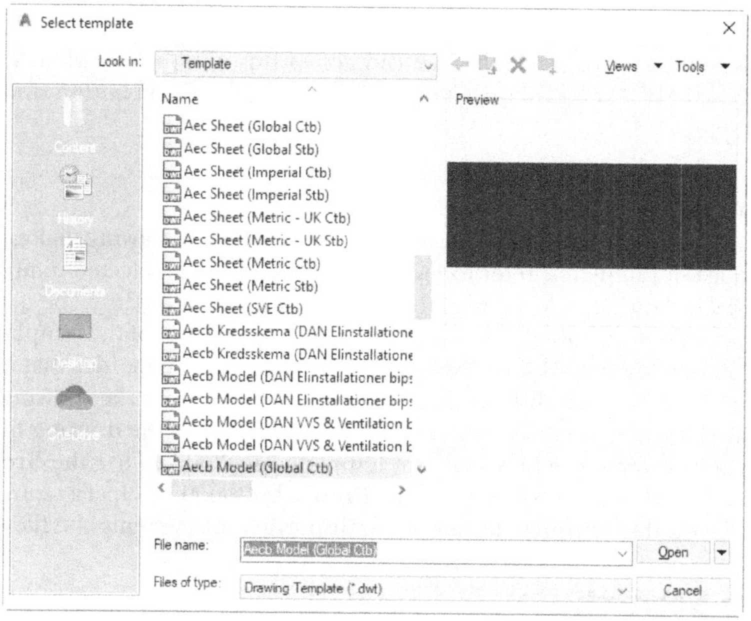

*Figure 1-16 The **Select template** dialog box*

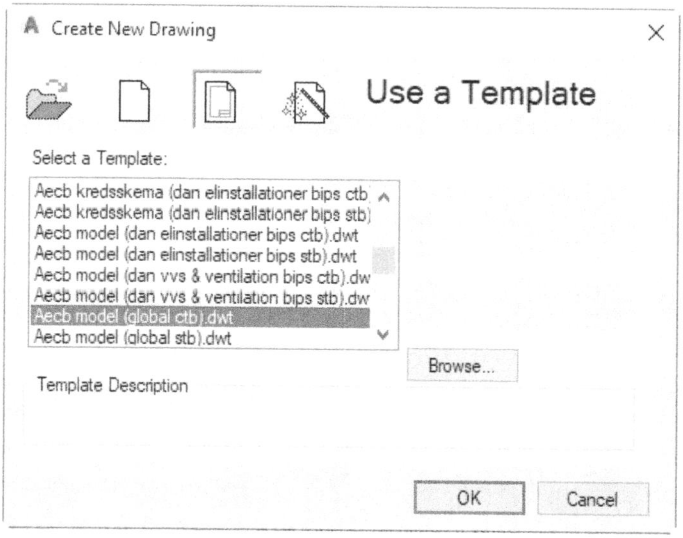

*Figure 1-17 The default templates displayed in the **Create New Drawing** dialog box on choosing the **Use a Template** button*

Note

*If you have started a new AutoCAD MEP session with the **STARTUP** variable set to 1 then the **Startup** dialog box will be displayed. The options in the **Startup** dialog box are same as that of the **Create New Drawing** dialog box with the only difference that in the **Startup** dialog box, the **Open a Drawing** button will be activated.*

Open a Drawing

By default, this option is not available. You can access this option only when you start a new session of AutoCAD MEP. You can open a drawing by using the **Open** button which is discussed later in this chapter.

Use a Template

When you choose the **Use a Template** button from the **Create New Drawing** dialog box, AutoCAD MEP displays a list of templates, refer to Figure 1-17. The default selected template file is *Aecb model (global ctb).dwt*. You can select any of the template files from the list. The new drawing will have the same settings as specified in the template file. The preview of the template file selected is displayed in the dialog box. You can also define your own template files that are customized to your requirements. You can differentiate the template files from the drawing files through their extensions. The template files have a *.dwt* extension whereas the drawing files have a *.dwg* extension. Any drawing file can be saved as a template file. You can use the **Browse** button to select other template files. When you choose the **Browse** button, the **Select a template file** dialog box is displayed with the **Template** folder open, displaying all the template files.

Start from Scratch

When you choose the **Start from Scratch** button, refer to Figure 1-18, AutoCAD MEP provides you with options to start a new drawing that contains the default AutoCAD MEP setup for Imperial or Metric drawing. If you select the **Imperial(feet and inches)** option from the **Default Settings** area, the limits are 12X9, text height is 0.20, and dimension and linetype scale factor is 1.

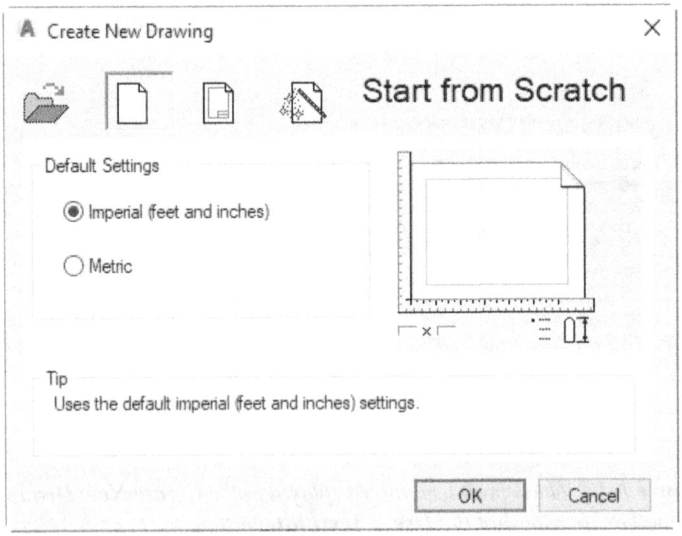

***Figure 1-18** The **Create New Drawing** dialog box with the **Start from Scratch** button chosen*

Use a Wizard

The **Use a Wizard** button allows you to set the initial drawing settings before actually starting a new drawing. When you choose the **Use a Wizard** button, the **Quick Setup** and **Advanced**

Setup options are displayed in the **Select a Wizard** area, refer to Figure 1-19. If you select the **Quick Setup** option, you can specify the units and the limits of the work area. If the **Advanced Setup** option is selected, then you can set the units, limits, and the other types of settings for a drawing. These options are discussed next.

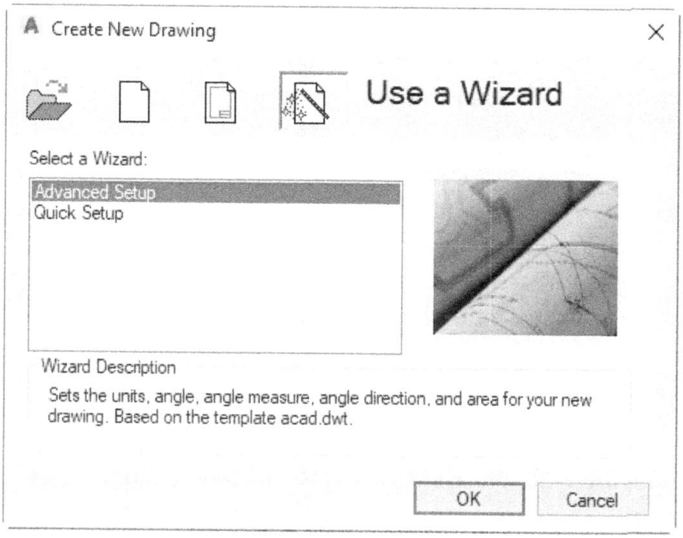

***Figure 1-19** The wizard options displayed on choosing the **Use a Wizard** button*

Advanced Setup

This option allows you to preselect the parameters of a new drawing such as the units of linear and angular measurements, type and direction of angular measurements, approximate area desired for the drawing, precision for displaying the units after decimal, and so on. When you select the **Advanced Setup** wizard option from the **Create New Drawing** dialog box and choose the **OK** button, the **Advanced Setup** wizard will be displayed. The **Units** page is displayed by default, as shown in Figure 1-20.

This page is used to set the units for measurement in the current drawing. The different units of measurement that you can choose from are Decimal, Engineering, Architectural, Fractional, and Scientific. You can select the required unit of measurement by selecting the respective radio button. You will notice that the preview image is modified accordingly. You can also set the precision for the measurement units by selecting it from the **Precision** drop-down list.

Choose the **Next** button to open the **Angle** page, as shown in Figure 1-21. You will notice that an arrow appears on the left of **Angle** in the **Advanced Setup** wizard. This suggests that this page is current.

This page is used to set the unit for angular measurements and its precision. The units for angle measurement are Decimal Degrees, Deg/Min/Sec, Grads, Radians, and Surveyor. The units for angle measurement can be set by selecting any one of these radio buttons as required. The preview of the selected angular unit is displayed on the right of the radio buttons. The precision format changes automatically in the **Precision** drop-down list depending on the angle measuring system selected. You can then select the precision from the drop-down list.

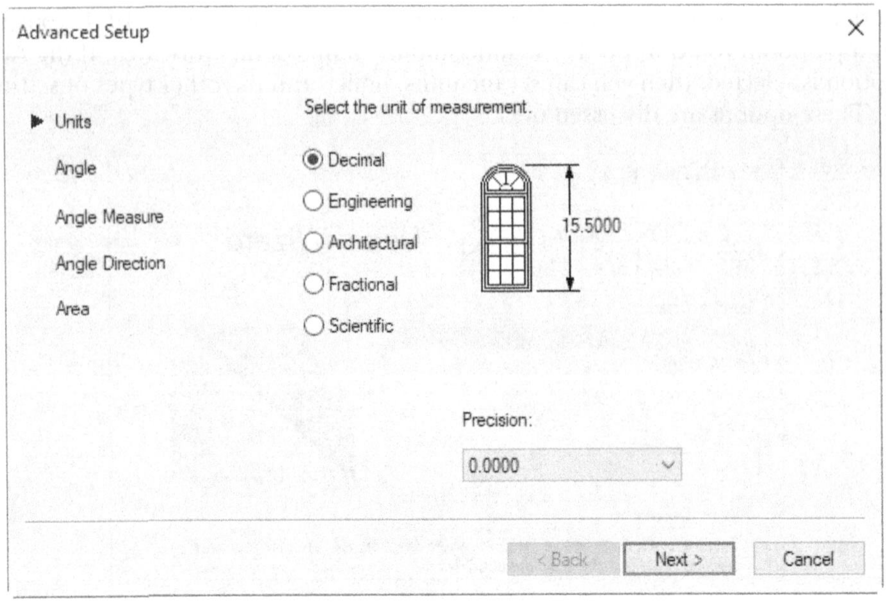

*Figure 1-20 The **Units** page of the **Advanced Setup** wizard*

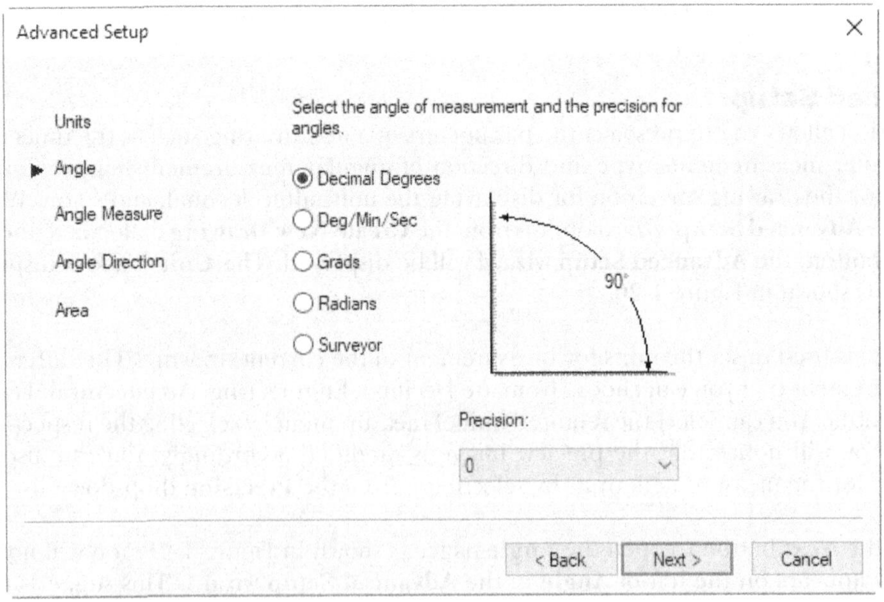

*Figure 1-21 The **Angle** page of the **Advanced Setup** wizard*

The next page is the **Angle Measure** page, as shown in Figure 1-22. This page is used to select the direction of the baseline from which the angles will be measured. You can also set your own direction by selecting the **Other** radio button and then entering the value in the edit box displayed below it. This edit box gets activated only when you select the **Other** radio button.

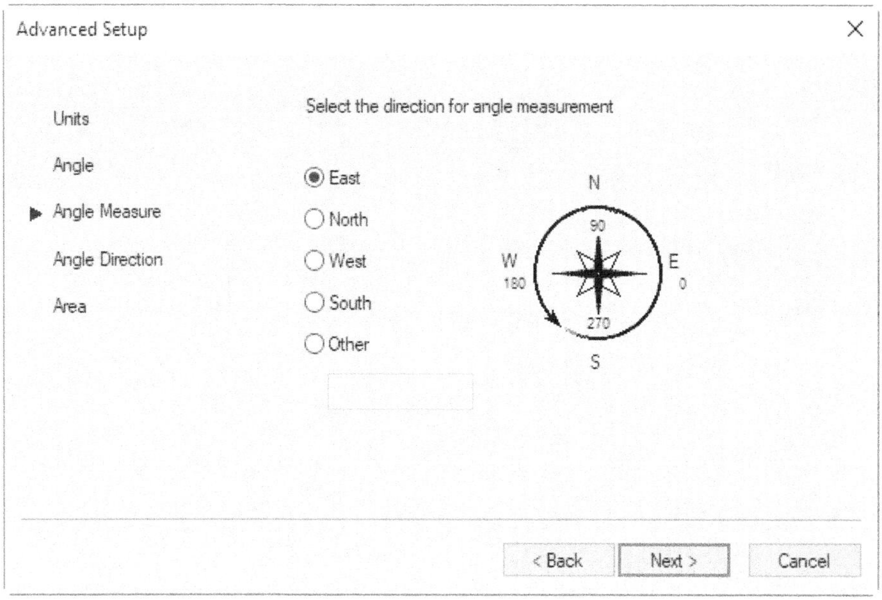

*Figure 1-22 The **Angle Measure** page of the **Advanced Setup** wizard*

Choose **Next** to display the **Angle Direction** page to set the orientation for the angle measurement, refer to Figure 1-23. By default the angles are positive if measured in a counterclockwise direction. This is because the **Counter-Clockwise** radio button is selected. If you select the **Clockwise** radio button, the angles will be considered positive when measured in the clockwise direction. To set the limits of the drawing, choose the **Next** button; the **Area** page will be displayed, as shown in Figure 1-24. You can enter the width and length of the drawing area in the respective edit boxes.

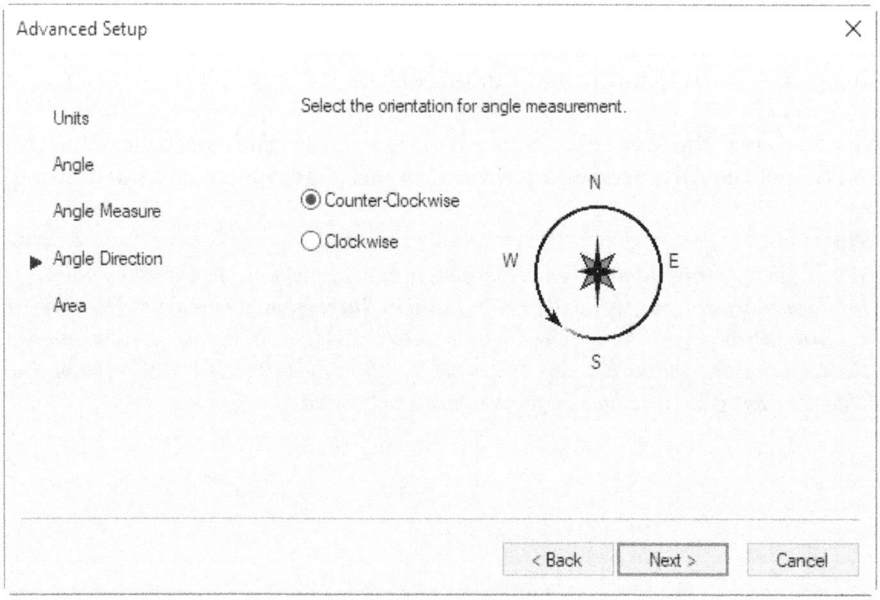

*Figure 1-23 The **Angle Direction** page of the **Advanced Setup** wizard*

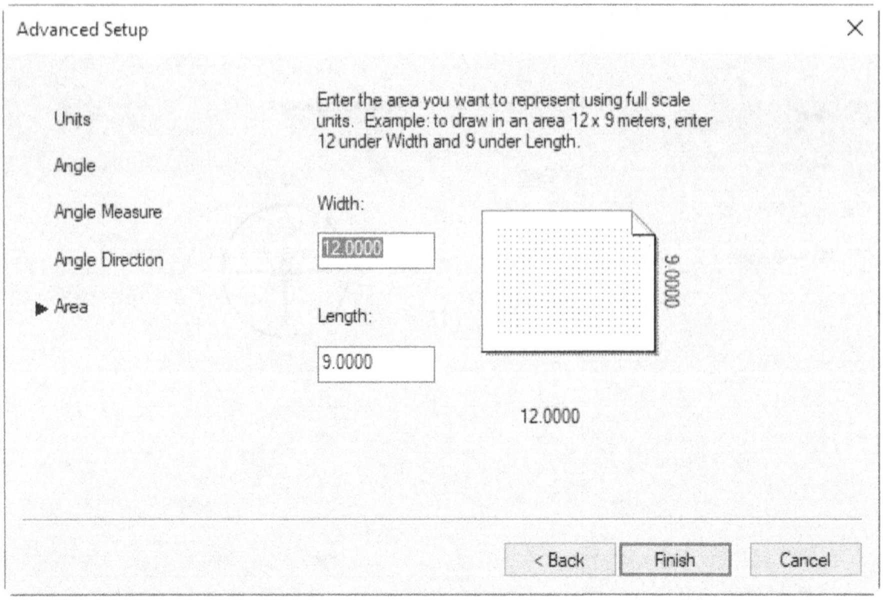

*Figure 1-24 The **Area** page of the **Advanced Setup** wizard*

Note

*Even after you increase the limits of the drawing, the drawing display area does not increase. You need to invoke the **Zoom All** tool from the Navigation Bar to increase the drawing display area.*

Quick Setup

When you select the **Quick Setup** option from the **Create New Drawing** dialog box and choose the **OK** button, the **QuickSetup** wizard is displayed. This wizard has two pages: **Units** and **Area**. The **Units** page is opened by default, as shown in Figure 1-25. The options in the **Units** page are similar to those in the **Units** page of the **Advanced Setup** wizard. The only difference is that you cannot set the precision for the units in this wizard.

Choose **Next** to display the **Area** page, as shown in Figure 1-26. The **Area** page of the **QuickSetup** is similar to that of the **Advanced Setup** wizard. In this page, you can set the drawing limits.

Tip

*When you open an AutoCAD MEP session, a drawing will be opened automatically. But you can open a new drawing using the options such as **Start from Scratch** and **Use a Wizard** from the **Startup** dialog box before entering into AutoCAD MEP environment. As mentioned earlier, the display of the **Startup** dialog box is turned off by default. Refer to the section **Starting a New Drawing** to know how to turn on the display of this dialog box.*

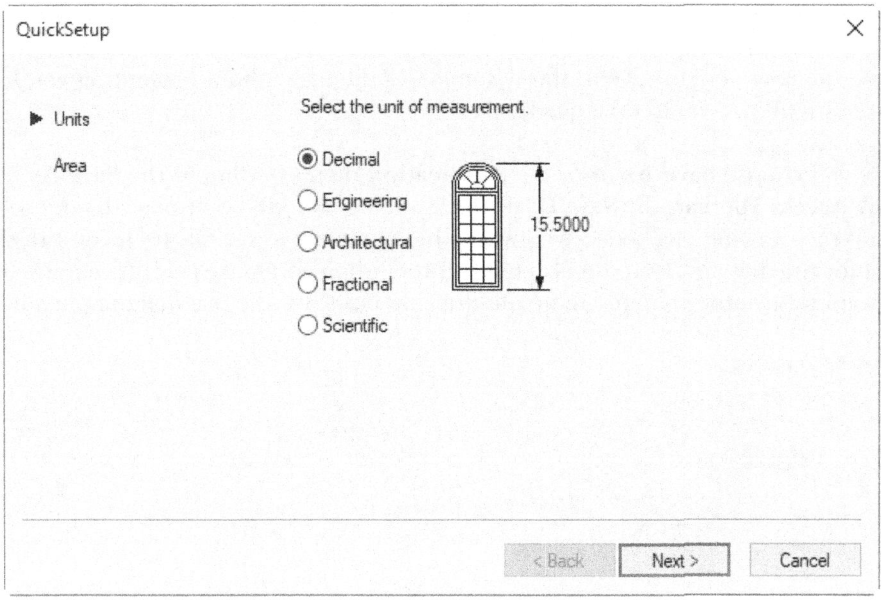

*Figure 1-25 The **Units** page of the **QuickSetup** wizard*

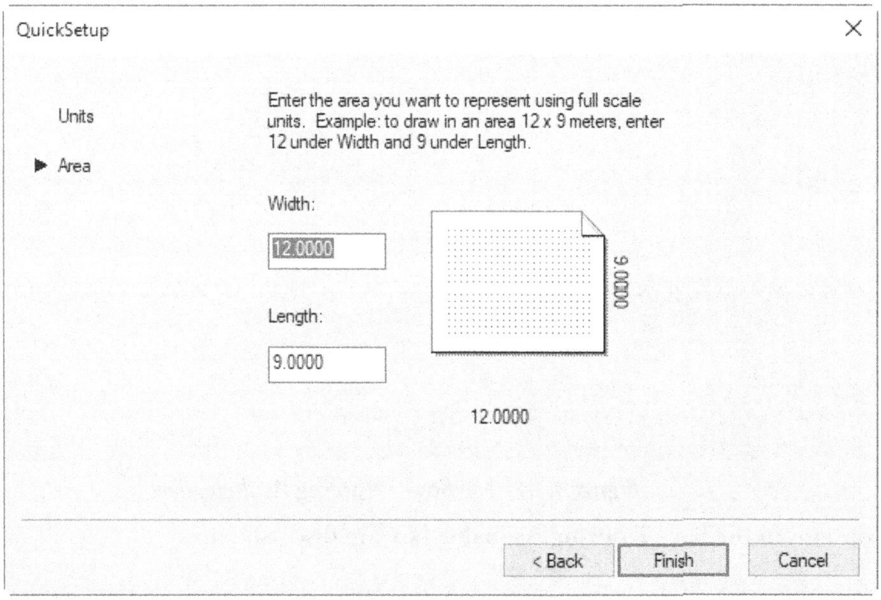

*Figure 1-26 The **Area** page of the **QuickSetup** wizard*

SAVING WORK

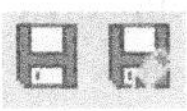

The **QSAVE**, **SAVEAS**, and **SAVE** commands allow you to save your work. When you choose the **Save** tool from the **Quick Access Toolbar**, the **QSAVE** command is invoked. If you are saving the drawing for the first time in the present session, the **SAVEAS** command will be invoked in place of the **QSAVE** command and you will be prompted to enter the file name in the **Save Drawing As** dialog box, as shown in Figure 1-27. You can enter the name for the drawing and then choose the **Save** button. If you have modified a drawing file, choose the **Save** tool to save it; the system saves the file without prompting you to enter a file name. This allows you to do a quick save.

When you choose **Save As** from the **Application** menu or choose the **Save As** tool from the **Quick Access Toolbar**, the **Save Drawing As** dialog box will be displayed, refer to Figure 1-27. Even if the drawing has been saved with a file name, by using this tool, you can specify a new name for the drawing. You can also use this tool when you make certain changes to a template and want to save the changed template drawing but leave the original template unchanged.

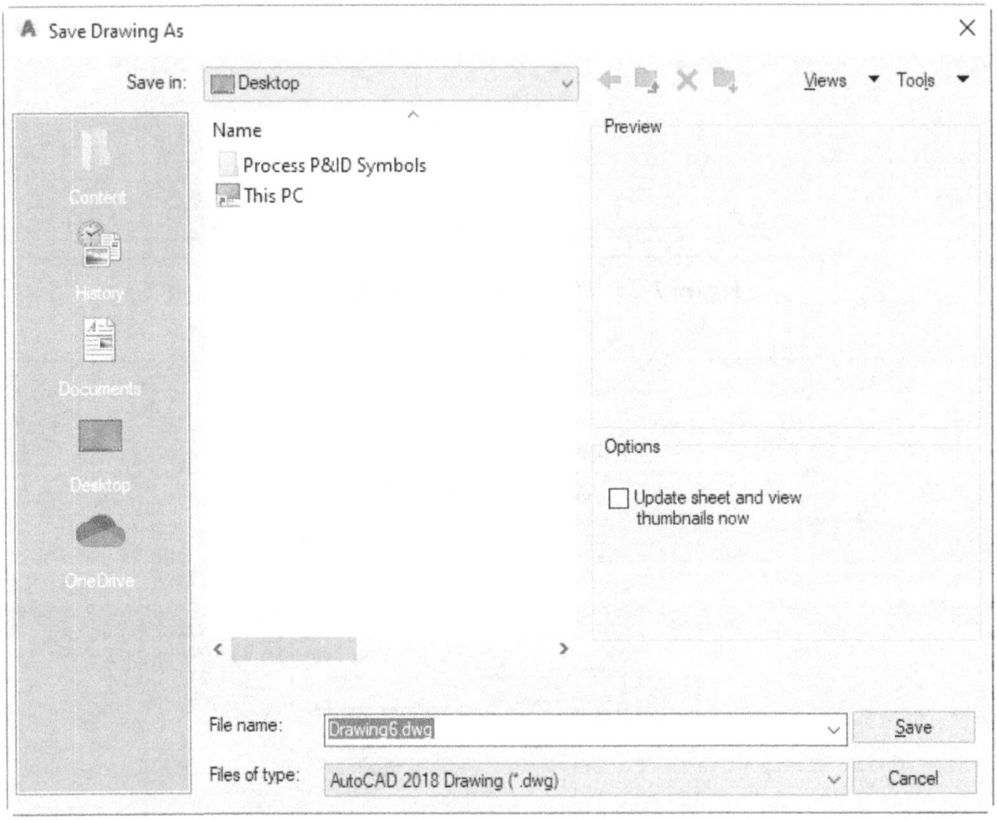

***Figure 1-27** The **Save Drawing As** dialog box*

The options in the **Save Drawing As** dialog box are discussed next.

Places List

A column of icons is displayed on the left side of the dialog box. These icons contain the shortcuts to the folders that are frequently used. You can quickly save your drawings in one of these folders. The **History** folder displays the list of the most recently saved drawings. You can save your personal drawings in the **Documents** or **Favorites** folder. The **FTP** folder displays the list of various FTP sites that are available for saving the drawing. By default, no FTP sites are shown in the dialog box. To add an FTP site to the dialog box, choose the **Tools** button on the upper-right corner of the dialog box to display a shortcut menu and select **Add/Modify FTP Locations**. The **Desktop** folder displays the list of contents on the desktop. The **Buzzsaw** icons connect you to their respective pages on the Web. You can add a new folder in this list for an easy access by simply dragging the folder on to the **Places List** area. You can rearrange all these folders by dragging them and then placing them at the desired locations. It is also possible to remove the folders which are not in frequent use. To do so, right-click on the particular folder and then choose **Remove** from the shortcut menu. Now, you can also save the document on Autodesk Cloud. The option for saving the document is discussed next.

The **A360** icon is available on the top left in the **Save Drawing As** dialog box, refer to Figure 1-27. It is used to share data online with the users who have an Autodesk account. When you choose this button, the **Autodesk-Sign In** window will be displayed. Now, you can sign in to upload your document or file in Autodesk Cloud.

File name

To save your work, enter the name of the drawing in the **File name** edit box by typing or by selecting it from the drop-down list. If you have already assigned a name to the drawing, it will be displayed in the edit box as the default name. If the drawing is unnamed, the default name *Drawing1* will be displayed in the **File Name** edit box.

Files of type

The options in the **Files of type** drop-down list are used to specify the drawing format in which you want to save the file, refer to Figure 1-28. For example, to save the file as an AutoCAD 2007 drawing file, select **AutoCAD 2007/LT 2007 Drawing (*.dwg)** from the drop-down list.

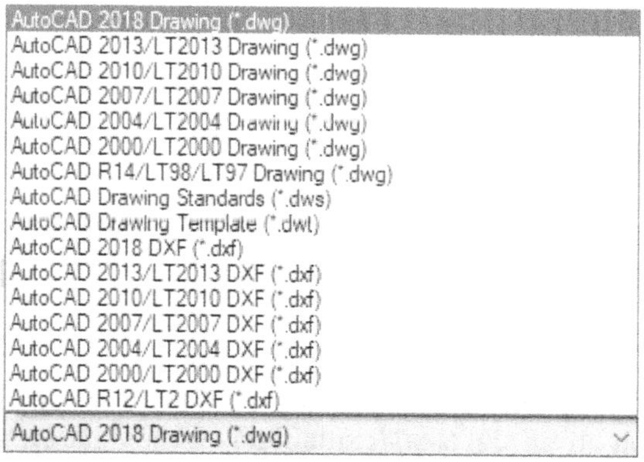

Figure 1-28 *The* ***File of type*** *drop-down list*

Save in

The current drive and path information is listed in the **Save in** drop-down list. AutoCAD MEP will initially save the drawing in the default folder, but if you want to save the drawing in a different folder, you have to specify the path. For example, to save the present drawing as *house* in the *C1* folder, choose the arrow button in the **Save in** drop-down list to display the drop-down list. Select **C**: from the drop-down list; all folders in the C drive will be listed in the **File** list box. Double-click on the **C1** folder, if it is already listed there or create a new folder with the name **C1** by choosing the **Create New Folder** button. Select *house* from the drop-down list, if it is already listed there, or enter it in the **File name** edit box and then choose the **Save** button. Your drawing (*house*) will be saved in the *C1* folder (*C:\C1\house.dwg*). Similarly, to save the drawing in the D drive, select **D:** from the **Save in** drop-down list.

> **Tip**
> *The file name you enter to save a drawing should match its contents. This helps you to remember the drawing details and makes it easier to refer to them later. Also, the file name can be 255 characters long and can contain spaces and punctuation marks.*

Views

The options in this drop-down list, refer to Figure 1-29, are used to set the appearance of the files and folders to specific view and they are discussed next.

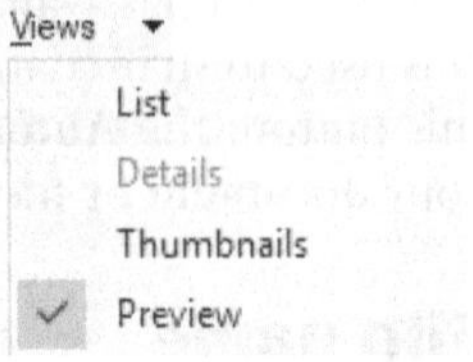

***Figure 1-29** The **Views** drop-down list*

List, Details, and Thumbnails Options

If you choose the **Details** option, it will display the detailed information about the files (size, type, date, and time of modification) in the **Files** list box. In the detailed information, if you click on the **Name** label, the files will be listed with the names in alphabetical order. If you double-click on the **Name** label, the files will be listed in reverse order. Similarly, if you click on the **Size** label, the files are listed according to their size in ascending order. Double-clicking on the **Size** label will list the files in descending order of size. Similarly, you can click on the **Type** label or the **Modified** label to list the files accordingly. If you choose the **List** option, all files present in the current folder will be listed in the **File** list box. If you select the **Thumbnails** option, the list box displays the preview of all the drawings, along with their names displayed at the bottom of the drawing preview. Also, the preview of the file is displayed in the **Preview** image box.

Create New Folder

If you choose the **Create New Folder** button, AutoCAD MEP creates a new folder with the name **New Folder**. The new folder is displayed in the **File** list box. You can change the name of the folder if required.

Up one level

When you choose the **Up one level** button, the folders that are up by one level are displayed. For example, if you are in the *Sample* subfolder of the *AutoCAD MEP 2022* folder, then choosing the **Up one level** button will open the *AutoCAD MEP 2022* folder.

Tools Drop-Down List

The **Add/Modify FTP Locations** option in the **Tools** drop-down list is used for adding or modifying the FTP sites. These sites can then be browsed from the FTP shortcut in the **Places** list. The **Add Current Folder to Places** and **Add to Favorites** options add the folder displayed in the **Save in** edit box to the **Places** list or to the favorites folder, respectively. The **Options** option displays the **Saveas Options** dialog box where you can save the proxy images of the custom objects. It has the **DWG Options** and **DXF Options** tabs.

AUTO SAVE

AutoCAD MEP allows you to save your work automatically at specific intervals. To change the time intervals, choose the **Options** button from the **Application Menu**; the **Options** dialog box will be displayed. In this dialog box, enter the duration after which the file will be saved automatically in the **Minutes between saves** text box in the **File Safety Precautions** area of the **Open and Save** tab. This duration depends on the power supply, hardware, and type of drawings. AutoCAD MEP saves the drawing with the file extension *.ac$*. You can also change the time interval by using the **SAVETIME** system variable.

Tip

*Although the automatic save feature saves your drawing upto a certain time interval, you should not completely depend on it because the procedure for converting the sv$ file into a drawing file is cumbersome. Therefore, it is recommended that you save your files regularly using the **QSAVE** or **SAVEAS** commands.*

BACKUP FILES

If a drawing file already exists and you use the **Save** or **Save As** tool to update the current drawing, AutoCAD MEP creates a backup file. AutoCAD MEP takes the previous copy of the drawing and changes it from *.dwg* to *.bak*. The updated drawing is saved as a drawing file with the *.dwg* extension. For example, if the name of the drawing is *myproj.dwg*, AutoCAD MEP will change it to *myproj.bak* and save the current drawing as *myproj.dwg*.

Using the DRAWING RECOVERY MANAGER to Recover Files

The files that are saved automatically can also be retrieved by using the Drawing Recovery Manager. You can open the **DRAWING RECOVERY MANAGER** by choosing **Drawing Utilities > Open the Drawing Recovery Manager** from the **Application Menu** or by entering **DRAWINGRECOVERY** at the command bar.

In case of a system crash, the **Drawing Recovery** message box will be displayed on starting AutoCAD MEP again, refer to Figure 1-30. The message box informs you that the program unexpectedly failed and you can open the most suitable among the backup files created by AutoCAD MEP. Choose the **Close** button from the **Drawing Recovery** message box; the **DRAWING RECOVERY MANAGER** will be displayed on the left of the drawing area, as shown in Figure 1-31.

Note

*The **DRAWING RECOVERY MANAGER** will be available only when the automatic save feature is active.*

The **Backup Files** rollout lists the original files, the backup files, and the automatically saved files. Select a file; its preview will be displayed in the **Preview** rollout. Also, the information corresponding to the selected file will be displayed in the **Details** rollout. To open a backup file, double-click on its name in the **Backup Files** rollout. Alternatively, right-click on the file name and then choose **Open** from the shortcut menu. It is recommended that you save the backup file at the desired location before you start working on it.

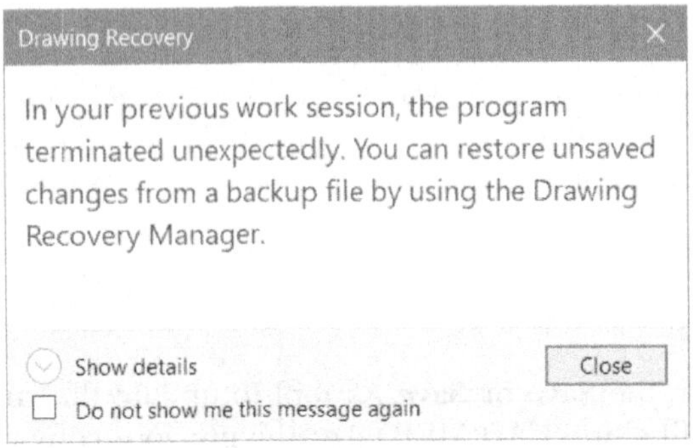

*Figure 1-30 The **Drawing Recovery** message box*

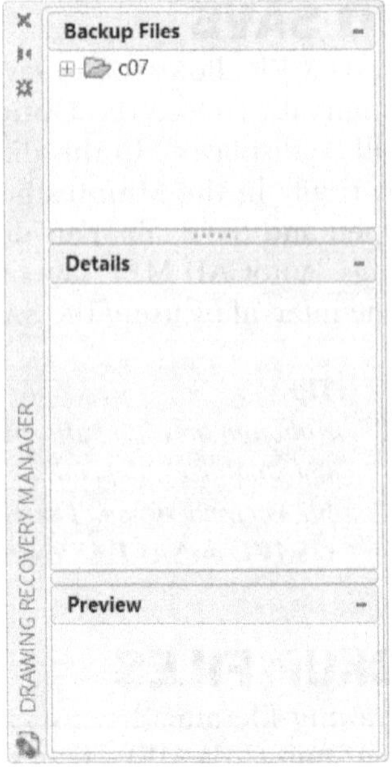

*Figure 1-31 The **DRAWING RECOVERY MANAGER***

EPD Backup Files

The Electrical Project Database is used to manage all drawings related to the electrical circuits for a project. As you create and modify electrical circuits for a project, you can use the circuit manager to view and manage panel and circuit information. By default, AutoCAD MEP creates a backup of all the EPD files. These backup files are used when the EPD files get corrupt due to system crash or when files get incorrectly linked. You can specify the number of data backup files in the **Electrical Preferences** dialog box displayed on choosing the **Electrical** button in the **Preferences** panel from the **Manage** tab of the **Ribbon**. You can create upto 99 backup files for a single Electrical Project Database.

CLOSING A DRAWING

You can use the **CLOSE** command to close the current drawing file without actually quitting AutoCAD MEP. To do so, choose **Close > Current Drawing** from the **Application Menu** or enter **CLOSE** at the command bar; the current drawing file will be closed. If multiple drawing files are open, choose **Close > All Drawings** from the **Application Menu**. If multiple drawing files of a single project are open, choose **Close > All Project Drawings** from the **Application Menu**. If you have not saved the drawing after making the last changes to it and you invoke the **CLOSE** command, AutoCAD MEP displays a dialog box that allows you to save the drawing before closing. This dialog box gives you an option to discard the current drawing or the changes made to it. It also gives you an option to cancel the command. After closing the drawing, you are still in AutoCAD MEP from where you can open a new or an already saved drawing file. You can also use the **Close** button (**X**) in the drawing area to close the drawing.

Note

You can close a drawing even if a command is active.

OPENING AN EXISTING DRAWING

You can open an existing drawing file by using one of the following three methods: by using the **Select File** dialog box, by using the **Create New Drawing** dialog box, and by dragging and dropping.

Opening an Existing Drawing Using the Select File Dialog Box

If you are already in the drawing editor and you want to open a drawing file, choose the **Open** tool from the **Quick Access Toolbar**; the **Select File** dialog box will be displayed. Alternatively, invoke the **OPEN** command to display the **Select File** dialog box, refer to Figure 1-32. You can select the drawing to be opened using this dialog box. This dialog box is similar to the standard dialog boxes. You can choose the file you want to open from the folder in which it is stored. You can change the folder from the **Look in** drop-down list. You can then select the name of the drawing from the list box or you can enter the name of the drawing file you want to open in the **File name** edit box. After selecting the drawing file, you can choose the **Open** button to open the file.

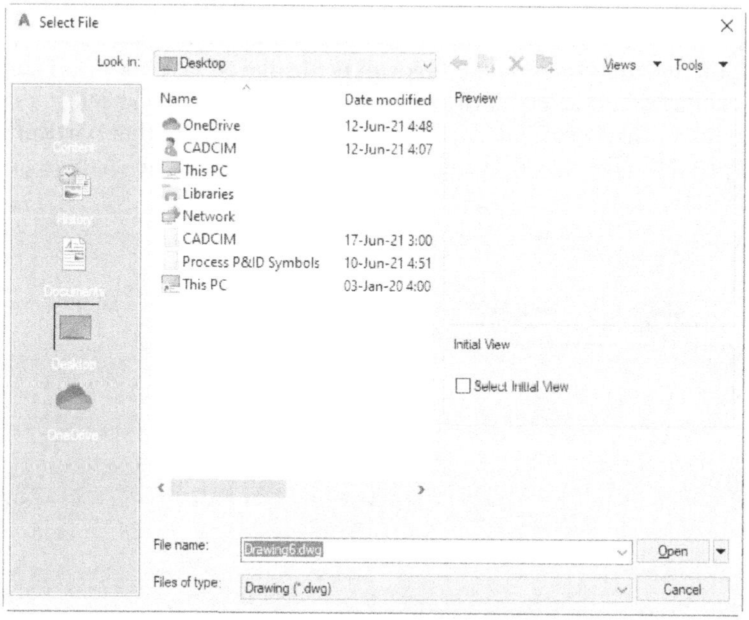

***Figure 1-32** The **Select File** dialog box*

When you select a file name, preview of the selected file is displayed in the **Preview** box. You can also use this box to identify the contents of a drawing. You can also change the file type by selecting it from the **Files of type** drop-down list. Apart from the *dwg* files, you can open the *dws* (standard), *dwt* (template) files or the *dxf* files. You have all the standard icons in the **Places** list that can be used to open drawing files from different locations. When you click on the down arrow adjacent to the **Open** button, a drop-down list is displayed, as shown in Figure 1-33. You can choose a method for opening the file using this drop-down list. These methods are discussed next.

*Figure 1-33 The **Files of type** drop-down list*

Open Read-Only

To view a drawing without modifying it, select the **Open Read-Only** option from the drop-down list. If you try to save the opened drawing with the original file name, AutoCAD MEP warns you that the drawing file is write protected. However, you can save the edited drawing with a different file name using the **SAVEAS** command. This way you can preserve your drawing.

Partial Open

The **Partial Open** option enables you to open only a selected view or a selected layer of a selected drawing. This option can be used to edit small portions of a complicated drawing and then save it with the complete drawing. When you select the **Partial Open** option from the **Open** drop-down list, the **Partial Open** dialog box will be displayed, as shown in Figure 1-34, which contains different views and layers of the selected drawing. When you select a check box for a layer and then choose the **Open** button, only the objects drawn in that particular layer for the drawing are displayed in the new drawing window. You can make the changes and then save it.

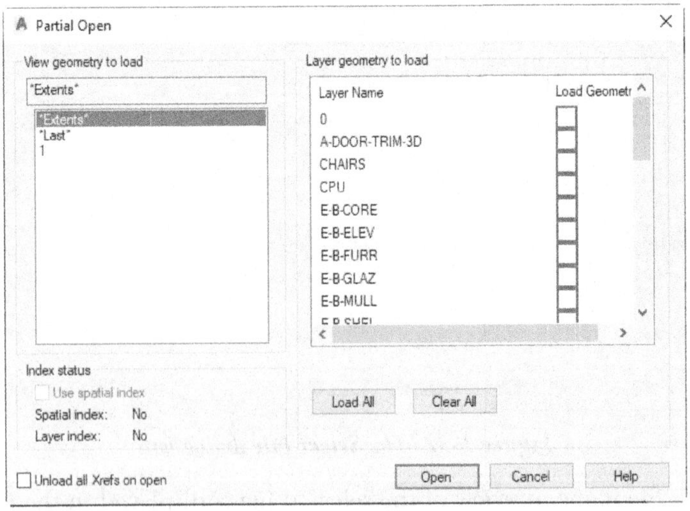

*Figure 1-34 The **Partial Open** dialog box*

Loading Additional Objects to Partially Opened Drawing

Once you have opened a part of a drawing and made the necessary changes, you may want to load additional objects or layers on the existing ones. To do so, enter **PARTIALOAD** at the command bar; the **Partial Load** dialog box will be displayed, which is similar to the **Partial Open** dialog box. You can choose another layer and the objects drawn in that layer will be added to the partially loaded drawing.

Note

1. *Loading a drawing partially is a good practice when you are working with objects on a specific layer in a large complicated drawing.*
2. *In the* ***Select File*** *dialog box, the preview of a drawing which was partially opened and then saved is not displayed.*

Tip

If a drawing is partially opened and saved previously, it is possible to open it again with the same layers and views. AutoCAD MEP remembers the settings, therefore when you open a partially opened drawing, a message box is displayed prompting you to fully open it or restore the partially opened drawing.

Select Initial View

Select the **Select Initial View** check box if you want to load a specific view initially when AutoCAD MEP loads the drawing. This option will work if the drawing has saved views. This is generally used while working on a large complicated drawing, in which you want to work on a particular portion. You can save that particular portion as a view and then select it to open the drawing next time. You can save the desired view by using the **VIEW** command. If the drawing has no saved views then on selecting this option, the last view will be loaded. If you select the **Select Initial View** check box and then the **OK** button, AutoCAD MEP will display the **Select Initial View** dialog box. You can select the view name from this dialog box, and AutoCAD MEP will load the drawing with the selected view.

Opening an Existing Drawing Using the Startup Dialog Box

If you have set the **STARTUP** system variable value as **1**, the **Startup** dialog box will be displayed whenever you start a new AutoCAD MEP session. The first button in this dialog box is the **Open a Drawing** button. When you choose this button, a list of the most recently opened drawings will be displayed for you to select from, refer to Figure 1-35. The **Browse** button displays the **Select File** dialog box, which allows you to browse to another file.

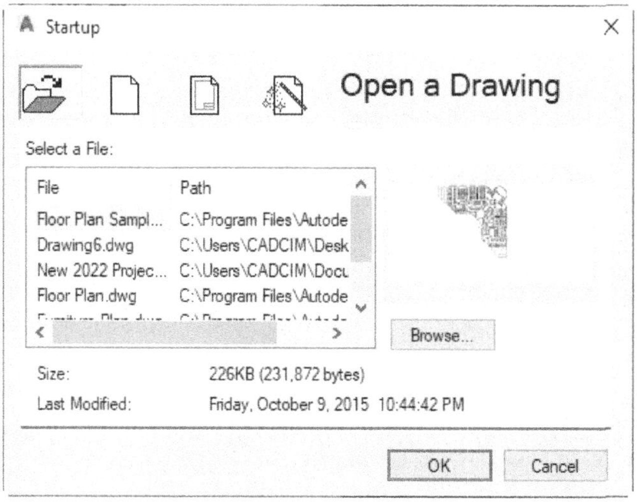

Figure 1-35 *List of the recently opened drawings*

Note

The display of the dialog boxes related to opening and saving drawings will be disabled, if the ***STARTUP*** *and the* ***FILEDIA*** *system variables are set to 0.*

Opening an Existing Drawing Using the Drag and Drop Method

You can also open an existing drawing in AutoCAD MEP by dragging it from the Window Explorer and dropping it into AutoCAD MEP. If you drop the selected drawing in the drawing area, the drawing will be inserted as a block. As a result, you cannot modify it. But if you drag the drawing from the Windows Explorer and drop it at any place other than the drawing area, AutoCAD MEP opens the selected drawing.

QUITTING AutoCAD MEP

You can exit the AutoCAD MEP program by using the **EXIT** or **QUIT** command. Even if you have an active command, you can choose **Exit AutoCAD MEP 2022** from the **Application Menu** to quit the AutoCAD MEP program. In case the drawing has not been saved, a dialog box is displayed with the **Yes** and **No** buttons. Choose the **Yes** button to save the drawing. Note that if you choose **No** in this dialog box, all the changes made in the current list till the last save will be lost. You can also use the **Close** button (**X**) of the main AutoCAD MEP window to end the AutoCAD MEP session.

CREATING AND MANAGING WORKSPACES

A workspace is defined as a customized arrangement of **Ribbon**, toolbars, menus, and window palettes in the AutoCAD MEP environment. You can create your own workspaces, in which only specified toolbars, menus, and palettes are available. When you start AutoCAD MEP, by default the **HVAC** workspace is displayed as the current workspace. However, you can select any other predefined workspace from the flyout displayed on choosing the **Workspace Switching** from the **Application Status Bar**, refer to Figure 1-36. You can also set the workspace by using the WORKSPACE command.

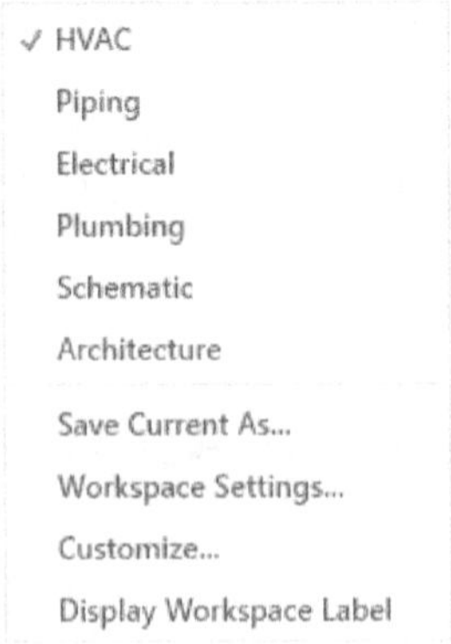

Figure 1-36 *The predefined workspaces*

Creating a New Workspace

To create a new workspace, customize the **Ribbon** and invoke the palettes to be displayed in the new workspace. Next, choose the **Save Current As** option from the flyout displayed on choosing the **Workspace Switching** button from the **Application Status Bar**; the **Save Workspace** dialog box will be displayed, as shown in Figure 1-37. Enter the name of the new workspace in the **Name** edit box and choose the **Save** button.

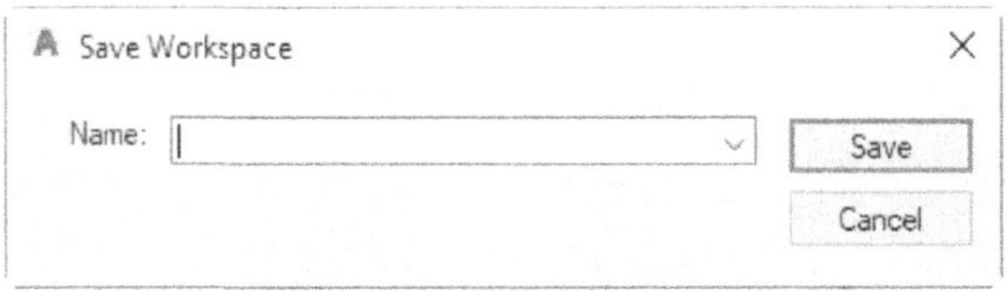

Figure 1-37 The ***Save Workspace*** *dialog box*

The new workspace is now the current workspace and is added to the drop-down list in the title bar. Similarly, you can create workspaces based on your requirement and switch from one workspace to another by selecting the name from the flyout displayed on choosing the **Workspaces Switching** button from the **Application Status Bar**.

Modifying the Workspace Settings

AutoCAD MEP allows you to modify the workspace settings. To do so, choose the **Workspace Settings** option from the flyout displayed on choosing the **Workspaces Switching** button from the **Application Status Bar**; the **Workspace Settings** dialog box will be displayed, as shown in Figure 1-38. All workspaces are listed in the **My Workspace** drop-down list. You can make any of the workspaces as My Workspace by selecting it from the **My Workspace** drop-down list. The options in the **Workspace Settings** dialog box are discussed next.

Menu Display and Order Area

The options in this area are used to control the display and the order of display of workspaces in the **Workspace Switching** drop-down list. By default, workspaces are listed in the sequence of their creation. To change the order, select a workspace and choose the **Move Up** or **Move Down** button. To control the display of the workspaces, you can select or clear the check boxes. You can also add a separator between workspaces by choosing the **Add Separator** button. A separator is a line that is placed between two workspaces in the flyout displayed on choosing the **Workspaces Switching** button from the **Application Status Bar**, as shown in Figure 1-39.

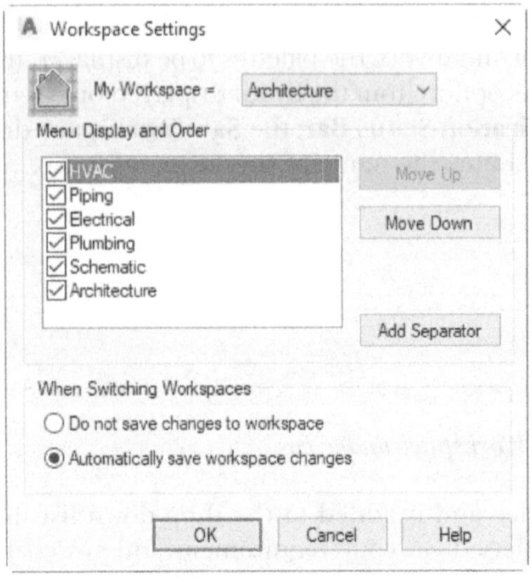

*Figure 1-38 The **Workspace Settings** dialog box*

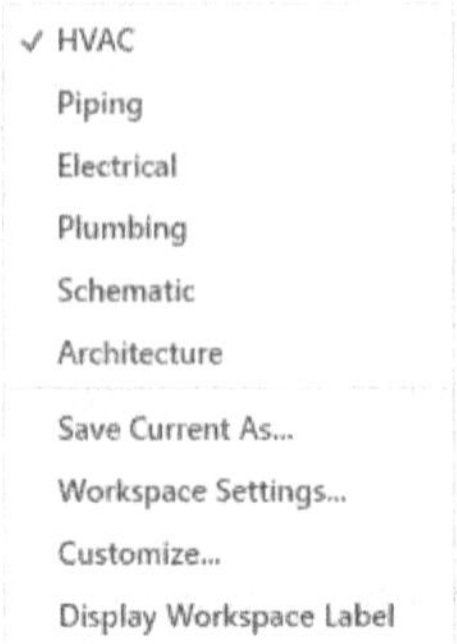

*Figure 1-39 The flyout displayed on choosing the **Workspaces Switching** button*

When Switching Workspaces Area

By default, the **Automatically save workspace changes** radio button is selected in this area, so the changes made in the current workspace will be automatically saved when you switch to the other workspace. If you select the **Do not save changes to workspace** radio button then while switching the workspaces, the changes made in the current workspace will not be saved. Therefore, when you invoke this workspace again, it will be displayed with default settings.

AutoCAD MEP HELP

You can get the on-line help and documentation about the working of AutoCAD MEP 2022 commands by using the options from the **Help** menu in the title bar, refer to Figure 1-40. You can access AutoCAD MEP's help by pressing the F1 function key. On pressing the F1 function key, the **AutoCAD MEP 2022 - Help** will be displayed, as shown in Figure 1-41. The entire help documentation on AutoCAD MEP 2022 is available on this page. You can search for information about any command or tool on this page. You can access this page without the internet connection also. But if you want to use the offline help then you need to download the help file first. You can download the offline help from Autodesk website. Some important options in the **Help** menu are discussed next.

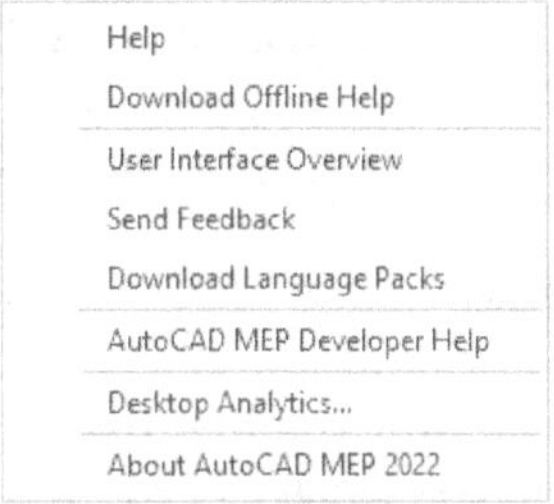

*Figure 1-40 The **Help** menu*

*Figure 1-41 The **Autodesk AutoCAD MEP 2022 - Help** window*

About AutoCAD MEP 2022

This option gives you information about the release, serial number, license number, and also the legal description about AutoCAD MEP.

InfoCenter BAR

An **InfoCenter** bar is displayed at the top right corner in the title bar that will help you sign into the Autodesk Online services, refer to Figure 1-42. You can also access AutoCAD MEP community by using certain keywords.

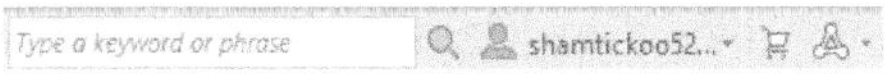

*Figure 1-42 The **InfoCenter** bar*

ADDITIONAL HELP RESOURCES

- You can get help for a command by pressing the F1 key while working. The help page thus obtained contains information about the selected command. You can exit the dialog box and continue with the command.
- You can get help about a dialog box by choosing the **Help** button in that dialog box.
- Autodesk has provided several resources that you can use to get assistance with your AutoCAD MEP questions. The following is a list of some of the resources:

  a. AutoCAD MEP Technical Assistance website: *https://knowledge.autodesk.com*
  b. AutoCAD MEP Discussion Groups website: *https://forums.autodesk.com/t5/autocad-forum/bd-p/706*

- You can also get help by contacting the author, Prof. Sham Tickoo, at *stickoo@pnw.edu* and *tickoo525@gmail.com*.

Self-Evaluation Test

Answer the following questions and then compare them to those given at the end of this chapter:

1. To restrict the movement of cursor along a specific angle, you need to turn on the __________ snap.

2. Using the __________ command, you can change the time interval of automatic save.

3. The **Startup** dialog box is displayed when the **STARTUP** variable is set to __________ .

4. You can sign into the Autodesk Online Services by using the options available in the __________ bar.

5. You can increase the display area of the screen by using the **Clean Screen** button available in the **Application Status Bar**. (T/F)

6. The **AutoCAD Text Window** is used to write text in the drawing area. (T/F)

7. The **Isolate Objects** button is used to display or hide the selected object. (T/F)

8. The **CLOSE** command is used to close the AutoCAD MEP application. (T/F)

Answers to Self-Evaluation Test

1. Polar Tracking, **2.** SAVETIME, **3.** 1, **4.** InfoCenter, **5.** T, **6.** F, **7.** T, **8.** F

Chapter 2

Getting Started with AutoCAD MEP

Learning Objectives

After completing this chapter, you will be able to:

- *Understand the workflow path*
- *Use the Project Browser*
- *Understand the concept of space*
- *Specify the space object settings*
- *Work with space styles and tools*
- *Understand the concept of zones*
- *Switch Workspaces in MEP*

INTRODUCTION

AutoCAD MEP, a software based on AutoCAD platform, is used to design, draft, and document electrical, mechanical, and piping system of buildings. The first step while creating such a system is to create a project. Thereafter drawings are added to this project to represent various components of the building like electrical system, ducts, and so on. These drawings are then arranged according to the workflow of the project.

WORKFLOW

Workflow is a sequence of connected steps required to create a specific type of system. It is dependent on the system to be created. For example, for an HVAC system, the workflow is shown in Figure 2-1. The steps involved in this workflow are discussed next.

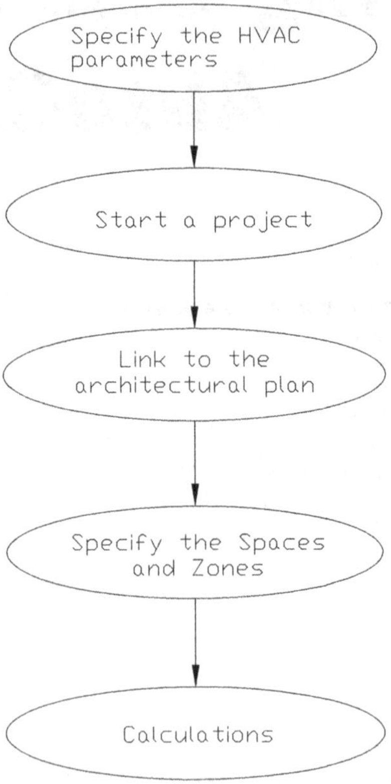

Figure 2-1 *Workflow for an HVAC system in AutoCAD MEP*

Specifying the HVAC Parameters

In this step, you need to specify all the parameters required to create an HVAC system. Some of the parameters are duct size, duct rise and drop, flow rate, cut length, and so on. On the basis of these parameters, the hierarchy of drawings in project will be decided.

Starting a Project

In this step, you need to create a project file to link the drawings of a system to each other. For example, the drawings related to HVAC system will be interlinked and will be in the same project. As a result, you can easily manipulate the parameters of the system.

Linking System File to the Architectural Plan

To create an HVAC system, you need to have an architectural plan. In this step, you will link the HVAC system file to the architectural plan file using the **PROJECT NAVIGATOR**. After the completion of this step, you can reroute the HVAC lines according to the architectural plan.

Specifying Spaces and Zones

In this step, you need to create spaces and zones using the tools available in AutoCAD MEP. These spaces are used for exporting the building information related to the heating and cooling loads. The spaces are further divided into zones which represent the actual heating and cooling loads.

Calculating Loads

In this step, you need to calculate the heating and cooling loads for the building. These calculations are performed by using the analysis tools available in AutoCAD MEP.

Note

In this textbook, the global unit system is followed, therefore you need to start AutoCAD MEP 2022 by double-clicking on the AutoCAD MEP 2022 - English (Global) icon available on the desktop.

PROJECT BROWSER

The **Project Browser** is used to manage project files. A project file contains the record of drawing files related to a category. For example, a building project file may have a record of drawing files related to piping, electrical, and different types of floors. You can create a new project file by using the options available in the **Project Browser**. Also, you can configure an existing project file. The **Project Browser** can be invoked by entering the **PROJECTBROWSER** command at the command prompt or by using the **Application** Menu. To invoke it from the **Application Menu**, hover the cursor on the **Open** option in the menu; a flyout will be displayed. Choose the **Project** button from the flyout; the **Project Browser** will be displayed, as shown in Figure 2-2.

In the **Project Browser**, the list of projects available in the selected directory is displayed in the left pane of the **Project Browser**. To change the current directory, click on **My Projects** from the left area of the dialog box; a drop-down list will be displayed having shortcuts to some common directories such as Documents and Desktop. Using these shortcuts, browse to the desired directory and select the category as the current directory; all the projects available in the selected directory will be displayed in the left pane of the **Project Browser**. In addition to the existing projects, you can also create a new project file by using the options available in the **Project Browser**. The procedure to create a new project file is discussed next.

Creating a New Project File

A new project file can be created by using the **New Project** tool available at the bottom left corner of the **Project Browser**. On choosing this tool, the **Add Project** dialog box will be displayed, as shown in Figure 2-3.

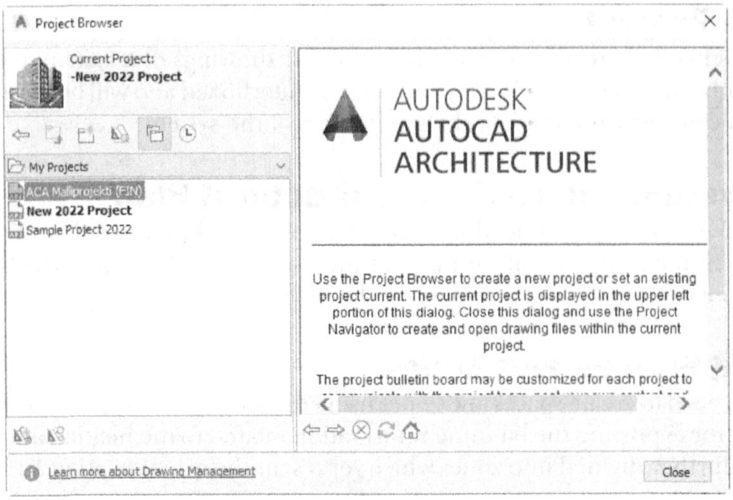

*Figure 2-2 The **Project Browser***

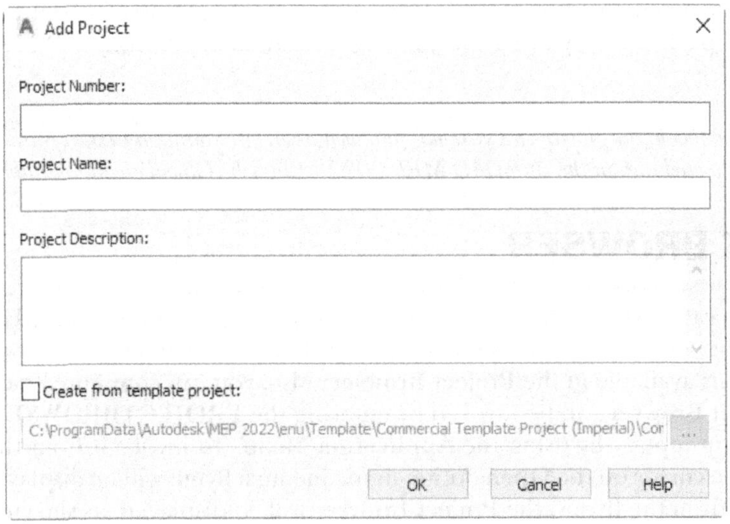

*Figure 2-3 The **Add Project** dialog box*

There are three edit boxes available in this dialog box namely: **Project Number**, **Project Name**, and **Project Description**. The **Project Number** edit box is used to specify a unique number for the project file. The **Project Name** edit box is used to specify the name for the project file. The **Project Description** edit box is used to specify the description about the project file. You can use any of standard templates for the project. To do so, select the **Create from template project** check box from the **Add Project** dialog box if not already selected; the edit box below the check box will be activated. Next, choose the **Browse** button available next to the edit box activated; the **Select Project** dialog box will be displayed, as shown in Figure 2-4.

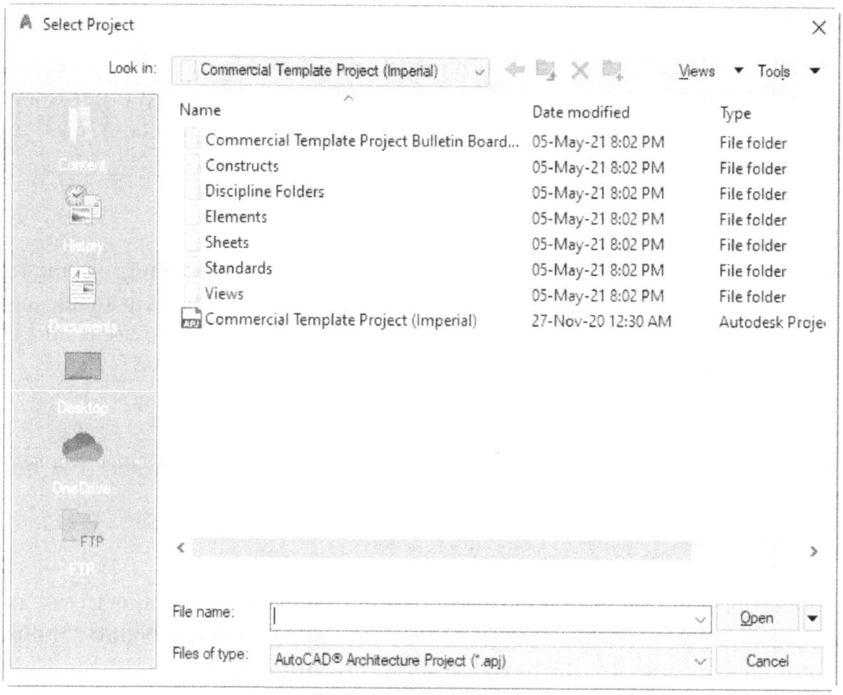

Figure 2-4 The **Select Project** dialog box

Browse to the location where template files are stored and then choose the **Open** button after selecting the desired template file. The selected template file will be used for the current project. Note that in this textbook, the standard template used is *Commercial Template Project (Metric).apj*. To select the template, browse to the location *C:\ProgramData\Autodesk\MEP 2022\enu\Template\Commercial Template Project (Metric)* and then select the *Commercial Template Project (Metric)* template file. Next, choose the **Open** button; the path of the selected file will be added to the edit box displayed below the **Create from template project** check box. Specify the name of project in the **Project Name** edit box and choose the **OK** button from the **Add Project** dialog box; a project file with the specified name will be created and also a copy of drawing files in the template project will be created in the new project folder. The extension of the project file is *.apt*. Now, close the **Project Browser** by choosing the **Close** button. On closing the **Project Browser**, the **PROJECT NAVIGATOR** will be displayed, refer to Figure 2-5.

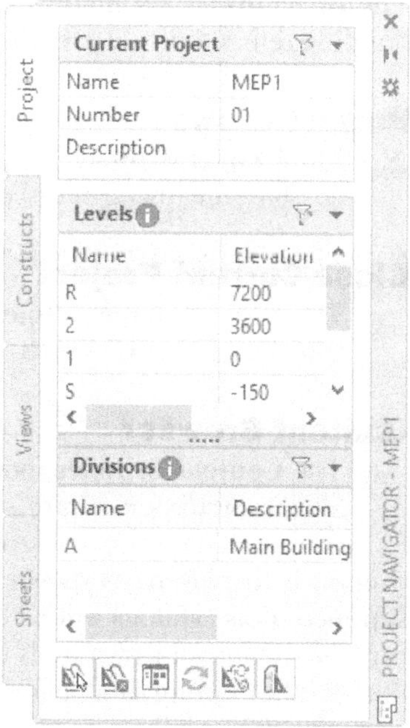

Figure 2-5 The ***PROJECT NAVIGATOR***

PROJECT NAVIGATOR

The **PROJECT NAVIGATOR** is used to navigate the drawing files of a project. Using the **PROJECT NAVIGATOR**, you can edit or create building drawings and other documentation data. The **PROJECT NAVIGATOR** has four tabs: **Project**, **Constructs**, **Views**, and **Sheets**. These tabs are discussed next.

Project Tab

The **Project** tab has three areas. These areas display the information about project name, number of levels in the building, and divisions of building of the project. The tools available at the bottom of the **PROJECT NAVIGATOR** are used to configure the project. The areas and the options available in the **Project** tab are discussed next.

Current Project

The **Current Project** area is used to store the project file name, project file number, and description of the project.

Levels

The **Levels** area contains information of various levels used in the project file. In case of AutoCAD MEP, level refers to floor. In this area, level names are displayed in the **Name** column and their corresponding height values are displayed in the **Elevation** column.

Divisions Area

The **Divisions** area contains information of various divisions of the building. A division of the building refers to its different segments and each segment contains its own name.

Project Browser

The **Project Browser** tool is used to invoke the **Project Browser** dialog box. This dialog box has already been discussed.

Close Current Project

The **Close Current Project** tool is used to close the current project file as well as the **PROJECT NAVIGATOR**. The tool palette opened in the current project will also get closed.

Content Browser

The **Content Browser** tool is used to display the content browser library of catalogs that allows you to store, share and exchange the AutoCAD Architecture contents, tools, and tool palettes. When you invoke the **Contents Browser** tool, the **Autodesk Content Browser 2022** window is displayed. as shown in Figure 2-6. By default, the items provided by the Autodesk supplied tools catalogs will be displayed in the **Autodesk Content Browser 2022** window. You can also create your own tools catalogs and can also copy other tool catalogs into your catalog library. The existing catalog library or website links also can be added into the **Autodesk Content Browser 2022** window. To create new catalog or to add an existing library, choose the **Click to add or create a catalog** button available in the bottom left corner of the dialog box; the **Add Catalog** dialog box will be displayed. Using this dialog box you can add or create new catalogs. When you double-click on the any of the standard catalogs in the **Autodesk Content Browser 2022** window, different catagories related to that catalog will be displayed, refer to Figure 2-7.

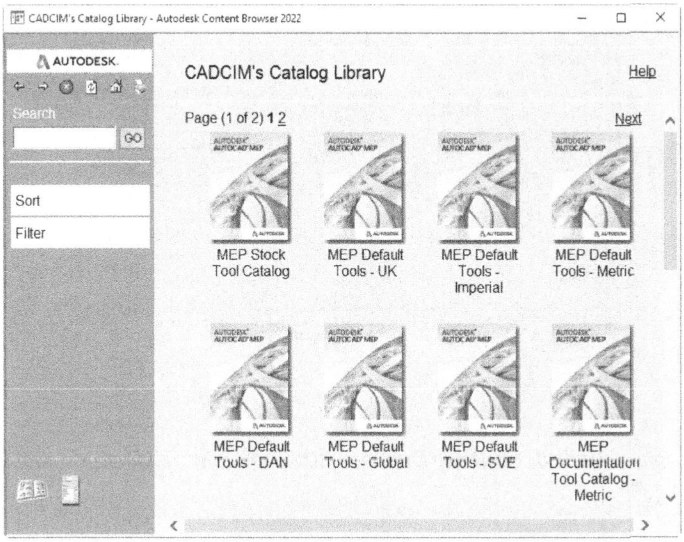

*Figure 2-6 The **Autodesk Content Browser 2022** window*

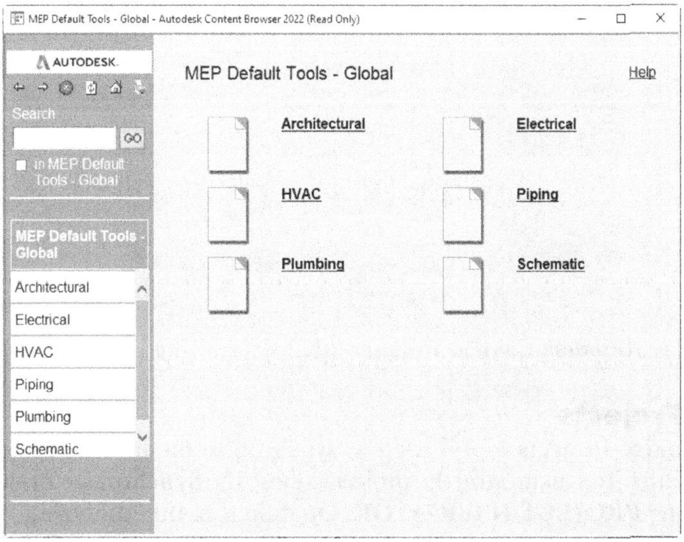

*Figure 2-7 The **Autodesk Content Browser 2022** window displaying component categories*

When you click on any of the categories shown in Figure 2-7, the palettes related to that category will be displayed in the **Autodesk Content Browser** window, refer to Figure 2-8. When you click on any of the palettes shown in Figure 2-8; the components related to that palette will be displayed in the **Autodesk Content Browser 2022** window, refer to Figure 2-9. You can import any of the components tool available in **Autodesk Content Browser 2022** to the **TOOL PALETTES**. To do so, press and hold the left mouse button on the icon of the component and then drag it to the **TOOL PALETTES**. The component will be placed in the **TOOL PALETTES**.

Note

*The **Tool Palettes** will be displayed only when you are in the Drawing environment.*

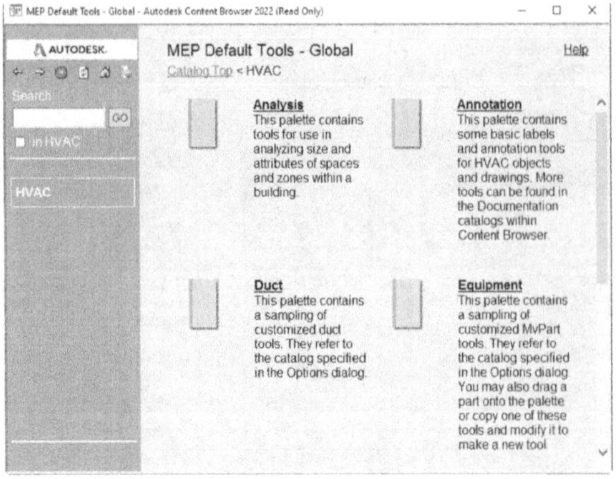

Figure 2-8 *The* ***Autodesk Content Browser 2022*** *window displaying component palettes*

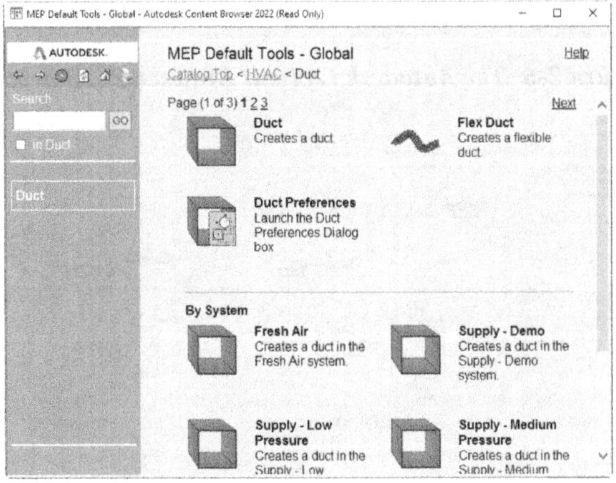

Figure 2-9 *The* ***Autodesk Content Browser 2022*** *window displaying component categories*

Synchronize Projects

The **Synchronize Projects** tool is used to synchronize the current project with the AEC project standards. To synchronize the project, choose the **Synchronize Projects** tool available at the bottom of the **PROJECT NAVIGATOR**. On doing so, the **Analyzing Project Drawings** window will be displayed showing the progress of synchronization of drawing files. When all the drawing files are synchronized to the AEC Project standards, the **Synchronize Project with Project Standards** dialog box will be displayed, refer to Figure 2-10. The upper half of the dialog box shows the objects in the drawing file of the project that do not match with the AEC Project standards and can be updated from the standards. The lower half shows the files that are not present in the project standards and can be skipped or ignored while synchronizing the project by selecting the appropriate option from the **Action** drop-down list.

The drawing files available in the current project are displayed in the **Host Drawing** column of this dialog box. For every file, the status for the availability of the updated version is displayed in the **Status** column of the dialog box. You can synchronize the drawing files which show **Newer Version** in their **Status** column. To synchronize a drawing file, click on its corresponding field in the **Action** column; a drop-down list will be displayed, refer to Figure 2-10. Select the **Update from Standard** option from the drop-down list; the selected file will be synchronized. Similarly, you can synchronize more than one file at a time by pressing and holding the CTRL key while selecting the files.

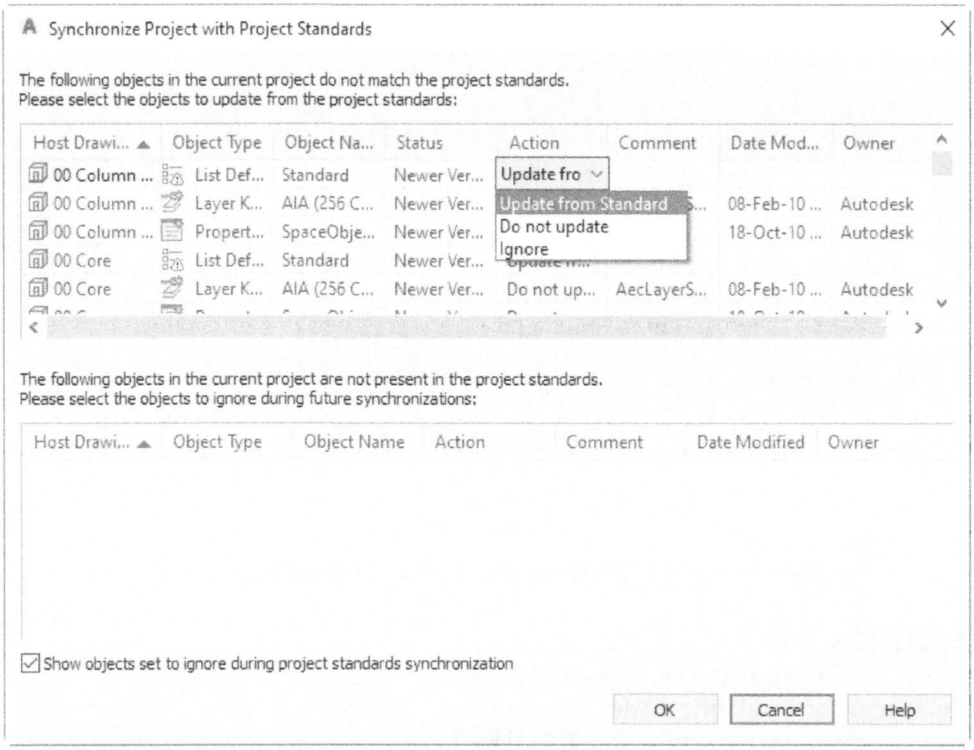

Figure 2-10 *The* ***Synchronize Project with Project Standards*** *dialog box*

Configure Project Standards

The **Configure Project Standards** tool is used to set up the project standard. These project standards are used to synchronize the project drawings. When you choose this tool, the **Configure AEC Project Standards** dialog box will be displayed, refer to Figure 2-11. The **Standard Styles** tab is chosen by default in the dialog box. You can standardize any of the objects available in the **Objects** list of this tab by selecting the check box corresponding to the object in the dialog box. If you choose the **Synchronization** tab, three radio buttons will be displayed: **Automatic**, **Semi-automatic**, and **Manual**.

The **Manual** radio button is selected by default. As a result, project drawings will not be synchronized with the project standards automatically and you would need to synchronize them manually. If you select the **Semi-automatic** radio button, the project standards will be applied only when the project drawing is opened. Also, you will be prompted to apply project standard on each opened project drawing. If you select the **Automatic** radio button, the project standards will be applied on each opened drawing without any prompt. Using the options in the **AutoCAD Standards** tab, you can load any AutoCAD Standard file to apply it as a standard on the project drawings.

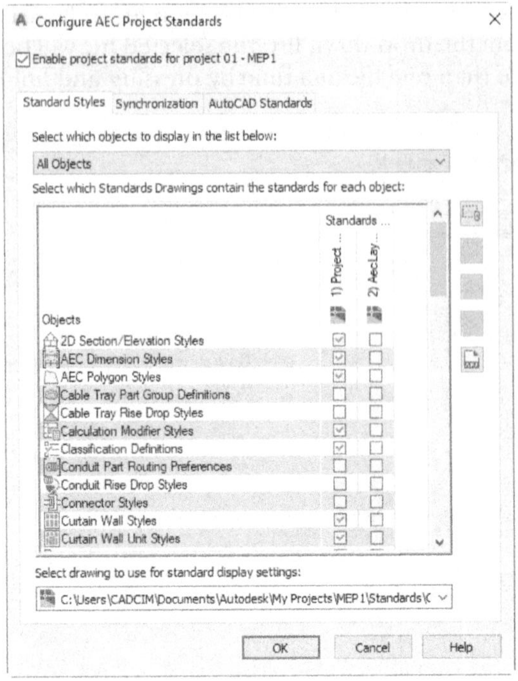

*Figure 2-11 The **Configure AEC Project Standards** dialog box*

Constructs Tab

The options in the **Constructs** tab are used to modify the drawing files available in the project. On choosing the **Constructs** tab, the **PROJECT NAVIGATOR** will be modified, as shown in Figure 2-12. Some of the options in this tab have already been discussed. The remaining options available in this tab are discussed next.

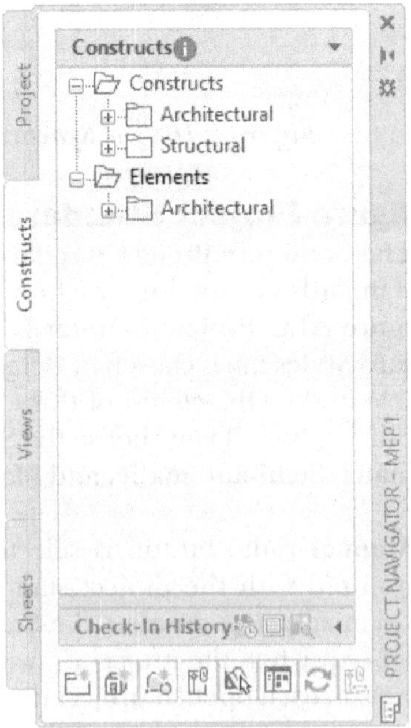

*Figure 2-12 The **PROJECT NAVIGATOR** with the **Constructs** tab chosen*

Constructs Area

The **Constructs** area has all the drawings of the current project arranged in a tree structure. In the tree, the drawing files are divided into two main categories: **Constructs** and **Elements**, which are further categorized according to their purpose/function. For example, the architectural drawings are stored in the Architectural category. You can open any of the drawings available in these folders by double-clicking on it.

Add Category

The **Add Category** tool is used to add a new category in the **PROJECT NAVIGATOR** to categorize the drawing files according to their usage. To do so, select a node from the **Constructs** rollout of the **PROJECT NAVIGATOR** and then choose the **Add Category** tool; the category will be added under the selected node.

Add Construct

The **Add Construct** tool is used to add a new construction in the project. When you choose this tool, the **Add Construct** dialog box will be displayed, as shown in Figure 2-13. You can add description about the new construct, change the name, edit category, and change the template using the fields available in the dialog box. In this dialog box, check boxes corresponding to each level of floor in the building are available in the **Assignments** area. Select the check boxes corresponding to the levels to which you want to add the construction. If you select multiple check boxes in this dialog box, then the objects created in the construction will span between the levels selected. Therefore, it is recommended to select only one check box. You can open the newly created construct by using the **Open in drawing editor** check box. When you select this check box and choose the **OK** button, the **Add Construct** dialog box will close and the newly created construction will open in AutoCAD MEP for editing.

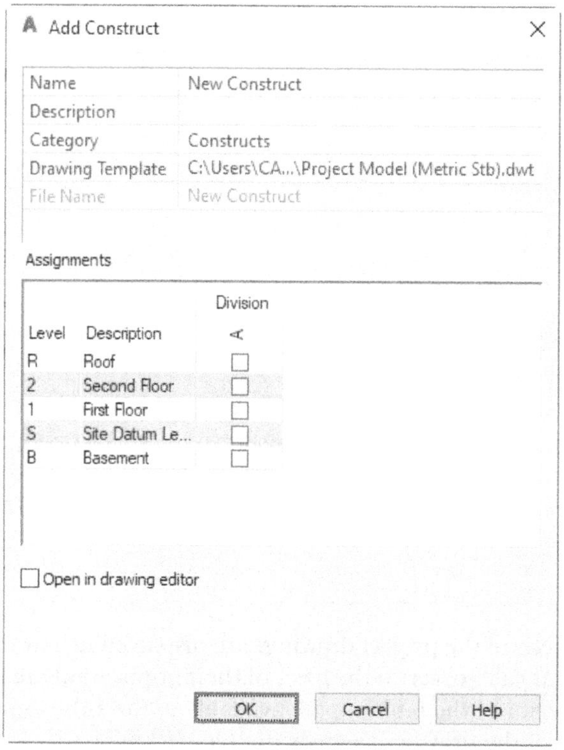

*Figure 2-13 The **Add Construct** dialog box*

Add Element

The **Add Element** tool is used to add a new element to the project. When you choose this tool, the **Add Element** dialog box will be displayed. Enter the required details in this dialog box and choose the **OK** button; a new element is added to the **Elements** category. You can edit the newly added element by selecting the **Open in drawing editor** check box.

Show External References

The **Show External References** tool is used to display external references for any drawing in the current project. When you select a drawing in the **PROJECT NAVIGATOR** and choose this button, the **External References** dialog box will be displayed. In the **Details** area of this dialog box, the information about the selected drawing is displayed, refer to Figure 2-14.

Views Tab

The options in the **Views** tab are used to add, modify, or delete a general, a detail, or a section view in the project. On choosing this tab, the **PROJECT NAVIGATOR** will be modified, refer to Figure 2-15. Some of the options in this tab have already been discussed. The remaining options in this tab are discussed next.

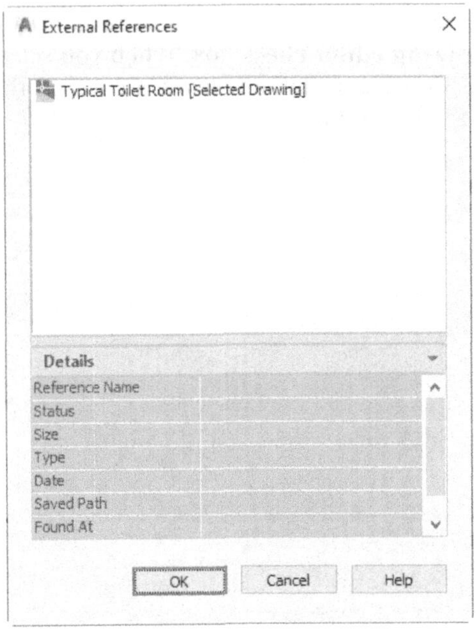

*Figure 2-14 The **External References** dialog box*

*Figure 2-15 The **PROJECT NAVIGATOR** with the **Views** tab chosen*

Views Area

In this area, different views of the project drawings are displayed in a tree structure. These views are divided into different categories on the basis of their application areas. For example, all the drawings related to interior of the building are available in the **Interiors** category in the **Views** tree. You can open any of the drawing views by double-clicking on it.

Add View

There are three types of views that can be added to the **View** area: General view, Section/Elevation view, and Detail view. The **Add View** tool is used to add a new view to the **View** area. On choosing the **Add View** tool, the **Add View** dialog box will be displayed, as shown in Figure 2-16.

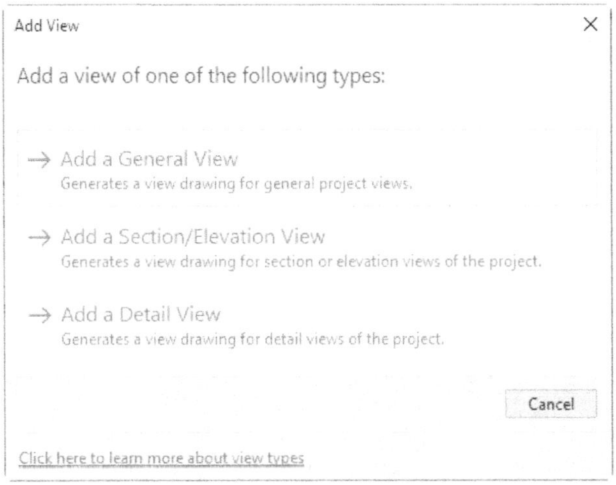

Figure 2-16 *The* ***Add View*** *dialog box*

There are three options available in this dialog box: **Add a General View**, **Add a Section/Elevation View**, and **Add a Detail View**. On choosing an option, the respective dialog box will be displayed. For example, when you choose the **Add a General View** option, the **Add General View** dialog box will be displayed, as shown in Figure 2-17.

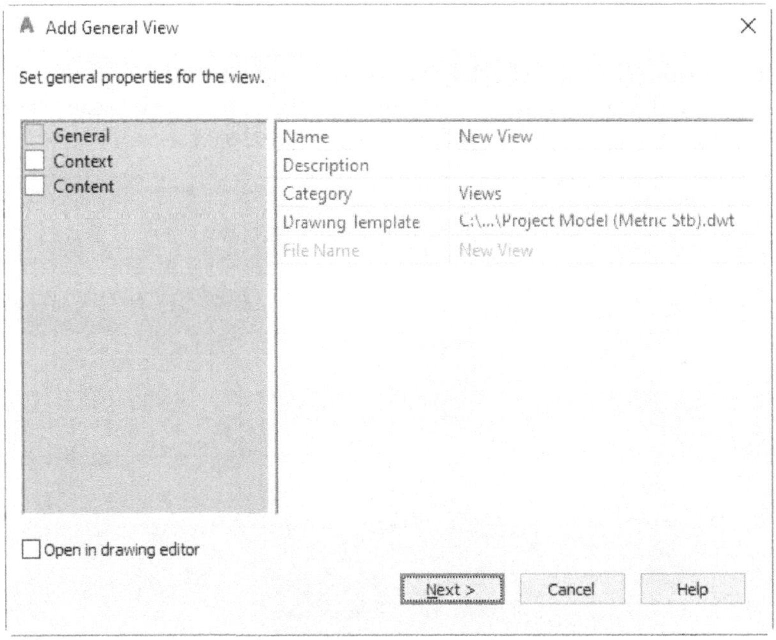

Figure 2-17 *The* ***Add General View*** *dialog box*

Using the options available in this dialog box, you can set the general properties of the view. Three pages are available in this dialog box: **General**, **Context**, and **Content**. The **General** page is displayed by default in this dialog box. In this page, you need to enter the general information about the view. After entering the general information, choose the **Next** button; the **Context** page will be displayed, refer to Figure 2-18.

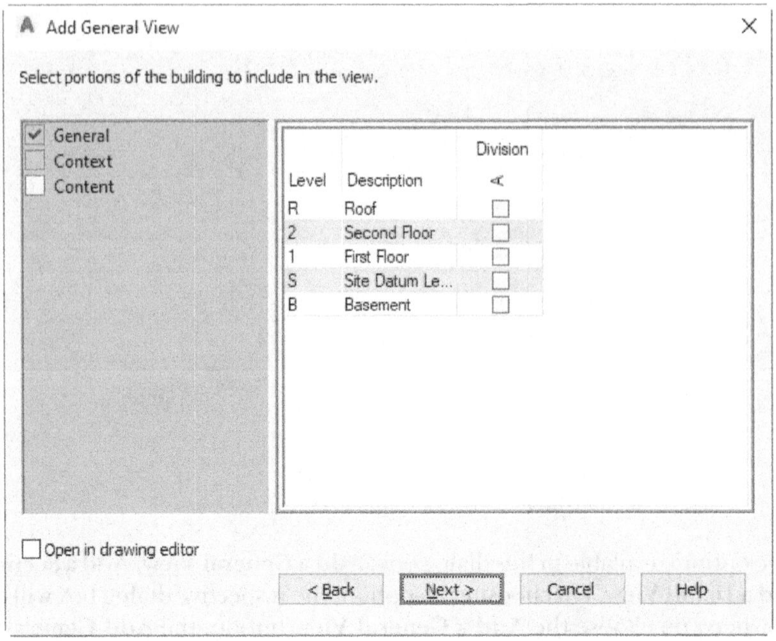

*Figure 2-18 The **Add General View** dialog box with the **Context** page displayed*

On this page, you can select the portions of the building that you want to include in the current view. To do so, you can select the check boxes corresponding to the portions of the building required to be included in the current view. After selecting the check boxes, choose the **Next** button; the **Content** page will be displayed, refer to Figure 2-19.

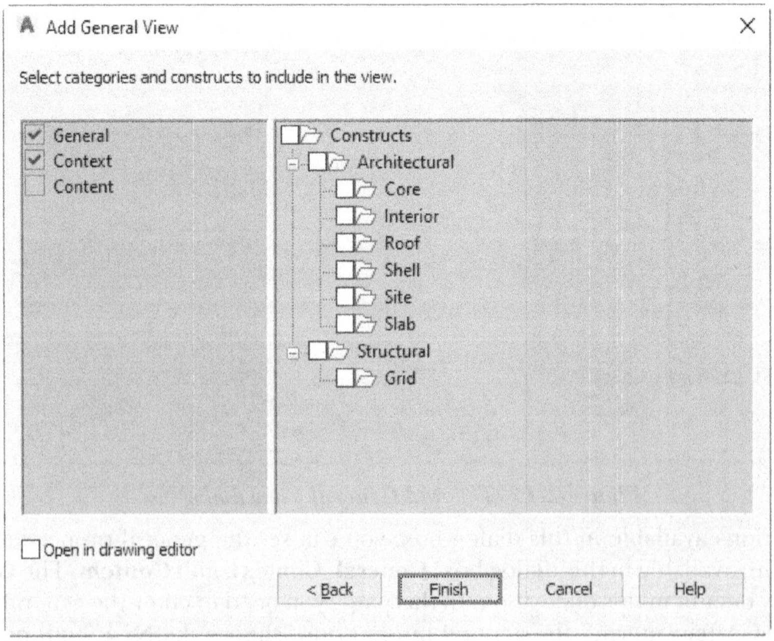

*Figure 2-19 The **Add General View** dialog box with the **Content** page displayed*

In this page, you can select the check boxes corresponding to those elements that you want to display in the current view. After specifying the required parameters, choose the **Finish** button to exit the dialog box. The newly created view will be displayed in the **Views** area of the **PROJECT NAVIGATOR**.

Regenerate View

The **Regenerate View** button is used to regenerate all the views so that you can get the updated version of the drawing views. This tool is also used to update the reference of the views.

Repath Xref

The **Repath Xref** tool is used to reconnect the external references whose names or locations have been changed.

Sheets Tab

On choosing this tab, the **PROJECT NAVIGATOR** will be modified, refer to Figure 2-20. The options in the **Sheets** tab are used to add, modify, or delete the sheets available in the project. Some of the options in this dialog box have already been discussed. The remaining options are discussed next.

***Figure 2-20** The **PROJECT NAVIGATOR** with the **Sheets** tab chosen*

Sheet Set View Area

All the drawing sheets available in the current project are displayed in the **Sheet Set View** area in a tree structure. You can open any of the drawing sheets by double-clicking on it.

Add Sheet

The **Add Sheet** tool is used to add a new sheet in the project. To do so, choose this tool; the **New Sheet** dialog box will be displayed, as shown in Figure 2-21. In this dialog box, you need to specify the sheet number, sheet title, and file name in their respective edit boxes. On specifying the sheet number and the sheet title in the edit boxes, a default file name is displayed in the **File name** edit box. You can change this file name or retain it. The folder path and the template path for the current sheet are displayed in the **Folder path** and **Sheet template** fields, respectively. These fields cannot be modified in this dialog box. After specifying the required parameters, choose the **OK** button from this dialog box; the newly created sheet will be added in the project and will be displayed at the bottom of the list in the **PROJECT NAVIGATOR**. You can edit this sheet by double-clicking on it.

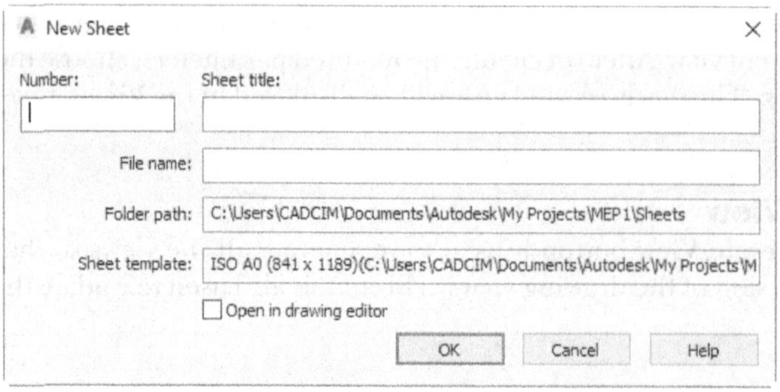

***Figure 2-21** The **New Sheet** dialog box*

Publish

The **Publish** tool is used to publish the complete sheet set in DWF file format. To publish a sheet set, choose the **Publish** tool from the **PROJECT NAVIGATOR**; the **AutoCAD MEP 2022** message box will be displayed, as shown in Figure 2-22. Choose the **OK** button from this message box; the **Specify DWF File** dialog box will be displayed, as shown in Figure 2-23. Choose the **Select** button from this dialog box; the **Publish Job Progress** message box will be displayed.

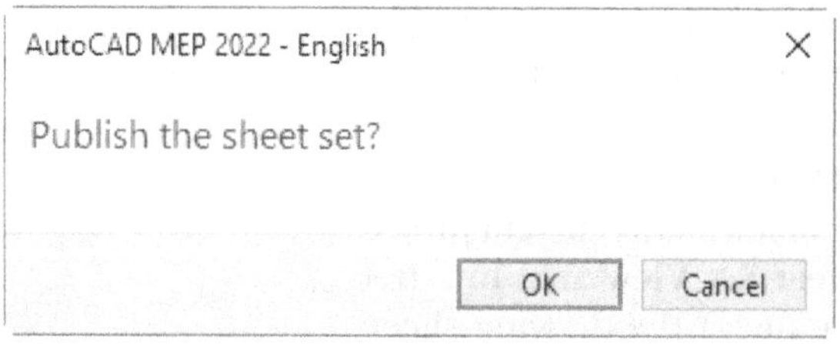

***Figure 2-22** The **AutoCAD MEP 2022** message box*

This message box shows the progress of plotting/publishing of the drawing sheets. When the process of publishing completes, the **Plot and Publish Job Complete** message will be displayed at the bottom right corner and the plot file will be created at the location specified in the **Specify DWF File** dialog box. To view the details of the plot file, click on the **Click to view plot and publish details** link in the message box displayed at the bottom right corner of the application window; the **Plot and Publish Details** dialog box will be displayed with the details of the plot file.

STYLES BROWSER

The **STYLES BROWSER** palette is used to import the styles and system definition to current drawing. This palette is invoked automatically when you start a new project. You can also invoke it manually by choosing **Home > Build > Tools** drop-down **> Styles Browser** or by typing **STYLESBROWSER** in the command prompt. You can also override the style or definition of an existing object in the drawing area by using this palette.

The options/drop-downs available in the **STYLES BROWSER** palette, refer to Figure 2-24, are discussed next.

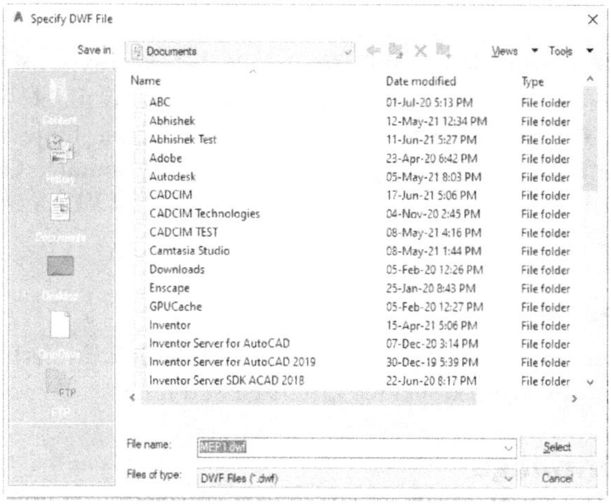

*Figure 2-23 The **Specify DWF File** dialog box*

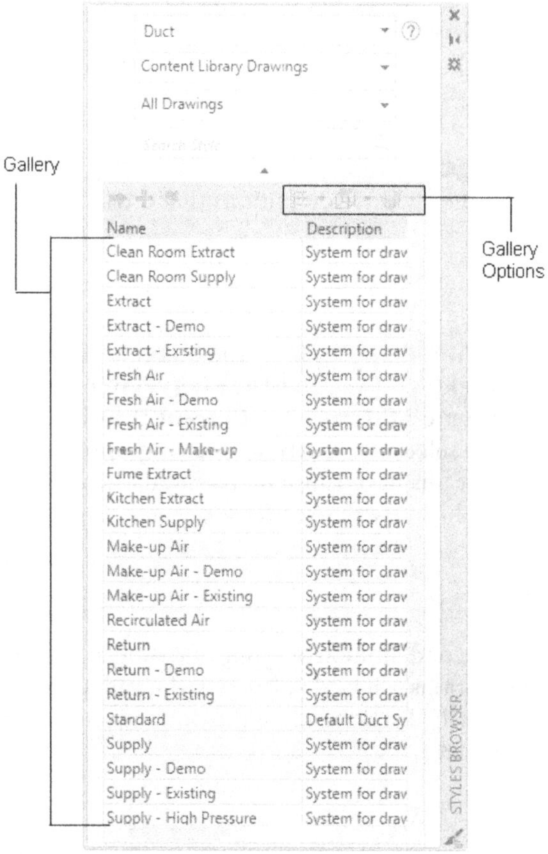

*Figure 2-24 The **STYLES BROWSER** palette*

Object Type

Using the options in this drop-down, you can select different type of objects for which you can choose different styles or definitions. The objects types available in this drop-down are **Architectural Objects**, **Documentation Objects**, **Multi-Purpose Objects**, **Electrical Objects**, **HVAC Objects**, **Piping Objects**, **Plumbing Objects**, and **Schematic Objects**. You can select an object from it, apply the desired style from the gallery of **STYLES BROWSER** palette and double-click on it to start the drawing with selected style.

Drawing Source

You can select the drawing source for different object styles or definitions by using this drop-down list. Options available in this drop-down list are discussed next.

Content Library Drawings

When this option is selected, all available styles or definitions for the selected object will be displayed in the gallery.

Project Standard Drawings

When this option is selected, the project standard styles or definitions for the selected object will be displayed in the gallery.

Currently Open Drawings

When this option is selected, the styles or definitions that are available for the currently open drawings will be displayed.

Drawing File

The options available in this drop-down list filter the object styles or definitions for an object depending upon the option selected from the **Drawing Source** drop-down list. The options available in this drop-down list are **All Drawings**, **Current Drawing**, and **All Without Current Drawing**. For example, if you select the **Current Drawing** option, only the object styles for currently open drawing will be displayed in gallery. Similarly, if you select the **All Without Current Drawing** option, all object styles excluding the style for currently open drawing will be displayed in gallery.

Search Style

You can search for an object style or definition by typing its name in the **Search Style** edit box. The search results of styles or definitions will be displayed in the gallery of the **STYLES BROWSER** palette. The results displayed will also depend on the options selected in the drop-down list in the **STYLES BROWSER** palette.

Import Styles

This button is used to directly start the drawing by importing the object styles or definitions which are not available in the current drawing. To import an object style or definition, select them from the gallery and then choose the **Import Styles** button; a green check mark will be displayed adjacent to selected style or definition. This green check mark indicates that the selected style will be imported to the current drawing.

Add object

This button is used to directly start the drawing without importing the object styles or definitions to the current drawing. To do so, select the object style from the gallery and choose the **Add object** button and start drawing in the drawing area. On choosing the desired style or definition, a green check mark will be displayed adjacent to selected style or definition. This green check mark indicates that the selected style is imported to the current drawing.

Apply style to selection

This button is used to override the object styles or definitions for the selected object from the drawing area. To override a style or definition, select the object from the drawing area. Next, select a different style or definition for that object from the gallery and choose the **Apply style to selection** button; the selected style or definition will override the existing style.

Gallery Options

These options are available at the right side of the **Apply style to selection** button, refer to Figure 2-24. By using these options, you can change the preview size, view direction, and background color of the styles available in the gallery.

SPACE

Space is an entity used in AutoCAD MEP to find out technical information about a specific section of an architectural drawing of a project. For example, if you want to make a specific section of a drawing as an office, then you need to assign corresponding space style to that section. The properties of that office such as area, airflow, height, equipment, and load are stored in the space style. To assign a space style to an area, first you need to create a space. The method to create a space is discussed next.

Creating Spaces

To create a space, choose the **Space** tool from the **Space** drop-down in the **Build** panel of the **Home** tab of the **Architecture** workspace. This tool is also available in the other workspaces. You can invoke this tool from any of the workspaces by entering the **SPACEADD** command at the command prompt. On invoking the **Space** tool, the **PROPERTIES** palette will also be displayed. By default, the **Rectangle** option is selected in the command prompt. Note that when you invoke the **Space** tool by entering the command at the command prompt, a default-sized space will be attached to the cursor automatically without selecting any option. You need to select **Create type** from the command prompt. On doing so, different options will be displayed. Select the **Insert** option; a space of default size will be attached to the cursor. You need to click in the drawing area to specify the position of the space. As soon as you specify the position of space, you will be prompted to specify the rotation value for the space. Specify the rotation value; the space will be positioned at the defined point. The command prompt using the **SPACEADD** command for creating the space is given next.

Start corner or [Name/STyle/Create type/Height]: **C**
Set create type [Insert/Polygon/Generate] <Rectangle>: **I**
Insertion point or [Name/STyle/Create type/Length/WIdth/Height/MOve/SIze/Drag point/MAtch]: *Enter the co-ordinates of the insertion point or click in the drawing area.*

Rotation or [Name/STyle/Create type/Length/WIdth/Height/MOve/SIze/Drag point/MAtch/Undo] <0>: *Enter the rotation angle of the space.*
Insertion point or [Name/STyle/Create type/Length/WIdth/Height/MOve/SIze/Drag point/MAtch/Undo]: *Press ENTER to exit the tool or select an option.*

The options available in the Command prompt are discussed next.

Name

The **Name** option is used to define a name for the space created by using the **SPACEADD** command. By default, the **Space** name is assigned to the newly created space.

STyle

The **STyle** option is used to change the style of the space. By default, the **Standard** style is selected. You can change the space style by using the **SPACESTYLE** command or by using the **STYLES BROWSER**. This command will be discussed later in this chapter.

Create type

The **Create type** option is used to change the type of space to be created. The space to be created can be a rectangle, a polygon, or it can be associative to the boundary objects. The command prompt after selecting the **Create type** option is given next.

Start corner or [Name/STyle/Create type/Height]: **C**
Set create type [Insert/Polygon/Generate] <Rectangle>:

According to the above command prompt, there are four options to create a space. These options are discussed next.

Insert: If you select the **Create type** command from the command prompt, a list of options will be displayed. Choose the **Insert** option or press I and then press the ENTER key; the space will be created according to the target dimensions specified. Figure 2-25 shows a space created by using the **Insert** option. The Command prompt for creating a space by using the **Insert** option is given next.

Insertion point or [Name/STyle/Create type/Length/WIdth/Height/MOve/SIze/Drag point/MAtch]: *Specify the insertion point.*
Rotation or [Name/STyle/Create type/Length/WIdth/Height/MOve/SIze/Drag point/MAtch/Undo] <default value>: *Specify the rotation value for the space, or press ENTER to accept the default values.*
Insertion point or [Name/STyle/Create type/Length/WIdth/Height/MOve/SIze/Drag point/MAtch/Undo]: *Press ENTER to exit the tool or select an option.*

*Figure 2-25 The space created by using the **Insert** option*

Polygon: By choosing this option, you can create a polygonal space by manually defining the segments of the polygon. You can create a polygon type space either by using the arcs or by using the lines. Figure 2-26 shows the polygon type space created by using the arcs and Figure 2-27 shows the polygon type space created by using the lines.

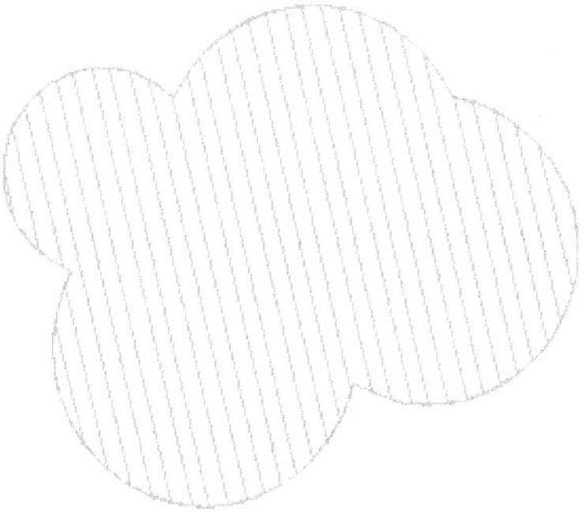

Figure 2-26 The polygon type space created by using arcs

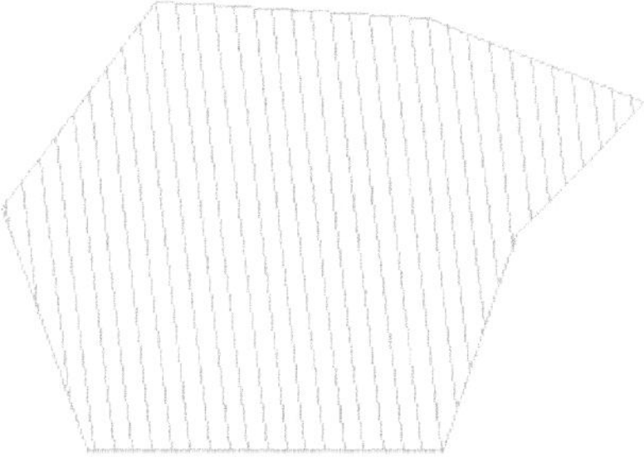

Figure 2-27 The polygon type space created by using lines

Generate: On choosing this option, the space created will be associative to the boundary objects. If you do not have any object with its space boundaries defined or with a valid space boundary, then the **Analyzing Potential Spaces** dialog box will be displayed, as shown in Figure 2-28. You can use all the visible objects to create a bounding space by choosing the **Use all visible objects to bound spaces** option from the dialog box. You can also select an object to create the bound space. To do so, choose the **Select objects that should bound spaces** option from the dialog box.

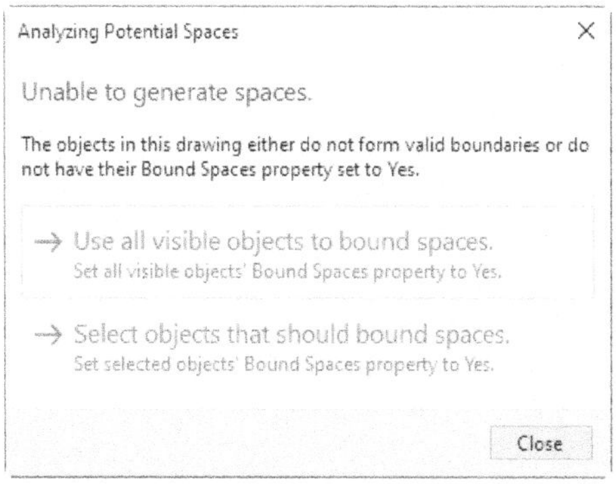

*Figure 2-28 The **Analyzing Potential Spaces** dialog box*

After selecting the **Create type** option from the command prompt, select the **Insert** option. The following options appear in the command bar.

Length

The **Length** option is used to change the length of the space to be created. By default, the target dimension of the space style is used as the length of the space. The Command prompt to change the length is given next.

Insertion point or [Name/STyle/Create type/Length/WIdth/Height/MOve/SIze/Drag point/MAtch]: **L**
Length <default value>: *Enter the desired value of length.*

WIdth

The **WIdth** option is used to change the width of the space to be created. By default, the target dimension of space style is used as the width of the space. The Command prompt to change the width is given next.

Insertion point or [Name/STyle/Create type/Length/WIdth/Height/MOve/SIze/Drag point/MAtch]: **WI**
Length <default value>: *Enter the desired value of width.*

Height

The **Height** option is used to change the height of the space to be created. By default, the target dimension of space style is used as the height of the space. The Command prompt to change the height is given next.

Insertion point or [Name/STyle/Create type/Length/WIdth/Height/MOve/SIze/Drag point/MAtch]: **H**
Length <default value>: *Enter the desired value of height.*

MOve

The **MOve** option is used to move the space created. This option is available only if you have chosen **Insert** from the **Create type** options. After moving the space, you can also rotate the space by a specified angle. The Command prompt to move the space is given next.

Insertion point or [Name/STyle/Create type/Length/WIdth/Height/MOve/SIze/Drag point/MAtch]: **MO**
Insertion point or [Name/STyle/Create type/Length/WIdth/Height/MOve/SIze/Drag point/MAtch]: *Specify the insertion point by clicking or entering the coordinates.*
Rotation or [Name/STyle/Create type/Length/WIdth/Height/MOve/SIze/Drag point/MAtch/Undo] <0>: *Specify the rotation angle by clicking or entering the value, and press ENTER.*

SIze

The **SIze** option is used to specify the size of the space to be created. This option is available only if you have selected **Insert** from the **Create type** option. The command prompt for specifying the size of the space is given next.

Insertion point or [Name/STyle/Create type/Length/WIdth/Height/MOve/SIze/Drag point/MAtch]: **SI**
Insertion point or [Name/STyle/Create type/Length/WIdth/Height/MOve/SIze/Drag point/MAtch]: *Specify the insertion point by clicking or entering the coordinates.*
New size or [Name/STyle/Create type/Length/WIdth/Height/MOve/SIze/Drag point/MAtch/Undo] <default value>: *Specify the insertion point by clicking or entering the dimensions.*
Rotation or [Name/STyle/Create type/Length/WIdth/Height/MOve/SIze/Drag point/MAtch/Undo] <0>: *Specify the rotation angle by clicking or entering the value.*

Drag point

The **Drag point** option is used to change the orientation of the space to be created. This option is available only if you have selected **Insert** from the **Create type** options. The command prompt to change the orientation of the space is given next.

Insertion point or [Name/STyle/Create type/Length/WIdth/Height/MOve/SIze/Drag point/MAtch]: **D**
Insertion point or [Name/STyle/Create type/Length/WIdth/Height/MOve/SIze/Drag point/MAtch]: *Enter **D** again if you want to change the orientation or press ENTER to exit.*

MAtch

The **MAtch** option is used to match the style of the newly created space with an existing space. This option is available only if you have selected **Insert** from the **Create type** options. The Command prompt to change the orientation of the space is given next.

Insertion point or [Name/STyle/Create type/Length/WIdth/Height/MOve/SIze/Drag point/MAtch]: **MA**

Select a space to match: *Select the space created earlier to use its properties for new space.*
Match [Style/Length/Width/Height] <All>: *Enter any of the options available in the prompt to match the properties. By default, the **All** option is selected, so all the properties of selected space are copied in the new space. Now, click in the drawing area to place it.*

Arc

This option is used to create an arc in a polygon type space. The **Arc** option is available only when **Polygon** is selected from the **Create type** options. The command prompt to create a polygon type space using an arc is discussed next.

Insertion point or [Name/STyle/Create type/Length/WIdth/Height/MOve/SIze/Drag point/MAtch]: **C**
Set create type [Rectangle/Polygon/Generate] <Insert>:**P**
Start point or [Name/STyle/Create type/Height/Arc]:**A**
Start point or [Name/STyle/Create type/Height/Line]: *Specify the first point of the arc.*
Second point or [Name/STyle/Create type/Height/Line/Undo]: *Specify the second point of the arc.*
Next point or [Name/STyle/Create type/Height/Line/Undo]: *Specify the third point to complete the arc.*
Second point or [Name/STyle/CReate type/Height/Line/Close/Ortho/Undo]: *Specify the next point.*
Next point or [Name/STyle/CReate type/Height/Line/Close/Ortho/Undo]: *Specify the next point or enter C to close the arc for creating the space.*

Line

This option is used to create a polygon by using the line. The **Line** option is available only when **Polygon** is selected from the **Create type** options and then **Arc** is chosen in the next prompt. The Command prompt to create a polygon type space using lines is discussed next.

Insertion point or [Name/STyle/Create type/Length/WIdth/Height/MOve/SIze/Drag point/MAtch]: **C**
Set create type [Rectangle/Polygon/Generate] <Insert>: **P**
Start point or [Name/STyle/Create type/Height/Arc]: **A**
Start point or [Name/STyle/Create type/Height/Line]: **L**
Start point or [Name/STyle/Create type/Height/Arc]: *Specify the start point of the polygon.*
Next point or [Name/STyle/Create type/Height/Arc/Undo]: *Specify the end point of the first line of the polygon.*
Next point or [Name/STyle/Create type/Height/Arc/Ortho/Undo]: *Specify the end point of the second line of the polygon.*
Next point or [Name/STyle/CReate type/Height/Arc/Close/Ortho/Undo]: *Specify the next point or enter C to close the polygon.*

Editing Spaces

You can perform various editing operations on the created spaces. For example, you can change the space style or divide a space. When you select a space from the drawing area, the **Space** contextual tab will be available in the **Ribbon**, refer to Figure 2-29. The options in this tab are discussed next.

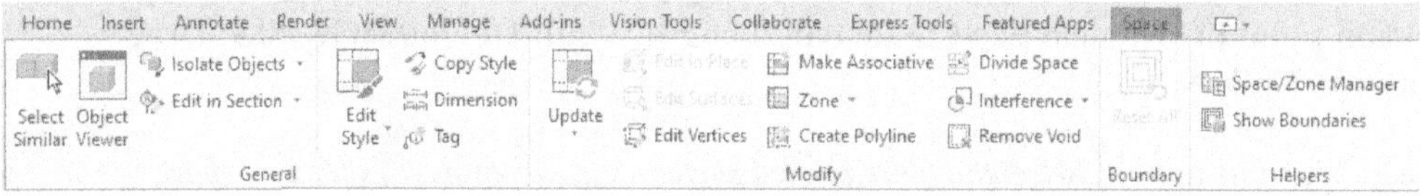

***Figure 2-29** The **Space** contextual tab*

Select Similar

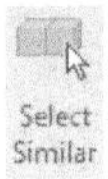

The **Select Similar** tool is used to select all those components from the drawing area which have the same style and layer as the selected object. The objects with the same style and properties but different layers will not be selected by this tool.

Object Viewer

The **Object Viewer** tool is used to display the selected object in a separate 3D preview window. When you choose this tool, the **Object Viewer** dialog will be displayed with selected object, as shown in Figure 2-30.

Various tools such as **Parallel**, **Perspective**, and **Zoom Window** are in the main toolbar of this dialog box. These tools are used to change the display of view.

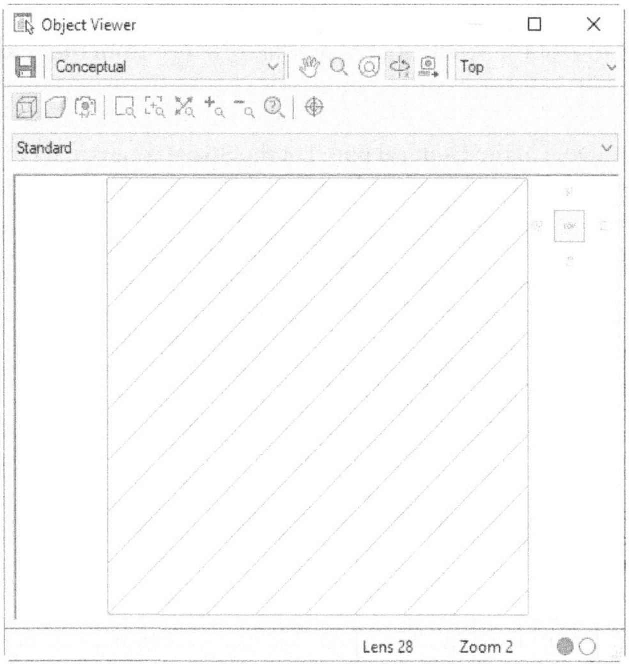

*Figure 2-30 The **Object Viewer** dialog box*

Isolate Objects Drop-down

This drop-down is available in the **General** panel of the **Space** contextual tab of the **Ribbon**. The tools in this drop-down are used to control the visibility of the objects. These tools are discussed next.

Isolate Objects

This tool is used to hide all the deselected objects from the drawing area.

Hide Objects

This tool is used to hide the selected objects from the drawing area.

End Isolation

This tool is used to display all the hidden objects.

Edit in Section

This drop-down is available in the **General** panel of the **Space** contextual tab in the **Ribbon**. The tools in this drop-down are used to edit the space created. These tools are discussed next.

Edit in Section

This tool is used to edit an object in a predefined section.

Edit in Elevation

This tool is used to edit the space at a certain elevation distance from the selected reference.

Edit in Plan

This tool is used to edit the space at certain plan distance from the selected reference.

Edit Style

This drop-down is available in the **General** panel of the **Space** contextual tab in the **Ribbon**. The tools in this drop-down are used to modify the style of the space. These tools are discussed next.

Edit Style

By using the options in this dialog box, you can change different properties of the selected space such as length and width of the space, target area, and various offset values. When you choose this tool, the **Space Style Properties - Standard** dialog box will be displayed, as shown in Figure 2-31. Using the options in the dialog box, you can modify the style of the selected space.

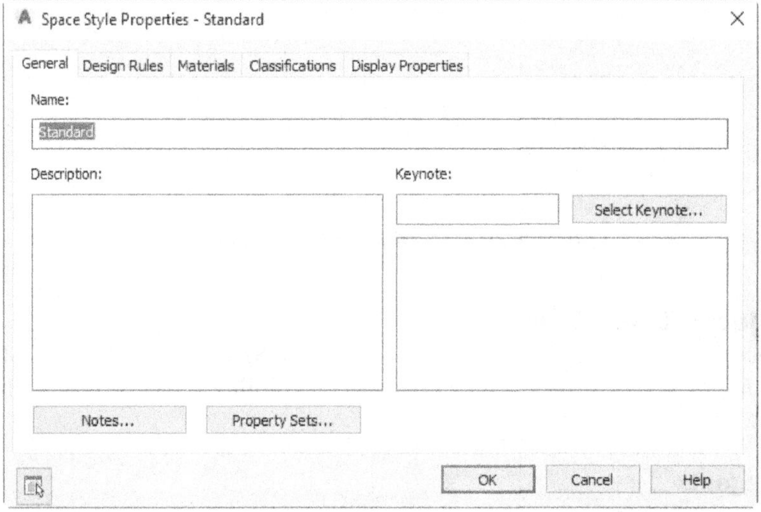

*Figure 2-31 The **Space Style Properties - Standard** dialog box*

Space Styles

When you choose this tool, the **Style Manager** dialog box will be displayed, as shown in Figure 2-32. The space styles available in the current drawing file are displayed in the left area of this dialog box under the **Space Styles** category. If you select any space style from this area, the options to change the space style will be displayed in the right area of the dialog box. These options are similar to the options displayed in the **Space Style Properties** dialog box.

Display Theme Styles

When you choose this tool, the **Style Manager** dialog box will be displayed, as shown in Figure 2-33. Various theme styles available in the drawing are displayed in the left area of this dialog box under the **Display Theme Styles** category. If you choose a theme style from this area, the options to change the properties of the selected theme are displayed in the right area. Using these options, you can change the properties of the selected theme such as title, text style, symbol, and so on.

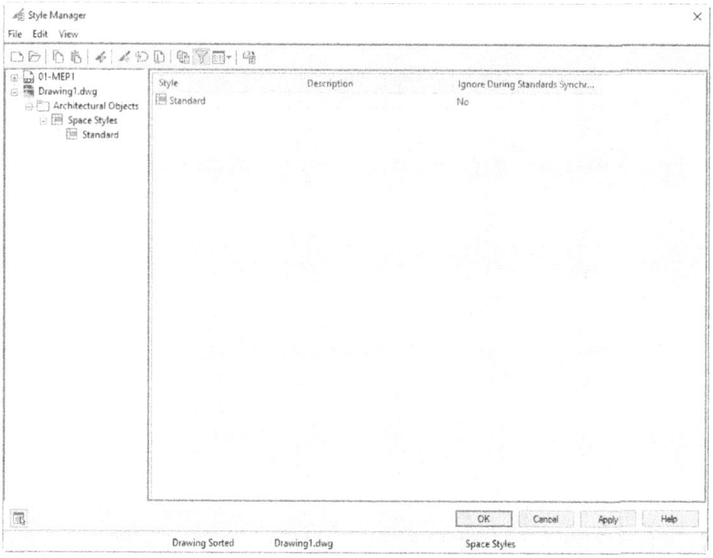

*Figure 2-32 The **Style Manager** dialog box*

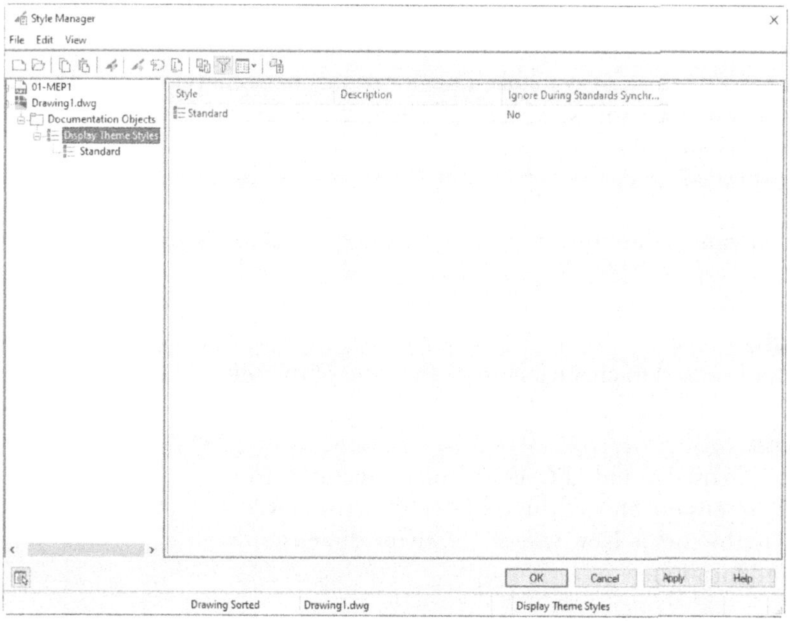

*Figure 2-33 The **Style Manager** dialog box with theme style options*

Zone Templates

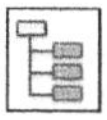

The **Zone Templates** tool is used to change the properties of the selected zone template such as its contents, modifiers, and name. To do so, choose the **Zone Templates** tool; the **Style Manager** dialog box will be displayed, as shown Figure 2-34.

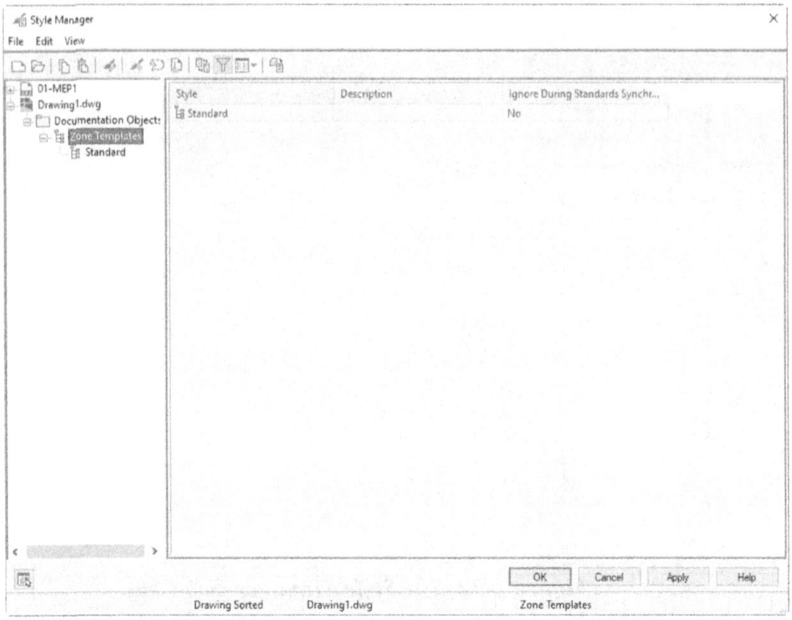

***Figure 2-34** The **Style Manager** dialog box with **Zone Templates** selected*

Various zone template styles available in the drawing are displayed in the left area of this dialog box under the **Zone Templates** category. When you choose a template style from the left area, the options to change the properties of the selected template style are displayed in the right area. Using these options, you can change the properties of the selected template style.

Similarly, you can change the zone style by using the **Zone Style** tool available in the same drop-down.

Copy Style

This tool is used to create a copy of the style of the selected object.

Dimension

This tool is used to add AEC dimension to an object. To add a dimension, choose this tool; the dimension will be attached to the cursor. Now, you can place the dimension at the desired location.

Tag

This tool is used to add a tag to the object. To add a tag, choose **Space > General > Tag** from the **Ribbon**; you will be prompted to select an object on which you want to add a tag. On selecting the object, the tag will be attached to the cursor. Now, place the tag at the desired location. When you click to place the tag, the **Edit Property Set Data** dialog box will be displayed, as shown in Figure 2-35.

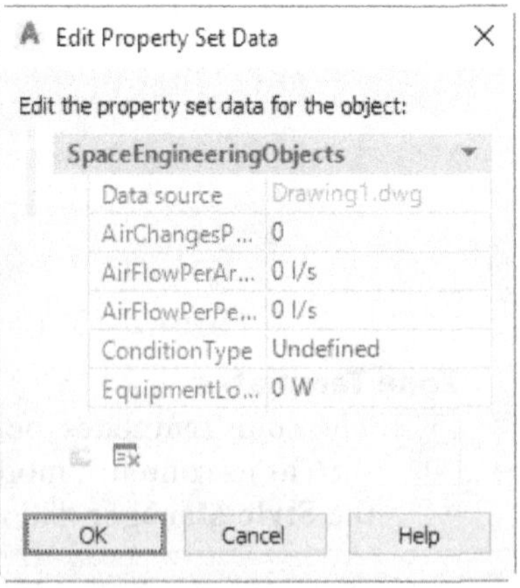

***Figure 2-35** The **Edit Property Set Data** dialog box*

Using the fields available in this dialog box, you can change the properties of the tag for the selected object.

Update

This drop-down is available in the **Modify** panel. The tools available in this drop-down are used to update spaces. There are two tools available in this drop-down: **Selected Space** and **All Associative Spaces**. The **Selected Space** tool is used to update the selected space. The **All Associative Spaces** tool is used to update all the spaces associated with the selected space.

Edit in Place

This tool is used to edit an extruded 3D space when you are in Isometric orientation. To do so, choose **Space > Modify > Edit in Place** from the **Ribbon**; the **Edit in Place: Space Body Modifier** contextual tab will be displayed and the selected space will be converted into a free form space. Now, using the vertices and control points available in the free form space, you can edit the shape and size of the space. When you hover the cursor over the center point of a selected face, a contextual menu with the editing options will be attached to the cursor, refer to Figure 2-36.

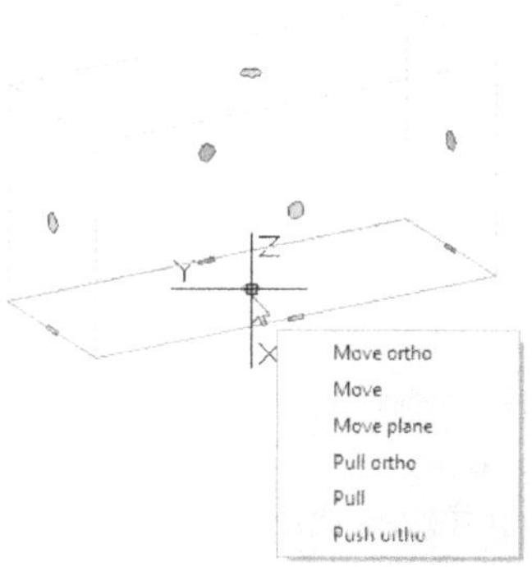

***Figure 2-36** The information box showing various editing options*

Edit Surfaces

This tool is used to edit only the faces of the space. Choose **Space > Modify > Edit Surfaces** from the **Ribbon**; the selected space will be converted into a free form space. Now, using the midpoints of edges, you can edit the faces of the selected space. Also, a plus icon will be displayed at the bottom face of the space, refer to Figure 2-37. Using this plus icon, you can add windows and doors to the selected space.

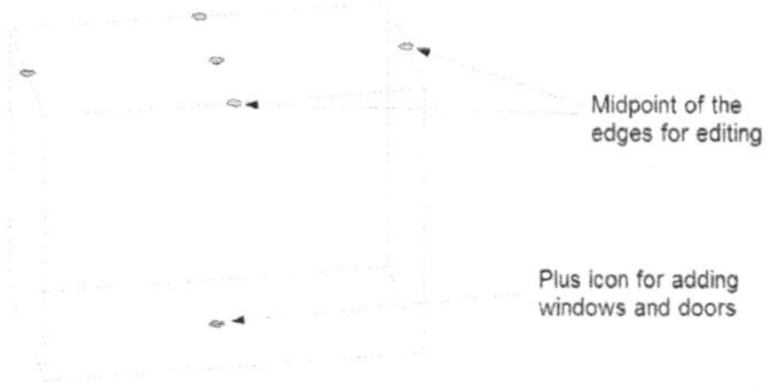

***Figure 2-37** Space with editing points*

Edit Vertices

This tool is used to add a vertex to the selected edge. To do so, choose **Space > Modify > Edit Vertices** from the **Ribbon**; the vertex will be attached to the cursor and you will be prompted to click in the drawing area to add the vertex, refer to Figure 2-38. Next, click in the drawing area; the vertex will be added to the corresponding edge. To remove the vertex, press and hold the CTRL or SHIFT key and then click on the vertex to be removed.

Note

To use the ***Edit in Place, Edit Surfaces,*** *and* ***Edit Vertices*** *tools, you need to switch to isometric view.*

Figure 2-38 *Space with its vertex attached to the cursor*

Make Associative

This tool is used to make the bounding objects associative to the selected space. To do so, choose **Space > Modify > Make Associative** from the **Ribbon**; the objects bounding the space will become associative with it. Note that for making space associative with the object, the boundary of the object must enclose the selected space.

Create Polyline

This tool is used to create a polyline around the selected space. To create a polyline around a selected space, choose **Space > Modify > Create Polyline** from the **Ribbon**; a polyline will be created around the selected space.

Divide Space

The **Divide Space** tool is available in the **Modify** panel of the **Space** tab. This tool is used to divide the selected space by using a line.

Interference

The tools available in this drop-down are used to add or remove an interference condition from a selected space.

Remove Void

The **Remove Void** tool is used to remove a selected void from non-associative space. To remove the voids, select the **Remove Void** tool; you will be promted to select the void. Now select the void to be removed and press ENTER.

Reset All

This option is used to revert all the changes taken place due to the grip editing of boundaries. To do so, choose **Space > Boundary > Reset All** from the **Ribbon** and select the spaces whose boundaries are to be reset to original state.

Space/Zone Manager

The **Space/Zone Manager** tool is available in the **Helpers** panel of the **Space** tab. This tool is used to change the properties of the selected space or zone.

Show Boundaries

The **Show Boundaries** tool is available in the **Helpers** panel of the **Space** tab. This tool is used to show only the objects in the drawing area that are currently defined as boundary objects. This tool is available only for associated spaces.

ZONE

A zone is a group of spaces which are used for a specific function; for example, a zone created for a specific temperature condition. You can create a zone or zones by using the **Zone** tool available in the **Space** drop-down of the **Build** panel in the **Home** tab of the **Ribbon**. When you choose this tool, a box will get attached to the cursor and you will be prompted to specify the location where the zone tag is to be inserted. Click in the drawing area; the zone will be created and name of the zone will be displayed along with the box. By default, **Zone** is displayed as the name for the created zone. You can change this name by using the **Name** field in the **PROPERTIES** palette. You can edit a zone by using the options available in the **Zone** contextual tab. The **Zone** contextual tab is displayed on selecting the zone. The options available in this tab have already been discussed this chapter.

WORKSPACES

A workspace is a combination of menus, toolbars, **Ribbon**, palettes, and control panels. It is used to represent a customized drawing environment based on the user requirement. In AutoCAD MEP, six default workspaces are available in the **Workspace Switching** flyout of the **Application Status Bar**, refer to Figure 2-39. These workspaces are **HVAC**, **Piping**, **Electrical**, **Plumbing**, **Schematic**, and **Architecture**.

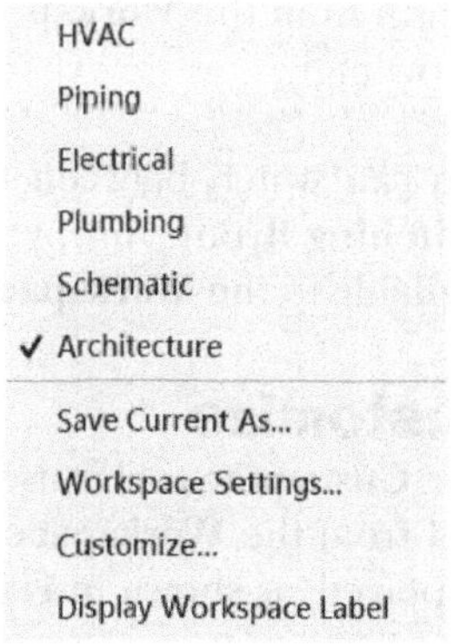

***Figure 2-39** The **Workspace Switching** flyout*

The options in the **Workspace Switching** flyout are discussed next.

HVAC

The tools in the **HVAC** workspace are used for designing heating, ventilation, and air conditioning system. Therefore, on invoking the **HVAC** workspace, the tools related to the HVAC design will be displayed.

Piping

The tools in the **Piping** workspace are used for routing and creating pipe lines in the building. To switch to this workspace, choose the **Piping** option from the **Workspace Switching** flyout;

the options in the **Ribbon** and **TOOL PALETTES** will change according to the workspace. Note that some options for plumbing are also available in this workspace.

Electrical

The tools in the **Electrical** workspace are used for creating electrical circuits, panels, devices, equipment, and cable trays. To switch to this workspace, choose the **Electrical** option from the **Workspace Switching** flyout; the options in the **Ribbon** and **TOOL PALETTES** will change according to the workspace.

Plumbing

Tools available in this workspace are similar to the tools in the **Piping** workspace. The tools in this workspace are used for routing and creating plumbing lines in the building. To switch to this workspace, choose the **Plumbing** option from the **Workspace Switching** flyout; the options in the **Ribbon** and **TOOL PALETTES** will change according to the workspace. Some of the options for piping are also available in this workspace. Plumbing is concerned with the drainage and other water related applications, whereas piping has a broad application area such as gas supply and petroleum lines.

Schematic

Schematics is the symbolic representation of an object. Using the **Schematic** workspace, you can represent MEP objects in the form of symbols. Some of the tools available in this workspace are schematic lines and schematic symbols.

Architecture

The tools in the **Architecture** workspace are used to create architectural objects such as walls, doors, windows, and stairs. An architectural layout creates foundation for other domains such as piping, HVAC, electrical, and so on. To switch to this workspace, choose the **Architecture** option from the **Workspace Switching** flyout; the **Ribbon** and **TOOL PALETTES** will change accordingly.

You can switch between the workspaces anytime during designing by using the **Workspace Switching** flyout. Also, you can customize any of the workspaces by using the **Customize** tool available in the **Workspace Switching** flyout. This tool is discussed next.

Customize

The **Customize** tool is used to customize the user interface of AutoCAD MEP. On invoking this tool from the **Workspace Switching** flyout, the **Customize User Interface** dialog box will be displayed, as shown in Figure 2-40. The areas in this dialog box are discussed next.

Customization in All Files

The options in this area are used to select the customization file to be used for modification. Also, you can change the properties of the selected item from this area. On selecting an option from this area, the related properties are displayed in the **Properties** area available on the right of this dialog box.

Command List

The options in this area are used to customize the selected command. On selecting a command from this area, the **Button Image** area is displayed at the top right corner of this dialog box. You can change the icon used for the selected button by using the options available in this area.

Properties

The options in this area are used to change the specifications of the selected option.

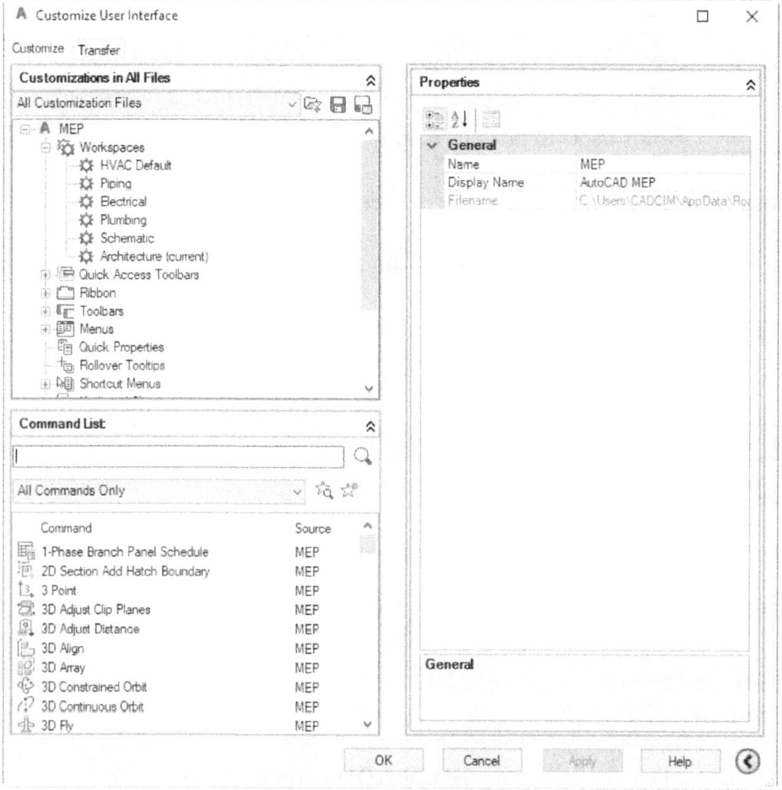

*Figure 2-40 The **Customize User Interface** dialog box*

Self-Evaluation Test

Answer the following questions and then compare them to those given at the end of this chapter:

1. In AutoCAD MEP, a level refers to a __________ .

2. The __________ tool is used to display the **Autodesk Content Browser** related to the current loaded project.

3. A zone is a division of __________ which is used for a specific function.

4. The __________ tool is used to add an instance of the selected object to the drawing.

5. The extension for AutoCAD MEP project files is *.apt*. (T/F)

6. You can create a category while changing the current directory of project files. (T/F)

7. The **PROJECT NAVIGATOR** is used to manage the drawing files of a project. (T/F)

Review Questions

Answer the following questions:

1. Schematics is the __________ representation of an object.

2. You can edit a 3D extruded space by using the __________ tool.

3. The **Synchronize Projects** tool is used to synchronize the current project with the previous project standards. (T/F)

4. You can create a space by using the **SPACEADD** command. (T/F)

5. The **Customize** tool is used to customize the user interface of AutoCAD MEP. (T/F)

Answers to Self-Evaluation Test

1. floor, **2. Content Browser**, **3.** space, **4. Add Selected**, **5.** F, **6.** T, **7.** T

Chapter 3

Working with Architecture Workspace

Learning Objectives

After completing this chapter, you will be able to:

- *Add columns and grids*
- *Add walls*
- *Add windows and doors*
- *Add stairs, railings, and stair tower*
- *Add roofs and slabs*
- *Create layouts*

INTRODUCTION

In AutoCAD MEP, before designing an MEP project, its architectural model is required. An architectural model consists of the following elements: Walls, Doors, Windows, Floors, Stairs, Roofs, Beams, and Columns. It also consists of standard views, sheets, and units. You can add these elements in the project using the Architecture workspace. In this chapter, you will learn to use various tools and options to add and create architectural elements using the Architecture workspace.

ARCHITECTURE WORKSPACE

To work with the architectural plans, you need to invoke the **Architecture** workspace. To do so, choose the **Architecture** option from the flyout displayed on choosing the **Workspace Switching** button available in the **Application Status Bar**; the tools required for performing architectural operations will be displayed in the **Ribbon**, refer to Figure 3-1.

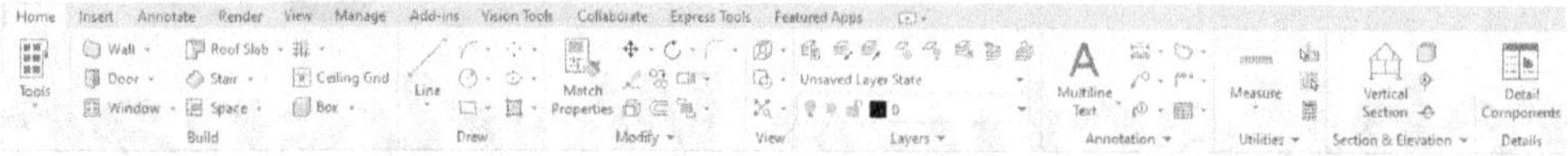

***Figure 3-1** The **Ribbon** displayed on invoking the **Architecture** workspace*

The procedure of creating various components of an architectural structure such as wall, door, window, grid, and so on are discussed next.

CREATING WALLS

Walls are the building blocks of a structure. The tools to create a wall are available in the **Wall** drop-down of the **Build** panel in the **Home** tab of the **Ribbon**, refer to Figure 3-2. There are three tools for creating walls: **Wall**, **Curtain Wall**, and **Curtain Wall Unit**. These tools are discussed next.

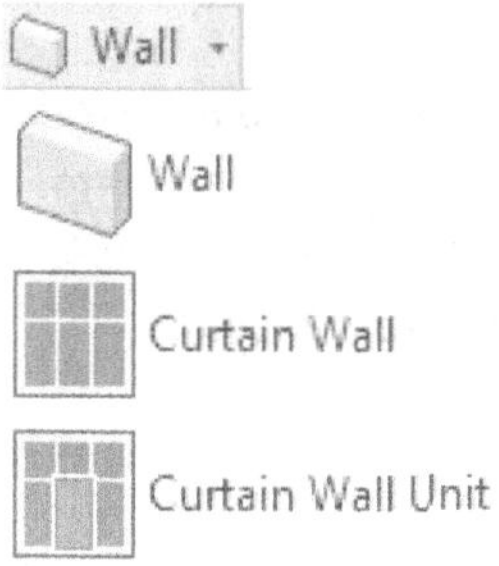

***Figure 3-2** The **Wall** drop-down*

Wall

This tool is used to create straight and curved walls. To create a wall, choose the **Wall** tool from the **Wall** drop-down available in the **Build** panel of the **Home** tab in the **Ribbon**; you will be prompted to specify the start point of the wall. Also, the **PROPERTIES** palette will be displayed. The prompt sequence for creating a wall by choosing the **Wall** tool is given next.

Start point or [STyle/Group/WIdth/Height/OFfset/Flip/Justify/Match/Arc/CReate type]: *Specify the start point of the wall segment.*
End point or [STyle/Group/WIdth/Height/OFfset/Flip/Justify/Match/Arc]: *Specify the end point of the current wall segment and starting point of the next wall segment.*
End point or [STyle/Group/WIdth/Height/OFfset/Flip/Justify/Match/Arc/Undo]: *Specify the end point of the current wall segment and starting point of the next wall segment.*
End point or [STyle/Group/WIdth/Height/OFfset/Flip/Justify/Match/Arc/Undo/Close/ORtho close]: *Specify the end point of the current wall segment and starting point of the next wall segment.*
End point or [STyle/Group/WIdth/Height/OFfset/Flip/Justify/Match/Arc/Undo/Close/ORtho close]: Enter

Note

*You can also invoke the tools given in the **Ribbon** by entering the corresponding command at the command prompt.*

There are various options available in the command prompt to change the properties of the wall. Alternatively, you can select these options from the shortcut menu displayed on right-clicking in the drawing area. These options are discussed next.

STyle

This option is used to change the style of the wall to be created. You can create a wall style by using the **Style Manager** which will be discussed later in this chapter. You can also choose a wall style from the **STYLES BROWSER** palette. By default, the **Standard** style is chosen as the wall style.

Group

This option is used to specify the cleanup group for the wall. These cleanup groups are created by using **Style Manager** which is discussed later. When two walls of the same group intersect each other, they get automatically cleaned up at the intersection point, refer to Figure 3-3. Figure 3-4 shows the intersecting walls of two different groups.

Figure 3-3 *The intersecting walls of same cleanup group*

Figure 3-4 *The intersecting walls of two different groups*

WIdth

This option is used to specify the width of a wall. The width specified using this option will be applicable for all the walls that are created after specifying this value. The prompt sequence for changing the width of a wall is given next.

Start point or [STyle/Group/WIdth/Height/OFfset/Flip/Justify/Match/Arc/CReate type]: **WI**
Width <240>: *Specify the desired width.* Enter
Start point or [STyle/Group/WIdth/Height/OFfset/Flip/Justify/Match/Arc/CReate type]: Enter

Height

This option is used to specify the height of the wall. The height specified using this option will be used for all the walls to be created afterwards. To view the height of wall, you need to switch to the isometric view. The prompt sequence for changing the height of wall is given next.

Start point or [STyle/Group/WIdth/Height/OFfset/Flip/Justify/Match/Arc/CReate type]: **H**
Height <3000>: *Specify the desired height.* Enter
Start point or [STyle/Group/WIdth/Height/OFfset/Flip/Justify/Match/Arc/CReate type]: Enter

OFfset

This option is used to set the distance of centerline of the wall from the wall edge. By default the value is set to zero. Figure 3-5 shows a wall being created using the **OFfset** option.

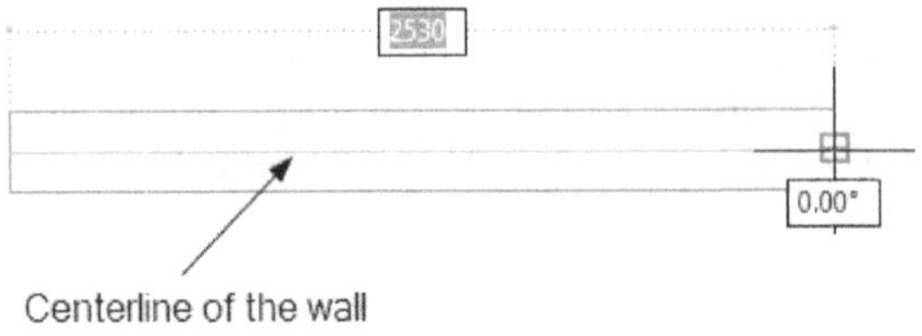

Figure 3-5 *The wall being created with centerline at its default position*

Flip

This option is used to flip the direction of wall creation to either side of the cursor. You can also press the CTRL key once to change the direction of the wall.

Note

*The **Flip** command works only if the **Justify** option selected from the **PROPERTIES** palette or from the command prompt is either **Left** or **Right**.*

Justify

This option is used to switch the cursor position to the right, center, and left points of the wall. When you choose this option, four options will be available at the command prompt to justify the wall. You can also switch between the justification option by pressing the SHIFT key. The command prompt for justifying the wall after choosing the **Wall** tool is given next.

Start point or [STyle/Group/WIdth/Height/OFfset/Flip/Justify/Match/Arc/CReate type]: **J**
Justification [Left/Center/Right/Baseline] <Baseline>: *Enter the justification option.*
Start point or [STyle/Group/WIdth/Height/OFfset/Flip/Justify/Match/Arc/CReate type]: Enter

The justification options available at the prompt are discussed next.

Left

The **Left** option is used to justify the wall on the left of the cursor.

Center

The **Center** option is used to justify the wall on the center of the cursor.

Right

The **Right** option is used to justify the wall on the right of the cursor.

Baseline

The **Baseline** option is used to justify the wall on the center of the baseline.

Match

This option is used to match the properties of the wall to be created with an existing wall. On choosing this option, you will be prompted to select a wall with which the properties will be matched. At the next prompt, enter the property names to be matched. The options available at this prompt are **Style**, **Group**, **Width**, **Height**, **Justify**, and **All**. After specifying the options, you will be prompted to specify the start point of the wall. Specify the start point and the end point of the wall to create a wall having properties similar to the one selected for matching.

Arc

This option is used to create a wall in the shape of an arc. The command prompt for creating an arc shaped wall is given next.

Command: **WALLADD** Enter
Start point or [STyle/Group/WIdth/Height/OFfset/Flip/Justify/Match/Arc/CReate type]: **A** Enter
Start point or [STyle/Group/WIdth/Height/OFfset/Flip/Justify/Match/Line/CReate type]: *Specify the Start point of the wall segment.*
Mid point or [STyle/Group/WIdth/Height/OFfset/Flip/Justify/Match/Line]: *Specify the Mid point of the wall segment.*
End point or [STyle/Group/WIdth/Height/OFfset/Flip/Justify/Match/Line]: *Specify the End point of the wall segment.*
Mid point or [STyle/Group/WIdth/Height/OFfset/Flip/Justify/Match/Line/Undo/Close]: *Specify the Mid point of the next wall segment or enter* ***Close*** *to close the wall segment.*
End point or [STyle/Group/WIdth/Height/OFfset/Flip/Justify/Match/Line/Undo/Close]: *Specify the Mid point of the next wall segment or enter* ***Close*** *to close the wall segment.*

Line

This option is used to create straight walls. This option will be available at the command prompt only when the **Arc** option is active. The command prompt for creating an arc shaped wall is already discussed.

Undo

This option is used to invert the changes made by the previous command. Using the **Undo** option, you can invert the changes made by the wall command in the current session.

Close

This option is used to create a wall that makes a closed boundary by joining the other walls. When you choose this option, a wall connecting the first and last walls is created.

ORtho close

This option is used to join two wall segments to make a closed boundary of walls. The command prompt for creating a wall using this option is given next.

Command: **WALLADD**
Start point or [STyle/Group/WIdth/Height/OFfset/Flip/Justify/Match/Arc/CReate type]: *Specify the Start point of the wall segment.*
End point or [STyle/Group/WIdth/Height/OFfset/Flip/Justify/Match/Arc]: *Specify the End point of the wall segment.*
End point or [STyle/Group/WIdth/Height/OFfset/Flip/Justify/Match/Arc/Undo]: *Specify the End point of the wall segment.*
End point or
[STyle/Group/WIdth/Height/OFfset/Flip/Justify/Match/Arc/Undo/Close/ORtho
close]: **ORtho** Enter
Point on wall in direction of close: *Click on the direction in which you want the two perpendicular connecting walls to meet; the joining walls will be created, refer to Figure 3-6 and Figure 3-7.*

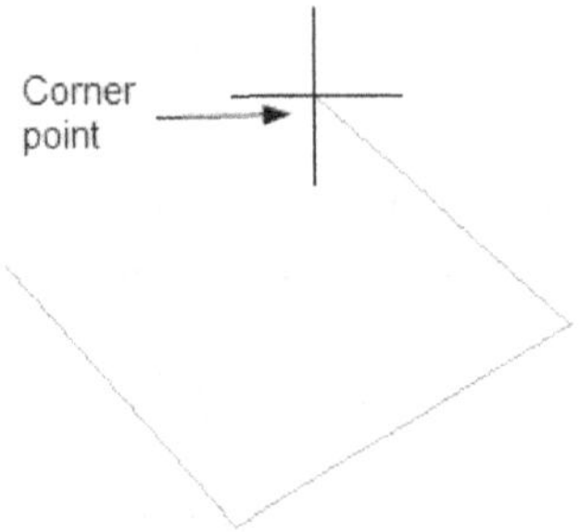

Figure 3-6 *The corner point to be selected for the perpendicular walls*

Figure 3-7 *The wall created after selecting the corner point using the **ORtho close** option*

You can also change the properties of a wall by using the **PROPERTIES** palette. Select the wall and then enter the **PR** command at the command prompt; the **PROPERTIES** palette will be displayed, as shown in Figure 3-8. Various rollouts available in this palette are discussed next.

BASIC Rollout

The options available in this rollout are used for basic settings. There are three options available in this rollout and they are discussed next.

General

The options in this rollout are used for specifying general settings such as the layer, description, style of the wall, and the segment type. When you click on the **Browse** area of this rollout, the **STYLES BROWSER** palette will be opened. Now you can change the wall style type directly by double-clicking on the required style in gallery of the **STYLES BROWSER** palette. The selected style will be added to the **Style** drop-down list and its preview will be displayed in the **Browse** area of the **PROPERTIES** palette. You can also change the cleanup properties for the intersecting walls by using the options in this rollout.

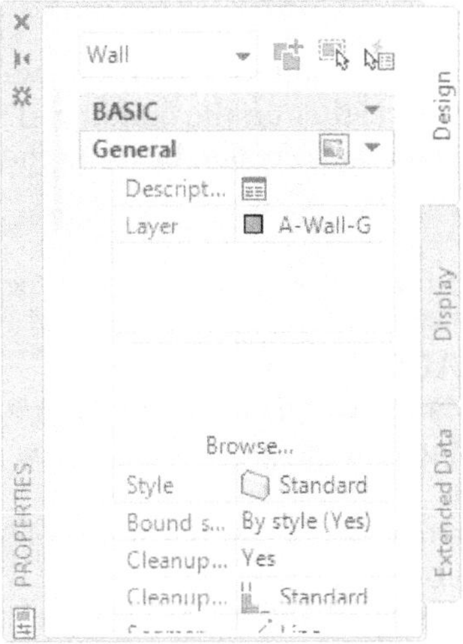

*Figure 3-8 The **PROPERTIES** palette displayed on selecting a wall*

Dimensions

The options in this rollout are used to specify the height, width, and length of the wall. You can also justify the wall by using the **Justify** option available in the rollout.

Location

The options available in this rollout are used to change the rotation angle and elevation of the wall. You can also change the insertion point and the orientation of wall by using the **Location** dialog box which is displayed on choosing the **Additional information** option available in this rollout.

ADVANCED Rollout

The options available in this rollout are used for changing the advanced settings such as cleanups, styles, overrides and worksheets. These options are discussed next.

Cleanups

The options in this rollout are used for changing the cleanup radius for intersecting walls. You can also apply overrides for the start and end cleanup radii by using the options available in this rollout.

Style Overrides

The options in this rollout are used to override the starting and ending endcap styles. You can also set the priority of a wall with respect to an intersecting wall by using the **Priority overrides** option available in this rollout.

Worksheets

The options in this rollout are used to modify the cross-section of the wall. You can also specify the start point and the end point of the modifiers by using the options in this rollout.

Curtain Wall

This tool is used to create a curtain wall. A curtain wall is a non-structural wall which is used to avoid the effect of weather on the building. This wall does not support any load in the building. The curtain walls created by using the **Curtain Wall** tool can be straight or curved.

The command prompt for creating a curtain wall is given next.

Command: **CURTAINWALLADD**
Start point or [STyle/Height/Match/Arc/CReate type]: *Specify the start point of the wall segment.*
End point or [STyle/Height/Match/Arc]: *Specify the end point of the current wall segment and start point of the next wall segment.*
End point or [STyle/Height/Match/Arc/Undo]: *Specify the end point of the current wall segment and start point of the next wall segment.*
End point or [STyle/Height/Match/Arc/Undo/Close/ORtho close]: *Specify the end point of the current wall segment and start point of the next wall segment or enter **Close** to create a closing wall.*

The options available in the command prompt have already been discussed. You can also use the **PROPERTIES** palette to change properties of the created wall. The options available in the **PROPERTIES** palette for a curtain wall are discussed next.

BASIC Rollout

The options available in this rollout are used for basic settings. Most of the options available in this rollout are same as discussed earlier. Rest of the options are discussed next.

Dimensions

The options in this rollout are used to change the base height, length, start miter, and end miter.

ADVANCED Rollout

The options available in this rollout are used to change the advanced settings. The options available in this rollout are already discussed.

Curtain Wall Unit

This tool is used to create a unit of curtain walls. On choosing this tool, you will be prompted to specify the start point of the wall. Specify the start point of the wall; you will be prompted to specify the end point of the wall. Specify the end point of the wall; you will be prompted to specify the height of the wall. On specifying the height, the **Curtain Wall Unit Styles** dialog box will be displayed, as shown in Figure 3-9.

*Figure 3-9 The **Curtain Wall Unit Styles** dialog box*

Select a curtain wall unit style from the dialog box and choose the **OK** button; the wall unit with the defined specifications will be created in the drawing area. Using the **PROPERTIES** palette, you can change the properties of a curtain wall unit. The options available for a curtain wall unit are the same as discussed earlier.

CREATING DOORS

Doors are movable structures used to close the entrance of a room or building. The tools to create a door are available in the **Door** drop-down of the **Build** panel in the **Home** tab of the **Ribbon**, refer to Figure 3-10. There are three tools available in the **Door** drop-down: **Door**, **Opening**, and **Door/Window Assembly**. These tools are discussed next.

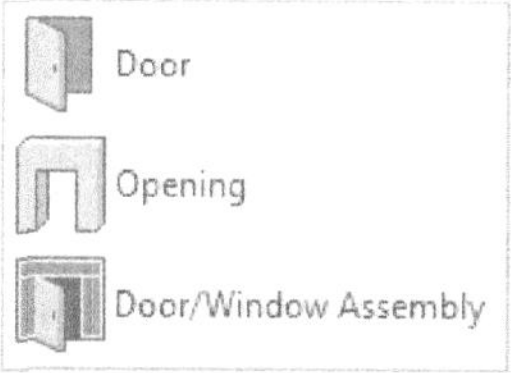

*Figure 3-10 The **Door** drop-down list*

Door

This tool is used to create doors of a specified profile. To create a door, choose the **Door** tool from the **Door** drop-down; the **PROPERTIES** palette will be displayed and you will be prompted to select a wall or a grid assembly. Figure 3-11 shows an expanded view of the **PROPERTIES** palette. You can press ENTER to create a door as an individual entity or you can attach the door with a wall. To attach a door to the wall, select an existing wall; you will be prompted to select an insertion point. Select the desired point on the wall; the door will be created with the parameters specified in the **PROPERTIES** palette. The options available in the **Dimensions** rollout of the palette are discussed next.

Standard sizes

This drop-down list displays various standard sizes available for the selected door style in the **General** rollout. You can change the door style in the same way as the wall style, which is already explained under the **Wall** tool. You can choose any of the standard sizes for the door or you can specify a custom size by using the options available in the **PROPERTIES** palette.

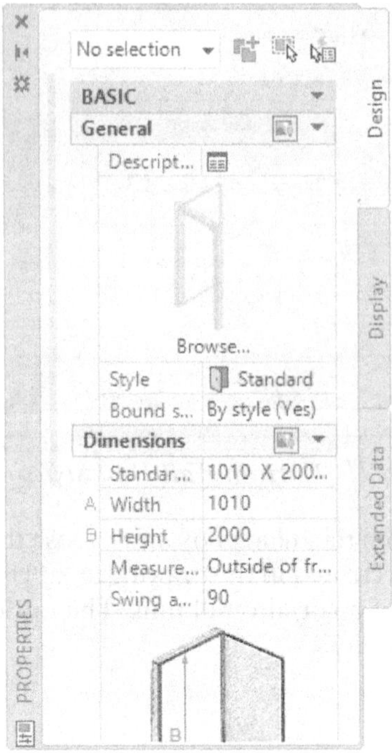

***Figure 3-11** The **PROPERTIES** palette displayed on choosing the **Door** tool*

Width

This option is used to specify the width of the door, refer to Figure 3-12. This option is used to customize a standard door. By default, the width specified by Door style is displayed in this field. You can change the value in this field as per your requirement.

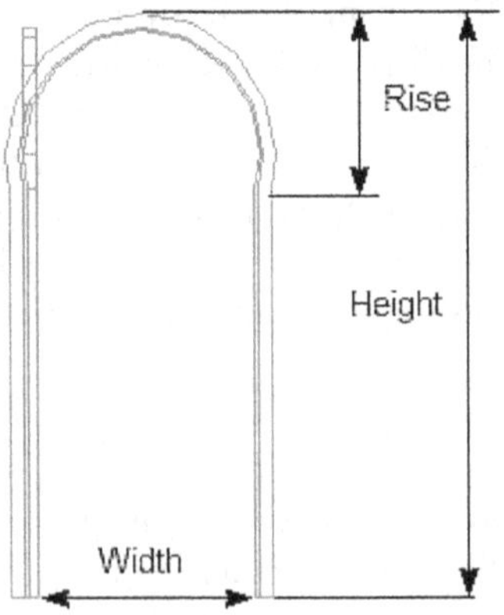

***Figure 3-12** Specifications of an arched door*

Height

This option is used to specify the height of the door, refer to Figure 3-12. This option is used to customize a standard door. By default, the height specified in the Door style is displayed in this field. You can change the value in this field as per your requirement.

Measure to

The options available in this drop-down list are used to specify whether the width and height of the door is measured from the inner edge of the frame or the outer edge of the frame.

Swing angle

This option is used to specify the maximum angle at which the door can be opened.

Opening percent

Using this edit box, you can specify the opening percentage of the door. This option will be available when you select the arch type or halfround type door.

You can change the parameters related to the location of a door by using the options available in the **Location** rollout. Some of the options available in the **Location** rollout of the palette are discussed next.

Vertical alignment

The options in this drop-down list will be available only if the selected door is anchored with wall. Using these options, you can specify whether the height of the door will be measured from the threshold of the door or from the head of the door.

Head height/Threshold height

The **Head height** or **Threshold height** option gets activated depending on the selection made in the **Vertical alignment** drop-down list. Using these options, you can specity the height of door from the head/threshold.

Rest of the options in the **PROPERTIES** palette have already been discussed.

Opening

This tool is used to create an opening of a specified profile in the wall. To create an opening, choose the **Opening** tool from the **Door** drop-down in the **Build** panel of the **Home** tab; you will be prompted to select a wall or press ENTER. Select the wall on which you want to create an opening; you will be prompted to specify the insertion point. Click to specify the insertion point on the wall; the opening will be created. On selecting an opening, the **PROPERTIES** palette will be displayed, as shown in Figure 3-13. Some of the options available in the **PROPERTIES** palette are used to change the properties of an opening. These options are discussed next.

Shape

This drop-down list is available in the **General** rollout of the **Basic** rollout. The options in this drop-down list are used to change the shape of the opening. There are 13 types of predefined shapes available in this drop-down list for creating an opening. You can customize the shape of an opening by selecting the **Custom** option from the drop-down list. On selecting the **Custom** option, the **Profile** drop-down list will be displayed below the **Shape** drop-down list. You can create the custom profiles of opening using this drop-down list.

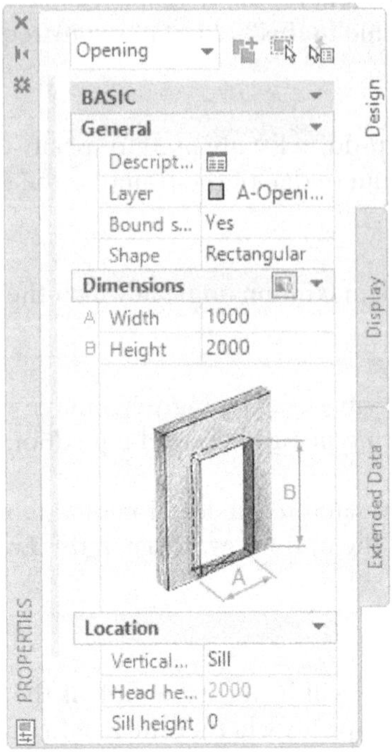

***Figure 3-13** The **PROPERTIES** palette displayed on selecting an opening*

Width

This option from the **Dimensions** rollout is used to specify the width of opening.

Height

This option from the **Dimensions** rollout is used to specify the height of opening.

Vertical alignment

This drop-down list is available in the **Location** rollout. The options in this drop-down list will be available only if the selected opening is anchored with wall. Using these options, you can specify whether the height of opening will be measured from the sill level of the opening or the head of the opening.

Door/Window Assembly

This tool is used to create a door or window assembly. The assembly contains required number of doors, windows, or both. To create a door/window assembly, choose the **Door/Window Assembly** tool from the **Door** drop-down available in the **Build** panel of the **Home** tab; you will be prompted to select a wall, a grid assembly, or press ENTER. Select a wall; you will be prompted to specify the insertion point for door/window assembly. Click at the desired point on the wall; an anchored door/window assembly will be created. The options available in the **PROPERTIES** palette for a door/window assembly are same as discussed earlier.

CREATING WINDOW

Windows are openings in a wall or door to facilitate the passage of light. If not closed, they also allow air and sound to pass through. In AutoCAD MEP, windows are created by using the tools available in the **Window** drop-down. This drop-down list is available in the **Build** panel of the **Home** tab. The tools available in this drop-down list are discussed next.

Window

This tool is used to create a standard window. To create a window, choose the **Window** tool from the **Window** drop-down available in the **Build** panel of the **Home** tab; you will be prompted to select a wall, a grid assembly, or press ENTER. Select a wall; you will be prompted to specify an insertion point. Click on the wall to specify the point; the window will be created at the specified point. Click on the wall to create more windows or press ENTER to exit the command. You can set the opening percentage of window by using the **Opening percent** field available in the **PROPERTIES** palette. The other options available in the **PROPERTIES** palette have already been discussed.

Corner Window

This tool is used to create a window at the point where two walls meet. This window can only be created on a cornered wall. To create a corner window, choose the **Corner Window** tool from the **Window** drop-down available in the **Build** panel; you will be prompted to select a wall. Select a wall which is connected to the other wall at the corner; you will be prompted to specify the insertion point. Click on the wall to place the window and press ENTER to exit the command.

There are three conditions for creating a corner window. They are:

1. The walls meeting to create a corner must be in "L" shape.
2. Wall joints must be created by linear walls only.
3. Wall will join with similar components of intersecting walls.

Various options available in the **Dimensions** rollout of the **PROPERTIES** palette are discussed next.

Standard sizes

The options in this drop-down list are used to change the standard size of the corner window. The pattern of size displayed in this drop-down list is given next.

(**Width 1** x **Width 2**) x **Height**

Here **Width 1** and **Width 2** represent width of the window in two different directions, and **Height** is the height of window from bottom edge to top edge.

Width
This field shows the total width of the window. This is the sum of the **Width 1** and **Width 2** values. You cannot change the value of this field.

Width 1
This edit box is used to change the value of the width in the first direction. When you click on this edit box, a button will be displayed on the right of the edit box. On choosing this button, you can specify the value of width by selecting two points in the drawing. The value changed in this edit box is also reflected in the **Width** field and the **Standard sizes** drop-down list.

Width 2
This edit box is used to change the value of width in the second direction. When you click on this edit box, a button will be displayed on the right of the edit box. On choosing this button, you can specify the value of width by selecting two points in the drawing. The value changed in this edit box is also reflected in the **Width** field and the **Standard sizes** drop-down list.

Height
This edit box is used to change the value of height of the window.

Measure to
The options available in this drop-down list are used to specify whether the value of width and height will be measured from inside of the frame or outside of the frame.

Opening measure
The options available in this drop-down list are used to specify the width measurement pattern. There are three options available in this drop-down list: **Inside of opening**, **Center of opening**, and **Outside of opening**.

Inside of opening
When you choose this option, the width of the first side of corner window is measured from the inner edge of the other side of the corner window.

Center of opening
When you choose this option, the width of first side of corner window is measured from the center of the edge of other side of the corner window.

Outside of opening
When you choose this option, the width of the first side of corner window is measured from the outer edge of the other side of the corner window.

Opening percent
Using this edit box, you can specify the opening percentage of the window.

CREATING ROOFS AND SLABS
The tools to create roofs and slabs are available in the **Roof Slab** drop-down, refer to Figure 3-14. The tools in this drop-down are **Roof Slab**, **Roof**, and **Slab**. These tools are discussed next.

Roof Slab

This tool is used to create a segment of roof. This segment does not have a direct connection with other entities. To create a roof slab, choose the **Roof Slab** tool from the **Roof Slab** drop-down available in the **Build** panel of the **Home** tab; you will be prompted to specify the start point of the roof slab. The command sequence for creating a roof slab is given next.

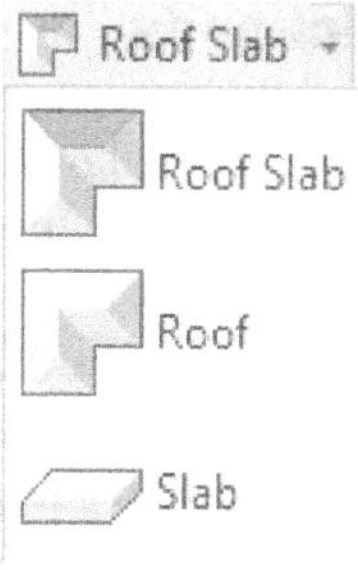

***Figure 3-14** The **Roof Slab** drop-down*

Specify start point or [STyle/MOde/Height/Thickness/SLope/OVerhang/Justify/MAtch/CReate type]: *Specify the Start point of the roof slab.*
Specify next point or [STyle/MOde/Height/Thickness/SLope/OVerhang/Justify/MAtch]: *Specify the next point of the roof slab.*
Specify next point or [STyle/MOde/Height/Thickness/SLope/OVerhang/Justify/MAtch/Undo/Ortho close]: *Specify the next point of the roof slab.*
Specify next point or [STyle/MOde/Height/Thickness/SLope/OVerhang/Justify/MAtch/Undo/Ortho close/Close]: *Specify the next point of the roof slab or enter **Close** to close the boundary.*
Specify next point or [STyle/MOde/Height/Thickness/SLope/OVerhang/Justify/MAtch/Undo/Ortho close/Close]: *Specify the next point of the roof slab or enter **Close** to close the boundary.*

After selecting a roof slab, the **PROPERTIES** palette will be displayed, as shown in Figure 3-15. Various options available in the **Dimensions** rollout of this palette are discussed next.

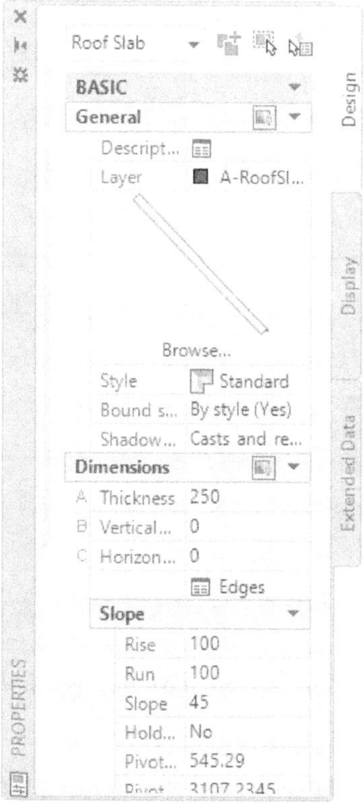

***Figure 3-15** The **PROPERTIES** palette displayed on selecting a roof slab*

Thickness

This edit box is used to specify the thickness of the roof slab. When you click on this edit box, a button is displayed on its right. On choosing this button, you can specify the value of thickness by selecting two points.

Vertical offset

This edit box is used to specify the offset value of the slab from the original position in vertical direction. You can also specify the offset value by selecting two points.

Horizontal offset

This edit box is used to specify the offset value of slab from the original position in the horizontal direction. You can also specify the offset value by selecting two points.

Edges

This button is available below the **Horizontal offset** edit box. When you choose this button, the **Roof Slab Edges** dialog box will be displayed, as shown in Figure 3-16. Also, a preview of the changes made in the edges are displayed in the Preview area on the right in the dialog box. You can change the parameters such as overhang value, edge style, and edge cut type by using the table displayed on the left in the dialog box. Various columns available in this table are discussed next.

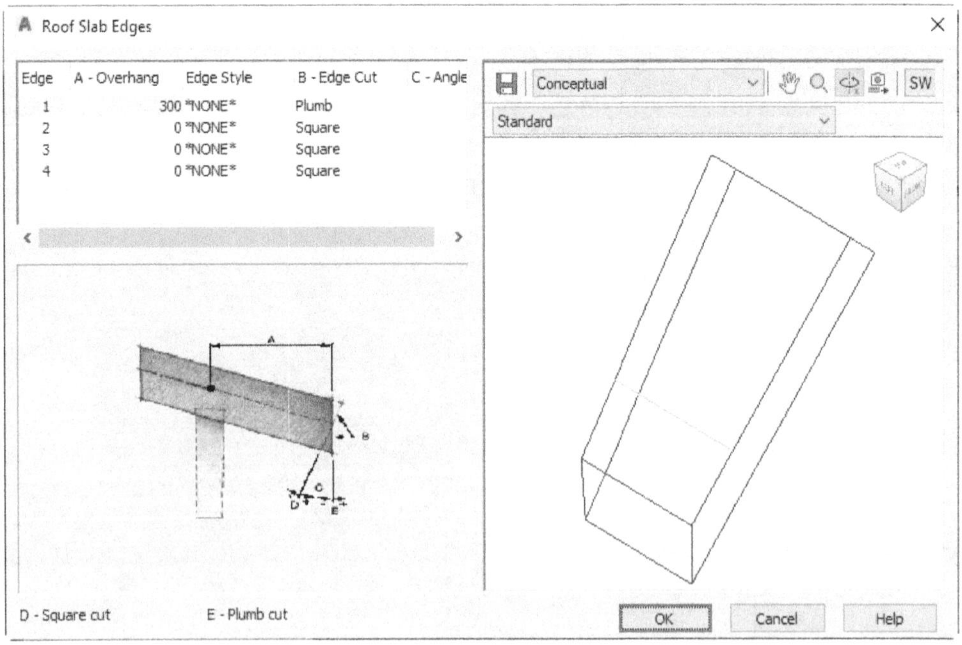

*Figure 3-16 The **Roof Slab Edges** dialog box*

Edge

All edges of the selected roof slab are displayed in this column by their sequence numbers. When you select any sequence number, its respective edge is highlighted in the **Preview** area.

A-Overhang

Using the fields available in this column, you can change the overhang value. Overhang is the area of slab which is out of the support boundary.

Edge Style

By default, the values in this column are set to **NONE**. You can choose any predefined style for slab edges. You can define an **Edge Style** by using the **Roof Slab Edge Style** node in the **Style Manager**. The options for a slab edge vary depending upon roof slab style chosen for it.

B-Edge Cut

In this column, edge cut methods are displayed. There are two options for edge cut: **Square** and **Plumb**. The **Square** option is used to cut the edge perpendicular to the roof slab whereas the **Plumb** option is used to cut the edge perpendicular to the ground.

C-Angle

In this column, you can specify an angle for the edge. If you enter a positive value, the bottom edge will extend. If a negative value is entered, then the top edge will extend.

Rise

This edit box is used to specify the value of rise for a roof slab. Rise is the slope difference between the start and end edges of the slope of roof slab along vertical direction. You can also specify the value of rise by selecting two points. To do so, choose the button displayed at the right of this edit box; you will be prompted to select points. Select the points to specify the rise value.

Run

This field is used to display the value of run for a roof slab. Run is the horizontal span of the slope. The value in this field is generally fixed.

Slope

This edit box is used to specify the value of slope for a roof slab. The value of slope is specified in degrees. Any change in the value specified in the **Rise** or **Run** edit box is reflected in the **Slope** edit box.

Hold fascia elevation

The options in this drop-down list are used to manage the fascia of roof. There are three options available in this drop-down list: **No**, **By adjusting overhang**, and **By adjusting baseline height**.

No

When you choose this option, the alignment of fascia is ignored.

By adjusting overhang

When you choose this option, the fascia is aligned with the roof slab by adjusting the overhang.

By adjusting baseline height

When you choose this option, the fascia is aligned with the roof slab by adjusting the baseline height.

Pivot Point X

This edit box is used to specify the position of pivot point of roof slab in X direction. You can calculate the value of position in X direction by using the **QuickCalc** button available on the right of the edit box. You can also use the **Pick Point** tool to specify the pivot point location which is discussed in the next section.

Pivot Point Y

This edit box is used to specify the position of pivot point of roof slab in Y direction. Alternatively, you can specify the position of point by using the **Pick Point** tool available on the right of the edit box. You can also use the **QuickCalc** button as discussed earlier.

Pivot Point Z

This edit box is used to specify the position of pivot point of roof slab in Z direction. Alternatively, you can specify the position of point by using the **Pick Point** tool available on the right of the edit box. You can also use the **QuickCalc** button as discussed earlier.

Roof

This tool is used to create a multi-peaked roof. To create a multi-peaked roof, invoke the **Roof** tool from the **Roof Slab** drop-down available in the **Build** panel of the **Home** tab; you will be prompted to specify the roof points. Specify the roof points; the roof will be created with the specified roof points. The **PROPERTIES** palette displayed on selecting a roof is shown in Figure 3-17.

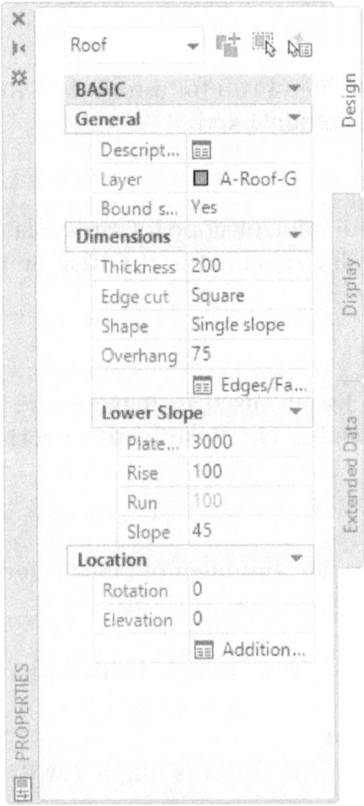

*Figure 3-17 The **PROPERTIES** palette displayed on selecting a roof*

The options available in the **General**, **Dimensions**, and **Location** rollouts are same as discussed earlier. The options available in the **Lower Slope** rollout are discussed next.

Plate height

This edit box is used to specify the height of the base point of roof from the ground. You can also specify the plate height by using two points. In this case, you need to choose the **Pick Point** button available on the right of the edit box.

Rise

This edit box is used to specify the value of rise for a roof. Rise is the difference in start and end edges of the slope of roof along vertical direction. You can also specify the value of rise by selecting two points. To do so, choose the button displayed at the right of this edit box; you will be prompted to select points. Select any two points on the screen to specify the rise value.

Run

This field is used to display the value of run for a roof. Run is the horizontal span of the slope.

Slope

This edit box is used to specify the value of slope for a roof. The value of slope is specified in degrees. Any change in the value specified in the **Rise** edit box or **Run** edit box is reflected in the **Slope** edit box.

You can also specify the plate height, rise, and slope value for the upper slope of the roof. To specify the values for the upper slope, you need to select the **Double slope** option from the **Shape** drop-down list in the **Dimensions** rollout. On doing so, the **Upper Slope** rollout will be displayed. The options in this rollout are similar to the options discussed for **Lower Slope** rollout.

Slab

This tool is used to create flat roofs or floors. The roofs or floors created by using this tool are in the form of a segment. This segment does not have a direct connection with other entities. To create a slab, choose the **Slab** tool from the **Roof Slab** drop-down available in the **Build** panel of the **Home** tab; you will be prompted to specify the start point of the slab. The command prompt for creating a slab is given next.

Specify start point or [STyle/MOde/Height/Thickness/SLope/OVerhang/Justify/MAtch/CReate type]: *Specify the Start point of the slab.*
Specify next point or [STyle/MOde/Height/Thickness/SLope/OVerhang/Justify/MAtch]: *Specify the next point of the slab.*
Specify next point or [STyle/MOde/Height/Thickness/SLope/OVerhang/Justify/MAtch/Undo/Ortho close]: *Specify the next point of the slab.*
Specify next point or [STyle/MOde/Height/Thickness/SLope/OVerhang/Justify/MAtch/Undo/Ortho close/Close]: *Specify the next point of the slab.*
Specify next point or [STyle/MOde/Height/Thickness/SLope/OVerhang/Justify/MAtch/Undo/Ortho close/Close]: **C**
Specify start point or [STyle/MOde/Height/Thickness/SLope/OVerhang/Justify/MAtch/Undo]: 

After selecting a slab, the **PROPERTIES** palette is displayed, as shown in Figure 3-18. The options in the palette have already been discussed.

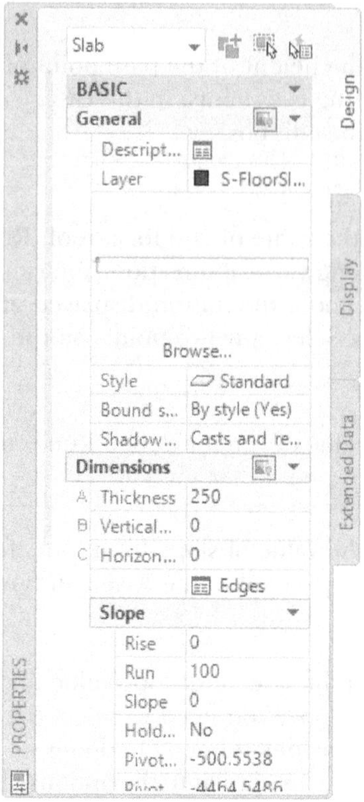

Figure 3-18 *The* ***PROPERTIES*** *palette displayed on selecting a slab*

CREATING STAIRS AND RAILINGS

Stairs are the structures that connect one floor to another, thus enabling easy movement. Railings are the structures which act as support or barrier on the stairs. The options to create stairs and railings are available in the **Stair** drop-down. These options are discussed next.

Stair

This tool is used to create stairs. There are various shapes of stairs such as straight, multi-landing, spiral, and U-shaped. While going on a curved path, the stairs can have curved landing. In such cases, the edges of stairs can also be curved. To create a stair, choose the **Stair** tool from the **Stair** drop-down available in the **Build** panel of the **Home** tab; you will be prompted to specify the start point of the stairs. Specify a point as the flight start point of the stairs; you will be prompted to specify the end point of the stairs. Specify a point as the flight end point to complete the stairs. While specifying the end point, you can specify the landing at desired position but this position must be within the specified limits. The limit of a stair is counted by the option chosen using the **Calculation rules** edit box. The **PROPERTIES** palette displayed after choosing the **Stair** tool is shown in Figure 3-19. Some important options available in the **General** rollout of the palette on choosing this tool are discussed next.

Shape

The options available in this drop-down list are used to specify the shape of the stairs. There are four options available in this drop-down list; **U-shaped**, **Multi-landing**, **Spiral**, and **Straight**. These options are discussed next.

U-shaped

Using this option, you can create U-shaped stairs, refer to Figure 3-20. In this type of stairs, the two rows of stairs run parallel and meet at the end points by a half-landing.

Multi-landing

Using this option, you can create stairs having multiple landings, refer to Figure 3-20. You can provide quarter landing or half landing. This landing can be flat or can have a turn.

Spiral

Using this option, you can create stairs in the shape of spiral, refer to Figure 3-20. In this type of stairs, the steps of stair revolve about a common center point from bottom to top. Spiral stairs can be in clockwise direction or counter-clockwise direction.

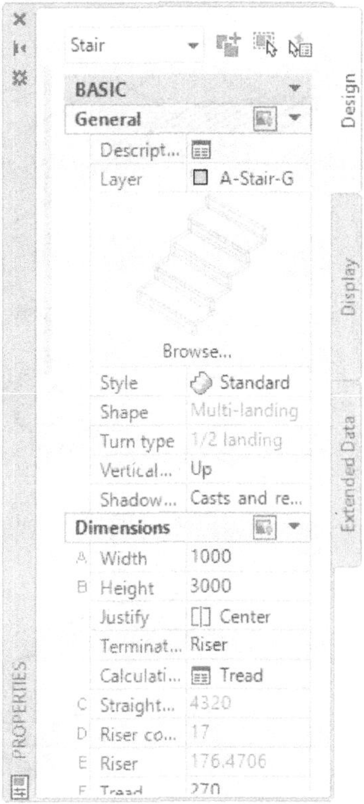

*Figure 3-19 The **PROPERTIES** palette displayed on choosing the **Stair** tool*

Straight

Using this option, you can create straight stairs, refer to Figure 3-20. In this type of stairs, the steps are created on a straight path that is inclined to the horizontal plane.

Turn type

This drop-down list is displayed only when **U-shaped** or **Multi-landing** is selected from the **Shape** drop-down list. The options available in this drop-down list are used to define the type of landing or turning for the U-shaped or multi-landing stairs. There are four options available in this drop-down list which are discussed next.

1/2 landing

Using this option, you can create the U-shaped or multi-landing stairs having a flat landing of user-defined length, refer to Figure 3-21.

1/2 turn

Using this option, you can create the U-shaped or multi-landing stairs having steps at the turn, refer to Figure 3-21. Note that there must be at least three segments in the stairs and direction of turn of all the segments must be the same.

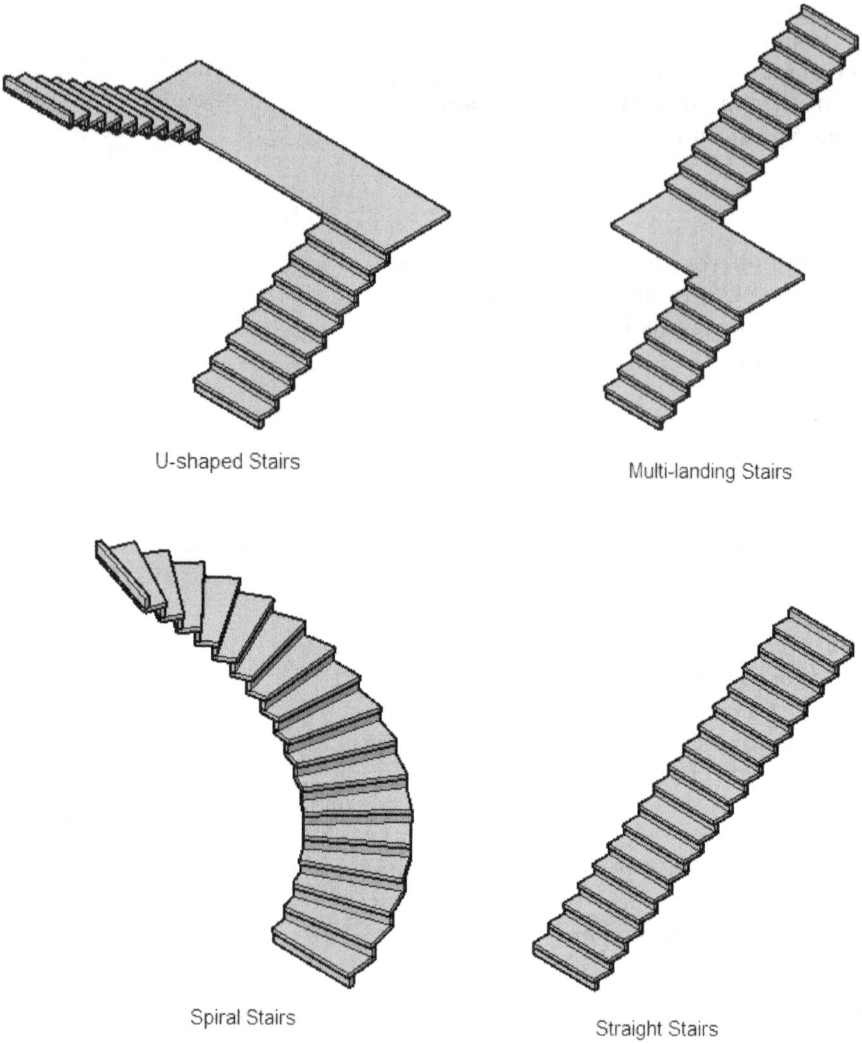

Figure 3-20 *Various type of stairs available in AutoCAD MEP*

1/4 landing

This option is available only when **Multi-landing** is selected from the **Shape** drop-down list. When you select this option, the width of landing created at turn will be equal to the width of the stair, refer to Figure 3-21. Generally, these type of stairs have two or more steps joined to the square landing.

1/4 turn

This option is available only when **Multi-landing** is selected from the **Shape** drop-down list. When you select this option, the resulting stairs will have steps at the turn, refer to Figure 3-21. These stairs can turn in both directions.

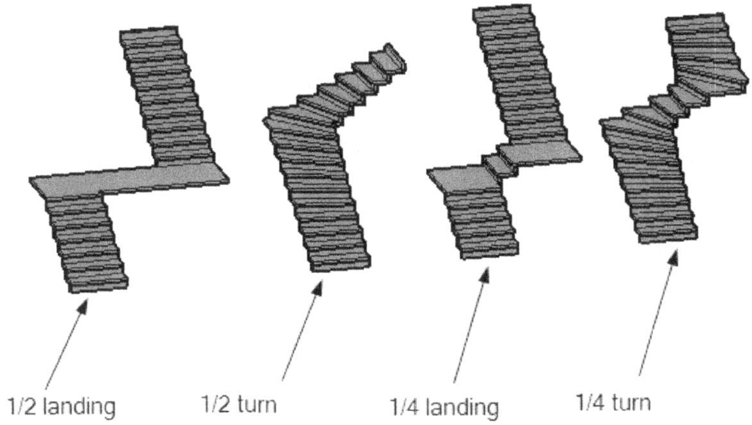

Figure 3-21 Stairs with different turning types selected

Winder Style

This drop-down list is available only when **1/2 turn** or **1/4 turn** is selected from the **Turn type** drop-down list. There is a single type of winder style available in AutoCAD MEP: **Balanced**. The **Balanced** winder style is used to distribute steps of stairs evenly throughout the run.

Horizontal orientation

This drop-down list is displayed only when **U-shaped** or **Spiral** is selected from the **Shape** drop-down list. The options available in this drop-down list are used to define the direction of turn of stairs. There are two options available in this drop-down list: **Clockwise** and **Counterclockwise**. Using these options, you can select the clockwise or counterclockwise direction of turn of the stairs.

Vertical orientation

The options in this drop-down list are used to specify the vertical direction of the stairs. There are two options available in this drop-down list: **Up** and **Down**. The **Up** option is selected when you need to create stairs from lower floor to higher floor. The **Down** option is selected when you need to create stairs from higher floor to lower floor.

The options in the **General** rollout are also used to control the shape of stairs. Some important terms used for defining the size of stairs are displayed in Figure 3-22. The options available in the **Dimensions** rollout of the palette are used to control the size of stairs. These options are discussed next.

Width

This edit box is used to specify the width of a step. You can also specify the width of a step by using two points. To do so, click on the button displayed on the right of the edit box; you will be prompted to select start point for width calculation. Select a start point; you will be prompted to select an end point for width calculation. Select a point; the width value for the specified points will be reflected in the edit box.

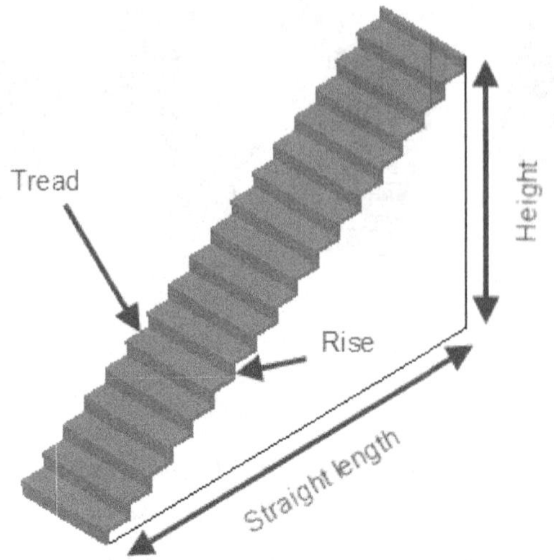

Figure 3-22 Some important terms for defining the size of stairs

Height

This edit box is used to specify total height of the stairs. You can also specify the total height of stairs by using two points. The method of using the points is already discussed.

Justify

The options in this drop-down list are used to change the justification of stairs. There are three options available in this drop-down list: **Left**, **Right**, and **Center**. These options change to **Inside**, **Outside**, and **Center** if the option selected from the **Shape** drop-down list is either **U-shaped** or **Spiral**.

Terminate with

The options in this drop-down list are used to change the justification of stairs. There are three options available in this drop-down list: **Riser**, **Tread**, and **Landing**. When you select the **Riser** option, the stairs end with a riser. When you select the **Tread** option, the stairs end with a tread. If the **Landing** option is selected, the stairs end with a landing. Figure 3-23 shows the output of various options selected from the **Terminate with** drop-down list.

Flight length

This drop-down list will be available when the **Multi-landing** option is selected from the **Shape** drop-down list. The options in this drop-down list are used to control the length of one segment of a staircase. There are two options available in this drop-down list: **Distance** and **Tread length**. Using the **Distance** option, you can specify the flight length by specifying total distance value. Using the **Tread length** option, you can specify the flight length by specifying the length of one tread. The total flight length is calculated on the basis of number of treads in the staircase.

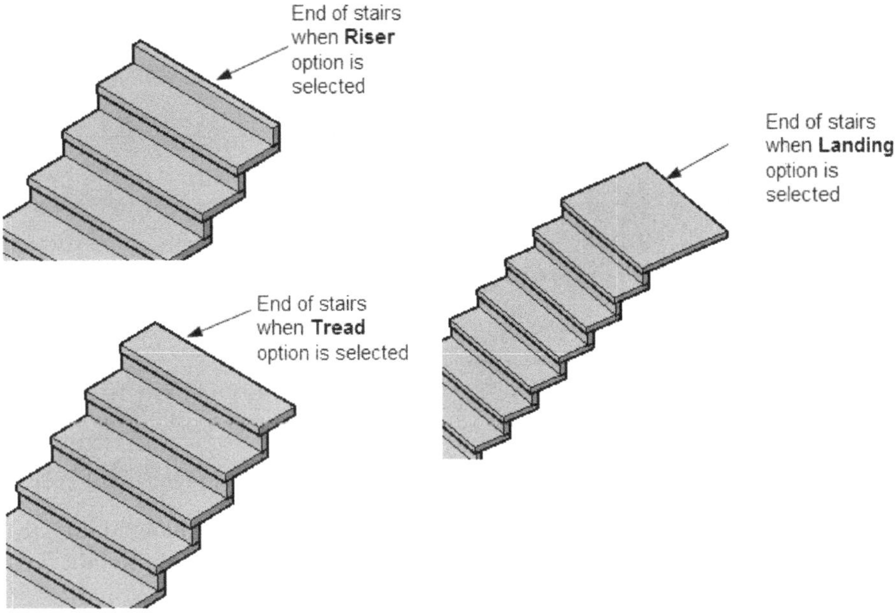

Figure 3-23 *The output of various options selected from the* ***Terminate with*** *drop-down list*

Calculation rules

When you click on the **Tread** button displayed in this field, the **Calculation Rules** dialog box will be displayed, as shown in Figure 3-24. By default, the **D-Tread** edit box is activated. On changing the value in this edit box, the value in the other edit boxes in this dialog box will change accordingly. To change values in other edit boxes manually, you need to lock the **D-Tread** edit box. To do so, choose the **lock** button; the **Calculation Rules** dialog box will be displayed, as shown in Figure 3-25. Now, you can change the value of any of the edit box in the dialog box by choosing the button adjacent to the respective edit box. In this dialog box, you can manually define the value in two edit boxes simultaneously. But if you choose the **C-Riser** edit box for defining the value of riser manually, then the other three edit boxes will be locked.

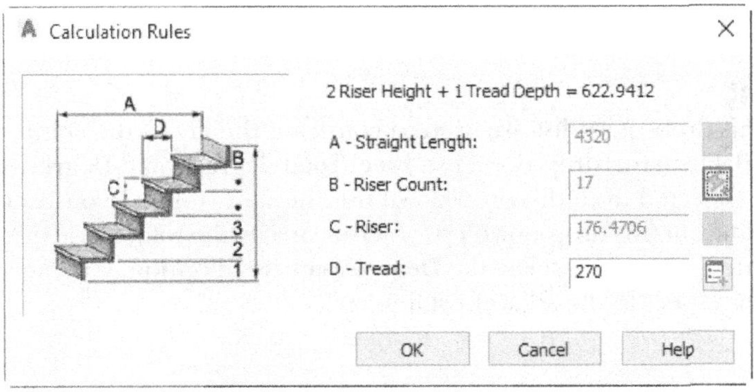

Figure 3-24 *The* ***Calculation Rules*** *dialog box*

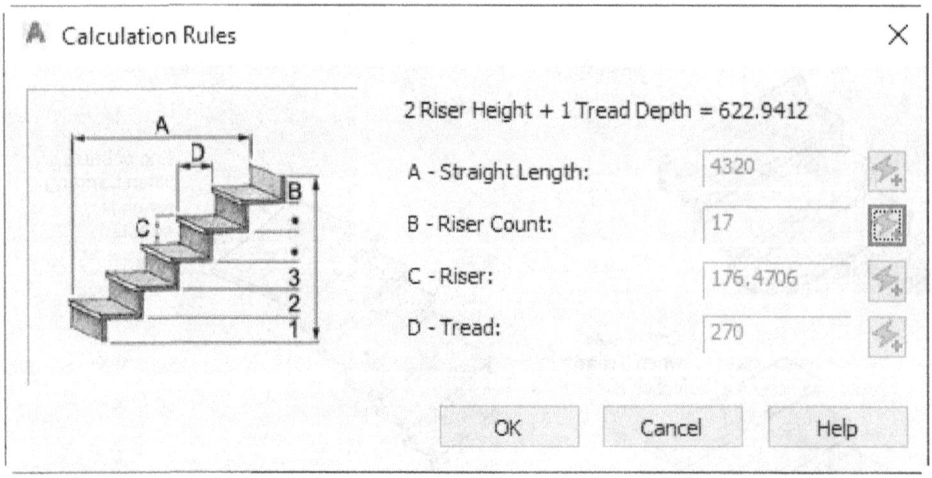

***Figure 3-25** The **Calculation Rules** dialog box displayed after locking the edit boxes*

The value of the edit boxes that are set to change manually can also be changed directly using the **PROPERTIES** palette. Note that in the **PROPERTIES** palette only those edit boxes will be active that are set to change manually in the **Calculation Rules** dialog box.

Some of the options in the **PROPERTIES** palette are displayed only when **Spiral** is selected from the **Shape** drop-down list of the palette. These options are discussed next.

Specify on screen

This option will be available only when **Spiral** is selected from the **Shape** drop-down list. The options in this drop-down list are used to specify whether the second point specifies the radius along the starting direction or not. There are two options available in this drop-down list: **Yes** and **No**. When you select **Yes** from this drop-down list, then you can specify the radius of stairs on the screen while creating the stairs.

Radius

This edit box is available only when you select the **No** option from the **Specify on screen** drop-down list. Using this edit box, you can specify the value of radius for the spiral stairs.

Arc constraint

The options in this drop-down list are used to constrain the arc of the spiral stairs. There are three options available in this drop-down list: **Free**, **Total degrees**, and **Degrees per tread**. When the **Free** option is selected from this drop-down list, the stair run is unconstrained. When **Total degrees** is selected from this drop-down list, you can specify the total angle of arc around which the stairs are created. When you select the **Degrees per tread** option, you can specify the angle of each tread with respect to the adjacent stairs.

Arc angle

This edit box is active only when the **Total degrees** or the **Degrees per tread** option is selected from the **Arc constraint** drop-down list. Using this edit box, you can specify the value of arc angle. The value specified in this edit box is linked to the option selected in the **Arc constraint** drop-down list. If you have selected the **Total degrees** option from the **Arc constraint** drop-down list, then the value specified in the **Arc angle** edit box is applicable for total degree of the spiral stairs. If the **Degrees per tread** is selected from the **Arc constraint** drop-down list, the angle value specified in the **Arc angle** edit box is applicable for each tread.

Other options in the **Dimensions** rollout have already been discussed. Some of the important options available in the **Advanced** rollout of the **PROPERTIES** palette are discussed next.

Top offset

This edit box is available in the **Floor Settings** rollout. This edit box is used to specify the value for thickness of the floor at the top of the stairs.

Bottom offset

This edit box is also available in the **Floor Settings** rollout and is used to specify the value of thickness of the floor at the bottom of the stairs.

Minimum limit type

This drop-down list is available in the **Flight Height** rollout. Using the options available in this drop-down list, you can change the minimum limit for the height of flight. There are three options available in this drop-down list: **NONE**, **Risers**, and **Height**. By default, the **NONE** option is selected in this drop-down list. As a result, no limit is set for height or risers of the stairs. You can specify the minimum limit of risers by selecting the **Risers** option from the drop-down list. You can also specify the minimum height of stairs by using the **Height** option from this drop-down list.

Minimum Risers

This edit box is available in the **Flight Height** rollout only when the **Risers** option is selected from the **Minimum limit type** drop-down list. You can specify the minimum number of riser by using this edit box.

Minimum Height

This edit box is available in the **Flight Height** rollout only when the **Height** option is selected in the **Minimum limit type** drop-down list. You can specify the minimum value for height of the stairs by using this edit box.

Maximum limit type

Using the options available in this drop-down list, you can change the maximum limit for the height of flight. There are three options available in this drop-down list: **NONE**, **Risers**, and **Height**. By default, the **NONE** option is selected in this drop-down list. As a result, no limit is set for height or risers of the stairs. You can specify the maximum limit of risers by selecting the **Risers** option from the drop-down list. You can also specify the maximum height of stairs by using the **Height** option from this drop-down list.

Maximum Risers

This edit box is available in the **Flight Height** rollout only when the **Risers** option is selected from the **Maximum limit type** drop-down list. You can specify the maximum number of riser by using this edit box.

Maximum Height

This edit box is available in the **Flight Height** rollout only when the **Height** option is selected from the **Maximum limit type** drop-down list. You can specify the maximum value for height for the stairs by using this edit box.

Headroom height

This edit box is available in the **Interference** rollout. This edit box is used to specify the height of ceiling around the stairs opening from the tread. This height is required so that people do not collide with the roof while going through the stairs.

Left clearance

This edit box will be available in the **Interference** rollout only when **Straight** or **Multi-landing** is selected from the **Shape** drop-down list. This edit box is used to specify the clearance value for stairs from the left edge of the opening in the roof.

Right clearance

This edit box will be available in the **Interference** rollout only when **Straight** or **Multi-landing** is selected from the **Shape** drop-down list. This edit box is used to specify the clearance value for stairs from the right edge of the opening in the roof.

Inside clearance

This edit box will be available in the **Interference** rollout only when **Spiral** or **U-shaped** is selected in the **Shape** drop-down list. This edit box is used to specify the clearance value for stairs from the inner edge of the opening in the roof.

Outside clearance

This edit box will be available in the **Interference** rollout only when **Spiral** or **U-shaped** is selected in the **Shape** drop-down list. This edit box is used to specify the clearance value for stairs from the outer edge of the opening in the roof.

Components

This option is available in the **Worksheets** rollout. It is used to edit the parameters for stairs. When you choose this option, the **Stair Components** dialog box will be displayed, as shown in Figure 3-26. The options available in this dialog box are discussed next.

Note

*You can edit the parameters in this dialog box only when you have selected the **Allow Each Stair to Vary** check box from the **Components** tab of the required **Stair Styles** in the **Style Manager**. The **Style Manager** is displayed on choosing the **Style Manager** tool from the **Style & Display** panel of the **Manage** tab in the **Ribbon**.*

Tread

This check box is available in the **Flight Dimensions** area. This check box is used to enable change in the value of tread thickness.

Riser

This check box is available in the **Flight Dimensions** area. This check box is used to enable change in the value of riser thickness.

A - Tread Thickness

This edit box is activated only when the **Tread** check box is selected. Using this edit box, you can specify the value for tread thickness.

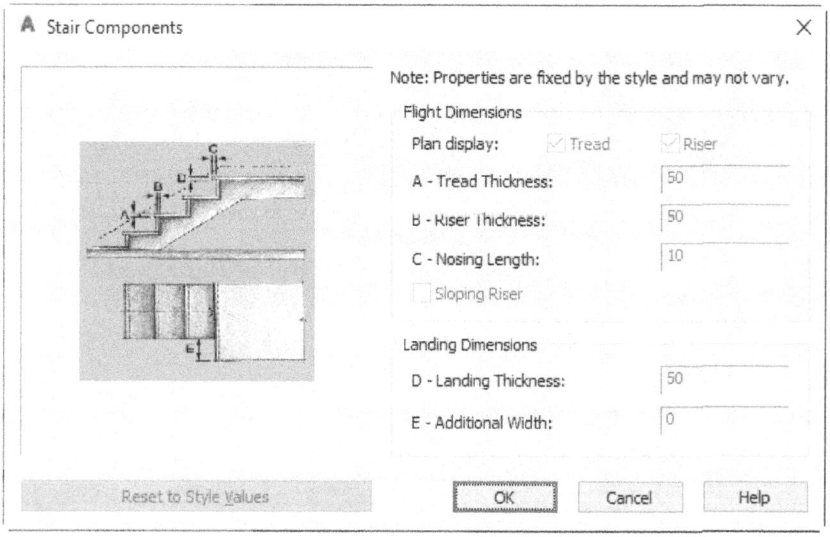

*Figure 3-26 The **Stair Components** dialog box*

B - Riser Thickness

This edit box is active only when the **Riser** check box is selected. Using this edit box, you can specify the value for riser thickness. An annotated preview of all the related parameters will be displayed on the left in the dialog box.

C - Nosing Length

This edit box is used to specify the length for extended portion of tread over the riser.

Sloping Riser

Select this check box if you want to create riser with a slope.

D - Landing Thickness

This edit box is available in the **Landing Dimensions** area. This edit box is used to specify the value for thickness of the landing.

E - Additional Width

This edit box is available in the **Landing Dimensions** area. This edit box is used to specify the value for additional width of landing.

Reset to Style Values

This button is used to reset the value of all the parameters to their original values. This button is available at the bottom of the dialog box.

Landing Extensions

This tool is available in the **Worksheets** rollout. This tool is used to edit the parameters for stairs related to landing extensions. When you choose this tool, the **Landing Extensions** dialog box will be displayed, as shown in Figure 3-27. The options available in this dialog box are discussed next.

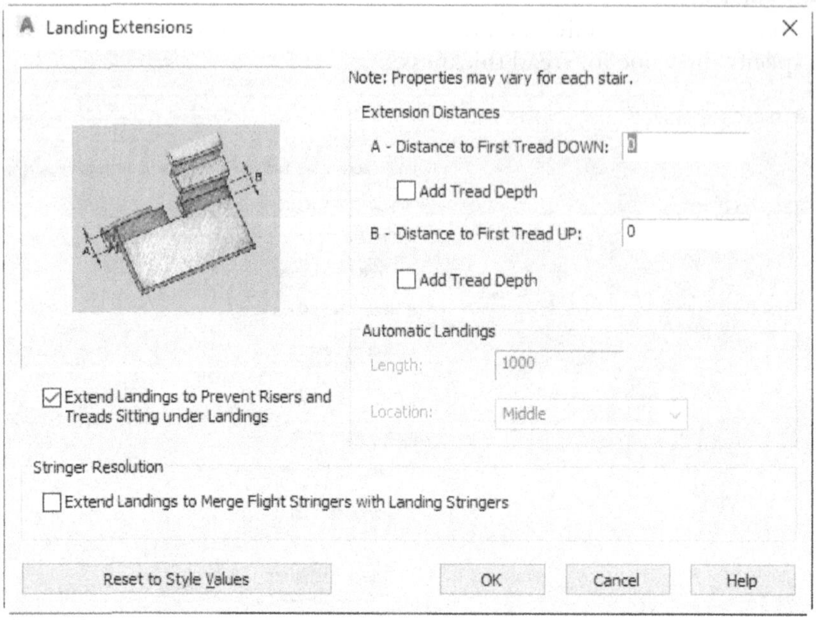

***Figure 3-27** The **Landing Extensions** dialog box*

Note

*You can edit the parameters in this dialog box only when you have selected the **Allow Each Stair to Vary** check box from the **Landing Extensions** tab of **Stair Styles** in the **Style Manager**. The **Style Manager** is displayed on choosing the **Style Manager** tool from the **Style & Display** panel in the **Manage** tab of the **Ribbon**.*

A - Distance to First Tread DOWN

This edit box is used to specify the value of extension of the tread attached to the lower riser. By specifying this value, you can extend the landing up to desired distance towards lower riser.

Add Tread Depth

Select this check box if you want to add tread depth to the value specified in the **Distance to First Tread DOWN** edit box.

B - Distance to First Tread UP

This edit box is used to specify the value for extension of the tread attached to the higher riser. By specifying this value, you can extend the landing up to desired distance towards higher riser.

Add Tread Depth

Select this check box if you want to add tread depth to the value specified in the **Distance to First Tread UP** edit box.

Extend Landings to Prevent Risers and Treads Sitting under Landings

This check box is available below the preview area. Select this check box if you want to create landing at the level of the adjacent riser and tread. If you clear this check box, you will get flush or rectangular landings.

Extend Landings to Merge Flight Stringers with Landing Stringers

This check box is available in the **Stringer Resolution** area of the dialog box. Select this check box to extend the landings so that the landing stringers merge with the flight stringer.

Railing

This tool is available in the **Stair** drop-down of the **Build** panel in the **Home** tab. This tool is used to create a stand-alone railing as well as a railing attached to stairs or some objects. To create a stand-alone railing, choose the **Railing** tool from the **Stair** drop-down; you will be prompted to specify the start point of the railing. Select a point as the start point; you will be prompted to specify the end point of the railing. Select a point as the end point; you will be prompted to specify the end point again. You can specify an end point for the next segment or you can press ESC to exit the command. Figure 3-28 shows an annotated railing created with guardrail, handrail, and bottomrail. Figure 3-29 shows the **PROPERTIES** palette displayed on selecting a railing.

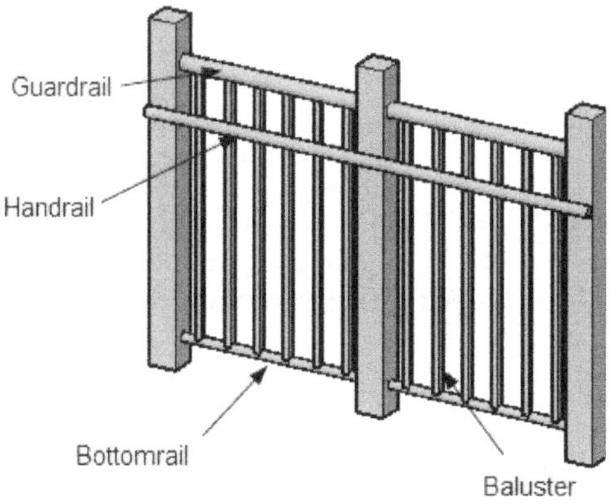

Figure 3-28 An annotated railing

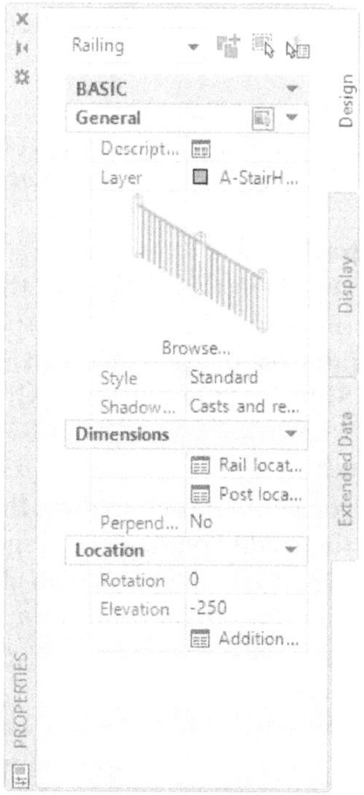

Figure 3-29 *The* ***PROPERTIES*** *palette displayed on selecting a stand-alone railing*

Some of the important options available in the **Dimension** rollout of the **PROPERTIES** palette are discussed next.

Rail locations

When you select this option, the **Rail Locations** dialog box will be displayed, as shown in Figure 3-30. Various options available in this dialog box are discussed next.

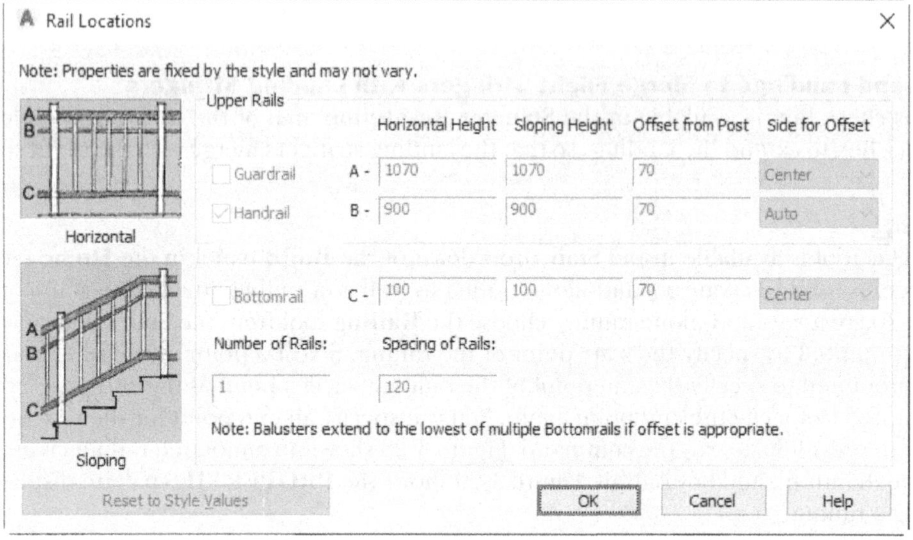

Figure 3-30 *The **Rail Locations** dialog box*

Note

*The options in this dialog box can be edited only when the **Allow Each Railing to Vary** check box is selected from the **Rail Locations** tab of the **Railing Styles** option in the **Style Manager**.*

Guardrail

When you select this check box, the edit boxes available next to the check box get activated. Using these edit boxes, you can specify horizontal height, sloping height, and offset value of guardrail from the post. You can also specify the side of offset by using the options available in the **Side for Offset** drop-down list.

Handrail

When you select this check box, the edit boxes available next to the check box get activated. Using these edit boxes, you can specify horizontal height, sloping height, and offset value of handrail from the post. You can also specify the side of offset by using the options available in the **Side for Offset** drop-down list.

Bottomrail

When you select this check box, the edit boxes available next to the check box get activated. Using these edit boxes, you can specify horizontal height, sloping height, and offset value for bottomrail from the post. You can also specify the side of offset by using the options available in the **Side for Offset** drop-down list. When you select the **Bottomrail** check box, then the **Number of Rails** and **Spacing of Rails** edit boxes get enabled. Using the **Num-**

ber of Rails edit box, you can specify the number of rails to be created from the bottom. Using the **Spacing of Rails** edit box, you can specify the value of spacing between two successive bottom rails. Note that the **Spacing of Rails** edit box gets activated only when the value in the **Number of Rails** edit box is greater than one.

Post locations

When you choose this tool, the **Post Locations** dialog box will be displayed, as shown in Figure 3-31. The options available in this dialog box are discussed next.

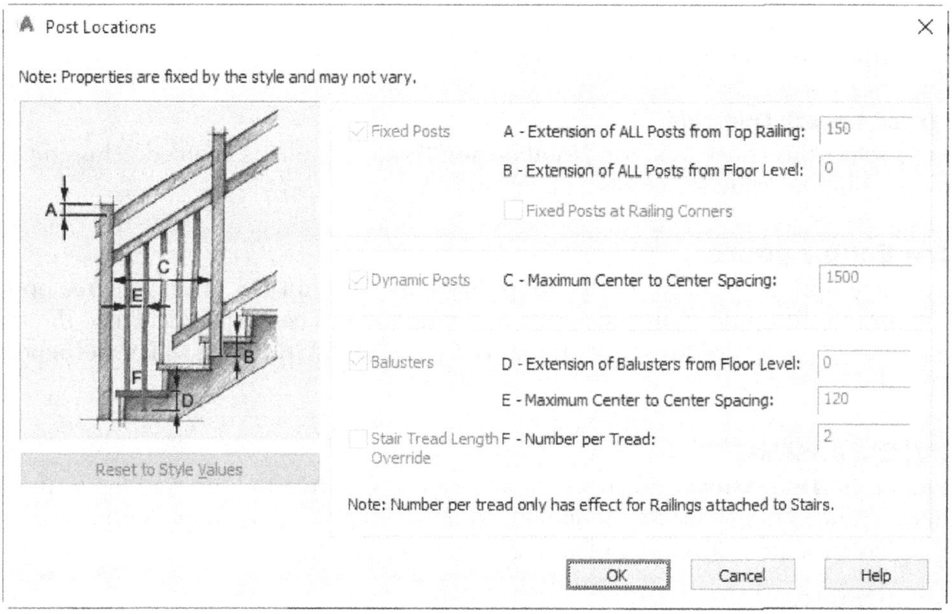

*Figure 3-31 The **Post Locations** dialog box*

Note

*The options in this dialog box can be edited only when the **Allow Each Railing to Vary** check box is selected from the **Post Locations** tab of Railing Styles in the **Style Manager**.*

Fixed Posts

This check box is used to enable the edit boxes that are used to modify the value of extension of the post. There are two edit boxes to change the value of extension: **Extension of ALL Posts from Top Railing** and **Extension of ALL Posts from Floor Level**. The **Extension of All Posts from Top Railing** edit box is used to specify the value of post above or below the top railing. The **Extension of ALL Posts from Floor Level** is used to specify the height of all the posts from the floor.

Fixed Posts at Railing Corners

This check box is used to include the posts present at the railing corners.

Dynamic Posts

When you select this check box, the **Maximum Center to Center Spacing** edit box is enabled. This edit box is used to modify the distance between two successive dynamic posts. Specify the value for distance between the dynamic posts in the edit box; the value will be taken as the maximum limit of distance between the two successive posts. When you create a railing having length more than this value, a new post is added to the railing.

Balusters

When you select this check box, the **Extension of Balusters from Floor Level** and **Maximum Center to Center Spacing** edit boxes are enabled. These check boxes are used to modify the values related to baluster. The **Extension of Balusters from Floor Level** edit box is used to specify the distance for bottom point of baluster from the level of corresponding tread. The **Maximum Center to Center Spacing** edit box is used to specify the center to center distance between the consecutive balusters.

Stair Tread Length Override

When you select this check box, the **Number per Tread** edit box is enabled. This edit box is used to override the value for number of balusters per tread.

Perpendicular posts

There are two options available in this drop-down list: **Yes** and **No**. When the **Yes** option is selected from this drop-down list, the posts in the railing will be perpendicular to the rails in the railing. If you select the **No** option from this drop-down list, the posts will be perpendicular to the tread.

Railing Extensions

This tool in the **Dimensions** rollout will be available only when railing is added to the stairs and there is a need to extend the railing ahead of the stairs. The railings can be extended at two levels, either at floor levels or at landings, refer to Figure 3-32.

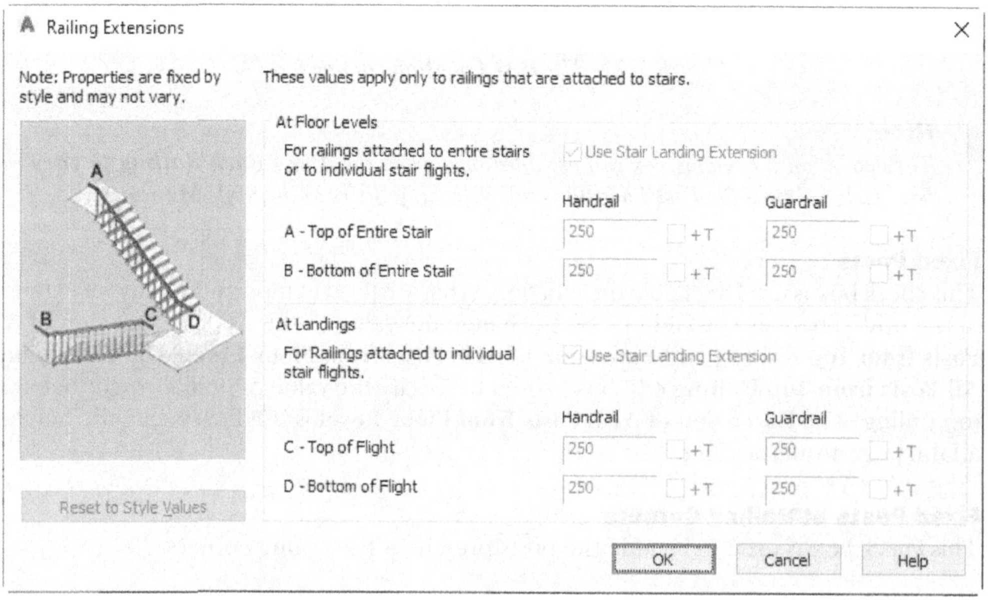

*Figure 3-32 The **Railing Extensions** dialog box*

At Floor Levels Area

When you deselect the **Use Stair Landing Extension** check box in the **At Floor Levels** area, the edit boxes given below get activated. You can specify the values for the **Top of Entire Stair** and **Bottom of Entire Stair** options in the **Handrail** and **Guardrail** edit boxes. Select the **+T** check box for adding the tread length to the extension value.

At Landings Area

When you deselect the **Use Stair Landing Extension** check box in the **At Landing** area, the edit boxes below it get activated. You can specify the values for **Top of flight** and **Bottom of flight** for the **Handrail** and **Guardrail** in the respective edit boxes. Select the **+T** check box for adding the tread length to the extension value.

Note

*1. To create a railing attached to stairs, choose the **Railing** tool from the **Stair** drop-down; the **PROPERTIES** palette will be displayed. Select the **Stairs** option from the **Attached to** drop-down list in the **Location** rollout; you will be prompted to select the stairs in the drawing area. Select the stairs; the railing will be created along the selected stairs.*

*2. The options in **Railing Extension** dialog box can be edited only when the **Allow Each Railing to Vary** check box is selected in the **Extensions** tab of the **Railing Styles** option in the **Style Manager**.*

Stair Tower

This tool is available in the **Stair** drop-down of the **Build** panel in the **Home** tab. This tool is used to create a stair tower from one stair. You can create a stair tower by using any stair shape except spiral. To create a stair tower, you need to fulfill the conditions given next.

1. A stair must already be created in the drawing.
2. You must have more than one level in the current project.

CREATING GRIDS, BEAMS, COLUMNS, AND BRACES

To create grids, beams, columns, or braces, the tools are available in the **Enhanced Custom Grid** drop-down in the **Build** panel of the **Home** tab in the **Ribbon**. The tools in this drop-down are discussed next.

Enhanced Custom Grid

This tool is available in the **Enhanced Custom Grid** drop-down. This tool is used to create column grids. When you choose this tool, the **Column Grid** dialog box will be displayed, as shown in Figure 3-33. Using the options in this dialog box, you can create two types of grids: orthogonal grids and radial grids. The methods to create these grids are discussed next.

Creating Orthogonal Grids

To create orthogonal grids, select the **Orthogonal** radio button from the top left corner of the **Grid Layout** area; the modified **Grid Layout** area will be displayed. By default, the **Top** tab is selected in the dialog box. As a result, the grid lines will be created in the Top plane. To create a grid line, select the desired distance value from the list available on the left in the **Grid Layout** area; the preview of the grid lines distanced as per the selected value will be displayed in the **Preview** area. Also, the parameters of the grid lines will be displayed in the table on the right in the **Grid Layout** area. Keep on clicking on the desired distance values in the list till you get the required number of grid lines. Figure 3-34 shows the **Column Grid** dialog box after selecting values from the list displayed on the left. Similarly, you can add desired number of grids to the Bottom, Left, and Right planes. You can change the pattern of labeling by using the options available in the **X-Labeling** and **Y-Labeling** drop-down lists. Similarly, you can change other parameters for grids by using the options available in the dialog box. After setting all the parameters, choose the **OK** button; the grid will be displayed attached to the cursor and you will be prompted to specify the insertion point. Specify the insertion point; you will be prompted to specify the rotation angle. Specify the rotation angle; the grid will be created at the specified location. Press ENTER to exit the command or you can specify an insertion point to create another grid with same specifications.

*Figure 3-33 The **Column Grid** dialog box*

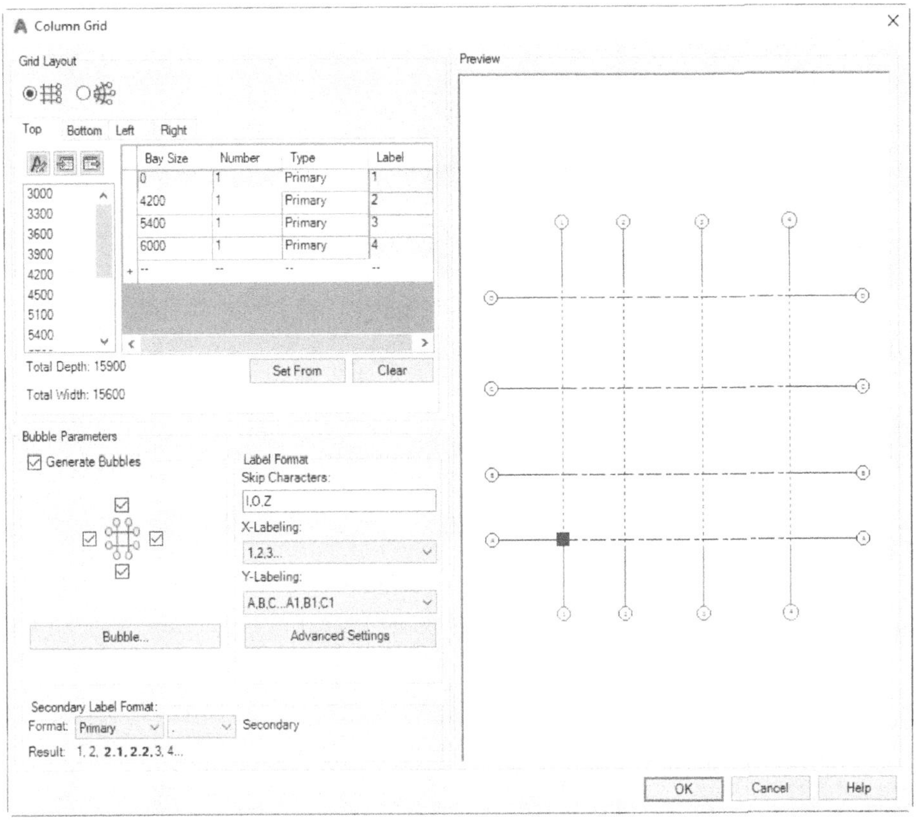

*Figure 3-34 The **Column Grid** dialog box displayed after adding grid lines*

Creating Radial Grids

To create radial grids, select the **Radial** radio button on the top left corner of the **Grid Layout** area; the modified **Grid Layout** area will be displayed, refer to Figure 3-35. By default, the **Radial** tab is selected in the dialog box, as a result the grid lines will be created in the radial direction. To create a grid line, select the desired angle value from the list available in the left of the dialog box; preview of the grid lines, at the selected value, will be displayed in the **Preview** area. Also, the parameters of the grid lines will be displayed in the table on the right in the **Grid Layout** area. You can add the desired number of grid lines by selecting them from the list. Similarly, you can add desired number of grids in the form of an arc by selecting the **Arcs** tab. Figure 3-36 shows the **Column Grid** dialog box after selecting values from the **Radial** tab and **Arcs** tab. You can change the pattern of labeling by using the options available in the **X-Labeling** and **Y-Labeling** drop-down lists. Similarly, you can change other settings for grids by using the options available in the dialog box. After setting all the parameters, choose the **OK** button; the grid will be displayed attached to the cursor and you will be prompted to specify the insertion point. Specify the insertion point; you will be prompted to specify the rotation angle. Specify the rotation angle; the grid will be created at the specified location. Press ENTER to exit the command or you can specify an insertion point to create another grid with same specifications.

Figure 3-35 *The modified* ***Column Grid*** *dialog box after selecting the* ***Radial*** *radio button*

Custom Grid Convert

This tool is available in the **Enhanced Custom Grid** drop-down. It is used to convert the network of lines into column grids. When you choose this tool, you will be prompted to select a network of lines. The command prompt for creating a grid from lines in given next.

Select linework: *Select the network of lines that you want to convert into grid.*
Select linework: Enter
Enter label extension or [No labels] <1200>: *Specify the length of extension line from the grid end point.*
Erase selected linework? [Yes/No] <No>: *Specify whether you want to delete the network of lines or not.*

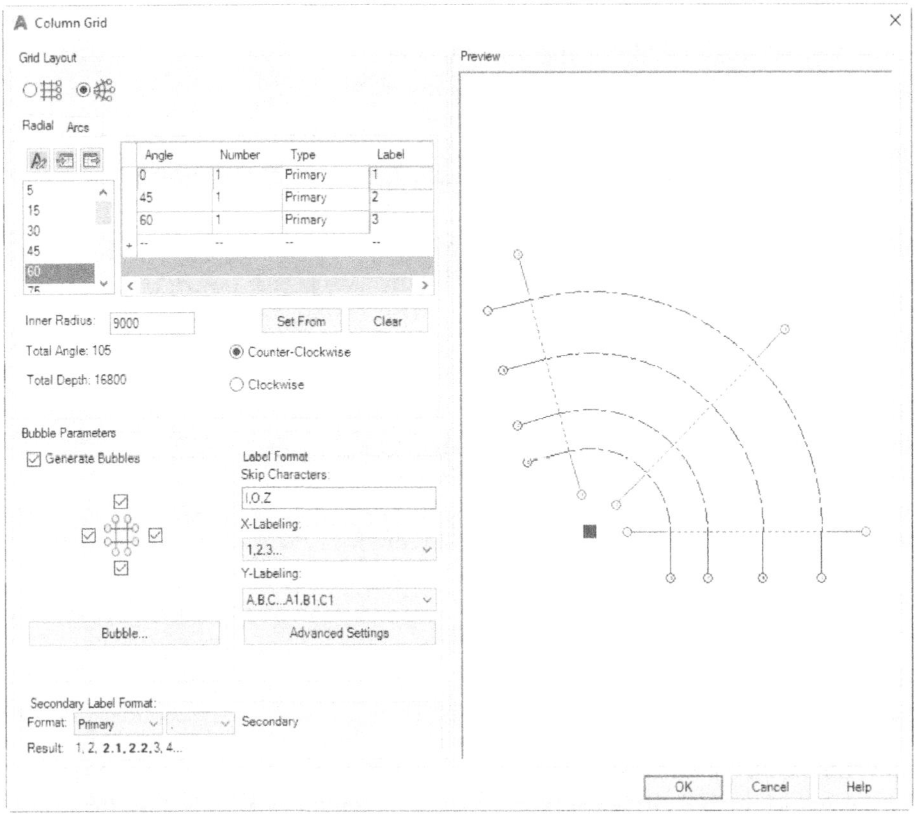

Figure 3-36 *The modified* ***Column Grid*** *dialog box after selecting values from the list*

Column Grid

This tool is available in the **Enhanced Custom Grid** drop-down. It is used to create a column grid with predefined parameters. To create a column grid, choose the **Column Grid** tool from the drop-down; you will be prompted to specify the insertion point for the grid. Specify the insertion point; you will be prompted to specify the rotation angle for the grid. Specify the rotation angle; the grid will be created at the specified insertion point. Again, you will be prompted to specify the insertion point for the grid. Press ENTER to exit the command. You can edit the parameters of a grid to be created by using the options available in the **PROPERTIES** palette, refer to Figure 3-37. Some important options in this palette are discussed next.

Shape

This drop-down list is available in the **General** rollout of the **PROPERTIES** palette. The options in this drop-down list are used to change the shape of the grid to be created. There are two options available in this drop-down list: **Rectangular** and **Radial**. When the **Rectangular** option is selected, the grid to be created will be rectangular in shape. There will be horizontal and vertical grid lines in the grid. When you select the **Radial** option, the grids will be in the form of arcs and in the radial direction.

Specify on screen

This drop-down list is available in the **Dimensions** rollout of the **PROPERTIES** palette. The options in this drop-down list are used to specify the method for dimensioning the column grids. There are two options available in this drop-down list: **Yes** and **No**. When you choose the **Yes** option, you will be prompted to specify the corner points of the column grids in the screen. If the **No** option is chosen, then you need to specify the dimensions in the edit boxes available in the **PROPERTIES** palette.

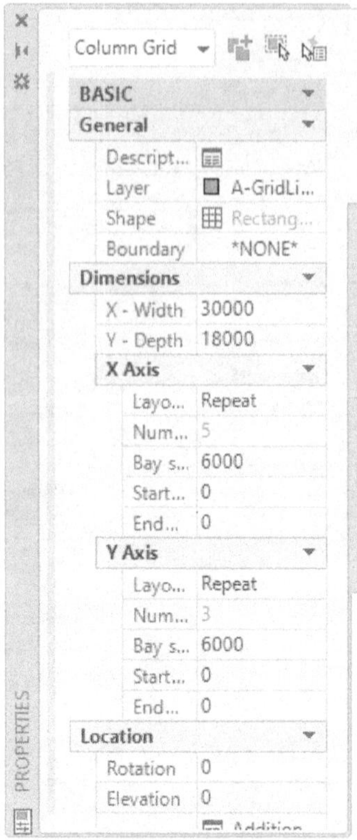

Figure 3-37 The ***PROPERTIES*** *palette displayed on choosing the* ***Column Grid*** *tool*

X - Width

This edit box is available for both rectangular shaped and radial shaped grids. This edit box in the **Dimensions** rollout of the **PROPERTIES** palette gets activated only when the **No** option is selected in the **Specify on screen** drop-down list. This edit box is used to specify the value for the width of the grid.

Y - Depth

This edit box is available for rectangular shaped grids only. This edit box in the **Dimensions** rollout of the **PROPERTIES** palette gets activated only when the **No** option is selected in the **Specify on screen** drop-down list. This edit box is used to specify the value for the depth of the grid.

A - Angle

This edit box is available for the radial shaped grids only. This edit box in the **Dimensions** rollout of the **PROPERTIES** palette gets activated only when the **No** option is selected in the **Specify on screen** drop-down list. This edit box is used to specify the value for angle of the grid.

Layout type

This drop-down list is available in both the **X Axis** rollout as well as the **Y Axis** rollout. There are two options available in this drop-down list: **Repeat** and **Space evenly**. When the **Repeat** option is selected, the distance between the two grids is fixed and depending on the total size specified, the number of grid lines are inserted. If the **Space evenly** option is selected in the **Layout type** drop-down list, the total number of grid lines will be fixed and depending on the total size of grid boundary, the distance between the two grid lines will be adjusted.

Bay size

This edit box is available in both the **X Axis** and the **Y Axis** rollouts. This edit box is available only when the **Repeat** option is selected in the **Layout type** drop-down list. You can specify the distance between two grid lines perpendicular to the X and Y axes by using the edit box in the respective rollout.

Number of bays

This edit box is available in both the **X Axis** rollout as well as the **Y Axis** rollout. This edit box is available only when the **Space evenly** option is selected in the **Layout type** drop-down list. You can specify the number of grid lines along X axis by using the edit box in the respective rollout.

Style

This drop-down list in the **Column** rollout of the **PROPERTIES** palette for the column grid will be available only after the custom convert column is applied to the drawing. It is used to change the type of column to be used for building the grid. The options available in this drop-down list are **NONE, 8mm Drop Rod Support, CH421 (40X20X1.5) Roll Formed Channel Profile,** and **Standard**.

Column

This tool is available in the **Enhanced Custom Grid** drop-down. This tool is used to create a column with predefined parameters. To create a column, choose the **Column** tool from the drop-down; you will be prompted to specify the position of the column in the drawing area. Select a point on the grid or specify a point in the drawing area; you will be prompted to specify the roll (rotation) of the column. Specify the roll by clicking in the drawing area or by specifying value in the command prompt; the column will be created at the specified point. You can change the parameters of the column to be created by using the options available in the **PROPERTIES** palette, refer to Figure 3-38. Some of the important options in the **PROPERTIES** palette are discussed next.

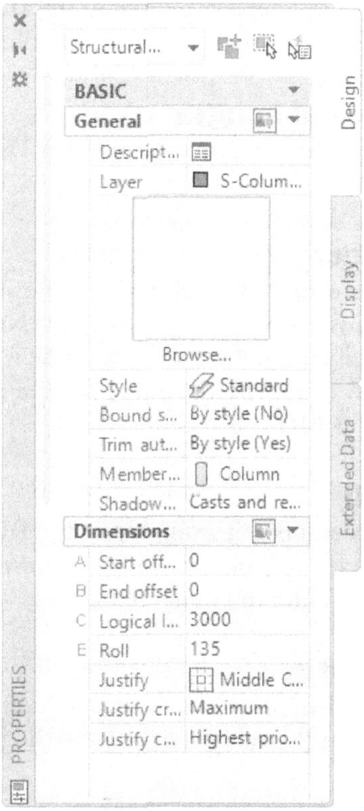

***Figure 3-38** The **PROPERTIES** palette displayed on choosing the **Column** tool*

Bound spaces

This drop-down list is available in the **General** rollout. There are three options available in this drop-down list: **Yes**, **No**, and **By style (NO)**. When the **Yes** option is selected in the drop-down list, the object to be created will act as a space boundary. When the **No** option is selected in the drop-down list, the object to be created will not act as a space boundary. When the **By style (NO)** option is selected in the drop-down list, the boundary conditions of the object are specified by the style of the object.

Trim automatically

This drop-down list is available in the **General** rollout. There are three options available in this drop-down list: **Yes**, **No**, and **By style (NO)**. When the **Yes** option is selected in the drop-down list, the object to be created will get automatically trimmed to join with the connecting object. When the **No** option is selected in the drop-down list, the object to be created will not get automatically trimmed to join with the connecting object. When the **By style (NO)** option is selected in the drop-down list, the trimming conditions of the object are specified by the style of the object.

On object

This drop-down list is available in the **General** rollout. There are two options available in this drop-down list: **Yes** and **No**. When you select the **Yes** option, the column will be attached to the base object. If you move the base, the column will also move accordingly. When you choose the **No** option, the column will be placed as a separate object having no link with other objects.

Start offset

This edit box is available in the **Dimensions** rollout. In this edit box, you can specify the offset value for the start point of the column from the insertion point.

End offset

This edit box is available in the **Dimensions** rollout. In this edit box, you can specify the offset value for the end point of the column from the insertion point.

Logical Length

This edit box is available in the **Dimensions** rollout. In this edit box, you can specify the value for the length of the column.

Specify roll on screen

This drop-down list is available in the **Dimensions** rollout. There are two options available in this drop-down list: **Yes** and **No**. When you select the **Yes** option, you will be prompted to specify the value for the rotation while placing the column. When you select the **No** option, you need to specify the value for the rotation of the column in the **Roll** edit box available in the **PROPERTIES** palette.

Roll

This edit box is available in the **Dimensions** rollout only when the **No** option is selected in the **Specify roll on screen** drop-down list. In this edit box, you can specify the value for rotation of the column being created.

Justify

This drop-down list is available in the **Dimensions** rollout. There are ten options available in this drop-down list to change the justification of the column.

Justify cross-section

This drop-down list is available in the **Dimensions** rollout. There are two options available in this drop-down list: **Maximum** and **At each node**. When you select the **Maximum** option from the drop-down list, the justification method is applied only to the columns having maximum cross section. When you choose the **At each node** option from the drop-down list, the justification method is applied to every column.

Justify components

This drop-down list is available in the **Dimensions** rollout. There are two options available in this drop-down list: **Highest priority only** and **All**. When you select the **Highest priority only** option from the drop-down list, the justification methods will be applied only to the columns having highest priority. When the **All** option is selected from the drop-down list, then the justification method is applied to all the columns.

Custom Column

This tool is available in the **Enhanced Custom Grid** drop-down. This tool is used to create a user defined column. To create a custom column, choose the **Custom Column** tool; you will be prompted to select a closed polyline, a closed spline, a circle, or an ellipse. Select a closed entity; you will be prompted to specify the insertion point or centroid. Select a point to specify as insertion point or centroid; the **Convert to Column** dialog box will be displayed, as shown in Figure 3-39. Specify the name of the column in the **New Name** edit box and choose the **OK** button from the dialog box; the custom column will be created at the specified location.

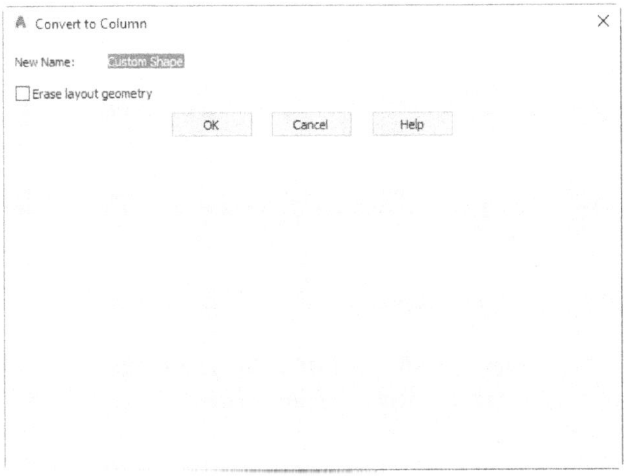

***Figure 3-39** The **Convert to Column** dialog box*

You can change the properties of a custom created column by using the **PROPERTIES** palette,

Beam

This tool is available in the **Enhanced Custom Grid** drop-down. This tool is used to create a beam. To create a beam, choose the **Beam** tool; you will be prompted to specify the start point of the beam. Specify the start point of the beam; you will be prompted to specify the end point of the beam. Specify the end point of the beam; the beam will be created with the specified parameters. You can specify the parameters of the beam in the **PROPERTIES** palette, refer to Figure 3-40. The options available in the **PROPERTIES** palette for beam are similar to the options available for column. The options that are available only for a beam are discussed next.

Array

This drop-down list is available in the **Layout** rollout. There are two options available in this drop-down list: **Yes** and **No**. The **No** option is selected by default in the drop-down list. When you select the **Yes** option, you can create multiple instances of the beam. On selecting the **Yes** option, the **Layout method** and **Number of bays** options become available in the **Layout** rollout. These options are used to specify the parameter for creating multiple instances of the beam.

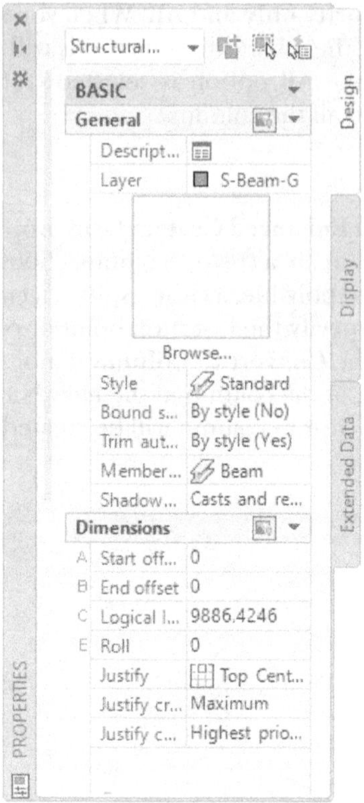

***Figure 3-40** The **PROPERTIES** palette displayed on choosing the **Beam** tool*

Layout method

This drop-down list is available in the **Layout** rollout. There are two options available in this drop-down list: **Space evenly** and **Repeat**. When you select the **Space evenly** option, the instances are spaced equally over the total distance. When you select the **Repeat** option, the instances are spaced according to the specified distance value specified.

Number of bays

This edit box is available in the **Layout** rollout. In this edit box, you can specify the value for number of instances of the beam.

Brace

This tool is available in the **Enhanced Custom Grid** drop-down. This tool is used to create a brace. To create a brace, choose the **Brace** tool; you will be prompted to specify the start point of the brace. Specify the start point of the brace; you will be prompted to specify the end point of the brace. Specify the end point of the brace; the brace will be created with the specified parameters. You can specify the parameters of the brace in the **PROPERTIES** palette. The options available in the **PROPERTIES** palette for brace are similar to the options available for the custom column. The options that are available only for a brace are discussed next.

Specify rise on screen

This drop-down list is available in the **Rise** rollout. There are two options available in this drop-down list: **Yes** and **No**. The **Yes** option is selected by default in the drop-down list. So you need to specify the value of rise on the screen while placing the braces. When you choose the **No** option, you can set the parameters related to rise by using the options available in the **PROPERTIES** palette.

Method

This drop-down list will be available in the **Rise** rollout only when you select the **No** option from the **Specify rise on screen** rollout. There are two options available in this drop-down list: **Angle** and **Distance**. On choosing the **Angle** option, you can set the value of rise by specifying angle value in the **Angle from first member** edit box.

Distance along first member

This edit box will be available in the **Rise** rollout only when you select the **No** option from the **Specify rise on screen** rollout. You can specify the value for distance of start point of the brace along the first member.

Angle from first member

This edit box is available only when the **Angle** option is selected in the **Method** drop-down list. You can specify the value for rotation of the brace with respect to the first member.

CREATING PRIMITIVES

You can create basic objects like box, cylinder, torus and so on by using the tools available in AutoCAD MEP. These basic objects are called primitives. The tools to create primitives are available in the **Box** drop-down of the **Build** panel. These tools are discussed next.

Note

*For better visualization, you may need to rotate the **ViewCube** while creating primitives shapes.*

Box

The **Box** tool is used to create a box with the specified dimensions. To create a box, choose the **Box** tool from the **Box** drop-down in the **Build** panel; you will be prompted to specify the first corner of the box. Specify the first corner of the box; you will be prompted to specify the second corner of the box. Specify the second corner of the box; you will be prompted to specify the height of the box. Specify the height of the box; you will be prompted to specify the rotation angle of the box. Specify the rotation value; the box will be created. Press the ESC key to exit the tool.

Pyramid

The **Pyramid** tool is used to create a pyramid with the specified dimensions. To create a pyramid, choose the **Pyramid** tool from the **Box** drop-down in the **Build** panel; you will be prompted to specify the first corner point of the pyramid. Specify the first corner point of the pyramid; you will be prompted to specify the second corner point. Specify the second corner point; you will be prompted to specify the height of the apex. Specify the height of the apex; you will be prompted to specify the rotation angle of the pyramid. Specify the value for rotation; a pyramid with specified settings will be created. Press the ESC key to exit the tool.

Cylinder

The **Cylinder** tool is used to create a cylinder of some specified dimensions. To create a cylinder, choose the **Cylinder** tool from the **Box** drop-down in the **Build** panel; you will be prompted to specify the insertion point of the cylinder. Specify the point in the drawing area; you will be prompted to specify the radius. Enter the radius value; you will be prompted to specify the height of the cylinder. Specify the height of the cylinder; you will be prompted to specify the rotation angle. Specify the value for rotation; a cylinder of specified dimensions will be created.

Right Triangle

The **Right Triangle** tool is used to create a right triangle mass of some specified dimensions. To create a right triangle, choose the **Right Triangle** tool from the **Box** drop-down in the **Build** panel; you will be prompted to specify the first corner point of the right triangle. Specify the point in the drawing area; you will be prompted to specify the second corner point of the right triangle. Specify the second corner point; you will be prompted to specify the height of the apex. Specify the height of the apex; you will be prompted to specify the rotation angle of the right triangle. Specify the value for rotation; a right triangle of specified dimensions will be created.

Isosceles Triangle

The **Isosceles Triangle** tool is used to create an isosceles triangle mass of some specified dimensions. The procedure to create an isosceles triangle is similar to the procedure of creating a right triangle mass.

Cone

The **Cone** tool is used to create a cone of some specified dimensions. To create a cone, choose the **Cone** tool from the **Box** drop-down in the **Build** panel; you will be prompted to specify the insertion point of the cone. Specify the point in the drawing area; you will be prompted to specify the radius. Enter the radius value; you will be prompted to specify height of the cone. Specify the height of the cone; you will be prompted to specify the rotation angle. Specify the value of rotation; a cone of specified dimensions will be created.

Dome

The **Dome** tool is used to create a dome of some specified dimensions. To create a dome, choose the **Dome** tool from the **Box** drop-down in the **Build** panel; you will be prompted to specify the insertion point of the dome. Specify the point in the drawing area; you will be prompted to specify the radius. Enter the radius value; you will be prompted to specify the rotation angle. Specify the value of rotation; a dome of specified dimensions will be created.

Sphere

The **Sphere** tool is used to create a dome of some specified dimensions. To create a sphere, choose the **Sphere** tool from the **Box** drop-down in the **Build** panel; you will be prompted to specify the insertion point of the sphere. Specify the point in the drawing area; you will be prompted to specify the radius. Enter the radius value; you will be prompted to specify the rotation angle. Specify the value of rotation; a sphere with dimensions will be created.

Arch

The **Arch** tool is used to create an arch with the specified dimensions. To create an arch, choose the **Arch** tool from the **Box** drop-down in the **Build** panel; you will be prompted to specify the first corner point of the base. Specify the point in the drawing area; you will be prompted to specify the second corner point of the base. Specify the second corner point; you will be prompted to specify the height of the arch. Specify the height of the arch; you will be prompted to specify the rotation angle of the arch. Enter the value of rotation angle; an arch will be created with the specified parameters.

Gable

The **Gable** tool is used to create a gable of some specified dimensions. To create a gable, choose the **Gable** tool from the **Box** drop-down in the **Build** panel; you will be prompted to specify the first corner point of the base. Specify the point in the drawing area; you will be prompted to specify the second corner point of the base. Specify the second corner point; you will be prompted to specify the height of the gable. Specify the height of the gable; you will be prompted to specify the rotation angle of the arch. Enter the value of the rotation angle; a gable of specified dimensions will be created.

Barrel Vault

The **Barrel Vault** tool is used to create a barrel vault of some specified dimensions. To create a barrel vault, choose the **Barrel Vault** tool from the **Box** drop-down in the **Build** panel; you will be prompted to specify the first corner point of the base. Specify the point in the drawing area; you will be prompted to specify the second corner point of the base. Specify the second corner point; you will be prompted to specify the rotation angle of the barrel vault. Enter the value of the rotation angle; a barrel vault of the specified dimensions will be created.

Drape

The **Drape** tool is used to create a drape of some specified parameters. A drape is used to show contour of the site. You can create a drape with the help of polylines or polygons. To create a drape, choose the **Drape** tool from the **Box** drop-down in the **Build** panel; you will be prompted to select objects representing the contour. Select polylines or other objects representing the contour and then press ENTER; you will prompted to erase or retain the selected contours. Enter **Y** or **N** at the command prompt; you will be prompted to generate a regular mesh. Enter **Y** or **N** at the command prompt. On specifying **N** at the command prompt, you will be prompted whether to generate a rectangular mesh. On entering **Y** at the command prompt; you will be prompted to specify the first corner of the rectangle to create a mesh. Specify a point in the drawing area; you will be prompted to specify the opposite corner of the rectangular mesh. Specify the opposite corner of the mesh; you will be prompted to specify the number of subdivisions along the X direction. Enter the desired number of subdivisions at the command prompt; you will be prompted to specify the number of subdivisions along the Y direction. Enter the number of subdivisions at the command prompt; you will be prompted to specify the thickness value of the base. Enter the value of thickness at the command prompt; the drape with the selected contours will be created.

Doric

The doric pillar is used for creating heritage type vertical structures. The **Doric** tool will be available only after **Box** is selected from the **Primitives** drop-down in the **Build** panel of the **Home** tab; the **Shape** option pops up in the command prompt. Select **Shape** in the command prompt; various options for different shapes get displayed in the command bar. Select the **DORic** option. Specify the center point of the doric shape in the drawing area; you will be prompted to specify the radius. Enter the radius value in the command bar; you will be prompted to specify the height of the doric shaped pillar. Specify the height for the pillar; you will be prompted to specify the rotation angle. Specify the value for the rotation angle; a doric pillar of specified dimensions will be created.

TUTORIALS

Tutorial 1

In this tutorial, you will create a model of a building, as shown in Figure 3-41. The plan of the building is given in Figure 3-42. **(Expected time: 30 min)**

Figure 3-41 *Model of a building*

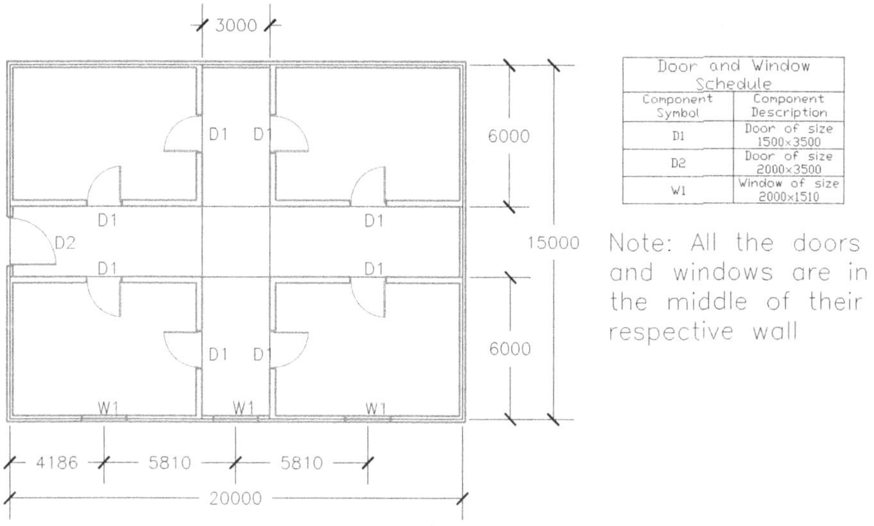

Figure 3-42 *Plan view of a building*

Examine the model to determine the number of features in it. The model consists of three features, refer to Figure 3-41.

The following steps are required to complete this tutorial:

a. Create a project file with the name Office.
b. Create a new construct plan with the name *C03_tut01*.
c. Create walls by using the reference of line diagram.
d. Create doors according to the plan.
e. Create windows according to the plan.

Starting a New Project File

1. Start AutoCAD MEP by double-clicking on the AutoCAD MEP 2022 - English (Global) icon from the desktop. Next, choose **New > Project** from the **Application Menu**; the **Project Browser** is displayed.

2. Choose the **New Project** button available at the bottom of the **Project Browser**; the **Add Project** dialog box is displayed.

3. Enter the project name as **Office** in the **Project Name** field. Also, enter the **Project Number** as **0001** and specify the description about the project as desired in their respective fields. Make sure that the **Create from template project** check box is selected.

4. Choose the **Browse** button and select the file *Commercial Template Project (Metric).apj* from the *C:\ProgramData\Autodesk\MEP 2022\enu\Template\Commercial Template Project (Metric)* directory

and then choose the **Open** button; the path of the selected file is added to the edit box displayed below the **Create from template project** check box.

5. Choose the **OK** button; the newly created project file name is displayed in the left pane of the **Project Browser**.

6. Choose the **Close** button from the **Project Browser**; the **PROJECT NAVIGATOR** palette is displayed in the drawing area and the new project is activated. By default, the **Constructs** tab is active in the **PROJECT NAVIGATOR**.

Adding a New Construct

1. Choose the **Construct** tab in the **PROJECT NAVIGATOR**.

2. Choose the **Add Construct** button available at the bottom of the **PROJECT NAVIGATOR**; the **Add Construct** dialog box is displayed.

3. Click in the **Name** field and specify the name of construct as *C03_tut01*. Make sure the **Open in drawing editor** check box is selected and choose the **OK** button; the *C03_tut01* drawing file is opened.

Creating Walls

Now, you will create walls.

1. Choose the **Architecture** option from the **Workspace Switching** flyout if not already selected.

2. Choose the **Wall** tool from the **Wall** drop-down available in the **Build** panel of the **Home** tab; you are prompted to specify the start point of the wall. Also, the corresponding **PROPERTIES** palette is displayed.

3. Specify the value for width, base height, and justify as **254**, **4000**, and **Center**, respectively, in their respective fields in the **Dimensions** rollout of the **PROPERTIES** palette.

4. Click to specify the start point of the wall and then create the walls, as shown in Figure 3-43. For dimensions, refer to Figure 3-42.

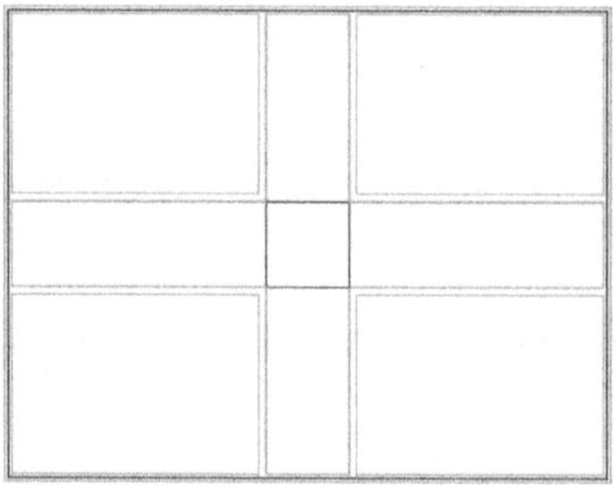

Figure 3-43 *Walls created*

Creating Doors

Now, you will create doors. For dimensions, refer to Figure 3-42.

1. Choose the **Door** tool from the **Door** drop-down available in the **Build** panel of the **Home** tab; you are prompted to select a wall or a grid assembly. Also, the **PROPERTIES** palette is displayed.

2. Specify the value for width and height as **1500** and **3500**, respectively, in their respective fields in the **Dimensions** rollout of the **PROPERTIES** palette. Also, select the **Offset/Center** option from the **Position along wall** field in the **Location** rollout of the **PROPERTIES** palette.

Note

*The **Offset/Center** option helps you to justify the position of the doors at the center of the wall.*

3. Click at the required locations to place the door D1, refer to Figure 3-42.

4. Now, specify width as **2000** in the **Width** field available in the **Dimensions** rollout of the **PROPERTIES** palette and create the main gate D2. For positioning the gates, refer to Figure 3-42.

   After creating the doors, the drawing is displayed, as shown in Figure 3-44.

Figure 3-44 *The drawing after creating gates*

Creating Windows

Now, you will create windows with the specifications given in Figure 3-42.

1. Choose the **Window** tool from the **Window** drop-down available in the **Build** panel of the **Home** tab; you are prompted to select a wall or a grid assembly. Also, the **PROPERTIES** palette with corresponding options is displayed.

2. Specify the value for width and height for the window as **2000** and **1510** respectively, in their corresponding fields in the **Dimensions** rollout of the **PROPERTIES** palette. Also, select the **Offset/Center** option from the **Position along wall** field in the **Location** rollout of the **PROPERTIES** palette.

3. Click at the required locations to create the windows W1, refer to Figure 3-42.

   The final model in the **SW Isometric** view and the **Conceptual** display style is shown in Figure 3-45.

Figure 3-45 *Model of a building*

Saving the Drawing File

1. Choose **Save** from the **Application Menu** to save the drawing file with the name *c03_tut1*.

Tutorial 2

In this tutorial, you will create a model of a building, as shown in Figure 3-46. The plan of the building is given in Figure 3-47. **(Expected time: 30 min)**

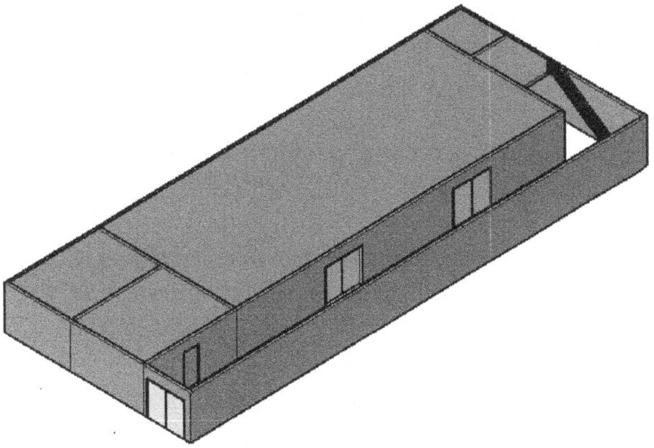

Figure 3-46 Model of a building

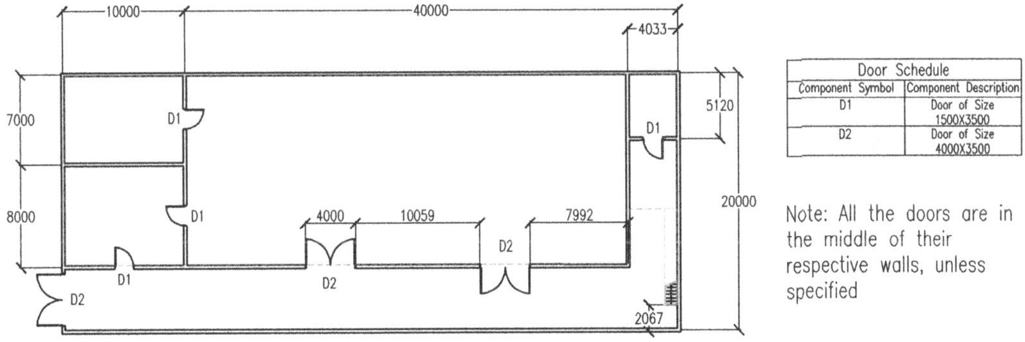

Figure 3-47 The plan of the building

The following steps are required to complete this tutorial:

a. Create a new project file.
b. Create a new construct with the name C03_tut02.
c. Create walls by using the reference of the line diagram.
d. Create doors according the plan.
e. Create the roof according to the plan.
f. Create the stairs.
g. Create a cut in the slab for railing.
h. Create railing on the stairs.

After starting the AutoCAD MEP session, the first task is to create a project.

Starting a New Project File

1. Start AutoCAD MEP by double-clicking on the AutoCAD MEP 2022- English (Global) icon from the desktop and then choose **New > Project** from the **Application Menu**; the **Project Browser** is displayed.

2. Choose the **New Project** button available at the bottom of the **Project Browser**; the **Add Project** dialog box is displayed.

3. Enter the project name as **Machining Plant** in the **Project Name** field. Also, enter the project number and description in their respective fields. Select *Commercial Template Project (Metric).apj* as the template for the project using the **Browse** button.

4. Choose the **OK** button; the newly created project file name is displayed on the left pane of the **Project Browser**.

5. Choose the **Close** button from the **Project Browser**; the **PROJECT NAVIGATOR** palette is displayed in the drawing area and the new project is activated.

Adding a New Construct

1. Choose the **Constructs** tab from the **PROJECT NAVIGATOR**. Choose the **Add Construct** button available at the bottom of the **PROJECT NAVIGATOR**; the **Add Construct** dialog box is displayed.

2. Click in the **Name** field and specify the name of the construct as *C03_tut02*. Make sure that the **Open in drawing editor** check box is selected and choose the **OK** button; the *C03_tut02* drawing file is opened.

Creating Walls

Now, you need to create walls. Make sure that the **Architecture** workspace is active.

1. Choose the **Wall** tool from the **Wall** drop-down available in the **Build** panel of the **Home** tab; you are prompted to specify the start point of the wall. Also, the **PROPERTIES** palette is displayed.

2. Specify width, base height, and justify as **254**, **4500**, and **Center**, respectively in their respective fields in the **Dimensions** rollout of the **PROPERTIES** palette if not specified.

3. Click to specify the start point of the wall and then create the walls, as shown in Figure 3-48. For dimensions, refer to Figure 3-47.

Figure 3-48 *Walls created using reference of line diagram*

Creating Doors

Now, you need to create doors. For dimensions, refer to Figure 3-47. Make sure that the **Architecture** workspace is active.

1. Choose the **Door** tool from the **Door** drop-down available in the **Build** panel of the **Home** tab; you are prompted to select a wall or a grid assembly.

   Note that the **PROPERTIES** palette with the corresponding options is displayed.

2. Specify width and height as **1500** and **3500** respectively, in their respective fields in the **Dimensions** rollout of the **PROPERTIES** palette.

3. Also, select the **Offset/Center** option from the **Position along wall** field in the **Location** rollout and make sure that the **Standard** option is selected in the **Style** drop-down list of the **PROPERTIES** palette.

4. Click at the required locations to create the doors D1, refer to Figure 3-47.

   Now, you need to create the hinged double doors. As these doors are not available by default, so you need to select the **Hinged-Double** door option from the **PROPERTIES** palette.

5. Select the **Door** tool from the **Door** drop-down available in the **Build** panel of the **Home** tab; you are prompted to select a wall or a grid assembly. Also, the **PROPERTIES** palette with the corresponding options is displayed.

6. Click on the **Browse** area in the **PROPERTIES** palette; the **STYLES BROWSER** palette is displayed. Choose the **Hinged-Double** door option from the gallery of **STYLE BROWSER** and double-click on it to select the door style.

7. Specify width and height as **4000** and **3500** in their respective fields in the **Dimensions** rollout of the **PROPERTIES** palette. Select the **Unconstrained** option from the **Position along wall** field in the **Location** rollout of the **PROPERTIES** palette.

Note

*The **Unconstrained** option is chosen in the **Position along wall** field of the **Location** rollout, so you can place the door D2 without any dimension reference.*

8. Click at the required location to position the doors D2, as shown in the Figure 3-47.

   After creating the doors, the drawing is displayed as shown in Figure 3-49.

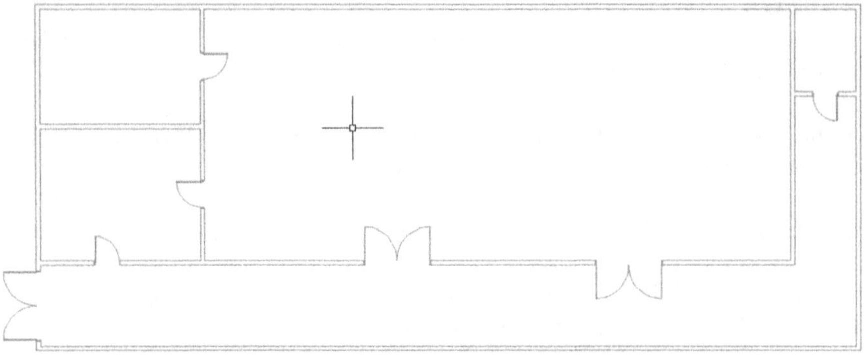

Figure 3-49 The drawing after creating all the doors

Creating Slab

Now, you need to create the slab with the specifications shown in Figure 3-50.

1. Choose the **Slab** tool from the **Roof Slab** drop-down available in the **Build** panel of the **Home** tab; you are prompted to specify the start point of the slab.

2. Select one of the corner points of the building displayed in Figure 3-50; you are prompted to specify the next point for the slab.

3. Select rest of the corner points as shown in Figure 3-50 and then press ENTER; the slab is created.

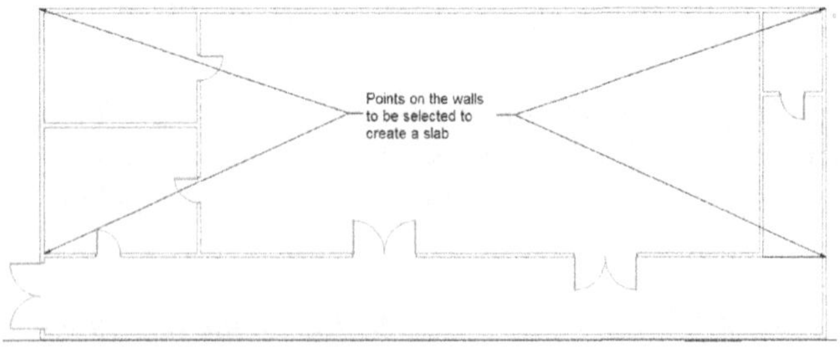

Figure 3-50 Corner points for the slab

Creating Stairs

Now, you will create stairs attached to the slab.

1. Choose the **Stair** tool from the **Stair** drop-down available in the **Build** panel of the **Home** tab; you are prompted to specify the flight start point. Also, the **PROPERTIES** palette is displayed with the options relevant to stairs.

2. Choose **Straight** from the **Shape** drop-down list in the **General** rollout. Specify width, height, justification, and termination as **1000**, **4500**, **Right**, and **Landing** in their respective fields in the **PROPERTIES** palette.

3. Select a starting point for stairs and align it with the adjacent wall, refer to Figure 3-51.

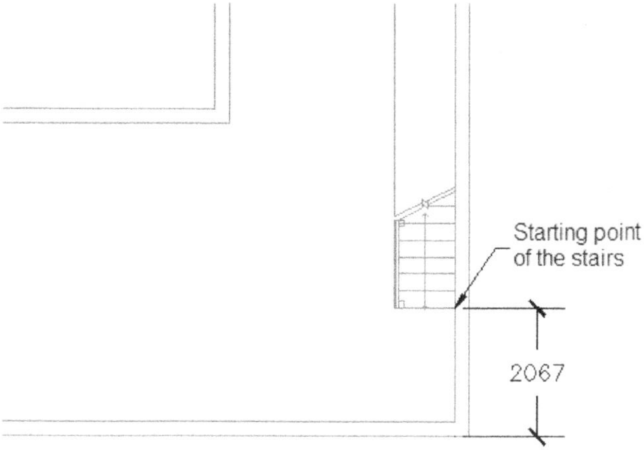

Figure 3-51 *Starting point of the stairs*

Now, you will create a cut on the slab to allow a passage through the stairs to the top of the roof.

Creating Cut in the Slab

1. Choose the **Rectangle** tool from the **Rectangle** drop-down available in the **Draw** panel of the **Home** tab; you are prompted to specify the first corner point. Specify the corner points for the rectangle, as shown in Figure 3-52.

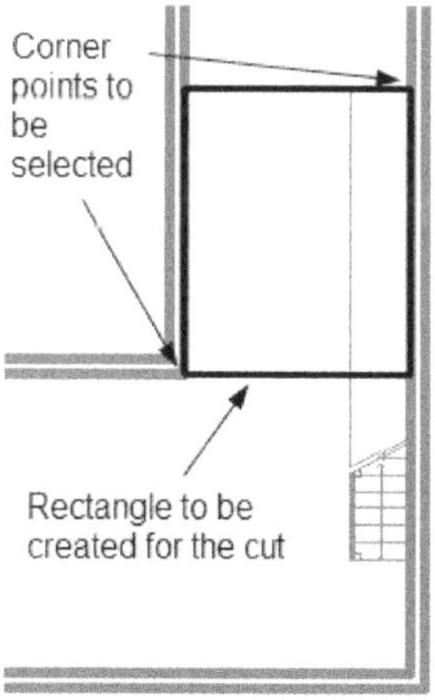

Figure 3-52 *Rectangle to be created for cut in the slab*

2. Select the slab and choose the **Trim** tool from the **Modify** panel in the **Slab** contextual tab; you are prompted to select a trimming object like a polygon or a solid object.

3. Select the rectangle created for the cut and press ENTER; you are prompted to specify the side to be deleted.

4. Click inside the rectangle, the area covered by the rectangle is trimmed. Press ESC to exit the tool.

   Now you need to hide the rectangle geometry created for trimming.

5. Right-click after selecting the rectangle; a shortcut menu is displayed. Move the cursor on the **Isloate Objects** option in the shortcut menu; a flyout is displayed. Choose the **Hide Objects** option to hide the rectangle. Isometric view of the drawing after creating the cut is shown in Figure 3-53.

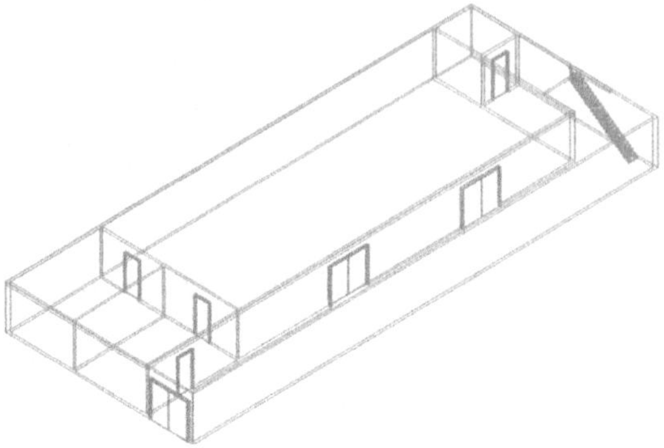

Figure 3-53 *Drawing after creating the cut in the slab*

Creating Railing on the Stairs

1. Choose the **Railing** tool from the **Stair** drop-down available in the **Build** panel of the **Home** tab; you are prompted to specify the start point for the railing.

2. Choose **Attach** and then the **Stair** option from the command prompt; you are prompted to select a stair.

3. Select the stairs created earlier; a railing with the standard settings is created in the drawing area.

4. Deselect all the entities, select the railing, and invoke the **PROPERTIES** palette.

5. Enter **900** in the **Side offset** field in the **Location** rollout of the **PROPERTIES** palette.

   After creating all the components, the final drawing (in conceptual view) is displayed, as shown in Figure 3-54.

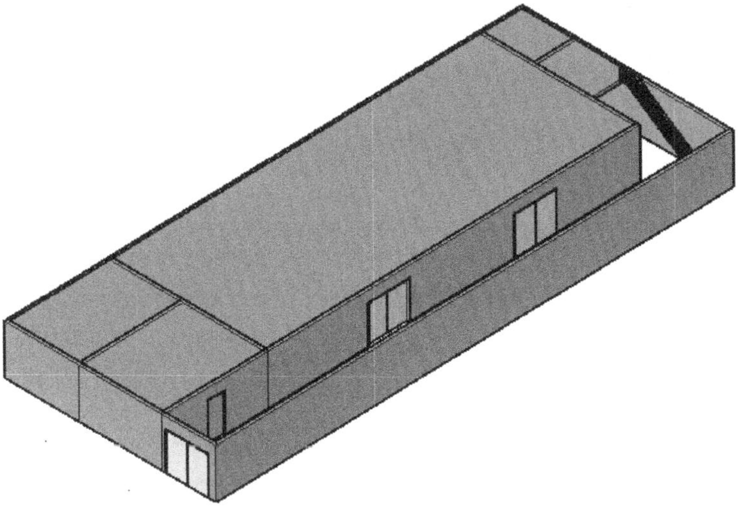

Figure 3-54 The final drawing

Saving the Drawing File

1. Choose **Save** from the **Application Menu** to save the drawing file with the name *c03_tut2*.

Self-Evaluation Test

Answer the following questions and then compare them to those given at the end of this chapter:

1. A __________ is an opening in a wall or door to facilitate the passage of air and light.

2. The __________ tool is used to create a segment of roof which is not connected with other entities.

3. A __________ window can be created on a cornered wall.

4. You cannot create a curved wall using the **Wall** tool. (T/F)

5. A curtain wall is a non-structural wall. (T/F)

6. Using the **Stair** tool, you can create only straight stairs. (T/F)

Review Questions

Answer the following questions:

1. On selecting a slab, the __________ contextual tab gets activated in the **Ribbon**.

2. The __________ tool is used to convert the network of lines into column grids.

3. **WALLADD** command is use to create curtain walls. (T/F)

4. Spiral stairs can be created only in clockwise direction. (T/F)

5. The **Railing** tool can be used to attach railing to a stair. (T/F)

EXERCISE

Exercise 1

Create the building model shown in Figure 3-55. The plan view of the building is shown in Figure 3-56. **(Expected time: 45 min)**

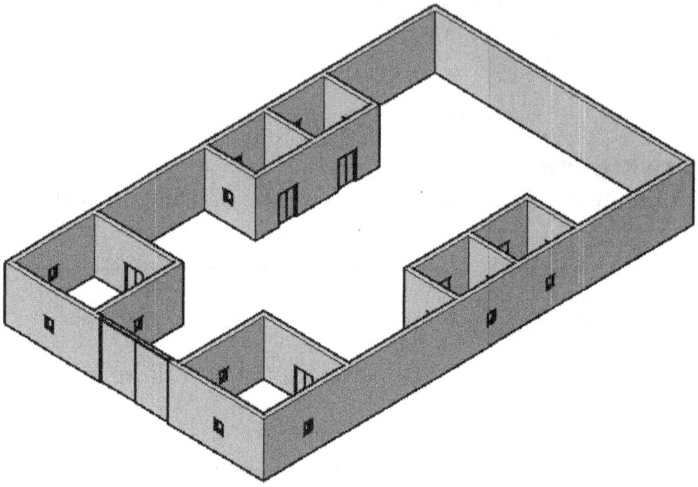

Figure 3-55 *Model for Exercise 1*

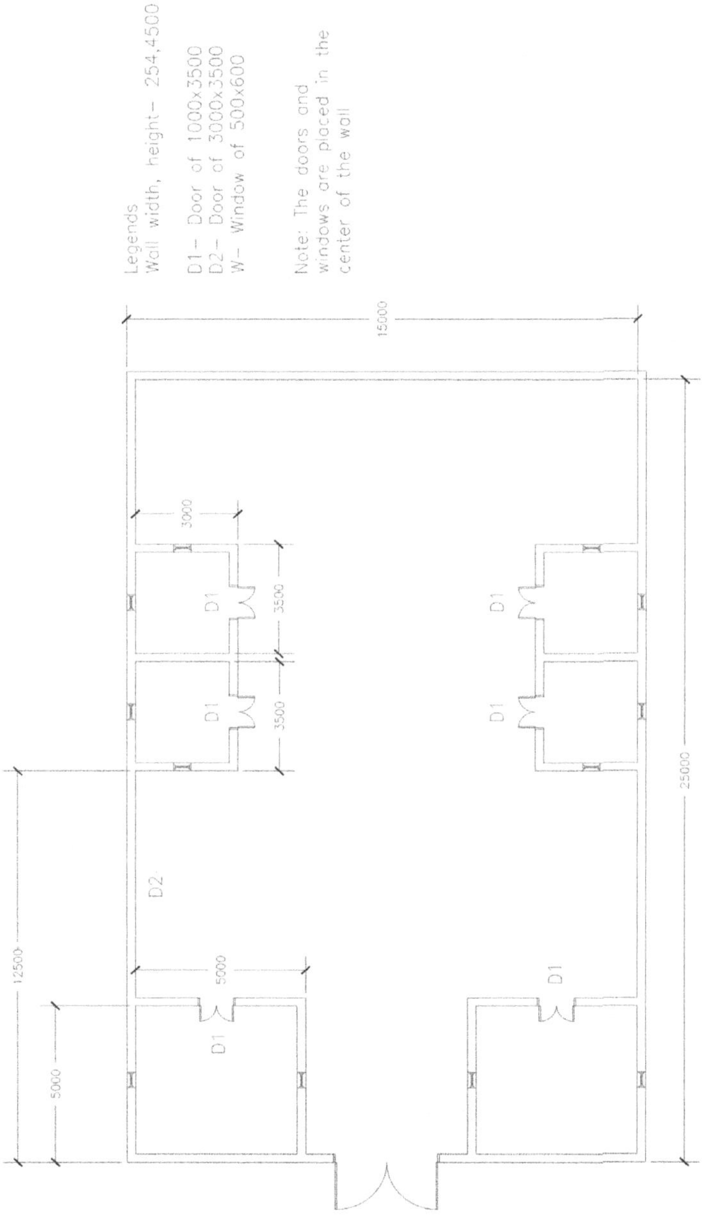

Figure 3-56 Plan of the building

Answers to Self-Evaluation Test

1. window, **2. Roof Slab**, **3.** cornered, **4.** F, **5.** T, **6.** F

Chapter 4

Creating an HVAC System

Learning Objectives

After completing this chapter, you will be able to:

- *Use HVAC tools*
- *Change the basic settings of an HVAC system*
- *Configure duct work options*
- *Route the duct line*
- *Create ducts*

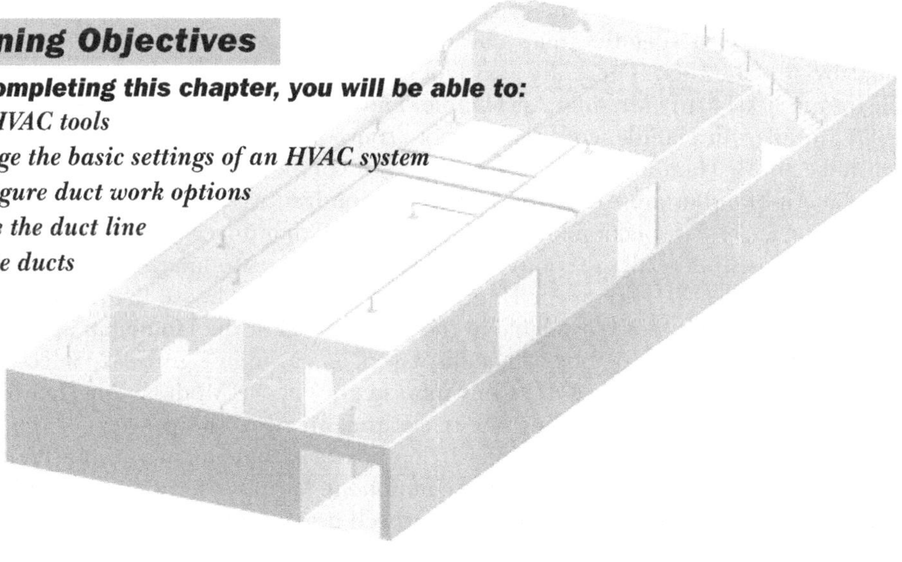

INTRODUCTION

In this chapter, you will learn about the use of mechanical equipments that are required for creating an HVAC system. An HVAC system is used to maintain desired environmental conditions at a specific area. It consists of the heating, ventilation, and air conditioning systems. To create an HVAC system, you need to know the heating load of the desired area by using thermodynamics, fluid mechanics, and heat transfer principles. These load settings are used to determine the capacity of equipment to be added for HVAC. To start working in the **HVAC** workspace, choose the **HVAC** option from the **Workspace Switching** flyout in the **Application Status Bar**. The equipments available in the **HVAC** workspace of AutoCAD MEP are discussed next.

EQUIPMENT

For creating an HVAC system, you need to add equipment related to the system to the building structure. All the equipments that can be added while working in the **HVAC** workspace are available in the **Equipment** drop-down of the **Build** panel in the **Home** tab of the **Ribbon**, refer to Figure 4-1. The tools available in this drop-down are discussed next.

*Figure 4-1 The **Equipment** drop-down*

Air Handler

Air Handler is an equipment or a device which is used to circulate air in a specific area. The quality of air is also controlled by Air Handler. There are two types of Air Handlers available in AutoCAD MEP: Modular Air Handler and Packaged Air Handler. A Modular Air Handler consists of various components that together make an Air Handler. Some of the important components in a Modular Air Handler are AHU Coils, AHU Economizer, AHU Fans, AHU Filters, AHU Inspection Modules, and AHU Mixing Boxes. A Packaged Air Handler is a closed unit consisting of all the components available in the Modular Air Handler but in an interconnected manner. To add an Air Handler in the drawing, choose the **Air Handler** tool from the **Equipment** drop-down available in the **Build** panel of the **Home** tab in the **Ribbon**; the **Add Multi-view Parts** dialog box will be displayed, as shown in Figure 4-2. Select the AHU Large Coils component from the AHU Coils sub-category of the Modular Air Handling Unit Components category of Air Handling Units equipment. Also, the preview of the selected component is displayed in the right of the dialog box. The blue arrows in the Preview area indicate the flow of fluid through the selected component. Various components in the Modular Air Handling Unit Components category are discussed next.

AHU Coils

The AHU Coil is a component of Modular Air Handler which is used to cool or heat the air coming through the duct. There are four ports of AHU Coil component: Duct inlet port, Duct outlet port, Heat Exchanging fluid inlet port, and Heat Exchanging fluid outlet port. To add an AHU Coil in the drawing, click on the + sign adjacent to **AHU Coils** in the **Modular Air Handling Unit Components** category of **Air Handling Units** equipment; three types of AHU Coils will be displayed below the **AHU Coils** sub-category.

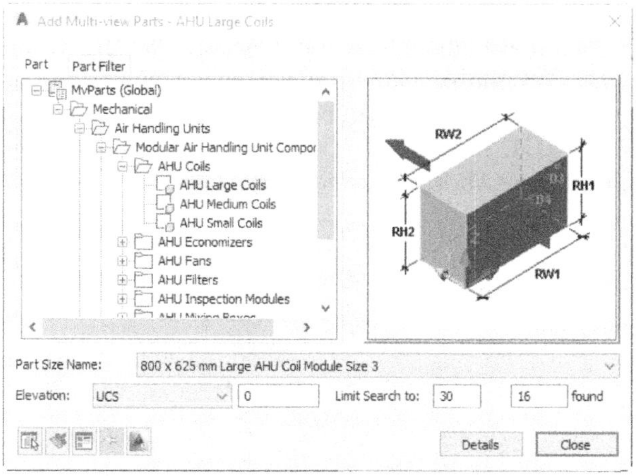

Figure 4-2 *The* ***Add Multi-view Parts*** *dialog box*

You can choose any of the three options: **AHU Large Coils**, **AHU Medium Coils**, and **AHU Small Coils**, as per the requirement. After choosing the desired option, select the required size from the **Part Size Name** drop-down list available below the Preview area. After selecting the respective size for AHU coil, click in the drawing area; the AHU Coils will be attached to the cursor. Now, click at the required position to place it; the AHU Coils will be placed at the selected position and a compass will be displayed below the AHU Coils. Orient the AHU Coils at the desired angle by using the compass. Figure 4-3 shows an annotated AHU Coils.

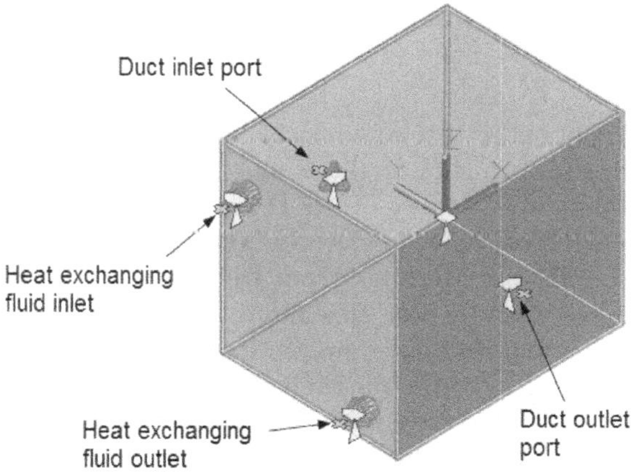

Figure 4-3 *An AHU Coils*

AHU Economizer

The AHU Economizer is a component of the AHU system which is used to increase the efficiency of an AHU system by using natural air. In an Economizer, natural air is used to heat or cool the air in a specific area. For example, if the temperature inside a room is higher than the temperature outside, then the economizer draws air from outside and mixes with the inside air to create an ambient temperature. To add an AHU Economizer in the drawing, click on the **+** sign adjacent to **AHU Economizers** in the **Modular Air Handling Unit Components** category of **Air Handling Units** equipment. On doing so, the **AHU Modular Economizers** will be displayed below the **AHU Economizers** sub-category. Next, select the required size from the **Part Size Name** drop-down list which is available below the Preview area. After selecting the size, click in the drawing area; the AHU Economizer will be attached to the cursor. Now, click at the required position to place it; the AHU Economizer will be placed at the selected position and a compass will be displayed below the AHU Economizer. Orient the AHU Economizer at the desired angle by using the compass. Figure 4-4 shows an annotated AHU Economizer.

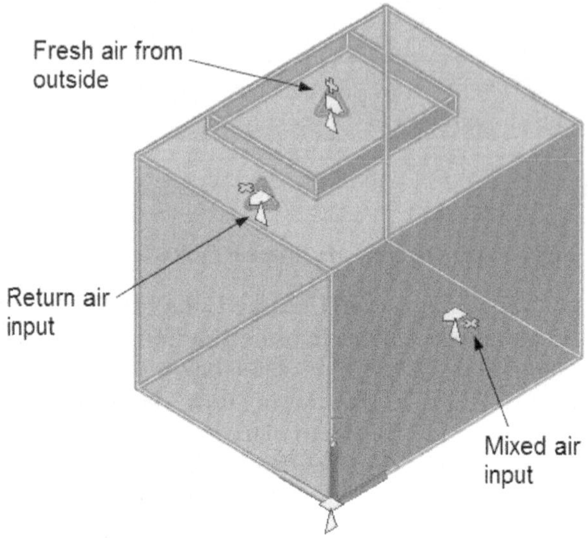

Figure 4-4 *An AHU Economizer*

AHU Fan

The AHU Fan is a component of the AHU system which forces the air to flow through the duct. To add an AHU Fan to the drawing, click on the + sign adjacent to **AHU Fans** in the **Modular Air Handling Unit Components** category of **Air Handling Units** equipment. On doing so, three types of AHU Fans will be displayed below the **AHU Fans** sub-category. You can choose any of the three options: **AHU Fan Modules Front Discharge Up**, **AHU Fan Modules Rear Discharge Up**, and **AHU Fan Modules Side Discharge**, as per the requirement. After choosing the desired option, select the required size from the **Part Size Name** drop-down list available below the Preview area. After selecting the required size for the AHU Fan, click in the drawing area; the AHU Fan will be attached to the cursor. Now, click at the required position to place it; the AHU Fan will be placed at the selected position and a compass will be displayed below it. Orient the AHU Fan at the desired angle by using the compass. Figure 4-5 shows an annotated AHU Fan Modules Side Discharge.

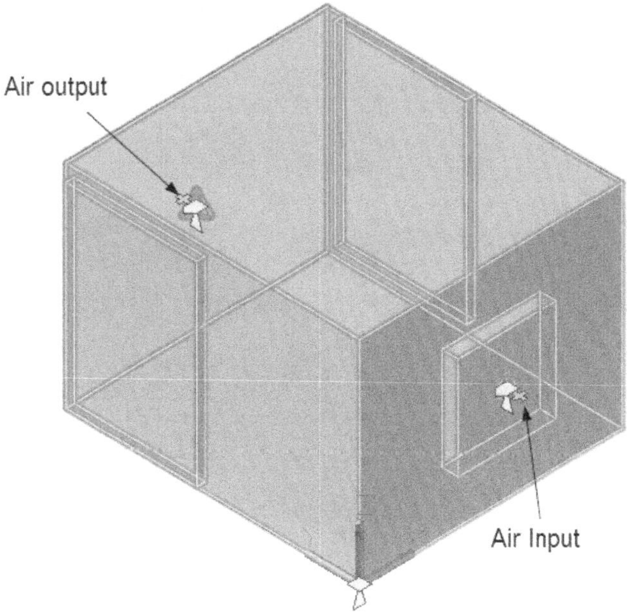

Figure 4-5 *An AHU Fan Modules Side Discharge*

AHU Filter

The AHU Filter is a component of the AHU system which filters the air coming from the input line. After filtering the air, it is passed to the AHU Inspection Module. To add an AHU Filter to the drawing, click on the **+** sign adjacent to **AHU Filters** in the **Modular Air Handling Unit Components** category of **Air Handling Units** equipment; four types of AHU Filters will be displayed below the **AHU Filters** sub-category. You can choose any of the following four options as per your requirement: **AHU Angle Filter**, **AHU Bag Filter**, **AHU Cartridge Filter**, and **AHU Panel Filter**. After choosing the required option, select the size from the **Part Size Name** drop-down list available below the Preview area. After selecting the required size for the AHU Filter, click in the drawing area; the AHU Filter will be attached to the cursor. Now, click at the required position to place it; the AHU Filter will be placed at the selected position and a compass will be displayed below it. Orient the AHU Filter at the desired angle by using the compass. Figure 4-6 shows an annotated AHU Bag Filter.

AHU Inspection Modules

The AHU Inspection Module is a component of the AHU system which is used to check the quality of air being spread in the desired area. To add an AHU Inspection Module to the drawing, click on the **+** sign adjacent to **AHU Inspection Modules** in the **Modular Air Handling Unit Components** category of **Air Handling Units**; the following three types of AHU Inspection Modules will be displayed: **Inspection Module Large**, **Inspection Module Medium**, and **Inspection Module Small**. These inspection module categories vary according to the size required for the system. After choosing the required option, select the required size from the **Part Size Name** drop-down list. Next, click in the drawing area; the AHU Inspection Module will be attached to the cursor. Now, click at the required position to place it; the AHU Inspection Module will be placed at the selected position and a compass will be displayed below it. Orient the AHU Inspection Module at the desired angle by using the compass. An AHU Inspection Module has two ports: one for inlet of air and the other for outlet of air.

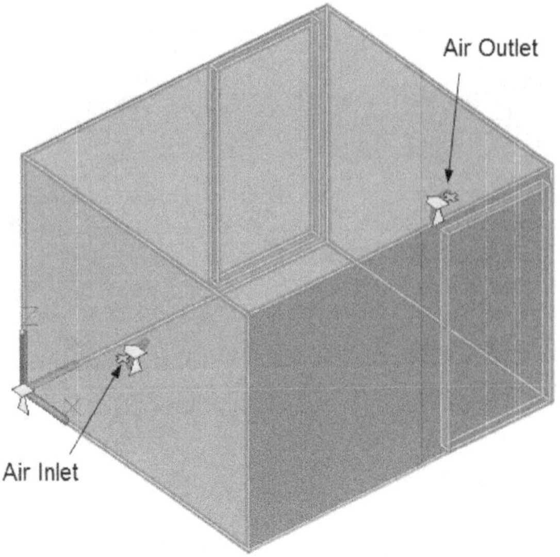

***Figure 4-6** An AHU Bag Filter*

AHU Mixing Boxes

The AHU Mixing Box is a component of the AHU system that mixes the returning air with the outside air as per the requirement. To add an AHU Mixing Box in the drawing, click on the **+** sign adjacent to **AHU Mixing Boxes** in the **Modular Air Handling Unit Components** category of **Air Handling Units** equipment. On doing so, the **AHU Mixing Boxes** will be displayed below the **AHU Mixing Boxes** sub-category. After selecting the required AHU mixing box, select the size from the **Part Size Name** drop-down list available below the Preview area. After selecting the required size, click in the drawing area; the AHU Mixing Box will be attached to the cursor. Now, click at the required position to place it; the AHU Mixing Box will be placed at the selected position and a compass will be displayed below it. Orient the AHU Mixing Box at the desired angle by using the compass. An AHU Mixing Box has three ports: for the inlet of returning air, for the inlet of fresh air, and for the outlet of mixed air.

Air Terminal

Air Terminal is a vent through which the fresh air is diffused in a specific area. To add a vent to the drawing, choose the **Air Terminal** tool from the **Equipment** drop-down in the **Build** panel of the **Home** tab; the **Add Multi-view Parts** dialog box will be displayed with the options for Air Terminals, as shown in Figure 4-7. There are three categories available for Air Terminals; **Diffusers**, **Grilles**, and **Registers**. Click on the **+** sign adjacent to the desired category in the dialog box; the available options will be displayed below that category. Select the required option; different sizes for the selected option will be displayed in the **Part Size Name** drop-down list. Select the required size from the list and then click in the drawing area; the Air Terminal will be attached to the cursor. Now, click at the required position to place the air terminal. On placing the Air Terminal, you will be prompted to specify the rotation angle by using the compass displayed below it. Specify the rotation angle either by entering the value at the command prompt or dynamically specify the value by clicking on the screen. On doing so, the air terminal will be placed at the desired point and angle. Close the dialog box by choosing the **Close** button after adding the required number of air terminals.

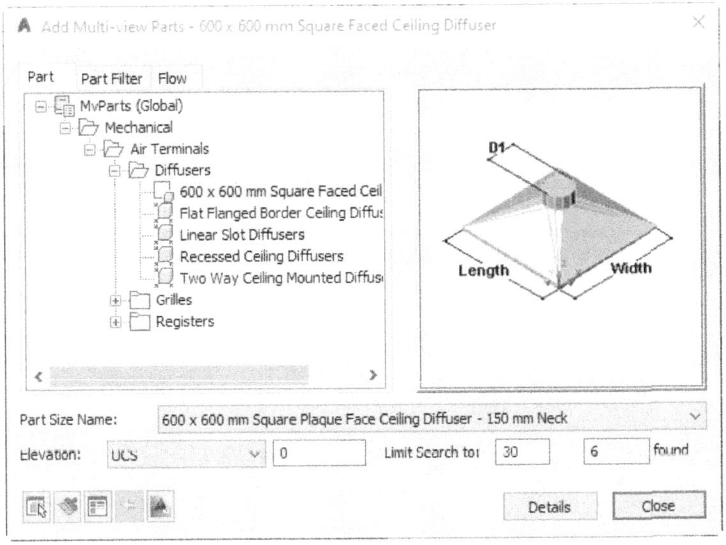

*Figure 4-7 The **Add Multi-view Parts** dialog box with options for Air Terminals*

Note

*You can specify the flow rate for the selected air terminal by using the **Flow (Each Terminal)** edit box available in the **Flow** tab of the **Add Multi-view Parts** dialog box. The unit for specifying the value should be l/s.*

Fan

Fan is an equipment that generates a current of air. To add a fan to the drawing, choose the **Fan** tool from the **Equipment** drop-down in the **Build** panel of the **Home** tab; the **Add Multi-view Parts** dialog box will be displayed with the options related to fans, as shown in Figure 4-8. Select the required fan from the list; various sizes for the selected fan will be displayed in the **Part Size Name** drop down list available below the Preview area. Select the required size from the list and click in the drawing area; the Fan will be attached to the cursor. Now, click at the required position to place it; the selected fan will be placed at the specified location and a compass will be displayed below the fan in the drawing area. Using this compass, you can specify the rotation value dynamically. On doing so, the fan will be placed at the desired point and angle. After adding the required number of fans, close the dialog box by choosing the **Close** button.

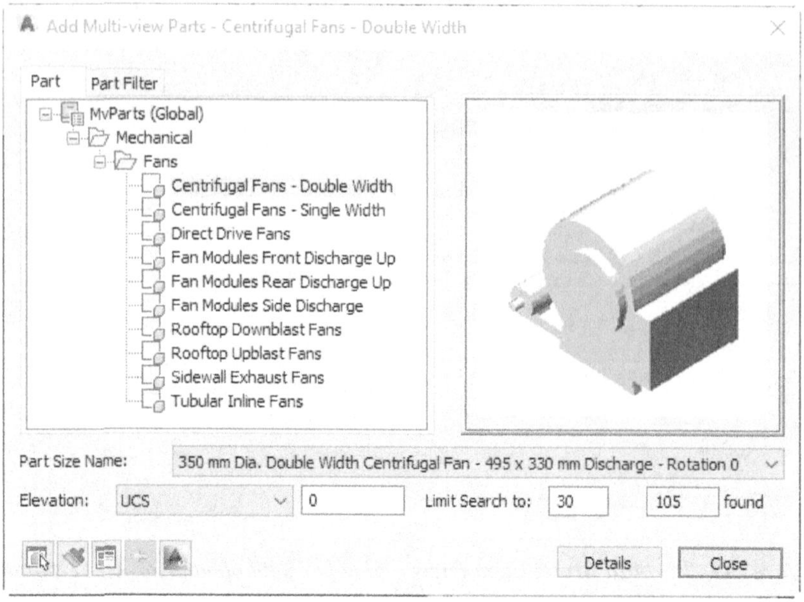

***Figure 4-8** The **Add Multi-view Parts** dialog box with options for fans*

Damper

Damper is an HVAC equipment that is used to regulate the flow of air in an HVAC system. To add a damper to a system, choose the **Damper** tool from the **Equipment** drop-down in the **Build** panel of the **Home** tab; the **Add Multi-view Parts** dialog box will be displayed with the options for dampers, as shown in Figure 4-9. There are four categories of dampers: **Balancing Dampers**, **Fire Dampers**, **Rectangular Curtain Fire Shield Damper**, and **Rectangular Smoke Shield Damper PTC**. The Balancing Damper is used to control the amount of air flowing through the duct. The Fire Damper is used to restrict the flow of fire through the duct, in case the building catches a fire. The Rectangular Curtain Fire Shield Damper is also used as a shield against fire but this type of fire dampers are in the form of curtains. The Rectangular Smoke Shield Damper PTC is used as a shield against smoke. PTC is a type of smoke shield damper which stands for Proportional Torque Control. Click on the **+** sign adjacent to the required category; a list with relative dampers will be displayed. Select the required damper from the list; various sizes for the selected damper will be displayed in the **Part Size Name** drop-down list available below the Preview area. Select the required size from the list and click in the drawing area; the Damper will be attached to the cursor. Now, click at required position to place it; the selected damper will be placed at the specified location and a compass will be displayed below the damper in the drawing area. Using this compass, you can specify the value of rotation dynamically. After specifying all the required parameters, the Damper will be placed at the desired point and angle. Close the dialog box by choosing the **Close** button from the **Add Multi-View Parts** dialog box.

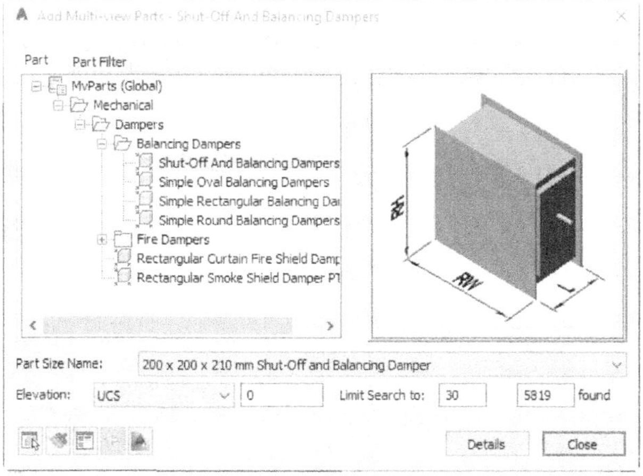

***Figure 4-9** The **Add Multi-view Parts** dialog box with options for dampers*

VAV Unit

A VAV unit is an equipment used for varying the speed of air flowing through the duct. The temperature of air to be supplied to VAV unit is constant; therefore, the air flow is regulated to meet the user requirements. To add a VAV Unit in the HVAC system, choose the **VAV Unit** tool from the **Equipment** drop-down in the **Build** panel of the **Home** tab; the **Add Multi-view Parts** dialog box will be displayed with the options for VAV unit, as shown in Figure 4-10. In this dialog box, there are two options available for selecting the type of VAV unit for the HVAC system Design: **Air Terminals** and **VAV Units**. The **Air Terminals** option has a sub option **Outlet Plenums**. The **VAV Units** has the sub option, **VAV Boxes** which can be opened in the Add Multi View Parts window. Click on the **+** sign adjacent to the required category; a list of relative VAV boxes will be displayed. Select the required VAV Unit from the **VAV Units** category; the standard sizes available for the selected VAV Unit will be displayed in the **Part Size Name** drop-down list. Choose the required size from the drop-down list and click in the drawing area; the VAV Unit will be attached with the cursor. Now, click at required position to place it; the VAV Unit will be placed at the selected position and a compass will be displayed attached to the VAV unit for specifying the angle. Specify the rotation angle and then choose the **Close** button from the **Add Multi-view Parts** dialog box.

Equipment

Using the **Equipment** tool, you can add any equipment available in AutoCAD MEP to the structure. When you choose the **Equipment** tool from the **Equipment** drop-down of the **Build** panel of the **Home** tab, the **Add Multi-view Parts** dialog box will be displayed, as shown in Figure 4-11. Click on the **+** sign adjacent to the **Mechanical** category in the dialog box; the various equipment categories available in AutoCAD MEP will be displayed in a tree structure, refer to Figure 4-12.

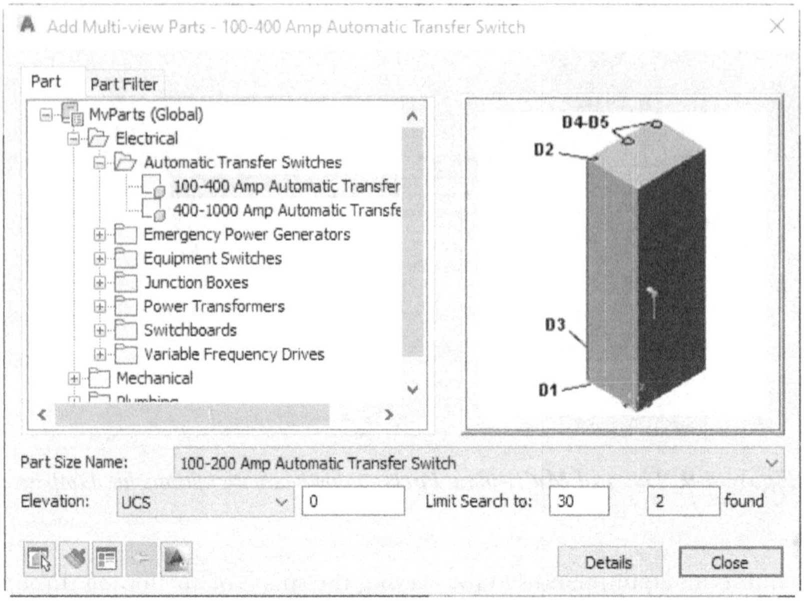

*Figure 4-10 The **Add Multi-view Parts** dialog box with options for VAV unit*

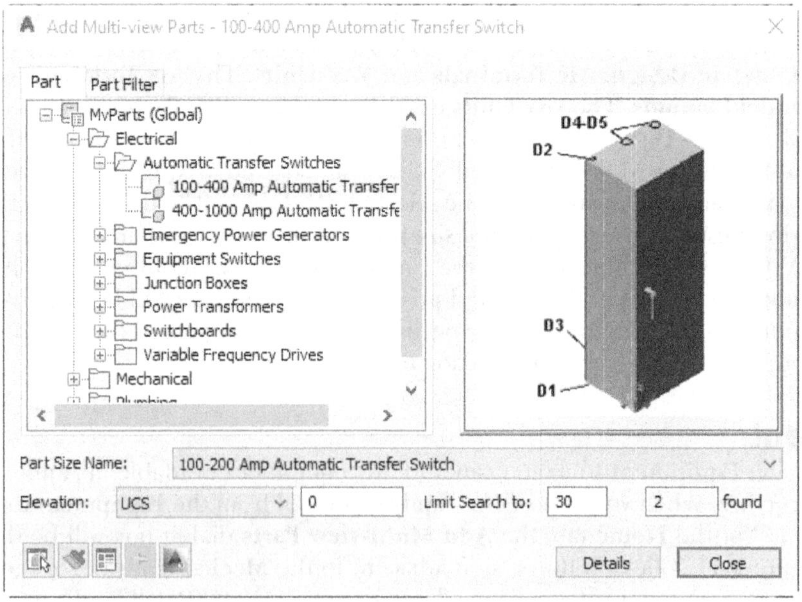

*Figure 4-11 The **Add Multi-view Parts** dialog box*

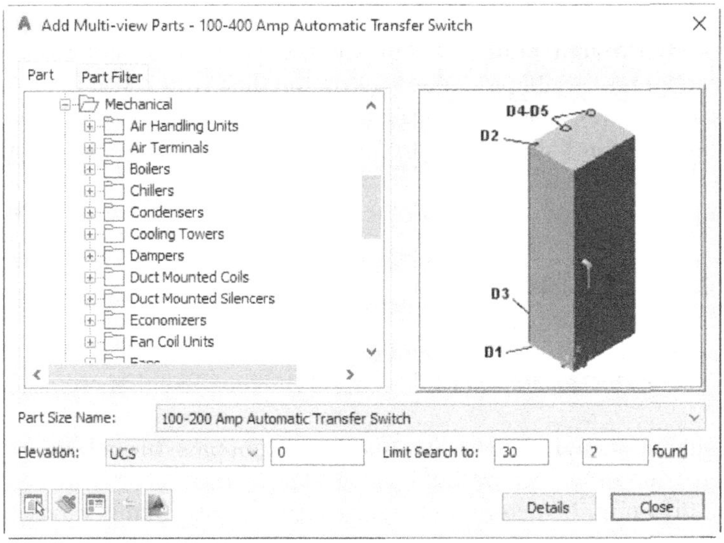

***Figure 4-12** The **Add Multi-view Parts** dialog box with mechanical equipment*

Click on the + sign adjacent to the required Equipment; various options related to the selected Equipment will be displayed in a list. Select the required option from the list and then click in the drawing area; the Equipment will be attached with the cursor. Now, click at the required position to place it; the Equipment will be placed at the selected position and a compass will also be displayed below the Equipment. Using this compass, you can rotate the Equipment at the required angle. After specifying the angle, choose the **Close** button from the **Add Multi-view Parts** dialog box to exit the dialog box.

DUCT LINE

Duct line is the circuit of ducts inserted in a particular area to create desired air and temperature conditions. Before creating a duct line, you must know about the specifications such as size of duct, air flow rate in the duct, number of branches required, and the size of duct in the branches. After entering these specifications, you will create the path of duct line. The methods of sizing the duct and creating a duct line are discussed next.

Sizing the Duct Line

In AutoCAD MEP, the duct size of main duct line is dependent on two parameters: the total amount of air to be circulated which is controlled by **Flow Rate** variable and the velocity of air in the duct which is controlled by **Velocity** variable. These two variables are discussed next.

Flow Rate

You can change the value of this variable by using the **Flow Rate** edit box available in the **Sizing** rollout of the **PROPERTIES** palette which is displayed on choosing the **1-Line** tool from the **By Shape** area in the **TOOL PALETTES- HVAC**. Flow rate is the total volume of air that is to be provided in a specific area. Enter the flow rate value in the **Flow Rate** edit box in the **PROPERTIES** palette; the value of friction and velocity will be calculated according to the rules specified in the design properties of duct type.

Velocity

Velocity of air flowing through a duct is a dependent variable. You cannot control the value of this variable directly. This variable is dependent on the duct size. If you increase the duct size, the value of velocity will automatically decrease and also the value of friction will decrease. If you decrease the size of duct, the value of velocity and friction will increase. In other words with the duct size, you can control the value of velocity. Note that the value of velocity and friction also changes according to the option selected in the **System** drop-down list in the **BASIC** rollout.

Routing the Duct Line

Routing is the process of creating a duct line in a layout. Routing of duct involves many factors such as position of handling units, position of diffusers, and layout of building. There are some major points that are to be considered while routing the duct line that are discussed next.

1. Duct line should be routed in such a way that it does not pass through an area that is having a large temperature difference from the air inside the duct.
2. Rise/Slope of duct must be determined after considering the temperature of air inside the duct.
3. Duct routes must be as straight as possible.
4. Duct must be larger at the opening point to the air filter entry and at the returning point of the unit.
5. Always try to route through either the basement or the attic so that you can support the ducts by using the duct hangers.
6. It is always good to position the air terminals and air handling unit first before routing the duct line.
7. For a vertical run, the duct must be fastened to a wall.

Note

You will be more clear about the usage of the 1-Line tool in Tutorial 1 of this chapter.

DUCT

Duct is an object which is used to deliver or remove air from an HVAC system. There are two types of ducts available in AutoCAD MEP: Duct and Flex Duct. Tools to create these ducts are available in the **Duct** drop-down in the **Build** panel of the **Home** tab in the **Ribbon**. These tools are discussed next.

Duct

This tool is used to create a rigid duct in the HVAC system. This duct can be rectangular, oval, round, or custom shaped. To create a rigid duct, choose the **Duct** tool from the **Duct** drop-down in the **Build** panel of the **Home** tab in the **Ribbon**; the **PROPERTIES** palette will be displayed, as shown in Figure 4-13. The options available in the **PROPERTIES** palette are discussed next.

Description

This field is available in the **BASIC > General** rollout in the **PROPERTIES** palette of the **Design** tab. When you click in this field, the **Description** dialog box will be displayed, as shown in Figure 4-14. You can enter description of the selected object in the **Edit the description for this object** text box. Choose **OK** to exit the dialog box.

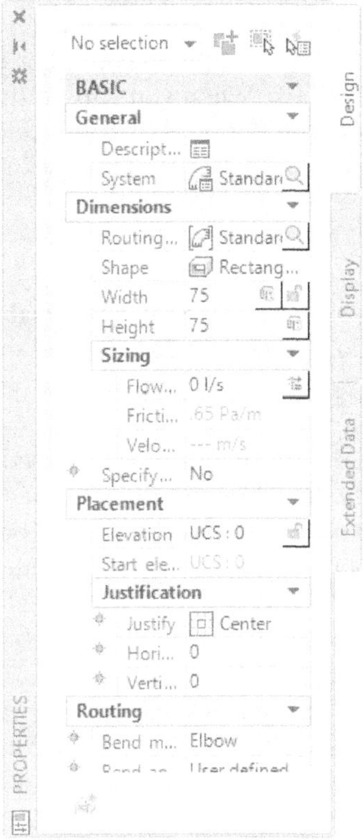

Figure 4-13 The ***PROPERTIES*** *palette displayed on choosing the* ***Duct*** *tool*

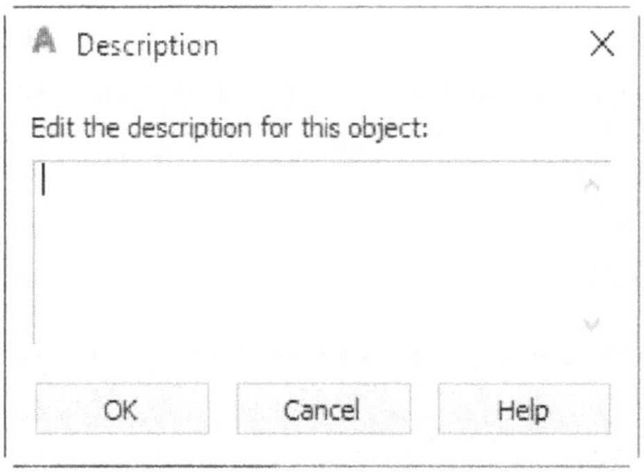

Figure 4-14 The ***Description*** *dialog box*

System

This drop-down list is available in the **BASIC > General** rollout in the **Design** tab of the **PROPERTIES** palette. This drop-down list contains various options for system definitions of the duct. By default, the **Standard (STD)** option is selected in this drop-down list.

Routing Preferences

This drop-down list is available in the **BASIC > Dimensions** rollout. The options available in this drop-down list are used for specifying the routing style of duct. By default, the **Standard** option is selected in this drop-down list.

Shape

This drop-down list is available in the **BASIC > Dimensions** rollout. This drop-down list contains options to change the shape of duct. There are four options available in this drop-down list: **Oval**, **Rectangular**, **Round**, and **Undefined**. Generally, round and rectangular ducts are used in industries.

Width

This edit box is available in the **Dimensions** rollout when the **Rectangular** or **Oval** option is selected from the **Shape** drop-down list. You can specify the value of width of the duct by using this edit box. When you click on the inverted triangle adjacent to this edit box, a drop-down list is displayed. You can select the standard sizes available for width from this edit box. The **Calculate size** toggle button is available on the right of this edit box. When you choose the button, the width of duct is automatically calculated on the basis of the flow rate, friction, velocity, and so on. The selected size for width of the duct can be locked by clicking on the lock button on the extreme right of this edit box.

Height

This edit box is available in the **Dimensions** rollout when the **Rectangular** or **Oval** option is selected from the **Shape** drop-down list. Using this edit box, you can specify the height of duct.

Diameter

This edit box is available in the **Dimensions** rollout when the **Round** option is selected from the **Shape** drop-down list. Using this edit box, you can specify the diameter of duct. The **Calculate Size** toggle button is available in the right of this edit box. When you choose this button, the diameter of duct is automatically calculated on the basis of parameters such as flow rate, friction, and velocity.

Flow Rate

This edit box is available in **Dimensions > Sizing** rollout. Using this edit box, you can specify the rate of flow of fluid through the duct. The flow rate is specified in liters per second.

Friction

This field is available in the **Dimensions > Sizing** rollout. This field shows the value of friction acting against the flow of fluid through the duct. The value in this field is controlled by the **Duct System Definitions** section in the **Style Manager**.

Velocity

This field is available in the **Dimensions > Sizing** rollout. This field shows the value of velocity of fluid passing through the duct. The value in this field is also controlled by **Duct System Definitions** section in the **Style Manager**.

Specify cut length

This drop-down list is available in the **Dimensions > Sizing** rollout. There are two options available in this drop-down list: **Yes** and **No**. By default, the **No** option is selected in this drop-down list. On selecting the **Yes** option, you can specify the cut length in the respective field.

Cut length

This edit box is available in the **Dimensions > Sizing** rollout only when the **Yes** option is selected from the **Specify Cut Length** drop-down list. You can specify the value of cut length in this edit box. Cut length is the maximum length of a piece of duct that is available for creating duct line.

Elevation
This edit box is available in the **BASIC > Placement** rollout. Using this edit box, you can specify the value of elevation of duct from the ground.

Start elevation
This field is available in the **BASIC > Placement** rollout. The value specified in this field is the same as the one specified in the **Elevation** edit box.

Justify
This drop-down list is available in the **Placement > Justification** rollout. Various options are available in this drop-down list to change the justification of duct.

Horizontal offset
This edit box is available in the **Placement > Justification** rollout. Using this edit box, you can specify the horizontal distance value by which the duct is placed from the selected justification point.

Vertical offset
This edit box is available in the **Placement > Justification** rollout. Using this edit box, you can specify the vertical distance value by which the duct is placed from the selected justification point.

Bend method
This drop-down list is available in the **Routing** rollout and is used to define the methods of bending applied on a bend in the duct system. There are three options available in this drop-down list: **Elbow**, **Offset**, and **Transition - Offset**. The **Elbow** option is selected by default.

Bend angle
This drop-down list is available in the **Routing** rollout and is used to specify the angle of bend that is to be applied to any bend while creating a duct.

Connection details
This button is available in the **ADVANCED** rollout. When you choose this button, the **Connection Details** dialog box will be displayed, as shown in Figure 4-15. There are two rollouts available in the dialog box that contain the details of the flow direction and the connection type of inlet and outlet connections.

Lining thickness
This edit box is available in the **ADVANCED** rollout. Using this edit box, you can specify the value of thickness of liner in the duct.

Insulation thickness
This edit box is also available in the **ADVANCED** rollout and is used to specify the thickness of insulation applied on the duct.

Slope format

This drop-down list is available in **ADVANCED > Routing Options** rollout. The options in this drop-down list are used to specify the format in which the slope value will be entered. There are four options available in this drop-down list: **Angle (Decimal Degrees)**; **Percentage, 100% = 45 degree**; **Percentage, 100% = 90 degree**; and **Rise/Run (Meters/Meters)**.

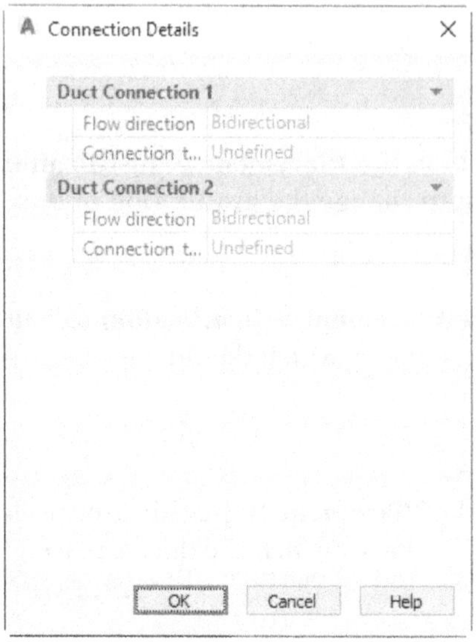

Figure 4-15 *The* ***Connection Details*** *dialog box*

Slope

This edit box is available in the **ADVANCED > Routing Options** rollout of the **PROPERTIES** palette. You can specify the value of slope in this edit box. The format in which the value will be specified in this edit box depends on the option selected in the **Slope format** drop-down list. If you change the slope value while adding more ducts, the fitting at joints will adjust automatically to provide the changed slope.

Branch fitting

This drop-down list is available in the **ADVANCED > Routing Options** rollout of the **PROPERTIES** palette. There are two options in this drop-down list: **Tee** and **Takeoff**. When the **Tee** option is selected in the drop-down list, then the branches to be created will be joined to the main duct through a Tee fitting. When the **Takeoff** option is selected in the drop-down list, the branches will be joined to the main duct through the Takeoff fitting.

Terminal-duct connection

This drop-down list is available in the **ADVANCED > Routing Options** rollout of the **PROPERTIES** palette. There are three options available in this drop-down list: **Flexible**, **Elbow with Rigid Duct**, and **Extended Duct**.

Fitting Settings

This option is available in the **ADVANCED > Routing Options** rollout of the **PROPERTIES** palette. When you click on this option, the **Fitting Settings** dialog box will be displayed, as shown in Figure 4-16. The options in this dialog box are used to change the type of fitting to be used while creating the branches in the duct.

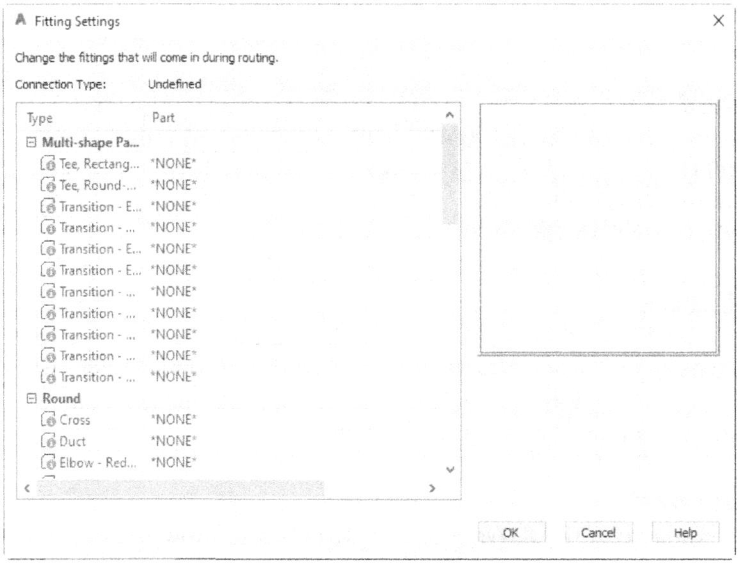

*Figure 4-16 The **Fitting Settings** dialog box*

Preferences

This option is available in the **ADVANCED > Routing Options** rollout of the **PROPERTIES** palette. When you click on this option, the **Duct Layout Preferences** dialog box will be displayed, as shown in Figure 4-17. The options in this dialog box are used to define the layout preferences for creating a duct. Using the options in this dialog box, you can set the preferences for variables such as **Slope**, **Elevation changes**, **Label style**, **Flow arrow style**, and **Elbow Layout Options**.

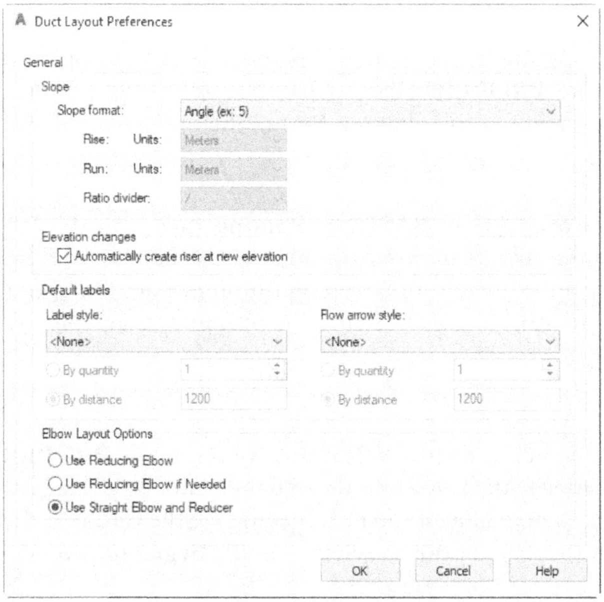

*Figure 4-17 The **Duct Layout Preferences** dialog box*

Style

This drop-down list is available in the **ADVANCED > Labels and Flow Arrows > Labels** rollout of the **PROPERTIES** palette. The options in this drop-down list are used to apply the label styles to duct.

Layout method

This drop-down list is available in the **ADVANCED > Labels and Flow Arrows > Labels** rollout of the **PROPERTIES** palette only when **NONE** is not selected from the **Style** drop-down list. There are two options available in this drop-down list: **By distance** and **By quantity**. These options are used to specify the layout method of ducts.

Number of Labels

This edit box is available in **ADVANCED > Labels and Flow Arrows > Labels** rollout of the **PROPERTIES** palette only when **NONE** is not selected from the **Style** drop-down list and **By quantity** is selected from the **Layout method** drop-down list. Using this edit box, you can specify the total number of labels applied on a segment duct.

Distance between

This edit box is available in the **ADVANCED > Labels and Flow Arrows > Labels** rollout of the **PROPERTIES** palette only when **NONE** is not selected from the **Style** drop-down list and **By distance** is selected from the **Layout method** drop-down list. Using this edit box, you can specify the distance between two consecutive labels applied on a duct.

The **Style**, **Layout method**, **Number of Labels**, and **Distance between** options are also available in the **Flow Arrows** rollout. These options work for flow arrows in the same way as for Labels.

Flex Duct

This tool is used to create flexible ducts in the HVAC system. To create a flexible duct, choose the **Flex Duct** tool from the **Duct** drop-down in the **Build** panel of the **Home** tab in the **Ribbon**; the **PROPERTIES** palette will be displayed, refer to Figure 4-18. Some of the options available in the **PROPERTIES** palette after selecting flex duct have already been discussed in the Duct section of this chapter. Rest of the options are discussed next.

Segment

This drop-down list is available in **BASIC > Routing** rollout in the **PROPERTIES** palette. There are three options available in this drop-down list: **Line**, **Arc**, and **Spline**. Using the **Line** option, you can create a flex duct in the form of a straight line. Using the **Arc** option, you can create a flex duct in the form of an arc. Using the **Spline** option, you can create a flex duct in the form of a spline.

Radius factor

This edit box is available in the **BASIC > Routing** rollout in the **PROPERTIES** palette. Using this edit box, you can specify the value of radius on the bend. The value entered in this edit box is multiplied by the diameter value of the flex duct to give the radius at the bend. This edit box is available only when the **Line** option is selected in the **Segment** drop-down list.

Graphics

This drop-down list is available in the **ADVANCED > Graphics** rollout in the **PROPERTIES** palette. This drop-down list is available for both **1-Line** and **2-Line** annotations in the respective rollouts. Using the options available in this drop-down list, you can specify the shape and pattern of the annotative representation of the duct in the 2-D drawing.

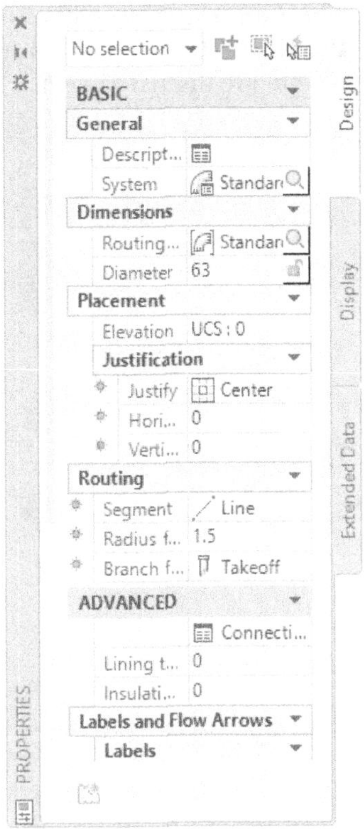

*Figure 4-18 The **PROPERTIES** palette displayed on choosing the **Flex Duct** tool*

Pitch

This edit box is available in **ADVANCED > Graphics** rollout in the **PROPERTIES** palette. This edit box is available for both **1-Line** and **2-Line** annotations in the respective rollouts. This edit box is used to specify the length of one piece flex duct.

Vertex

This edit box is available in **ADVANCED > Geometry** rollout in the **PROPERTIES** palette when you select an already created flex duct. Using this edit box, you can select an available vertex of the flexible duct. You can also change the selected vertex by using the spinner available in the right of the edit box. On doing so, the options relevant to the selected vertex will be displayed.

Vertex X

This edit box is available in **ADVANCED > Geometry** rollout in the **PROPERTIES** palette. Using this edit box, you can specify X coordinate of the selected vertex.

Vertex Y

This edit box is available in **ADVANCED > Geometry** rollout in the **PROPERTIES** palette. Using this edit box, you can specify Y coordinate of the selected vertex.

Vertex Z

This edit box is available in **ADVANCED > Geometry** rollout in the **PROPERTIES** palette. Using this edit box, you can specify Z coordinate of the selected vertex.

DUCT FITTING

Duct fitting is used to connect multiple ducts. The tools to add duct fitting are available in the **Duct Fitting** drop-down in the **Build** panel of the **Home** tab in the **Ribbon**. There are three tools available in this drop-down: **Duct Fitting**, **Duct Custom Fitting**, and **Duct Transition Utility**. These tools are discussed next.

Duct Fitting

This tool is used to add a user specified fitting in the duct. On choosing this tool, the **PROPERTIES** palette is displayed, refer to Figure 4-19. Various options available in this palette are discussed next.

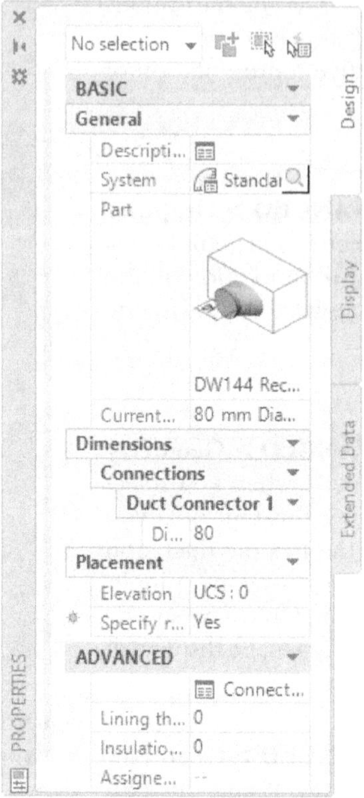

*Figure 4-19 The **PROPERTIES** palette displayed after choosing the **Duct Fitting** tool*

Description

This field is available in the **BASIC > General** rollout in the **PROPERTIES** palette. When you click in this field, the **Description** dialog box will be displayed. You can write description about the fitting in this text box.

System

This drop-down list is available in the **BASIC > General** rollout of the **PROPERTIES** palette. There are various options available in this drop-down list. These options are used to change the standard of fitting to be created. By default, the **Standard** option is selected in this drop-down list.

Part

This field is available in the **BASIC > General** rollout of the **PROPERTIES** palette. When you click in this field, the **Select Part** dialog box will be displayed, refer to Figure 4-20. There are various types of fittings available for duct in this dialog box. All these fittings are displayed in the **SELECT PART FROM CATALOG** rollout. The fittings in this rollout are divided into groups in a tree structure. You can filter the available parts depending on your requirements by using the options in the **FILTER** rollout of this dialog box. The filtered options will be displayed in the **SELECT PART SIZE** area of this dialog box. You can also select the required fitting from the **TOOL PALETTE - HVAC**. These fittings are available in the **Fitting** tab of the palette.

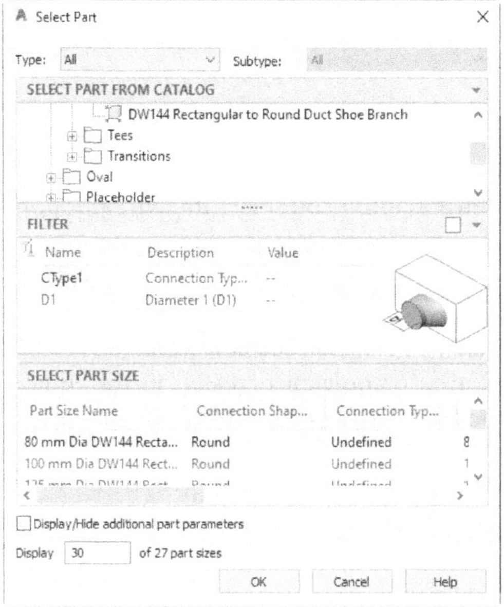

*Figure 4-20 The **Select Part** dialog box*

Current size

This drop-down list is available in the **BASIC > General** rollout of the **PROPERTIES** palette. The options available in this drop-down list are used to change the size of the current selected fitting.

Connections Rollout

This rollout is available in the **BASIC > Dimensions** rollout in the **PROPERTIES** palette. The options in this rollout are used to change the dimensions of a selected fitting. The options in this rollout may vary depending on the selected fitting.

Elevation

This edit box is available in the **BASIC > Placement** rollout in the **PROPERTIES** palette. Using this edit box, you can specify the value of height of fitting from the ground level. By default, **UCS : 0** is displayed in this edit box.

Specify rotation on screen

This drop-down list is available in the **BASIC > Placement** rollout in the **PROPERTIES** palette. There are two options available in this drop-down list: **Yes** and **No**. If you select the **Yes** option, you will be prompted to specify the rotation value on screen while creating the fitting. If you select the **No** option, then you need to specify the rotation value in the **Rotation** edit box available in the **PROPERTIES** palette.

Rotation

This edit box is available in the **BASIC > Placement** rollout in the **PROPERTIES** palette. Using this edit box, you can specify the value of rotation of the fitting before placing it in the drawing. This edit box is available only when the **No** option is selected in the **Specify rotation on screen** drop-down list.

Vanes

This drop-down list is available in the **ADVANCED** rollout in the **PROPERTIES** palette. There are two options available in this drop-down list: **Yes** and **No**. If you select the **Yes** option, the vanes will be added to the fitting and if you select the **No** option, the vanes will not be added to the fitting.

Duct Custom Fitting

This tool is used for creating custom fittings in the duct line. To create a custom fitting, you must have lines, arcs, or polylines created in the drawing area. Choose the **Duct Custom Fitting** tool from the **Duct Fitting** drop-down; you will be prompted to select lines, arcs, or polylines. Select lines, arcs, or polylines from the drawing area and then press ENTER; the **Create Duct Custom Fitting** dialog box will be displayed, refer to Figure 4-21.

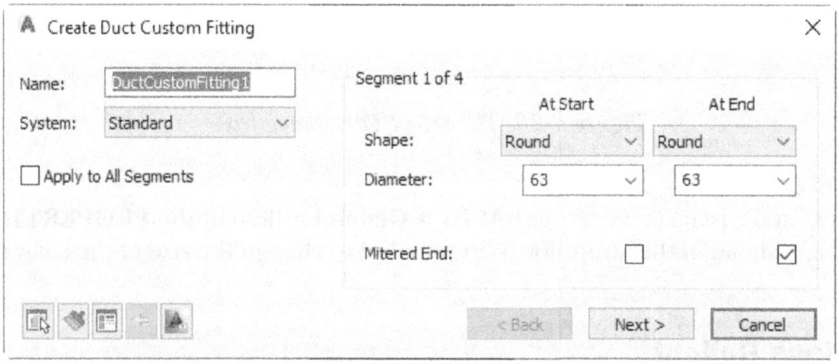

*Figure 4-21 The **Create Duct Custom Fitting** dialog box*

Depending on the entities selected, the segments will be displayed in the dialog box as Segment n of m, where n is the serial number of the current segment and m is the total number of segments in the fitting. Using the **Shape** drop-down list available in the **Segment *n* of *m*** area, you can change the shape of segments in the fitting. There are three options available in this drop-down list: **Rectangular**, **Round**, and **Oval**. After selecting the required option, you can specify the relevant parameters in the edit boxes available below this drop-down list. After specifying the parameters, you can choose the **Next >** button to change the parameters of next segment. You can also select the **Apply to All Segments** check box, if you want to keep same parameters for the other segments. You can create mitered ends at the start point or the end point by selecting the corresponding **Mitered End** check boxes. After specifying parameters for all the segments, choose the **Finish** button; you will be prompted whether to delete the base geometry or not. Enter **Yes** or **No** at the command prompt; the custom fitting will be created.

Duct Transition Utility

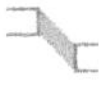

This tool is used to connect two parallel ducts, duct fittings, or equipment. Various shapes that can be connected by using this tool are given next.

Round	to	Round
Round	to	Rectangular
Round	to	Oval
Rectangular	to	Rectangular
Rectangular	to	Oval
Rectangular	to	Round
Oval	to	Oval
Oval	to	Rectangular
Oval	to	Round

To create a duct transition, choose the **Duct Transition Utility** tool from the **Duct Fitting** drop-down; you will be prompted to select the first duct, duct fitting, or MvPart. Select the first entity; you will be prompted to select the second entity. Select the duct, duct fitting, or MvPart to be joined; a transition fitting will be created, joining both the entities.

TUTORIAL

Tutorial 1

In this tutorial, you will add a mechanical system (HVAC system) to the building created in Tutorial 2 of Chapter 3. You can download the architectural input file used in this tutorial from *www.cadcim.com*. Path of the file is: *Textbooks > CAD/CAM > AutoCAD MEP > AutoCAD MEP 2022 for Designers > Input Files.* The building after adding the mechanical system is shown in Figure 4-22. The plan for the mechanical system is given in Figure 4-23. Assume the missing dimensions.

(Expected time: 45 min)

Zone-wise Airflow:
Zone1 = 144 m^3/h = 40 l/s
Zone2 = 180 m^3/h = 50 l/s
Zone3 = 720 m^3/h = 200 l/s

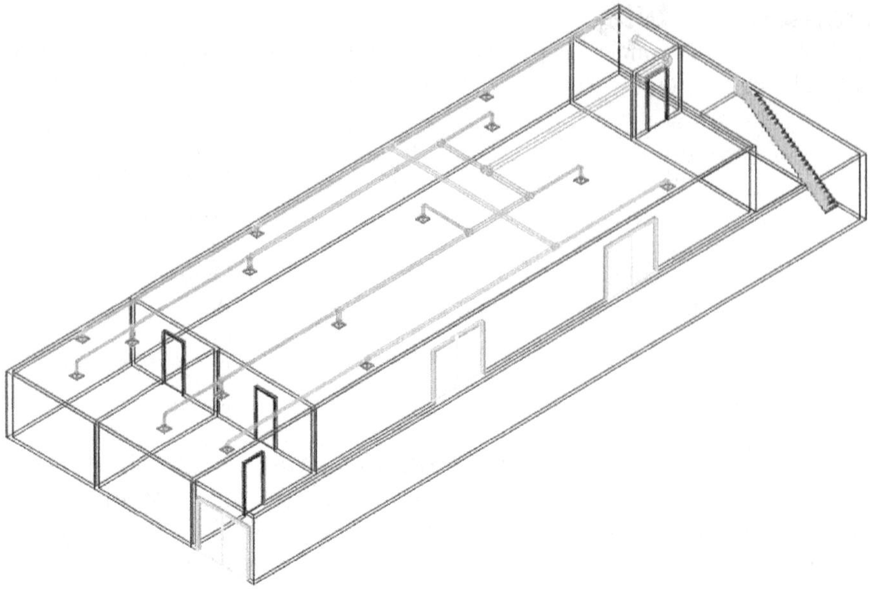

Figure 4-22 The drawing after adding the mechanical system

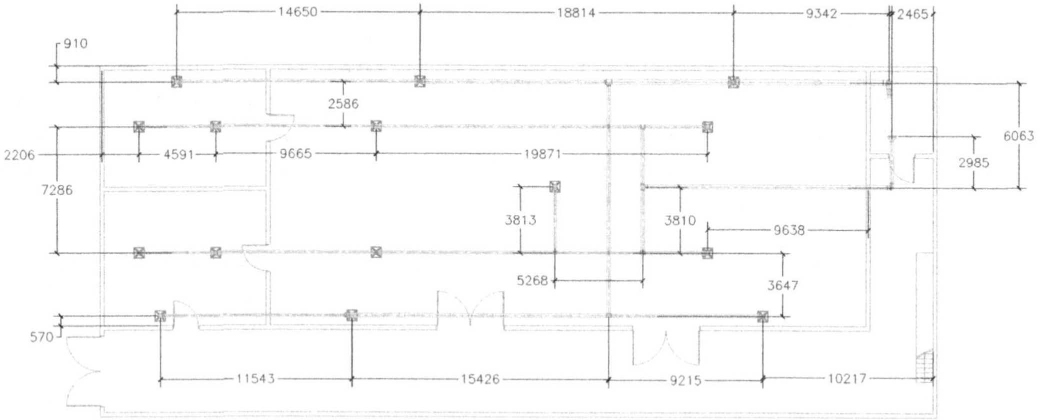

Figure 4-23 The plan for mechanical system

The following steps are required to complete this tutorial:

a. Opening the drawing file.
b. Install the Air Terminals on the basis of airflow required in a zone.
c. Add the duct line to the Air Terminals.
d. Install the AHU on the basis of requirement.
e. Calculate the size of duct on the basis of requirements.
f. Install the duct lines and duct fittings in the system.

Now, you need to open the project file created in Tutorial 2 of Chapter 3.

Opening the Drawing File

1. Choose **Open > Drawing** from the **Application Menu**; the **Select File** dialog box is displayed.

2. Select the file created in Tutorial 2 of Chapter 3 and choose the **Open** button; the file is opened and displayed, as shown in Figure 4-24.

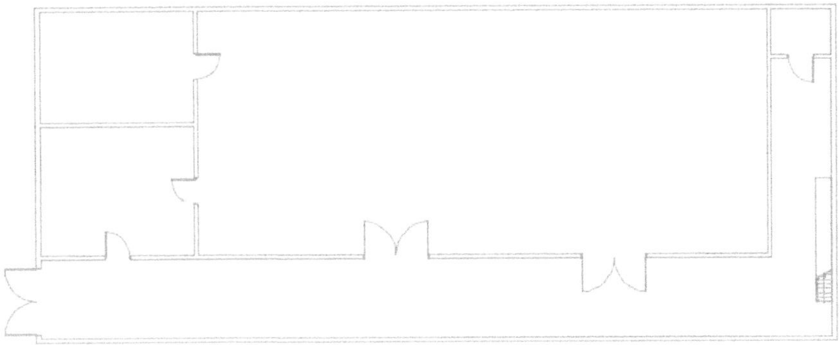

Figure 4-24 *The drawing after dividing into sections*

Note

*If the file opened, as mentioned in the previous step, is not displayed in the same orientation and visual style as shown in Figure 4-24, choose the **Top** option from the **View Controls** and **2D Wireframe** option from the **Visual Style Controls** drop-down list of the In-Canvas Viewport Controls.*

Placing Air Terminals

Depending upon the air flow required for each zone and the area to be covered, you need to install the diffusers.

1. Choose the **Air Terminal** tool from the **Equipment** drop-down in the **Build** panel of the **Home** tab in the **Ribbon**; the **Add Multi-view Parts** dialog box is displayed with the options related to diffusers.

2. Select **600 x 600 mm Square Faced Ceiling Diffuser** from the part list displayed in the **Part** tab of the dialog box; the parts for the selected category are displayed in the **Part Size Name** drop-down list.

3. Select the part with 150mm neck from the drop-down list, set the value of elevation as **4500**, and place the diffusers according to the air flow requirements in the zones, refer to Figure 4-23.

   Now, you need to assign flow rate to the diffusers.

4. Select diffusers **4, 5** in **Zone1** and **1** in **Zone2**, as shown in Figure 4-25.

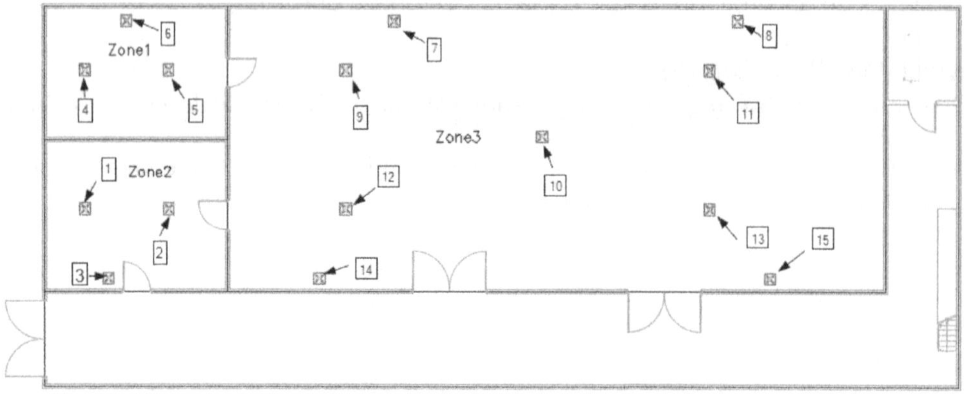

Figure 4-25 The drawing after adding diffusers

5. Right-click and choose the **MvPart Properties** option from the shortcut menu displayed; the **Multi-view Part Properties** dialog box is displayed, as shown in Figure 4-26. Enter the value **20 l/s** in the **Flow (Each Terminal)** edit box in the **Flow** tab and then choose the **OK** button to close the dialog box.

6. Similarly, assign flow rate **40 l/s** to diffusers **9, 10, 11, 12,** and **13** in **Zone3**, refer to Figure 4-25.

7. Assign flow rate **50 l/s** to diffusers **7, 8, 14,** and **15** in **Zone3**, refer to Figure 4-25.

8. Assign flow rate **30 l/s** to diffuser **2** in **Zone 2**, **50 l/s** to diffuser **3** in **Zone2**, and **40 l/s** to diffuser **6** in **Zone1**, refer to Figure 4-25.

Adding the Duct Line to the Diffusers

Now, you need to route the duct line by using the **1-Line** tool.

1. To create routing of the duct line, choose the **1-Line** tool from the **By Shape** area of the **Duct** tab in the **TOOL PALETTE - HVAC**; you are prompted to specify the starting point of the duct line.

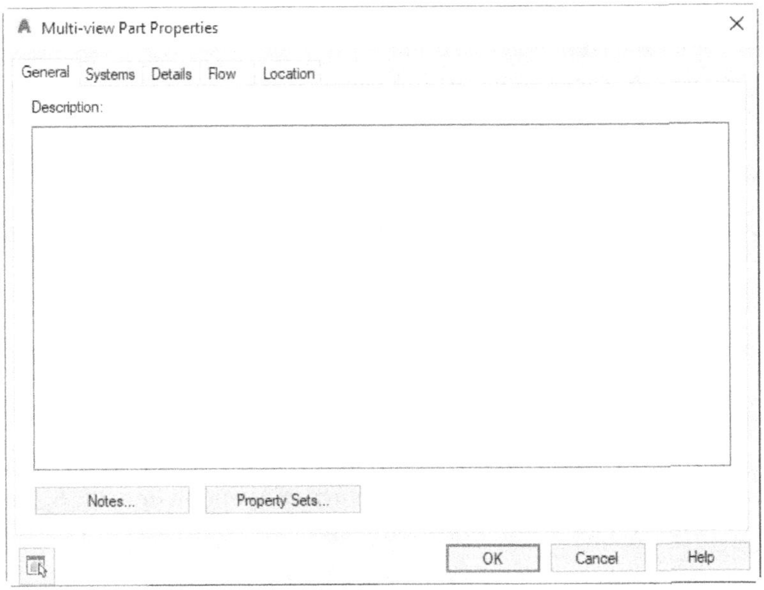

Figure 4-26 *The **Multi-view Part Properties** dialog box*

2. Select the **Fresh Air - Make-up (FA MAKE-UP)** option from the **System** drop-down list in the **BASIC > General** rollout of the **Design** tab in the **PROPERTIES** palette and create a supply duct line, as shown in Figure 4-27.

Note

*The **Fresh Air - Make-up (FA MAKE-UP)** option is not available by default in the **System** drop-down list. To add this option to the drop-down list, choose the **Select a system** button available at the right of the **System** edit box; the **STYLES BROWSER** palette will be displayed. Next, double-click on the **Fresh Air - Make-up** option in the **Name** column of the **STYLES BROWSER**; it will be added to the drop-down list and displayed in the **System** edit box.*

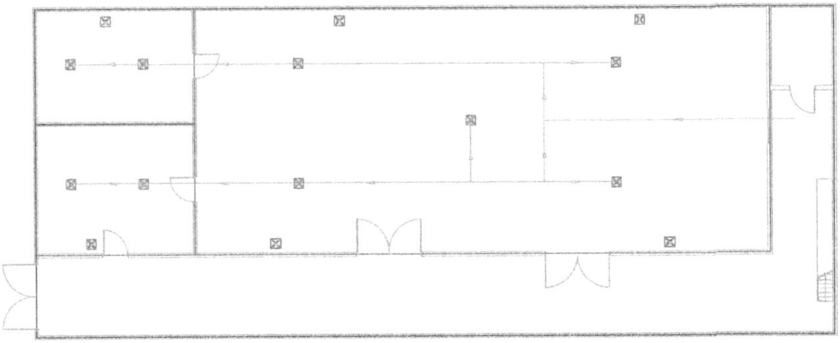

Figure 4-27 *The drawing after creating fresh air duct line*

Note

*1. After choosing the **1-Line** tool, you are prompted to specify the start point. Specify the start point by selecting the center point of the air terminal from where you want to start the route; you are prompted to specify the next point. Specify the next point at the center of the next air terminal you want to connect with the previous air terminal. As you select the center of the next air terminal, the **Choose a Part** dialog box is displayed. Choose the **Duct Elbows Placeholder** option of the **Duct (Global)** node available in the list box at the left of the dialog box and then choose the **OK** button. Next, choose the **Accept** option from the command line and press ENTER or ESC to exit the tool.*

2. After connecting two air terminals, if you want to connect a third air terminal, select the placeholder (duct) line; a + sign is displayed. Click on the + sign, the placeholder (duct) line is attached to the cursor. Specify the center point of the next air terminal that you want to connect and follow the same procedure explained above to connect the air terminal.

3. Again, choose the **1-Line** tool and select the **Return (RA)** option from the **System** drop-down list in the **General** rollout of the **BASIC** rollout of the **Design** tab in the **PROPERTIES** palette.

4. Create the return duct line, as shown in Figure 4-28.

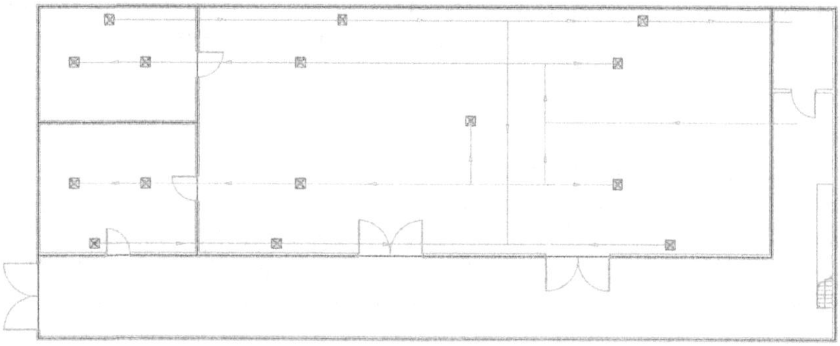

Figure 4-28 *The drawing after creating the return duct line*

5. After creating the duct lines, choose the **Accept** option from the command prompt.

Adding an Air Handler

Now, you need to add an Air Handler to the drawing to complete the duct line.

1. Choose the **Air Handler** tool from the **Equipment** drop-down in the **Build** panel of the **Home** tab in the **Ribbon**; the **Add Multi-view Parts** dialog box is displayed.

2. Select the **Air Handling Units - Floor Mounted Front Discharge** equipment from the Part list in the **Part** tab of this dialog box, refer to Figure 4-29; a preview of the equipment is displayed on the right of the Part list.

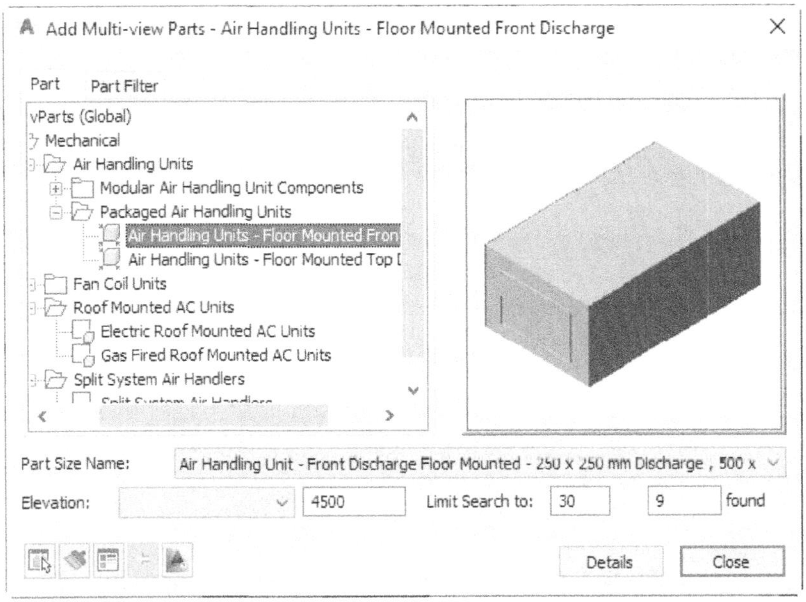

Figure 4-29 *The* ***Add Multi-view Parts*** *dialog box with the* ***Air Handling Units - Floor Mounted Front Discharge*** *option selected*

3. Specify the elevation value as **4500** in the **Elevation** edit box.

4. Click in the drawing area to specify the location of equipment; you are prompted to specify the rotation angle for equipment.

5. Enter the angle value **0**; the equipment is placed at the specified location, refer to Figure 4-30. Choose the **Close** button from the **Add Multi-view Parts** dialog box.

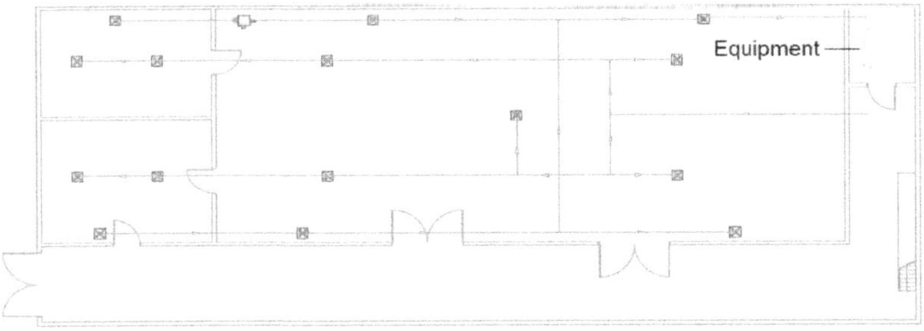

Figure 4-30 *The drawing after adding equipment*

Now, you need to add a duct line to the equipment.

6. Choose the **1-Line** tool from the **By Shape** area of the **Duct** tab in the **TOOL PALETTE - HVAC** and connect the 'A' port of Air Handler with Return duct line, refer to Figure 4-31.

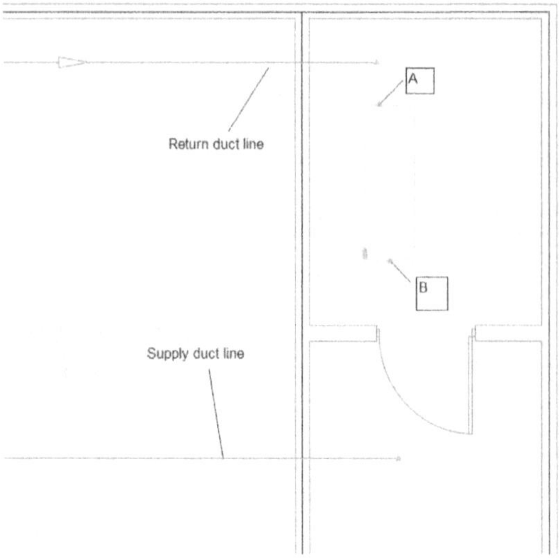

Figure 4-31 Connection for Air Handler with ducts

7. Similarly, connect the 'B' port of Air Handler with Supply duct line, refer to Figure 4-31.

   The drawing after connecting the equipment with the duct line is shown in Figure 4-32.

Calculating the Duct Size

Now, you need to calculate the duct size of each segment.

1. Select the Return duct lines, as shown in Figure 4-33 and choose the **Calculate Duct Sizes** button from the **Calculations** panel of the **Duct** contextual tab in the **Ribbon**; the **Duct System Size Calculator** dialog box is displayed.

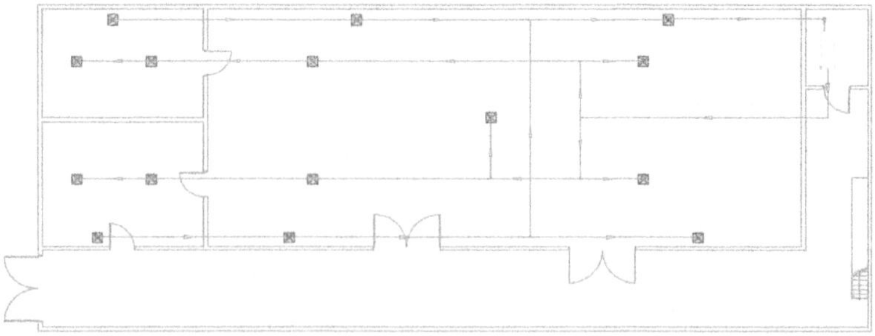

Figure 4-32 The drawing after connecting the equipment with the duct line

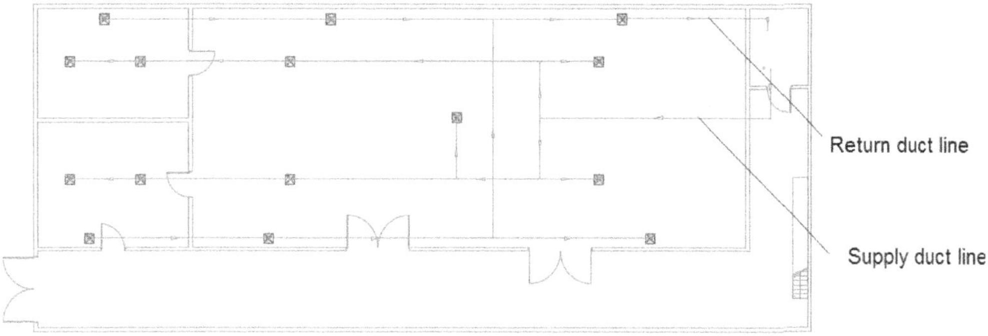

Figure 4-33 *The duct lines to be selected for calculating the duct size*

2. Change all the settings in the dialog box according to Figure 4-34.

3. Choose the **Start** button from the **4** area of the dialog box; the **Multiple Parts Found** dialog box is displayed, as shown in Figure 4-35.

Note

*Sometimes, the **Choose a Part** dialog box is displayed before the **Multiple Parts Found** dialog box if the part specified for the layout connection is not connected due to size or angle of layout of duct line. So, you need to select the required part from the dialog box and choose the **OK** button. Similarly, you can add other parts whenever this dialog box appears.*

4. Select the part of appropriate size from the **Select a detailed part** area of the dialog box and choose the **OK** button; the selected part is added at the prompted position.

5. Similarly, add all the parts at the prompted locations one after the other.

After adding all the parts, the **Duct System Size Calculator** dialog box is displayed, as shown in Figure 4-36.

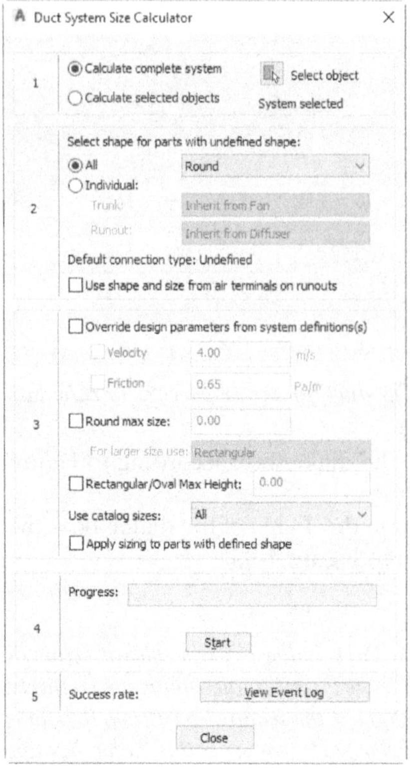

*Figure 4-34 The **Duct System Size Calculator** dialog box*

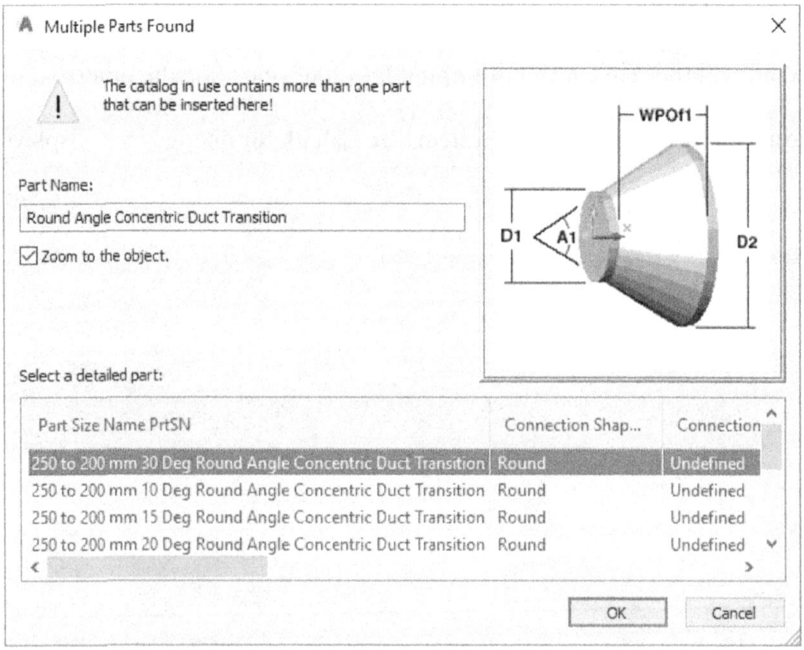

*Figure 4-35 The **Multiple Parts Found** dialog box*

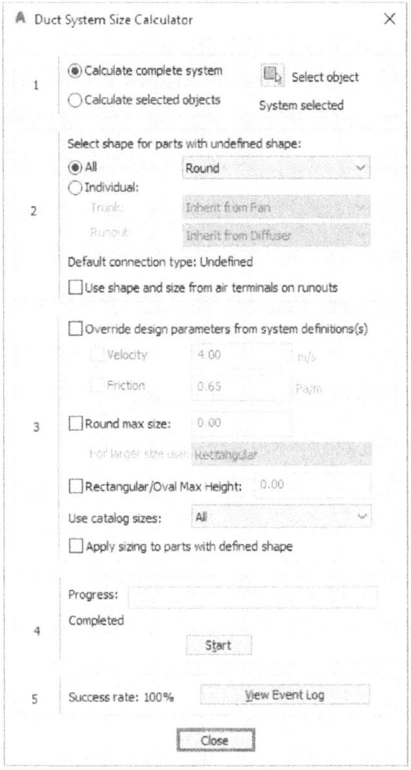

*Figure 4-36 The **Duct System Size Calculator** dialog box after completing calculations*

6. If the success rate is displayed as 100%, choose the **Close** button and exit the dialog box.

7. If success rate is not displayed as 100%, choose the **View Event Log** button from the **5** area of the dialog box; the **Event Log** dialog box is displayed, refer to Figure 4-37.

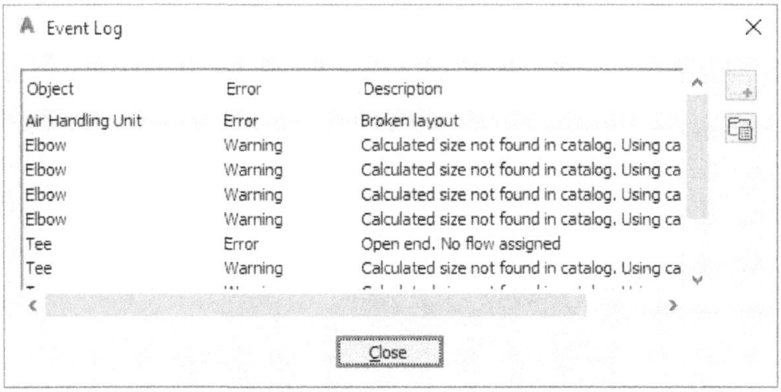

*Figure 4-37 The **Event Log** dialog box*

8. Select the object in the **Object** column that shows an error in the **Error** column, refer to Figure 4-37, and then choose the **Highlight and Zoom the selected object** button from the dialog box; the selected object is highlighted in the drawing area, refer to Figure 4-38.

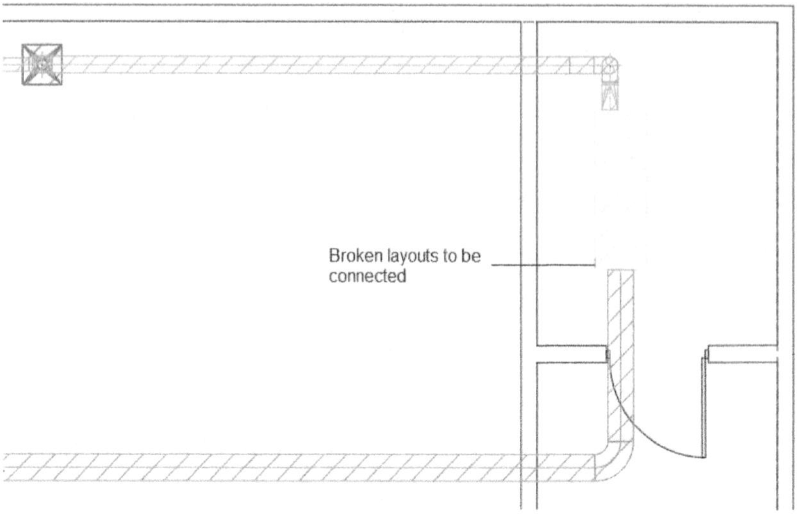

Figure 4-38 *The object causing error highlighted in the drawing area*

9. Rectify the errors according to the description given in the **Description** column of the **Event Log** dialog box and then choose the **Start** button again after all the errors are rectified.

Note

Sometimes, you may need to rearrange the duct system to rectify errors. In that case, your final drawing may look different from the drawing shown in Figure 4-39.

10. Similarly, select the Supply duct line, refer to Figure 4-33 and calculate the duct size for Supply duct.

The drawing after calculating the duct size is displayed, as shown in Figure 4-39.

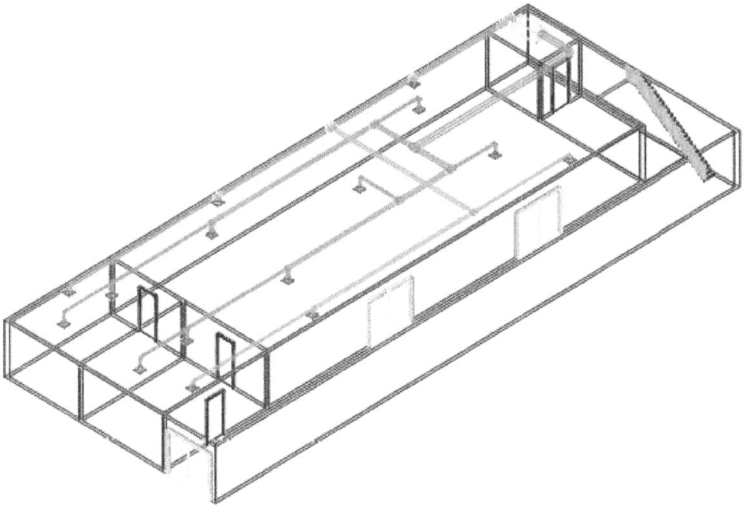

Figure 4-39 The drawing after calculating duct size

Saving the Drawing File

1. Choose **Save** from the **Application Menu** to save the drawing file.

Self-Evaluation Test

Answer the following questions and then compare them to those given at the end of this chapter:

1. In which of the following drop-downs is the **Fan** tool available?

   (a) **Equipment** (b) **Duct Fitting**
   (c) **Duct** (d) **Pipe**

2. An AHU Mixing Box has three ports, one for the inlet of _________ , one for the inlet of fresh air, and one for the __________ of mixed air.

3. You can specify the flow rate for an air terminal by using the _________ edit box.

4. The **Air Handler** option is available in the **Equipment** drop-down of the **Build** panel. (T/F)

5. The AHU Inspection Module is used to check the quantity of air to be spread in the desired area. (T/F)

Review Questions

Answer the following questions:

1. Which of the following buttons is used to calculate the duct size of a duct system?

   (a) **Calculate Duct Sizes** (b) **Duct**
   (c) **Flexible Duct** (d) **Detail Components**

2. There are three options available in AutoCAD MEP for specifying bends of a duct: __________, __________, and __________.

3. For branch fitting, you can use two options, __________ and __________ .

4. The AHU Mixing Box is an equipment that is used to vary the speed of air flowing through the duct. (T/F)

5. Using the **Elevation** edit box, the value of elevation from the ground can be specified for an object. (T/F)

EXERCISE

Exercise 1

In this exercise, you will add an HVAC system to an office. The office after adding the HVAC system is shown in Figure 4-40. The plan for the HVAC system is given in Figure 4-41. You can download the architecture model of the office from *www.cadcim.com*. The complete path for downloading the file is: *Textbook > CAD/CAM > AutoCAD MEP > AutoCAD MEP 2022 for Designers> Input Files.* **(Expected time: 30 min)**

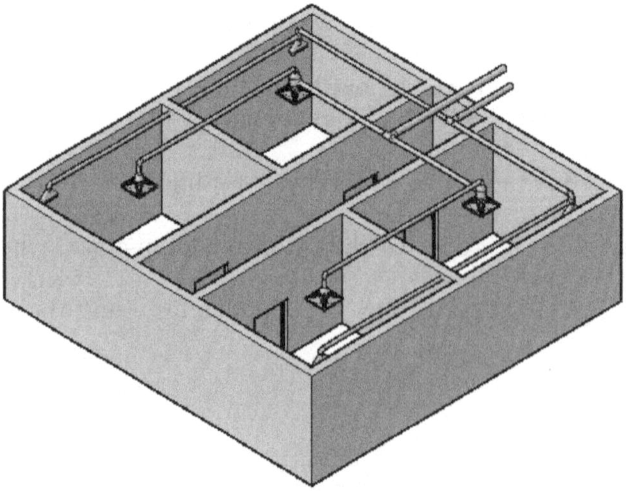

Figure 4-40 *The HVAC system in the office*

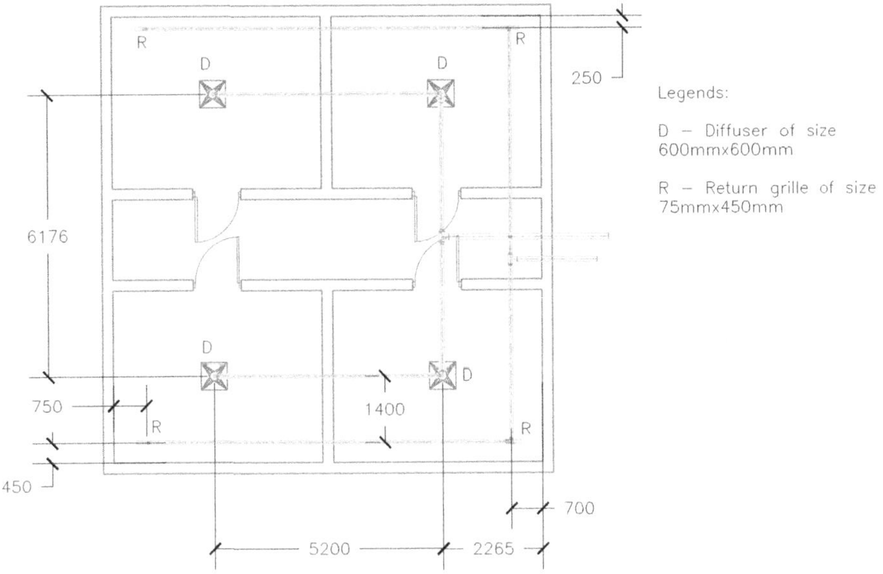

***Figure 4-41** The plan for the HVAC system*

Answers to Self-Evaluation Test

1. A, **2.** Returning air, outlet, **3.** **Flow (Each Terminal)**, **4.** T, **5.** F

Chapter 5

Creating Piping Systems

Learning Objectives

After completing this chapter, you will be able to:

- *Add equipment required in a piping system*
- *Change basic settings of a piping system*
- *Configure pipe line options*
- *Route the pipe line*
- *Create pipe and flex pipe*
- *Create a custom multi-view part*

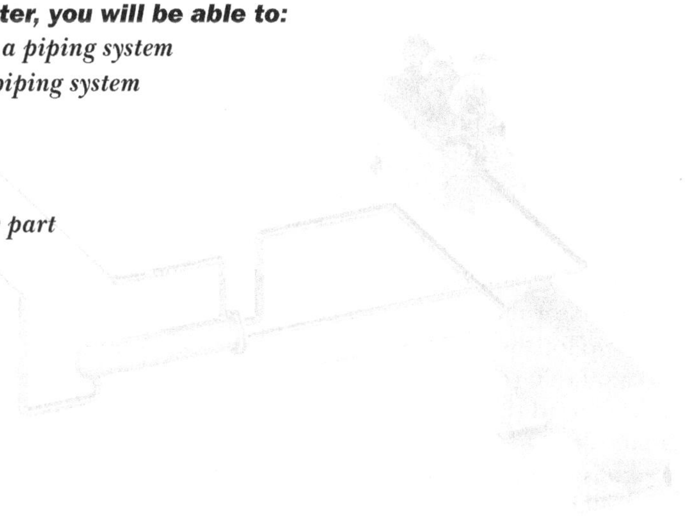

INTRODUCTION

In this chapter, you will learn the use of various equipment for creating a piping system. A piping system is used to supply the desired amount of water to a specific location. A piping system is composed of piping equipment and pipes. Piping equipment and pipes together control the temperature, pressure, and flow rate of the fluid passing through the pipes. To create a piping system, you need to know the vertical heads, pressure, temperature, and flow rate of the fluid. These variables are used for deciding the capacity of the equipment that are to be added to the piping system. To create a piping system, choose the **Piping** option from the **Workspace Switching** flyout; the **Piping** workspace will be invoked. The equipment available in the **Piping** workspace of AutoCAD MEP are discussed next.

ADDING EQUIPMENT

For creating a piping system, you need to add related equipment to the given structure. All the equipment that can be added while working in the **Piping** workspace are available in the **Equipment** drop-down of the **Build** panel in the **Home** tab of the **Ribbon**, refer to Figure 5-1. The tools available in this drop-down are discussed next.

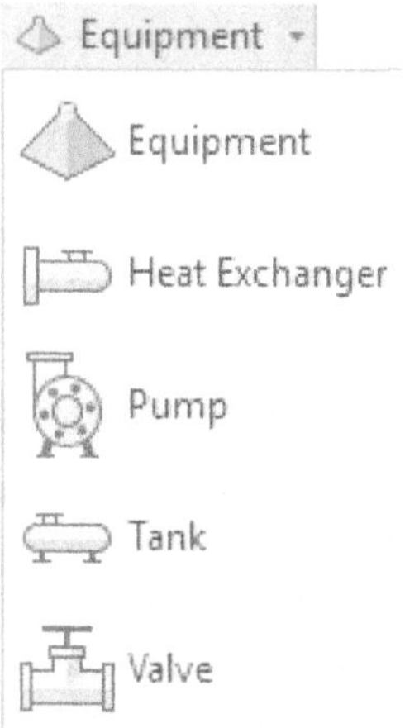

***Figure 5-1** The **Equipment** drop-down*

Heat Exchanger

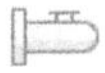

A heat exchanger is an equipment or a device which is used to transfer heat efficiently between two fluids. This heat transfer can occur through conduction or convection. To add a heat exchanger to a drawing, choose the **Heat Exchanger** tool from the **Equipment** drop-down available in the **Build** panel of the **Home** tab in the **Ribbon**; the **Add Multi-view Parts** dialog box will be displayed, as shown in Figure 5-2. Select the **Shell and Tube Heat Exchangers** from the **Heat Exchangers** category of the **Mechanical** node; a preview of the selected component will be displayed on the right in the dialog box. The D1, D2, D3, and D4 in the **Preview area** indicate the diameters of the ports available on the heat exchanger. Additionally, you can select the required size for the heat exchanger from the **Part Size Name** drop-down list. You can specify the elevation value of heat exchanger from the ground or UCS by using the **Elevation** edit box available below the **Part Size Name** drop-down list. After specifying the required parameters, click in the drawing area; the heat exchanger will be attached with the cursor. Now, click at the required position to place it; the heat exchanger will be placed at the selected position and a compass will be displayed below it. Using this compass, you can rotate the heat exchanger at the required angle. After specifying the angle, choose the **Close** button from the **Add Multi-view Parts** dialog box to exit it. Figure 5-3 shows a Shell and Tube Heat Exchanger.

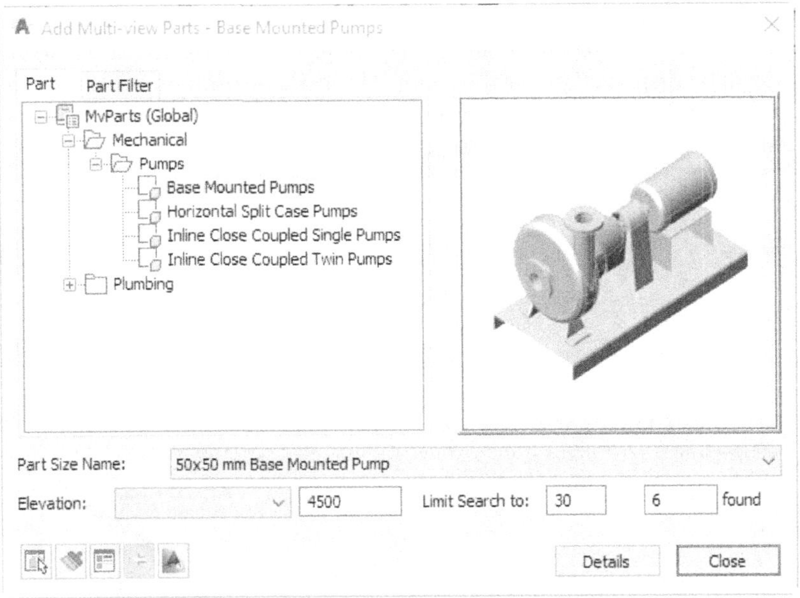

Figure 5-2 *The* ***Add Multi-view Parts*** *dialog box*

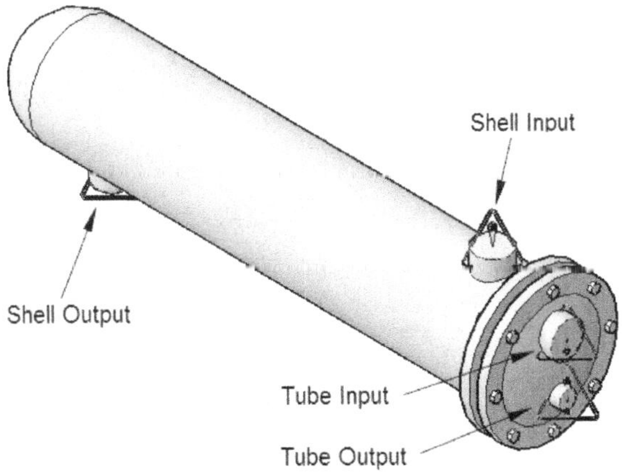

Figure 5-3 *The Shell and Tube Heat Exchanger*

Pump

A pump is a mechanical device that is used to supply fluid to the desired point by using mechanical force. To add a pump to the drawing, choose the **Pump** tool from the **Equipment** drop-down available in the **Build** panel of the **Home** tab in the **Ribbon**; the **Add Multi-view Parts** dialog box will be displayed, as shown in Figure 5-4. Select the required part in the sub-category from the **Pumps** category of the **Mechanical** node in the dialog box; various sizes available for that part are displayed in the **Part Size Name** drop-down list. Select the required size from the drop-down list; you will be prompted to specify a point in the drawing area to place the pump. Click in the drawing area; the pump will be attached with the cursor. Now, click at the required position to place it; the pump will be placed at the selected position and a compass will be displayed below the pump. Using this compass, you can rotate the pump at the required angle. After specifying the angle, choose the **Close** button from the **Add Multi-view Parts** dialog box to exit it. Figure 5-5 shows a base mounted pump.

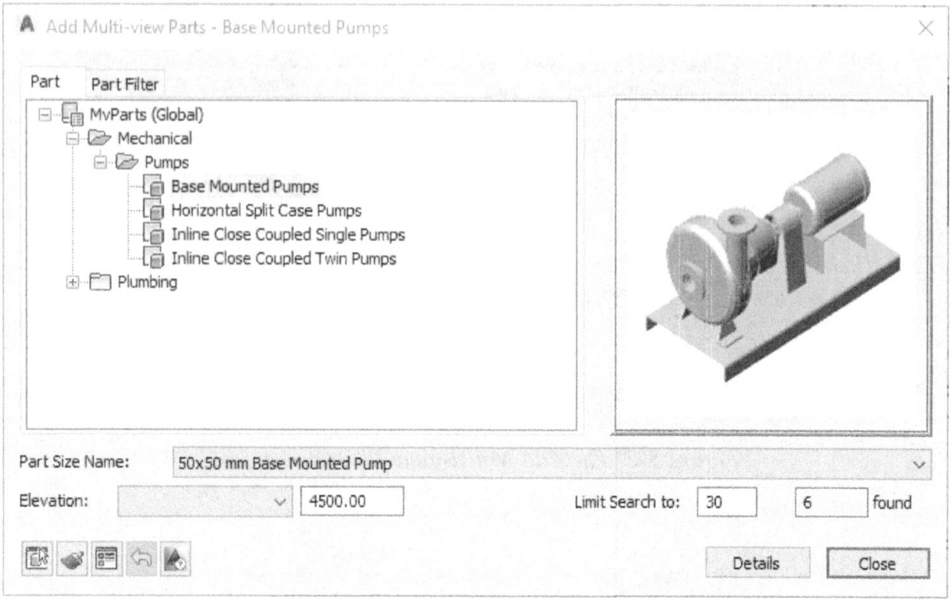

Figure 5-4 *The **Add Multi-view Parts** dialog box displayed after invoking the **Pump** tool*

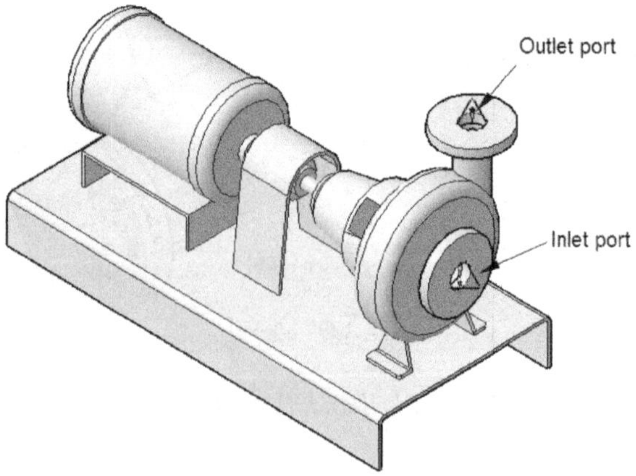

Figure 5-5 *A base mounted pump*

Tank

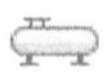

A tank is a hollow space created in a structure to store the fluid for later use. There are two types of tanks available in AutoCAD MEP: Expansion Tank and Storage Tank. The expansion tank acts as a safety tank for fluid heating system. This tank allows the fluid to expand so that it can release pressure. The storage tank is used to store the fluid for later use. To add a tank to a drawing, choose the **Tank** tool from the **Equipment** drop-down available in the **Build** panel of the **Home** tab in the **Ribbon**; the **Add Multi-view Parts** dialog box will be displayed, as shown in Figure 5-6. Select the required part from the **Tanks** category of the **Mechanical** node in the dialog box; various sizes available for that sub-category are displayed in the **Part Size Name** drop-down list. Select the required size from the drop-down list and click in the drawing; the tank will be attached with the cursor. Now, click at required position to place it; the tank will be placed at the selected position and a compass will be displayed below the tank. Using this compass, you can rotate the component at the required angle. After specifying the angle, choose the **Close** button from the **Add Multi-view Parts** dialog box to exit the dialog box. Figure 5-7 shows the tanks available in AutoCAD MEP.

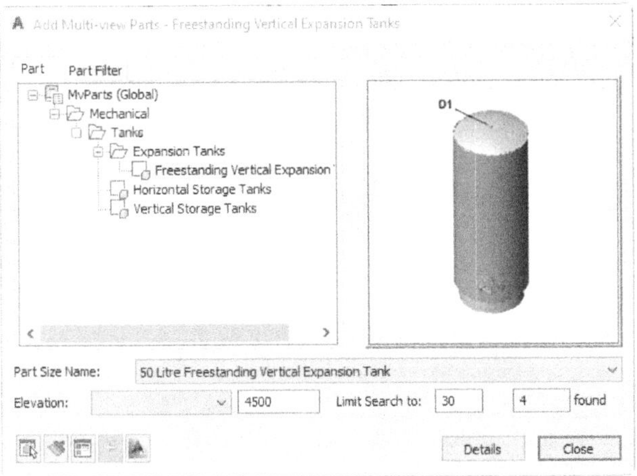

***Figure 5-6** The **Add Multi-view Parts** dialog box displayed after choosing the **Tank** tool*

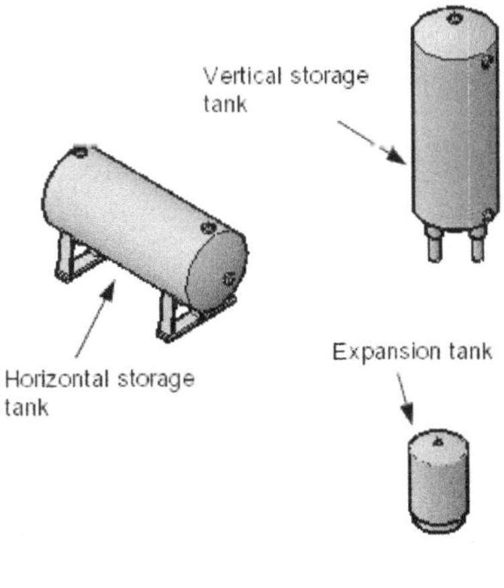

***Figure 5-7** The tanks available in AutoCAD MEP*

Valve

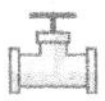

A valve is a device that is used to regulate or direct the flow of fluid through a passage. There are various types of valves available in AutoCAD MEP. These valves are available in two main categories: Fire Protection and Valves. To add a valve to the drawing, choose the **Valve** tool from the **Equipment** drop-down available in the **Build** panel of the **Home**

tab in the **Ribbon**; the **Add Multi-view Parts** dialog box will be displayed, as shown in Figure 5-8. Select the **Gate Valves Hose Connection** part from the **Hose Connections** sub-category of the **Fire Protection** category in the **Mechanical** node; various sizes available for it will be displayed in the **Part Size Name** drop-down list. Select the required size from the drop-down list and click in the drawing area; the valve will be attached with the cursor. Now, click at the required position to place it; the valve will be placed at the selected position and a compass will be displayed below it. Using this compass, you can rotate the valve at the required angle. After specifying the angle, choose the **Close** button from the **Add Multi-view Parts** dialog box to exit it.

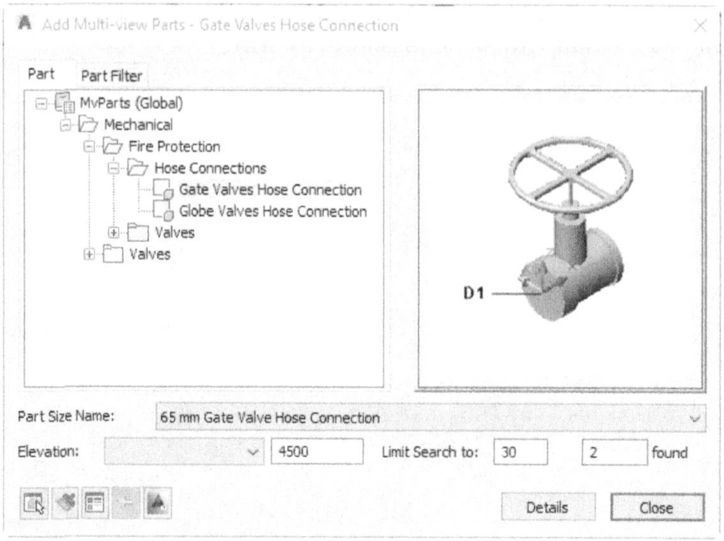

Figure 5-8 The ***Add Multi-view Parts*** *dialog box displayed after choosing the* ***Valve*** *tool*

Equipment

When you choose the **Equipment** tool from the **Equipment** drop-down of the **Build** panel of the **Home** tab, the **Add Multi-view Parts** dialog box will be displayed, refer to Figure 5-9. In this dialog box, all the equipment related to Electrical, Mechanical, and Plumbing categories will be displayed.

Click on the + sign adjacent to the required category; various equipment related to the selected category will be displayed in a list. Select the required equipment from the list and select the size of that equipment from the **Part Size Name** drop-down list. Click in the drawing area; the equipment will be attached with the cursor. Now, click at required position to place it; the equipment will be placed at the selected position and a compass will also be displayed below the equipment. Using this compass, you can rotate the equipment at any required angle. After specifying the angle, choose the **Close** button from the **Add Multi-view Parts** dialog box to exit.

CREATING PIPE LINES

In a piping system, pipe is a mechanical object through which the fluid flows. There are two types of pipes available in AutoCAD MEP: Pipe and Parallel Pipes. The tools to create these pipes are available in the **Pipe** drop-down in the **Build** panel of the **Home** tab in the **Ribbon**. These tools are discussed next.

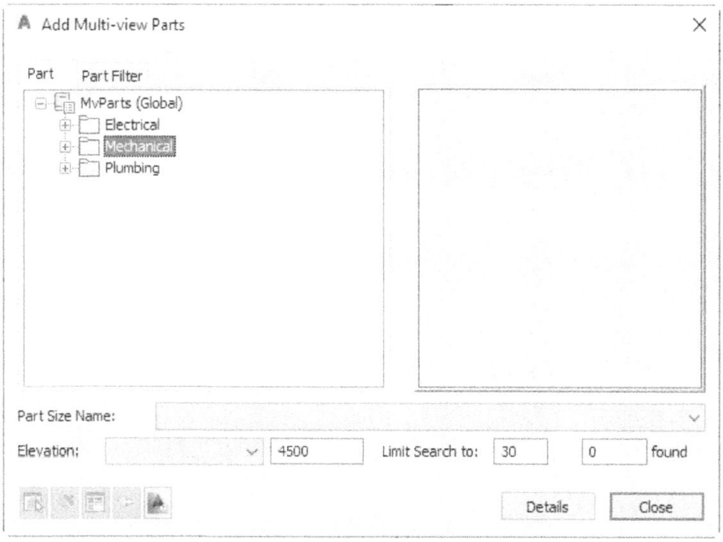

*Figure 5-9 The **Add Multi-view Parts** dialog box*

Pipe

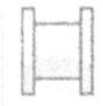
This tool is used to create a pipe line in the piping system. The shape of the pipe created by using this tool is round. When you choose this tool, the **Choose a Part** dialog box will be displayed. Choose the **OK** button; the dialog box will exit and the **PROPERTIES** palette will be displayed, as shown in Figure 5-10. Also, you will be prompted to specify the start point of the pipe line. Click in the drawing area to specify the start point of the pipe line; you will be prompted to specify the next point of the pipe line. Specify the next point to create the pipe line. The options available in the **PROPERTIES** palette are discussed next.

Description

This field is available in the **BASIC > General** rollout in the **PROPERTIES** palette. When you click in this field, the **Description** dialog box will be displayed, as shown in Figure 5-11. You can enter description for the pipe in the **Edit the description for this object** text box in this dialog box. Choose **OK** to exit the dialog box.

System

This drop-down list is available in the **BASIC > General** rollout of the **PROPERTIES** palette. This drop-down list contains various system definitions for the pipe.

Routing preference

This drop-down list is available in the **BASIC > Dimensions** rollout. The options available in this drop-down list are used for selecting routing style for the pipe. By default, the **Standard** option is selected in this drop-down list.

Nominal size

This drop-down list is available in the **BASIC > Dimensions** rollout. This drop-down list contains options to change the size of a pipe. The options available in this drop-down list will change depending upon the option selected from the **Routing preference** drop-down list.

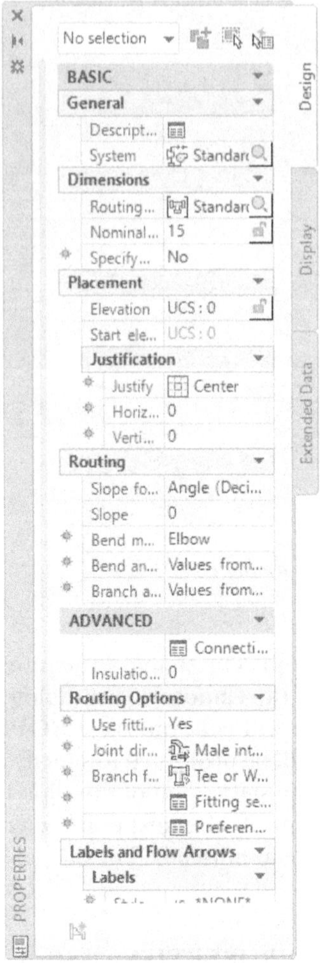

*Figure 5-10 The **PROPERTIES** palette displayed on choosing the **Pipe** tool*

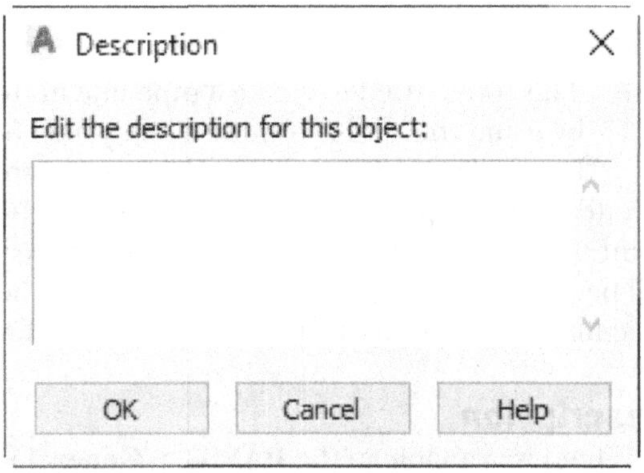

*Figure 5-11 The **Description** dialog box*

Specify cut length

This drop-down list is available in the **General > Dimensions** rollout. There are two options available in this drop-down list: **Yes** and **No**. By default, the **No** option is selected in this drop-down list. On selecting the **Yes** option, you can specify the cut length in the respective field.

Cut length

This edit box is available in the **Dimensions** rollout only when the **Yes** option is selected in the **Specify cut length** drop-down list. You can specify the value of cut length in this edit box. Cut length is the maximum available length of a piece of pipe.

Elevation

This edit box is available in the **BASIC > Placement** rollout. Using this edit box, you can specify the value of elevation of pipe from the ground.

Start elevation

This field is available in the **BASIC > Placement** rollout. The value in this field is the same as specified in the **Elevation** edit box.

Justify

This drop-down list is available in the **Placement > Justification** rollout. The options in this drop-down list are used to change the justification of pipe.

Horizontal offset

This edit box is available in the **Justification** rollout of the **Placement** rollout. Using this edit box, you can specify the horizontal distance value by which the pipe is distant from the selected justification point.

Vertical offset

This edit box is available in the **Justification** rollout of the **Placement** rollout. Using this edit box, you can specify the vertical distance value by which the pipe is distant from the selected justification point.

Slope format

This drop-down list is available in the **BASIC > Routing** rollout of the **PROPERTIES** palette. The options in this drop-down list are used to specify the format in which the slope value will be entered. There are seven options available in this drop-down list: **Angle (Decimal Degrees)**; **Percentage, 100%=45 degree**; **Percentage, 100%=90 degree**; **Rise/Run (Millimeters/Millimeters)**; **Run (Millimeters), Rise=(1 Millimeters)**; **Rise (Millimeters), Run= (10 Millimeters)**; and **Fractional Rise (Millimeters), Run= (10 Millimeters)**. In AutoCAD MEP, the slope also includes the gravity factor in it.

Slope

This edit box is available in the **BASIC > Routing** rollout of the **PROPERTIES** palette. You can specify the value of slope in this edit box. The format in which the value will be specified depends upon the option selected from the **Slope format** drop-down list. If you change the slope value while adding more pipes, the fitting at joints will adjust automatically to provide the changed slope.

Bend method

This drop-down list is used to specify the method of bending that is to be applied on any bend while creating a pipe line. There are two methods of bending available in this drop-down list: **Elbow** and **Offset**.

Bend angle

This drop-down list is used to specify the angle of bend that is to be applied on any bend while creating a pipe. By default, the **Values from catalog** option is selected in this drop-down list. Therefore, the bend angle specified in the catalog is used. You can specify a desired value by clicking on this drop-down list.

Branch angle

This drop-down list is used to specify the lateral angle of Tee that is to be applied on any bend while creating a pipe. By default, the **Values from catalog** option is selected in this drop-down list. Therefore, the bend angle specified in the catalog is used. You can specify a desired value by clicking on this drop-down list.

Connection details

This button is available in the **ADVANCED** rollout. When you choose this button, the **Connection Details** dialog box will be displayed, refer to Figure 5-12. There are two rollouts available in the dialog box which contain the details about both the connections.

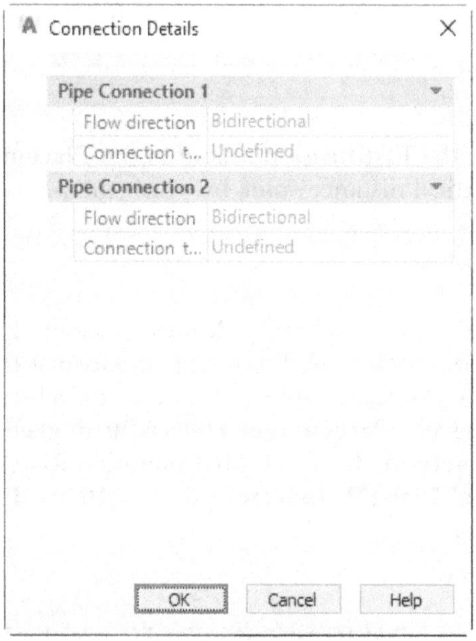

Figure 5-12 The ***Connection Details*** *dialog box*

Insulation thickness

This edit box is also available in the **ADVANCED** rollout and is used to specify the thickness of insulation applied in the pipe.

Use fitting tolerance

This drop-down list is available in the **ADVANCED > Routing Options** rollout of the **PROPERTIES** palette. There are two options in this drop-down list: **Yes** and **No**. When the **Yes** option is selected in the drop-down list, the branch fittings will be connected to the main pipe, considering the fitting tolerances. If the **No** option is selected in the drop-down list, the branches will be joined to the main pipe without considering the fitting tolerances.

Joint direction

This drop-down list is available in the **ADVANCED > Routing Options** rollout of the **PROPERTIES** palette. There are two options available in this drop-down list: **Male into Female** and **Female out to Male**.

Branch fitting

This drop-down list is available in the **ADVANCED > Routing Options** rollout of the **PROPERTIES** palette. The options in this drop-down list are used to specify the type of fitting to be applied on a branch. There are five options available in this drop-down list: **Takeoff only**, **Tee only**, **Tee or Wye (Lateral)**, **Wye (Lateral) only**, and **Wye (Lateral) or Tee**.

Fitting Settings

This option is available in the **ADVANCED > Routing Options** rollout of the **PROPERTIES** palette. When you click on this option, the **Fitting Settings** dialog box will be displayed, as shown in Figure 5-13. The options in this dialog box are used to change the type of fitting to be applied while creating the branches in the pipe.

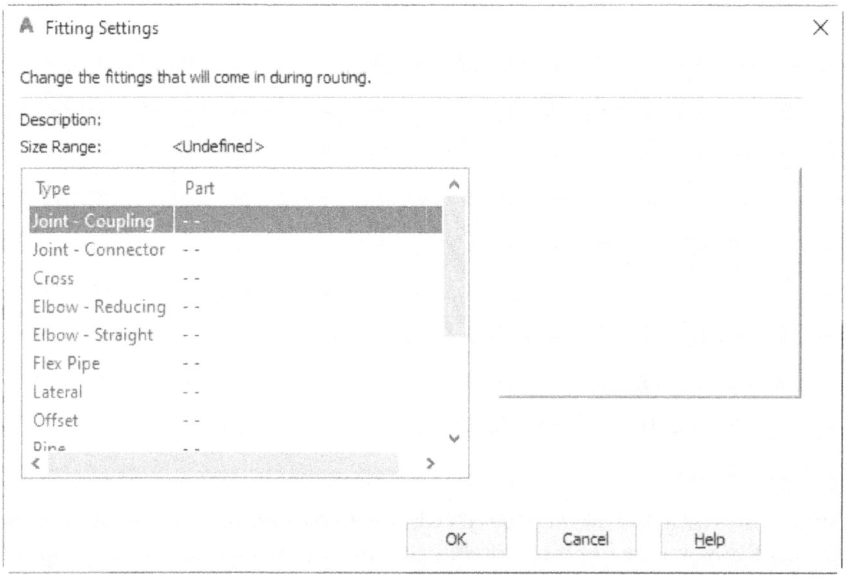

*Figure 5-13 The **Fitting Settings** dialog box*

Preferences

This option is available in the **ADVANCED > Routing Options** rollout of the **PROPERTIES** palette. When you click on this option, the **Pipe Layout Preferences** dialog box will be displayed, as shown in Figure 5-14. The options in this dialog box are used to define the layout preferences for creating a pipe. Using the options in this dialog box, you can set the preferences for parameters such as Slope, Elevation, Label style, Flow arrow style, and Elbow layout.

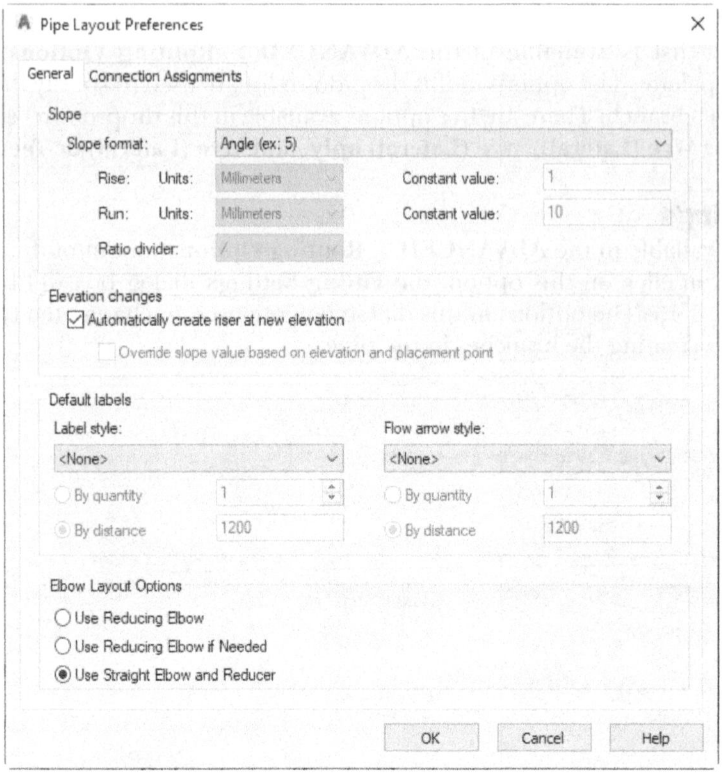

*Figure 5-14 The **Pipe Layout Preferences** dialog box*

Style

This drop-down list is available in the **ADVANCED > Labels and Flow Arrows > Labels** rollout of the **PROPERTIES** palette. The options in this drop-down list are used to apply the label styles to pipe.

Layout method

This drop-down list is available in the **ADVANCED > Labels and Flow Arrows > Labels** rollout of the **PROPERTIES** palette only when **NONE** is not selected from the **Style** drop-down list. The options in this drop-down list are used to specify the type of layout for pipes. There are two options available in this drop-down list: **By distance** and **By quantity**.

Number of Labels

This edit box is available in the **ADVANCED > Labels and Flow Arrows > Labels** rollout of the **PROPERTIES** palette only when **NONE** is not selected in the **Style** drop-down list and **By quantity** is selected in the **Layout method** drop-down list. Using this edit box, you can specify the total number of labels on a segment pipe.

Distance between

This edit box is available in the **ADVANCED > Labels and Flow Arrows > Labels** rollout of the **PROPERTIES** palette only when **NONE** is not selected in the **Style** drop-down list and **By**

distance is selected in the **Layout method** drop-down list. Using this edit box, you can specify the distance between two consecutive labels on a pipe.

The **Style**, **Layout method**, **Number of Labels**, and **Distance between** options are also available for Flow Arrows. These options have already been discussed in this chapter.

Parallel Pipes

This tool is used to create parallel pipes in the Piping system. To create a parallel pipe, choose the **Parallel Pipes** tool from the **Pipe** drop-down in the **Build** panel of the **Home** tab in the **Ribbon**; you will be prompted to select a baseline object. Select a base line object (like an earlier created pipe) from the drawing area; you will be prompted to select pipe parallel to it. Select parallel pipe from the drawing area and press ENTER; you will be prompted to specify the next point for creating parallel pipes. The options available in the **PROPERTIES** palette for parallel pipes are same as discussed in the Pipe section of this chapter.

ADDING PIPE FITTINGS

A pipe fitting is used to join two or more pipes. You can add pipe fittings by using the tools available in the **Pipe Fitting** drop-down. This drop-down is available in the **Build** panel of the **Home** tab in the **Ribbon**. The tools in this drop-down are discussed next.

Pipe Fitting

This tool is used to add a user specified fitting to the pipe line. On choosing this tool, the **PROPERTIES** palette will be displayed, refer to Figure 5-15. The options available in this palette are discussed next.

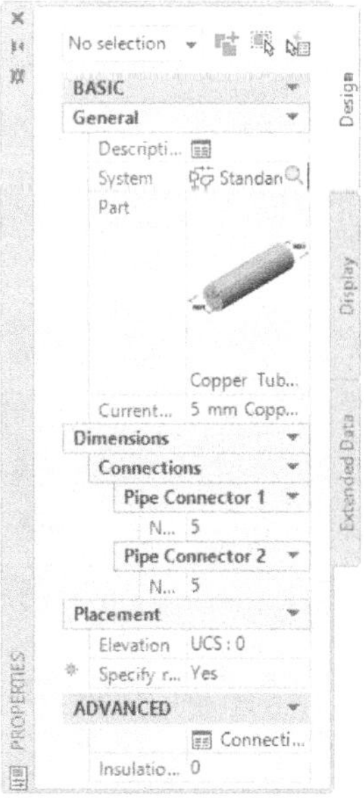

*Figure 5-15 The **PROPERTIES** palette for pipe fittings*

Description

This field is available in the **BASIC > General** rollout in the **PROPERTIES** palette. When you click in this field, the **Description** dialog box will be displayed. You can write description about the fitting in the text box available in this dialog box.

System

This drop-down list is available in the **BASIC > General** rollout of the **PROPERTIES** palette. The options in this drop-down list are used to change the standard of fitting to be created. By default, the **Standard (STD)** option is selected in this drop-down list.

Part

This field is available in the **BASIC > General** rollout of the **PROPERTIES** palette. When you click in this field, the **Select Part** dialog box will be displayed, refer to Figure 5-16. There are various types of fittings available for pipe in this dialog box. All these fittings are displayed in the **SELECT PART FROM CATALOG** rollout. The fittings in this rollout are divided into groups in a tree structure. You can filter the available parts depending on your requirements by using the options available in the **FILTER** rollout of this dialog box. The filtered options will be displayed in the **SELECT PART SIZE** area of this dialog box. You can also select the required fitting from the **TOOL PALETTE - Piping**. These fittings are available in the **Fitting** tab of the palette.

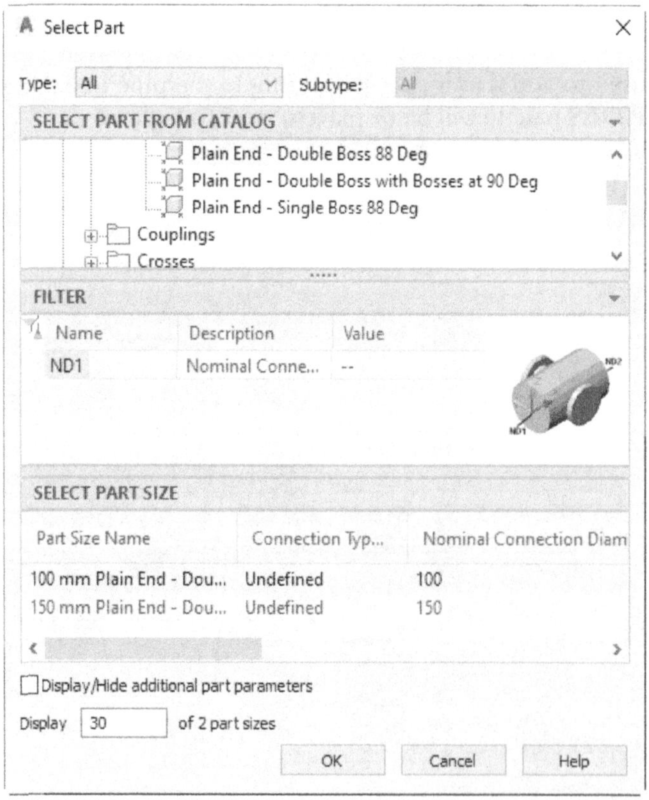

***Figure 5-16** The **Select Part** dialog box*

Current size

This drop-down list is available in the **BASIC > General** rollout of the **PROPERTIES** palette. There are various options available in this drop-down list to change the size of the current fitting.

Connections rollout

This rollout is available in the **BASIC > Dimensions** rollout in the **PROPERTIES** palette. There are various options available in this rollout to change the dimensions of a selected fitting. The options in this rollout vary depending on the selected fitting.

Elevation

This edit box is available in the **BASIC > Placement** rollout in the **PROPERTIES** palette. Using this edit box, you can specify the value of height of fitting from the ground level.

Specify rotation on screen

This drop-down list is available in the **BASIC > Placement** rollout in the **PROPERTIES** palette. There are two options available in this drop-down list: **Yes** and **No**. If you select the **Yes** option, then you will be prompted to specify the rotation value while creating the fitting. If you select the **No** option, then you need to specify the rotation value in the edit box available in the **PROPERTIES** palette.

Rotation

This edit box is available in the **BASIC > Placement** rollout in the **PROPERTIES** palette. Using this edit box, you can specify the value of rotation of the fitting before placing it in the drawing. This edit box is available only when the **No** option is selected from the **Specify rotation on screen** drop-down list.

Connection details

This button is available in the **ADVANCED** rollout. When you choose this button, the **Connection Details** dialog box will be displayed. There are two rollouts available in the dialog box that contain the details about both the connections.

Insulation thickness

This edit box is also available in the **ADVANCED** rollout and is used to specify the thickness of insulation applied to the pipe.

Pipe Custom Fitting

This tool is used for creating custom fittings in the pipe line. To create a pipe custom fitting, you must have lines, arcs, or polylines created in the drawing area. To create a custom fitting, choose the **Pipe Custom Fitting** tool from the **Pipe Fitting** drop-down list; you will be prompted to select lines, arcs, or polylines. Select lines, arcs, or polylines from the drawing area and press ENTER; the **Create Pipe Custom Fitting** dialog box will be displayed, refer to Figure 5-17. Depending on the selected entities, the segments will be displayed in the dialog box as ***Segment n of m***, where ***n*** is the serial number of current segment and ***m*** is the total number of segments in the fitting. There are various system definitions available in the **System** drop-down. After selecting the desired system, choose the **Next >** button to change the parameters of next segment. You can also select the **Apply to All Segments** check box if you want to keep the same parameters for other segments. After specifying parameters for all the segments, choose the **Finish** button; you will be prompted whether to delete the base geometry or not. Enter **Yes** or **No** at the command prompt; the custom fitting will be created. The open end points of entities will be the connection ports for fitting.

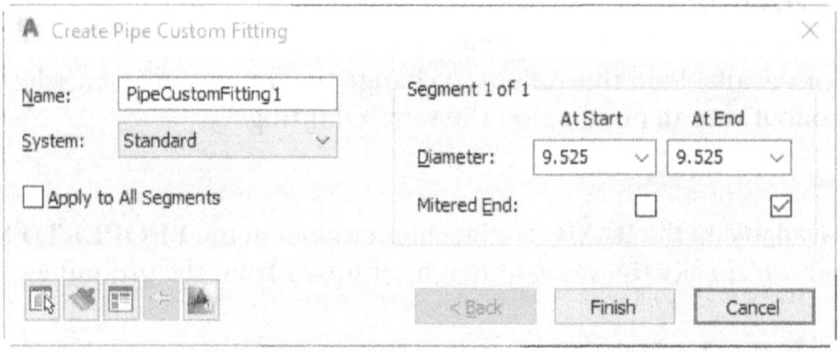

Figure 5-17 *The* ***Create Pipe Custom Fitting*** *dialog box*

CREATING A CUSTOM MULTI-VIEW PART

While creating models in AutoCAD MEP, you may need to create some custom parts that can be frequently used in the drawing. The procedure to create a Custom Multi-View Part is given next. To create a Custom Multi-View Part, you need to create a solid component and convert it into a block using the **Create Block** tool from the **Insert** tab in the **Ribbon**. The steps to create a custom multi view part are given below:

Before creating a Custom Multi-View Part, you need to add the **Solids** tab to the **Ribbon** by customizing the tab. To do so, right-click anywhere on the **Ribbon**; a shortcut menu is displayed. Choose **Show Tabs > Solids** from the shortcut menu; the **Solids** tab is added to the **Ribbon**. Next, you can create any required solid component by using the tools in the **Solids** tab.

1. Create a model of the custom part that you want to add to the Multi-view Part list, refer to Figure 5-18 and save it as a block.

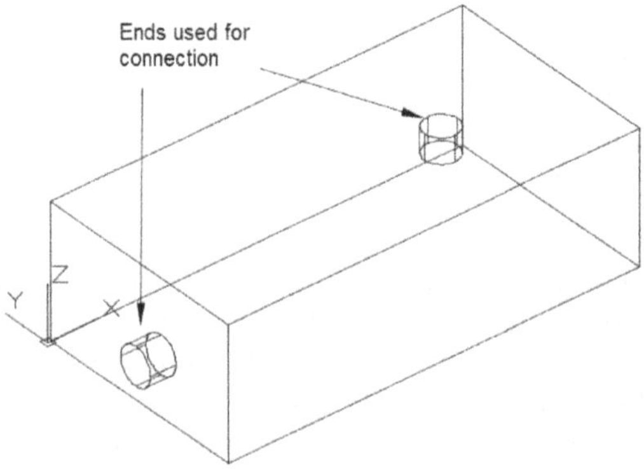

Figure 5-18 *Waste water tank used as custom part*

2. Choose the **Content Builder** tool from the **MEP Content** panel in the **Manage** tab of the **Ribbon**; the **Getting Started - Catalog Screen** dialog box will be displayed, as shown in Figure 5-19.

3. Select the **Multi-view Part** option from the **Part Domain** drop-down list available at the top of the dialog box; the options in the dialog box will be modified according to Multi-view parts.

4. Select **Mechanical** from the part tree displayed in the dialog box to add a new equipment range and choose the **New Chapter** button available at the right of the part tree; the **New Chapter** dialog box will be displayed, as shown in Figure 5-20.

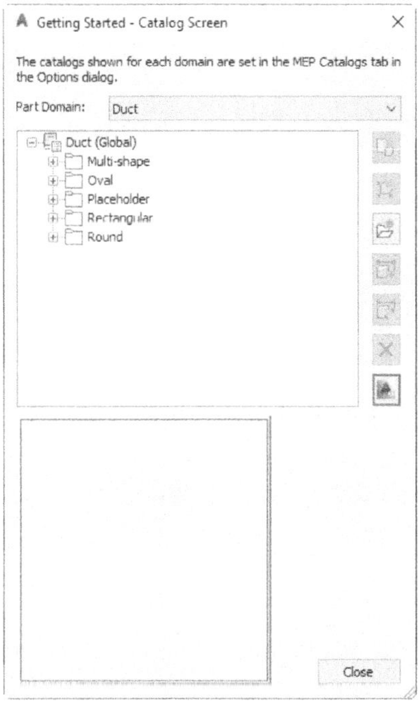

Figure 5-19 The ***Getting Started - Catalog Screen*** *dialog box*

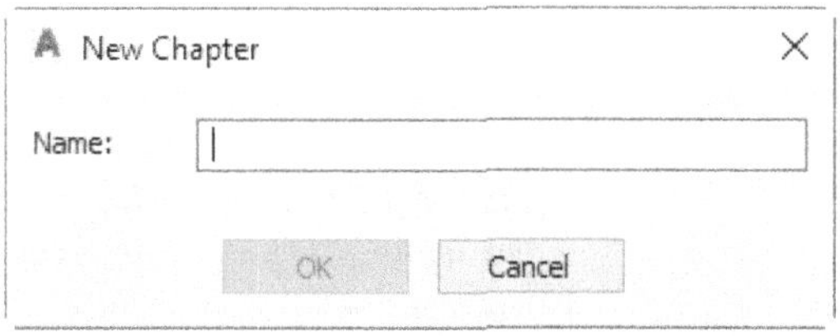

Figure 5-20 The ***New Chapter*** *dialog box*

5. Enter **Waste Water Tank** as name for the category in the **Name** edit box of the dialog box and choose **OK**; a new category will be added to the Mechanical part list. Figure 5-21 shows the **Waste Water Tank** category added in the Mechanical part list.

6. Choose the **New Block Part** button from the **Getting Started - Catalog Screen** dialog box; the **New Part** dialog box is displayed, as shown in Figure 5-22.

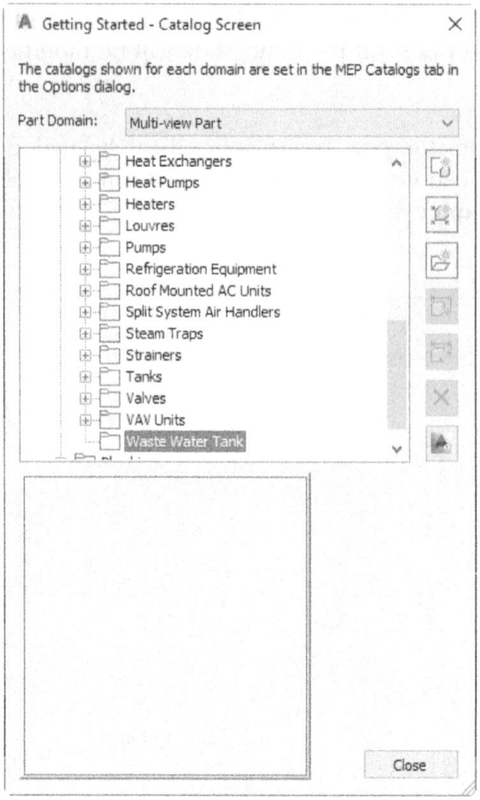

Figure 5-21 *The* ***Getting Started - Catalog Screen*** *dialog box with waste water tank added as a new chapter*

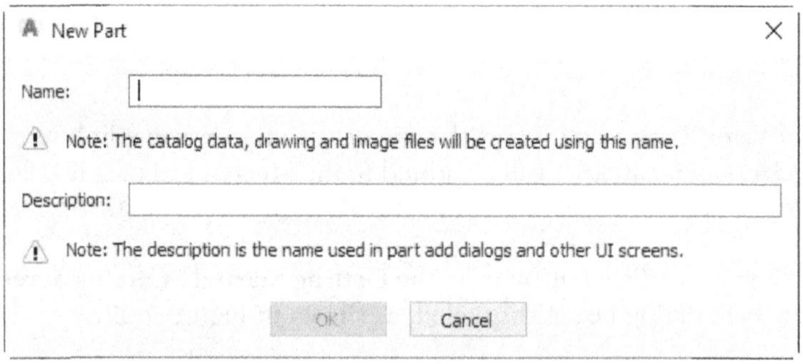

Figure 5-22 *The* ***New Part*** *dialog box*

7. Enter **Rectangular waste water tank** and the **Rectangular waste water tank- 2 end connections** in the **Name** and **Description** edit boxes, respectively and choose **OK**; the **MvPart Builder (New Part)** dialog box will be displayed, refer to Figure 5-23.

8. Select an option from the **Type** drop-down list whose properties are matching the part you want to create. In this case, select the **Tank** option from this drop-down list. Next, select **Horizontal Storage Tank** option from the **Subtype** field.

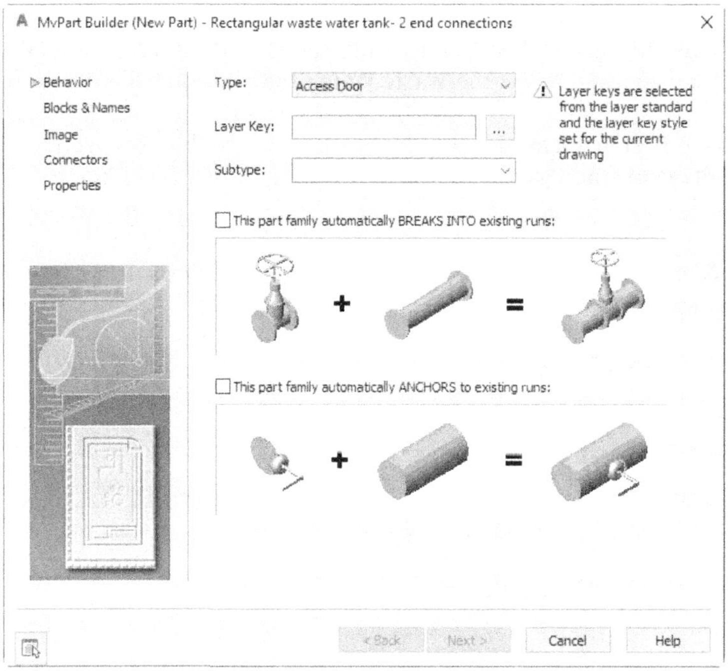

Figure 5-23 *The* ***MvPart Builder (New Part)*** *dialog box*

9. Choose the **Next** button from the dialog box; the **Blocks & Names** page of the dialog box will be displayed, as shown in Figure 5-24.

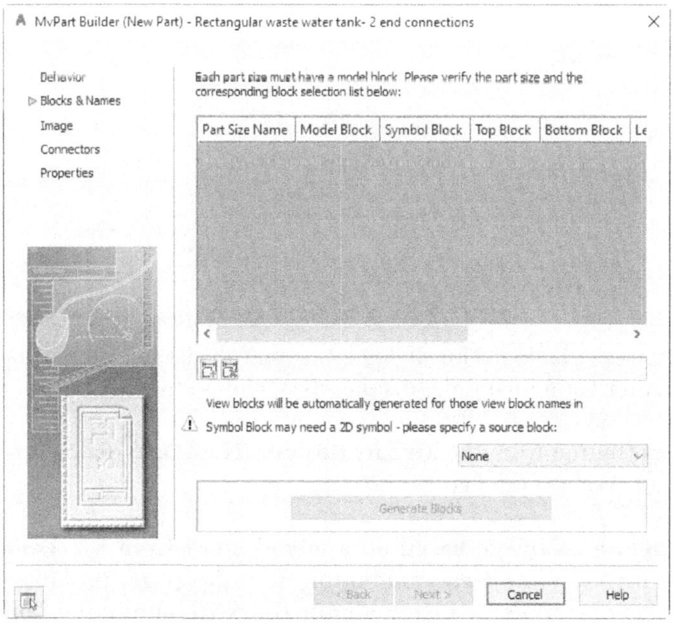

Figure 5-24 *The* ***MvPart Builder (New Part)*** *dialog box with the* ***Blocks & Names*** *page displayed*

10. Choose the **Add Part Size** button available below the part sheet; a new part will be added to the list and you will be prompted to select an option from the **Model Block** drop-down list displayed. Select the **Waste Water Tank** option from the drop-down list.

11. Click below the **Part Size Name** field; the block name will be displayed under all the fields and block will be assigned as the new part. (In this case, the block is created with the name Waste water tank).

12. Choose the **Generate Blocks** button to create the part; the **Views** dialog box will be displayed, as shown in Figure 5-25.

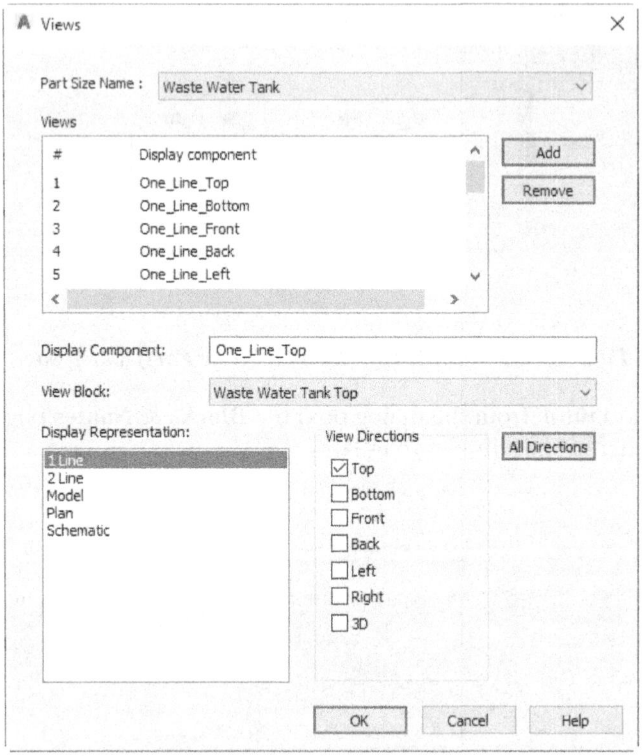

***Figure 5-25** The **Views** dialog box*

13. Using the options available in this dialog box, you can change the display style of the part to be created. After configuring the display style, choose the **OK** button to exit.

14. Choose the **Next** button from the **MvPart Builder (New Part)** dialog box; the **Image** page will be displayed, as shown in Figure 5-26.

15. Select the **Generate an image based on a model block from SW Isometric View** radio button and then choose the **Generate** button from this page; the image of block will be generated. After generating the image, choose the **Next** button; the **Connectors** page will be displayed, as shown in Figure 5-27.

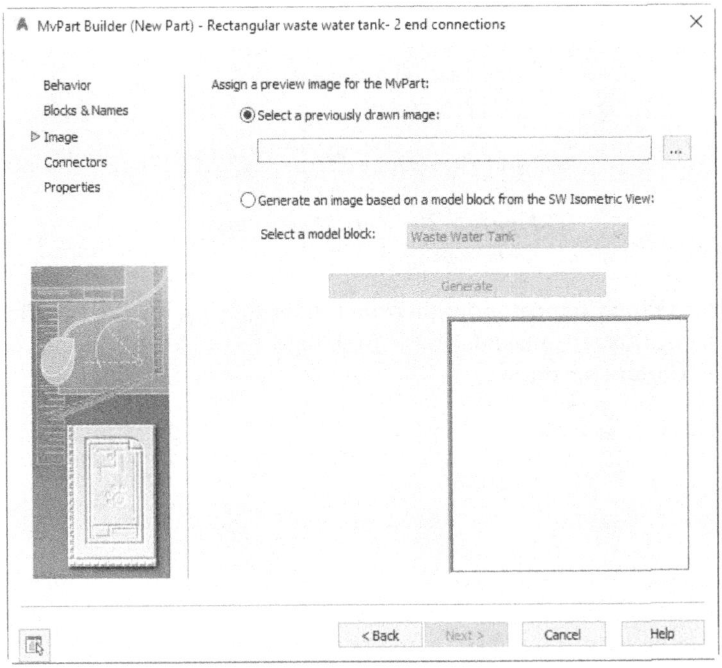

Figure 5-26 The ***MvPart Builder (New Part)*** *dialog box with the* ***Image*** *page*

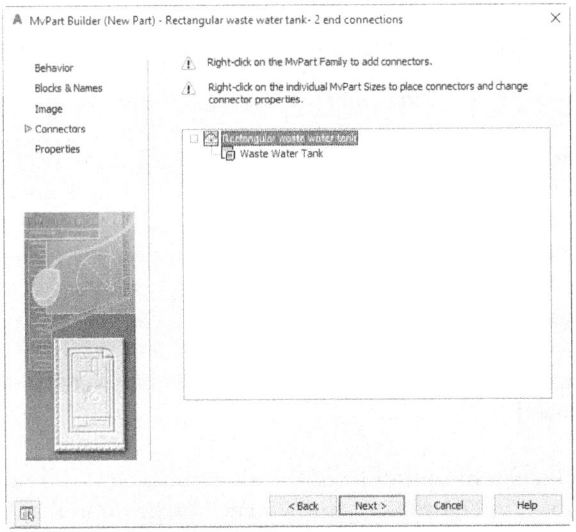

Figure 5-27 The ***MvPart Builder (New Part)*** *dialog box with the* ***Connectors*** *page*

16. Using the options available in this page, you can specify the connectors to be added to the Multi-view part. To add a connector to the part (Rectangular waste water tank), right-click on the **Rectangular waste water tank** in the dialog box; a shortcut menu will be displayed, as shown in Figure 5-28.

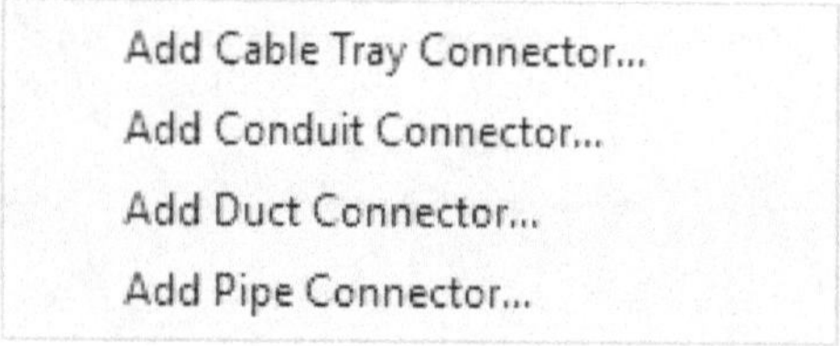

Figure 5-28 Shortcut menu to add connectors

17. Choose the **Add Pipe Connector** option from the shortcut menu; the **Part Family Connector Properties** dialog box is displayed. Figure 5-29 shows the dialog box displayed after choosing the **Add Pipe Connector** option.

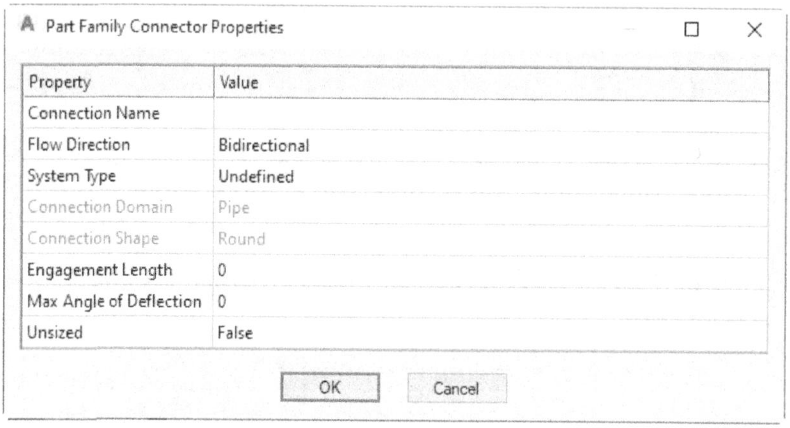

*Figure 5-29 The **Part Family Connector Properties** dialog box*

18. Click on the field adjacent to **Flow Direction**; a drop-down list will be displayed. Select the **In** option from the drop-down list and choose the **OK** button from the dialog box.

19. Similarly, add one more pipe connector with the **Out** option and choose the **OK** button from the dialog box; the **MvPart Builder (New Part)** dialog box after adding the connectors will be displayed, as shown in Figure 5-30.

20. Select and right-click on **Connector1** available below **Waste water tank** in the list; a shortcut menu will be displayed.

21. Choose the **Edit Placement** option from the shortcut menu; the Application window will be displayed, as shown in Figure 5-31, and you will be prompted to specify the position or normal of connector. Also, the **MvPartBuilder - Connector Editor** palette is displayed.

22. Choose the **Position** option from the command prompt and specify the location of the connector1 on the block in the drawing area, refer to Figure 5-31 .

23. Next, select the **Connector2** from the **MvPartBuilder - Connector Editor** palette and select the **Normal** option from the command prompt. Now, define the normal direction by selecting both the centers of the pipe, refer to Figure 5-32.

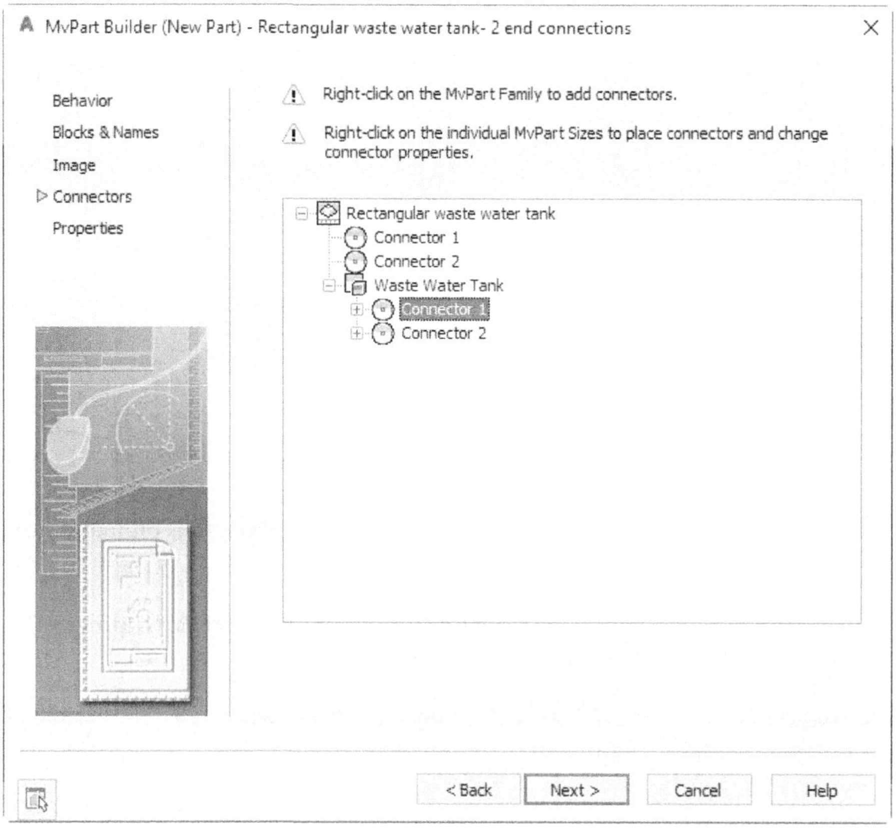

Figure 5-30 *The* **MvPart Builder (New Part)** *dialog box after adding connectors*

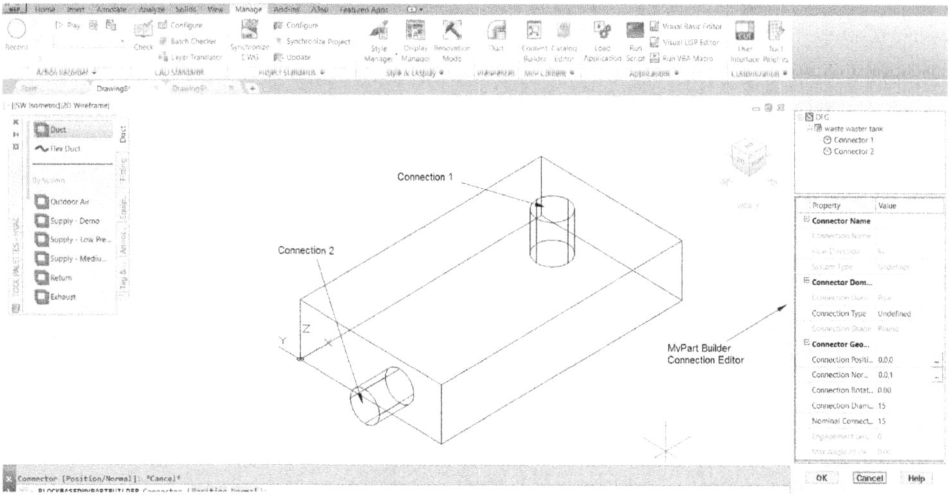

Figure 5-31 *The Application window*

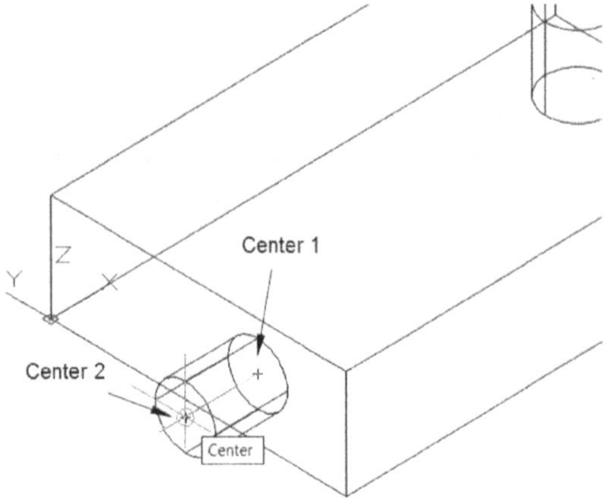

Figure 5-32 *Centers of the pipe*

24. After selecting both the centers, choose the **Position** button from the command prompt and specify the location of the connector2 on the block in the drawing area, refer to Figure 5-31.

25 After specifying the locations, choose the **OK** button from the **MvPartBuilder - Connector Editor** palette; the **MvPart Builder** dialog box will be displayed again.

26. Choose the **Next** button from the dialog box; the **Properties** page will be displayed, as shown in Figure 5-33.

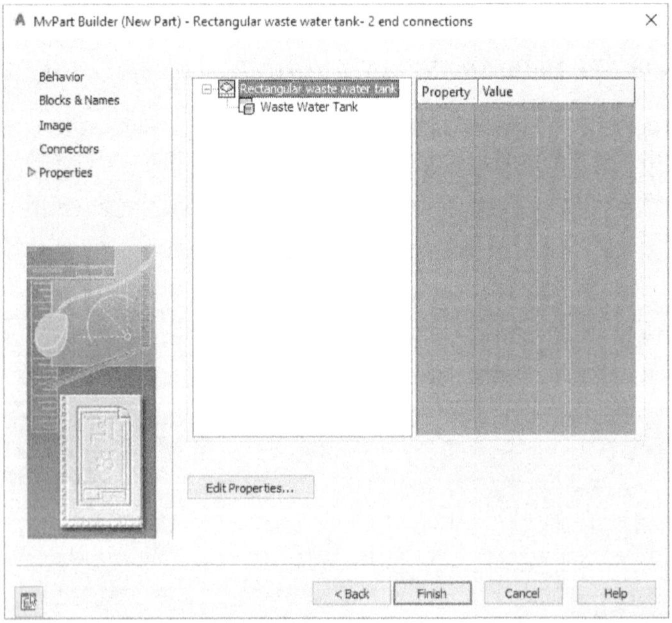

Figure 5-33 *The* ***MvPart Builder (New Part)*** *dialog box with the* ***Properties*** *page displayed*

27. Choose the **Edit Properties** button from the dialog box; the **Property Editor** dialog box will be displayed, refer to Figure 5-34. Using the options available in this dialog box, you can add desired property variables to the new part.

28. After configuring the property variables, choose the **OK** button and then choose the **Finish** button from the **MvPart Builder(New Part)** dialog box; the part will be created and added to the equipment list.

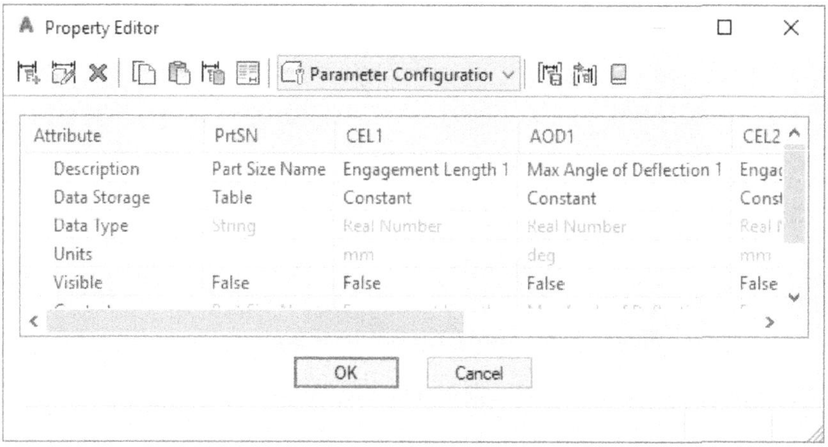

*Figure 5-34 The **Property Editor** dialog box*

TUTORIAL

TUTORIAL 1

In this tutorial, you will create the pipe system shown in Figure 5-35. The plan view for creating the pipe system is given in Figure 5-36. Note that to complete this piping system, you also need to create a custom part named steam turbine component. **(Expected time: 30 min)**

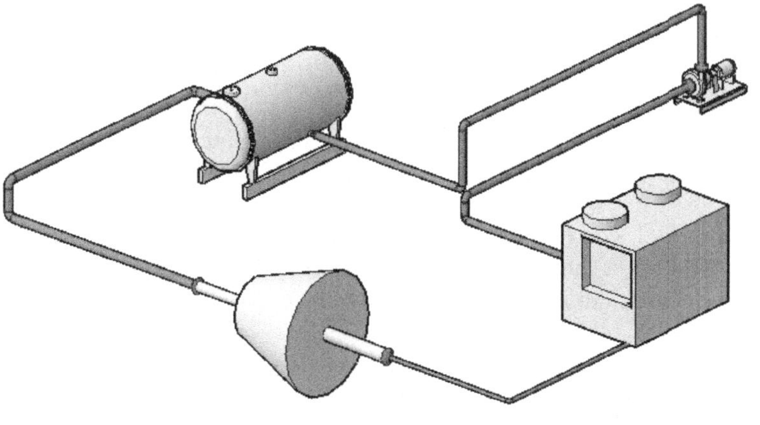

Figure 5-35 The piping system

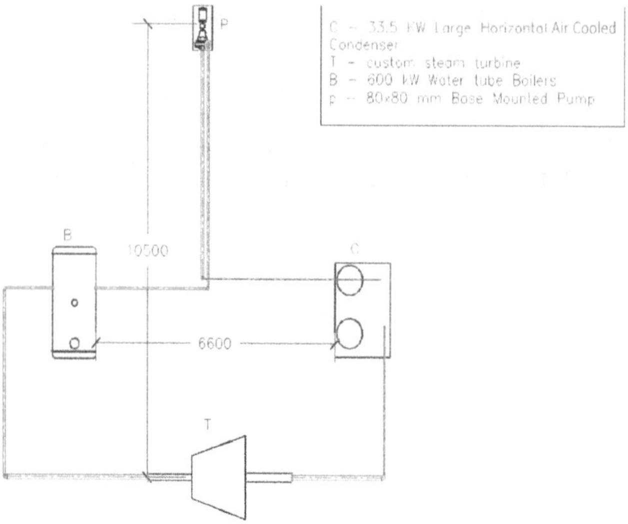

Figure 5-36 *Plan for creating the piping system*

The following steps are required to complete this tutorial:

Examine the model to determine equipment to be added and parameters of piping.

a. Create a custom part named Turbine.
b. Add the equipment according to the model.
c. Create piping between various equipment.

Creating the Drawing File

1. Choose **New > Drawing** from the **Application Menu**; the **Select Template** dialog box is displayed.

2. Select the **Aecb Model (Global Ctb).dwt** template from the dialog box and then choose the **Open** button; a blank drawing file is created.

Creating a Block

To create a custom part, you must have a model of the part created as a block. So, before creating a custom part, you need to create a model of the part and save it as a block.

Before creating a model, you need to add the **Solids** tab to the **Ribbon**. To do so, right-click anywhere on the **Ribbon**; a shortcut menu is displayed. Choose **Show Tabs** > **Solids** from the shortcut menu; the **Solids** tab is added to the **Ribbon**.

1. Choose the **Cone** tool from the **Solid Primitives** drop-down in the **Modeling** panel of the **Solids** tab in the **Ribbon**; you will be prompted to specify the center of the base.

2. Enter **0,0,0** at the command prompt and create a cone with the base radius **1000**, top radius **500**, and height **1000**. Also, create the inlet and outlet pipes on the cone.

3. Select the created model and then choose the **Create Block** tool from the **Block** panel of the **Insert** tab in the **Ribbon**; the **Block Definition** dialog box is displayed, as shown in Figure 5-37.

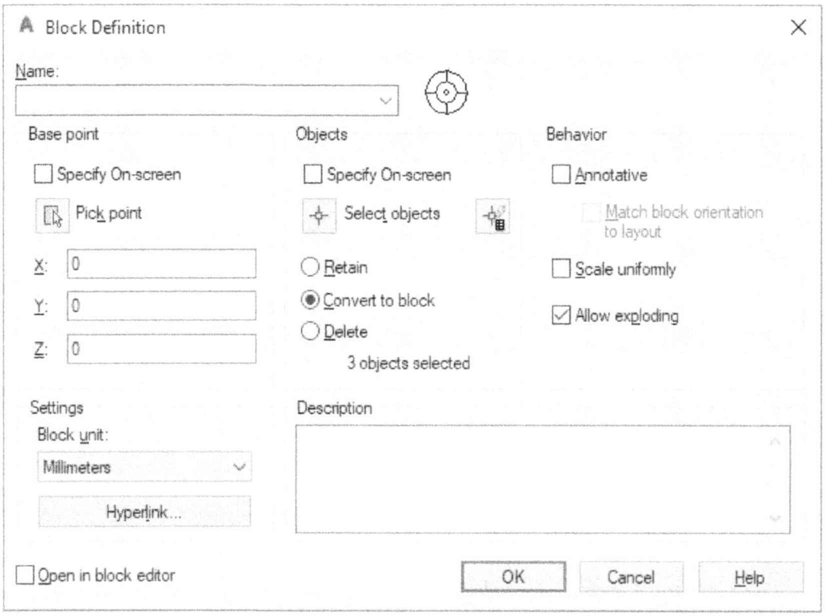

***Figure 5-37** The **Block Definition** dialog box*

4. Specify the name of the block as **Steam Turbine** in the **Name** edit box available at the top left corner of the dialog box. Now, choose the **OK** button from the dialog box; the model is added as a block.

Creating Custom Part by Using the Block

1. Choose the **Content Builder** tool from the **MEP Content** panel in the **Manage** tab of the **Ribbon**; the **Getting Started-Catalog Screen** dialog box is displayed, as shown in Figure 5-38. Select the **Multi-view Part** option from the **Part Domain** drop-down list, if it is not already selected.

2. Click on **Mechanical** in the part tree and choose the **New Chapter** button at the right in the dialog box; the **New Chapter** dialog box is displayed, as shown in Figure 5-39.

3. Specify the name as **Turbine1** in the **Name** edit box of the dialog box and then choose the **OK** button to exit; **Turbine1** is added to the Mechanical part list.

4. Select **Turbine1** from the list and choose the **New Block Part** button at the right in the dialog box; the **New Part** dialog box is displayed, as shown in Figure 5-40.

5. Specify the name of the part as **Steam Turbine1** in the **Name** edit box and then click in the **Description** edit box; the text specified in the **Name** edit box is copied in the **Description** edit box.

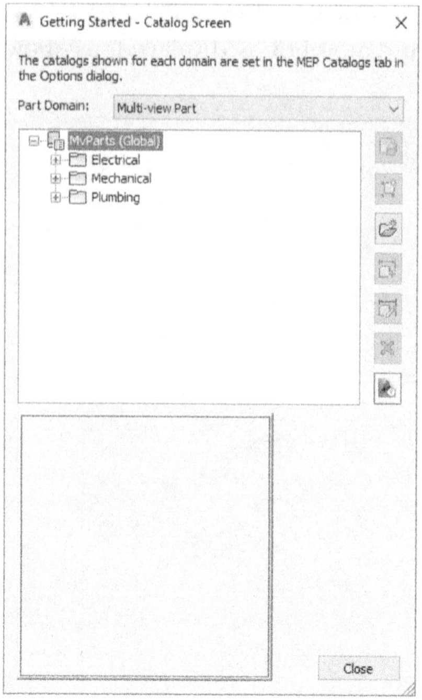

*Figure 5-38 The **Getting Started- Catalog Screen** dialog box*

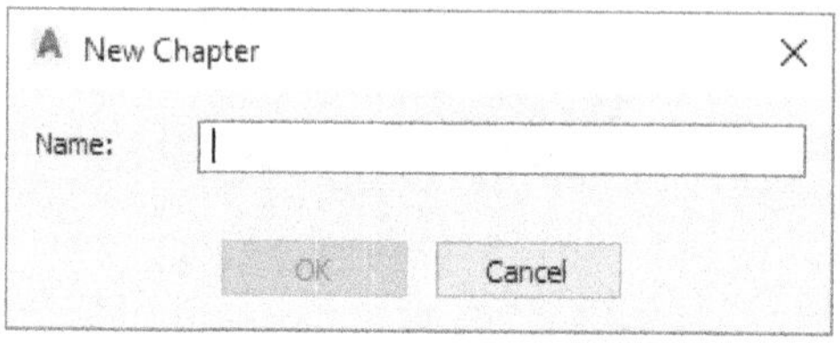

*Figure 5-39 The **New Chapter** dialog box*

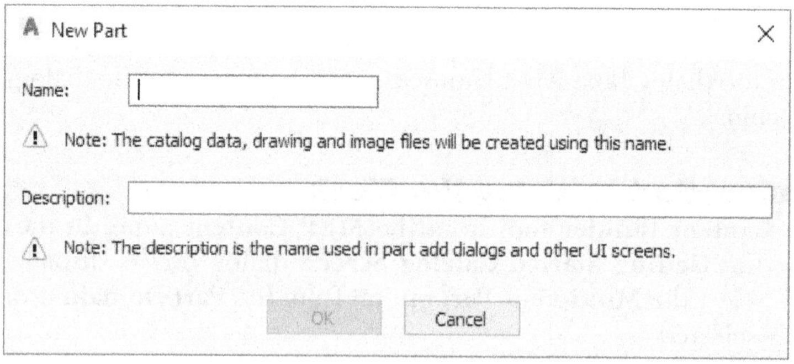

*Figure 5-40 The **New Part** dialog box*

6. Choose the **OK** button from the **New Part** dialog box; the **MvPart Builder (New Part)** dialog box is displayed, refer to Figure 5-41.

7. Select the **Pump** option from the **Type** drop-down list and select the **Inline Pump** option from the **Subtype** drop-down list.

8. Choose the **Next** button from the dialog box; the **Blocks & Names** page of the dialog box is displayed, as shown in Figure 5-42.

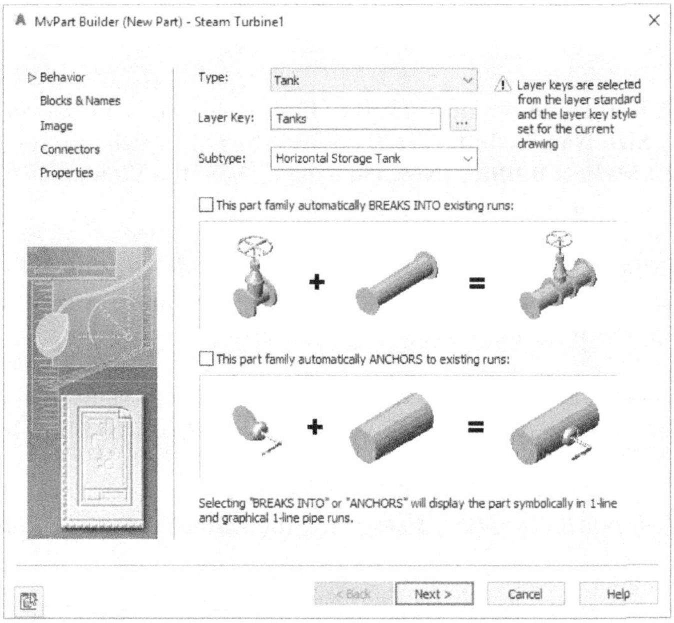

Figure 5-41 *The* ***MvPart Builder (New Part)*** *dialog box*

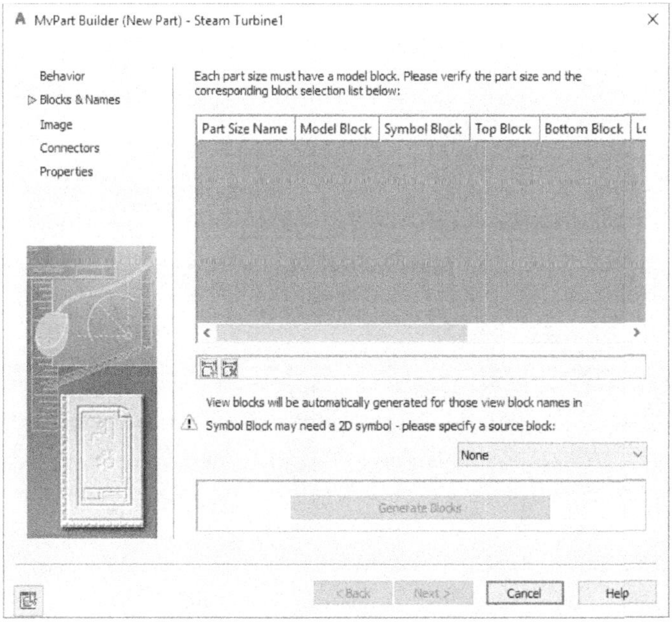

Figure 5-42 *The* ***MvPart Builder (New Part)*** *dialog box with the* ***Blocks & Names*** *page displayed*

9. Choose the **Add Part Size** button available below the part size sheet; a drop-down list is displayed.

10. Select the **Steam Turbine** option from the drop-down list and click on the empty space below the **Part Size Name** edit box in the dialog box. Then choose the **Generate Blocks** button from the **MvPart Builder (New Part)** dialog box; the **Views** dialog box is displayed, as shown in Figure 5-43.

11. Choose the **OK** button from the **Views** dialog box; the **MvPart Builder (New Part)** dialog box is displayed. Choose the **Next** button from it; the **Image** page of the dialog box is displayed, as shown in Figure 5-44.

12. Select the **Generate an image based on a model block from the SW Isometric View** radio button, and then choose the **Generate** button; a preview of the block is displayed in the **Preview** area of the dialog box.

13. Choose the **Next** button from the dialog box; the **Connectors** page is displayed, refer to Figure 5-45.

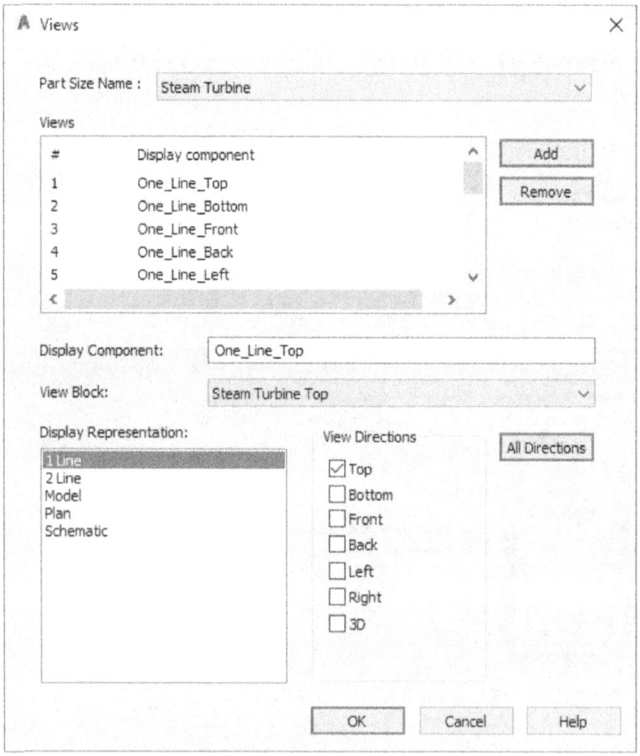

***Figure 5-43** The **Views** dialog box*

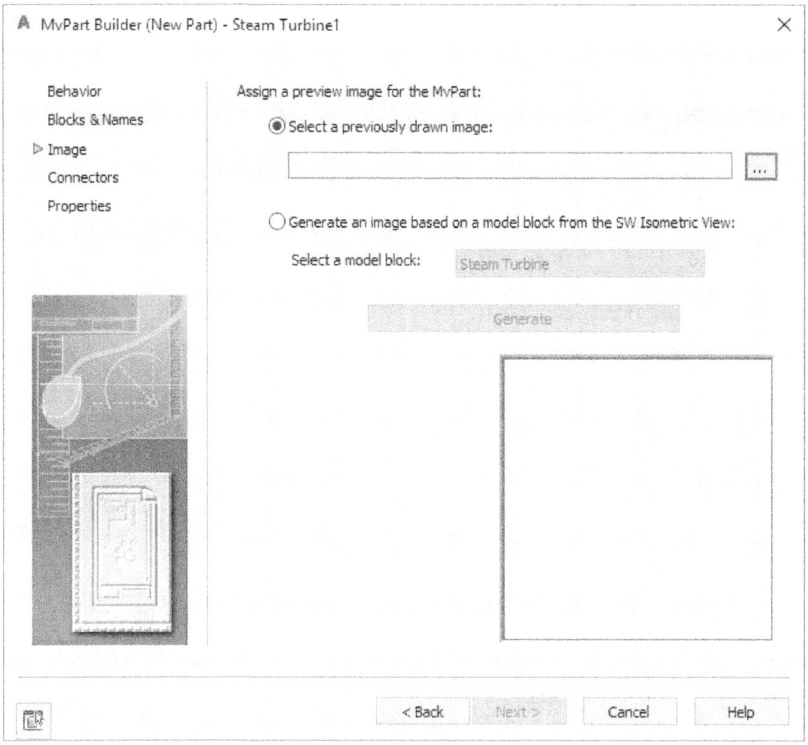

***Figure 5-44** The **MvPart Builder (New Part)** dialog box with the **Image** page*

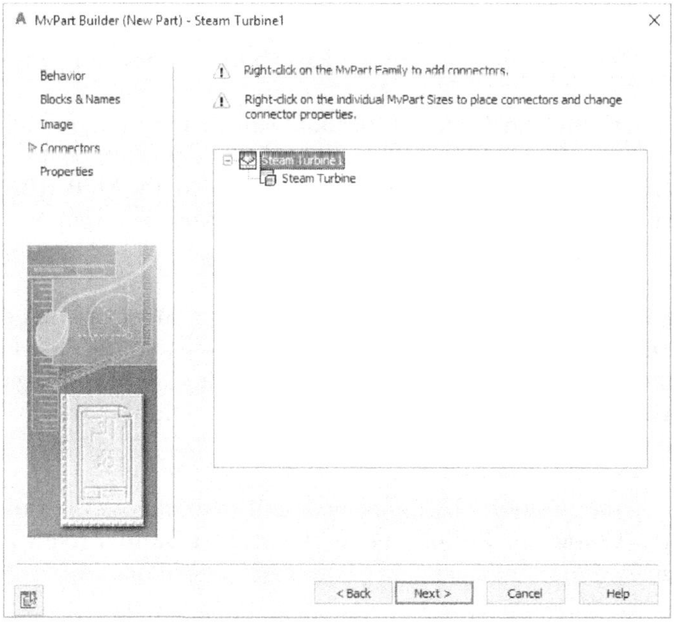

***Figure 5-45** The **MvPart Builder (New Part)** dialog box with the **Connectors** page displayed*

14. Right-click on the **Steam Turbine1** symbol in the dialog box, refer to Figure 5-45; a shortcut menu is displayed. 

15. Choose the **Add Pipe Connector** option from the shortcut menu; the **Part Family Connector Properties** dialog box is displayed, as shown in Figure 5-46.

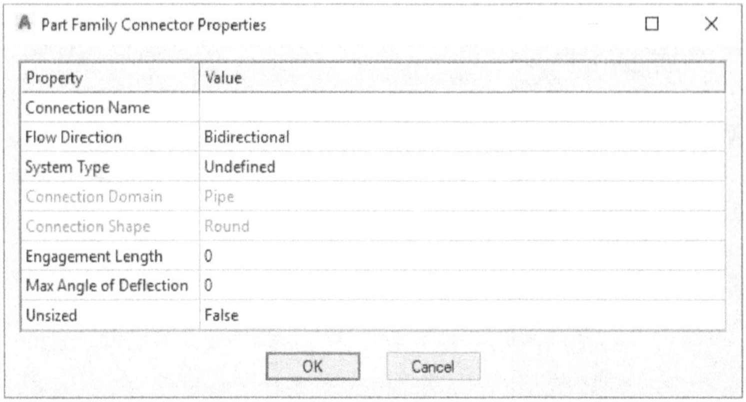

***Figure 5-46** The **Part Family Connector Properties** dialog box*

16. Select the **In** option from the **Flow Direction** drop-down list and the **Hot Water** option from the **System Type** drop-down list.

17. Choose the **OK** button to close the dialog box; **Connector 1** is added to the new part.

18. Similarly, add another pipe connector to the part and then select the **Out** option from the **Flow Direction** drop-down list and the **Hot Water** option from the **System Type** drop-down list. Choose the **Ok** button to exit from the **Part Family Connector Properties**.

19. Right-click on the **Connector 1** available below **Steam Turbine**; a shortcut menu is displayed.

20. Choose the **Edit Placement** option from the shortcut menu; the **MvPartBuilder - Connector Editor** palette is displayed, as shown in Figure 5-47 and you are prompted to specify position of connector or normal to connector.

21. Choose the **Position** button from the command prompt; you are prompted to select position for the first connector. Click on the In Connector available on the model, as shown in Figure 5-48, and then select the **Flange** option from the **Connection Type** drop-down list in the **MvPartBuilder - Connector Editor** palette. Click in the drawing area and choose the **OK** button to accept the results.

22. Similarly, specify the position of Connector 2 and then choose the **OK** button from the **MvPartBuilder - Connector Editor** palette; the **MvPart Builder (New Part)** dialog box is displayed again.

Figure 5-47 *The* ***MvPartBuilder - Connector Editor*** *palette*

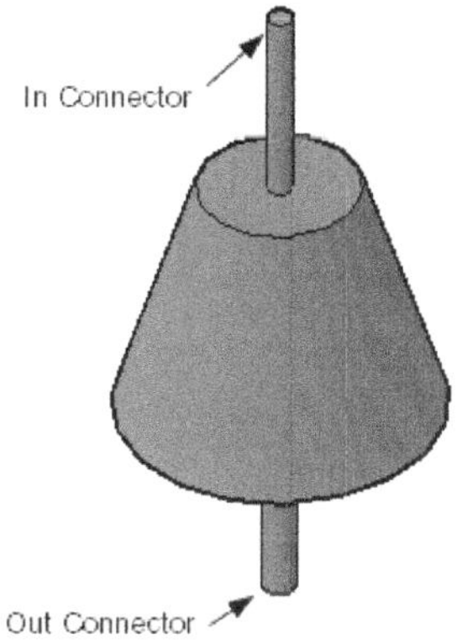

Figure 5-48 *The model with In Connector and Out Connector*

23. Choose the **Next** button from the dialog box; the **Properties** page of the dialog box is displayed, as shown in Figure 5-49.

24. Choose the **Finish** button; the custom part is created with the name **Steam Turbine1** in the **Turbine1** category of equipment in the equipment list. Close the drawing file.

Adding the Equipment

1. Choose **New > Drawing** from the **Application Menu**; the **Select Template** dialog box is displayed.

2. Select the **Aecb Model (Global Ctb).dwt** template from the dialog box and then choose the **Open** button; a blank drawing file is created. Choose the **Piping** workspace, if not already selected.

3. Choose the **Equipment** tool from the **Equipment** drop-down available in the **Build** panel of the **Home** tab in the **Ribbon**; the **Add Multi-view Parts** dialog box is displayed.

4. Expand the **Mechanical** category, if not already expanded; the list of all the available mechanical equipment is displayed.

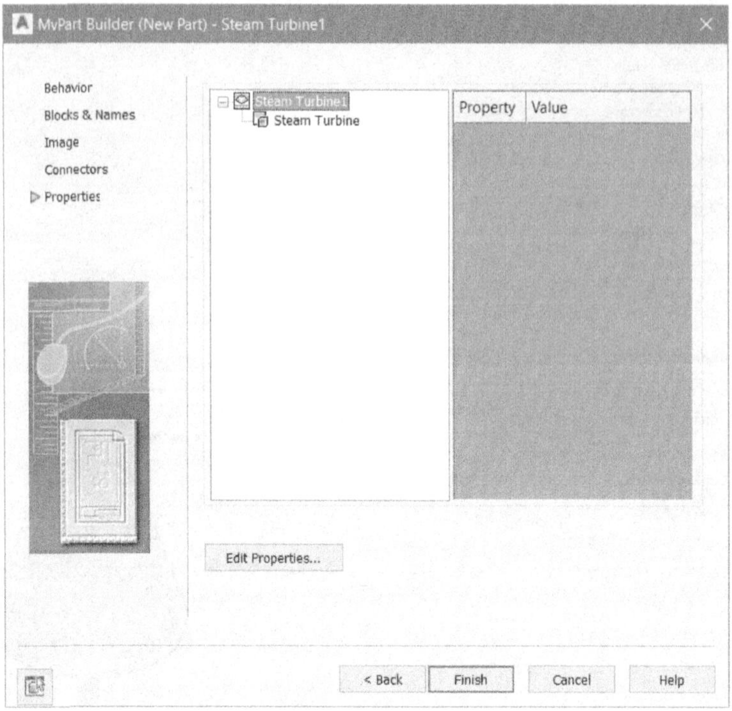

***Figure 5-49** The **MvPart Builder (New Part)** dialog box with the **Properties** page displayed*

5. Click on the + sign adjacent to **Boilers**; various types of boilers are displayed.

6. Select **Firetube Boilers** from the list. Next, select the **600 kW Firetube Boilers** option from the **Part Size Name** drop-down list and click anywhere in the drawing area; the boiler will be attached with the cursor. Now, type **0,0,0** in the command line and press ENTER. Next, ENTER **0** in the command line to specify the rotation angle value; the boiler is placed.

7. Similarly, add 80x80mm Base Mounted Pump, 33.5 KW Large Horizontal Air-Cooled Condenser, and the Steam Turbine1 created earlier. For position, refer to Figure 5-50.

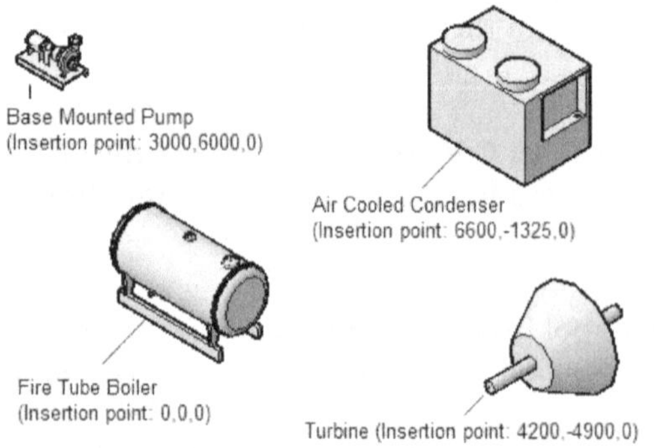

***Figure 5-50** The drawing after adding equipment*

8. Choose the **Close** button to exit the dialog box.

Note

*1. **Steam Turbine1** is available in the **Turbine1** category of equipment in the Mechanical node of the **Add Multi-view Part** dialog box.*

*2. You need to rotate the **Turbine** to set it at the required orientation before you place it at the location, refer to Figure 5-50, by using the **3DROTATE** command.*

Creating Piping between Various Equipment

1. Choose the **Pipe** tool from the **Pipe** drop-down in the **Build** panel of the **Home** tab in the **Ribbon**; you are prompted to specify the start point of the pipe.

2. Select **80** in the **Nominal Size** drop-down list in the **Dimensions** rollout of the **PROPERTIES** palette.

3. Click on the Pipe End Connector available on the pump, refer to Figure 5-51, move the cursor in a vertical direction, and enter **1000** at the dynamic prompt displayed; the **Choose a Part** dialog box is displayed, refer to Figure 5-52.

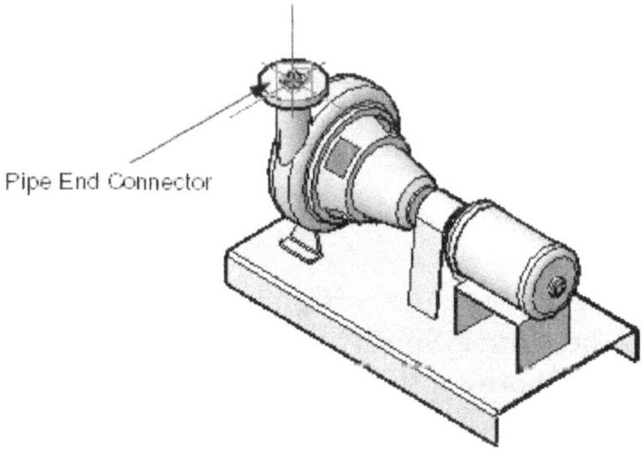

Figure 5-51 *The Pipe End Connector on the pump*

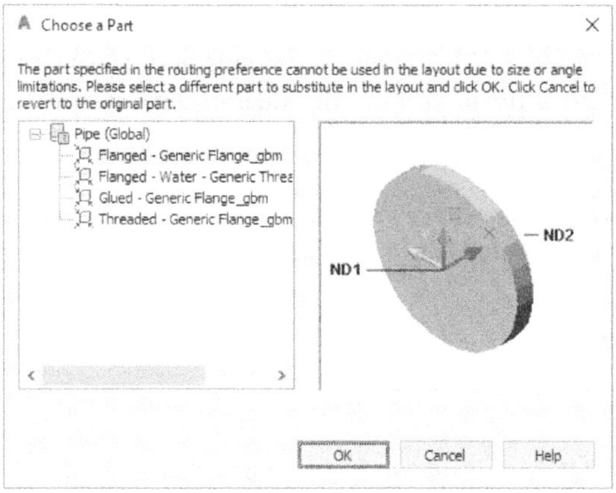

Figure 5-52 *The **Choose a Part** dialog box*

4. Choose the **OK** button from the dialog box; a pipe with the length of **1000** is created. Select the Pipe End Connector of the boiler, as shown in Figure 5-53; you are prompted to accept the connection or want to undo the connection made. Choose the **Accept** option from the command prompt; a pipeline is created between the Pump and the Boiler. Press ENTER to exit the command.

Figure 5-53 *The pipe connector end to be selected*

5. Select **Steam Turbine1** and click on the **+** sign available at the inlet of turbine; a rubber band pipe is attached to the cursor. Specify **80** in the **Nominal Size** drop-down list in the **PROPERTIES** palette; the **Choose a Part** dialog box is displayed. Choose the **OK** button from the dialog box. Move the cursor in the left direction and enter **4000** at the command prompt; the **Choose a Part** dialog box is displayed again. Choose the **OK** button from the dialog box; the pipe line is created, refer to Figure 5-54.

6. Connect the pipe with pipe end connector of boiler, as shown in Figure 5-55; the options related to possible layouts are displayed at the command prompt. Choose the **Next** button from the command prompt till you get the desired layout, refer to Figure 5-35.

Note

*If the **Custom size** message box is displayed while connecting the turbine and the boiler, choose the **No** button from the dialog box and try again to connect the pipe with the boiler.*

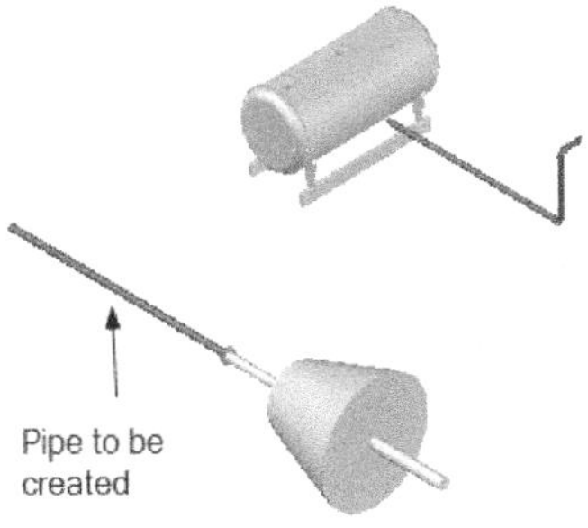

Figure 5-54 *The pipeline created*

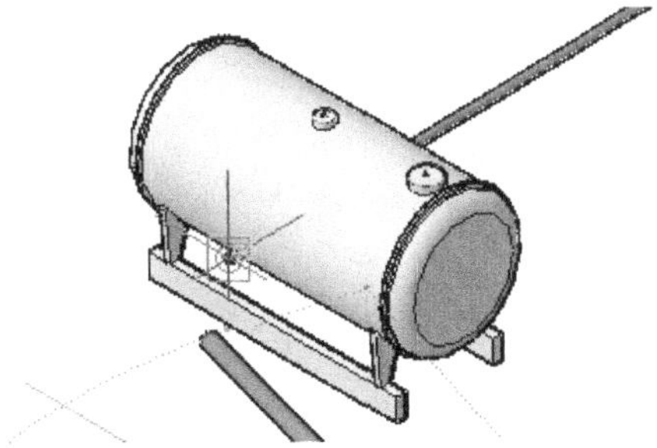

Figure 5-55 *The Pipe End Connector in the model*

7. Choose the **Accept** option from the command prompt; the pipe line is created between the boiler and the turbine. Next, press ENTER to exit the command.

8. Select pump and then select +sign on the horizontal connector of the pump, move the cursor in a horizontal direction, and specify the distance as **1500** at the command prompt; the **Choose a Part** dialog box is displayed. Choose the **OK** button from the dialog box and click on the Pipe End Connector available below the condenser, as shown in Figure 5-56; a pipe line is created, as shown in Figure 5-57.

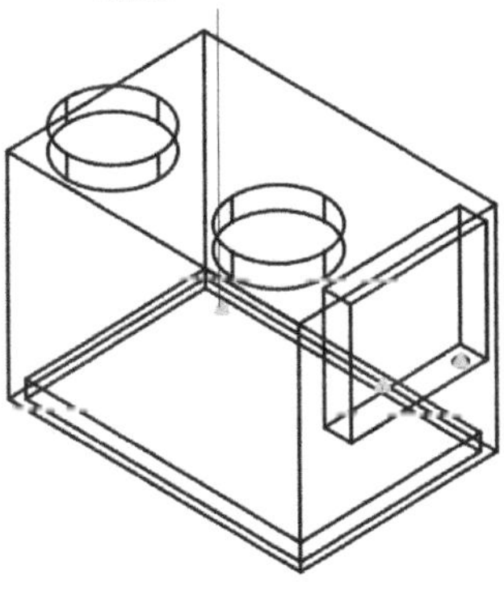

Figure 5-56 *The Pipe End Connector to be selected*

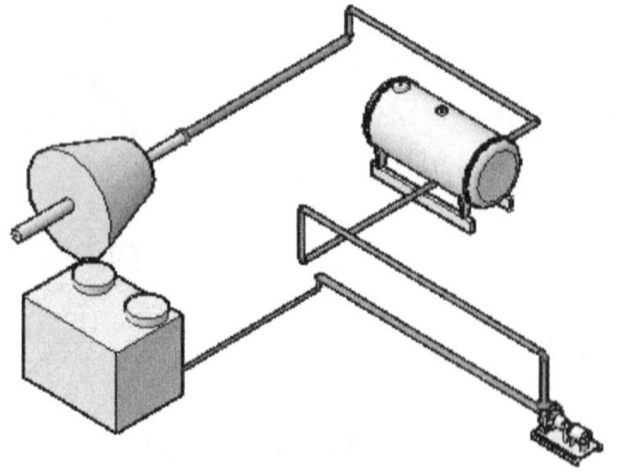

Figure 5-57 *The drawing after creating pipeline between the condenser and pump*

9. Choose the **Accept** button from the Command prompt to accept the pipe line; the **Custom Sizes** dialog box is displayed. Choose the **Yes** option from the dialog box. Press ENTER to exit the tool.

10. Select the Condenser and click on the **+** sign displayed below the condenser, refer to Figure 5-58 and specify **80** in the **Nominal Size** drop-down list in the **PROPERTIES** palette; a rubber band pipe is attached to the cursor. Now, click on the Pipe End Connector displayed on the turbine. Accept the default settings. The pipe line is created and the final model is displayed, as shown in Figure 5-59. Press ENTER to exit the tool.

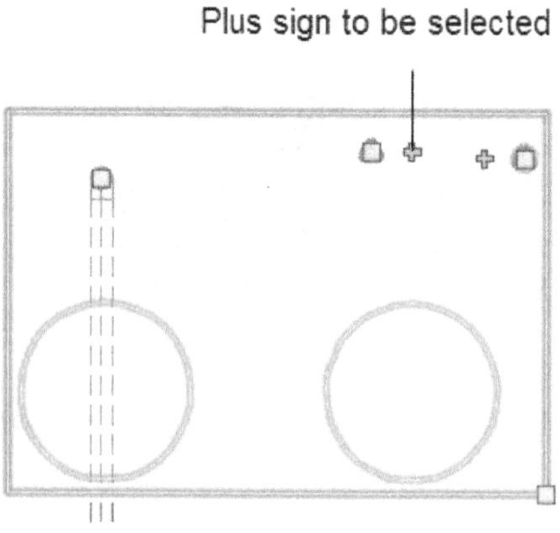

Figure 5-58 *The Pipe End Connector to be selected*

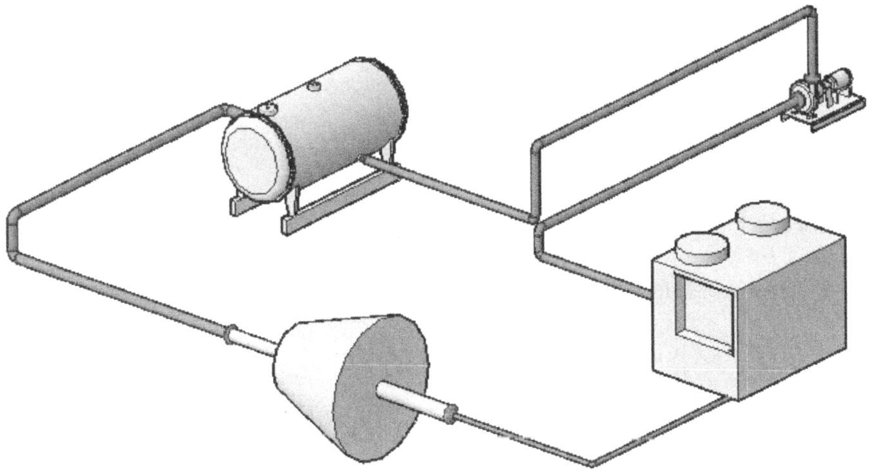

Figure 5-59 The final model

Saving the Drawing File

1. Choose **Save** from the **Application Menu** to save the drawing file.

Self-Evaluation Test

Answer the following questions and then compare them to those given at the end of this chapter:

1. Which of the following tools is used to create a custom part ?

   (a) **Equipment** (b) **Content Builder**
   (c) **Catalog Editor** (d) **Style Manager**

2. The cut length of a pipe can be specified in the _________ edit box.

3. The **Equipment** drop-down is available in the _________ panel of the **Home** tab.

4. The elevation value of an equipment can be specified only from the ground. (T/F)

5. You need to choose the **Plumbing** option from the **Workspace Switching** flyout to activate the **Piping** workspace. (T/F)

Review Questions

Answer the following questions:

1. Which of the following panels contains the **Cone** tool?

   (a) **Build** (b) **Draw**
   (c) **Block** (d) **Modeling**

2. To create a custom Multi-view Part, you must have a _________ of the model.

3. The _________ tool is used to add valve to a pipeline.

4. The **Pipe Custom Fitting** tool is available in the **Pipe** drop-down of the **Build** panel. (T/F)

5. The **Branch angle** option is used to specify the lateral angle of a Tee at the bend. (T/F)

EXERCISE

Exercise 1

In this exercise, you will create model of a piping system, as shown in Figure 5-60. Figure 5-61 shows the plan of the piping system. **(Expected time: 30 min)**

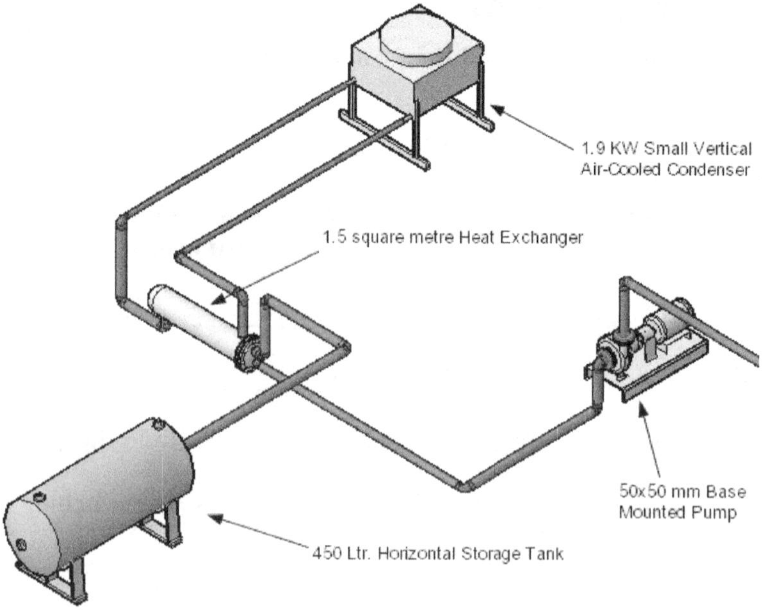

Figure 5-60 *Model of the piping system*

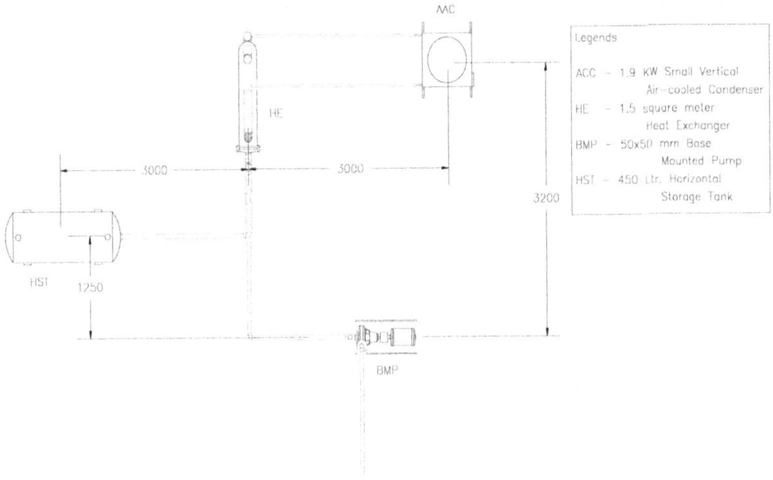

Figure 5-61 Plan of the piping system

Answers to Self-Evaluation Test

1. b, **2. Cut length**, **3. Build**, **4.** F, **5.** F

Chapter 6

Creating Plumbing System

Learning Objectives

After completing this chapter, you will be able to:

- *Create a plumbing system*
- *Use equipment required in plumbing system*
- *Change basic settings of a plumbing system*
- *Configure plumbing options*
- *Route the plumbing line*

INTRODUCTION

In this chapter, you will learn the usage of various mechanical equipment required for creating a plumbing system. A plumbing system is used to drain the waterborne waste from different locations and to supply water to different locations. It consists of plumbing equipment and plumbing line which together control the flow of water at various locations in a building. To create a plumbing system, first you need to figure out variables such as the vertical heads, pressure required at various locations, and the flow rate of water. These variables are used to determine the capacity of equipment to be added to the plumbing system.

PLUMBING WORKSPACE

To create a plumbing system, you first need to invoke the Plumbing Workspace. To invoke this workspace, choose the **Workspace Switching** button from the **Application Status Bar**; a flyout will be displayed. Choose the **Plumbing** option from the flyout; the **Plumbing** workspace will be activated. The equipment that can be added while working in the **Plumbing** workspace are available in the **Equipment** drop-down of the **Build** panel in the **Home** tab of the **Ribbon**, refer to Figure 6-1. The tools available in this drop-down are discussed next.

***Figure 6-1** The **Equipment** drop-down*

Filter

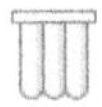

A filter is an equipment or a device which is used to filter fluid before making it flow through an outlet. To add a filter to the drawing, choose the **Filter** tool from the **Equipment** drop-down available in the **Build** panel of the **Home** tab in the **Ribbon**; the **Add Multi-view Parts** dialog box will be displayed, as shown in Figure 6-2. Select the **Panel Filters** sub-category in the **Filters** category of Mechanical equipment in this dialog box; preview of the selected component is displayed on the right pane in the dialog box. Various sizes for the filter are available in the **Part Size Name** drop-down list in this dialog box. Select the required size from this drop-down list. You can specify the elevation value of the filter from the ground or UCS by using the **Elevation** edit box available below the **Part Size Name** drop-down list. Click in the drawing area; the filter will be attached to the cursor. Now, click at required position to place it; the filter will be placed at the selected position and a compass will be displayed below the component. Using this compass, you can rotate the component at any required angle. After specifying the angle, choose the **Close** button from the **Add Multi-view Parts** dialog box to exit.

Pump

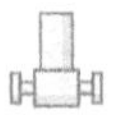

A pump is a mechanical device that is used to supply fluid to a desired point by using mechanical force. The method to place a pump has already been discussed in Chapter 5.

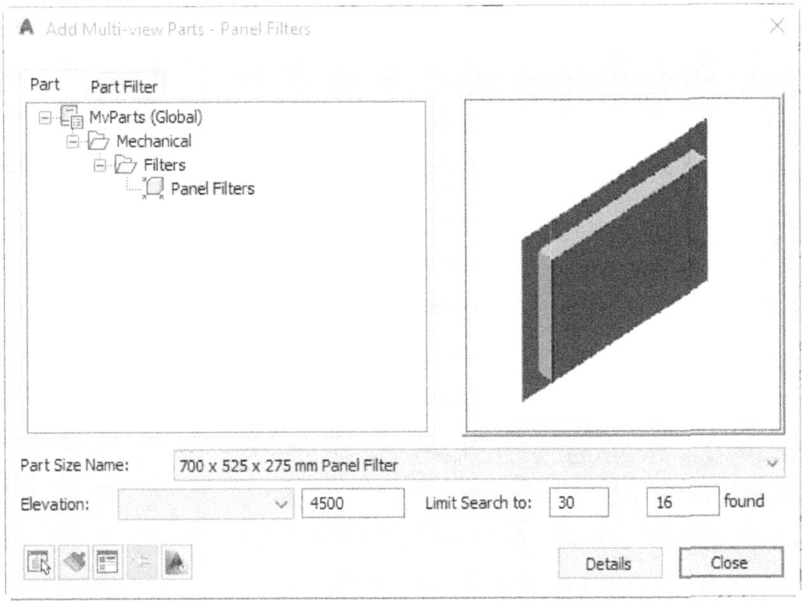

*Figure 6-2 The **Add Multi-view Parts** dialog box*

Shower

A shower is used to convert a stream of water into spray. To add a shower to a drawing, choose the **Shower** tool from the **Equipment** drop-down available in the **Build** panel of the **Home** tab in the **Ribbon**; the **Add Multi-view Parts** dialog box will be displayed. Choose the **Part** tab; the **Rectangular Shower Stall** part is selected by default in the **Showers** category of the Plumbing equipment, refer to Figure 6-3. Select the required part from the dialog box; various sizes available for that part are displayed in the **Part Size Name** drop-down list. Select the required size from the drop-down list and click in the drawing area; the shower will be attached to the cursor. Now, click at any required position; the shower will be placed at the selected position and a compass will be displayed below the shower. Using this compass, you can rotate the shower at any required angle. After specifying the angle, choose the **Close** button from the **Add Multi-view Parts** dialog box to exit the dialog box. Figure 6-4 shows the annotated shower stall. You can set various parameters for the fixture attached to the Multi-view Parts. The options to change these parameters are available in the **Fixture Units** tab of the **Add Multi-view Parts** dialog box, refer to Figure 6-5. These options are discussed next.

Fixture Unit Table

The **Fixture Unit Table** drop-down list is available in the **Fixture Units** tab of the **Add Multi-view Parts** dialog box. The options in this drop-down list are used to change the fixture unit table style which in turn changes the options available for fixture type and occupancy type.

Fixture

The options in this drop-down list are used to specify the type of fixture to be applied to the multi-view part.

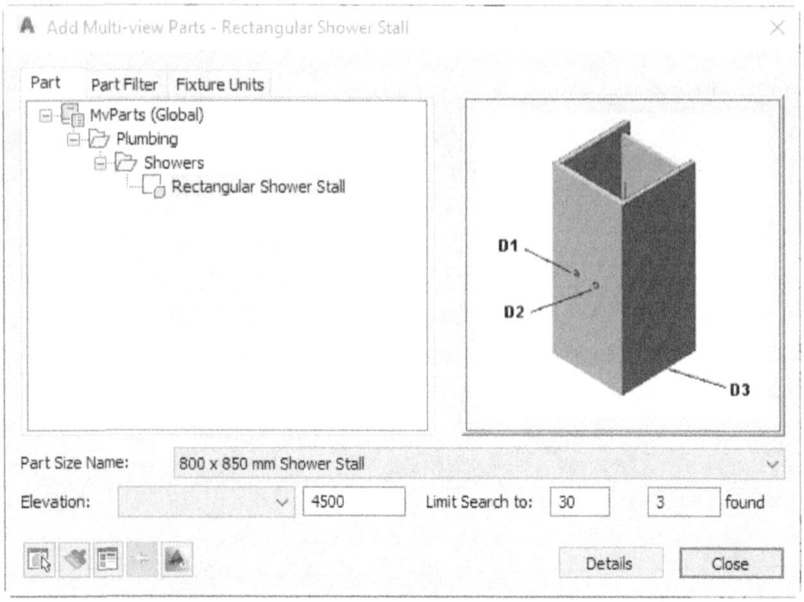

Figure 6-3 *The* ***Add Multi-view Parts*** *dialog box*

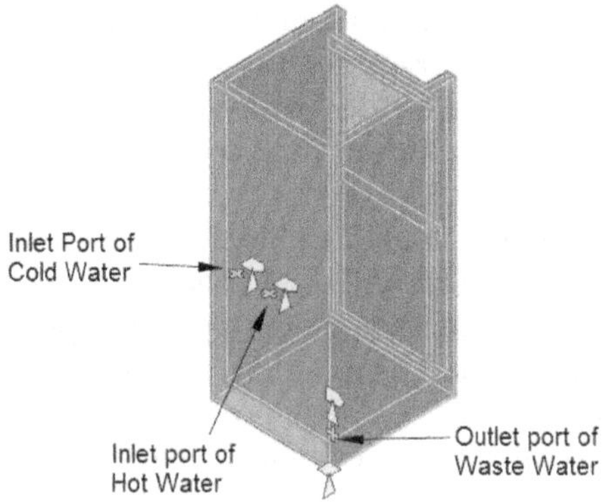

Figure 6-4 *The shower stall*

Occupancy

The options in this drop-down list are used to specify the occupancy type of the Multi-view part. There are two options available in this drop-down list: **Public** and **Private**.

Fixture Units for Connectors

There are various options available in this area to change the properties of various connectors available for the component. The options in this area are displayed based on the part selected.

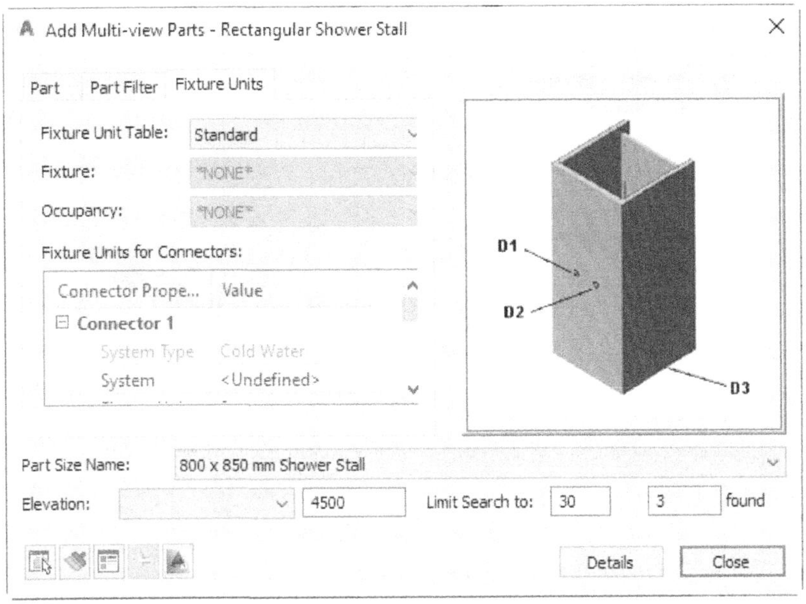

Figure 6-5 The ***Add Multi-view Parts*** *dialog box with the* ***Fixture Units*** *tab selected*

Sink

A sink is a plumbing equipment that is used to wash utensils or any other small object. There are various types of sinks available in AutoCAD MEP. These sinks are available in four main categories: Oval Basin, Rectangular Basin, Vanity Basin, and Wall Mounted Basin. To add a sink to the drawing, choose the **Sink** tool from the **Equipment** drop-down available in the **Build** panel of the **Home** tab in the **Ribbon**; the **Add Multi-view Parts** dialog box will be displayed, as shown in Figure 6-6. By default, the **Oval Basin** part is selected in the **Basins** category of the Plumbing equipment. Select the required part from the dialog box; various sizes available for the category are displayed in the **Part Size Name** drop-down list. Select the required size from the drop-down list and click in the drawing area; a sink will be attached to the cursor. Now, click at any required position; the shower will be placed at the selected position and a compass will be displayed below the component. Using this compass, you can rotate the component at any required angle. After specifying the angle, choose the **Close** button from the **Add Multi-view Parts** dialog box to exit.

Water Closet and Urinal

You can add water closet and urinal to the drawing area in the same way as other equipment discussed earlier in this chapter. After choosing the **Water Closet** and **Urinal** tools from the **Equipment** drop-down available in the **Build** panel of the **Home** tab in the **Ribbon**, the corresponding **Add Multi-view Parts** dialog boxes will be displayed, as shown in Figures 6-7 and 6-8.

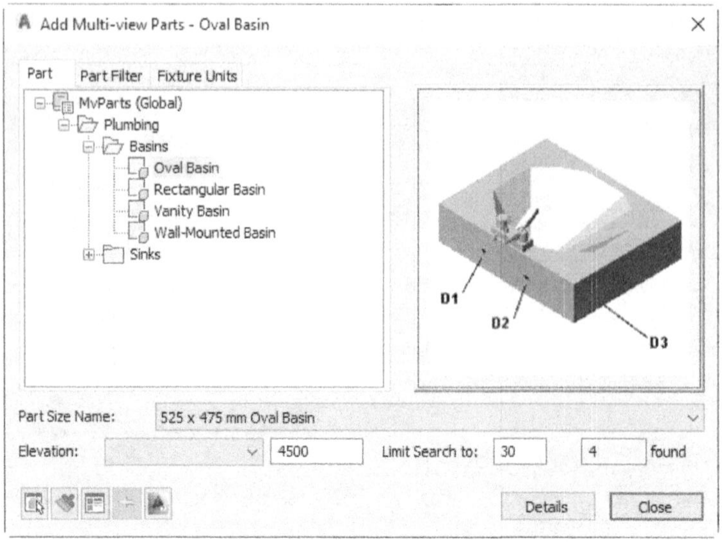

Figure 6-6 *The* ***Add Multi-view Parts*** *dialog box*

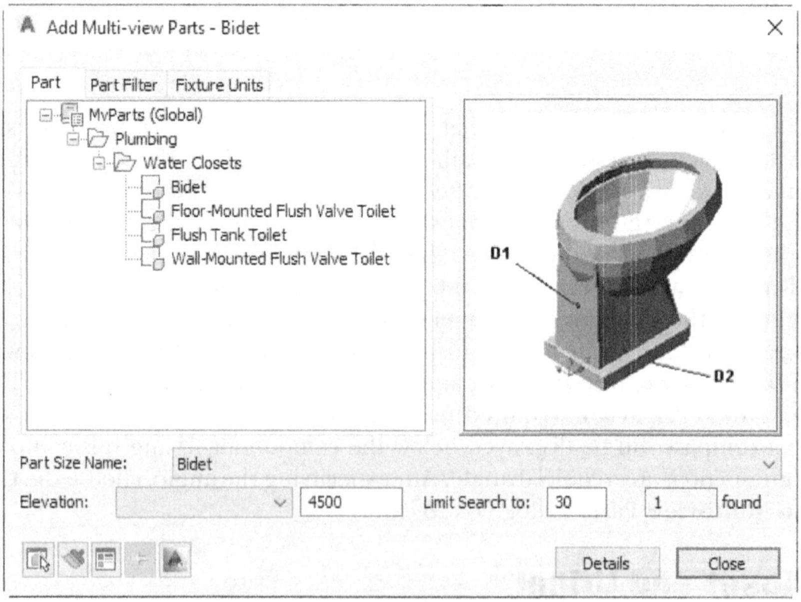

Figure 6-7 *The* ***Add Multi-view Parts*** *dialog box displayed after choosing the* ***Water Closet*** *tool*

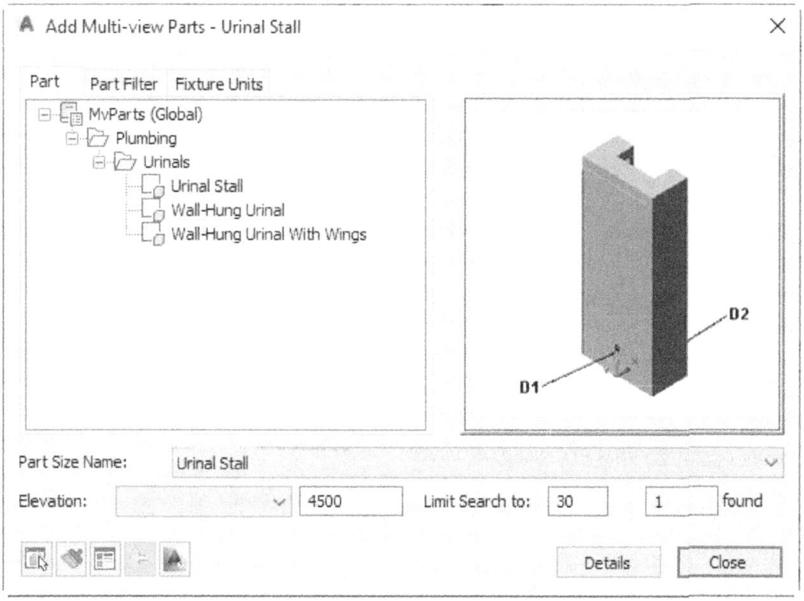

Figure 6-8 *The* ***Add Multi-view Parts*** *dialog box displayed after choosing the* ***Urinal*** *tool*

Equipment

When you choose the **Equipment** tool from the **Equipment** drop-down of the **Build** panel of the **Home** tab in the ribbon; the **Add Multi-view Parts** dialog box will be displayed, refer to Figure 6-9; the related equipment available for Plumbing in AutoCAD MEP will be displayed in a tree structure.

Select the Equipment option from the list and click in the drawing area; selected equipment will be attached to the cursor. Now, click at any required position to place it; the Equipment will be placed at the selected position and a compass will also be displayed below the Equipment. Using this compass, you can rotate the component at any required angle. After specifying the angle, choose the **Close** button from the **Add Multi-view Parts** dialog box to exit.

PLUMBING LINE

After adding all the required equipment to the drawing, you need to add the plumbing line. To add a plumbing line, choose the **Plumbing Line** tool from the **Build** panel in the **Home** tab; you will be prompted to specify the start point of the plumbing line. Click in the drawing area to specify the start point; you will be prompted to specify the next point. Click in the drawing area to specify the next point or enter the distance at the command prompt; a plumbing line will be created and you will be prompted to specify the next point. Click in the drawing area to specify the next point or press ENTER to exit the command. The options related to the plumbing line are displayed in the **PROPERTIES** palette, refer to Figure 6-10.

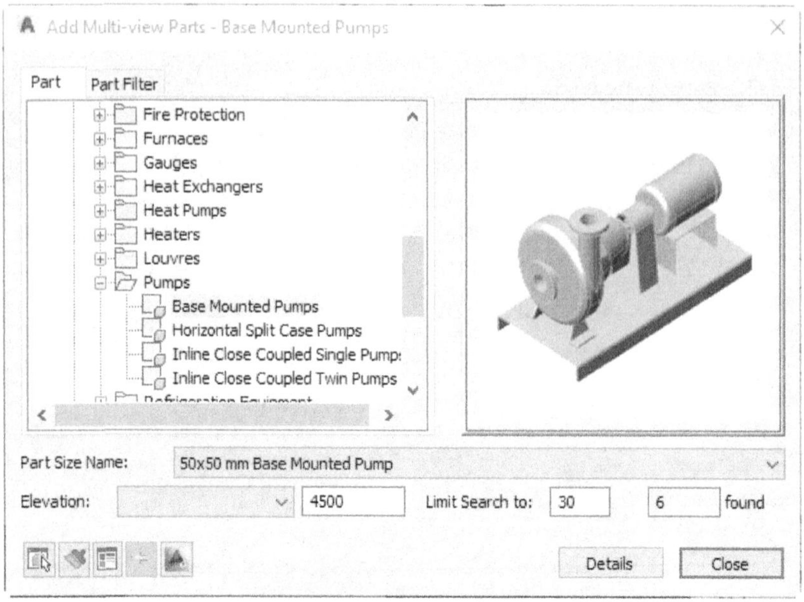

*Figure 6-9 The **Add Multi-view Parts** dialog box*

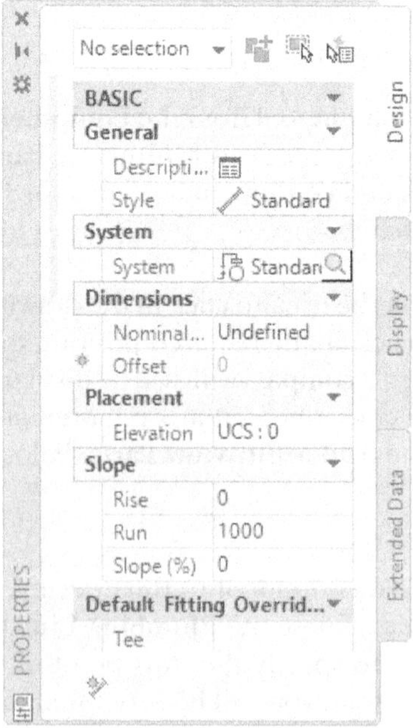

*Figure 6-10 The **PROPERTIES** palette displayed on choosing the **Plumbing Line** tool*

PROPERTIES Palette

The options in the **PROPERTIES** palette are used to change the parameters of the plumbing line. The options displayed in the **PROPERTIES** palette after choosing the **Plumbing Line** tool are discussed next.

Description

This field is available in the **General** rollout in the **BASIC** rollout of the **PROPERTIES** palette. When you click on this field, the **Description** dialog box will be displayed, as shown in Figure 6-11. Enter description for the plumbing line in the **Edit the description for this object** text box in this dialog box and choose the **OK** button to exit.

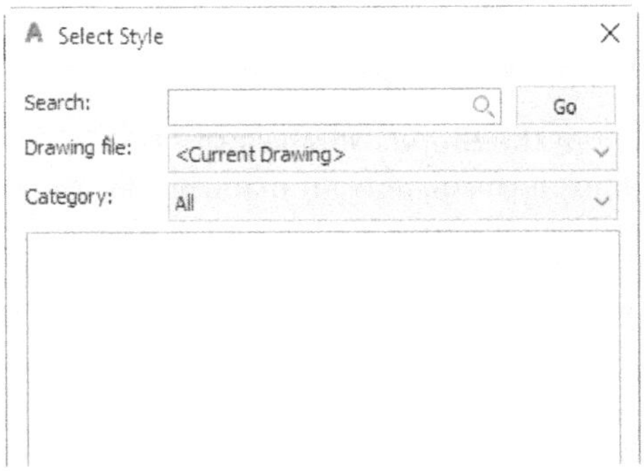

***Figure 6-11** The **Description** dialog box*

Style

This drop-down list is available in the **General** rollout in the **BASIC** rollout of the **PROPERTIES** palette. The options in this drop-down list are used to define the appearance and purpose of the plumbing line. By default, the **Standard** option is selected in the drop-down list. You can select any of the options such as **Black Pipe** and **Copper Tube - Table W**.

System

This drop-down list is available in the **System** rollout in the **BASIC** rollout of the **PROPERTIES** palette. It contains various system definitions for the plumbing line layout. When you choose the **Select a System** button available next to this drop-down list, the **STYLES BROWSER** palette will be displayed. You can select a system for the plumbing line according to the equipment to be connected from the gallery of the **STYLES BROWSER** palette.

Nominal size

This drop-down list is available in the **Dimensions** rollout of the **BASIC** rollout. It contains options to change the size of a pipe. The options available in this drop-down list change according to the option selected in the **Style** drop-down list.

Offset

This edit box is available in the **Dimensions** rollout of the **BASIC** rollout. Using this edit box, you can create the plumbing line at some specified offset distance.

Elevation

This edit box is available in the **Placement** rollout of the **BASIC** rollout. Using this edit box, you can specify the value of elevation of plumbing line, from the ground.

Rise

This edit box is available in the **Slope** rollout in the **BASIC** rollout in the **PROPERTIES** palette. You can specify the value of total rise in this edit box.

Run

This edit box is available in the **Slope** rollout of the **BASIC** rollout in the **PROPERTIES** palette. You can specify the value of total run in this edit box.

Slope (%)

This edit box is also available in the **Slope** rollout of the **BASIC** rollout in the **PROPERTIES** palette. The value in this edit box is calculated automatically depending upon the values specified in the **Run** edit box and the **Rise** edit box. If you enter the desired value in the **Slope (%)** edit box, the values in the **Rise** and **Run** edit boxes will change accordingly.

Default Fitting Overrides Rollout

The options in this rollout are used to override the type of fitting to be chosen while creating the plumbing line. The options available in this rollout are Tee, Tee up, Tee down, and so on. To override any of the available plumbing fittings, click in the field next to the desired plumbing fitting; the **Select Style** dialog box will be displayed, refer to Figure 6-12. Select a drawing file from the **Drawing file** drop-down list; the related categories will be displayed in the **Category** drop-down list. On selecting the desired category from the drop-down list, the relevant components will be displayed in the area below the **Category** drop-down list. Select the desired component and choose the **OK** button from the dialog box; the selected component will be used as an override for the desired fitting. You can also search the default override fitting by entering its name in the **Search** edit box at the top in the **Select Style** dialog box and then choose the **Go** button to get the desired fitting.

*Figure 6-12 The **Select Style** dialog box*

Assigned engineering ID

This drop-down list is available in the **Engineering Data** rollout of the **ADVANCED** rollout of the **PROPERTIES** palette. If the component to be added in the drawing area has an ASHRAE number, then the engineering ID for the component will be displayed in the drop-down list. You can assign any of the available engineering IDs to the component by selecting it from the drop-down list.

Style

This drop-down list is available in the **Labels** rollout of the **Labels and Flow Arrows** rollout in the **ADVANCED** rollout of the **PROPERTIES** palette. The options in this drop-down list are used to apply the label styles to plumbing line.

The **Style** drop-down list is also available in **Flow Arrows** rollout. The options in this drop-down list have already been discussed.

PLUMBING FITTING

The **Plumbing Fitting** tool is used to add fitting to a plumbing line. To add a plumbing fitting, choose this tool from the **Build** panel of the **Home** tab in the **Ribbon**; you will be prompted to specify the insertion point. Also, the **PROPERTIES** palette will be displayed, as shown in Figure 6-13. Click on the plumbing line to add the plumbing fitting to the line; you will be prompted to specify the rotation value. Specify the desired rotation value at the command prompt or click in the drawing area to specify the rotation value; the plumbing fitting will be added. The **PROPERTIES** palette displayed on choosing the **Plumbing Fitting** tool is discussed next.

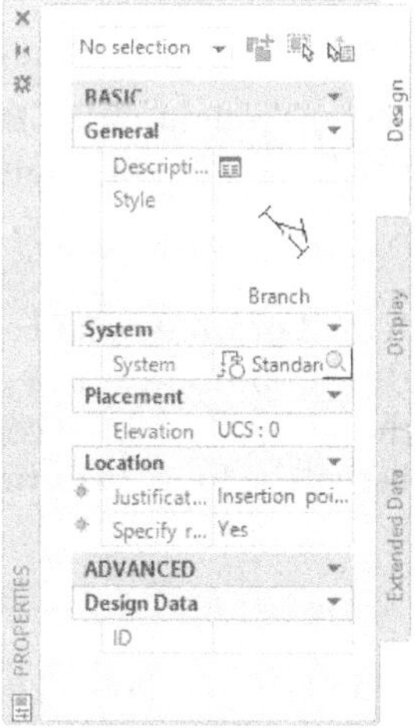

*Figure 6-13 The **PROPERTIES** palette displayed on choosing the **Plumbing Fitting** tool*

Note

*The symbols in the **Style** field and the **Select Style** dialog box are displayed in a black background if the background color of the drawing area is set to black.*

PROPERTIES Palette

The options available in the **PROPERTIES** palette displayed on choosing the **Plumbing Fitting** tool are used to change the parameters of plumbing fitting. These options are discussed next.

Description

This field is available in the **General** rollout in the **BASIC** rollout in the **PROPERTIES** palette. When you click on this field, the **Description** dialog box will be displayed. You can write description about the fitting in the text box available in this dialog box.

Style

This option is available in the **General** rollout in the **BASIC** rollout of the **PROPERTIES** palette. Using this option, you can specify the type of fitting to be applied to a plumbing line. To change the style, click on the field next to the **Style** option; the **STYLE BROWSER** will be displayed. Select the desired fitting from the **STYLE BROWSER**.

System

This drop-down list is available in the **System** rollout in the **BASIC** rollout of the **PROPERTIES** palette. There are various options available in this drop-down list to change the application area of the fitting to be created. By default, the **Anti-Syphon (ASP)** option is selected in this drop-down list.

Elevation

This edit box is available in the **Placement** rollout of the **BASIC** rollout in the **PROPERTIES** palette. Using this edit box, you can specify the value of height of the fitting from the ground level.

Justification

This drop-down list is also available in the **Location** rollout and is used to specify the justification for plumbing line. The options in this drop-down list depend on the number of connectors available on the selected fitting. If the fitting has three connectors, then the total number of options available in this drop-down list will be four: **Insertion point**, **Connector1**, **Connector2**, and **Connector3**.

Specify rotation on screen

This drop-down list is available in the **Location** rollout. There are two options available in this drop-down list. If you select the **Yes** option then you can specify the rotation value while adding the fitting in the drawing area. If you select the **No** option, then you need to specify the value of rotation in the edit box available in the **PROPERTIES** palette.

Rotation

This edit box is available in the **Location** rollout only when the **No** option is selected in the **Specify rotation on screen** drop-down list. Using this edit box, you can specify the value of rotation of the fitting.

ID

This edit box is available in the **Design Data** rollout in the **ADVANCED** rollout of the **PROPERTIES** palette. You can specify a design ID to the fitting using this edit box.

TUTORIAL

Tutorial 1

In this tutorial, you will create a plumbing system, as shown in Figure 6-14. You can download the architectural file from *www.cadcim.com*. Path of the file is: *Textbooks > CAD/CAM > AutoCAD MEP > AutoCAD MEP 2022 for Designers > Input Files*. **(Expected time: 30 min)**

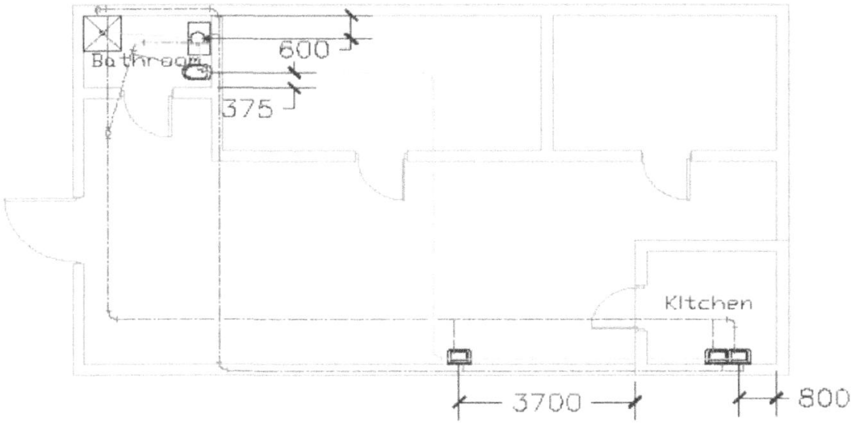

Figure 6-14 *The plumbing system to be created*

The following steps are required to complete this tutorial:

a. Open the drawing downloaded from the website.
b. Add the equipment according to the model.
c. Create plumbing line between various equipment.

Downloading and Opening the Drawing File

1. Download the *c06_amep_prt.zip* file from *https://www.cadcim.com*. The path of the file is as follows: *Textbooks > CAD/CAM > AutoCAD MEP > AutoCAD MEP 2022 for Designers > Input Files*.

2. Extract this file to desired location.

3. Open the drawing file *c06_amep_prt.dwg* from the specified location by double-clicking on it. The drawing file is displayed, as shown in Figure 6-15.

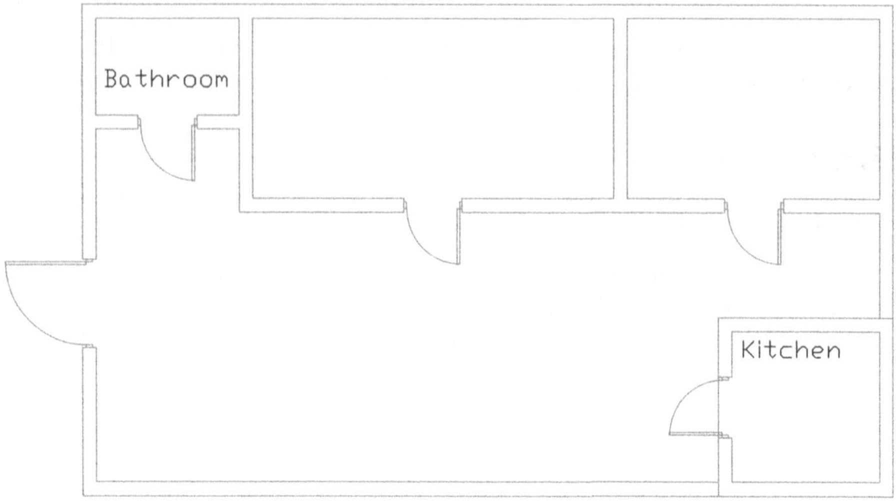

Figure 6-15 The downloaded drawing file

Adding the Equipment

1. Change the workspace to **Plumbing** and choose the **Shower** tool from the **Equipment** drop-down available in the **Build** panel of the **Home** tab in the **Ribbon**; the **Add Multi-view Parts** dialog box is displayed, as shown in Figure 6-16. Also, the shower stall is displayed attached to the cursor.

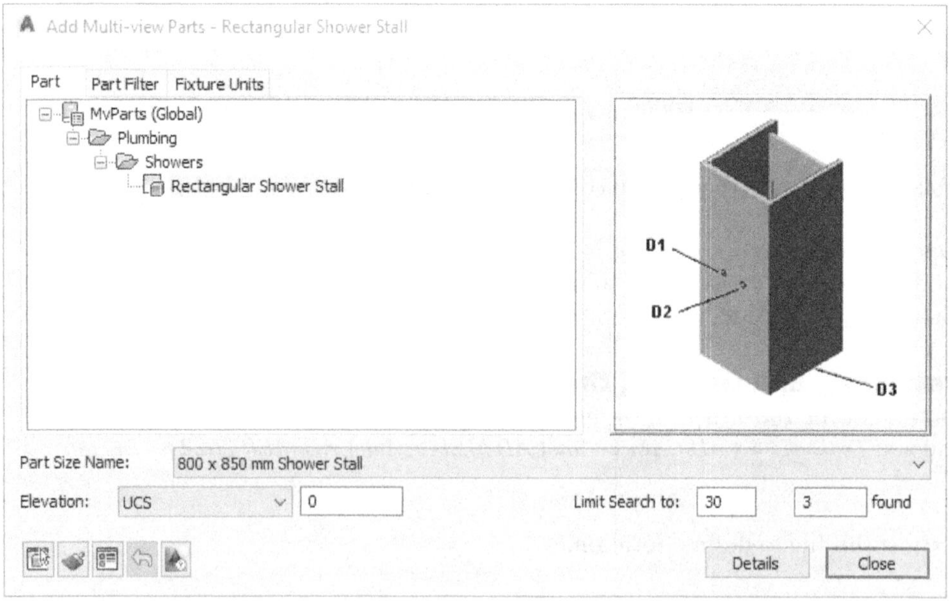

Figure 6-16 The ***Add Multi-view Parts*** *dialog box*

2. Specify **800 x 850 mm Shower Stall** in the **Part Size Name** drop-down list and **0** in the **Elevation** edit box in the dialog box.

3. Place the shower stall in the bathroom, aligned to the corner, refer to Figure 6-17. Make sure that you specify the rotation value as 0 when prompted. Also, specify the elevation value as **0** in the **Elevation** edit box of the **Location** rollout of the **PROPERTIES** palette while placing the shower stall. After placing the shower stall, choose the **Close** button from the **Add Multi-view Parts** dialog box to close it.

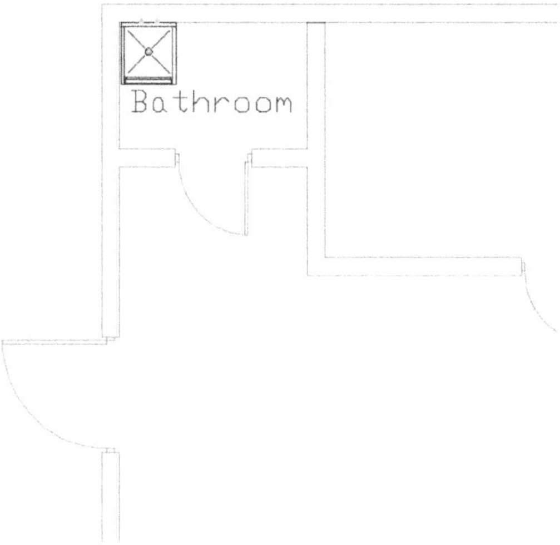

Figure 6-17 *The drawing after adding equipment*

4. Choose the **Sink** tool from the **Equipment** drop-down; the **Add Multi-view Parts** dialog box is displayed, as shown in Figure 6-18.

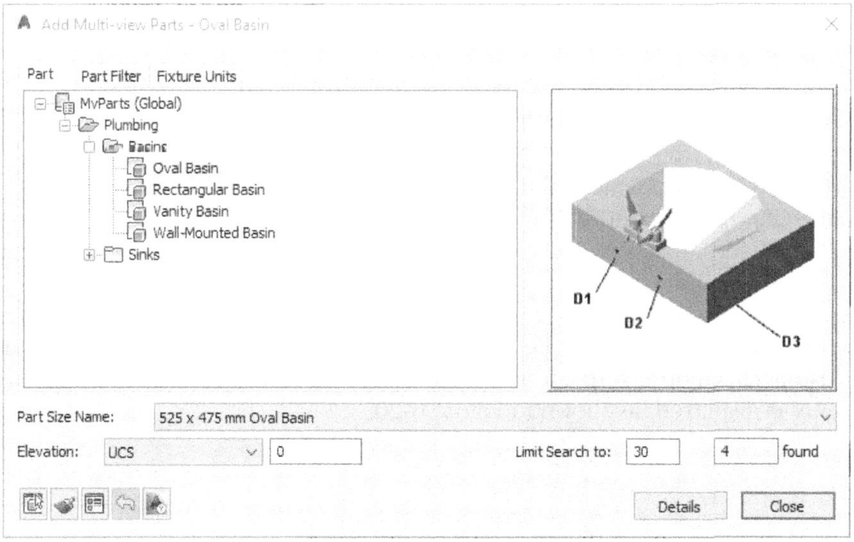

Figure 6-18 *The* ***Add Multi-view Parts*** *dialog box displayed after choosing the* ***Sink*** *tool*

5. Select **Vanity Basin** from the left area of the dialog box, and then select part size as **750mm x 750mm Vanity Basin**. Click anywhere in the drawing area; the **Vanity Basin** is attached with the cursor. Again click anywhere in the drawing area to place it; you are prompted to specify the rotation value. Specify the rotation value as **180** in order to orient the Vanity Basin in the required manner. Next, use the **MOVE** command to place it at the required location, refer to Figure 6-14 for positioning the vanity basin. Make sure the elevation value is set to **0** in the **Elevation** edit box of the **Location** rollout of the **PROPERTIES** palette . The Vanity Basin after placement is shown in Figure 6-19. After pacing the Vanity Basin choose the **Close** button from the the **Add Multi-view Parts** dialog box or press ESC to exit the dialog box.

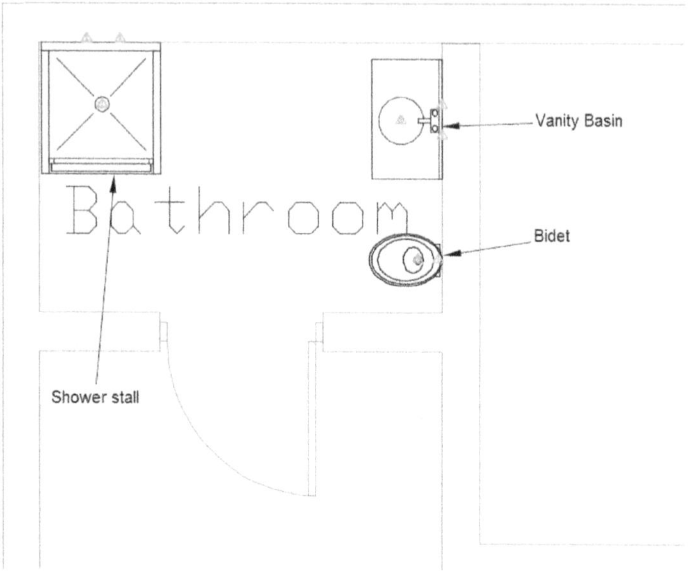

Figure 6-19 *The drawing after adding equipment*

6. Similarly, add **Bidet** available in the **Add Multi-view Parts** dialog box displayed on choosing the **Water Closet** tool from the **Equipment** drop-down, refer to Figures 6-14 and 6-19 for placing the Bidet. Make sure the rotation value is set to **180** and elevation value is set to **0** while placing the Bidet.

7. Choose the **Sink** tool from the **Equipment** drop-down; the **Add Multi-view Parts** dialog box is displayed. Choose **Wall-Mounted Basin** from the left area; the **Add Multi-view Parts** dialog box is displayed, as shown in Figure 6-20.

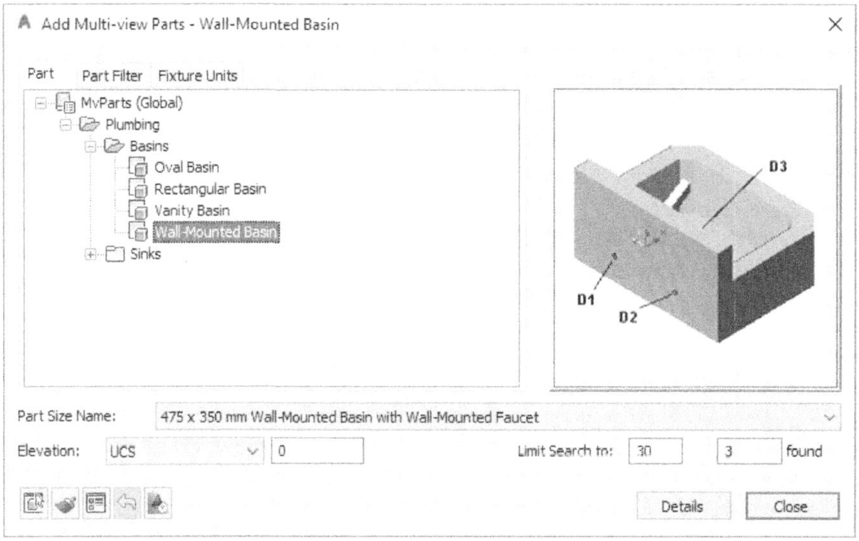

*Figure 6-20 The **Add Multi-view Parts** dialog box displayed after choosing **Wall-Mounted Basin***

8. Place the basins in the drawing area at an elevation value of **1000** and set the rotation value to **90**. The basins after placement are shown in Figure 6-21.

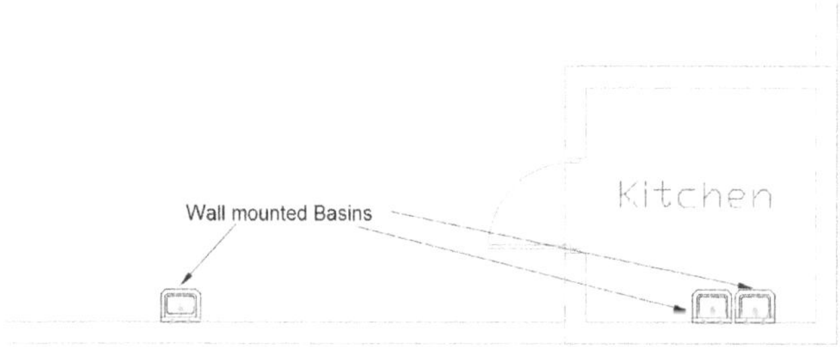

Figure 6-21 The drawing area after adding the basins

Creating Plumbing Line Between Various Equipment

There are three plumbing lines to be added to the system: Waste (WP), Domestic Cold Water, and Domestic Hot Water.

1. Choose the **Waste (WP)** tool from the **TOOL PALETTES - PLUMBING** displayed at the right in the AutoCAD MEP window, refer to Figure 6-22; you are prompted to select the starting point for Waste plumbing line.

2. Select the Waste Pipe End Connector of the shower stall in the Bathroom area; the other end of the waste plumbing line gets attached to the cursor and you are prompted to specify the next end point.

3. Select the Pipe End Connector of the vanity basin placed in the Bathroom area; the **Select Connector** dialog box is displayed, as shown in Figure 6-23.

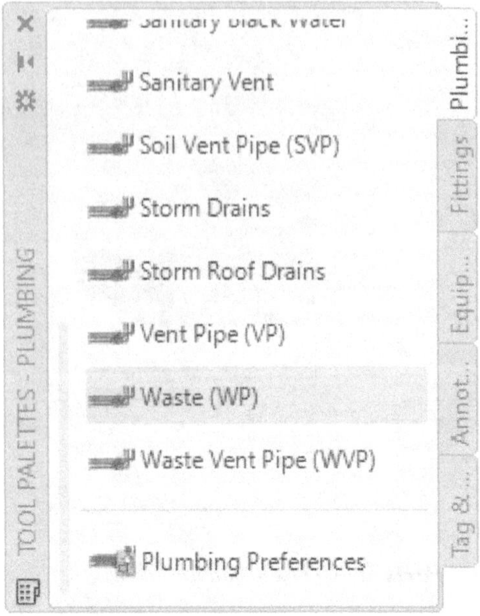

Figure 6-22 The ***TOOL PALETTES - PLUMBING***

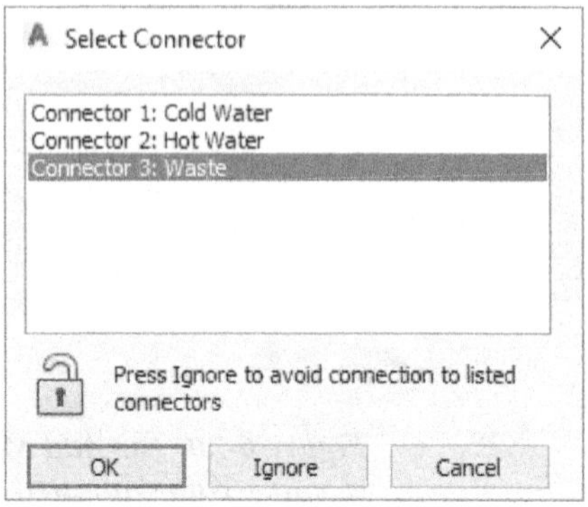

Figure 6-23 The ***Select Connector*** *dialog box*

4. Choose the **Connector 3: Waste** option from the dialog box and choose the **OK** button; the **Plumbing Line - Elevation Mismatch** dialog box is displayed, as shown in Figure 6-24.

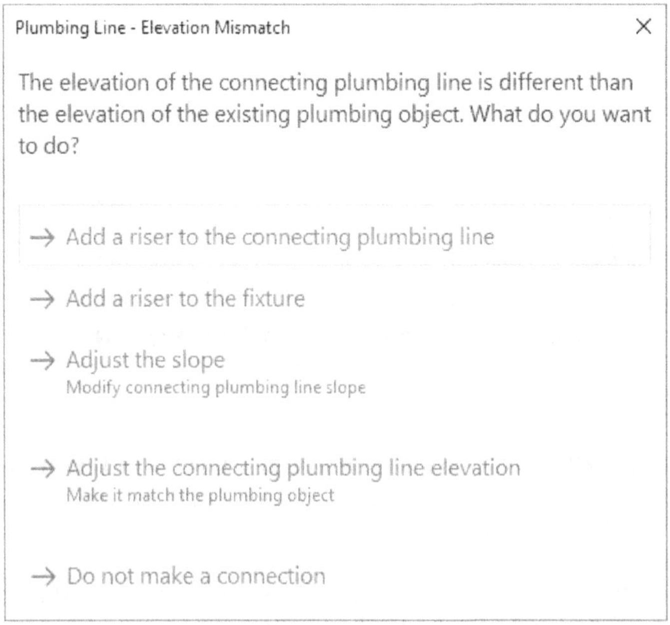

Figure 6-24 The ***Plumbing Line - Elevation Mismatch*** *dialog box*

5. Choose the **Adjust the slope** option from the dialog box and press ENTER; the slope of the plumbing line is automatically adjusted to permit the flow of water and a plumbing line is created.

6. Similarly, create a plumbing line from the waste line of vanity basin to waste line of bidet in the Bathroom area and then to the waste lines of the wall mounted basins. The drawing after adding all the waste plumbing lines is displayed, as shown in Figure 6-25.

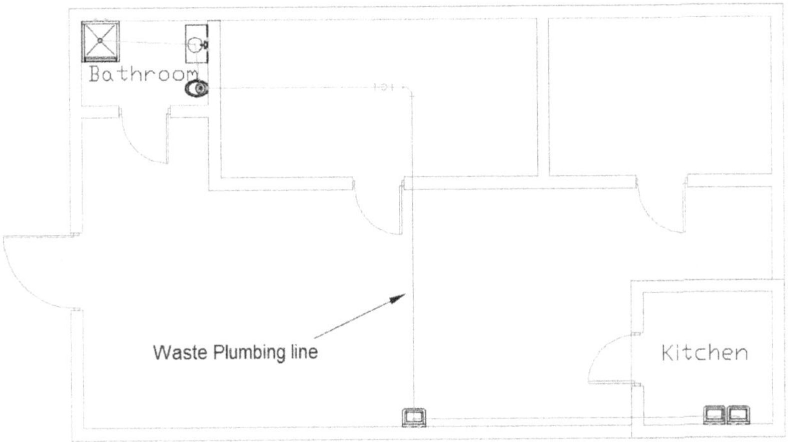

Figure 6-25 *The drawing after adding all the waste plumbing lines*

7. Choose the **Domestic Hot Water** tool from the **TOOL PALETTES - PLUMBING** and add the hot water plumbing line, as shown in Figure 6-26.

Note

1. Choose the ***Connector 2: Hot Water*** *from the* ***Select Connector*** *dialog box when it is displayed while connecting hot water plumbing line.*

2. Choose the ***Connector 3: Cold Water*** *from the* ***Select Connector*** *dialog box when it is displayed while connecting the cold water plumbing line.*

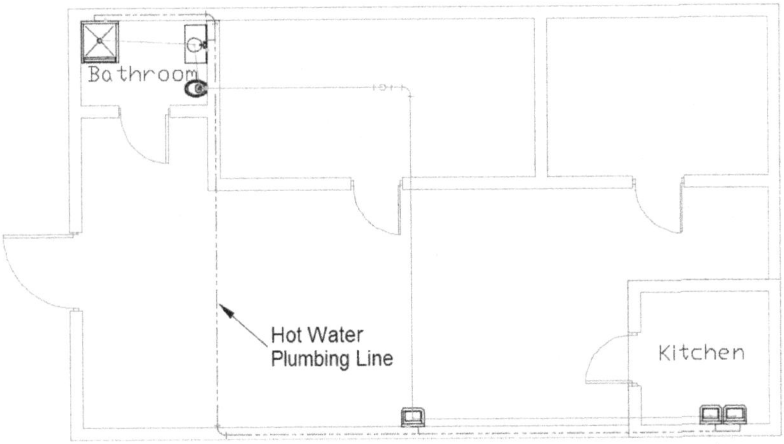

Figure 6-26 *The drawing after adding all the hot water plumbing lines*

8. Choose the **Domestic Cold Water** tool from the **TOOL PALETTES - PLUMBING** and add the cold water plumbing line, as shown in Figure 6-27.

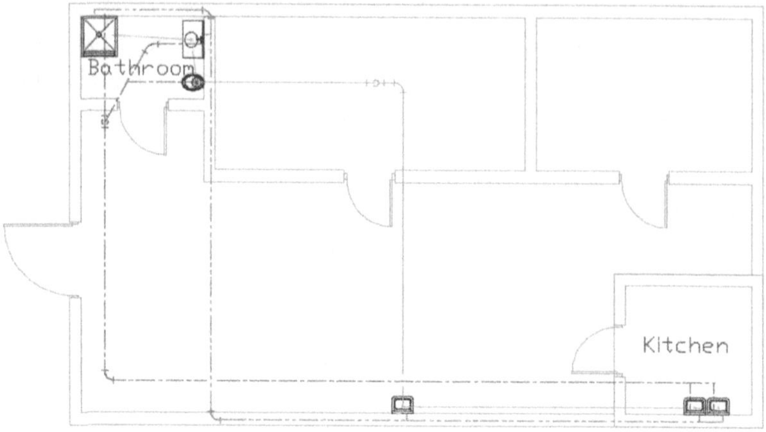

Figure 6-27 *The drawing after adding all the cold water plumbing lines*

The drawing after adding all the plumbing lines is displayed, refer to Figure 6-27.

Saving the Drawing File

1. Choose **Save** from the **Application Menu** to save the drawing file.

Self-Evaluation Test

Answer the following questions and then compare them to those given at the end of this chapter:

1. Which of the following equipment does not require a fixture?

   (a) **Water Closet** (b) **Shower**
   (c) **Sink** (d) **Pump**

2. The __________ drop-down list in the **PROPERTIES** palette is used to specify the type of system for plumbing line.

3. The value in the **Slope (%)** edit box is calculated automatically depending upon the values specified in the __________ and __________ edit boxes.

4. Rotation of a fitting can be specified either by using an edit box or by dynamically rotating it. (T/F)

5. You cannot change the type of fitting after adding it in the plumbing line. (T/F)

Review Questions

Answer the following questions:

1. Which of the following is not a type of plumbing fitting?

   (a) **Tee** (b) **Cross**
   (c) **Elbow** (d) **Shower**

2. To create a custom multi-view part, you must have a __________ of the model in the current drawing.

3. The **Domestic Hot Water** tool is available in the **TOOL PALETTES -** __________ .

4. The **End Cap** option is available in the **STYLES BROWSER** palette. (T/F)

5. The **Pipe Custom Fitting** tool is not available in the **Plumbing** workspace. (T/F)

EXERCISE

Exercise 1

In this exercise, you will create the model of a plumbing system using the drawing shown in Figure 6-28. You can download the architectural file from *www.cadcim.com*. Path of the file is: *Textbooks > CAD/CAM > AutoCAD MEP > AutoCAD MEP 2022 for Designers > Input files.*

(Expected time: 30 min)

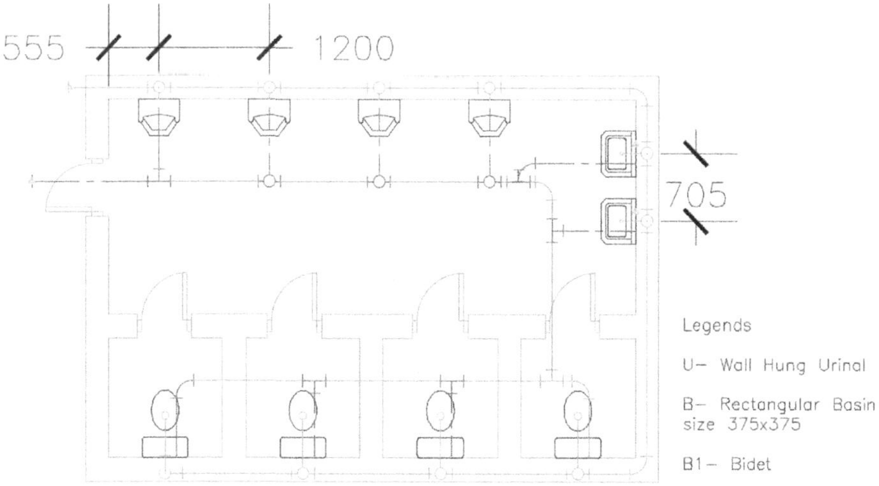

Figure 6-28 *The drawing of plumbing system*

Answers to Self-Evaluation Test

1. d, **2. System**, **3. Rise**, **Run**, **4.** T, **5.** F

Chapter 7

Creating Electrical System Layout

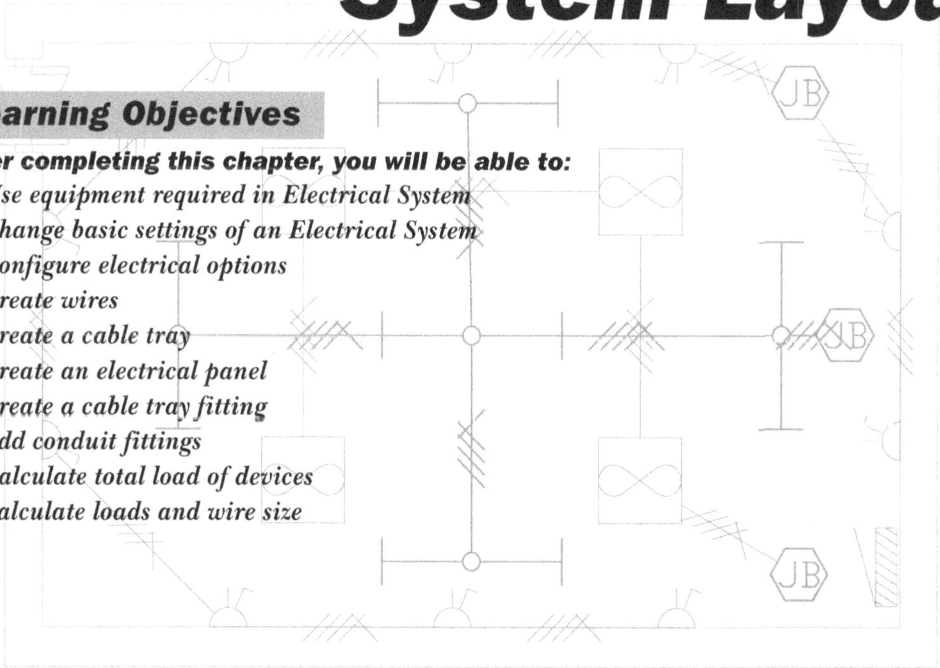

Learning Objectives

After completing this chapter, you will be able to:

- *Use equipment required in Electrical System*
- *Change basic settings of an Electrical System*
- *Configure electrical options*
- *Create wires*
- *Create a cable tray*
- *Create an electrical panel*
- *Create a cable tray fitting*
- *Add conduit fittings*
- *Calculate total load of devices*
- *Calculate loads and wire size*

INTRODUCTION

In this chapter, you will learn the usage of various electrical equipment for creating an electrical system. An electrical system is used to transmit power from one location to the other. It is composed of equipment, panels, cable trays, wires, conduits and so on. For creating an electrical system, choose the **Electrical** option from the **Workspace Switching** flyout, the **Electrical** workspace will be activated. The equipments available in the **Electrical** workspace of AutoCAD MEP are discussed next.

ADDING EQUIPMENT

For creating an electrical system, you need to add related equipment to the structure. All the equipment that can be added while working in the **Electrical** workspace are available in the **Equipment** drop-down of the **Build** panel in the **Home** tab of the **Ribbon**, refer to Figure 7-1. Some of the options available in this drop-down are discussed next.

***Figure 7-1** The **Equipment** drop-down*

Generator

A generator is an equipment or a device, which is used to convert mechanical energy into electrical energy. To add a generator to the drawing, choose the **Generator** tool from the **Equipment** drop-down of the **Build** panel in the **Home** tab of the **Ribbon**; the **Add Multi-view Parts** dialog box will be displayed, as shown in Figure 7-2. By default, **200-600kW Emergency Power Generator - Diesel** is selected in the **Part** tab. Preview of the selected component is displayed in the right of the dialog box. Various sizes for the generator, depending on their load capacity, are available in the **Part Size Name** drop-down list of this dialog box. Select the required size from this drop-down list. Click in the drawing area; the generator will be attached with the cursor. Now, click at the required position to place it; the generator is placed at the selected position and a compass will be displayed below the component. Using this compass, you can rotate the component at any specific angle. After specifying the angle, choose the **Close** button from the **Add Multi-view Parts** dialog box to exit the dialog box.

You can also specify the elevation value of the Generator from the ground or UCS by using the **Elevation** edit box available below the **Part Size Name** drop-down list.

Junction Box

A junction box is a metallic or plastic container that is used to hide the electrical connections. To add a junction box, choose the **Junction Box** tool from the **Equipment** drop-down of the **Build** panel in the **Home** tab of the **Ribbon**; the **Add Multi-view Parts** dialog box will be displayed, as shown in Figure 7-3. Select the desired junction box from the **Junction Boxes** node in the **Part** tab of the dialog box. Various sizes of the selected junction box are displayed in the **Part Size Name** drop-down list. By default, **13 Hole Large Outlet Boxes** is selected in the **Part** tab. Select the required size from the drop-down list. Now, click in the drawing area; the junction box will be attached with the cursor. Next, click at required position to place it; the junction box will be placed at the selected position and a compass is displayed below the junction box. Using this compass, you can rotate the component at any specific angle. After specifying the angle, choose the **Close** button from the **Add Multi-view Parts** dialog box to exit the dialog box.

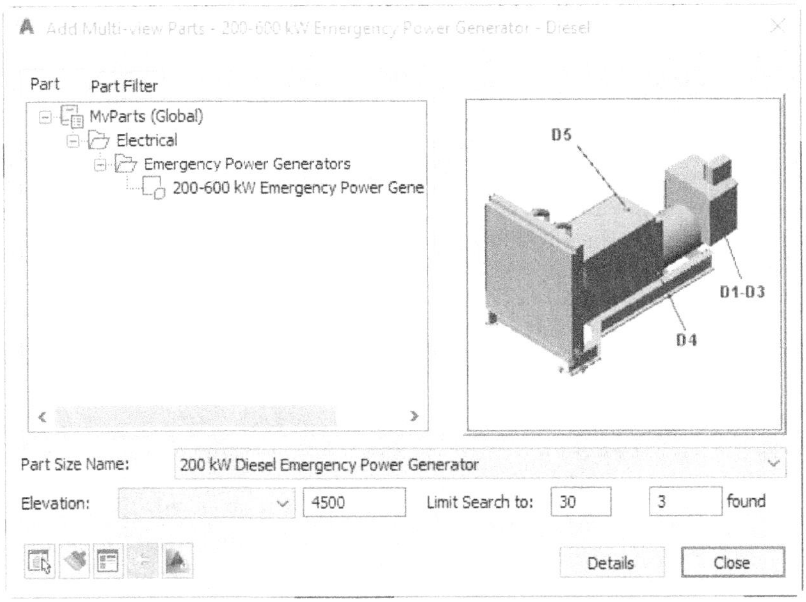

*Figure 7-2 The **Add Multi-view Parts** dialog box with the **200-600 kW Emergency Power Generator - Diesel** part selected*

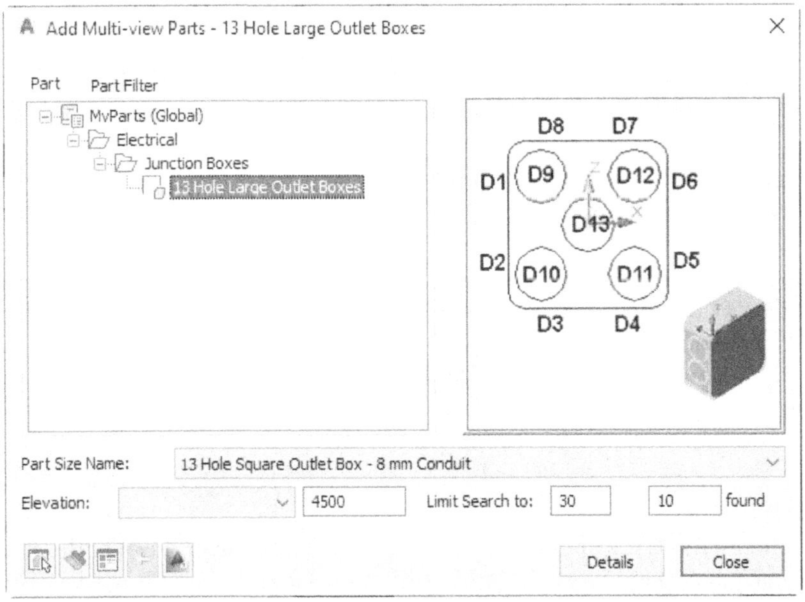

*Figure 7-3 The **Add Multi-view Parts** dialog box with the **13 Hole Large Outlet Boxes** part selected*

Switchboard

A switchboard is an arrangement of electrical switches connected to each other in a close packed unit. A switch board controls the power of various areas of a serving unit. To add a switchboard, choose the **Switchboard** tool from the **Equipment** drop-down of the **Build** panel in the **Home** tab of the **Ribbon**; the **Add Multi-view Parts** dialog box will be displayed, as shown in Figure 7-4. Expand the **Switchboards** node if not already expanded and click on the desired switchboard type; preview of the selected switch board will be displayed in the Preview area of the dialog box. You can select the desired size from the **Part Size Name** drop-down list displayed below the Preview area of the dialog box. Next, click in the drawing area; the switchboard will be attached with the cursor. Now, click at the required position to place it; the switchboard will be placed at the selected position and a compass is displayed below the component. Using this compass, you can rotate the component at any specific angle. After specifying the angle, choose the **Close** button from the **Add Multi-view Parts** dialog box to exit the dialog box.

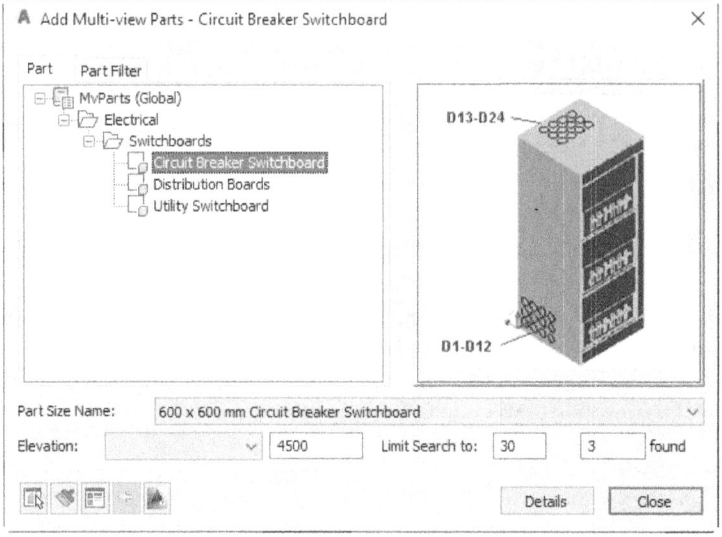

Figure 7-4 *The **Add Multi-view Parts** dialog box with the **Circuit Breaker Switchboard** part selected*

There are three types of switchboards available in AutoCAD MEP by default: circuit breaker switchboard, distribution board, and utility switchboard. The circuit breaker switchboard consists of switches that are automatically operated to protect the circuit from the damage caused by overload or short circuit. The distribution boards are used to distribute the power coming from source to various outlets. The utility switchboards are used to transmit power for a specific purpose.

Equipment

If you choose the **Equipment** tool from the **Equipment** drop-down of the **Build** panel in the **Home** tab of the ribbon; the **Add Multi-view Parts** dialog box will be displayed, refer to Figure 7-5. Click on the + sign adjacent to the desired category in the **Add Multi-view Parts** dialog box; the related equipment available in AutoCAD MEP will be displayed in a tree structure. Select the required option from the list and click in the drawing area; the Equipment will be attached with the cursor. Now, click at the required position to place it; the Equipment will be placed at the selected position and a compass is displayed below the equipment. Using this compass, you can rotate the equipment at any specific angle. After specifying the angle, choose the **Close** button from the **Add Multi-view Parts** dialog box to exit.

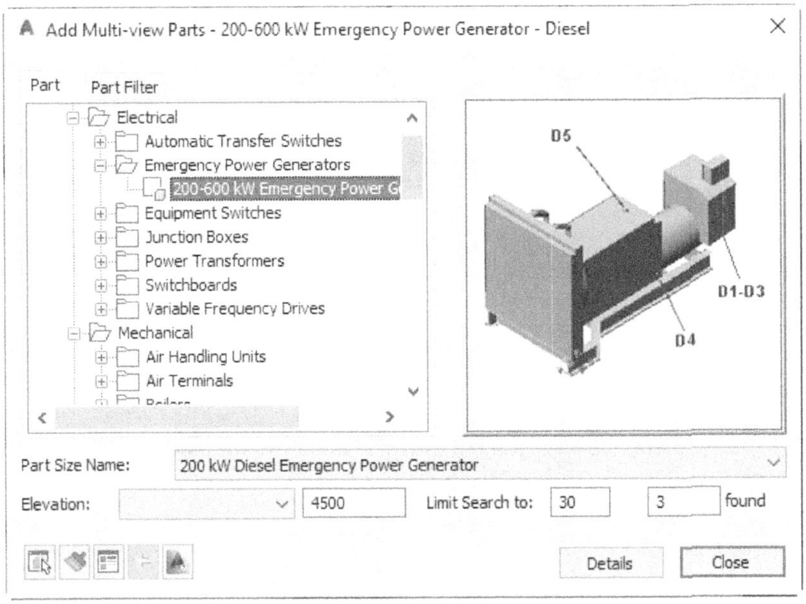

Figure 7-5 *The* ***Add Multi-view Parts*** *dialog box*

PANEL

Panels are the distribution boxes in which various switches are arranged for a specific purpose. To add a panel to the drawing, choose the **Panel** tool from the **Build** panel of the **Home** tab in the **Ribbon**; preview of a panel will be displayed attached to the cursor, refer to Figure 7-6.

Figure 7-6 *Preview of the panel*

Also, on choosing this tool, the **PROPERTIES** palette will be displayed, as shown in Figure 7-7. Now, click in the drawing area to place the panel. You will be prompted to specify the rotation value for the panel. Specify the rotation value and press ENTER; the panel will be created at the specified location.

The options available in the **PROPERTIES** palette after choosing the **Panel** tool are discussed next.

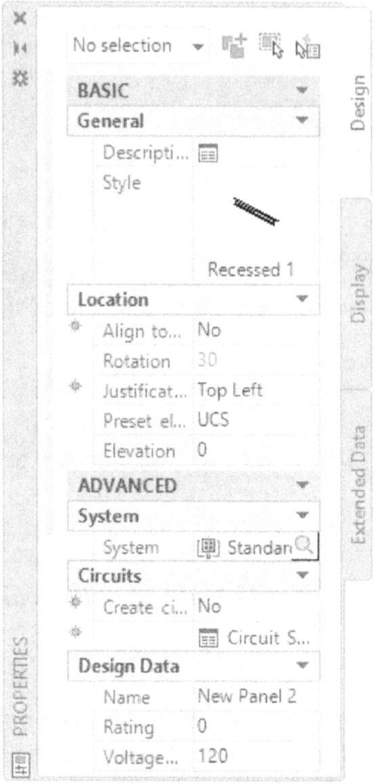

***Figure 7-7** The **PROPERTIES** palette displayed on choosing the **Panel** tool*

Description

This option is available in the **General** rollout of the **BASIC** rollout. It is used to specify the description about the object. When you click in the field corresponding to this option, the **Description** dialog box will be displayed, as shown in Figure 7-8. You can enter the description about the component in the **Edit the description for this object** text box of the dialog box. After specifying the description, choose the **OK** button to exit the dialog box.

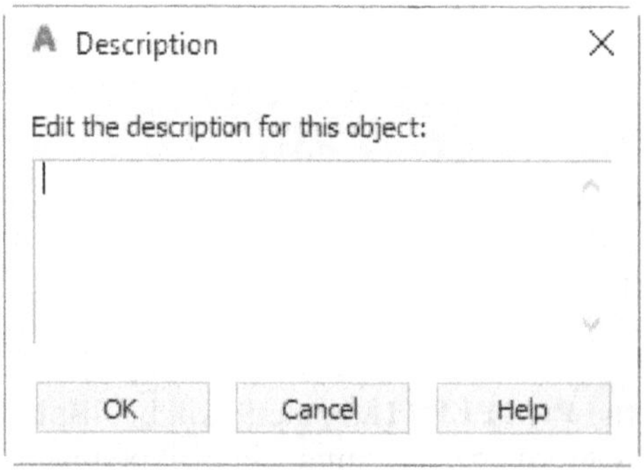

***Figure 7-8** The **Description** dialog box*

Style

This option is available in the **General** rollout of the **BASIC** rollout and is used to choose a desired style of the panel to be created. Click in the field corresponding to this option; the **STYLES BROWSER** will be displayed. Select the desired style from the **STYLES BROWSER**; the selected style will be assigned to the panel.

Align to objects

This drop-down list is available in the **Location** rollout of the **BASIC** rollout. The options in this drop-down list are used to specify whether the panel will be aligned to the selected object or not. There are two options available in this drop-down list: **Yes** and **No**. The **Yes** option is used to specify that the panel will be aligned to the selected object.

Rotation

This edit box is available in the **Dimensions** rollout of the **BASIC** rollout. It is used to specify the rotation angle value of the panel.

Justification

This drop-down list is available in the **Location** rollout of the **BASIC** rollout. It is available only when the **No** option is selected in the **Align to objects** drop-down list. The options in this drop-down list are used to specify the position of the panel with respect to the insertion point.

Preset elevation

This drop-down list is available in the **Location** rollout of the **BASIC** rollout. The options in this drop-down list are used to set the elevation of the panel. By default, **UCS** is selected in this drop-down list.

Elevation

This edit box is available in the **Location** rollout of the **BASIC** rollout. It is used to specify the value of elevation from the selected preset.

System

This drop-down list is available in the **System** rollout of the **ADVANCED** rollout. The options in this drop-down list are used to specify the type of system for which the panel is being created.

Create circuits

This drop-down list is available in the **Circuits** rollout of the **ADVANCED** rollout. The options in this drop-down list are used to specify whether to create a circuit for the panel or not. There are two options available in this drop-down list: **Yes** and **No**. If you select the **Yes** option from this drop-down list, then the circuit will also be created along with the panel.

Circuit Settings

This field is available in the **Circuits** rollout of the **ADVANCED** rollout. On clicking in this field, the **Circuit Settings** dialog box will be displayed, as shown in Figure 7-9. Using the options in this dialog box, you can define various settings for the circuit. Choose the **OK** button after defining the settings.

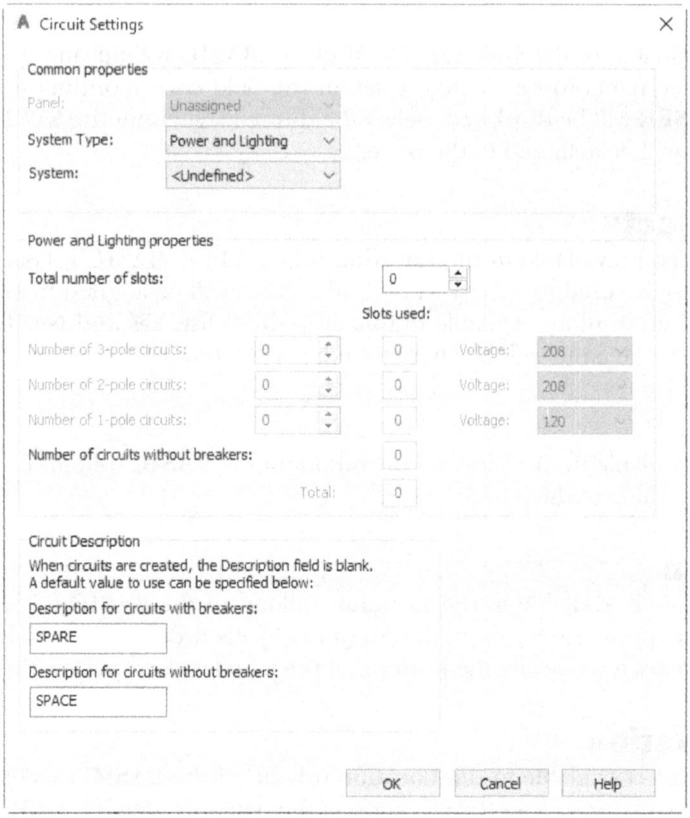

*Figure 7-9 The **Circuit Settings** dialog box*

The options in the **Design Data** rollout of the **ADVANCED** rollout are discussed next.

Name

The **Name** edit box is used to specify the name of the panel.

Rating

This edit box is used to specify the rating of the panel.

Voltage phase-to-neutral

The options in this drop-down list are used to specify the voltage value between phase line and neutral line.

Voltage phase-to-phase

The options in this drop-down list are used to specify the voltage value between two phase lines.

Phases

The options in this drop-down list are used to specify whether the selected panel is for single phase supply or three phase supply. There are two options available in this drop-down list: **1** and **3**. If you select the **1** option from this drop-down list, the panel will be created for single phase supply. If you select the **3** option from this drop-down list, the panel will be created for three phase supply.

Wires

The options in this drop-down list are used to specify the number of cables to be attached with the panel after creation. The options in this drop-down list will be available only when the **3** option is selected in the **Phases** drop-down list.

Note

*If the 3 option is selected in both the **Phases** and the **Wires** drop-down lists, then the **Voltage phase-to-neutral** edit box will not be available in the **PROPERTIES** palette.*

Main type

There are two options available in this drop-down list: the **Main lugs only (MLO)** and **Main circuit breaker (MCB)**. These options are used to specify whether the panel is of main lug only or main circuit breaker.

Main size (amps)

This edit box is used to specify the value of Current (I) running through the main supply. It has the same value as specified in the **Rating** edit box of the panel.

Design capacity (amps)

This edit box is used to specify the designed capacity of the panel.

Panel type

The options in this drop-down list are used to specify the type of panel to be used. There are two options available in this drop-down list: **ANSI** and **ISO**.

Enclosure type

This edit box is used to specify the type of enclosure for the panel.

Mounting

The options in this drop-down list are used to specify the type of mounting required for the panel. There are three options available in this drop-down list: **Surface**, **Recessed**, and **Floor**.

AIC rating

This option is used to specify the short circuit rating. You can specify the maximum value of current that can flow without causing damage to the breaker.

Fed from

This option is used to specify the source of power for the current panel.

Notes

This option is used to specify important notes that are to be taken care of while handling the panel.

DEVICE

This tool is used to insert an electrical device in the drawing area. This tool is available in the **Build** panel of the **Home** tab in the **Ribbon**. To insert an electrical device, choose the **Device** tool; you will be prompted to specify an insertion point for the device. Also, the **PROPERTIES** palette will be displayed, as shown in Figure 7-10. Click in the drawing area; the device will be placed at the specified point and a compass will be displayed below the device. Using this compass, you can rotate the device at any specific angle. The options available in the **PROPERTIES** palette after choosing the **Device** tool are discussed next.

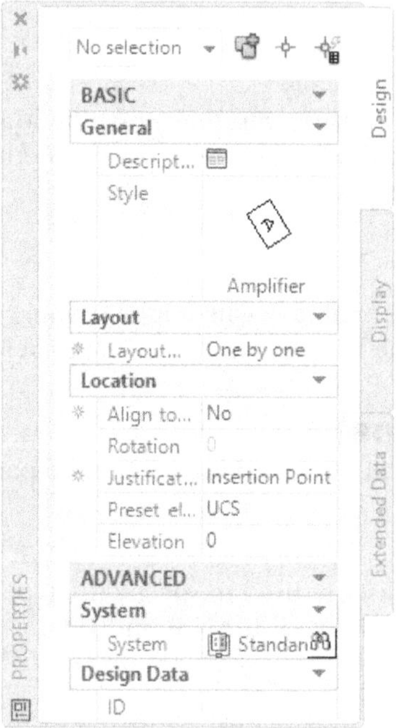

*Figure 7-10 The **PROPERTIES** palette displayed on choosing the **Device** tool*

Description

This option is available in the **General** rollout of the **BASIC** rollout. It is used to enter the description of the device to be added.

Style

This option is available in the **General** rollout of the **BASIC** rollout and is used to choose a desired style of the panel to be created. Click in the field corresponding to this option; the **STYLES BROWSER** will be displayed. Select the desired style from the **STYLES BROWSER**; the selected style will be assigned to the panel.

Layout method

This drop-down list is available in the **Layout** rollout of the **BASIC** rollout. The options in this drop-down list are used to specify the method of insertion of the device. There are three options available in this drop-down list: **One by one**, **Distance around space**, and **Quantity around space**. If you select the **One by one** option from this drop-down list then you need to insert the devices one by one.

If the **Distance around space** option is selected then you can specify the distance around the boundary by using the edit boxes displayed below it. On selecting the **Distance around space** option, the **Distance between** and the **Number of devices** edit boxes will be displayed below the option. The **Distance between** and the **Number of devices** edit boxes cannot be activated at the same time. On selecting the **Distance around space** option, only the **Distance between** edit box is activated. If you choose the **Quantity around space** option from the drop-down list, the **Distance between** edit box will be deactivated whereas the **Number of devices** edit box will be activated. You can specify the number of devices in the **Number of devices** edit box.

Align to objects

This drop-down list is available in the **Location** rollout of the **BASIC** rollout. The options in this drop-down list are used to specify whether the device is to be aligned to the selected object or not. There are two options available in this drop-down list: **Yes** and **No**. Choose the **Yes** option from this drop-down list to align the device with the selected object. This drop-down list is available only if **One by one** is selected from the **Layout Method** drop down list in the **Layout** rollout.

Rotation

This option is used to specify the rotation angle value for the device.

Justification

This drop-down list is available in the **Location** rollout of the **BASIC** rollout. The options in this drop-down list are used to justify the device with respect to its insertion point.

Preset Elevation

This drop-down list is available in the **Location** rollout of the **BASIC** rollout. The options in this drop-down list are used to set elevation of the device. By default, **UCS** is selected in this drop-down list.

Elevation

This option is used to specify the value of elevation from the selected preset.

System

This drop-down list is available in the **System** rollout of the **ADVANCED** rollout. The options in this drop-down list are used to specify the system type in which the device is inserted.

ID

This edit box is available in the **Design** rollout of the **ADVANCED** rollout. This option is used to assign an ID to the current device.

Insert tag

This drop-down list is available in the **Tag** rollout of the **ADVANCED** rollout. The options in this drop-down list are used to specify the tag to be added to the selected device.

Electrical Properties

This field is available in the **Circuits** rollout of the **ADVANCED** rollout. On clicking in this field, the **Electrical Properties** dialog box will be displayed, as shown in Figure 7-11. While adding a new device, you can change the number of connectors and other related properties by using the options available in this dialog box.

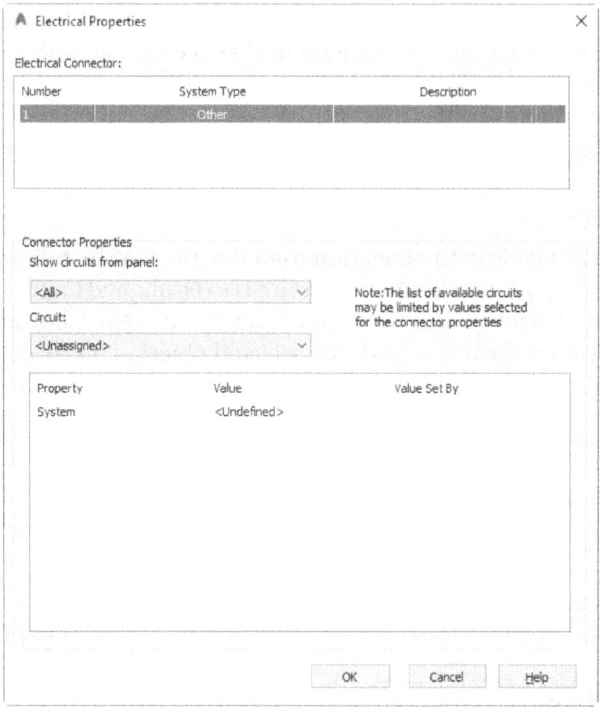

Figure 7-11 *The* ***Electrical Properties*** *dialog box*

CABLE TRAY

This tool is used to add a cable tray for supporting the cables. To add a cable tray, choose the **Cable Tray** tool from the **Build** panel in the **Home** tab of the **Ribbon**; you will be prompted to specify start point of the cable tray. Also, the **Add Cable Trays** dialog box will be displayed, as shown in Figure 7-12. Now, click in the drawing area to specify the start point of the cable tray; you will be prompted to specify the end point of the cable tray. Click to specify the end point of the cable tray; you will be prompted to specify the end point of the cable tray again. You can specify the end point of the next section or you can press ENTER to exit.

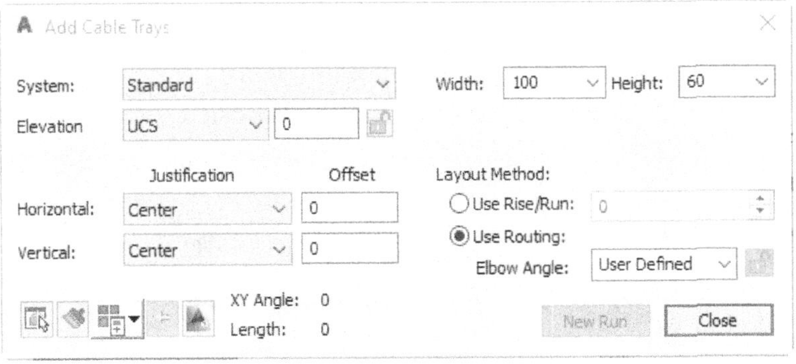

*Figure 7-12 The **Add Cable Trays** dialog box*

The options available in the **Add Cable Trays** dialog box are discussed next.

System

The options in this drop-down list are used to specify the system type in which the cable tray is being added.

Elevation

You can specify the elevation of the cable tray in this dialog box by using the **Elevation** drop-down list or the **Elevation** edit box. The **Elevation** edit box is used to specify the value of elevation of the cable tray from the reference. The options in the **Elevation** drop-down list are used to specify reference for the elevation. The elevation value thus specified can be locked or kept unlocked by clicking on the button available next to the **Elevation** edit box.

Horizontal

You can position the cable tray horizontally with respect to the insertion point by using the **Justification** drop-down list and the **Offset** edit box. The options in the **Justification** drop down list are used to specify the justification method for the cable tray in horizontal direction. The **Offset** edit box is used to specify the distance of the cable tray from the cursor.

Vertical

You can vertically position the cable tray with respect to the insertion point by using the **Justification** drop-down list and the **Offset** edit box. The options in the **Justification** drop-down list are used to specify the justification method for the cable tray in vertical direction. The **Offset** edit box is used to specify the distance of the cable tray from the cursor.

Width

The **Width** option in the **Add Cable Trays** dialog box is used to specify the width of the cable tray. If you specify the width other than the predefined value, a **Custom Size** message box will be displayed, refer to Figure 7-13, with the message: **This part is not available in the size needed. Would you like to create a custom size of this part ?** If you choose the **Yes** button from the message box, a part of custom size is created, but if you choose the **No** button; the **Choose a Part** dialog box will be displayed, refer to 7-14. Select the required part from the dialog box.

Figure 7-13 The ***Custom Size*** *message box*

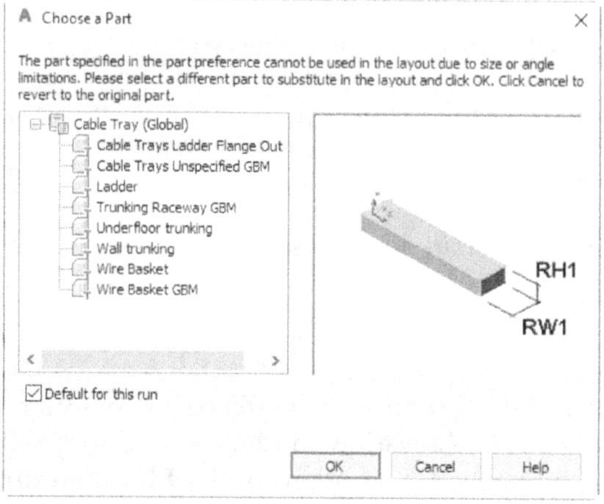

Figure 7-14 The ***Choose a Part*** *dialog box*

Height

The **Height** option in the **Add Cable Tray** dialog box is used to specify the height of the cable tray. You can specify the height using the same method that was used for specifying the width.

Use Rise/Run

This radio button is used to specify the rise/run value for the cable tray. On selecting this radio button, an edit box adjacent to this radio button will be activated. You can specify the value for rise and run in this edit box.

Use Routing

By default, this radio button is selected in the **Layout Method** area. As a result, the **Elbow Angle** edit box will be activated. You can specify the elbow angle value in this edit box. This elevation value can be locked or kept unlocked by clicking on the button available next to the **Elbow Angle** edit box.

CABLE TRAY FITTING

This tool is used to add a user defined cable tray fitting. To create a cable tray fitting, choose the **Cable Tray Fitting** tool from the **Build** panel in the **Home** tab of the **Ribbon**; the **Add Cable Tray Fittings** dialog box will be displayed, as shown in Figure 7-15. By default, the last used cable tray fitting is selected in this dialog box. Select the desired part from the **Part** tab of the dialog box; a preview of the selected cable tray fitting will be displayed on the right in the dialog box and the selected part will get attached to the cursor. Select the desired size of the selected part from the **Part Size Name** drop-down list in the dialog box and click in the drawing area to place the cable tray fitting. You can create a cable tray fitting as a separate entity or can join it with the cable tray.

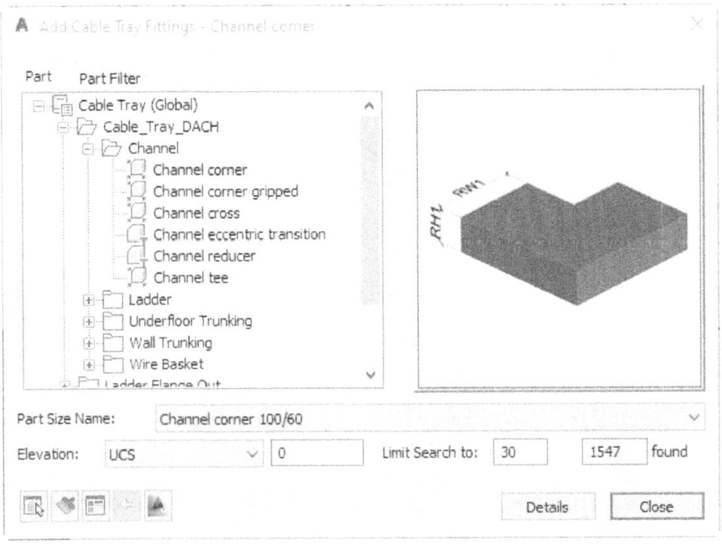

*Figure 7-15 The **Add Cable Tray Fittings** dialog box*

WIRE

This tool is used to add a wire on the drawing area. To do so, choose the **Wire** tool from the **Build** panel in the **Home** tab of the **Ribbon**; you will be prompted to specify the start point of the wire and the corresponding **PROPERTIES** palette will be displayed, as shown in Figure 7-16. Click in the drawing area to specify the first point of the wire; you will be prompted to specify the next point of the wire. Click to specify the next point of the wire; the wire will be created. You can specify more points or you can press ENTER to exit the tool.

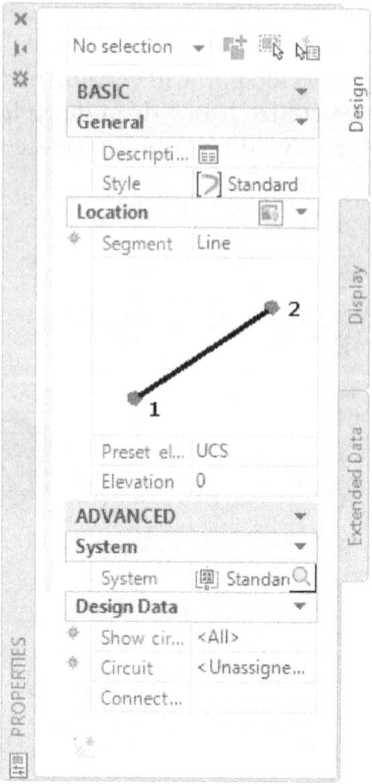

*Figure 7-16 The **PROPERTIES** palette displayed on choosing the **Wire** tool*

Tip

*You can also convert a line into a wire. To do so, select a line and right-click on it; a shortcut menu will be displayed. Hover the cursor over the **Convert To** option and choose the **Wire** option from the flyout displayed; you will be prompted to delete or retain the line after creating the wire. Enter **Y** or **N** as per the requirement.*

The options available in the **PROPERTIES** palette, after choosing the **Wire** tool, are discussed next.

Description

This option is available in the **General** rollout of the **BASIC** rollout. It is used to specify the description of the wire.

Style

This drop-down list is available in the **General** rollout of the **BASIC** rollout. The options in this drop-down list are used to specify the wire type.

Segment

This drop-down list is available in the **Location** rollout of the **BASIC** rollout. The options in this drop-down list are used to specify the segment type to be used while creating the wire system. There are six options available in this drop-down list: **Line**, **Arc**, **Snake**, **Polyline**, **Chamfer**, and **Spline**. On choosing an option from this drop-down list, the preview of the corresponding segment type is displayed.

Height

This option is available below the **Segment** drop-down list only when the **Arc**, **Snake**, **Chamfer**, or the **Spline** option is selected in the **Segment** drop-down list. It is used to specify the height of the segment.

Offset

This drop-down list is available below the **Height** edit box only when the **Arc**, **Snake**, **Chamfer**, or the **Spline** option is selected in the **Segment** drop-down list. The options in this drop-down list are used to specify the alignment of the segment. There are two options available in this drop-down list: **Left** and **Right**. The **Left** option is used to align the segment to the left. The **Right** option is used to align the segment to the right.

Radius

This option is available only when the **Polyline** option is selected in the **Segment** drop-down list. This option is used to specify the radius at corners of the polyline segment.

Preset Elevation

This drop-down list is available in the **Location** rollout of the **BASIC** rollout. The options in this drop-down list are used to set the value for elevation. By default, **UCS** is selected in this drop-down list.

Elevation

This drop-down list is available in the **Location** rollout of the **BASIC** rollout. The option in this drop-down list is used to specify the value of elevation from the selected preset.

System

This drop-down list is available in the **System** rollout of the **ADVANCED** rollout. The options in this drop-down list are used to specify the system type in which the wire will be added.

Show circuits from panels

This drop-down list is available in the **Design Data** rollout of the **ADVANCED** rollout. The options in this drop-down list are used to specify whether you want to display the circuit from the panels or not.

Circuit

This drop-down list is available in the **Design Data** rollout of the **ADVANCED** rollout. The options in this drop-down list are used to specify the circuit for which the wire is being created.

Connected circuits

This field is available in the **Design Data** rollout of the **ADVANCED** rollout. It displays the circuits that are connected to the wire.

Connected load

This field is available in the **Design Data** rollout of the **ADVANCED** rollout. It displays the total load in the circuit connected to the wire.

Hot size

This drop-down list is available in the **Dimension** rollout of the **ADVANCED** rollout. The options in this drop-down list are used to specify the size of the hot wire in the wiring system.

Neutral size

This option is used to specify the size of the neutral wire in the wiring system.

Ground size

This option is used to specify the size of the ground wire in the wiring system.

New Run

This tool is used to start a new run of wire system. This tool is available at the bottom of the **PROPERTIES** palette. It will be active after making one run of wire. On choosing this tool, you can start creating a new wiring system by specifying the start point.

CONDUIT

The **Conduit** tool is used to add conduits to the drawing area. To do so, choose this tool from the **Conduit** drop-down of the **Build** panel in the **Home** tab of the **Ribbon**; the **PROPERTIES** palette will be displayed, as shown in Figure 7-17 and you will be prompted to specify the start point of the conduit. Click in the drawing area to specify the start point of the conduit; you will be again prompted to specify the next point of the conduit. Click to specify the end point of the conduit; you will be again prompted to specify the next point of the conduit. You can specify the next point or you can press ENTER to exit the tool. Most of the options in this palette have already been discussed. Remaining options are discussed next.

Routing preference

This drop-down list is available in the **Dimension** rollout of the **BASIC** rollout The options in this drop-down list are used to specify the preferred routing system for the conduit creation.

Nominal size

This drop-down list is available in the **Dimension** rollout of the **BASIC** rollout. The options in this drop-down list are used to specify the diameter of the conduit pipe.

Specify cut length

This drop-down list is available in the **Dimension** rollout of the **BASIC** rollout. The options in this drop-down list are used to specify whether the conduit has a cut length or not.

Cut length

This option is available only when the **Yes** option is selected in the **Specify cut length** drop-down list. It is used to specify the maximum length of one segment of the conduit.

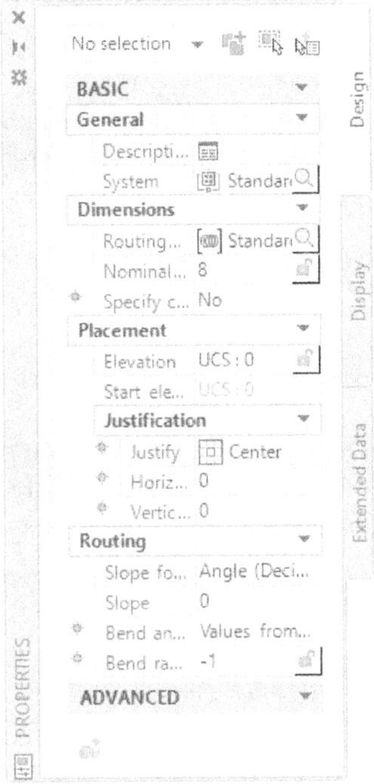

*Figure 7-17 The **PROPERTIES** palette displayed on choosing the **Conduit** tool*

Justify

This drop-down list is available in the **Placement** rollout of the **BASIC** rollout. The options available in this drop-down list are used to specify the justification method for the conduit.

Horizontal offset

This edit box is available in the **Placement** rollout of the **BASIC** rollout. Using it, you can specify the value of horizontal distance from the conduit to the selected justification point.

Vertical offset

This edit box is available in the **Placement** rollout of the **BASIC** rollout. Using it, you can specify the value of vertical distance from the conduit to the selected justification point.

Slope format

This drop-down list is available in the **Routing** rollout of the **BASIC** rollout. The options in this drop-down list are used to specify the format in which the slope value will be entered. There are four options available in this drop-down list: **Angle (Decimal Degrees)**, **Percentage, 100%=45 Degrees**, **Percentage, 100%=90 Degrees**, and **Rise /Run (Meters / Meters)**.

Slope

This edit box is used to specify the value of slope. The format of the slope value specified in this edit box will depend on the option selected in the **Slope format** drop-down list. If you change the slope value while adding more ducts, then the fitting at joints will adjust accordingly.

Bend angle

This drop-down list is available in the **Routing** rollout of the **BASIC** rollout. It is used to specify the angle of bend that is to be applied on the bend while creating conduit.

Bend radius

This edit box is used to specify the radius of bend that is to be applied on a bend while creating conduit.

Connection details

This field is available in the **ADVANCED** rollout. When you click in this field, the **Connection Details** dialog box will be displayed, as shown in Figure 7-18. There are two rollouts available in the dialog box containing details of both the connections.

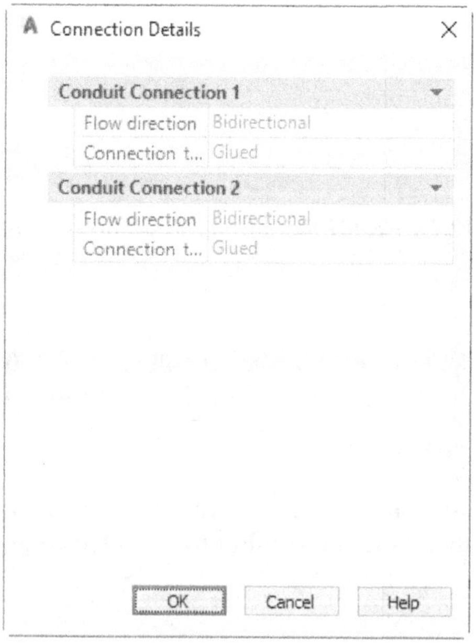

*Figure 7-18 The **Connection Details** dialog box*

Preferences

When you click in this field, the **Conduit Layout Preferences** dialog box will be displayed, as shown in Figure 7-19. The options in this dialog box are used to define the layout preferences for creating a conduit. Using the options in this dialog box, you can set the preferences for Slope, Elevation, Label style, Flow arrow style, and other parameters.

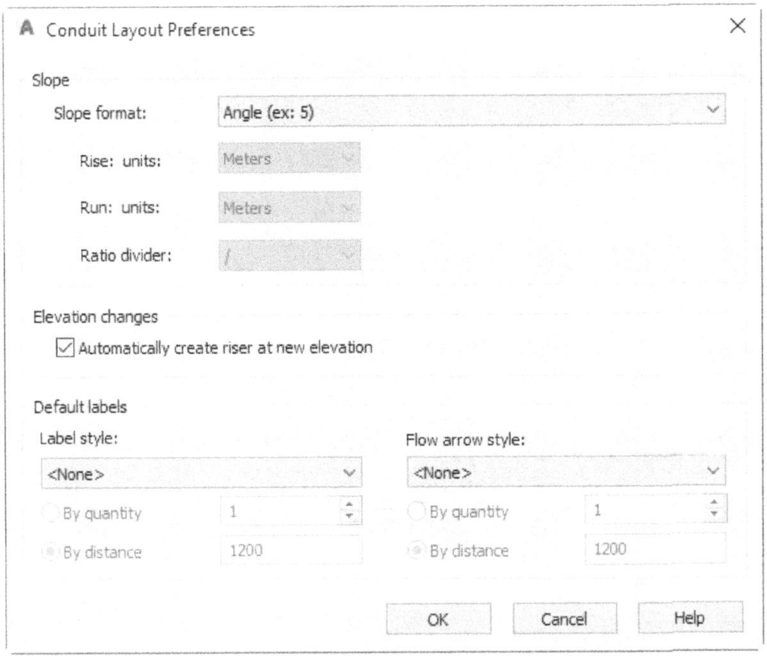

*Figure 7-19 The **Conduit Layout Preferences** dialog box*

Style

There are two drop-down lists with the name Style: one in the **ADVANCED** > **Label and Flow Arrows** > **Labels** rollout of the **PROPERTIES** palette and the other in the **ADVANCED** > **Label and Flow Arrows** > **Flow Arrows** rollout of the **PROPERTIES** palette. The options in these drop-down lists are used to apply styles to the labels and flow arrows of the conduit.

PARALLEL CONDUITS

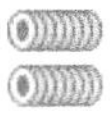

The **Parallel Conduits** tool is used to add parallel conduits to the drawing area. To do so, choose this tool from the **Conduit** drop-down in the **Build** panel of the **Home** tab in the **Ribbon**; you will be prompted to select baseline objects. Select the baseline objects, refer to Figure 7-20; you will be prompted to select the parallel conduits. Select the conduits parallel to the selected baseline and press ENTER; you will be prompted to specify the next point for the conduit. Click in the drawing area to specify the next point of the conduit; a parallel conduit consisting of the selected conduit lines is displayed, as shown in Figure 7-21.

CONDUIT FITTING

The **Conduit Fitting** tool is used to add fittings to the conduit. To add a conduit fitting, choose this tool from the **Build** panel in the **Home** tab of the **Ribbon**; you will be prompted to specify an insertion point. Also, the **PROPERTIES** palette will be displayed, as shown in Figure 7-22. Click in the drawing area or on a conduit line to add the conduit fitting. The options in the **PROPERTIES** palette after choosing the **Conduit Fitting** tool are discussed next.

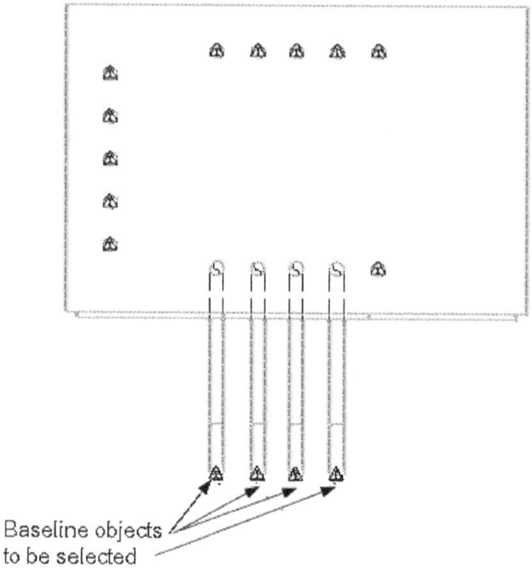

Figure 7-20 *The baseline objects to be selected*

Figure 7-21 *The parallel conduits created*

Description

This option is available in the **General** rollout of the **BASIC** rollout. It is used to specify description about the conduit fitting.

System

This drop-down list is available in the **General** rollout of the **BASIC** rollout. The options in this drop-down list are used to specify the system for which the conduit is being added.

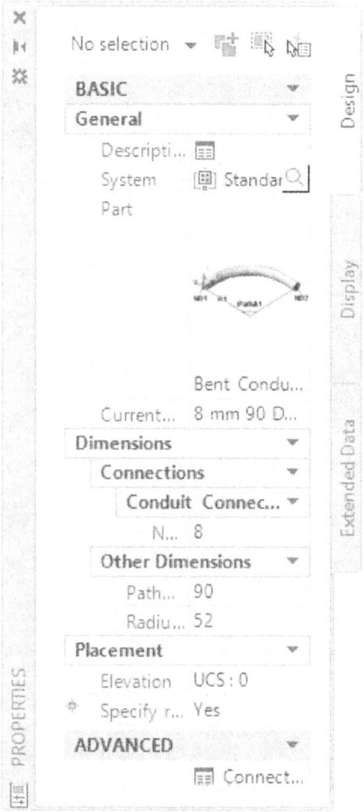

***Figure 7-22** The **PROPERTIES** palette displayed after choosing the **Conduit Fitting** tool*

Part

This option is available in the **General** rollout of the **BASIC** rollout. It is used to select the required fitting type to be used. Click in the field next to the **Part** option in the **PROPERTIES** palette; the **Select Part** dialog box will be displayed, as shown in Figure 7-23. Select the desired part from the dialog box and choose the **OK** button; the selected conduit fitting gets attached to the cursor. The options available in this dialog box are discussed next.

Type

The options in this drop-down list are used to specify the part type to be used as conduit fitting. There are five options available in this drop-down list: **All**, **Conduit Body**, **Elbow**, **Tee**, and **Transition**. Choose any of the options from the drop-down list: the related options are displayed in the dialog box.

Subtype

The options in this drop-down list are used to choose the subtypes available for the selected type. On choosing a subtype from the drop-down list, the related options are displayed in the **SELECT PART FROM CATALOG** area of the dialog box.

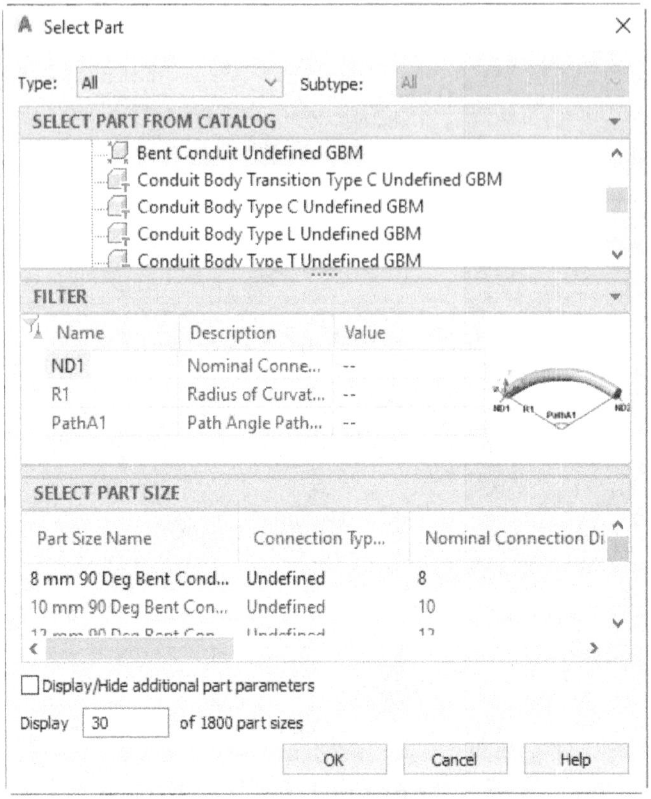

*Figure 7-23 The **Select Part** dialog box*

SELECT PART FROM CATALOG

The parts available for selected type and subtype are displayed in this area. Choose the required part from this area and then choose the **OK** button from the dialog box; the selected part gets attached to the cursor.

FILTER

The options in this area are used to filter the parts available for selected type and subtype depending on their size and parameters.

SELECT PART SIZE

The options in this area are used to select required size of the selected part. The options displayed in this area are confined by the values selected in the **Filter** area of the dialog box. Select the part having required size from this area and choose the **OK** button from this dialog box; the part will get attached to the cursor.

Current size

This drop-down list is available in the **General** rollout. The options in this drop-down list are used to specify the size for the selected part. These options are also available in the **SELECT PART SIZE** area of the **Select part** dialog box which has been discussed earlier.

Nominal diameter

This edit box is available in the **Dimension** rollout. It is available for each connector added to the part. Using this edit box, you can change the nominal diameter of the connector.

Other Dimensions Rollout

The options in this rollout are used to specify various dimensions for the part. The options in this rollout change depending upon the selected part.

Elevation

This edit box is available in the **Placement** rollout. It is used to specify the value of elevation for the selected part.

Specify rotation on screen

The options in this drop-down list are used to specify whether the rotation of the part will be specified on the screen or in the edit box available in the **PROPERTIES** palette. If you choose the **No** option from the drop-down list, the **Rotation** edit box will be displayed.

Rotation

This edit box is used to specify the value of rotation. It will be available only when the **No** option is selected from the **Specify rotation on screen** drop-down list.

Connection details

This button is available in the **ADVANCED** rollout. When you choose this button, the **Connection Details** dialog box will be displayed, as shown in Figure 7-24. There are two rollouts available in the dialog box containing the details about both the ends of the conduit.

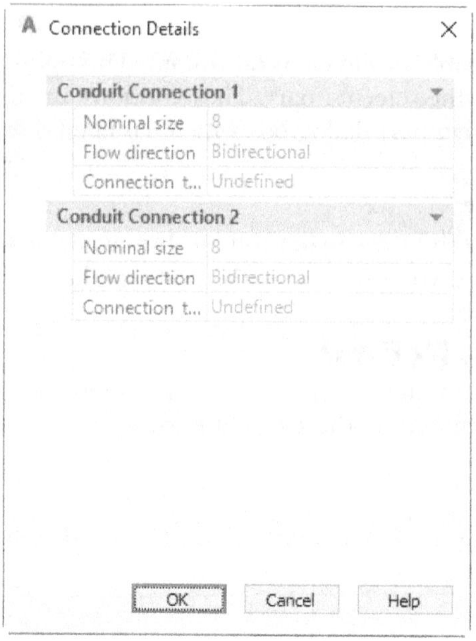

***Figure 7-24** The **Connection Details** dialog box*

CIRCUIT MANAGER

In an electrical layout, all the appliances are connected to the power sources with the help of a circuit. In AutoCAD MEP, circuits are used for calculating circuit loads, checking circuit overloads, or calculating wire sizes. There can be more than one circuit in a single electrical layout. To create and manage circuits in AutoCAD MEP, the Circuit Manager is used. To invoke the CIRCUIT MANAGER, choose the **CIRCUIT MANAGER** tool from the **Electrical** panel in the **Analyze** tab of the **Ribbon**; the **CIRCUIT MANAGER** palette will be displayed, as shown in Figure 7-25. The options available in the **CIRCUIT MANAGER** palette are discussed next.

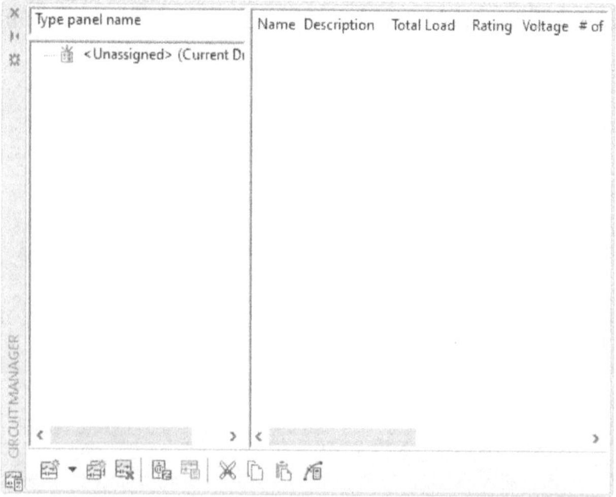

***Figure 7-25** The **CIRCUIT MANAGER** palette*

Create New Circuit

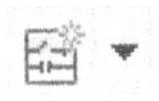

This drop-down is available at the bottom of the **CIRCUIT MANAGER** palette. The options in this drop-down are used to create new circuits to supply power to appliances depending on the required load, refer to Figure 7-26. The options available in this drop-down are discussed next.

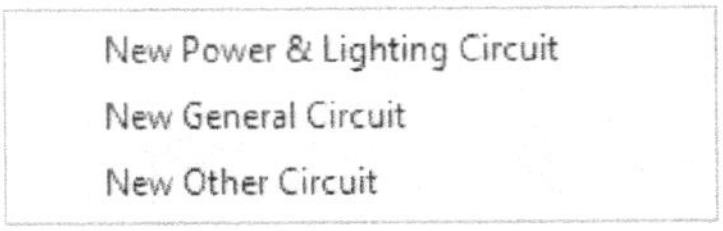

Figure 7-26 *The* ***Create New Circuit*** *drop-down*

New Power & Lighting Circuit

This option is used to create a circuit for power and lighting. To create such type of circuits, choose the **New Power & Lighting Circuit** option from the **Create New Circuits** drop-down; the **AutoCAD MEP - Electrical Project Database** dialog box will be displayed, as shown in Figure 7-27, and you will be prompted to create a new electrical project database (EPD) or open an existing database.

Choose the **Create a new EPD file** option from the dialog box; the **Save As** dialog box will be displayed, as shown in Figure 7-28. Specify the desired file name and choose the **Save** button from the dialog box. A circuit will be created and then displayed under the **Power and Lighting** node in the **CIRCUIT MANAGER** palette. Also, the related parameters will be displayed on the right side of the dialog box. You can change the parameters as per your requirement.

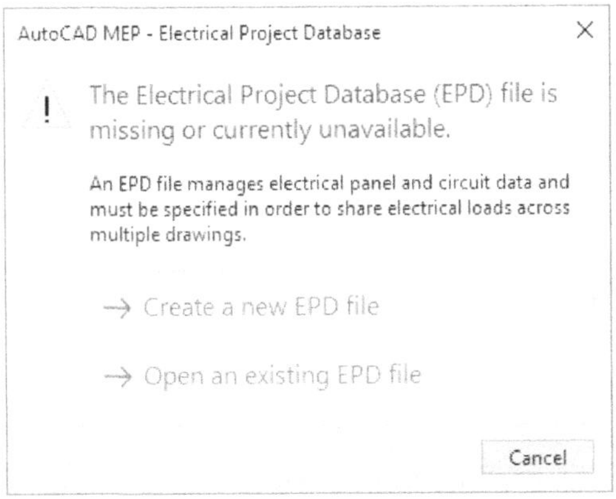

Figure 7-27 *The* ***AutoCAD MEP - Electrical Project Database*** *dialog box*

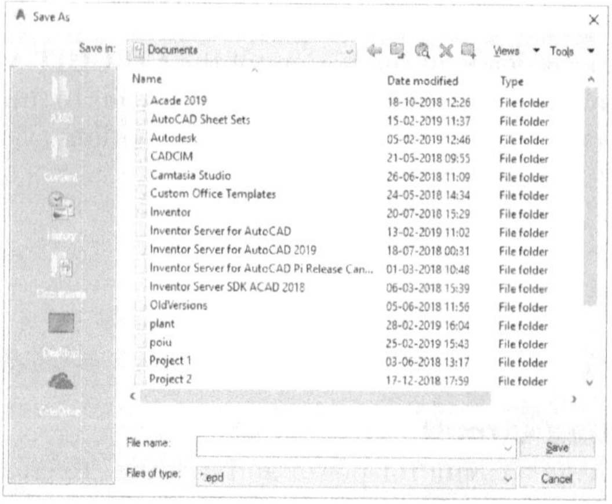

*Figure 7-28 The **Save As** dialog box*

New General Circuit

This option is used to create general circuits. General circuits are used for general application. Figure 7-29 shows a circuit created by using the **New General Circuit** option in the **CIRCUIT MANAGER** palette. There are four parameters available in the right side of the **CIRCUIT MANAGER** palette for a general circuit. You can change these parameters as per your requirement.

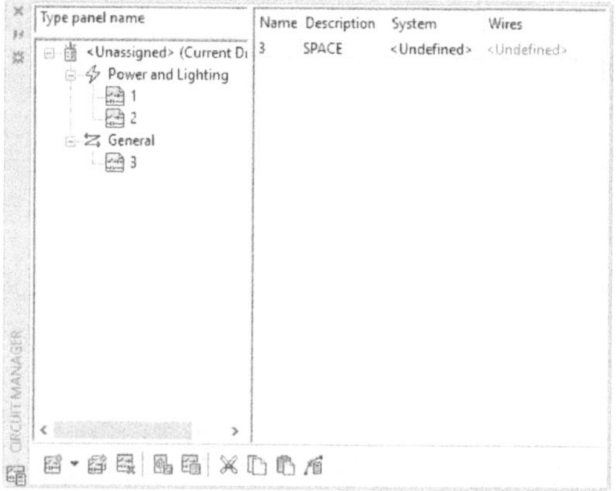

*Figure 7-29 The **CIRCUIT MANAGER** palette with the General circuit*

New Other Circuit

This option is used to create new circuits for special purposes like a circuit to run air conditioner. The working of this tool is similar to the **New General Circuit** tool.

Create Multiple Circuits

This tool is used to create multiple circuits at a time. To do so, choose the **Create Multiple Circuits** tool available at the bottom of the **CIRCUIT MANAGER** palette; the **Create Multiple Circuits** dialog box will be displayed, as shown in Figure 7-30. Select the desired options and choose the **OK** button from the dialog box to create multiple circuits. The options available in this dialog box are discussed next.

*Figure 7-30 The **Create Multiple Circuits** dialog box*

Panel

The options in this drop-down list are used to select the panel to be created. All the panels created in the current drawing are displayed in this drop-down list.

System Type

The options in this drop-down list are used to select the system type for the circuits to be created. There are three options available in this drop-down list: **Power and Lighting**, **General**, and **Other**.

System

The options in this drop-down list are used to specify the system for which the circuit is to be created. The options in this drop-down list change according to the option selected in the **System Type** drop-down list.

Total number of slots

This option is used to specify the number of slots required for current electrical layout. You cannot change the value of this spinner directly. The value in this spinner is changed automatically depending on the values selected in the **Number of circuits** spinner if the **Other** option or the **General** option is selected in the **System Type** drop-down list. If the **Power and Lighting** option is selected in the **System Type** drop-down list, then the value in the **Total number of slots** changes according to the values specified in the **Number of 3-pole circuits**, **Number of 2-pole circuits**, and **Number of 1-pole circuits** spinners.

Number of 3-pole circuits

This option is available only when the **Power and Lighting** option is selected in the **System**

Type drop-down list, refer to Figure 7-30. Using this option, you can specify the total number of circuits that will use three pole electric supply.

Number of 2-pole circuits

This option is also available only for the Power and Lighting system type. Using this option, you can specify the total number of circuits that will use the two pole electric supply.

Number of 1-pole circuits

This option is also available only for the Power and Lighting system type. Using this option, you can specify the total number of circuits that will use the one pole electric supply.

Voltage

These options are also activated only when the **Power and Lighting** option is selected in the **System Type** drop-down list. The **Voltage** options are available for 1-pole circuits, 2-pole circuits, and 3-pole circuits. You can change the value of voltage for a specific circuit by using this spinner, refer to Figure 7-31.

***Figure 7-31** The **Create Multiple Circuits** dialog box with circuits selected*

Description for circuits with breakers

This edit box is used to specify the default description about the circuit having circuit breakers.

Description for circuits without breakers

This edit box is used to specify the default description about the circuits having no circuit breaker.

Delete Circuit

This tool is used to delete the circuits that are created earlier. To delete a circuit, select the circuit to be deleted from the left area and then choose the **Delete Circuit** tool from the bottom of the **CIRCUIT MANAGER** palette; the selected circuit will be deleted.

Show Circuited Devices

This tool is used to display the devices that are attached to the current circuit. On choosing this tool; the devices attached to the current circuit are highlighted in the drawing area.

Circuit Report

This tool is used to display a report for the current circuit containing the data related to its various parameters. To display a circuit report, choose this tool from the bottom of the **CIRCUIT MANAGER** palette; the **Circuit Report** dialog box will be displayed, refer to Figure 7-32. This report consists of all the information for a circuit such as load, voltage, and length.

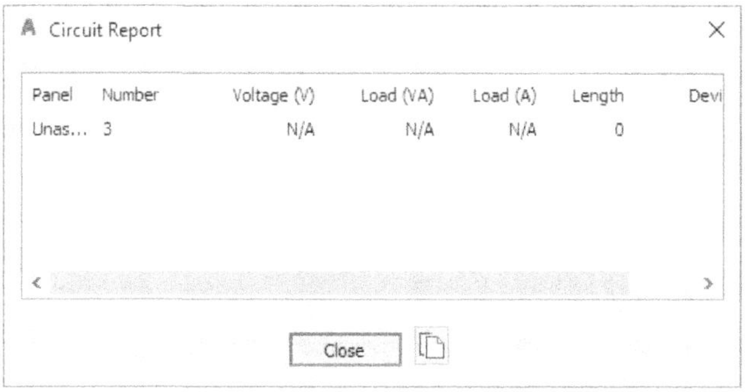

*Figure 7-32 The **Circuit Report** dialog box*

Cut Circuit

This tool is used to remove a circuit from a panel system and place it in another panel system. To do so, select the circuit from one panel and choose this tool from the bottom of the **CIRCUIT MANAGER** palette, refer to Figure 7-33.

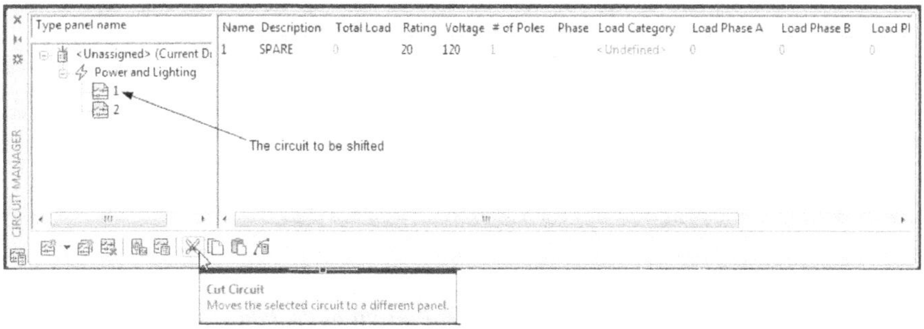

*Figure 7-33 The **Circuit Manager** palette with the circuit to be shifted*

Copy Circuit

This tool is used to copy the selected circuit. The circuit selected is copied to the clipboard and then it can be pasted in any of the panels. To copy a circuit, select the circuit from the left area of the **CIRCUIT MANAGER** palette and then choose the **Copy Circuit** tool from the toolbar available at the bottom; the circuit will be copied to the clipboard.

Paste Circuit

This tool is used to paste an already copied circuit. This tool is also used to paste a circuit copied by using the **Cut Circuit** tool or the **Copy Circuit** tool. To paste a circuit, select the panel in which you want to copy the circuit and then choose the **Paste Circuit** tool from the toolbar available at the bottom of the **CIRCUIT MANAGER** palette; the circuit in the clipboard will be pasted in the selected panel.

Calculate Wires

This tool is used to calculate the size of the wire to be used in the selected circuit.

TUTORIAL

Tutorial 1

In this tutorial, you will create the electrical layout of an office, refer to Figure 7-34. You can download the architectural file of the office from *www.cadcim.com*. The path of the file is: *Textbooks > CAD/CAM > AutoCAD MEP > AutoCAD MEP 2022 for Designers > Input Files.*

(Expected time: 30 min)

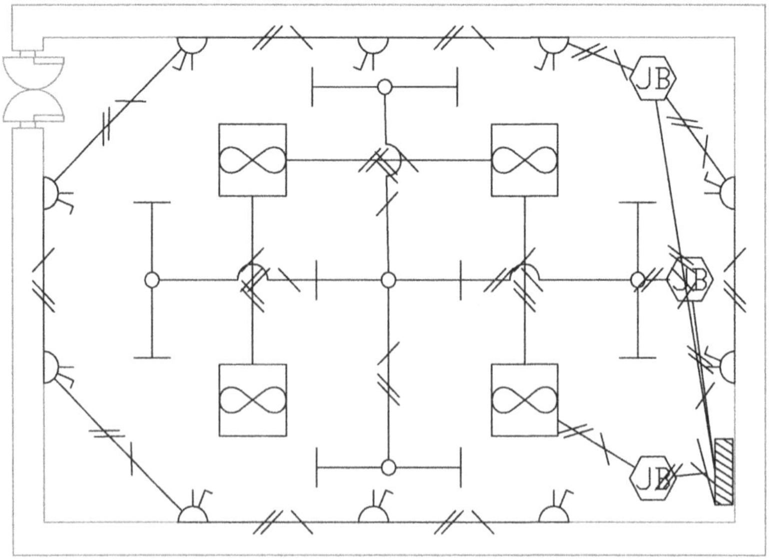

Figure 7-34 *An electrical layout of the office*

Power Factor is **0.8** for all the devices and the parameters of the electrical devices of the office are given in the Table 7-1.

Table 7-1 Parameters of the devices

Device	Fan	1200 Long Linear Floroscent	Single Switch Socket
Load	180VA	150VA	300VA
Voltage	230	230	230
Phases	1	1	1
Maximum Overcurrent Rating	10	8	10

The following steps are required to complete this tutorial:

a. Open the drawing downloaded from the website.
b. Add the devices according to the layout.
c. Create Panel.
d. Configure the Panel.
e. Configure the devices to apply specific load.
f. Create a wiring line between devices.
g. Calculate load and wire size of the circuits

Downloading and Opening the Drawing File

1. Download the *c07_amep_prt.zip* file from *https://www.cadcim.com*. The path of the file is as follows: *Textbooks > CAD/CAM > AutoCAD MEP > AutoCAD MEP 2022 for Designers > Input Files.*

2. Extract this file at the desired location.

3. Open the drawing file *c07_amep_prt.dwg* from the specified location by double-clicking on it. The drawing file is displayed, as shown in Figure 7-35.

Figure 7-35 *Architectural layout of the office*

Adding Devices

1. Open the **Electrical** workspace and choose the **Device** tool from the **Build** panel in the **Home** tab of the **Ribbon**; the **PROPERTIES** palette is displayed, as shown in Figure 7-36.

2. Click in the **Style** field in the **BASIC** rollout of the **PROPERTIES** palette; the **STYLES BROWSER** is displayed, refer to Figure 7-37.

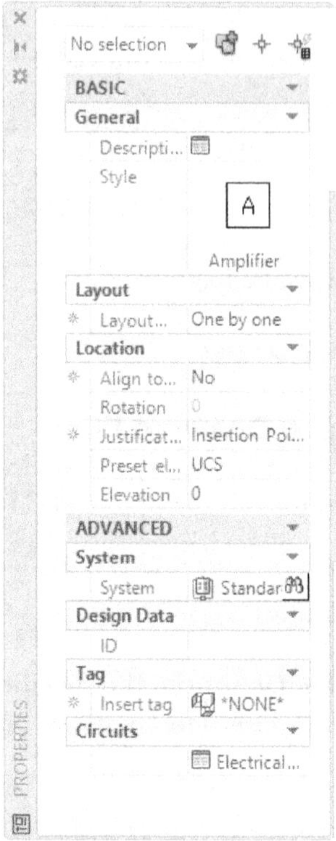

***Figure 7-36** The **PROPERTIES** palette displayed after choosing the **Device** tool*

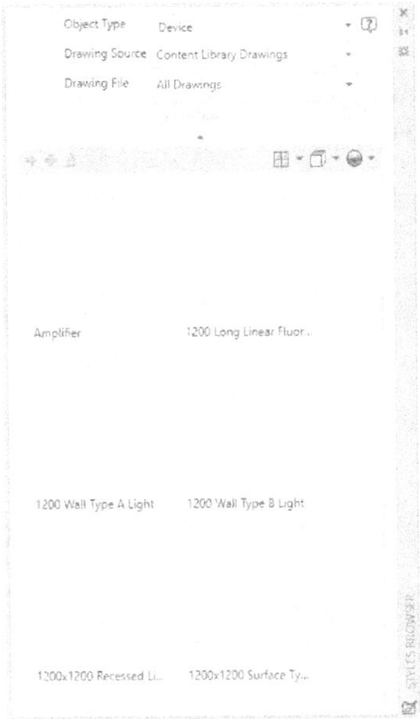

Figure 7-37 *The* ***STYLES BROWSER*** *palette*

3. Select the **Lighting Fluorescent (Global).dwg** option from the **Drawing File** drop-down list and double click on the **1200 Long Linear Fluorescent** device from the gallery area in the **STYLES BROWSER** palette; the **1200 Long Linear Fluorescent** device will be added to the **PROPERTIES** palette.

4. Enter **3500** in the **Elevation** edit box and select the **230V Lighting Devices(Ceiling) (230V CEILING LIGHTS)** option from the **System** drop-down of the **PROPERTIES** palette.

5. Now, place the lights, as shown in Figure 7-38.

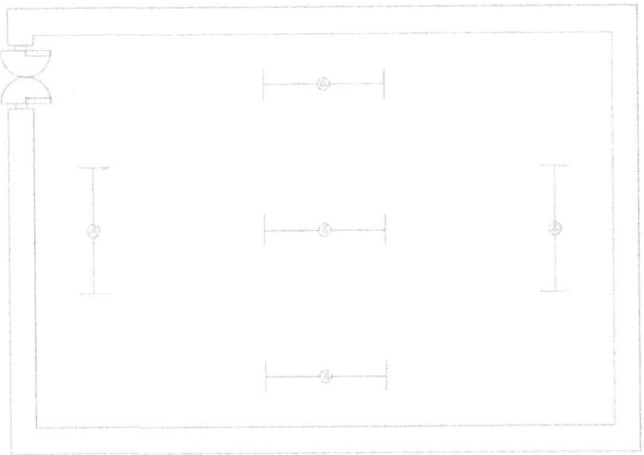

Figure 7-38 *The drawing after placing lights*

6. Similarly, place the **Single Switched Socket Outlet** and **Fan** devices in the drawing area at **2000** and **3000** elevation, respectively, refer to Figure 7-39. Make sure that **230V Power (230V POWER)** is selected from the **System** drop-down list in the **PROPERTIES** palette while placing both the devices.

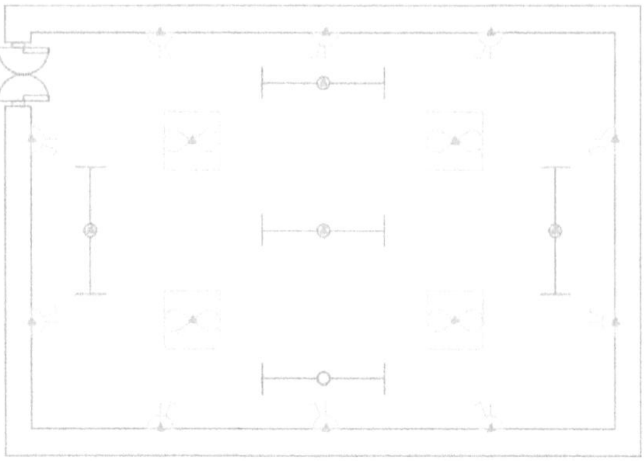

Figure 7-39 *The drawing after placing fans and sockets*

Note

*1. When you select the **Sockets(Global).dwg** option from the **Drawing File** drop-down list; the **Single Switched Socket Outlet** gets available in the gallery area of the **STYLES BROWSER** palette.*

*2. When you select the **Power(Global).dwg** option from the **Drawing File** drop-down list; the **Fan** gets available in the gallery area of the **STYLES BROWSER** palette.*

Now, you need to place junction boxes in the drawing.

7. Choose the **Device** tool from the **Build** panel in the **Home** tab of the **Ribbon**; the **PROPERTIES** palette is displayed.

8. Click in the **Style** field of the **PROPERTIES** palette; the **STYLES BROWSER** palette is displayed. Select the **Junction Boxes (Global).dwg** option from the **Drawing File** drop-down list; the junction boxes are displayed in the gallery area of **STYLES BROWSER** palette.

9. Double-click on the **Hexagon 3 Junction Box** device in the gallery; the **Hexagon 3 Junction Box** device is selected as style.

10. Now, place the junction boxes at an elevation of 3000, as shown in Figure 7-40.

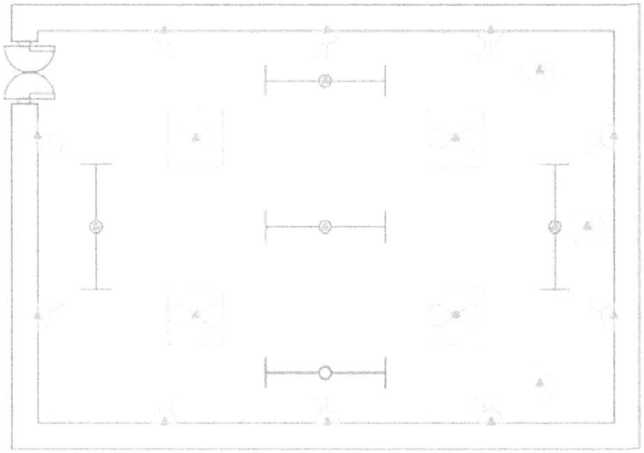

Figure 7-40 The drawing after adding the junction boxes

Creating the Panel

1. Choose the **Panel** tool from the **Build** panel in the **Home** tab of the **Ribbon**; you are prompted to specify an insertion point for the panel. Also the **PROPERTIES** palette is displayed, as shown in Figure 7-41.

2. Click in the **Style** field in the **BASIC** rollout of the **PROPERTIES** palette; the **STYLES BROWSER** palette is displayed.

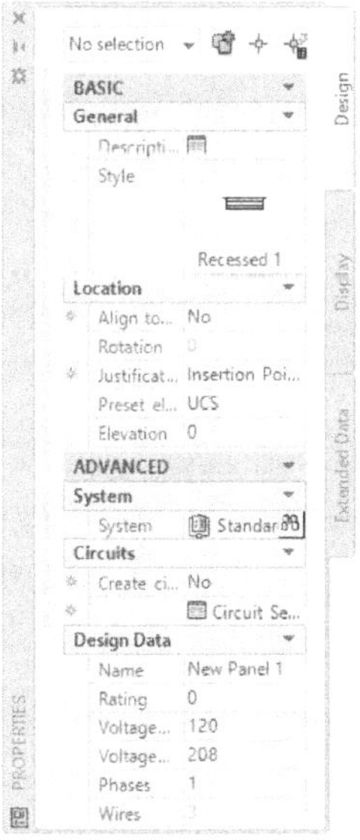

*Figure 7-41 The **PROPERTIES** palette displayed after choosing the **Panel** tool*

3. Select the **Panels (global).dwg** option from the **Drawing File** drop-down list in the dialog box and double click on the **Surface Door 3** option from the gallery area of the palette; the device gets attached to the cursor. Specify the name as **Main Panel** in the **Name** edit box in the **ADVANCED >Design Data** rollout of the **PROPERTIES** palette.

4. Specify **800** in the **Rating** edit box.

5. Select the **230** option from the **Voltage phase-to-neutral** drop-down list.

6. Select the **240** option from the **Voltage phase-to-phase** drop-down list.

7. Specify **Main type** as **main circuit breaker(MCB)**, **Main size (amps)** as **15**, **Design capacity (amps)** as **20**, **AIC rating** as **800**, and **Panel type** as **ISO** in the **PROPERTIES** palette.

   Now, you need to create circuits for the panel.

8. Make sure that the **Yes** option is selected from the **Create circuits** drop-down list and click in the **Circuit Settings** field in the **Circuits** rollout of the **PROPERTIES** palette; the **Circuit Settings** dialog box is displayed, refer to Figure 7-42.

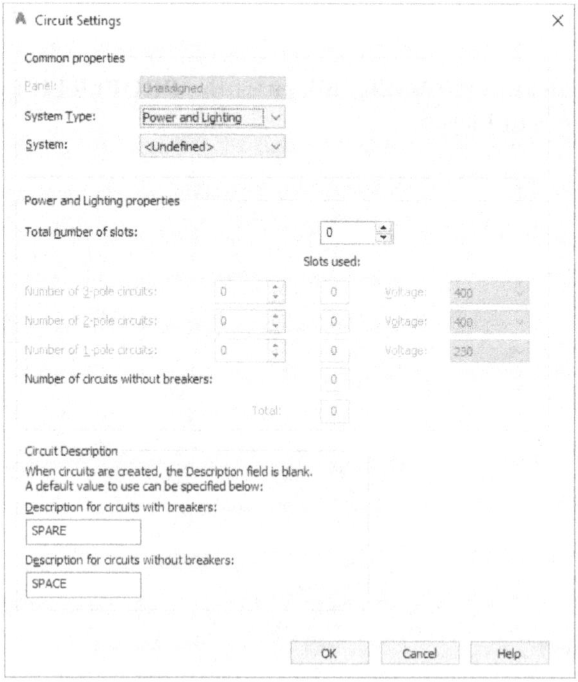

Figure 7-42 The ***Circuit Settings*** *dialog box*

9. Make sure that **Power and Lighting** is selected in the **System Type** drop-down list and **230V Power** is selected in the **System** drop-down list. Set the value **3** in both the **Total number of slots** and **Number of 1-pole circuits** spinners and select the **230** option from the **Voltage** drop-down lists adjacent to the spinners.

10. Choose the **OK** button box to exit the dialog box.

11. Click in the drawing area to place the panel, refer to Figure 7-43; the **AutoCAD MEP - Electrical Project Database** dialog box is displayed, refer to Figure 7-44.

12. Choose the **Create a new EPD file** option from the dialog box and save the file at the desired location with the name **Panel**; the panel is created at the specified location. Next, choose ESC to exit the tool.

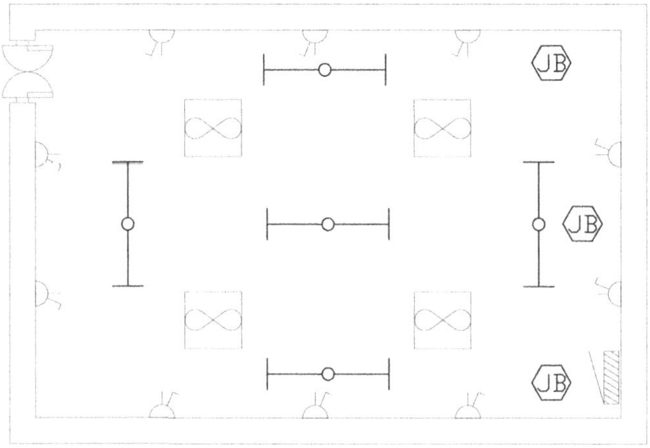

Figure 7-43 *The drawing after adding the panel*

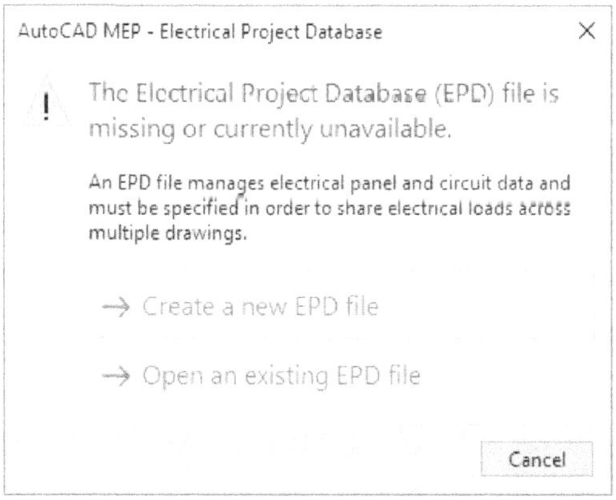

Figure 7-44 *The **AutoCAD MEP - Electrical Project Database** dialog box*

Configuring Circuits

1. Select the panel created and then choose the **Circuit Manager** tool from the **Circuits** panel in the **Panel** tab of the **Ribbon**; the **CIRCUIT MANAGER** is displayed.

2. Double-click in the field 1 in the **Name** column of the **CIRCUIT MANAGER** and enter the name as **Lights**.

3. Click in the field 2 in the **Name** column of the **CIRCUIT MANAGER** and enter the name as **Fans**.

4. Similarly, click in the field 3 in the **Name** column of the **CIRCUIT MANAGER** and enter the name as **Sockets**.

5. Double-click in the **System** field for **Lights** and select the **230V Lighting Devices (Ceiling)** option from the drop-down list displayed.

6. Double-click in the **Voltage** field and select the **230** option from the drop-down list displayed for all the devices. The **CIRCUIT MANAGER** after applying the above configuration is displayed, as shown in Figure 7-45. Then, close the **CIRCUIT MANAGER**.

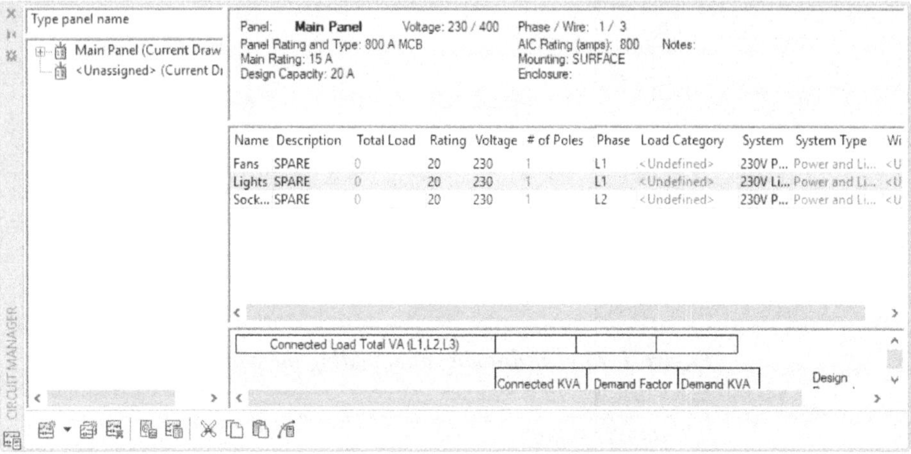

*Figure 7-45 The **CIRCUIT MANAGER** after applying configuration*

Configuring Devices

1. Select a socket from the drawing area; the **Device** contextual tab is displayed in the **Ribbon**. Next, select the **Select Similar** option from the **Select Similar** drop-down list of the **General** panel; all the sockets available in the drawing area are selected.

2. Right click on the selected items; shortcut menu is displayed. Choose the **Properties** option from the shortcut menu. Click in the **Electrical properties** field in the **Circuit** rollout of **ADVANCED** rollout in the **PROPERTIES** palette; the **Electrical Properties** dialog box is displayed, as shown in Figure 7-46.

   Now, you need to specify the parameters as per the table.

3. Select the **230V Power** option from the **System** drop-down list.

4. Specify **300** in the **Load Phase 1** edit box, refer to Table 7-1.

5. Select the **230** option from the **Voltage** drop-down list.

6. Similarly, select the **1** option from the **Number of Poles** drop-down list in the dialog box.

7. Specify **10** in the **Maximum Overcurrent Rating (amps)** edit box in the dialog box.

8. Specify **0.8** in the **Power Factor** edit box.

9. Select the **Main Panel (Current Drawing)** option from the **Show Circuits from panel** drop-down list and also select the **Sockets [Load: 0 VA]** option from the **Circuit** drop-down list. Choose the **OK** button to exit the dialog box.

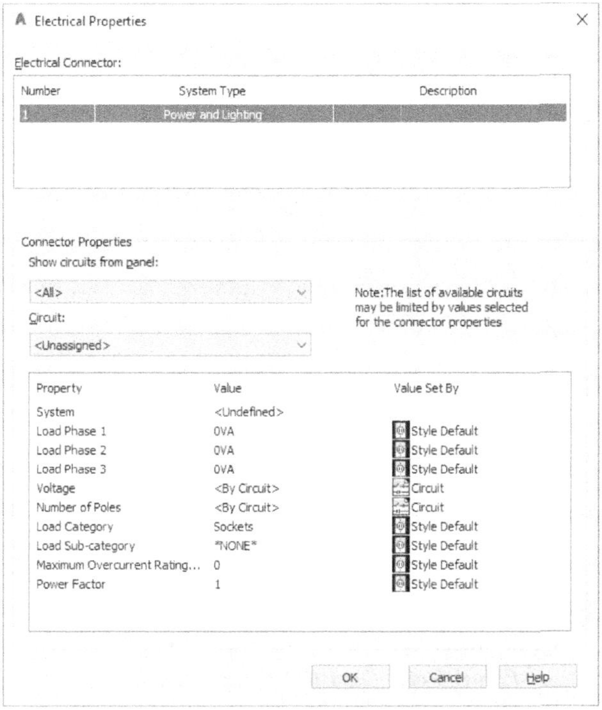

Figure 7-46 *The **Electrical Properties** dialog box*

10. Similarly, specify the parameters for other devices, refer to the Table 7-1, in the **Electrical Properties** dialog box by following the steps discussed above. Note that the power factor will be same for all the devices. Select **230 V Power** for fans and **230 V Lighting Devices (ceiling)** for lights from the **System** drop-down list in the **Electrical Properties** dialog box.

11. Also, select the **Main Panel (Current Drawing)** option from the **Show Circuits from panel** drop-down list for all the devices and select the **Lights [Load: 0 VA]** for lights and **Fan [Load: 0 VA]** for fans from the **Circuit** drop-down list in the **Electrical Properties** dialog box.

Note

*The **Sockets [Load: 0 VA]** option when selected from the **Circuit** drop-down list is modified to **Sockets [Load: 3000 VA]**. This happens because the software automatically calculates the load of the sockets according to the number of sockets added to the drawing. Similarly, **Lights [Load: 0 VA]** changes into **Lights [Load: 750 VA]** and **Fan [Load: 0 VA]** changes into **Fan [Load: 720 VA]**.*

Adding Wires

1. Choose the **Wire** tool from the **Build** panel in the **Home** tab of the **Ribbon**; you are prompted to specify the start point of the wire on an electrical device. Also, the **PROPERTIES** palette is displayed, as shown in Figure 7-47.

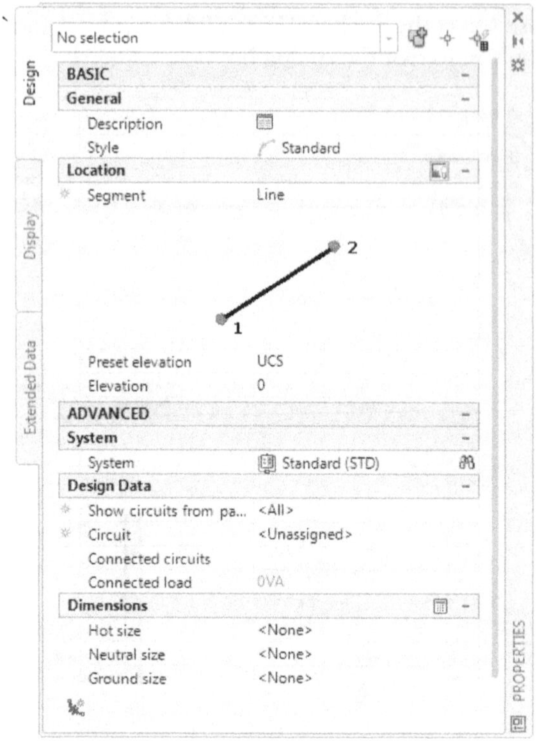

Figure 7-47 *The **PROPERTIES** palette displayed on choosing the **Wire** tool*

2. Click in the **System** drop-down list and select the **230V Power(230V POWER)** from the options displayed.

3. Connect all the sockets to the junction box using wires, refer to Figure 7-48. Make sure that the **Line** option is selected in the **Segment** drop-down list and the **PVC Multi** option is selected from the **Style** drop-down list.

4. Similarly, connect all the fans and lights to the junction boxes using the wires, refer to Figure 7-49. Make sure that the system selected for fans is **230V Power(230V POWER)** and for lights is **230V Lighting Devices(Ceiling) (230V CEILING LIGHT)**.

Note

*A device or wire related to the **230V Power** system is displayed in cyan color and a device or wire related to the **230V Lighting Devices (Ceiling)** is displayed in brown color in the drawing area. Make sure that all the devices connected to a specific circuit are in the same system.*

5. Connect all the junction boxes to the panel, refer to Figure 7-50.

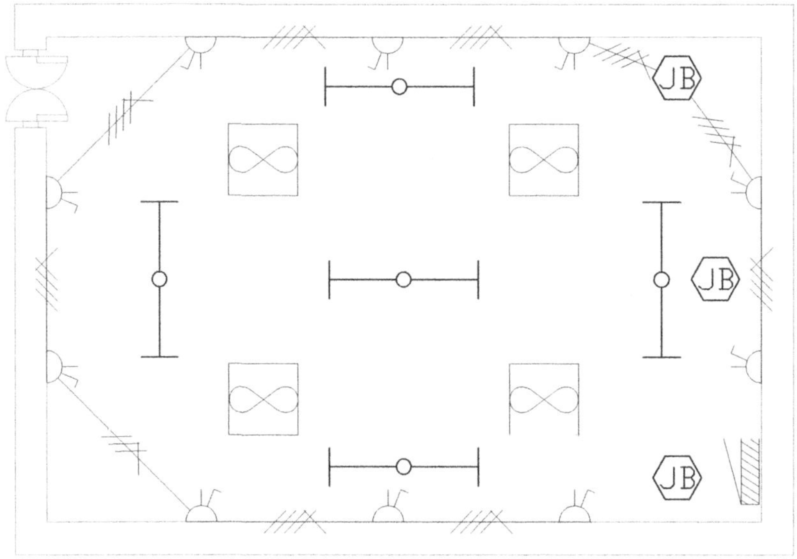

Figure 7-48 The drawing after adding wires to the sockets

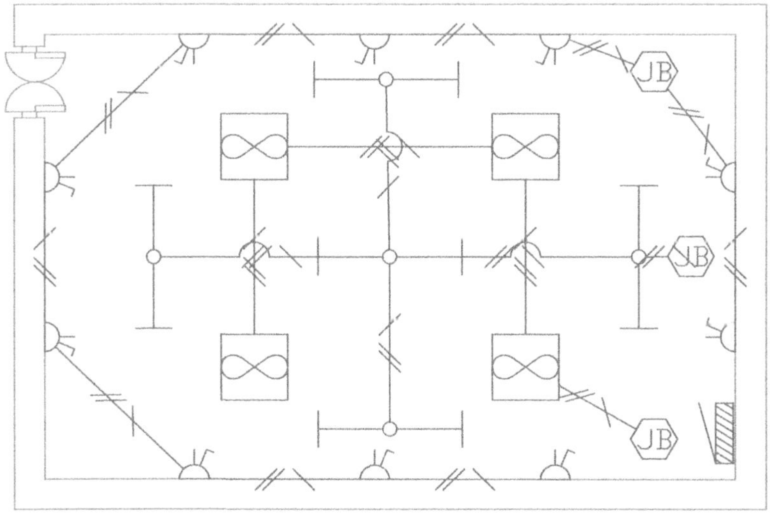

Figure 7-49 The drawing after adding wires to lights and fans

Calculating Loads and Wire Sizes

1. To calculate the total load of all the devices in the drawing area, choose the **Power Totals** tool from the **Electrical** panel in the **Analyze** tab of the **Ribbon**; you are prompted to select the devices.

2. Select all the devices available in the drawing area and press ENTER; the **Power Totals** dialog box is displayed, refer to Figure 7-51.

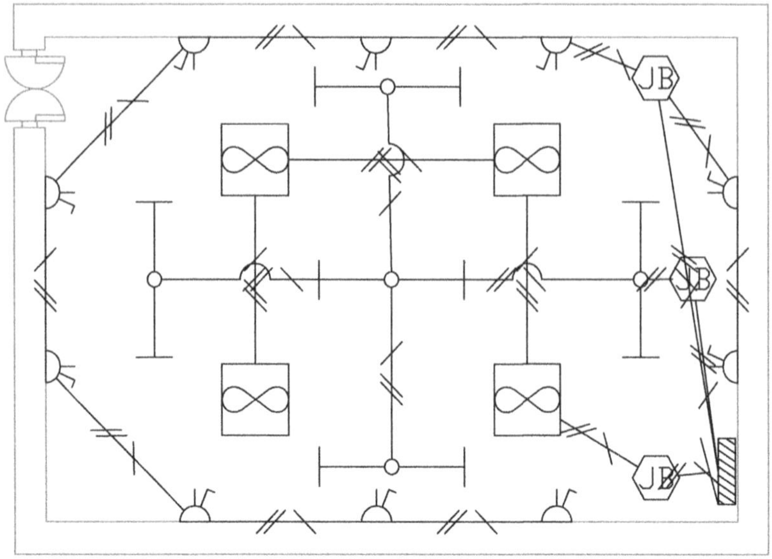

***Figure 7-50** The drawing after connecting junction boxes to the panel*

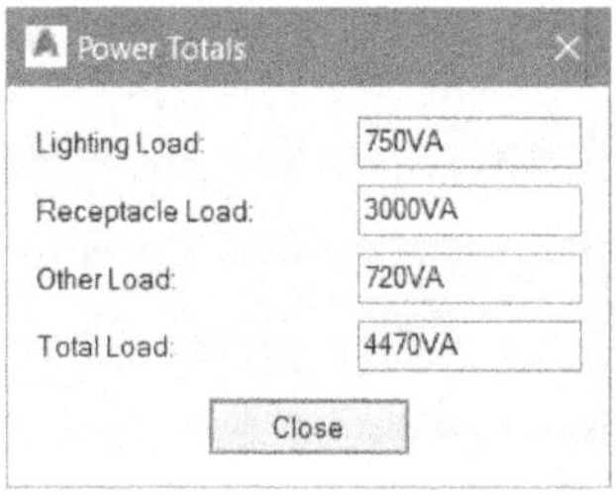

***Figure 7-51** The **Power Totals** dialog box*

The total load is displayed in the **Total Load** field of the dialog box. Now, you need to calculate the wire size of the circuit.

3. Select all the wires in the drawing area; the **PROPERTIES** palette is displayed.

4. Choose the **Calculate sizes for the wire** button available at the right of the **Dimensions** rollout in the **ADVANCED** rollout of the **PROPERTIES** palette; the wire sizes are displayed in the **Hot size**, **Neutral size**, and **Ground size** edit boxes in the **Dimensions** rollout.

Saving the Drawing File

1. Choose **Save** from the **Application Menu** to save the drawing file.

Self-Evaluation Test

Answer the following questions and then compare them to those given at the end of this chapter:

1. In which of the following tabs is the **Circuit Manager** tool available?

    (a) **Home** (b) **Analyze**
    (c) **View** (d) **Manage**

2. The ________ is used to create and manage circuits in AutoCAD MEP.

3. The **Create Circuits** drop-down list is available in the **PROPERTIES** palette displayed while creating a ________.

4. The cable tray is used to support the cables in the system. (T/F)

5. A line can be converted into a wire. (T/F)

Review Questions

Answer the following questions:

1. In which of the following tools is the **Cut Length** option available?

    (a) **Conduit** (b) **Cable Tray**
    (c) **Wire** (d) **Panel**

2. The Circuit Report is used to display data related to various parameters of a ________.

3. You can select a wire type from the ________ tab of the **TOOL PALETTE - ELECTRICAL.**

4. The **Hair Drier** option is not available in the **STYLES BROWSER palette**. (T/F)

5. The **Space** tool is not available in the **Electrical** workspace. (T/F)

EXERCISE

Exercise 1

In this exercise, you will create a model of an electrical system, refer to Figure 7-52. The architectural drawing for creating this exercise is available at *www.cadcim.com*. Download the *c06_amep_prt.zip* file from *https://www.cadcim.com*. The path of the file is as follows: *Textbooks > CAD/CAM > AutoCAD MEP > AutoCAD MEP 2022 for Designers > Input Files*. Table 7-2 contains the parameters of the devices to be added to the layout. **(Expected time: 30 min)**

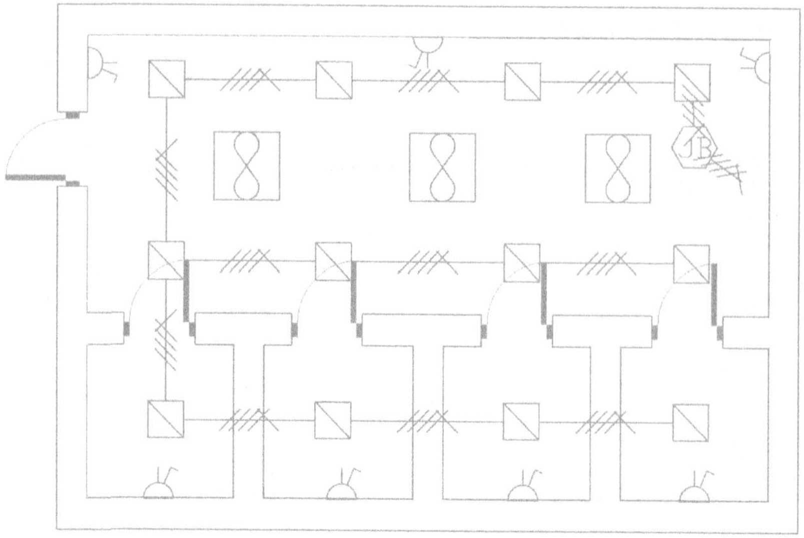

Figure 7-52 *The final model*

Power Factor is **0.8** for all the devices and the parameters of the electrical devices of the given office are given in the Table 7-2.

Table 7-2 *Parameters for the devices*

Device	Fan	300x300 Recessed Light	Single Switch Socket
Load	180VA	100	300VA
Voltage	230	230	230
Phases	1	1	1
Maximum Overcurrent Rating	10	8	10

Answers to Self-Evaluation Test

1. b, **2.** panel, **3. Circuit Manager**, **4.** T, **5.** T

Chapter 8

Representation and Schedules

Learning Objectives

After completing this chapter, you will be able to:
- *Create vertical section of the model*
- *Create horizontal section of the model*
- *Create section line for creating section views*
- *Create elevation line*
- *Create hidden line projections*
- *Slice a 3D object for extracting a profile*
- *Create schedules and tables*

INTRODUCTION

In this chapter, you will learn to create different views of a building model for representation. These views represent every minute detail of the building model. You will also learn to create various schedules and tables to document the equipment required for the building.

CREATING VERTICAL SECTIONS

Vertical Section of an object is created by passing a vertical plane through the objects. To create a section, choose the **Vertical Section** tool from the **Section & Elevation** panel of the **Home** tab in the **Ribbon**; you will be prompted to specify the start point of the section line. Click in the drawing area to specify the start point of the section; you will be prompted to specify the next point of the section line. Click in the drawing area to specify the end point of the section line; you will be prompted again to specify the next point for the section line. Press ENTER; you will be prompted to specify the length of the bounding box. Enter the length of the section area at the command prompt; a section line will be created. Now, press the ESC key to exit the tool. Figure 8-1 shows a drawing with the section line created. The vertical extent of the object is automatically set as the height of the section. You can assign a user defined value as the height. To do so, select the line and click in the **Use model extents for height** field in the **Dimensions** rollout of the **PROPERTIES** palette. Select the **No** option from the drop-down list; the **Height** and **Lower extension** fields will be displayed below the **Use model extents for height** field. Click in the **Height** field and specify a value for the section height. You can also specify a value for lower extension in the **Lower extension** field.

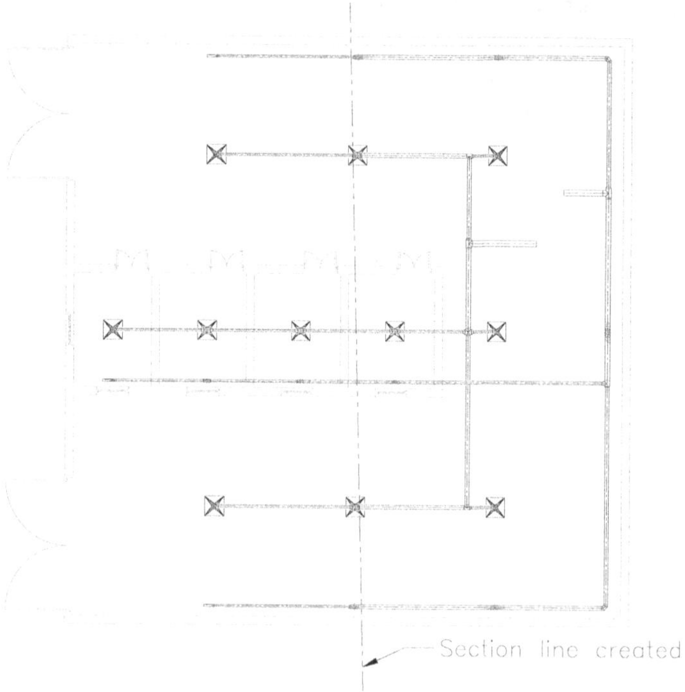

Figure 8-1 *The drawing after creating the section line*

After specifying the section line, you can create a vertical section view by using the section line. To create a vertical section view, select the section line; the **Building Section Line** contextual tab will be displayed, as shown in Figure 8-2. The options available in the contextual tab are discussed next.

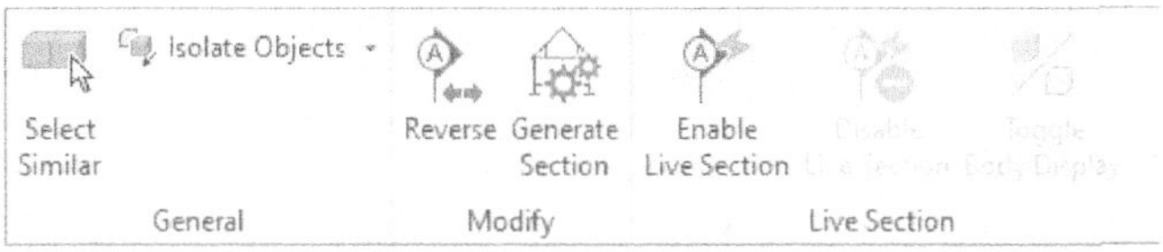

Figure 8-2 *The **Building Section Line** contextual tab*

Enable Live Section

This tool is used to create live sections by using the current section line. This type of section is a dynamic section of the building and gets modified as you modify the section line. To create a live section, select the section line and then choose the **Enable Live Section** tool from the **Live Section** panel of the **Building Section Line** contextual tab in the **Ribbon**; the live section will be created. To display the live section you must switch to any of the isometric view such as SW Isometric and NE Isometric. Figure 8-3 shows a drawing with the live section created.

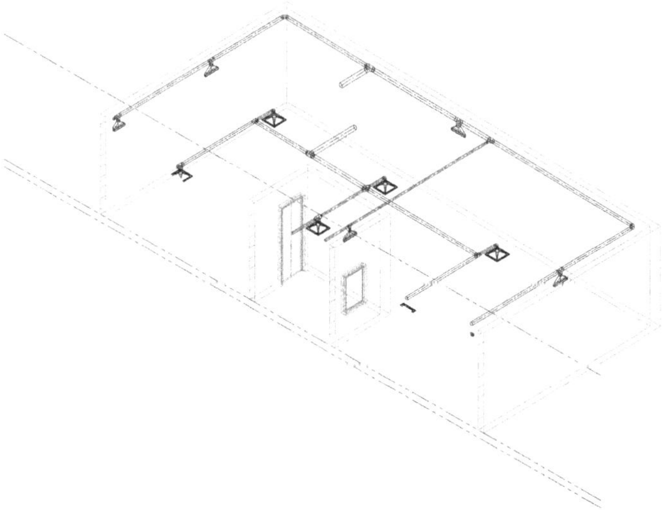

Figure 8-3 *The drawing with live section created*

Disable Live Section

This tool will get enabled only when a live section is created. This tool is used to remove the live sections created earlier. To remove a live section, select the section line that was used to create it; the **Building Section Line** contextual tab will be displayed. Choose the **Disable Live Section** tool from the **Live Section** panel of the **Building Section Line** contextual tab in the **Ribbon**; the live section will be removed.

Toggle Body Display

This tool is used to toggle the display of the object that is not displayed in the section when the live section is created.

Reverse

This tool is used to reverse the side of the bounding box with respect to the section line. To reverse the side of the bounding box, choose the **Reverse** tool from the **Modify** panel in the **Building Section Line** contextual tab of the **Ribbon**; the bounding box will be created on the reverse side of the section line.

Generate Section

This tool is used to generate section view of a building with respect to the section line selected. To generate a section, choose the **Generate Section** tool from the **Modify** panel of the **Building Section Line** contextual tab in the **Ribbon**; you will be prompted to specify the insertion point. Choose the **Dialog** option from the command prompt; the **Generate Section/Elevation** dialog box will be displayed, as shown in Figure 8-4. Choose the **Select Objects** button in the **Selection Set** area of the dialog box; you will be prompted to select the objects that are to be included in the section view. After selecting the object to be sectioned, press ENTER. Now, you need to define the type of section result. In AutoCAD MEP, you can display two types of section results by selecting their respective radio buttons from the **Result Type** area of the dialog box. Both these options of generating section views are discussed next.

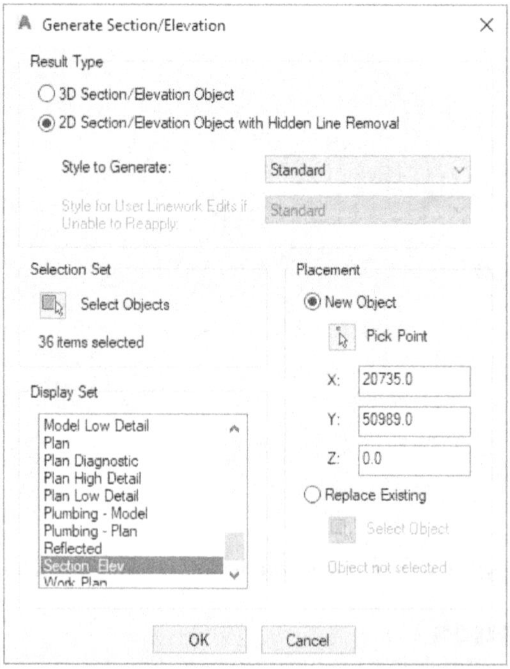

Figure 8-4 *The* ***Generate Section/Elevation*** *dialog box*

3D Section/Elevation Object

This radio button is used for creating 3D section view of a building. If you select this radio button while creating the section view, the section will be created three dimensionally, as shown in Figure 8-5.

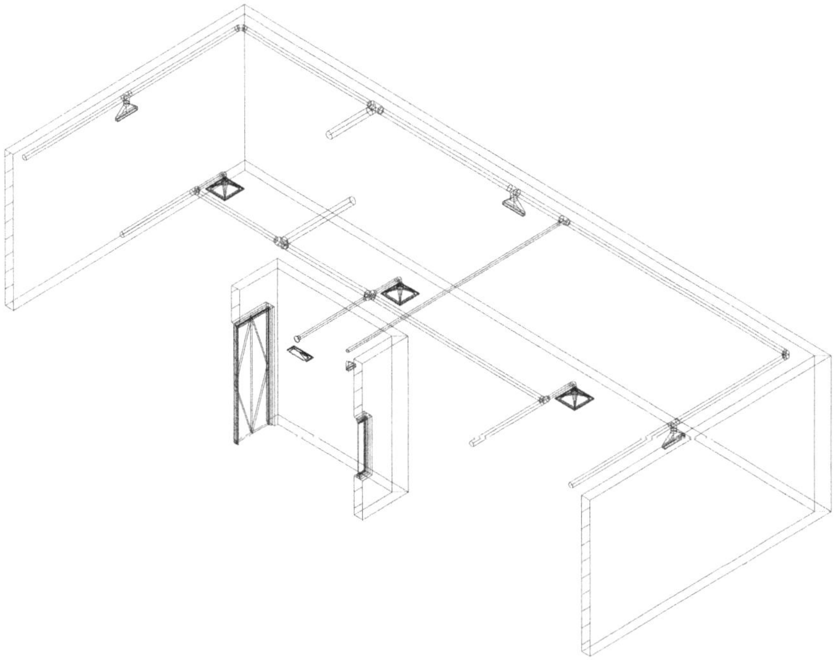

Figure 8-5 The 3D section view of the building

2D Section/Elevation Object with Hidden Line Removal

This radio button is used for creating 2D section view of the building. Figure 8-6 shows a 2D section created.

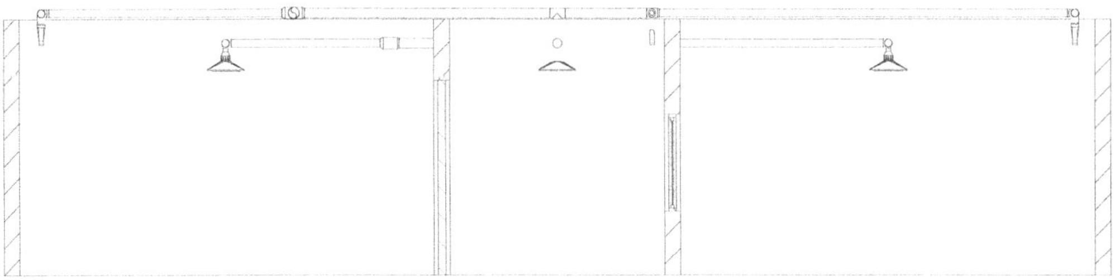

Figure 8-6 The drawing after creating 2D section

CREATING HORIZONTAL SECTION

The **Horizontal Section** tool is used to create a section of the building bounded by two horizontal planes. To create a horizontal section, choose the **Horizontal Section** tool from the **Section & Elevation** panel of the **Home** tab in the **Ribbon**; you will be prompted to select a corner for horizontal section. Click in the drawing area to specify the first corner of the section plane; you will be prompted to specify the other diagonal corner point of the section plane. Click to specify the point; you will be prompted to specify elevation of the current section plane. Enter the elevation value at the command prompt; you will be prompted to specify the depth of the section. Enter the desired value at the command bar; section lines will be created. Now, press the ESC key to exit the tool. To create a section, select the created section lines from the drawing area; the **Building Section Line** contextual tab will be displayed in the **Ribbon**. Choose the **Generate Section** tool from the **Modify** panel in the contextual tab; you will be prompted to specify the insertion point. Choose the **Dialog** option from the command prompt; the **Generate Section/Elevation** dialog box will be displayed. Create the section as discussed earlier. The options in the **Building Section Line** contextual tab have already been discussed.

CREATING A SECTION LINE

The **Section Line** tool is used to create a section line passing through any user defined points. To create a section line, choose the **Section Line** tool from the **Section & Elevation** panel of the **Home** tab in the **Ribbon**; you will be prompted to specify start point of the section line. Click in the drawing area to specify the start point of the section; you will be prompted to specify the next point of the section line. End the section line by specifying the end point of section line; you will be prompted again to specify the next point for the section line. Press ENTER to exit creating section line; you will be prompted to specify length of the bounding box. Enter the length of the bounding box in the command prompt; the section line will be created. Now, press the ESC key to exit the tool. By default, model extent is used as the bounding box height. You can specify the height of the bounding box as discussed earlier. To create section view, select the section line; the **Building Section Line** contextual tab will be displayed in the **Ribbon**. Rest of the procedure to create section view is same as discussed earlier.

CREATING ELEVATION LINE

The **Elevation Line** tool is used to create an elevation line passing through user defined points. To create an elevation line, choose the **Elevation Line** tool from the **Section & Elevation** panel of the **Home** tab in the **Ribbon**; you will be prompted to specify the start point of the elevation line. Click in the drawing area to specify the start point of the elevation line; you will be prompted to specify the end point of the elevation. Click in the drawing area to specify the end point of the elevation line; the elevation line and the elevation plane will be created. Now, press the ESC key to exit the tool. Select the elevation line; the **PROPERTIES** palette will be displayed. The plane created is square in shape. You can change the length of Side1 and Side2 by using the corresponding options in the **PROPERTIES** palette, as shown in Figure 8-7. You can also change the angle values of the plane by using the **Angle1** and **Angle2** edit boxes.

Now, select the elevation line; the **Building Section Line** contextual tab will be displayed in the **Ribbon**. Using the options available in the contextual tab, you can create the section as discussed earlier.

CREATING HIDDEN LINE PROJECTION

The **Hidden Line Projection** tool is used to create 2D projections with hidden projection lines of the model. To create the projection, choose the **Hidden Line Projection** tool from the expanded **Section & Elevation** panel of the **Home** tab in the **Ribbon**; you will be prompted to select objects for creating a projection. Select all objects of the model to generate the 2D projections with hidden lines and then press ENTER; you will be prompted to specify the insertion point for the projection. Click in the drawing area to specify the insertion point; you will be prompted to specify whether the projection is to be inserted in plan view or not. Enter **Y** at the command prompt if you want to insert it in the plan view. Otherwise an isometric view will be inserted in the drawing. Figure 8-8 shows a model with its hidden line projection.

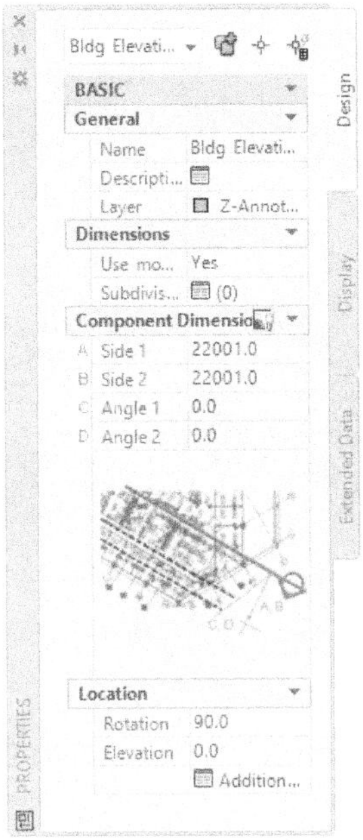

*Figure 8-7 The **PROPERTIES** palette*

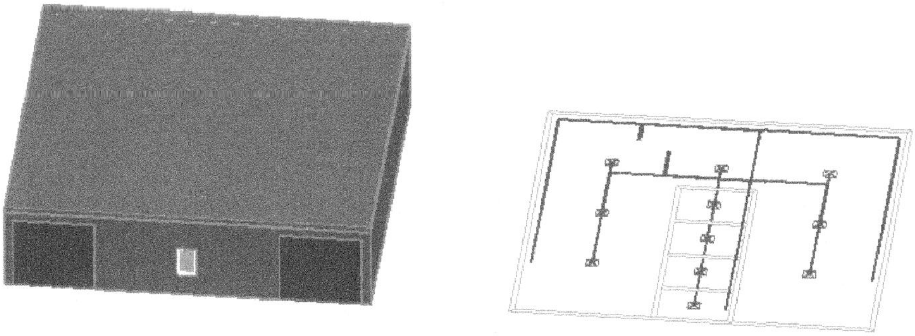

Figure 8-8 The model with its hidden line projection

SLICING THE MODEL

The **Quick Slice** tool is used to extract a polyline outline of the slice created using the model. To extract the outline, choose the **Quick Slice** tool from the expanded **Section & Elevation** panel in the **Home** tab of the **Ribbon**; you will be prompted to select the objects to be sliced. Select the objects to be sliced and press ENTER; you will be prompted to select first point for slicing. Click in the drawing area to specify the first point; you will be prompted to specify the second point for slicing. Click to specify the second point; the slice will be created through the specified points. Figure 8-9 shows a model sliced using the **Quick Slice** tool.

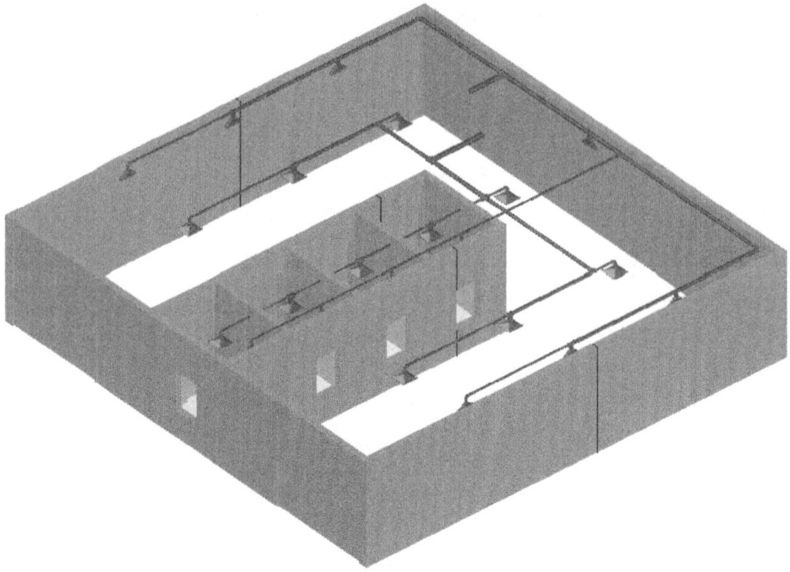

Figure 8-9 *The model sliced using the* ***Quick Slice*** *tool*

REFRESHING SECTIONS AND ELEVATIONS IN A BATCH

The **Batch Refresh** tool is used to refresh all the 2D sections and elevations created in the current project or in the specified folder. To refresh the 2D sections and elevations, choose the **Batch Refresh** tool from the expanded **Section & Elevation** panel of the **Home** tab in the **Ribbon**; the **Batch Refresh 2D Section/Elevations** dialog box will be displayed, as shown in Figure 8-10. There are two radio buttons available in this dialog box: **Current Project** and **Folder**. Select the **Current Project** radio button if you want to refresh all the 2D sections and elevations created in the current project. If you want to refresh all the 2D sections and elevations in the drawings of a specific folder then select the **Folder** radio button. After selecting the desired radio button, choose the **Begin** button; all the section and elevation views available in the selected drawings will be updated and its status will be displayed in the **Status** area of the dialog box.

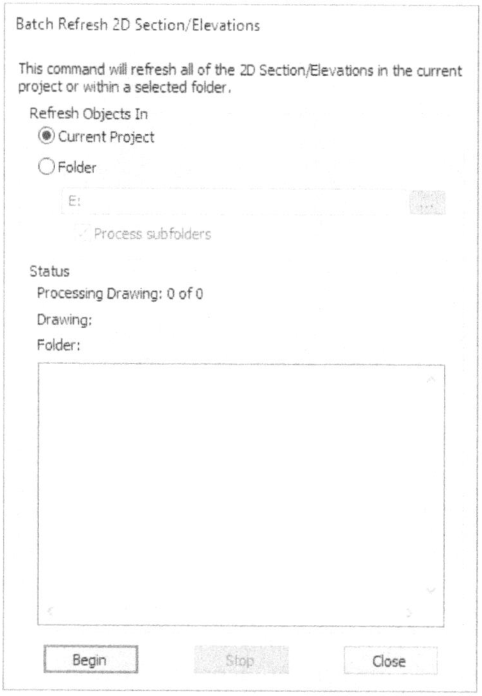

Figure 8-10 *The* ***Batch Refresh 2D Section/Elevations*** *dialog box*

INSERTING DETAIL COMPONENTS

The detail components are used to represent AutoCAD MEP components with detailed parameters. To insert detail components, choose the **Detail Components** tool from the **Details** panel of the **Home** tab in the **Ribbon**; the **Detail Component Manager** dialog box will be displayed, as shown in Figure 8-11. In the left area of this dialog box, various categories of the detail components are displayed. Click on the plus sign adjacent to the desired category; the sub-categories available in it will be displayed. Click on the plus sign adjacent to the desired sub-category; various components in that sub-category will be displayed, as shown in Figure 8-12. Select a component from the list; various sizes for the selected component will be displayed in the table available at the bottom of the dialog box. Select the desired size from the table; the **Insert Component** button will be activated. Choose the **Insert Component** button from the dialog box; you will be prompted to specify the insertion point for the component. Click on the desired location in the drawing area to specify the insertion point; you will be prompted again to specify the insertion point. Click to specify the insertion point for another component if required or press ENTER to exit the tool. You can change the view of the component while placing it by using the options in the **View** drop-down list in the **PROPERTIES** palette.

Some of the options available in the **Detail Component Manager** are discussed next.

Edit Database

This button is available at the right of the **Current detail component database** drop-down list. On choosing this button, you can edit the database available for detail components. After choosing this button, the buttons available below will be activated.

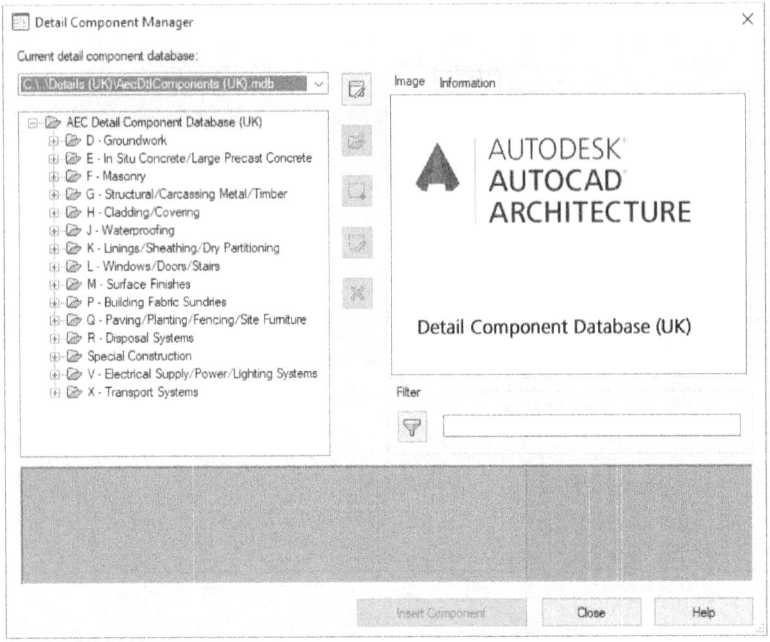

Figure 8-11 The ***Detail Component Manager*** *dialog box*

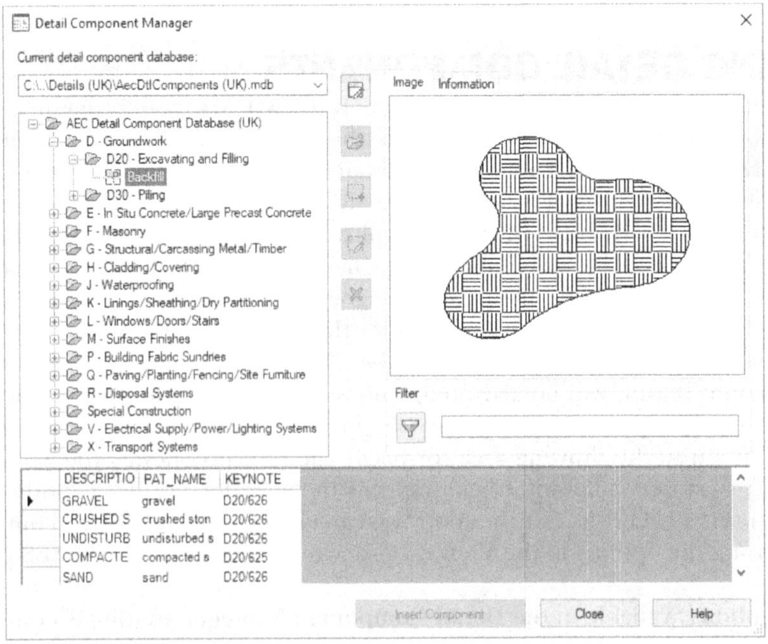

Figure 8-12 The ***Detail Component Manager*** *dialog box with the component selected*

Add Group

This button is available below the **Edit Database** button and is used to add groups to the database. To add groups, choose the **Add Group** button; the **Add Group** dialog box will be displayed, as shown in Figure 8-13. The options available in this dialog box are discussed next.

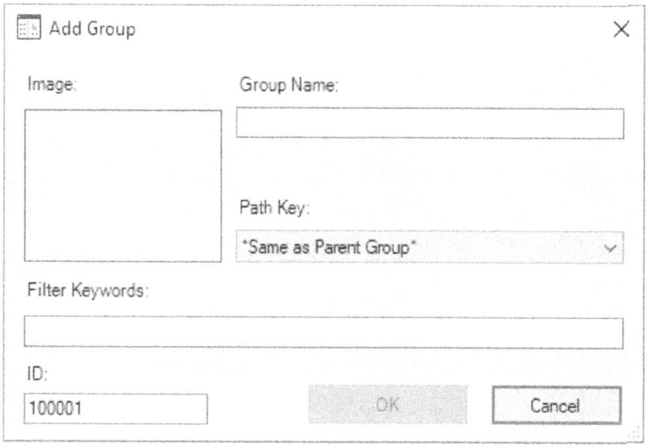

*Figure 8-13 The **Add Group** dialog box*

Group Name

This edit box is used to specify the name of the detail components group.

Path Key

The options in this drop-down list are used to identify the location of images and drawings for this group. By default, the **Same as Parent Group** option is selected in this drop-down list, so the path key is same as for the parent group.

Filter Keywords

This edit box is used to specify the keywords for searching components in the current group.

Add Component

This button is available below the **Add Group** button and is used to add components to the selected group. To add a component, choose the **Add Component** button; the **New Component** dialog box will be displayed, as shown in Figure 8-14. The options available in the **General** tab of this dialog box are discussed next.

Display Name

This edit box is used to specify the name of the component that will be displayed in the **Detail Component Manager** dialog box.

Table Name

This edit box is used to specify the name of the size table of the current component.

Recipe

This edit box is used to specify the name of the file that contains the method for creating the current component. Files having the **xml** extension can be inserted in this edit box.

Units

The options in this drop-down list are used to specify whether the current unit system is in mm or inches.

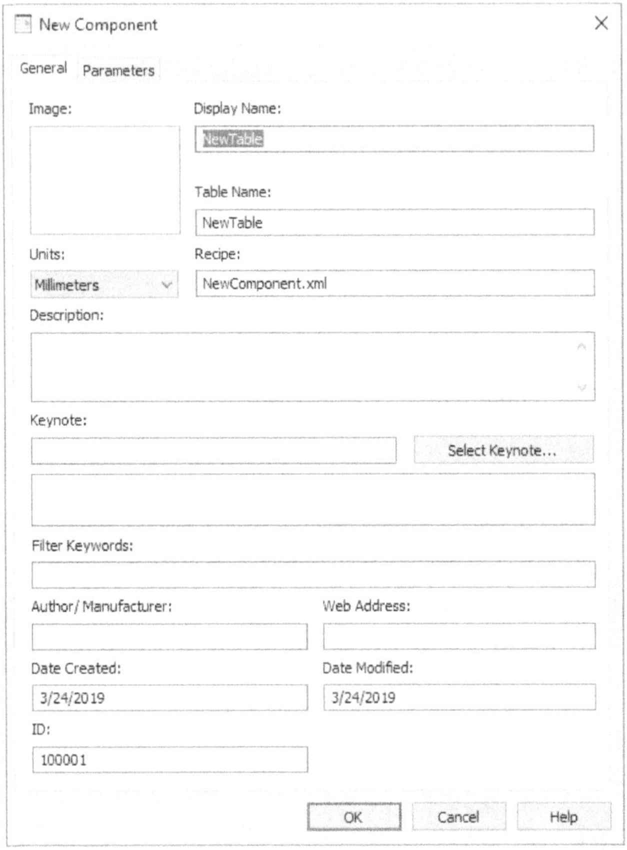

***Figure 8-14** The **New Component** dialog box*

Description

This edit box is used to specify the description about the component being created.

Keynote

This edit box is used to assign key notes about the component being created. You can also assign the key notes by selecting them from the **Select Keynote** dialog box. The **Select Keynote** dialog box will be displayed on choosing the **Select Keynote** button from the **New Components** dialog box, as shown in Figure 8-15. Click on the plus sign adjacent to the desired category and then the sub-category; the keynotes for various components in that sub-category will be displayed. Select the desired keynote and then choose the **OK** button to add the selected keynote. On adding the keynote, the description about the selected keynote will be displayed in the display box just below the **Keynote** edit box.

Filter Keywords

This edit box is used to specify keywords for the created component which will be displayed in the search list.

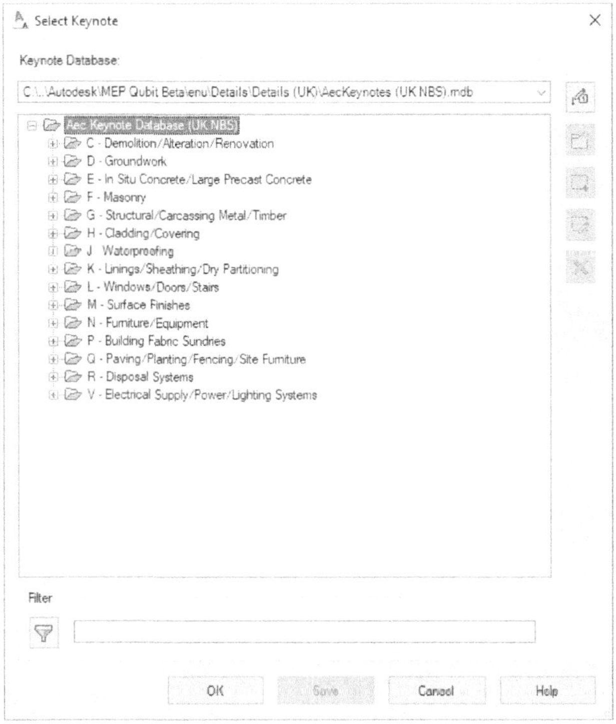

*Figure 8-15 The **Select Keynote** dialog box*

Author/Manufacturer

This edit box is used to specify the name of the author/manufacturer of the current component.

Web Address

This edit box is used to specify the website url of the component to be created.

Date Created

This display box is used to display the date on which the component was created.

Date Modified

This display box is used to display the date on which the component was modified. If you have created a new component, then the current date is displayed in this edit box.

ID

This edit box is used to assign a unique identity number to the current component. By default, the system provides a unique number in this edit box.

After specifying the desired values in the **General** tab, click on the **Parameters** tab to display the options related to the parameters of the current component, as shown in Figure 8-16. The options available in the **Parameters** tab of the dialog box are discussed next.

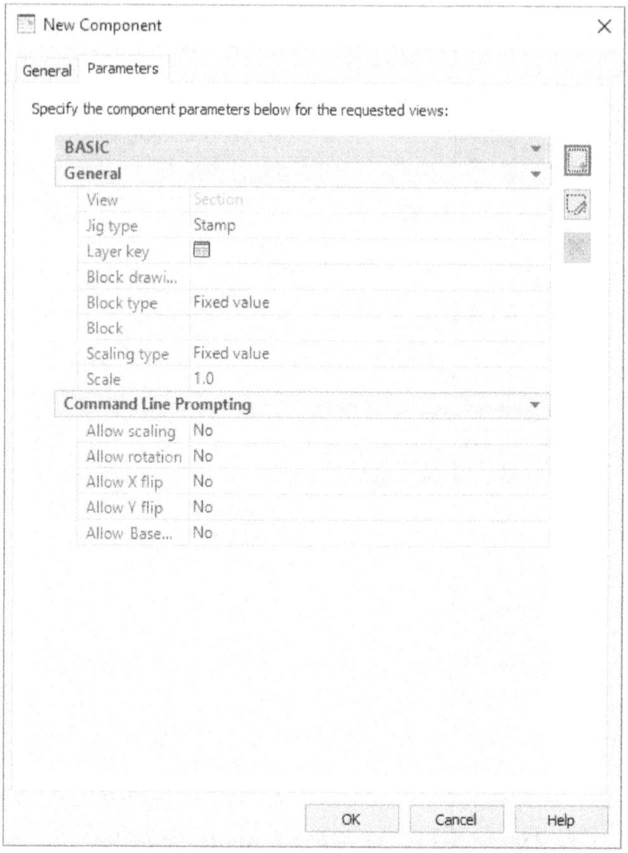

*Figure 8-16 The **New Component** dialog box with the **Parameters** tab chosen*

View

This field is used to specify the name of the view for which the current component will be available.

Jig type

The options in this drop-down list are used to specify the pattern in which the current component will be inserted in the drawing. There are six options available in this drop-down list: **Stamp**, **Bookends**, **Linear Array**, **Surface**, **Surface Linetype**, and **Surface Top**.

Layer Key

This field is used to specify a layer key for the current component. Click on this field; the **Select Layer Key** dialog box will be displayed, as shown in Figure 8-17. Select a layer key from the **Layer Key** column of the dialog box and choose the **OK** button to exit the dialog box. The **Layer Key** option is also available in the **Hatching** and **Linetype** rollouts of the dialog box and has the same function. These rollouts are displayed depending on the selection from the **Jig type** drop-down list.

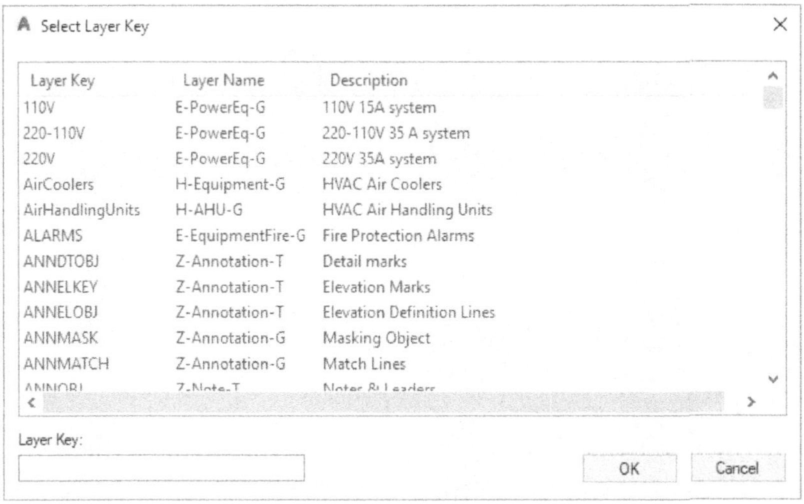

*Figure 8-17 The **Select Layer Key** dialog box*

Note

*1. The **Hatching** rollout will become available in the **Parameters** tab of the **New Components** dialog box when the **Surface** or **Surface Top** option is selected from the **Jig type** drop-down list.*

*2. The **Linetype** rollout will become available in the **Parameters** tab of the **New Components** dialog box when **Surface Linetype** is selected from the **Jig type** drop-down list.*

Block drawing location

The options in this drop-down list are used to select the location of block drawing for the component. Select the **Browse** option from the drop-down list to select a block drawing file from a user defined location; the **Select Block Library** dialog box will be displayed, as shown in Figure 8-18. Select the block drawing and then choose the **Open** button from the dialog box; the selected drawing will be used as a block for the current component.

Block type

The options in this drop-down list are used to select the type of block to be used for current component while inserting in the drawing. There are two options available in this drop-down list: **Fixed value** and **Database**. The **Fixed value** option is selected if the current block is fixed. The **Database** option is selected if you want to create the block of sizes dependent on the option selected in the database.

Block/Block field

This edit box is used to specify a name for the current drawing block.

Scaling type

The options in this drop-down list are used to specify the type of scaling to be used for scaling the current component. By default, the **Fixed value** option is selected in this drop-down list. You can select the **Database** option if you want to change the scale value depending on the option selected in the database.

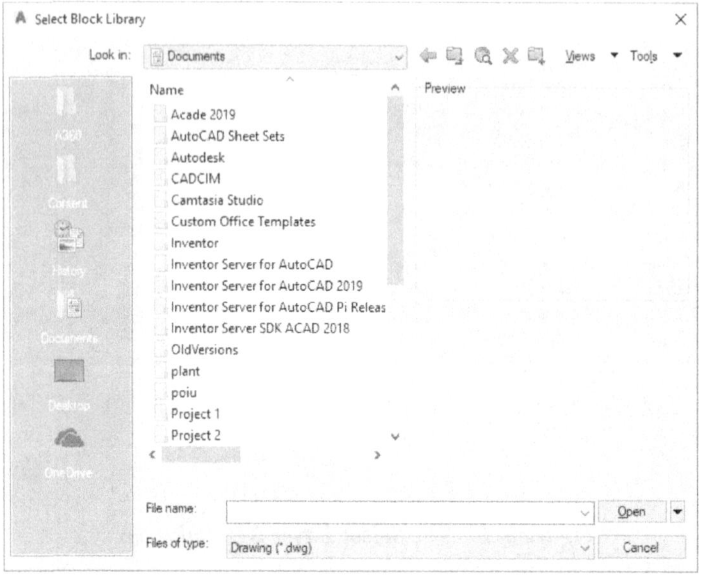

Figure 8-18 *The* ***Select Block Library*** *dialog box*

Scale/Scale field

These edit boxes are used to specify the value of scale. If the **Fixed value** option is selected in the **Scaling type** drop-down list then the **Scale** edit box will be displayed. You can specify an integral value in the **Scale** edit box. If the **Database** option is selected in the **Scaling Type** drop-down list, then the **Scale field** edit box will be displayed. By default, the **S_SCALE** value is displayed in this edit box.

Allow scaling

There are two options available in this drop-down list: **Yes** and **No**. If you select the **Yes** option in this drop-down list, you will be prompted to scale the component while inserting it in the drawing.

Allow rotation

There are two options available in this drop-down list: **Yes** and **No**. If you select the **Yes** option in this drop-down list, you will be prompted to rotate the component while inserting it in the drawing.

Allow X flip

There are two options available in this drop-down list: **Yes** and **No**. If you select the **Yes** option in this drop-down list, you will be prompted to flip the component about X axis while inserting it in the drawing.

Allow Y flip

There are two options available in this drop-down list: **Yes** and **No**. If you select the **Yes** option in this drop-down list, you will be prompted to flip the component about Y axis while inserting it in the drawing.

Allow Base point

There are two options available in this drop-down list: **Yes** and **No**. If you select the **Yes** option, you will be prompted to specify the base point for the component while inserting it in the drawing.

Create new view

This button is available at the top right corner of the **New Component** dialog box in the **Parameters** tab. This tool is used to create more views of the component. To create more views, choose the **Create new view** button from the dialog box; the **New Component View** dialog box will be displayed, as shown in Figure 8-19.

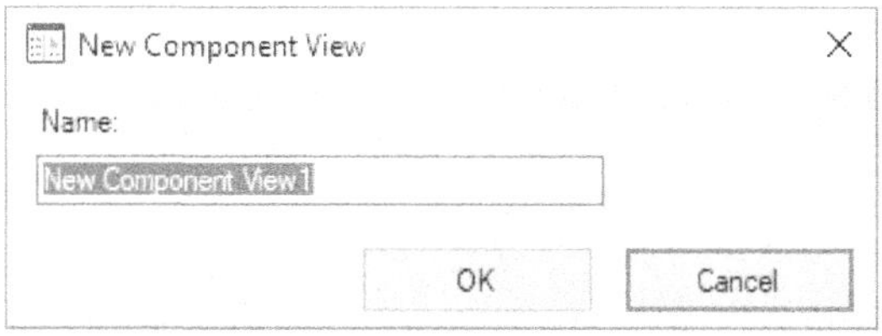

***Figure 8-19** The **New Component View** dialog box*

Specify the name of the view in the **Name** edit box available in this dialog box and choose the **OK** button from the dialog box; a new component view with the specified name will be added to the **View** drop-down list.

Rename view

This button is available below the **Create new view** tool. This tool is used to rename the current selected view of the component. To rename the view, choose the **Rename view** button; the **Rename View** dialog box will be displayed, as shown in Figure 8-20. Specify the name of the view and then choose the **OK** button; the current view will be renamed.

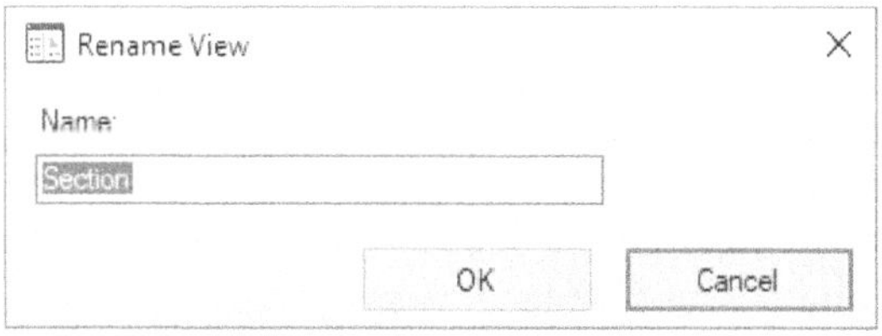

***Figure 8-20** The **Rename View** dialog box*

Delete view

This button is available below the **Rename view** tool. This tool is used to delete the current selected view of the component. To delete the current view, choose the **Delete view** button; the **Delete Component View** dialog box will be displayed, as shown in Figure 8-21. Choose the **Yes** button if you want to delete the current view. This tool cannot be used to delete the default Section view.

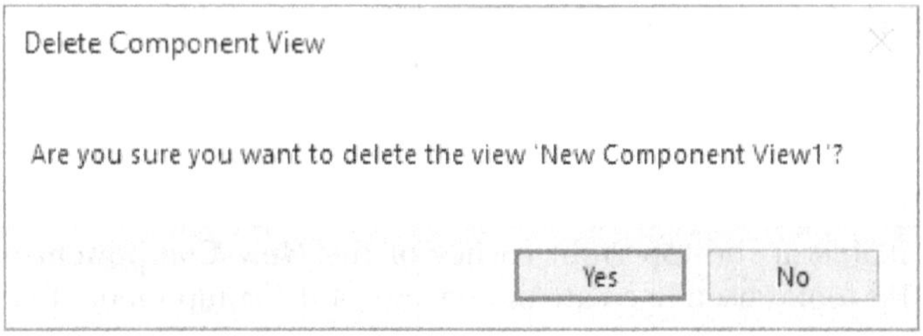

Figure 8-21 The ***Delete Component View*** *dialog box*

After specifying the desired options, choose the **OK** button from the **New Component** dialog box; the component will be added to the selected category of components in the **Detail Component Manager** dialog box.

Edit

This button is available below the **Add Component** tool. It is used to edit current component. To edit the selected component, choose the **Edit** button; the **Component Properties** dialog box will be displayed, as shown in Figure 8-22. Alternatively, this tool can be accessed by right-clicking on the component and selecting the **Edit** option or by clicking the component in the data base when the **Edit Database** option is active. The options in this dialog box are similar to those discussed for the **New Component** dialog box.

Figure 8-22 The ***Component Properties*** *dialog box*

Delete

This button is used to delete the selected component from the **Detail Component Manager** dialog box. To delete a component, choose the **Delete** button; the **Confirm Component Delete** dialog box will be displayed, as shown in Figure 8-23. Choose the **Yes** button from the dialog box; the selected component will be deleted.

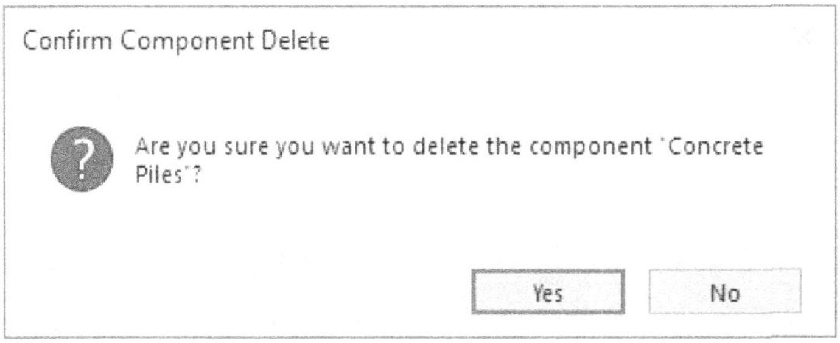

***Figure 8-23** The **Confirm Component Delete** dialog box*

CREATING SCHEDULES

The schedules are the tables that are used to represent the information regarding the selected components. Some of the schedules available in AutoCAD MEP are: Plumbing Fixture Schedule, Air Terminal Devices Schedules, and Fan Schedules. The tools to create these schedules are discussed next.

Air Terminal Devices Schedule

This tool is available in the **Schedules** drop-down in the **Annotation** panel of the **Home** tab of the **Ribbon** when the **HVAC** option is selected in the **Workspace Switching** flyout. To create an air terminal device schedule, choose the **Air Terminal Devices Schedule** tool from the **Schedules** drop-down; you will be prompted to select objects or press ENTER to schedule external drawings. Select the air terminals that you want in the schedule and then press ENTER; the schedule will get attached to the cursor and you will be prompted to specify the upper left corner of the table. Click in the drawing area to specify the upper left corner of the schedule; you will be prompted to specify the lower right corner of the schedule. Click in the drawing area to specify the lower right corner of the schedule; the table will be created, as shown in Figure 8-24. By default, the ? mark is displayed in all the fields of the table. To update the entries in this schedule, select the schedule; the **Schedule Table** contextual tab will be added in the **Ribbon**, as shown in Figure 8-25. Choose the **Add All Property Sets** tool from the **Modify** panel of the **Schedule Table** contextual tab in the **Ribbon**; the fields in the table will display the parameters related to the selected devices. The options available in the contextual tab are discussed next.

General Panel

The tools in this panel are used to modify the general parameters of a schedule. The options in this panel are discussed next.

Select Similar

This tool is used to select all the items in the current drawing similar to the selected one.

MECHANICAL AIR TERMINAL DEVICES SCHEDULE								
TAG	SIZE	DESCRIPTION	CONSTRUCTION			BASIS OF DESIGN		NOTES
			MATERIAL	FINISH	DISCHARGE PATTERN	MANUFACTURER	MODEL OR SERIES	
?	?	?	?	?	?	?	?	?
?	?	?	?	?	?	?	?	?
?	?	?	?	?	?	?	?	?
?	?	?	?	?	?	?	?	?
?	?	?	?	?	?	?	?	?
?	?	?	?	?	?	?	?	?
?	?	?	?	?	?	?	?	?
?	?	?	?	?	?	?	?	?
?	?	?	?	?	?	?	?	?
?	?	?	?	?	?	?	?	?
?	?	?	?	?	?	?	?	?
?	?	?	?	?	?	?	?	?
?	?	?	?	?	?	?	?	?
?	?	?	?	?	?	?	?	?
?	?	?	?	?	?	?	?	?
?	?	?	?	?	?	?	?	?
?	?	?	?	?	?	?	?	?
?	?	?	?	?	?	?	?	?
?	?	?	?	?	?	?	?	?
?	?	?	?	?	?	?	?	?
?	?	?	?	?	?	?	?	?
?	?	?	?	?	?	?	?	?

***Figure 8-24** The Air Terminal Devices Schedule*

***Figure 8-25** The **Schedule Table** contextual tab*

Isolate Objects

The tools in this drop-down are used to display/hide objects in the drawing area and are discussed next.

Isolate Objects

This tool is used to display only the objects that are selected in the drawing. This tool is available in the **Isolate Objects** drop-down list.

Hide Objects

This tool is used to hide the selected object in the drawing. This tool is available in the **Isolate Objects** drop-down list.

End Isolation

This tool is used to end the isolation in the drawing. This tool is available in the **Isolate Objects** drop-down list.

Edit Style

The tools in this drop-down are used to edit styles and definitions of the schedule tables. You can also change the text styles and property data formats used in the schedule tables. The tools available in this drop-down are discussed next.

Edit Style

This tool is used to change the style of the selected table. To change the style of the selected schedule, choose the **Edit Style** tool from the **Edit Style** drop-down; the

Schedule Table Style Properties dialog box will be displayed, as shown in Figure 8-26. The options in this dialog box are discussed next.

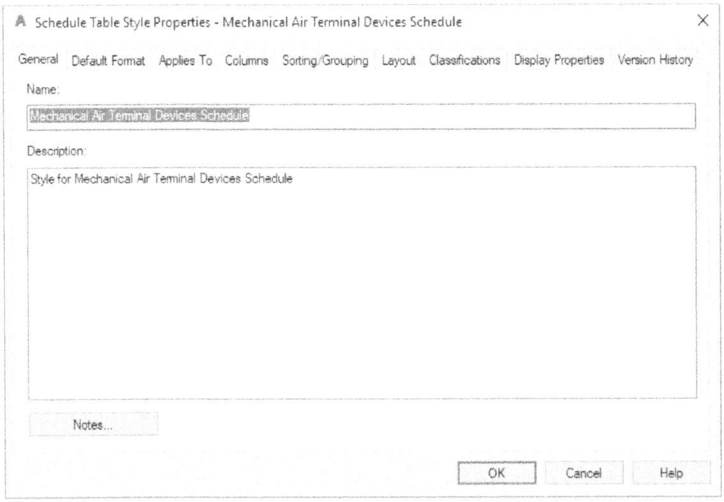

***Figure 8-26** The **Schedule Table Style Properties** dialog box*

The options in the **General** tab are used to specify the name and description of the current table style.

The options in the **Default Format** tab are used to specify the format such as text style, text height, text alignment, and cell size of the table.

The options in the **Applies To** tab are used to select the categories for which the current selected style will be applied.

The options in the **Columns** tab are used to add or delete columns in the table.

The options in the **Sorting/Grouping** tab are used to sort or group the values specified in the table.

The options in the **Layout** tab are used to change layout of the table. Using these options, you can change the format of the title, column header, rows header, and so on.

The options in the **Classifications** tab are used to classify the values in the table.

The options in the **Display Properties** tab are used to edit the display style of the table. Using these options, you can change properties such as colors and layers.

The options in the **Version History** tab are used to display or edit the version history of the current table.

Schedule Table Style

This tool is used to change the style of the selected schedule table. To change the style of the selected schedule table, choose the **Schedule Table Styles** tool from the **Edit**

Style drop-down; the **Style Manager** dialog box will be displayed. Click on the + sign adjacent to the **Schedule Table Style** node and choose the require schedule style, as shown in Figure 8-27.

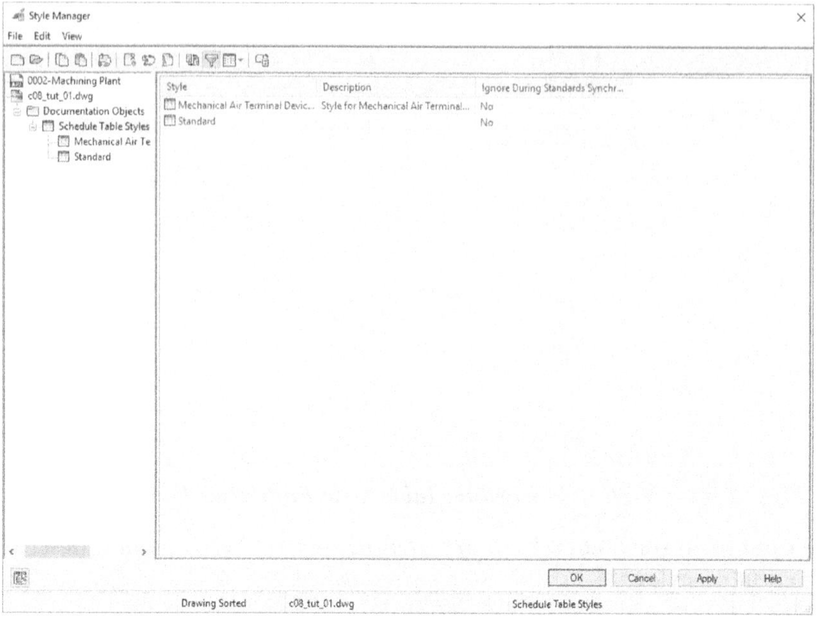

Figure 8-27 *The* ***Style Manager*** *displayed on choosing the* ***Schedule Table Styles*** *tool*

The options in various tabs in the **Style Manager** are same as those discussed in the **Schedule Table Style Properties** dialog box.

Classification Definitions

This tool is used to change the classification style used in the current table. To change the classification style, choose the **Classification Definitions** tool from the **Edit Style** drop-down; the **Style Manager** will be displayed, as shown in Figure 8-28. Select a type from the left pane of the **Style Manager** and the related options will be displayed in the right pane of the dialog box. Using these options, you can change the style of classification of the components in the table.

Property Set Definitions

This tool is used to change the definitions of property set for the selected property. To change the definition of the property sets, choose the **Property Set Definitions** tool from the **Edit Style** drop-down; the **Style Manager** will be displayed, as shown in Figure 8-29. On selecting a part from the left pane, the options related to the selected part are displayed in the right area of dialog box. Using these options, you can change the definition of the property sets used in the schedule table.

Property Data Formats

This tool is used to change the format data specified in the schedule table. To change the data format, choose the **Property Data Formats** tool from the **Edit Style** drop-down; the **Style Manager** dialog box will be displayed, as shown in Figure 8-30. Using the options available in this dialog box, you can change the format of the properties.

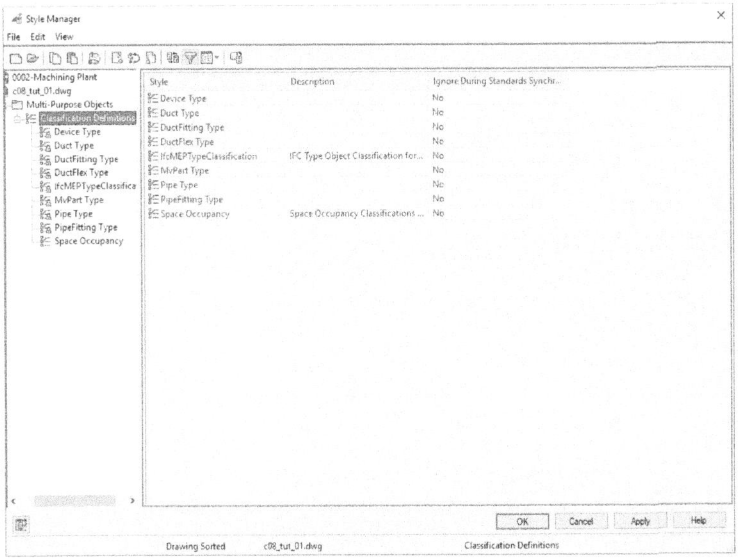

Figure 8-28 The ***Style Manager*** *displayed on choosing the* ***Classification Definitions*** *tool*

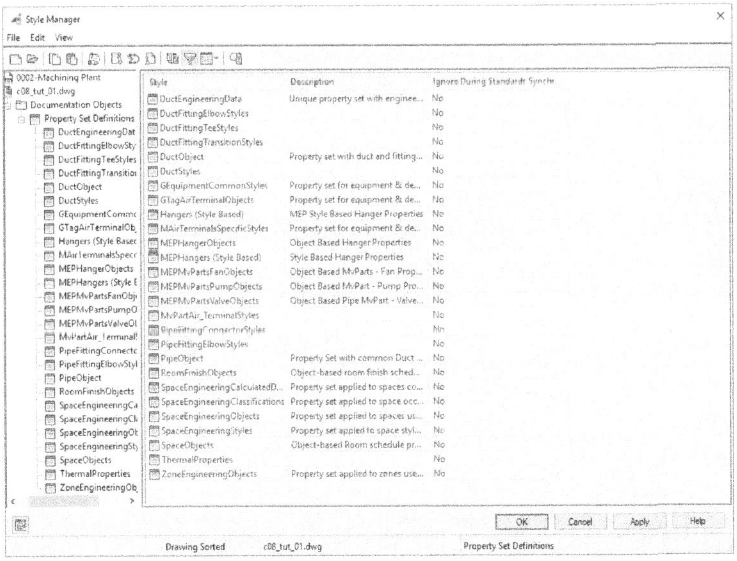

Figure 8-29 The ***Style Manager*** *displayed on choosing the* ***Property Set Definitions*** *tool*

Text Styles

This tool is used to change the text style in the schedule table. To change the text style, choose the **Text Styles** tool from the **Edit Style** drop-down; the **Text Style** dialog box will be displayed, as shown in Figure 8-31. Using the options in this dialog box, you can change the style of the text in the table.

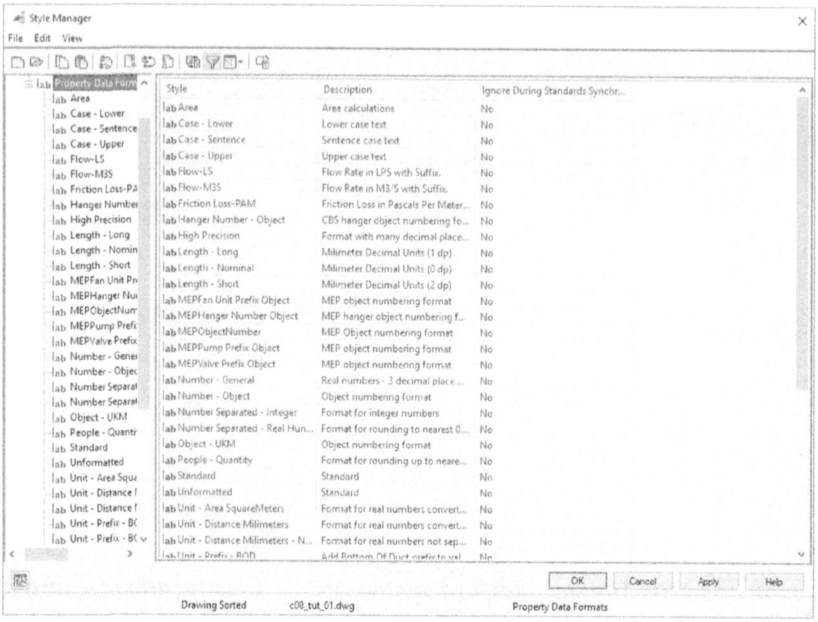

*Figure 8-30 The **Style Manager** displayed on choosing the **Property Data Formats** tool*

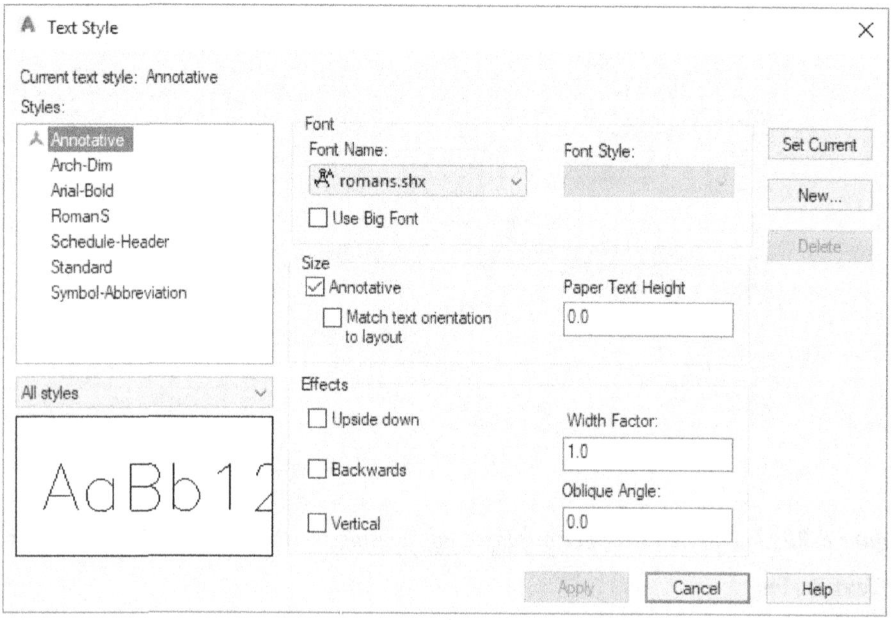

*Figure 8-31 The **Text Style** dialog box*

Copy Style

This tool is used to copy the style of an existing object and then create a new style based on that style. To copy a style, choose the **Copy Style** tool from the **General** panel of the **Schedule table** tab; the **Schedule Table Style Properties** dialog box, as shown in Figure 8-32. The options in this dialog box have already been discussed.

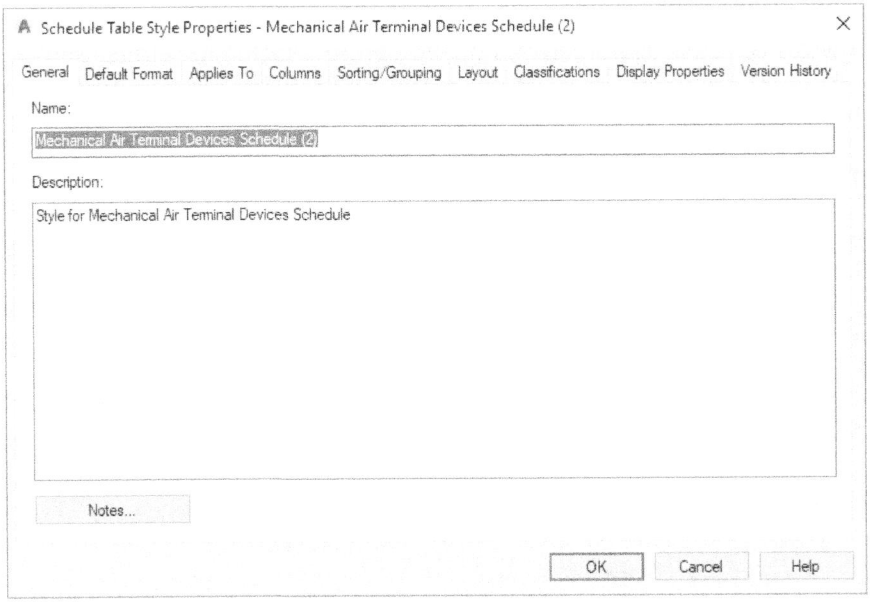

Figure 8-32 The ***Schedule Table Style Properties*** *dialog box*

Modify Panel

The tools in this panel are used to modify the properties of a schedule. The tools in this panel are discussed next.

Update

This tool is used to update the fields in the table that are not up to date.

Edit Table Cell

This tool is used to edit a table cell in the schedule. To do so, choose the **Edit Table Cell** tool; you will be prompted to select a schedule table cell. Select a cell from the table; the **Edit Referenced Property Set Data** dialog box will be displayed, as shown in Figure 8-33. Using the fields available in this dialog box, you can change the properties of a table cell.

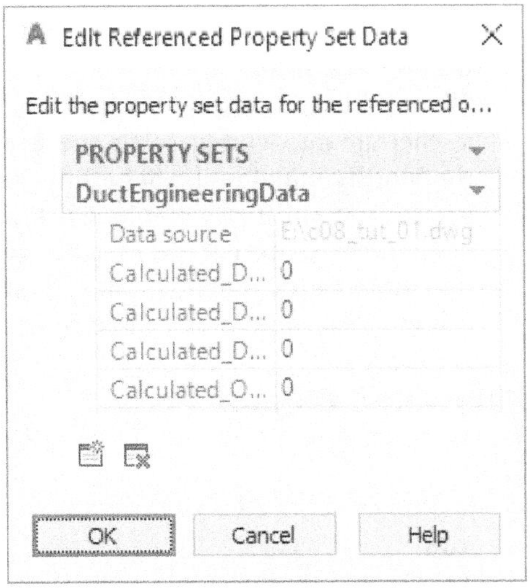

Figure 8-33 The ***Edit Referenced Property Set Data*** *dialog box*

Note

If you select the cell in which the data comes from a referenced style or definition, then the ***AutoCAD MEP 2022 - English*** *message box will be displayed. The message box will prompt you to edit the data affecting the other data. Choose the* ***Yes*** *button from the message box; the* ***Edit Property Set Data*** *dialog will be displayed.*

Add All Property Sets

This tool is used to add all property sets in the table for which ? mark will be displayed in the table. To add the property sets, choose the **Add All Property Sets** tool from the contextual tab; the property sets in the table will be displayed automatically.

Export

This tool is used to export the selected table in external formats. To export a table, select the table and then choose the **Export** tool from the **Modify** panel in the **Schedule Table** contextual tab; the **Export Schedule Table** dialog box will be displayed, as shown in Figure 8-34. Choose the desired file format from the **Save As Type** drop-down list in the **Export Schedule Table** dialog box and then choose the **OK** button; the table will be exported to the format selected in the **Save As Type** drop-down list. To change the location of the file to be exported, choose the **Browse** button and specify the desired location.

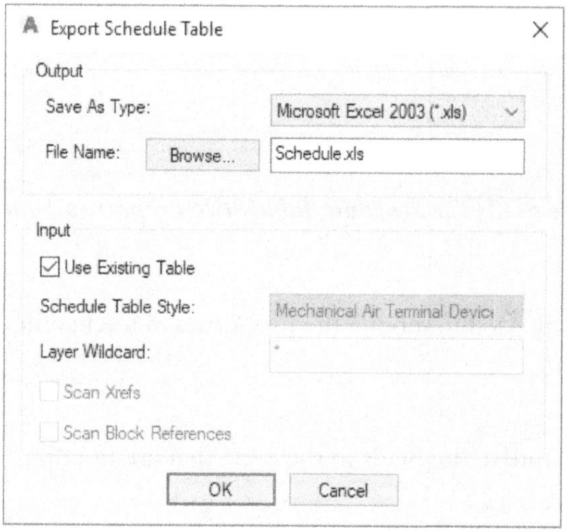

*Figure 8-34 The **Export Schedule Table** dialog box*

Convert to Table

This tool is used to convert a schedule into a table which can be edited directly. To convert a schedule into a table, select the schedule and then choose the **Convert to Table** tool from the **Modify** panel in the **Schedule Table** contextual tab; you will be prompted to specify an insertion point for the table. Click in the drawing area to specify the insertion point; the table will be placed at the specified point. To edit any of the cell in the table, select the cell; the **Table Cell** contextual tab will be added in the **Ribbon**. Using the options available in this tab, you can edit the table cells.

Scheduled Objects Panel

The tools in this panel are used to modify the objects in the schedule. These tools are discussed next.

Add

This tool is used to add an object into the selected schedule table. To do so, choose the **Add** tool; you will be prompted to select the objects to be added to the table. Select the air terminals that you want to add to the schedule table and then press ENTER; the selected objects will be added to the schedule table.

Remove

This tool is used to remove an object from the selected schedule table. To do so, choose the **Remove** tool; you will be prompted to select the objects to be removed from the table. Select the air terminals that you want to remove from the schedule table and then press ENTER; the selected objects will be removed from the schedule table.

Reselect

This tool is used to clear all entries in the selected schedule table. To do so, choose the **Reselect** tool; you will be prompted to select the new objects that you want to add to the table. Select the air terminals and then press ENTER; the selected objects will be added to the schedule table and all the previous entries will be removed.

Show

This tool is used to show the selected entity from the schedule table in the drawing area. To do so, choose the **Show** tool; you will be prompted to select schedule table entity. Select the entity; the selected entity will be highlighted in the drawing area.

Fan Schedule

This tool is available in the **Schedules** drop-down of the **Annotation** panel in the **Home** tab of the **Ribbon** when the **HVAC** option is selected in the **Workspace Switching** flyout. To create a fan schedule, choose the **Fan Schedule** tool; you will be prompted to select the objects. The procedure for creating a fan schedule is similar to the procedure for creating an air terminal devices schedule.

VAV Fan Powered Box (Electric Heat) Schedule

This tool is available in the **Schedules** drop-down of the **Annotation** panel in the **Home** tab of the **Ribbon** when the **HVAC** option is selected in the **Workspace Switching** flyout. To create a VAV fan powered box (electric heat) schedule, choose the **VAV Fan Powered Box (Electric Heat) Schedule** tool; you will be prompted to select the objects. The procedure for creating this type of schedule is similar to the procedure for creating an air terminal devices schedule.

Space Engineering Schedule

This tool is available in the **Schedules** drop-down of the **Annotation** panel in the **Home** tab of the **Ribbon** when the **HVAC** option is selected in the **Workspace Switching** flyout. To create a space engineering schedule, choose the **Space Engineering Schedule** tool; you will be prompted to select the objects. The procedure for creating a space engineering schedule is similar to the procedure for creating an air terminal devices schedule.

Duct Quantity Schedule

This tool is available in the **Schedules** drop-down of the **Annotation** panel in the **Home** tab of the **Ribbon** when the **HVAC** option is selected in the **Workspace Switching** flyout. To create a duct quantity schedule, choose the **Duct Quantity Schedule** tool; you will be prompted to select the objects. The procedure for creating a duct quantity schedule is similar to the procedure for creating an air terminal devices schedule.

Duct Fabrication Contract Schedule

This tool is available in the **Schedules** drop-down of the **Annotation** panel in the **Home** tab of the **Ribbon** when the **HVAC** option is selected in the **Workspace Switching** flyout. To create a duct fabrication contract schedule, choose the **Duct Fabrication Contract Schedule** tool; you will be prompted to select the objects. The procedure for creating a duct fabrication contract schedule is similar to the procedure for creating an air terminal devices schedule.

You can create a user defined schedule using the **Table** tool. This tool is discussed next.

Table

The **Table** tool is available in all the workspaces. To create a table, choose this tool from the **Schedule** drop-down in the **Annotation** panel of the **Home** tab in the **Ribbon**; the **Insert Table** dialog box will be displayed, as shown in Figure 8-35. The options in this dialog box are discussed next.

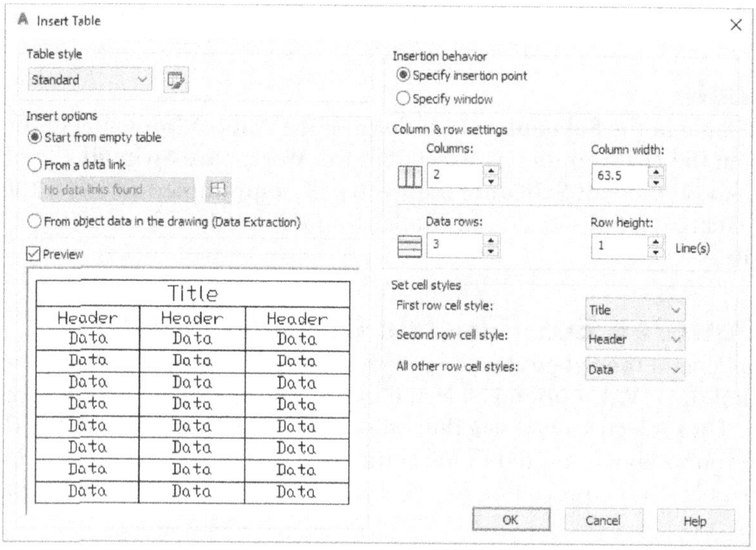

***Figure 8-35** The **Insert Table** dialog box*

Table style

The options in the **Table style** drop-down list are used to select a table style for the current table. You can edit the selected table style by using the options available in the **Table Style** dialog box. To invoke the **Table Style** dialog box, choose the **Launch the Table Style dialog** button adjacent to the **Table style** drop-down list; the **Table Style** dialog box will be displayed, as shown in Figure 8-36.

Insert options

The radio buttons in this area are used to specify the insertion method of the table. There are three radio buttons available in this area: **Start from empty table**, **From a data link**, and **From**

object data in the drawing (Data Extraction). If the **Start from empty table** radio button is selected then the table inserted will be empty. If you select the **From a data link** radio button then the table inserted will have the data linked to an excel sheet created earlier. If the **From object data in the drawing (Data Extraction)** radio button is selected then the table inserted consists of data extracted by using the **Data Extraction** dialog box.

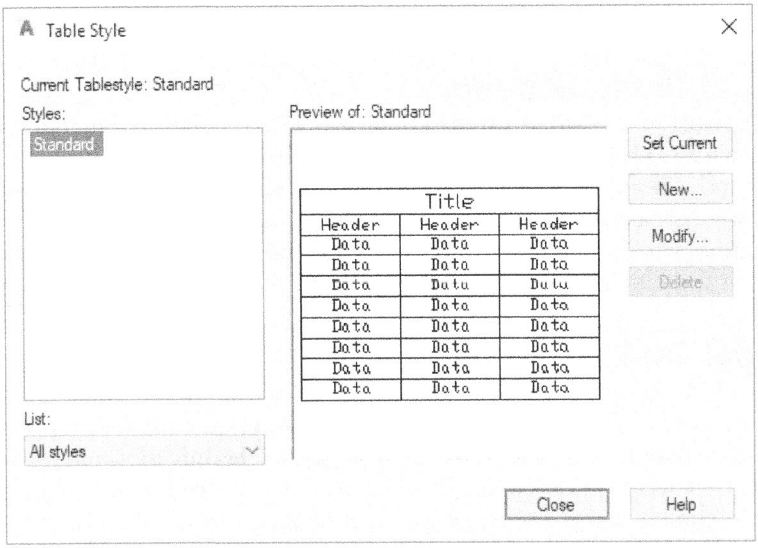

*Figure 8-36 The **Table Style** dialog box*

Insertion behavior

There are two radio buttons available in this area: **Specify insertion point** and **Specify window**. If the **Specify insertion point** radio button is selected then you will be prompted to specify the insertion point for the table. If you select the **Specify window** radio button from the **Insertion behavior** area then you will be prompted to create a window for inserting the table.

Column & row settings

The options in this area are used to specify the number of columns and rows for the table. You can also specify the width of the column, the number of rows, and the height of the rows by using the related spinners.

Set cell styles

The options in this area are used to specify the styles for the cells. By default, the style of first row cell is set for Title, cell style of second row is set for Header and the cell style of all the other rows is set for Data.

Pipe & Fitting Schedule

This tool is available in the **Schedules** drop-down of the **Annotation** panel in the **Home** tab of the **Ribbon** when the **Piping** option is selected in the **Workspace Switching** flyout. To create a pipe and fitting schedule, choose the **Pipe & Fitting Schedule** tool; you will be prompted to select the objects. Select the pipes and fittings. The procedure for creating a pipe and fitting schedule is similar to the procedure for creating an air terminal devices schedule.

Pipe Quantity

This tool is available in the **Schedules** drop-down of the **Annotation** panel in the **Home** tab of the **Ribbon** when the **Piping** option is selected in the **Workspace Switching** flyout. To create a pipe quantity schedule, choose the **Pipe Quantity** tool; you will be prompted to select the objects. Select the pipes in the drawing area. The procedure for creating a pipe quantity schedule is similar to the procedure for creating an air terminal devices schedule.

Mechanical Pump Schedule

This tool is available in the **Schedules** drop-down of the **Annotation** panel in the **Home** tab of the **Ribbon** when the **Piping** option is selected in the **Workspace Switching** flyout. To create a mechanical pump schedule, choose the **Mechanical Pump Schedule** tool; you will be prompted to select the objects. Select the pumps from the drawing area. The procedure for creating a mechanical pump schedule is similar to the procedure for creating an air terminal devices schedule.

Mechanical Tank Schedule

This tool is available in the **Schedules** drop-down of the **Annotation** panel in the **Home** tab of the **Ribbon** when the **Piping** option is selected in the **Workspace Switching** flyout. To create a mechanical tank schedule, choose the **Mechanical Tank Schedule** tool; you will be prompted to select the objects. Select the tanks in the drawing area. The procedure for creating a mechanical tank schedule is similar to the procedure for creating an air terminal devices schedule.

Device Schedule

This tool is available in the **Schedules** drop-down of the **Annotation** panel in the **Home** tab in the **Ribbon** when the **Electrical** option is selected in the **Workspace Switching** flyout. To create a device schedule, choose the **Device Schedule** tool; you will be prompted to select the objects. The procedure for creating a device schedule is similar to the procedure for creating an air terminal devices schedule.

Lighting Device Schedule

This tool is available in the **Schedules** drop-down of the **Annotation** panel in the **Home** tab of the **Ribbon** when the **Electrical** option is selected in the **Workspace Switching** flyout. To create a lighting device schedule, choose the **Lighting Device Schedule** tool; you will be prompted to select the objects. The procedure for creating a lighting device schedule is similar to the procedure for creating an air terminal devices schedule.

Conduit & Fitting Schedule

This tool is available in the **Schedules** drop-down of the **Annotation** panel in the **Home** tab of the **Ribbon** when the **Electrical** option is selected in the **Workspace Switching** flyout. To create a conduit and fitting schedule, choose the **Conduit & Fitting Schedule** tool; you will be prompted to select the objects. The procedure for creating a conduit and fitting schedule is similar to the procedure for creating an air terminal devices schedule.

Electrical & Mechanical Equipment Schedule

This tool is available in the **Schedules** drop-down of the **Annotation** panel in the **Home** tab of the **Ribbon** when the **Electrical** option is selected in the **Workspace Switching** flyout. To create an electrical and mechanical equipment schedule, choose the **Electrical & Mechanical Equipment Schedule** tool; you will be prompted to select the objects. The procedure for creating an electrical and mechanical equipment schedule is similar to the procedure for creating an air terminal devices schedule.

3-Phase Branch Panel Schedule

This tool is available in the **Schedules** drop-down of the **Annotation** panel in the **Home** tab of the **Ribbon** when the **Electrical** option is selected in the **Workspace Switching** flyout. To create a 3-phase branch panel schedule, choose the **3-Phase Branch Panel Schedule** tool; the **Panel Schedule** dialog box will be displayed, as shown in Figure 8-37. The options in this dialog box are discussed next.

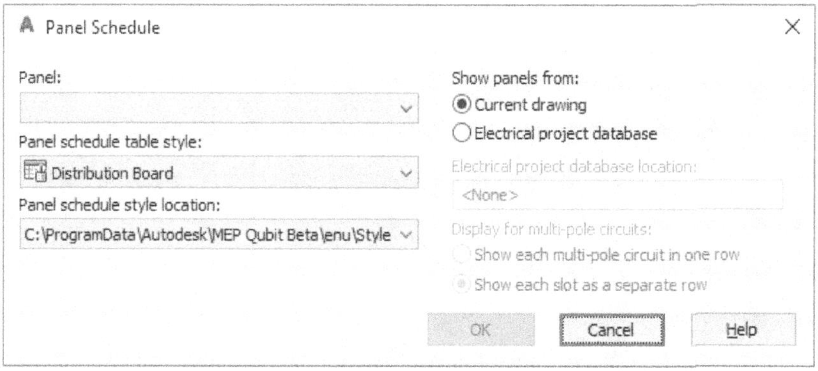

*Figure 8-37 The **Panel Schedule** dialog box*

Panel

The options in this drop-down list are used to select the panel for which the panel schedule is being created.

Panel schedule table style

The options in this drop-down list are used to specify the style of panel schedule. There are two options available in this drop-down list: **Distribution Board** and **Panel**. Select the **Distribution Board** option if you want to use the distribution board as the panel schedule table style. If you want to use panel as panel schedule table style then select the **Panel** option from the drop-down list.

Panel schedule style location

The options in this drop-down list are used to specify the location of panel schedule style. To specify a user defined location, choose the **Browse** option from the drop-down list; the **Select a file** dialog box will be displayed, as shown in Figure 8-38. Select the file and then choose the **Open** button; the panel schedule styles will be fetched from the selected file.

Show panels from

There are two radio buttons in this area: **Current drawing** and **Electrical project database**. Select the **Current drawing** radio button if you want to use the panels available in the current drawing. You can also use the electrical project database for displaying panel. To do so, select the **Electrical project database** radio button; the system will automatically display the panels available in the electrical project database. If an electrical project database file is missing or unavailable then it will prompt you to create a new EPD file or open an existing EPD file. After specifying the desired parameters in the dialog box, choose the **OK** button; the panel schedule will get attached to the cursor. Click in the drawing area to specify the insertion point; the schedule will be placed at the specified point. You can edit any of the cells in the schedule by double clicking on it.

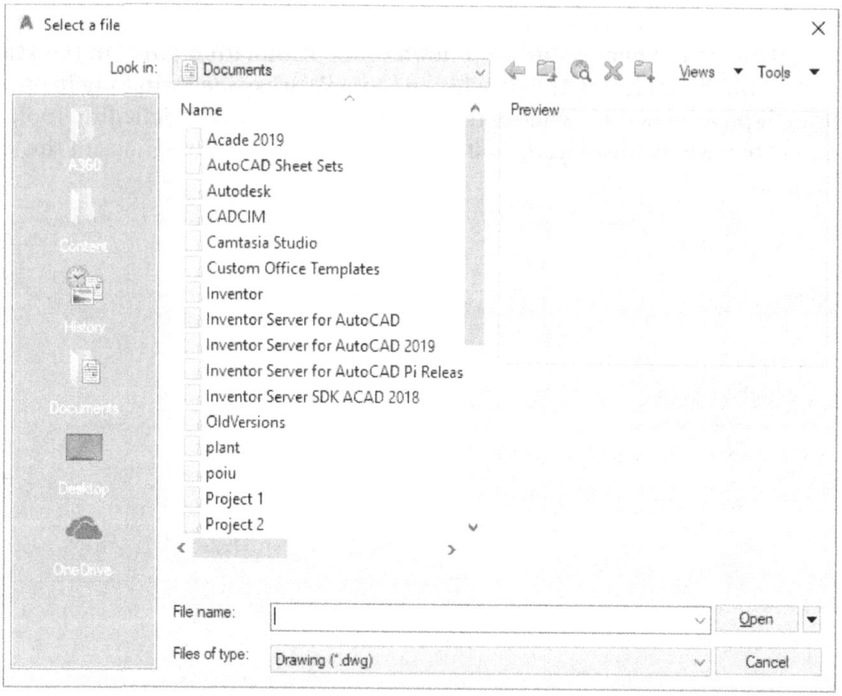

*Figure 8-38 The **Select a file** dialog box*

1-Phase Branch Panel Schedule

This tool is also available in the **Schedules** drop-down of the **Annotation** panel in the **Home** tab of the **Ribbon** when the **Electrical** option is selected in the **Workspace Switching** flyout. To create a 1-phase branch panel schedule, choose the **1-Phase Branch Panel Schedule** tool; the **Panel Schedule** dialog box will be displayed. The options in this dialog box have already been discussed.

Distribution Board Schedule

This tool is also available in the **Schedules** drop-down of the **Annotation** panel in the **Home** tab of the **Ribbon** when the **Electrical** option is selected in the **Workspace Switching** flyout. To create a distribution board schedule, choose the **Distribution Board Schedule** tool; the **Panel Schedule** dialog box will be displayed. The options in this dialog box have already been discussed.

Switchboard Schedule

This tool is also available in the **Schedules** drop-down of the **Annotation** panel in the **Home** tab of the **Ribbon** when the **Electrical** option is selected in the **Workspace Switching** flyout. To create a switchboard schedule, choose the **Switchboard Schedule** tool; the **Panel Schedule** dialog box will be displayed. The options in this dialog box have already been discussed.

Panel Schedule

This tool is also available in the **Schedules** drop-down of the **Annotation** panel in the **Home** tab of the **Ribbon** when the **Electrical** option is selected in the **Workspace Switching** flyout. Select this tool; the **Panel Schedule** dialog box will be displayed with the **Panel** option selected in the **Panel schedule table style** drop-down list by default.

Plumbing Fixture Schedule

This tool is available in the **Schedules** drop-down of the **Annotation** panel in the **Home** tab of the **Ribbon** when the **Plumbing** option is selected in the **Workspace Switching** flyout. To create a plumbing fixture schedule, choose the **Plumbing Fixture Schedule** tool; you will be prompted to select the objects. The procedure for creating a plumbing fixture schedule is similar to the procedure for creating an air terminal devices schedule.

Plumbing Fixture & Pipe Connection Schedule

This tool is available in the **Schedules** drop-down of the **Annotation** panel in the **Home** tab of the **Ribbon** when the **Plumbing** option is selected in the **Workspace Switching** flyout. To create a plumbing fixture and pipe connection schedule, choose the **Plumbing Fixture & Pipe Connection Schedule** tool; you will be prompted to select the objects. The procedure for creating a plumbing fixture and pipe connection schedule is similar to the procedure for creating an air terminal devices schedule.

Water Heater (Gas) Schedule

This tool is available in the **Schedules** drop-down of the **Annotation** panel in the **Home** tab of the **Ribbon** when the **Plumbing** option is selected in the **Workspace Switching** flyout. To create a water heater schedule, choose the **Water Heater (Gas) Schedule** tool; you will be prompted to select the objects. The procedure for creating a water heater (gas) schedule is similar to the procedure for creating an air terminal devices schedule.

Door Schedule

This tool is available in the **Schedules** drop-down of the **Annotation** panel in the **Home** tab of the **Ribbon** when the **Architecture** option is selected in the **Workspace Switching** flyout. To create a door schedule, choose the **Door Schedule** tool; you will be prompted to select the objects. The procedure for creating a door schedule is similar to the procedure for creating an air terminal devices schedule.

Door Schedule - Project Based

This tool is available in the **Schedules** drop-down of the **Annotation** panel in the **Home** tab of the **Ribbon** when the **Architecture** option is selected in the **Workspace Switching** flyout. To create a project based door schedule, choose the **Door Schedule - Project Based** tool; you will be prompted to select the objects. The procedure for creating a project based door schedule is similar to the procedure for creating an air terminal devices schedule.

Window Schedule

This tool is available in the **Schedules** drop-down of the **Annotation** panel in the **Home** tab of the **Ribbon** when the **Architecture** option is selected in the **Workspace Switching** flyout. To create a window schedule, choose the **Window Schedule** tool; you will be prompted to select the objects. The procedure for creating a window schedule is similar to the procedure for creating an air terminal devices schedule.

Room Schedule

This tool is available in the **Schedules** drop-down of the **Annotation** panel in the **Home** tab of the **Ribbon** when the **Architecture** option is selected in the **Workspace Switching** flyout. To create a room schedule, choose the **Room Schedule** tool; you will be prompted to select the objects. The procedure for creating a room schedule is similar to the procedure for creating an air terminal devices schedule.

Space Schedule - BOMA

This tool is available in the **Schedules** drop-down of the **Annotation** panel in the **Home** tab of the **Ribbon** when the **Architecture** option is selected in the **Workspace Switching** flyout. To create a space schedule, choose the **Space Schedule - BOMA** tool; you will be prompted to select the objects. The procedure for creating a space schedule is similar to the procedure for creating an air terminal devices schedule.

Space Inventory Schedule

This tool is available in the **Schedules** drop-down of the **Annotation** panel in the **Home** tab of the **Ribbon** when the **Architecture** option is selected in the **Workspace Switching** flyout. To create a space inventory schedule, choose the **Space Inventory Schedule** tool; you will be prompted to select the objects. The procedure for creating a space inventory schedule is similar to the procedure for creating an air terminal devices schedule.

Wall Schedule

This tool is available in the **Schedules** drop-down of the **Annotation** panel in the **Home** tab of the **Ribbon** when the **Architecture** option is selected in the **Workspace Switching** flyout. To create a wall schedule, choose the **Wall Schedule** tool; you will be prompted to select the objects. The procedure for creating a wall schedule is similar to the procedure for creating an air terminal devices schedule.

Schedule Styles

This tool is available in the **Schedules** drop-down of the **Annotation** panel in the **Home** tab of the **Ribbon** when the **Architecture** option is selected in the **Workspace Switching** flyout. This tool is used to open the **Style Manager** with the options related to schedule styles only. The options in the **Style Manager** have already been discussed.

Table Editing

Table editing can be done after selecting the table schedule created by the user. You can edit a schedule table in the same way as done in an Excel sheet. On selecting a cell from the table, the **Table Cell** contextual tab will be displayed in the **Ribbon**, as shown in Figure 8-39. The options in this tab are discussed next.

***Figure 8-39** Partial view of the **Table Cell** contextual tab*

Rows

The tools in this panel are used to add or delete rows from the table. The tools available in this pancl arc discussed next.

Insert Above

This tool is used to insert a row above the selected cell.

Insert Below

This tool is used to insert a row below the selected cell.

Delete Row(s)

This tool is used to delete the row of the selected cell.

Columns

The tools in this panel are used to add or delete columns from the table. The tools available in this panel are discussed next.

Insert Left

This tool is used to insert a column on the left of the selected cell.

Insert Right

This tool is used to insert a column on the right of the selected cell.

Delete Column(s)

This tool is used to delete columns in the selected cell.

Merge

The tools in this panel are used to merge or separate the cells in the table. The tools available in this panel are discussed next.

Merge Cells

The tools in this drop-down are used to merge cells in some desired pattern. The tools in the drop-down are discussed next.

Merge All

This tool is used to merge all the selected cells of the table.

Merge By Row
This tool is used to merge all the selected cells row wise.

Merge By Column
This tool is used to merge all the selected cells column wise.

Unmerge Cells
This tool is used to separate the merged cells in the table.

Cell Styles
The tools in this panel are used to manage cell styles. These tools are discussed next.

Match Cell
This tool is used to match the properties of other cells to the selected cell. To use this option, select a cell and then choose the **Match Cell** tool; you will be prompted to select the destination cell. Click in the destination cell; the properties of the selected cell will be applied to the destination cell.

Cell Alignment
The tools available in this drop-down are used to justify the text in the table cells. The tools available in this drop-down are discussed next.

Top Left
It is used to align the text at the top left of the cell.

Top Center
It is used to align the text at the top center of the cell.

Top Right
It is used to align the text at the top right of the cell.

Middle Left
It is used to align the text at the middle left of the cell.

Middle Center
It is used to align the text at the middle center of the cell.

Middle Right
It is used to align the text at the middle right of the cell.

Bottom Left
It is used to align the text at the bottom left of the cell.

Bottom Center
It is used to align the text at the bottom center of the cell.

Bottom Right

It is used to align the text in the bottom right of the cell.

Create new cell styles

The options in this drop-down list are used to apply a cell style to the selected cell. The cell styles displayed in this drop-down list are the cell styles available in the current table style. You can also create a new cell style. To do so, select the **Create new cell style** option from the drop-down list; the **Create New Cell Style** dialog box will be displayed, as shown in Figure 8-40. A default name is displayed in the **New Style Name** edit box of this dialog box. You can specify the desired name in this edit box. The options in the **Start With** drop-down list are used to select a template for the cell style to be created.

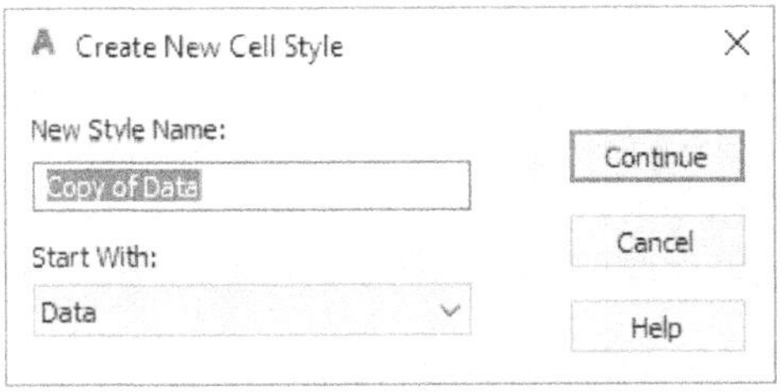

***Figure 8-40** The **Create New Cell Style** dialog box*

After specifying the desired options, choose the **Continue** button; a new style will be created and displayed in the **Table Cell Styles** drop-down list.

Table Cell Background Color

The options in this drop-down list are used to change the background color of the selected cell.

Edit Borders

This button is used to modify borders of the selected cell. To do so, choose the **Edit Border** button; the **Cell Border Properties** dialog box will be displayed, as shown in Figure 8-41. The options used for editing the borders are shown in the **Border properties** area. Using the options available in the **Border properties** area, you can change the properties of borders like line weight, line type, color and so on. To change the border type, choose the corresponding button available around the Preview area. Preview of the changes made in the selected border are displayed in the Preview area. After specifying the desired options, choose the **OK** button from the dialog box; the changes will be applied to the selected cell.

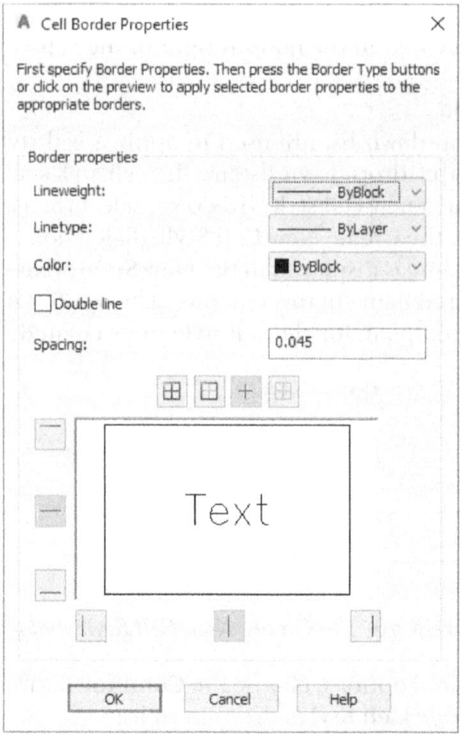

Figure 8-41 *The* ***Cell Border Properties*** *dialog box*

Cell Format

The tools in this panel are used to modify the format of data to be entered in a cell. Also, you can lock/unlock the selected cells by using the tools in this panel. These tools are discussed next.

Cell Locking

The tools in this drop-down are used to lock/unlock the format, content, or both of a cell. The tools in this drop-down are discussed next.

Unlocked

This tool is used to unlock the selected cell so that it can be edited format wise as well as content wise.

Content Locked

This tool is used to lock the content of the selected cell so that it cannot be edited.

Format Locked

This tool is used to lock the format of the selected cell so that it cannot be edited.

Content and Format Locked

This tool is used to lock the content as well as the format of the selected cell so that it cannot be edited.

Data Format
The options available in this drop-down list are used to specify the format of the selected cell .

Insert
The tools available in this panel are used to insert various types of objects in the table. These tools are discussed next.

Block
This tool is used to insert a block in the current cell. To do so, choose the **Block** tool; the **Insert a Block in a Table Cell** dialog box will be displayed, as shown in Figure 8-42. Using the options available in this dialog box, you can specify the values for the parameters such as **Scale**, **Rotation angle**, and **Overall cell alignment** for the selected block in the cell. Also, a preview of the block to be inserted will be displayed on the right in the dialog box. After specifying the desired options in this dialog box, choose the **OK** button; the block will be inserted in the selected cell.

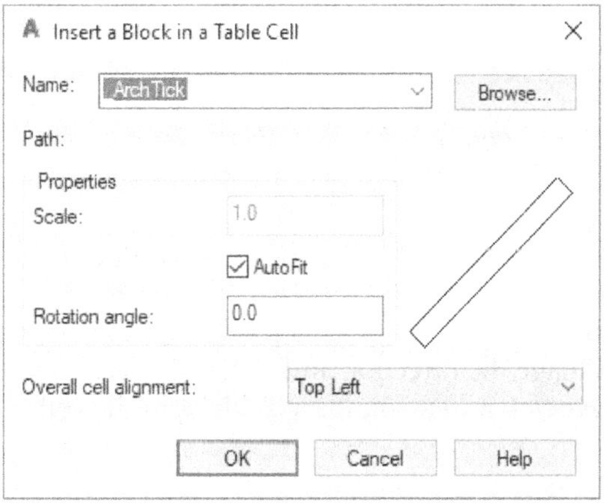

*Figure 8-42 The **Insert a Block in a Table Cell** dialog box*

Field
This tool is used to insert a text field in the current cell. To insert a text field, choose the **Field** tool; the **Field** dialog box will be displayed, as shown in Figure 8-43. Select a category from the **Field category** drop-down list in the dialog box; the options related to the selected category are displayed in the **Field names** list box. Select an option from this list box; the related options will be displayed in the right of the dialog box. Specify the desired option from the right area and then choose the **OK** button; the specified field will be inserted in the current cell.

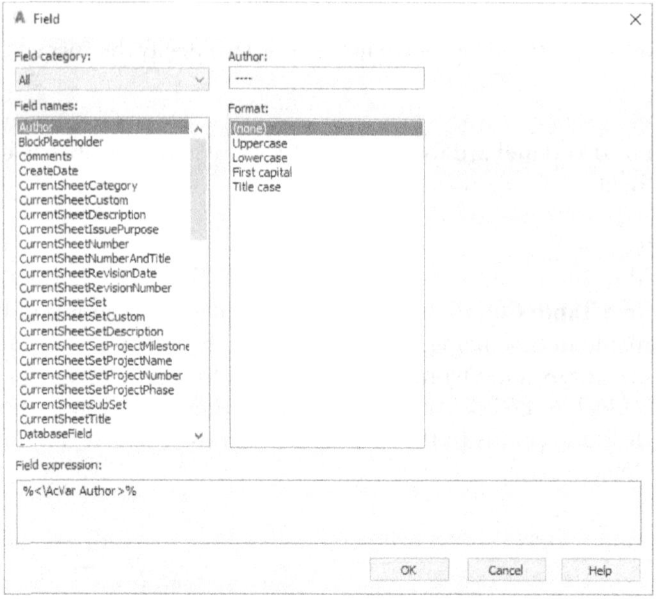

Figure 8-43 *The **Field** dialog box*

Formula

The options available in this drop-down are used to apply a formula to the selected cell.

Manage Cell Contents

This tool is used to manage the direction and order of the content in the selected cell of the table. This tool is active only when you insert a block in the cell.

Data

The tools in this panel are used to manage data links of the selected cell. The tools available in this panel are discussed next.

Link Cell

This tool is used to link the selected cell in the table to a field in the excel sheet. To do so, choose the **Link Cell** tool from the contextual tab; the **Select a Data Link** dialog box will be displayed, as shown in Figure 8-44. Click on the **Create a new Excel Data Link** node in the **Links** area of the dialog box; the **Enter Data Link Name** dialog box will be displayed, as shown in Figure 8-45. Specify the name of the data link in the **Name** edit box and then choose the **OK** button from the dialog box; the **New Excel Data Link** dialog box will be displayed, as shown in Figure 8-46. Click on the Browse button next to the **Browse for a file** drop-down list in the dialog box; the **Save As** dialog box will be displayed and you will be prompted to open an already existing excel file. Select an already existing excel file and then choose the **Open** button from the dialog box; the **New Excel Data Link** dialog box will be displayed, refer to Figure 8-47.

Figure 8-44 *The* ***Select a Data Link*** *dialog box*

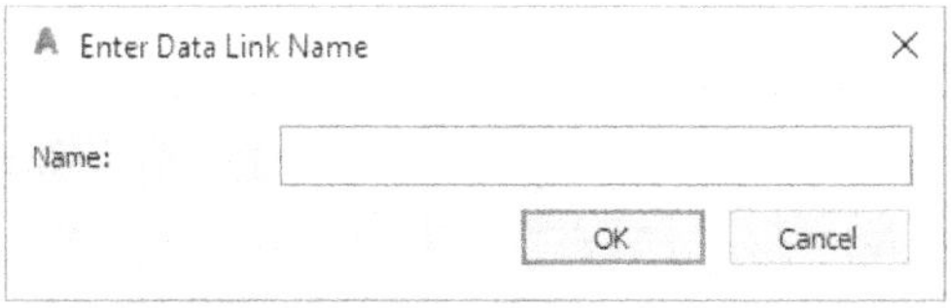

Figure 8-45 *The* ***Enter Data Link Name*** *dialog box*

This dialog box is divided into three areas: **File**, **Link options**, and **Preview**. The options in the **File** area are used to specify the location of excel file and its path type. The options in the **Link options** area are used to specify the data that is to be linked from the excel sheet. The **Preview** area is used to display preview of the selected data that is to be linked.

After specifying the desired settings in the dialog box, choose the **OK** button from the dialog box to apply the settings; the **Select a Data Link** dialog box will be displayed again with the newly created data link selected. Choose the **OK** button from the dialog box; the selected link will be applied to the selected cell.

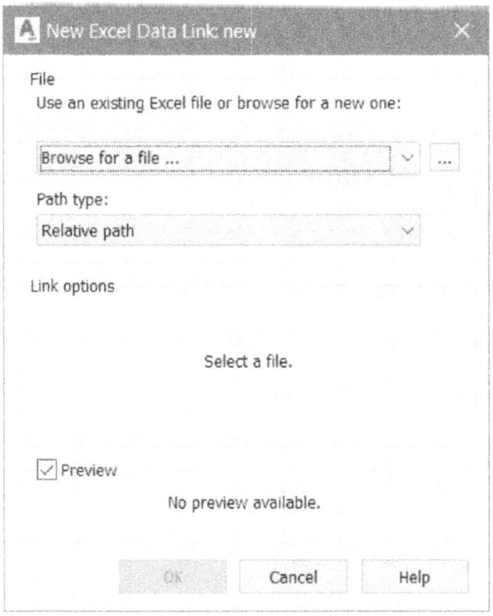

Figure 8-46 *The* ***New Excel Data Link*** *dialog box*

Figure 8-47 *The* ***New Excel Data Link*** *dialog box*

Download from Source

This tool is available in the **Data** panel of the **Table Cell** contextual tab. This tool is used to update the link from the source file. This tool is active only when you select a link from the table.

TUTORIAL

Tutorial 1

In this tutorial, you will create an air terminal device schedule for the mechanical system created in Exercise 1 of Chapter 4, as shown in Figure 8-48. **(Expected time: 30 min)**

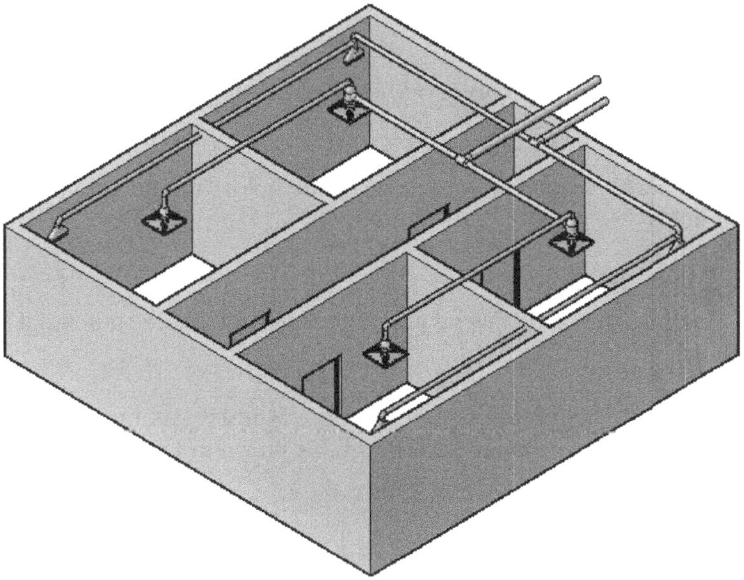

Figure 8-48 *The mechanical system created in Chapter 4*

The following steps are required to complete this tutorial:

a. Open the drawing created in Exercise1 of Chapter 4.
b. Add the Air Terminal Device Schedule.
c. Update the Property Data and Schedule Details.

Opening the Drawing File in HVAC Workspace

1. Start AutoCAD MEP and choose the **Open** tool from the **Quick Access Toolbar**; the **Select File** dialog box is displayed.

2. Select the drawing file created in Exercise 1 of Chapter 4 and then choose the **Open** button; the file will open in the application window.

3. Choose the **Workspace Switching** button in the **Application Status Bar**; a flyout is displayed.

4. Choose the **HVAC** option from the flyout; the **HVAC** workspace is activated.

Adding Air Terminal Devices Schedule

1. Choose the **Air Terminal Devices Schedule** tool from the **Schedule** drop-down in the **Annotation** panel of the **Home** tab in **Ribbon**; you are prompted to select the objects to be included in the schedule.

2. Select all the Diffusers and Return Air Grilles available in the drawing area and then press ENTER; the schedule gets attached to the cursor.

3. Click to specify the upper left corner of the schedule; you are prompted to specify the lower right corner.

4. Click to specify the lower right corner of the schedule; the schedule is placed at the specified position.

   By default, "?" marks are displayed in each of the fields. You need to update the property sets in these fields.

Updating the Schedule

1. Select the schedule from the drawing area; the **Schedule Table** contextual tab is displayed in the **Ribbon**.

2. Choose the **Add All Property Sets** tool from the **Modify** panel in the contextual tab; the properties in the schedule change accordingly, as shown in Figure 8-49.

MECHANICAL AIR TERMINAL DEVICES SCHEDULE								
TAG	SIZE	DESCRIPTION	CONSTRUCTION			BASIS OF DESIGN		NOTES
			MATERIAL	FINISH	DISCHARGE PATTERN	MANUFACTURER	MODEL OR SERIES	
D-1			Aluminum		4-Way			
D-2			Aluminum		4-Way			
D-3			Aluminum		4-Way			
D-4			Aluminum		4-Way			
D-5			Aluminum		4-Way			
D-6			Aluminum		4-Way			
D-7			Aluminum		4-Way			
D-8			Aluminum		4-Way			

Figure 8-49 *The mechanical air terminal devices schedule*

You can also edit the schedule to include more information in the blank fields.

Saving the Drawing

1. Choose **Save** from the **Application Menu** to save the drawing file at an appropriate location.

Self-Evaluation Test

Answer the following questions and then compare them to those given at the end of this chapter:

1. In which of the following panels is the **Detail Components** tool available?

   (a) **Build** (b) **Details**
   (c) **Modify** (d) **Draw**

2. To create a horizontal section, choose the __________ tool from the **Section & Elevation** panel of the **Home** tab in the **Ribbon**.

3. The __________ tool is used to extract a polyline outline of the slice created through the model.

4. Vertical section is a section created by a plane perpendicular to the object to be sectioned. (T/F)

5. The **Generate Section** tool is used to create live sections by using the current section line. (T/F)

Review Questions

Answer the following questions:

1. In which of the following dialog boxes, the **Recipe** option is available?

   (a) **Generate Section/Elevation** (b) **Batch Refresh Section/Elevations**
   (c) **Component Properties** (d) **Schedule Table Style Properties**

2. The **Space Inventory Schedule** option becomes available in the **Schedules** drop-down in the **Annotation** panel of the **Home** tab in the **Ribbon** when the __________ option is selected in the **Workspace Switching** flyout.

3. The __________ tool is used to refresh all the 2D sections and elevations created in the current project or in the specified folder.

4. The **Detail Components** tool is not available in the **Schematic** workspace. (T/F)

5. The **Space Engineering Schedule** tool is available in the **Schedules** drop-down in the **Annotation** panel of the **Home** tab in the **Ribbon** when the **HVAC** option is selected in the **Workspace Switching** flyout. (T/F)

EXERCISE

Exercise 1

In this exercise, you will create a 1-Phase Branch Panel schedule for the panel in the drawing, as shown in Figure 8-50. The drawing file is created in Tutorial 1 of Chapter 7. The schedule is given for your reference in Figure 8-51. **(Expected time: 30 min)**

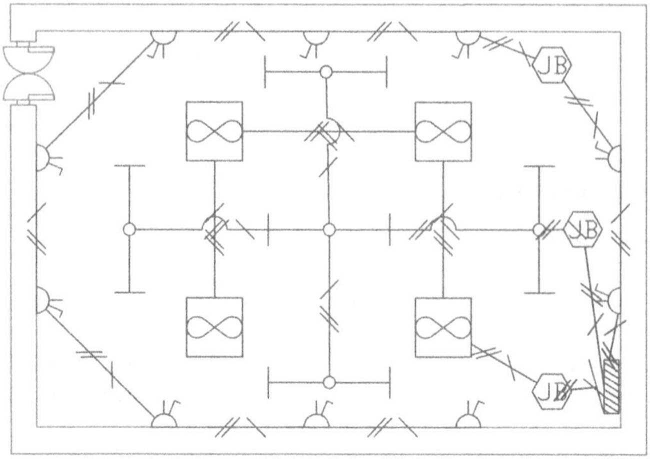

Figure 8-50 *The mechanical air terminal devices schedule*

Panel Ref Nr.:	Main Panel	Supply Voltage:	240/230
Service:	20 A	Incomer Type/Rating:	MCB/15 A
Location:		Number of Ways:	3
Fed From:	----	Feed Cable Details:	

Circuit Ref.	Circuit Description	Protective Device			Cable mm²	Load (Watts)		
		Type	Amps	Curve		L1	L2	L3
Fans	SPARE		20		1x50;1x50;1x25;–	720	0	0
Lights	SPARE		20		1x50;1x50;1x25;–	750	0	0
Sockets	SPARE		20		1x50;1x50;1x25;–	0	3000	0
					Totals	1470	3000	0
					Total Installed Load:	4.5		KW

Figure 8-51 *The 1-Phase Branch Panel schedule for the drawing*

Answers to Self-Evaluation Test

1. Details, **2.** Horizontal Section, **3.** Quick Slice, **4.** T, **5.** F

Chapter 9

Working with Schematics

Learning Objectives

After completing this chapter, you will be able to:

- *Understand the use of schematics*
- *Add schematic symbols to the drawings*
- *Create schematic lines in the drawing*
- *Display schematic representation of existing drawing*

INTRODUCTION

In this chapter, you will learn about various tools that are used for creating a schematic drawing for a building system. You will also learn the use of equipment and schematic lines in a schematic drawing. The tools to create a schematic drawing are available in the **Schematic** workspace. This workspace is discussed next.

SCHEMATIC WORKSPACE

To invoke this workspace, choose the **Schematic** option from the **Workspace Switching** flyout; the **Schematic** workspace will be activated. Figure 9-1 shows partial view of the **Ribbon** in the **Schematic** workspace. The tools to create a schematic drawing are available in the **Build** panel of the **Home** tab in the **Ribbon**. The usage of these tools are discussed next.

***Figure 9-1** Partial view of the **Ribbon** in the **Schematic** workspace*

Equipment

This tool is available in the **Build** panel of the **Home** tab in the **Ribbon**. This tool is used to add equipment to the drawing. To add an equipment, choose the **Equipment** tool from the **Ribbon**; the **Add Multi-view Parts** dialog box will be displayed. The options in this dialog box are the same as discussed in previous chapters.

Schematic Symbol

Schematic symbols are the symbolic representations of physical objects required in a building system. In AutoCAD MEP, there are two types of schematic symbols: In-line symbols and End-of-line symbols. The In-line symbols are those that can be added in between the schematic line. Note that when you delete a schematic line in which the In-line symbols are attached, the symbols also get deleted with the line. The End-of-line symbols are those that can be added either at the start point or at the end point of a schematic line. To add a schematic symbol, choose the **Schematic Symbol** tool from the **Build** panel of the **Home** tab in the **Ribbon**; the symbol will get attached to the cursor and you will be prompted to specify the insertion point for the symbol. Also, the **PROPERTIES** palette will be displayed, as shown in Figure 9-2. Click in the drawing area to place the symbol and then specify the rotation. The options in the **PROPERTIES** palette are discussed next.

Description

This field is available in the **BASIC > General** rollout of the **Design** tab in the **PROPERTIES** palette. When you click on this field, the **Description** dialog box will be displayed, as shown in Figure 9-3. Enter description for the symbol in the **Edit the description for this object** text box in this dialog box. Choose the **OK** button to exit the dialog box.

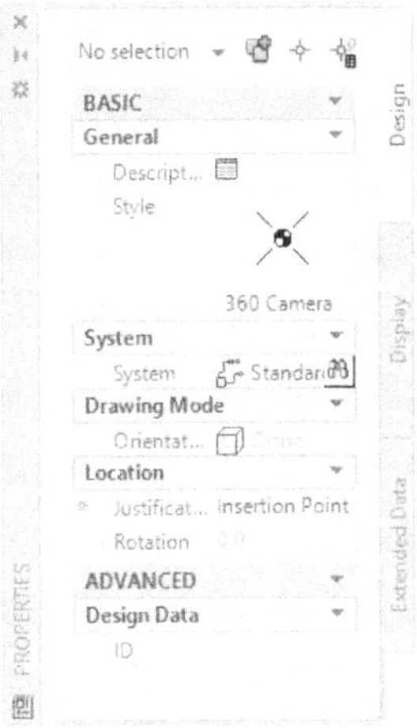

*Figure 9-2 The **PROPERTIES** palette displayed on choosing the **Schematic Symbol** tool*

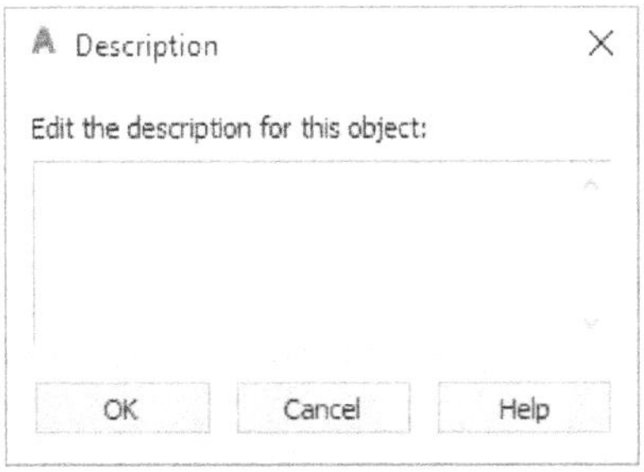

*Figure 9-3 The **Description** dialog box*

Style

This option is available in the **BASIC > General** rollout of the **PROPERTIES** palette. This option is used to select a schematic symbol from the list of symbols available in AutoCAD MEP. To select a symbol, choose the **Style** option from the **PROPERTIES** palette; the **STYLES BROWSER** will be displayed, as shown in Figure 9-4. Select the desired style from the **STYLES BROWSER**.

System

This drop-down list is available in the **BASIC > System** rollout. This drop-down list contains various system definitions for building systems. The option selected in this drop-down list specifies the system to which the symbol belongs.

Orientation

This drop-down list is available in the **BASIC > Drawing Mode** rollout. The options in this rollout are used to specify the orientation in which the symbol will be placed in the drawing. There are two options available in this drop-down list: **Ortho** and **Isometric**. The **Ortho** option is used to place the symbols in orthographic mode, while the **Isometric** option is used to place the symbol in isometric orientation. The **Isometric** option will get activated only when an isometric schematic symbol is selected in the **STYLES BROWSER** palette.

Isoplane

This drop-down list will be available in the **PROPERTIES** palette only when the **Isometric** option is selected in the **Orientation** drop-down list. There are three options in this drop-down list: **Left**, **Right**, and **Top**. Select an option from this drop-down list; the symbol will be oriented along the plane corresponding to the selected option.

Justification

This drop-down list is available in the **Location** rollout. The options in this drop-down list are used to position the symbol with respect to the insertion point.

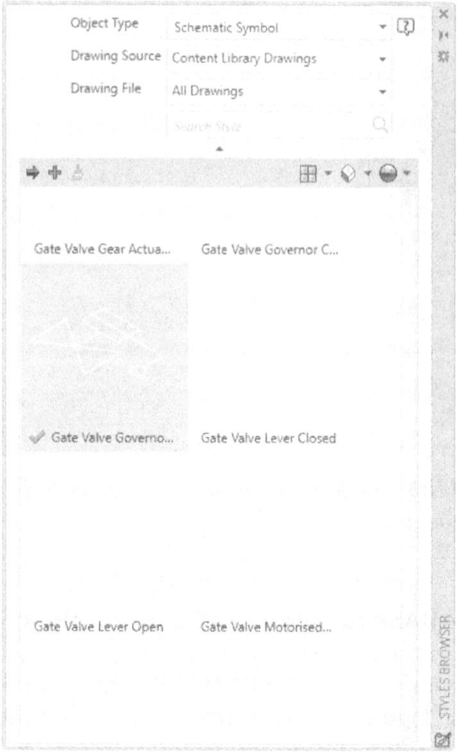

Figure 9-4 *The* ***STYLES BROWSER*** *palette*

Rotation

This field will be available in the **Location** rollout for the symbols in ortho mode only when the **Ortho** option is selected from the **Orientation** drop-down list in the **Drawing Mode** rollout. To activate this field, you need to specify the insertion point. The value in this field changes according to the position of the cursor.

Rotation in isoplane

This field is available in the **Location** rollout for the symbols in isometric mode only when the **Isometric** option is selected from the **Orientation** drop-down list in the **Drawing Mode** rollout. To activate this field, you need to specify the insertion point for the symbol in the isometric view mode. The value in this field changes according to the position of the cursor.

ID

This edit box is available in the **ADVANCED > Design Data** rollout in the **PROPERTIES** palette. You can assign a unique ID to the symbol being inserted in the drawing area.

After placing a symbol in the drawing area, you can change the orientation of the symbol dynamically. Figure 9-5 shows the **2 Port Pneumatic Valve** symbol placed in the isometric mode with its orientation handles. The handles displayed on the symbols are discussed next.

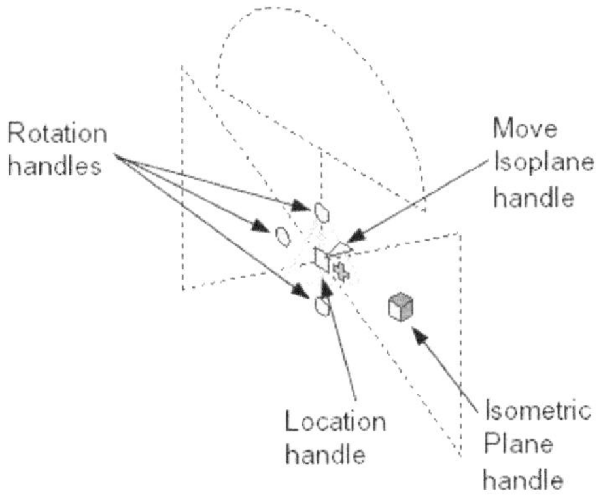

*Figure 9-5 The **2 Port Pneumatic Valve** symbol with its orientation handles*

Rotation handles
These handles are used to rotate the symbol. When you click on a handle, the symbol is rotated with respect to the insertion point.

Location handle
This handle is used to modify the location of the symbol. When you click on this handle and move the cursor, the symbol moves along the cursor in the selected isoplane.

Move Isoplane handle
This handle is used to change the location of the symbol perpendicular to the isoplane selected.

Isometric Plane handle
This handle is used to change the current isometric plane of the symbol. Click on this symbol to switch between Left, Right, and Top planes.

Schematic Line
Schematic lines are used to represent various types of connections in a building system. To create a schematic line, choose the **Schematic Line** tool from the **Build** panel in the **Home** tab of the **Ribbon**; you will be prompted to specify the start point for the schematic line. Also, the **PROPERTIES** palette will be displayed, as shown in Figure 9-6. Click to specify the start point of the line; you will be prompted to specify the next point of the schematic line.

Click to specify the second point of the line; you will be again prompted to specify the next point of the line. Click to specify the third point or press ENTER to exit the tool. Except the **Length** edit box, the options displayed in the **PROPERTIES** palette on choosing the **Schematic Line** tool have already been discussed.

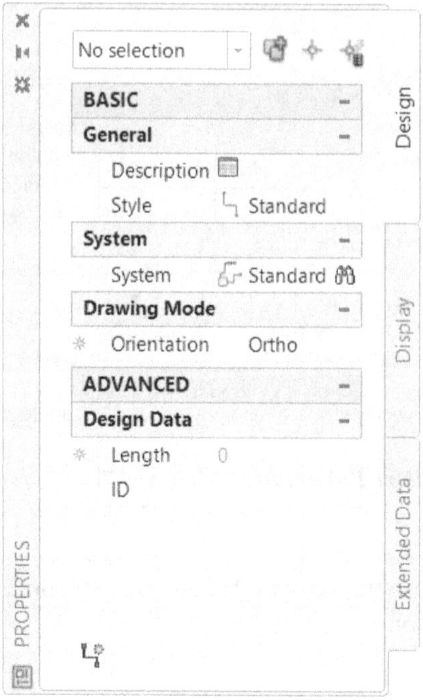

Figure 9-6 *The* ***PROPERTIES*** *palette displayed on choosing the* ***Schematic Line*** *tool*

The **Length** edit box is used to specify the length of the schematic line. You cannot modify the value of length once you have created the schematic line. Also, you cannot specify the value of length directly in this edit box. To specify a value in this edit box, you need to specify the desired value in the dynamic prompt displayed along the cursor while creating the schematic line.

Schematic Line Styles

While creating a schematic diagram, you might require to change the style of the schematic lines. The style of schematic lines can be changed by using the **Style Manager**. To invoke the **Style Manager** for modifying the schematic line style, choose the **Schematic Line Styles** tool from the **Style Manager** drop-down in the **Style & Display** panel of the **Manage** tab in the **Ribbon**; the **Style Manager** will be displayed, as shown in Figure 9-7. Select a line style from the list available on the left in the dialog box; the options related to that line style will be displayed on the right in the dialog box, refer to Figure 9-8. The options displayed in the **Style Manager** on selecting a line style are discussed next.

General Tab

This tab is selected by default in the **Style Manager**, refer to Figure 9-8. The options in this tab are used to change the general settings for the line style. These options are discussed next.

Name

This edit box is used to change the name of the schematic line style selected.

Description

This edit box is used to specify the description about the selected line style.

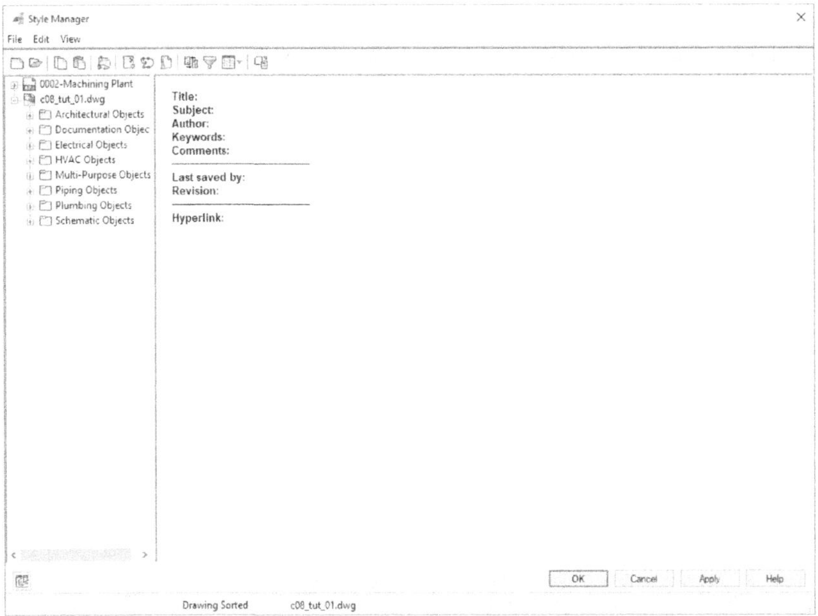

Figure 9-7 The ***Style Manager*** *with schematic line styles*

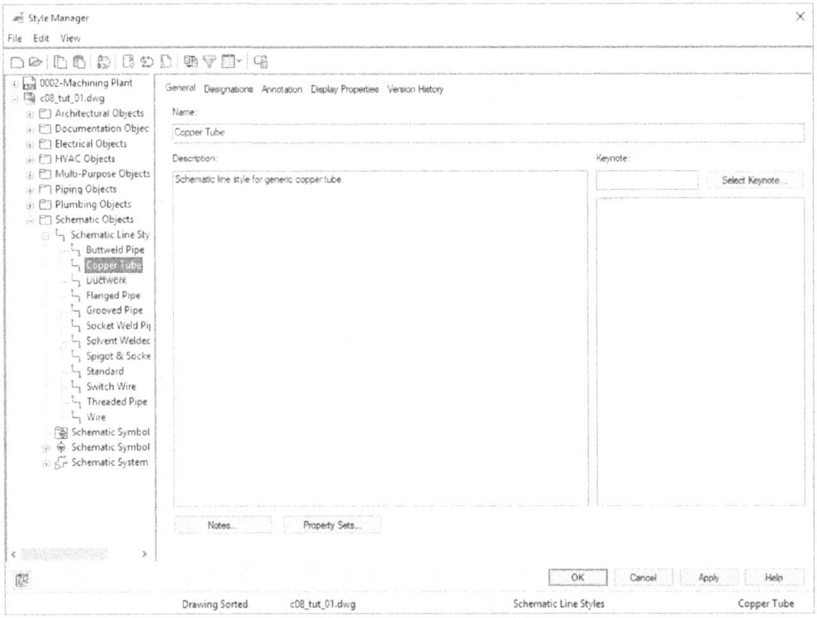

Figure 9-8 The ***Style Manager*** *with options related to a line style*

Keynote

This edit box is used to specify key notes for the schematic line style. You can enter the desired key notes in the edit box or you can choose the **Select Keynote** button next to the edit box to select a keynote from the list of predefined keynotes. On choosing this button, the

Select Keynote dialog box will be displayed, refer to Figure 9-9. To specify any predefined keynote, open the desired category by clicking on the plus sign adjacent to the category and double-click on the desired keynote; the name of the selected keynote will be displayed in the **Keynote** edit box. The description of the keynote is also displayed in the edit box available below the **Keynote** edit box.

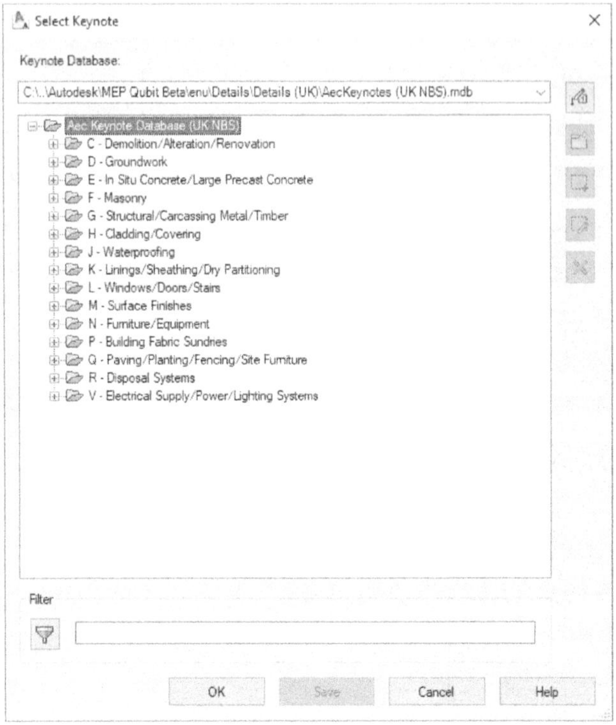

Figure 9-9 *The* ***Select Keynote*** *dialog box*

Notes

This button is used to specify notes for the selected line style. To specify the notes, choose the **Notes** button from the bottom of the **General** tab; the **Notes** dialog box will be displayed, as shown in Figure 9-10. There are two tabs available in this dialog box: **Notes** and **Reference Docs**. In the **Notes** tab, you can specify notes regarding the line style in the edit box displayed below it. You can also add a reference document to the selected line style. To do so, choose the **Reference Docs** tab, refer to Figure 9-11. Choose the **Add** button from the dialog box; the **Select Reference Document** dialog box will be displayed, as shown in Figure 9-12.

Figure 9-10 *The **Notes** dialog box*

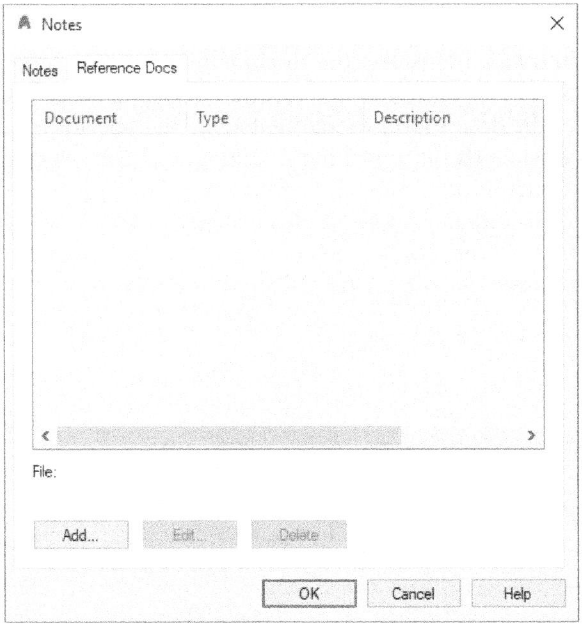

Figure 9-11 *The **Notes** dialog box with the **Reference Docs** tab chosen*

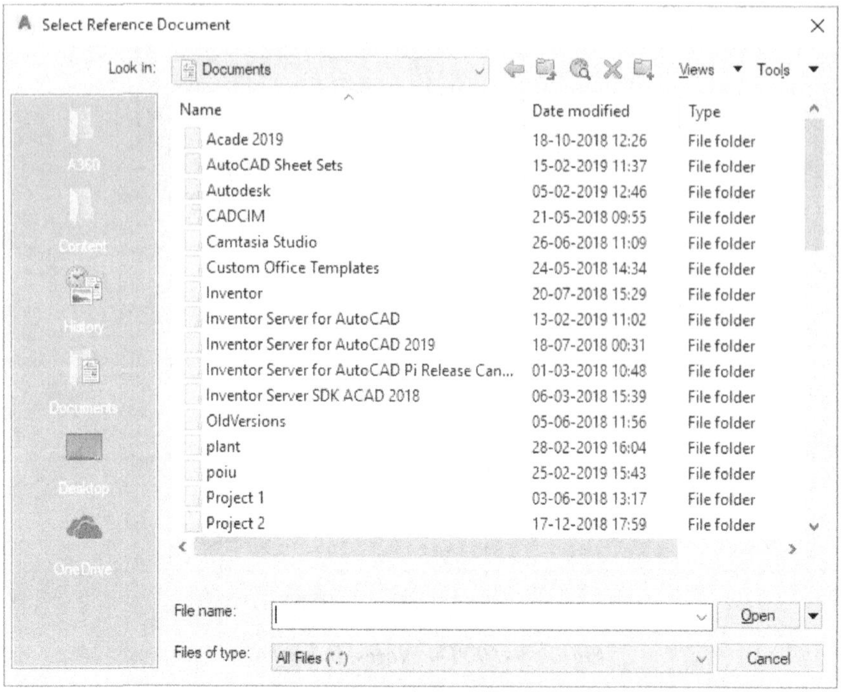

***Figure 9-12** The **Select Reference Document** dialog box*

Browse to the desired location, select the document to be attached, and choose the **Open** button from the dialog box; the **Reference Document** dialog box will be displayed, as shown in Figure 9-13. Enter the description about the document to be added in the **Description** edit box and then choose the **OK** button from the dialog box; the selected file will be displayed in the list of documents in the **Notes** dialog box. You can edit or delete the document by choosing the **Edit** or **Delete** button, respectively. You can add more documents by choosing the **Add** button from the **Notes** dialog box. Choose the **OK** button from the dialog box; the selected file will be added as note for the selected line style.

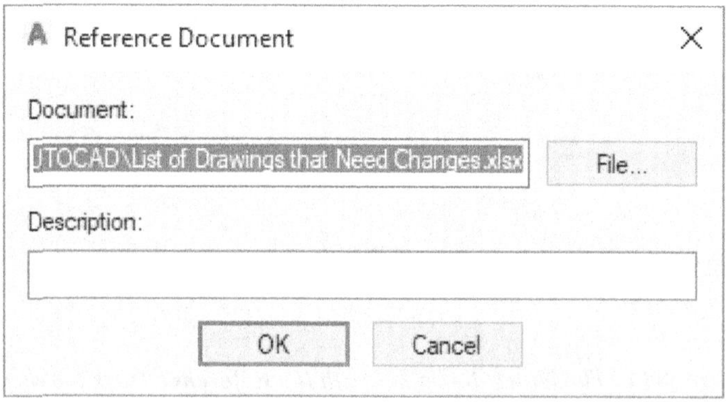

***Figure 9-13** The **Reference Document** dialog box*

Property Sets

This option is used to specify property set data for the selected style. Property sets are the parameters that can be changed for each instance of the object created using the specific style.

Designations Tab

The options in this tab are used to specify designations for the schematic lines, refer to Figure 9-14. Designations are used to create unique IDs for the schematic lines. To specify designations, choose the **New Designation (ID)** button  from the tab; **1** will be displayed under the **Index** column of the list. Click in the field corresponding to **1** in the **Designation (ID)** column and specify the desired designation in the field. You can also create more than one designation for a schematic line by choosing the **New Designation (ID)** button.

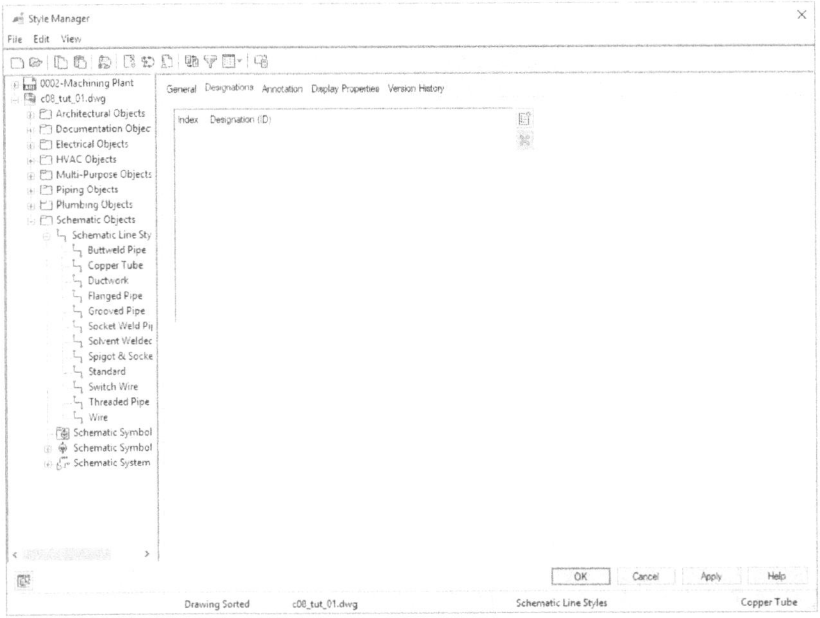

*Figure 9-14 The **Style Manager** with the **Designations** tab chosen*

Annotation Tab

The options in this tab are used to modify annotation style for a schematic line, refer to Figure 9-15. The options available in this tab are discussed next.

Crossings Area

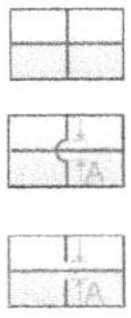

There are three buttons available in this area: **Do Nothing**, **Overlap Graphics**, and **Break Existing Line**. The **Do Nothing** button is used to create the crossing at the intersection point of the schematic lines. The **Overlap Graphics** button is used to create an overlapping graphic at the intersection point of the schematic lines. The **Break Existing Line** button is used to break the existing line at the intersection point. The **A - Break/Overlap Paper Width** edit box, available adjacent to the **Break Existing Line** button, is used to change the width of overlap or break. The **Break/Overlap Priority** edit box is available below the **A - Break/Overlap Paper Width** edit box. This edit box is used to set overlap or break priority.

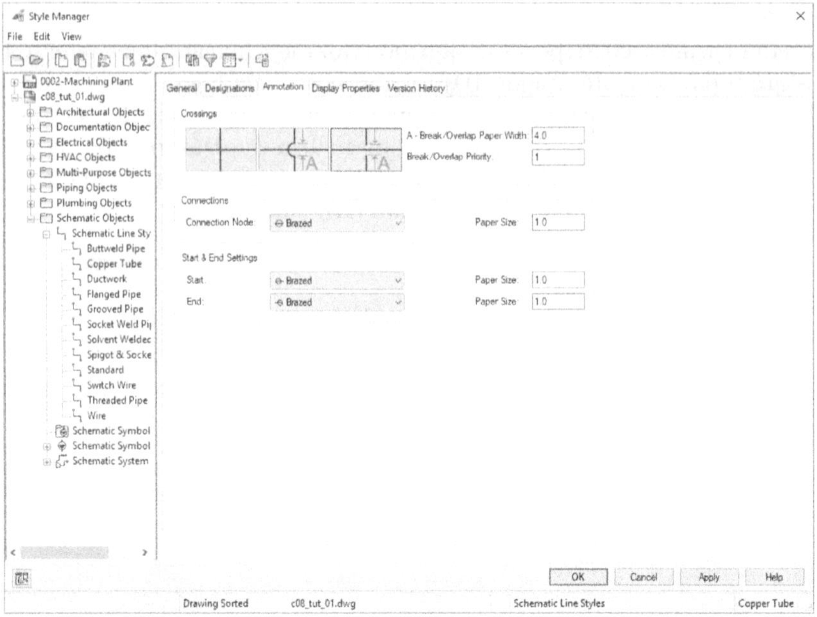

*Figure 9-15 The **Style Manager** with the **Annotation** tab chosen*

Connections Area

The **Connection Node** drop-down list in this area is used to specify the style of nodes created at the connections. You can specify the size of connection node in the **Paper Size** edit box.

Start & End Settings Area

There are two drop-down lists in this area: **Start** and **End**. The options in this drop-down lists are used to specify the shape nodes created at the start and end of the schematic lines. You can specify the sizes of the nodes in the corresponding **Paper Size** edit boxes.

Display Properties Tab

The options in this tab are used to modify the display representations of schematic lines, refer to Figure 9-16. There are various templates for display representations available in this tab. You can override any of the representations by using the options available in this tab.

Version History Tab

The options in this tab are used to record the history of the selected line style, refer to Figure 9-17. You can check the versions of the selected line style with the date of modification listed at the bottom of the dialog box. You can also remove any of the versions by using the **Remove** button.

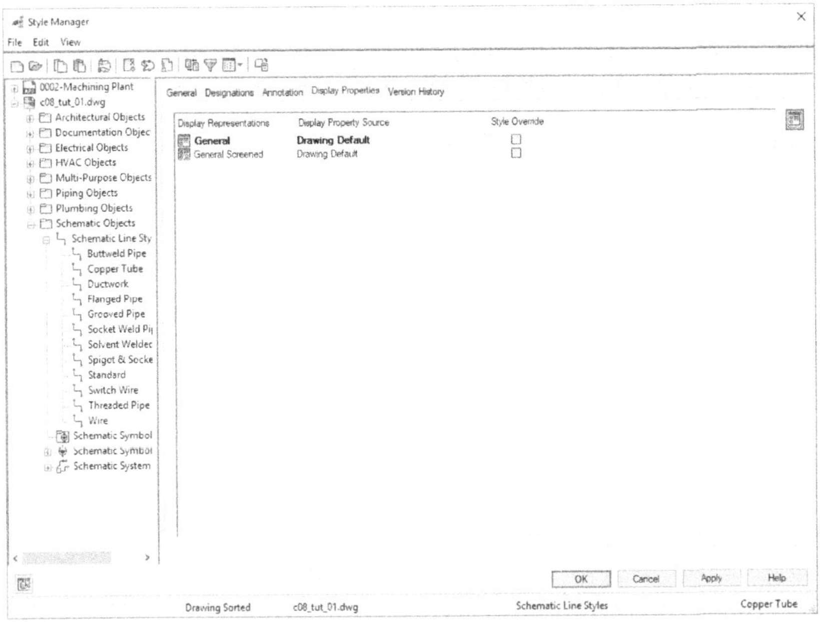

Figure 9-16 The ***Style Manager*** *with the* ***Display Properties*** *tab chosen*

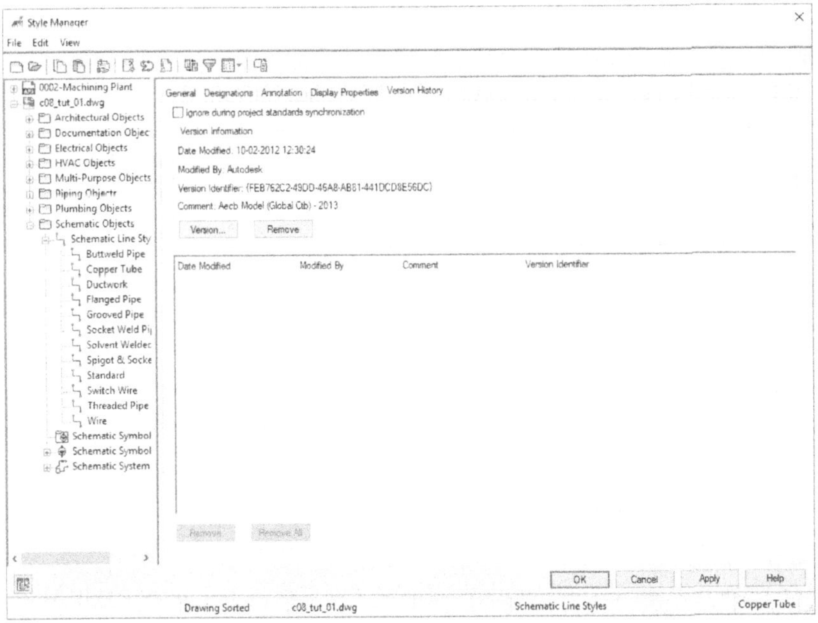

Figure 9-17 The ***Style Manager*** *with the* ***Version History*** *tab chosen*

There are some common tools available in the **Style Manager** which one used to create or edit line styles. These tools are discussed next.

New Drawing

This tool is used to add a new drawing in the **Style Manager**. You can add various line styles in a drawing by copying them.

Open Drawing

This tool is used to add an existing drawing in the **Style Manager**. Some styles available in the drawing are automatically imported in the **Style Manager**.

Copy

This tool is used to copy the selected line style. To do so, select a line style from the list at the left in the **Style Manager** and then choose the **Copy** tool from the **Style Manager**; the style will be copied in the clipboard.

Paste

This tool is used to paste the line style copied from the list by using the **Copy** tool. To paste a line style, choose the **Paste** tool from the **Style Manager**; the line style will be pasted in the selected drawing.

Edit Style

This tool is used to switch to the editing mode.

New Style

This tool is used to create a new line style. To do so, choose the **New Style** tool from the toolbar displayed in the **Style Manager**; a new line style will be created and added in the list with the name **New Style**. Also, you will be prompted to change the name of the style. The options corresponding to the style will be displayed at the right in the **Style Manager**.

Set From

This tool is used to set the shape of the style by using an existing drawing file.

Purge Styles

This tool is used to remove the unused styles from the list displayed in the **Style Manager**. To remove styles, select the styles to be removed and then choose the **Purge Styles** tool from the toolbar; the selected styles will be removed from the list.

Toggle View

This tool is used to toggle between the display styles available in the **Style Manager**. There are two display styles available in the **Style Manager**: **Display per category and Display per drawing**. The Display per drawing display style is selected by default in the **Style Manager**. If this style is selected, the line styles are displayed as per the drawings. If the **Display per category** style is selected, the styles will be displayed according to their categories.

Filter Style Type

This tool is used to toggle between the display styles available in the **Style Manager**. If this tool is chosen then the styles corresponding only to the selected type will be displayed.

Inline Edit Toggle

This tool is used to toggle between the symbolic view/list and properties of a line style. On choosing this toggle button, the options in the **Style Manager** will get modified, as shown in Figure 9-18.

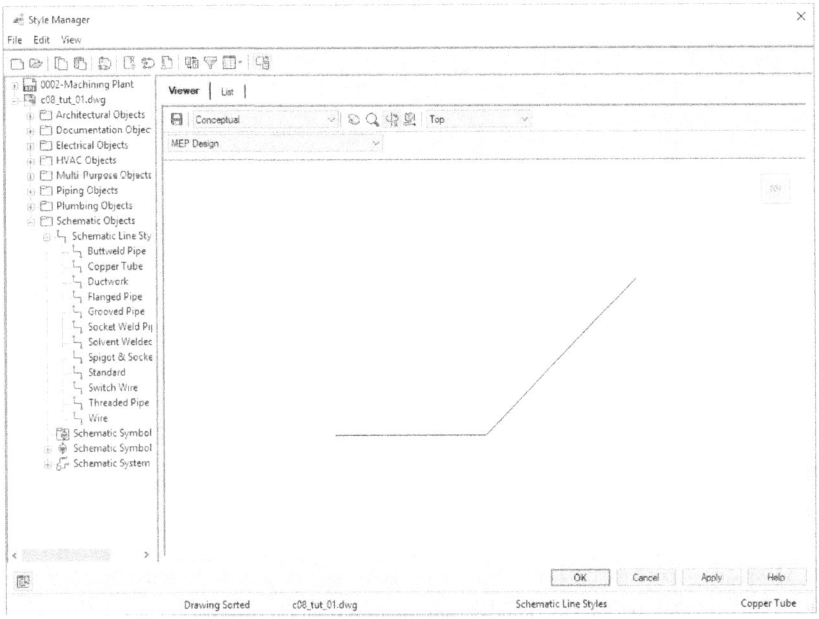

Figure 9-18** The **Viewer** tab displayed on choosing the **Inline Edit Toggle** button from the **Style Manager

There are two tabs in the right area of the dialog box, the **Viewer** tab and the **List** tab. The options in the **Viewer** tab are used to view the current line style in various orientations. On choosing the **List** tab, the options in the **Style Manager** will get modified, refer to Figure 9-19. Also, the information regarding the selected line style will be displayed in this tab.

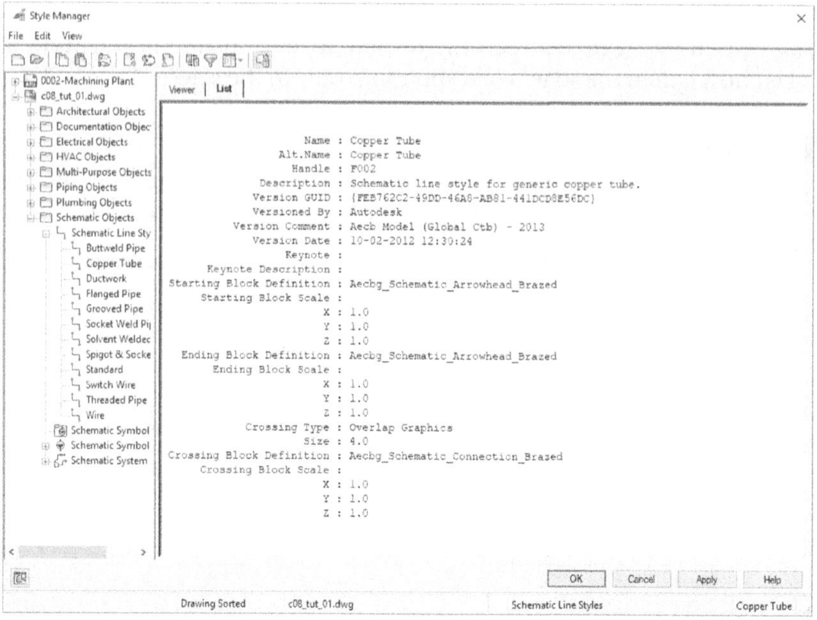

Figure 9-19** The **List** tab displayed on choosing the **Inline Edit Toggle** button from the **Style Manager

Schematic Representation of an Existing System

MEP Design ▾ You can display the schematic representation of any system created in other workspaces. To display the schematic representation, open the desired file and then click on the **Display Configuration** button in the **Application Status Bar**; a flyout will be displayed, as shown in Figure 9-20.

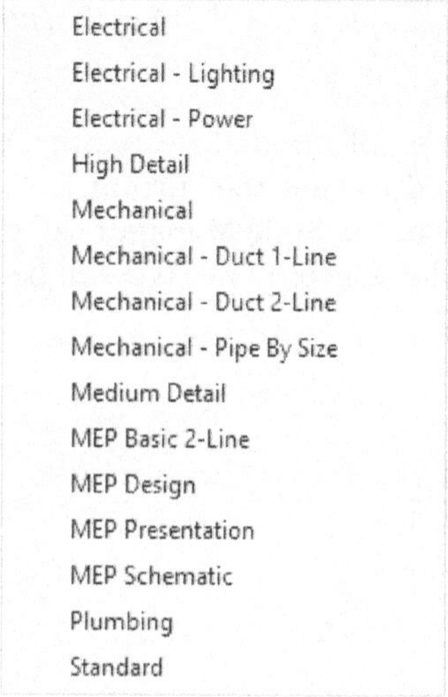

***Figure 9-20** The flyout displayed on choosing the **Display Configuration** button*

Choose the **MEP Schematic** option from the flyout; the current drawing will be displayed with schematic representations, refer to Figure 9-21.

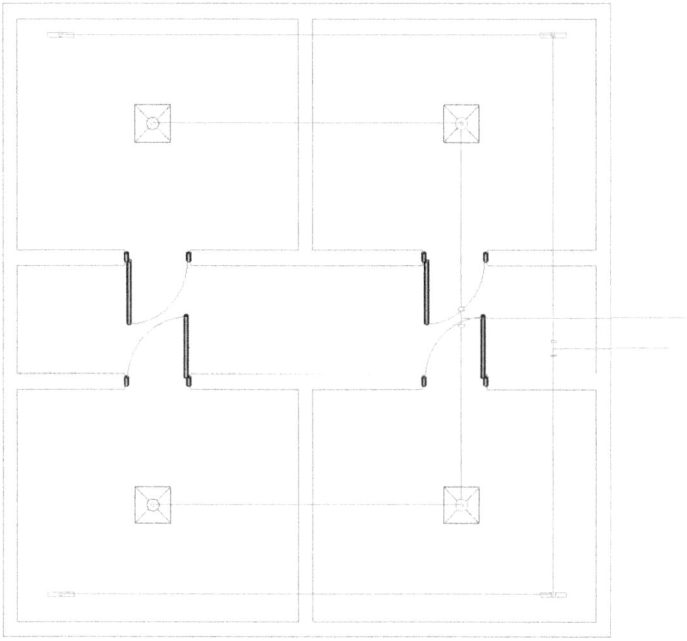

Figure 9-21 *The schematic representation of an HVAC system*

TUTORIAL

TUTORIAL 1

In this tutorial, you will create a schematic diagram of a computer lab, refer to Figure 9-22.

(Expected time: 30 min)

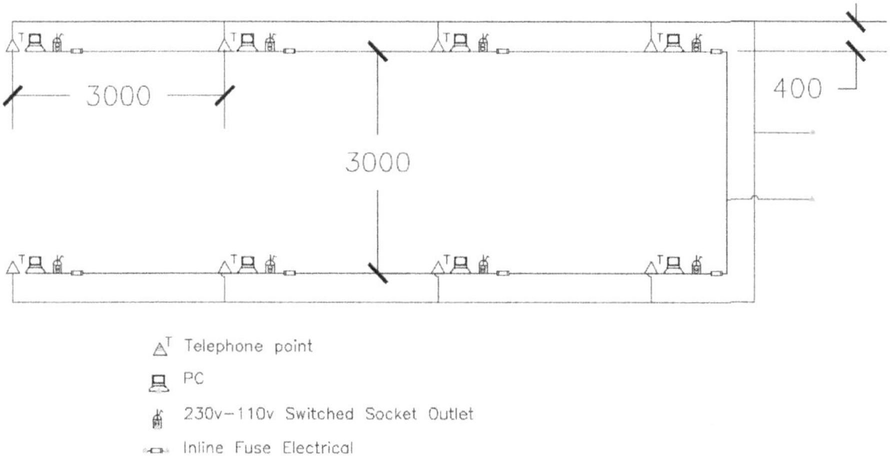

Figure 9-22 *The schematic representation of a computer lab*

Examine the model to determine the schematic symbols to be added.

The following steps are required to complete this tutorial:

a. Start a new drawing in the **Schematic** workspace.
b. Add schematic symbols.
c. Change the system of symbols.
d. Connect symbols with schematic lines.

Starting a New Drawing File in Schematic Workspace

1. Start AutoCAD MEP; a new drawing file with the default name *Drawing1* is opened.

2. Click on the **Workspace Switching** button in the **Application Status Bar**; a flyout is displayed.

3. Choose the **Schematic** option from the flyout; the **Schematic** workspace is activated.

Adding Schematic Symbols

1. Choose the **Schematic Symbol** tool from the **Build** panel of the **Home** tab in the **Ribbon**; the **PROPERTIES** palette is displayed, as shown in Figure 9-23. Also, you are prompted to specify the location of the symbol.

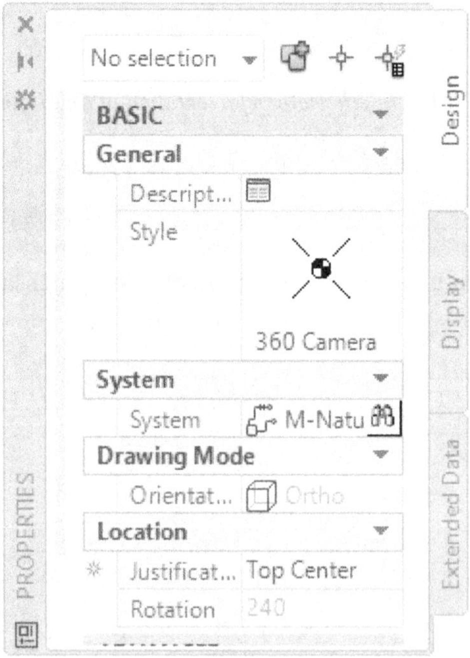

***Figure 9-23** The **PROPERTIES** palette displayed on choosing the **Schematic Symbol** tool*

2. Click in the **Style** field of the **PROPERTIES** palette; the **STYLES BROWSER** palette is displayed, as shown in Figure 9-24.

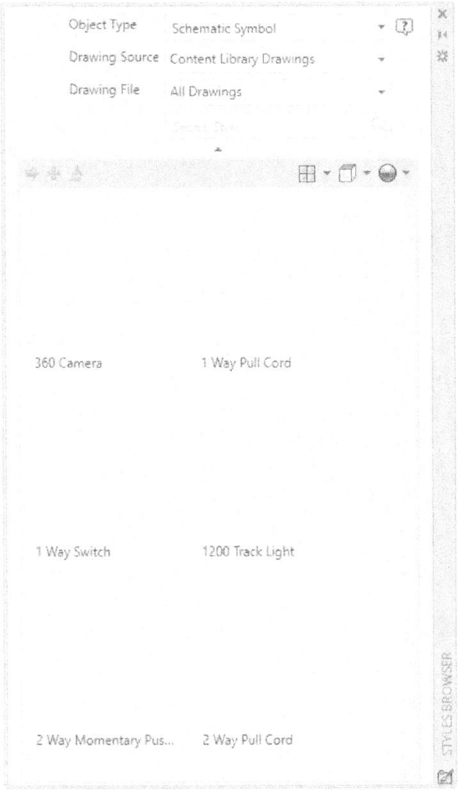

*Figure 9-24 The **STYLES BROWSER** palette*

3. Select the **Electrical Communications (Global).dwg** option from the **Drawing File** drop-down list and double-click to select the **Telephone Point** symbol from the gallery of the **STYLES BROSWER** palette, refer to Figure 9-25; the symbol gets attached to the cursor.

4. Click in the drawing area to place the symbol; you are prompted to specify the rotation value.

5. Specify the value of rotation as **0** at the command prompt; the symbol is placed at the specified location. Press ESC to exit the tool.

6. Select the symbol from the drawing area and right-click; a shortcut menu is displayed. Choose the **Array** tool from the **Basic Modify Tools** flyout. Make sure the **Dynamic Input** button in the **Application Status Bar** is deactivated.

7. Choose the **Rectangular** option from the command prompt; a preview of the array of telephone points is displayed, refer to Figure 9-26. Also, the **Array Creation** contextual tab is displayed, as shown in Figure 9-27.

Figure 9-25 *The* ***STYLES BROWSER*** *palette with* ***Telephone Point*** *symbol selected*

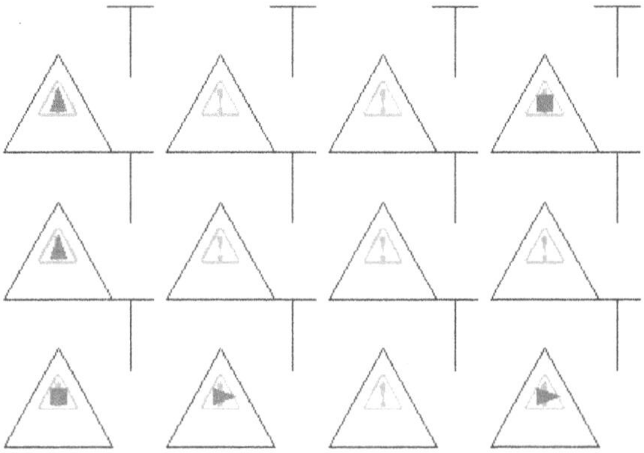

Figure 9-26 *The preview of the array of telephone points*

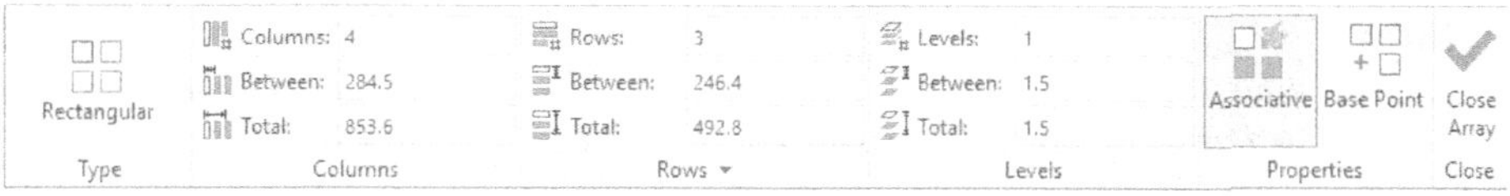

***Figure 9-27** The **Array Creation** contextual tab*

8. Specify **4** in the **Columns** edit box and **3000** in the **Between** edit box in the **Columns** panel of the contextual tab; the preview of the array is displayed.

9. Specify **2** in the **Rows** edit box and **3000** in the **Between** edit box in the **Rows** panel; the preview of the array is displayed.

10. Choose the **Close Array** tool from the **Close** panel of the contextual tab; the **Associative Array** message box is displayed. Choose the **OK** button; the array of telephone points is created, as shown in Figure 9-28.

11. Similarly, add other symbols according to Figure 9-22. The drawing after adding other symbols is displayed, refer to Figure 9-29.

***Figure 9-28** The preview of array*

***Figure 9-29** The drawing after adding other symbols*

Note

1. *Symbol for **PC** will be available only when the **Electrical Power (Global).dwg** is selected from the **Drawing File** drop-down list in the **STYLES BROWSER** palette.*

2. *Symbol for **240v-110v Switched Socket Outlet** will be available only when the **Electrical Power (Global).dwg** is selected from the **Drawing File** drop-down list in the **STYLES BROWSER** palette.*

3. *Symbol for **Inline Fuse Electrical** will be available only when the **Electrical Schematic (Global).dwg** is selected from the **Drawing File** drop-down list in the **STYLES BROWSER** palette.*

Changing the System of Symbols

Now, you need to change the system of symbols available in the drawing area as per their application.

1. Select all the symbols of **PC, 240v-110v Switched Socket Outlet**, and **Inline Fuse Electrical** from the drawing. Next, invoke the **PROPERTIES** palette, refer to Figure 9-30.

2. Select the **E-230V Power (230-PWR)** option from the **System** drop-down list in the **System** rollout of the **PROPERTIES** palette and select **Z-Schematics-G** from the **Layer** drop-down list in the **General** rollout. The **PROPERTIES** palette after specifying the parameters appears as shown in Figure 9-31. After specifying properties, press ESC.

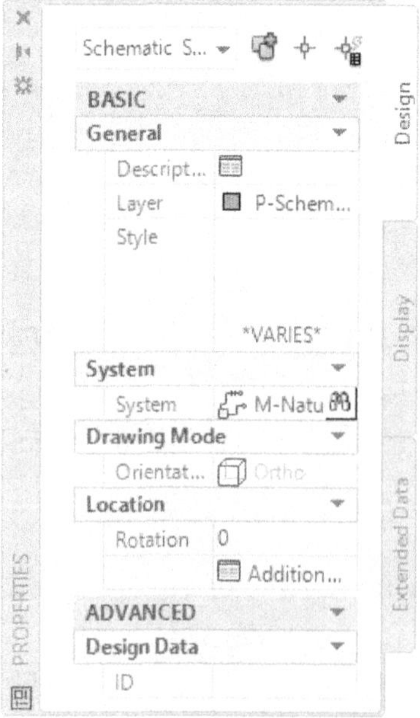

***Figure 9-30** The **PROPERTIES** palette*

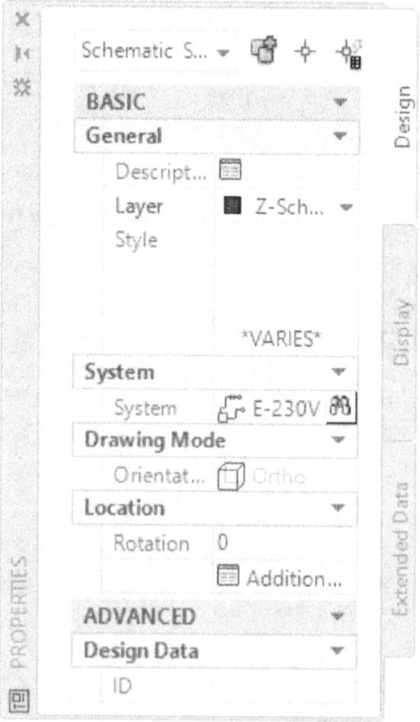

***Figure 9-31** The **PROPERTIES** palette after specifying the parameters*

3. Similarly, select all the Telephone Points in the **PROPERTIES** palette, and then select the **E-Telephone (TELEPHONE)** option from the **System** drop-down list. Also, select the

Z-Schematics-G option from the **Layer** drop-down list. After specifying properties, press ESC.

Connecting Symbols with Schematic Line

Now, you need to connect all schematic symbols to their corresponding schematic lines.

1. Choose the **Schematic Line** tool from the **Build** panel in the **Home** tab of the **Ribbon**; the **PROPERTIES** palette is displayed, as shown in Figure 9-32.

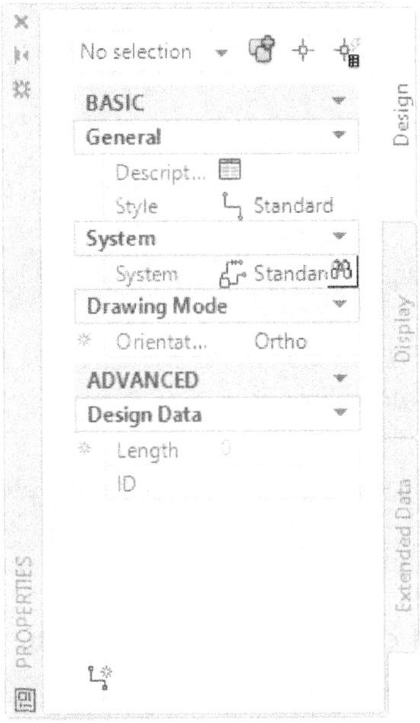

Figure 9-32 The ***PROPERTIES*** *palette after choosing the* ***Schematic Line*** *tool*

2. Select the **E-230V Power (230-PWR)** option from the **System** drop-down list and the **Wire** option from the **Style** drop-down list.

3. Click on schematic end connector of the **PC** at the top-left in the drawing, refer to Figure 9-33; the schematic line gets attached to the cursor.

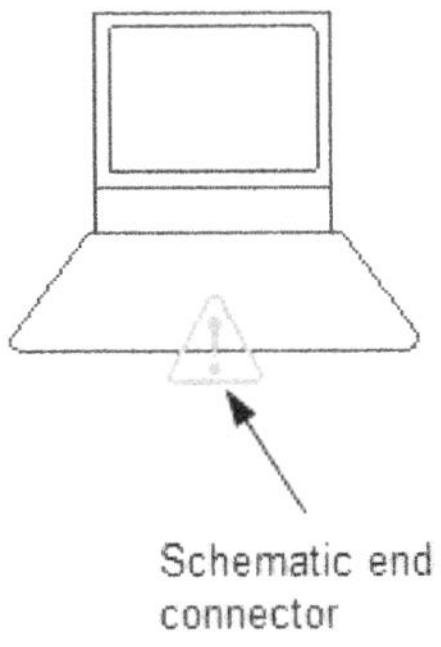

Figure 9-33 The schematic end connector to be selected

4. Move the cursor towards right and select the schematic end connector of the **240v-110v Switched Socket Outlet** adjacent to the selected PC. Similarly, connect the **Inline Fuse Electrical** in the drawing area.

5. Similarly, connect rest of the symbols, refer to 9-34, and press ESC key.

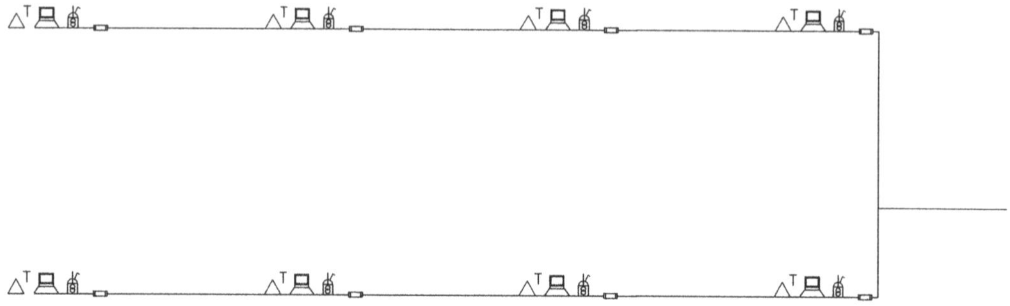

*Figure 9-34 The drawing after connecting all the symbols of the **Electrical Power (Global)** and **Electrical Schematic (Global)** categories*

6. Choose the **Schematic Line** tool again and select the **E-Telephone (TELEPHONE)** option from **System** drop-down list and the **Wire** option from the **Style** drop-down list in the **PROPERTIES** palette; you are prompted to specify the start point of the line.

7. Click on the schematic end connector of the **Telephone Point**; the schematic line gets attached to the cursor.

8. Connect all the telephone points with the schematic lines, as shown in Figure 9-35.

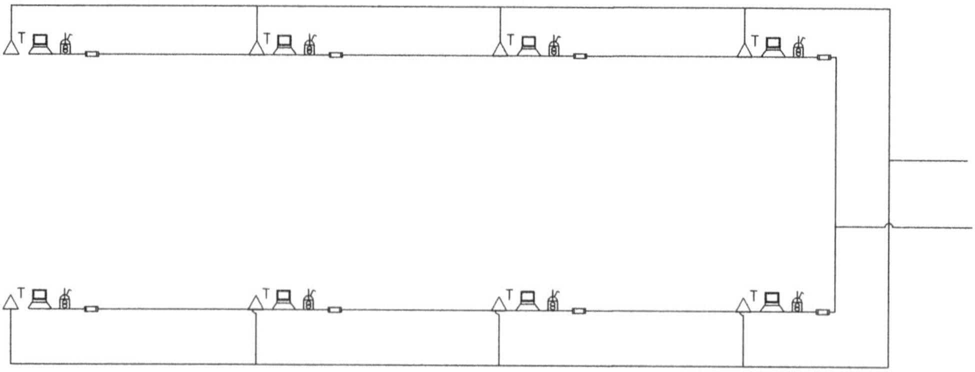

Figure 9-35 The drawing after connecting all the telephone points with the schematic lines

Saving the Drawing File

1. Choose **Save** from the **Application Menu** to save the drawing file.

Self-Evaluation Test

Answer the following questions and then compare them to those given at the end of this chapter:

1. In which of the following drawing files, the **360 Camera** symbol will be available in the **STYLES BROWSER** palette?

   (a) **Electrical Communications (Global)** (b) **Electrical Lighting (Global)**
   (c) **Mechanical Equipment (Global)** (d) **Electrical Schematic (Global)**

2. The **System** drop-down list is available in the __________ rollout of the **Design** tab in the **PROPERTIES** palette.

3. The __________ handle is used to modify the location of a symbol.

4. Schematic symbols are the symbolic representation of physical objects required in a building system. (T/F)

5. When you delete a schematic line in which the In-line symbols are attached, the symbols do not get deleted with the line. (T/F)

Review Questions

Answer the following questions:

1. In which of the following drawing files, the **Card Reader** symbol is available in the **Style** dialog box?

   (a) **Electrical Communications (Global)** (b) **Electrical Lighting (Global)**
   (c) **Mechanical Equipment (Global)** (d) **Electrical Schematic (Global)**

2. The __________ option is used to select a schematic symbol from the list of symbols available in AutoCAD MEP.

3. The __________ tool in the **Display Configuration** flyout is used to display the schematic representation of a drawing.

4. The **Ortho** option is used to place the symbols perpendicular to the insertion point. (T/F)

5. The style of schematic lines can be changed by using the **Style Manager**. (T/F)

EXERCISE

Exercise 1

In this exercise, you will create a schematic drawing, as shown in Figure 9-36. The schematic line for connecting the symbols should be of the **E-230V Power (230-PWR)** system.

(Expected time: 30 min)

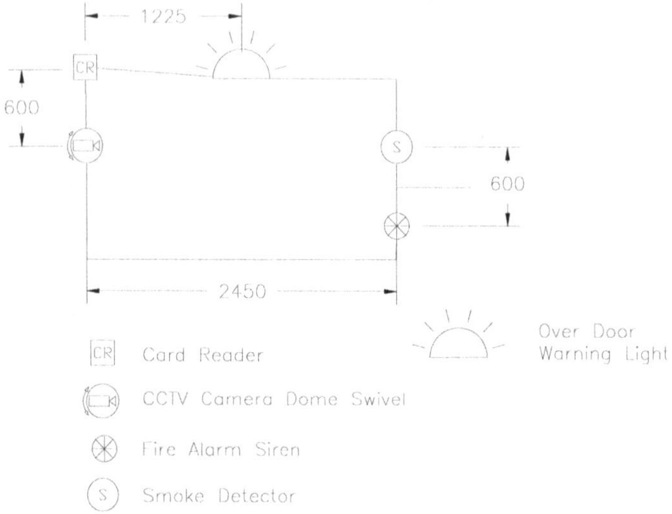

Figure 9-36 *Schematic drawing for Exercise 1*

Answers to Self-Evaluation Test

1. Electrical Communications (Global), **2. System**, **3.** Location, **4.** T, **5.** F

Project 1

Creating Complete System of a Forging Plant

Project Description

In this project, you will create complete system of a forging plant. Figure Prj1-1 shows the architectural drawings, Figure Prj1-2 shows the HVAC drawings, Figure Prj1-3 shows the piping drawings, and Figure Prj1-4 shows the electrical drawings of the plant. Table Prj1-1 shows the parameters required for various devices. **(Expected time: 4 hr)**

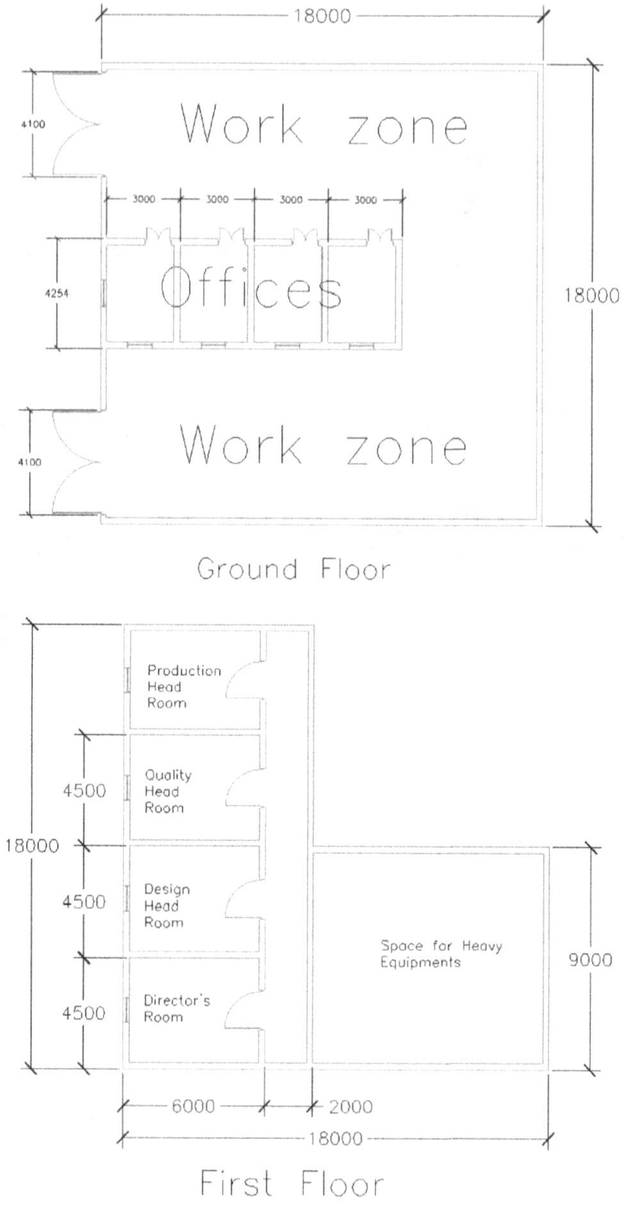

Figure Prj1-1 *Architectural drawings of the plant*

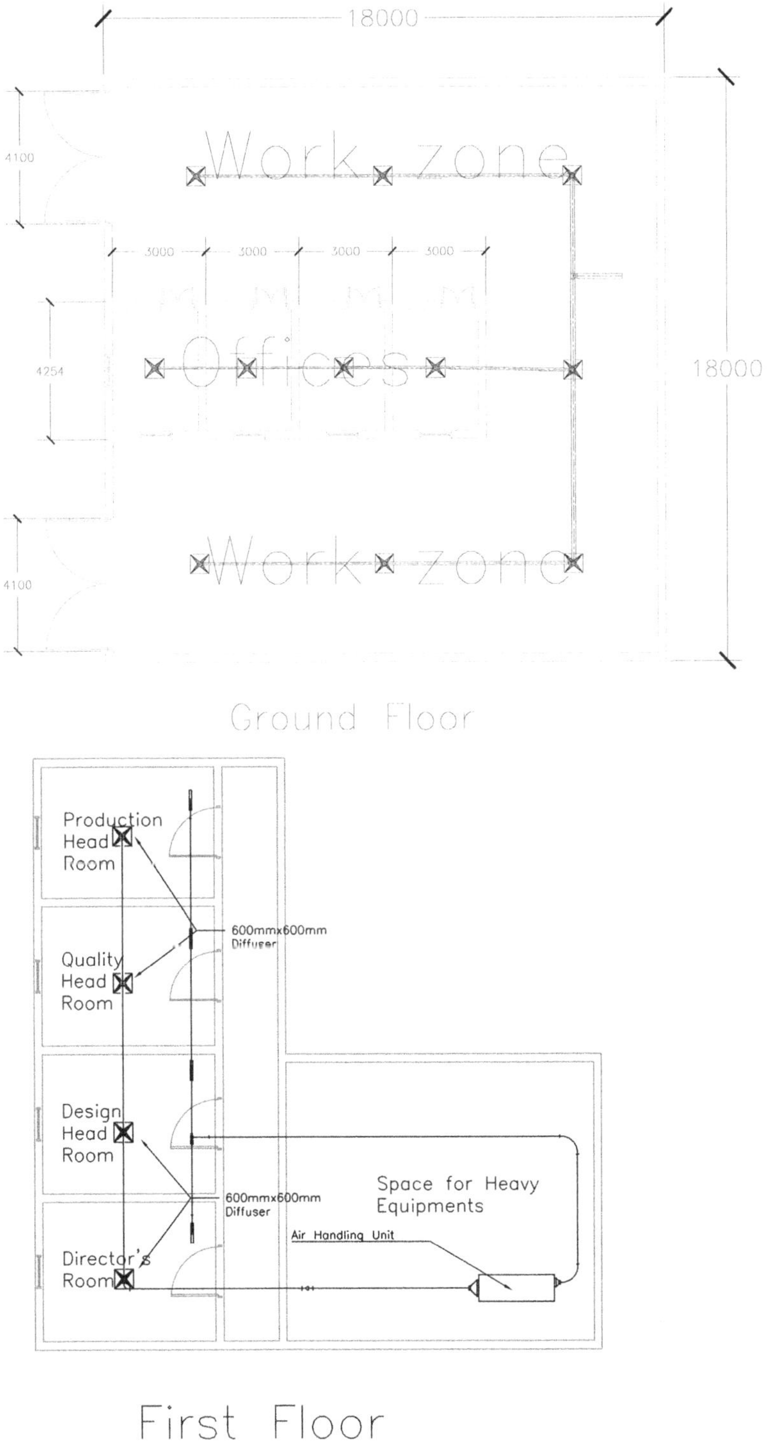

Figure Prj1-2 *HVAC drawings of the plant*

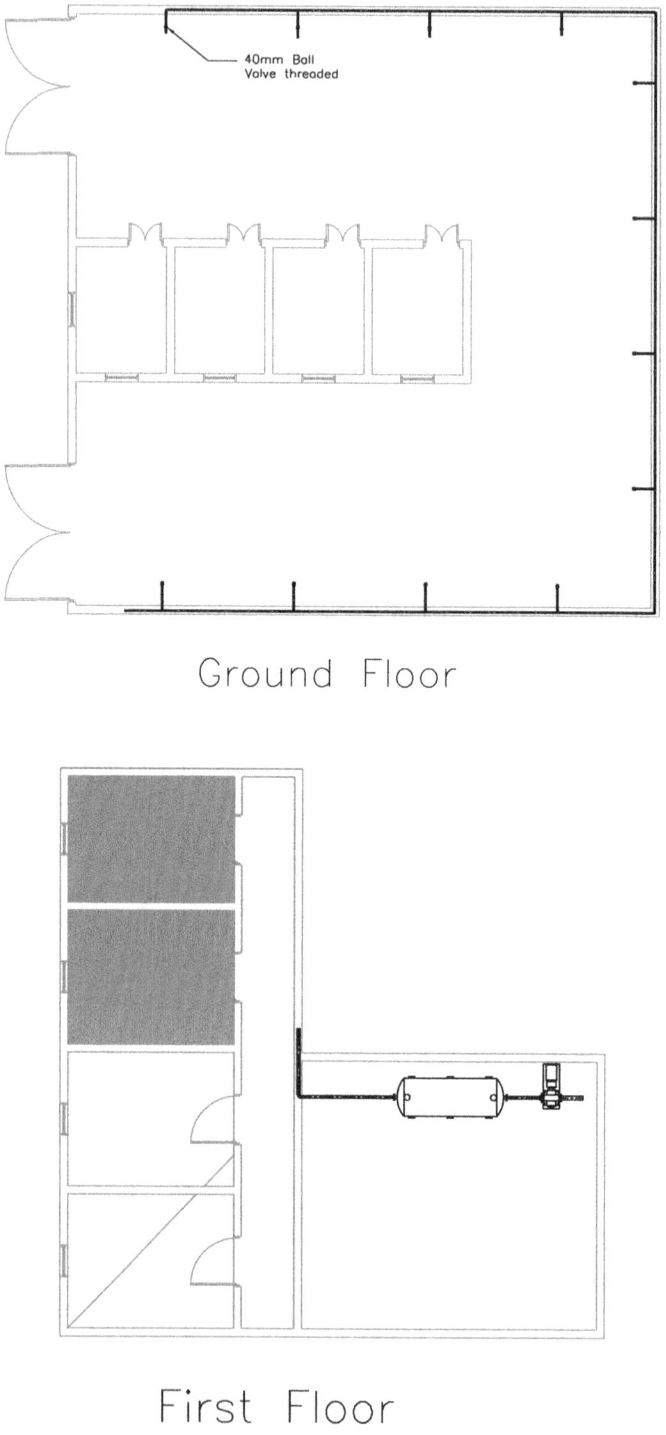

Figure Prj1-3 *Piping drawings of the plant*

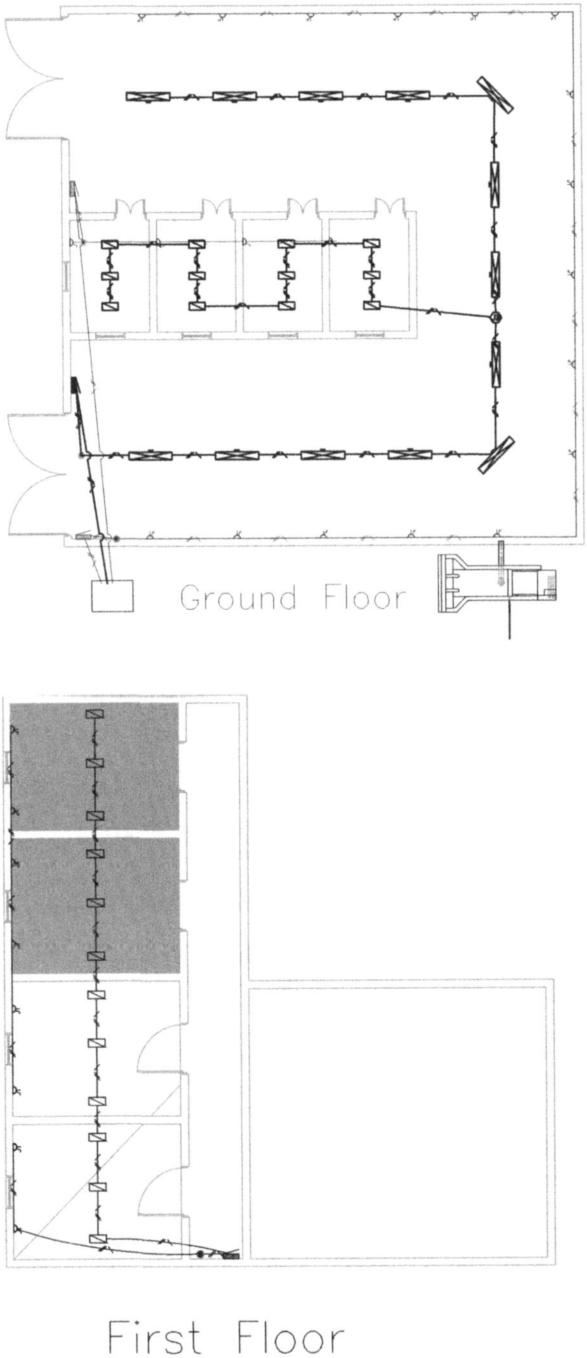

Figure Prj1-4 *Electrical drawings of the plant*

Table Prj1-1 *The parameters required for various devices*

Device	300x1200 Surface Type A Light	300x600 Recessed Light	Single Switch Socket
Load	180VA	100	300VA
Voltage	230	230	230
Phases	1	1	1
Maximum Overcurrent Rating	10	8	10
Power Factor	0.8	0.8	0.8

The following steps are required to complete this project:

1. Start a new project file
2. Create categories in the project
3. Create levels in the project
4. Create architectural drawings
    - Create architectural drawing of ground floor
    - Create walls in the architectural drawing for ground Floor
    - Change the door style in the architectural drawing
    - Create doors in the architectural drawing of ground floor
    - Create windows in the architectural drawing of ground floor
    - Create architectural drawing of first floor
    - Create walls in the architectural drawing for first floor
    - Create doors in the architectural drawing of first floor
    - Create windows in the architectural drawing of first floor
5. Create HVAC drawings
    - Create HVAC drawing of ground floor
    - Import the architectural drawing of ground floor
    - Add air terminals in the architectural drawing of ground floor
    - Create the duct line of ground floor
    - Calculate the duct sizes of ground floor
    - Create return duct for the ground floor
    - Create return duct line for the ground floor
    - Calculate the duct sizes of ground floor
    - Create HVAC drawing of first floor
    - Import the architectural drawing of first floor
    - Add air terminals in the architectural drawing of first floor
    - Add duct line to the diffusers
    - Add air handling unit
    - Add return grilles in the architectural drawing of first floor
    - Create return duct line for the first floor
    - Calculate the duct sizes of first floor
6. Create piping drawings
    - Create piping drawing of ground floor
    - Import the architectural drawing of ground floor
    - Add ball valves in the architectural drawing of ground floor
    - Add pipe line in the architectural drawing of ground floor
    - Connect ball valves with the pipe line
    - Create piping drawing of first floor
    - Import the architectural drawing of first floor

   - Add tank in the first floor
   - Add pumps in the first floor
   - Add pipe line in the first floor
7. Create electrical drawings
   - Create electrical drawing of ground floor
   - Import the architectural drawing of ground floor
   - Add **300x1200 surface type lights** to the drawing
   - Add sockets to the drawing
   - Add **300x600 recessed lights** to the drawing
   - Create panel of ground floor
   - Configure circuits of ground floor
   - Configure devices of ground floor
   - Add wires of ground floor
   - Calculate load and wire sizes of ground floor
   - Add transformer and emergency generator to the drawing based on total load
   - Create electrical drawing of first floor
   - Import the architectural drawing of first floor
   - Add lights in the drawing of first floor
   - Add sockets in the drawing of first floor
   - Create panel of first floor
   - Configure circuits of first floor
   - Configure devices of first floor
   - Add wires of first floor
   - Calculate loads and wire sizes of first floor

Starting a New Project File

1. Start AutoCAD MEP by using the *AutoCAD MEP 2022 - English (Global)* icon displayed on your desktop.

2. Choose **New > Project** from the **Application Menu**; the **Project Browser** is displayed.

3. Choose the **New Project** button available at the bottom of the **Project Browser**; the **Add Project** dialog box is displayed.

4. Enter the project name as **Forging Plant** in the **Project name** field, **0001** in the **Project Number** field and other descriptions in their respective fields. Make sure that the **Create from template project** check box is clear.

5. Choose the **OK** button; the newly created project file name is displayed in the left pane of the **Project Browser**, refer to Figure Prj1-5.

6. Choose the **Close** button from the **Project Browser**; the **PROJECT NAVIGATOR** is displayed in the drawing area and the new project gets activated.

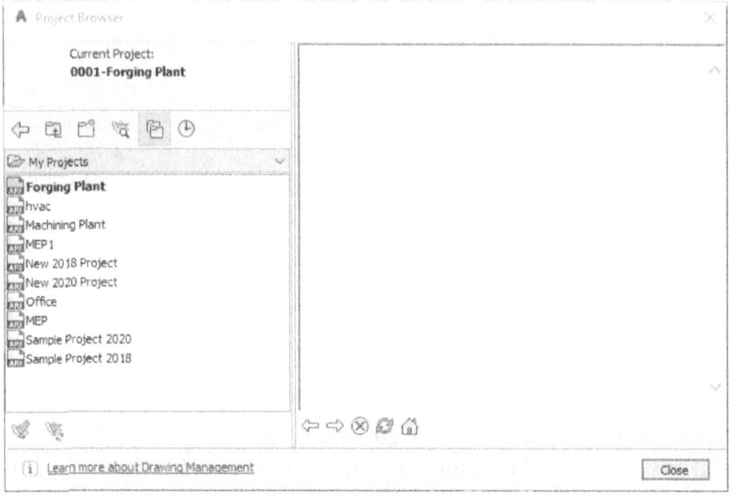

Figure Prj1-5 The Project Browser

Creating Categories in the Project

Now, you need to categorize the project.

1. To categorize a project, choose the **Constructs** tab and then click on the **Construct** category in it. Choose the **Add Category** button from the bottom of the **PROJECT NAVIGATOR** in the **Constructs** tab; a new category is added to the **Constructs** node.

2. Specify the name of the category as **Architectural** and press ENTER.

3. Similarly, add other categories and name them as **Mechanical**, **Piping**, and **Electrical**.

Creating Levels in the Project

Now, you need to create levels in the project.

1. To create levels, choose the **Project** tab from the **PROJECT NAVIGATOR**; the **PROJECT NAVIGATOR** is displayed, as shown in Figure Prj1-6.

2. Choose the **Edit Levels** button from the **Levels** rollout of the **PROJECT NAVIGATOR**; the **Levels** dialog box is displayed, as shown in Figure Prj1-7.

3. Enter **4000** in the **Floor to Floor Height** column and **1** in the **Name** column.

4. Choose the **Add Level** button on the right in the dialog box; a new level is added with the name **2** to the list displayed in the dialog box.

5. Choose the **OK** button in the dialog box to exit. If you get a message box with the message that do you want AutoCAD MEP to regenerate all the views in this project, as shown in Figure Prj1-8, choose the **Yes** button from the message box.

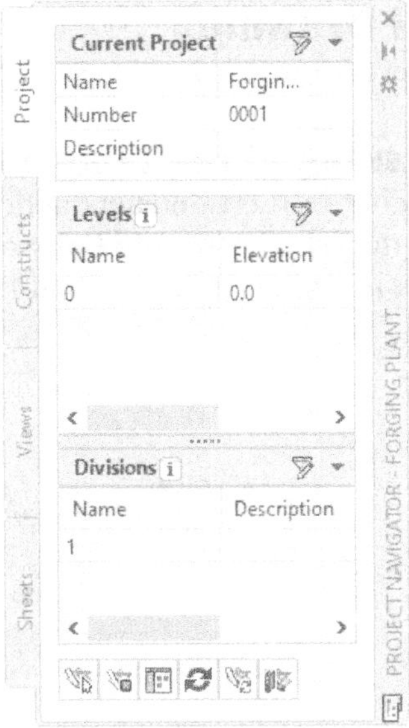

*Figure Prj1-6 The **PROJECT NAVIGATOR** with the **Project** tab chosen*

*Figure Prj1-7 The **Levels** dialog box*

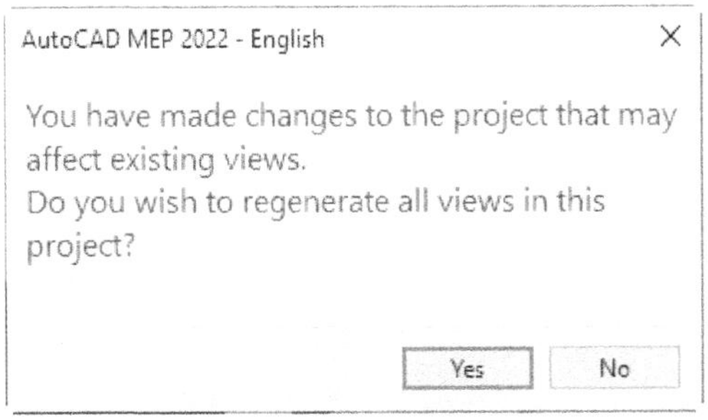

*Figure Prj1-8 The **AutoCAD MEP 2022** message box*

Creating Architectural Drawings

Now, you need to create architectural drawings for the ground floor and first floor.

Creating Architectural Drawing of the Ground Floor

1. Select the **Architectural** category in the **Contructs** node from the **Constructs** tab in the **PROJECT NAVIGATOR** and then choose the **Add Construct** button available at the bottom; the **Add Construct** dialog box is displayed, as shown in Figure Prj1-9.

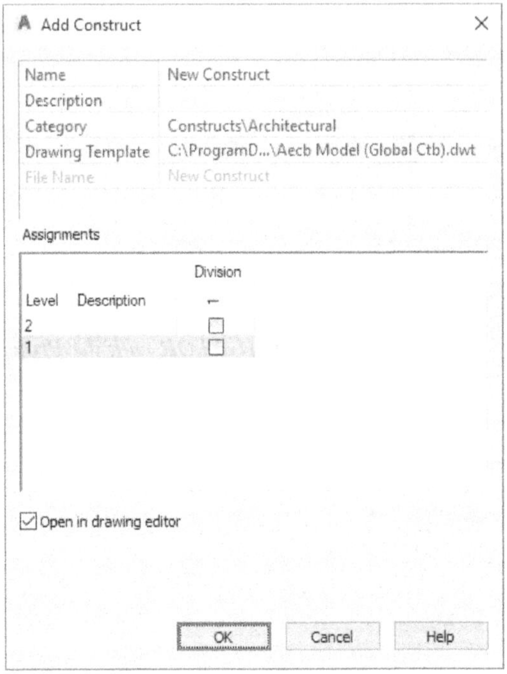

*Figure Prj1-9 The **Add Construct** dialog box*

2. Select the **Open in drawing editor** check box from the bottom of the dialog box.

3. Enter **Ground Floor Architectural** in the **Name** field of the dialog box.

4. Click in the **Description** field; the **Description** dialog box is displayed, as shown in Figure Prj1-10.

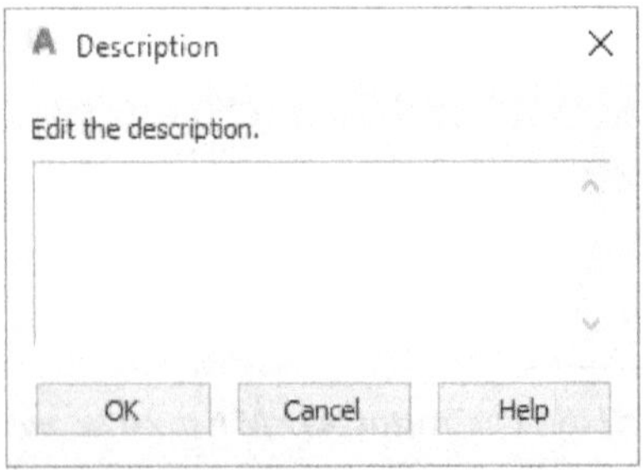

*Figure Prj1-10 The **Description** dialog box*

5. Enter the description as **This drawing is meant for architectural plan of the ground floor** in the **Edit the description** edit box and then choose the **OK** button from the dialog box.

6. Select the check box corresponding to level **1** in the **Division** column in the **Add Construct** dialog box. Also, make sure that the **Open in drawing editor** check box is selected and then choose the **OK** button from the dialog box; the drawing is opened in AutoCAD MEP. Also, the Ground Floor Architectural drawing is displayed with a lock icon adjacent to it in the **PROJECT NAVIGATOR**.

Note

*If the **PROJECT NAVIGATOR** is not displayed, you can invoke it by entering the command **PROJECTNAVIGATOR** in the command prompt.*

7. Choose the **Workspace Switching** option from the **Application Status Bar** and then choose the **Architecture** option from the flyout displayed; the **Architecture** workspace is activated.

Creating Walls in the Architectural Drawing

1. Choose the **Wall** tool from the **Wall** drop-down in the **Build** panel of the **Home** tab in the **Ribbon**; you are prompted to specify the starting point of the wall. Also, the **PROPERTIES** palette is displayed, refer to Figure Prj1-11.

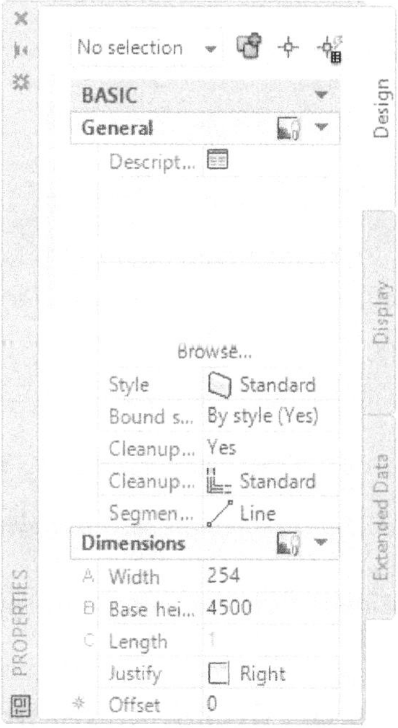

*Figure Prj1-11 The **PROPERTIES** palette*

2. Enter the base height of the wall as **4000**, width as **254**, and set the **Justify** option as **Right** in the **PROPERTIES** palette. Make sure the **Dynamic Input** option in the **Application Status Bar** is turned off.

3. Enter the coordinates **0,0,0** at the command prompt and press ENTER to specify the start point; a rubber band wall is displayed with its other end attached to the cursor.

4. Press F8 to work in the ORTHOMODE and specify the horizontal length of the wall **18000** at the command prompt. Next, press ENTER.

5. Move the cursor vertically upward and specify the value **18000** at the command prompt. Next, press ENTER.

6. Move the cursor toward the left and specify the value **18000** at the command prompt. Next, press ENTER.

7. Enter **C** at the command prompt to create the last wall. The drawing displays the architectural outer boundary of the plant, refer to Figure Prj1-12.

Figure Prj1-12 *The architectural outer boundary of the plant*

8. Similarly, create the walls inside the plant, as shown in Figure Prj1-13. For dimensions of the walls, refer to Figure Prj1-1.

Changing the Door Style in the Architectural Drawing

1. Choose the **Style Manager** tool from the **Style & Display** panel of the **Manage** tab in the **Ribbon**; the **Style Manager** is displayed, as shown in Figure Prj1-14.

2. Click on the plus sign adjacent to **Architectural Objects** on the left in the **Style Manager**; a list of architectural objects is displayed under the **Architectural Objects** category.

3. Click on the plus sign adjacent to **Door Styles** in the list; the **Standard** door style is displayed in the list.

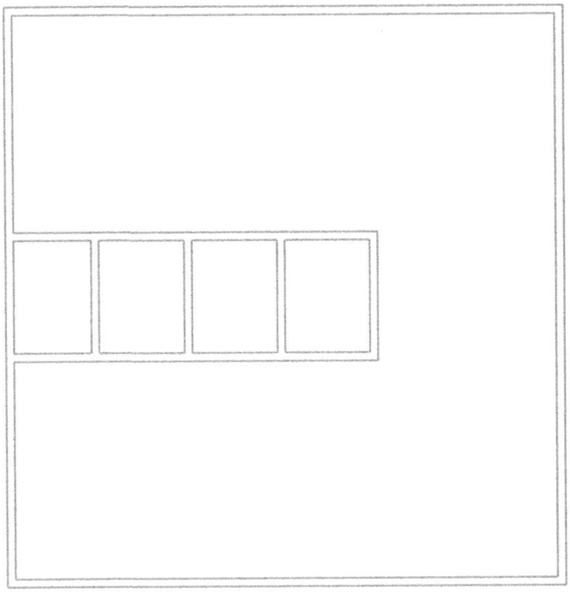

Figure Prj1-13 The drawing after creating all walls

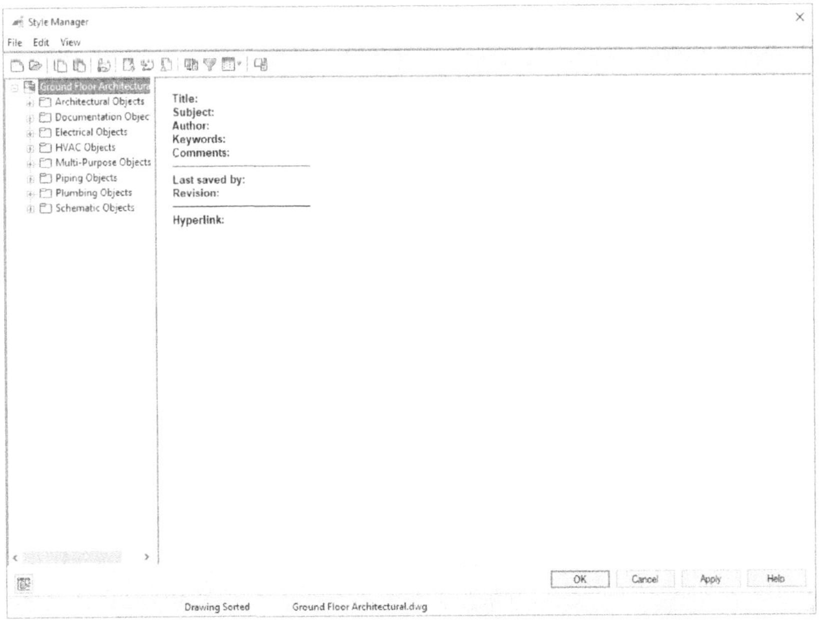

Figure Prj1-14 The ***Style Manager***

4. Select the **Standard** door style; the options related to the door style are displayed on the right in the **Style Manager**, refer to Figure Prj1-15.

5. Choose the **Design Rules** tab in the **Style Manager**; the options related to the shape of the door are displayed.

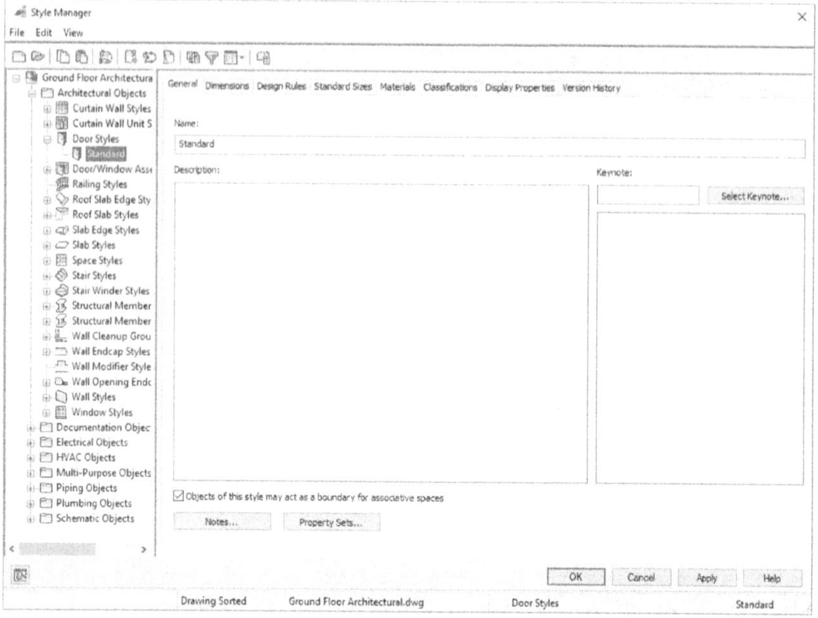

*Figure Prj1-15 The **Style Manager** with door style selected*

6. Select the **Rectangular** option from the **Predefined** drop-down list of the **Shape** area in the **Style Manager**.

7. Select the **Double** option from the **Door Type** area.

8. Choose the **Standard Sizes** tab; the options related to the size of door are displayed on the right in the **Style Manager**.

9. Choose the **Add New Standard Size** button from the right in the **Style Manager**; the **Add Standard Size** dialog box is displayed, as shown in Figure Prj1-16.

10. Enter the description as **Inner Door** in the **Description** edit box of the dialog box.

11. Specify the width and height as **1000** and **3000** in the respective fields of the dialog box and then choose the **OK** button.

12. Choose the **Add New Standard Size** button again and create a door style with width and height as **4000** and **3500**, respectively. Specify **Main Door** in the **Description** edit box.

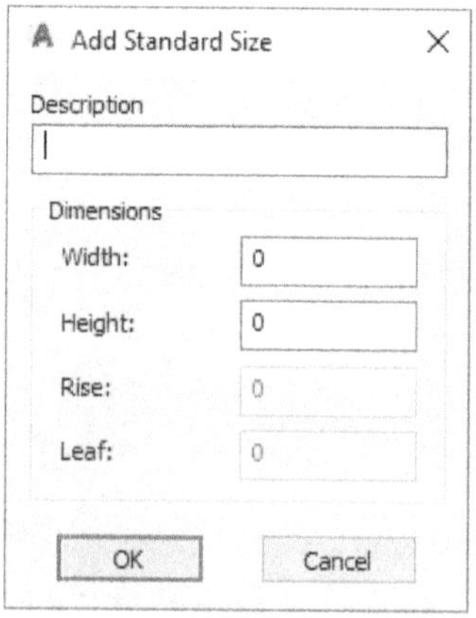

*Figure Prj1-16 The **Add Standard Size** dialog box*

13. Choose the **OK** button to exit the **Style Manager**.

Creating Doors in the Architectural Drawing of the Ground Floor

1. Choose the **Door** tool from the **Door** drop-down in the **Build** panel of the **Home** tab in the **Ribbon**; you are prompted to specify the insertion point of the door. Also, the **PROPERTIES** palette is displayed, as shown in Figure Prj1-17.

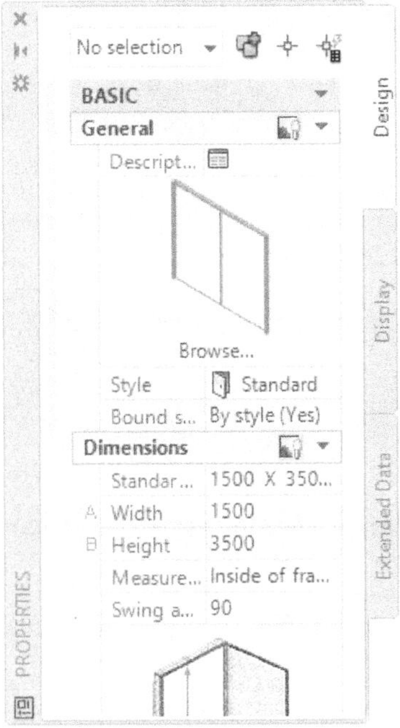

*Figure Prj1-17 The **PROPERTIES** palette displayed on choosing the **Door** tool*

2. Select the **1000 X 3000** option from the **Standard sizes** drop-down list in the **Dimensions** rollout of the **PROPERTIES** palette.

3. Select the **Offset/Center** option from the **Position along wall** drop-down list in the **Location** rollout and specify **150** in the **Automatic offset** edit box. Add all the inner doors with the respective walls, as shown in Figure Prj1-18. Press ENTER to exit the tool.

4. Again, choose the **Door** tool; you are prompted to select a wall or grid. Also, the **PROPERTIES** palette is displayed.

5. Select the **4000 X 3500** option from the **Standard sizes** drop-down list in the **Dimensions** rollout.

6. Click on the walls to create main doors, refer to Figure Prj1-19.

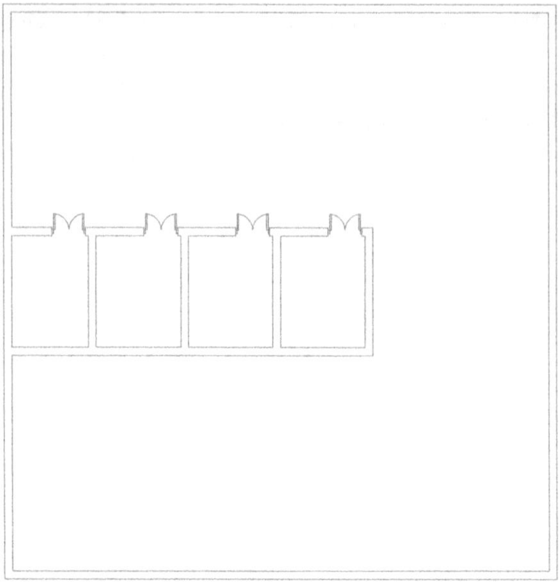

Figure Prj1-18 The drawing after adding inner doors

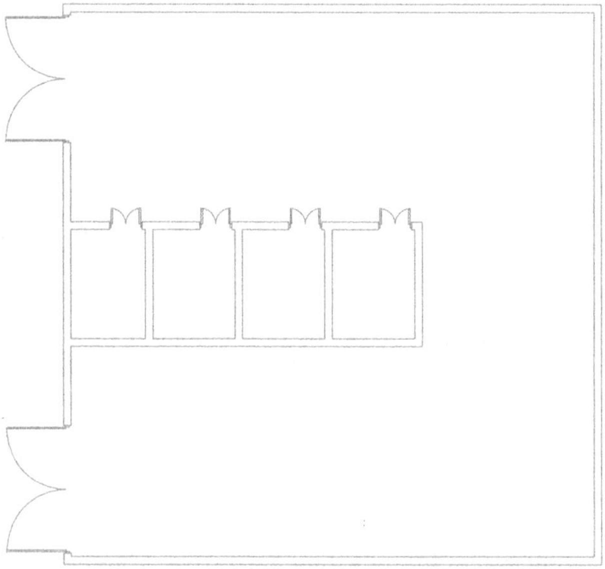

Figure Prj1-19 The drawing after adding main and inner doors

Creating Windows in the Architectural Drawing of the Ground Floor

1. Choose the **Window** tool from the **Window** drop-down in the **Build** panel of the **Home** tab in the **Ribbon**; you are prompted to select a wall or a grid assembly. Also, the **PROPERTIES** palette is displayed, as shown in Figure Prj1-20.

2. Choose the **Offset/Center** option from the **Position along wall** drop-down list in the **Location** rollout of the **PROPERTIES** palette and enter **0** in the **Automatic offset** edit box. Choose the window size **1010 X 1510** from the **Standard sizes** drop-down list in the **Dimensions** rollout. Also, select **Yes** from the **Relative to grid** drop-down list in the **Location** rollout.

Note

*If the window size 1010 X 1510 is not available in the **Standard sizes** drop-down list in the **Dimensions** rollout, manually enter **1010** and **1510** in the **Width** and **Height** edit boxes available below the **Standard sizes** drop-down list.*

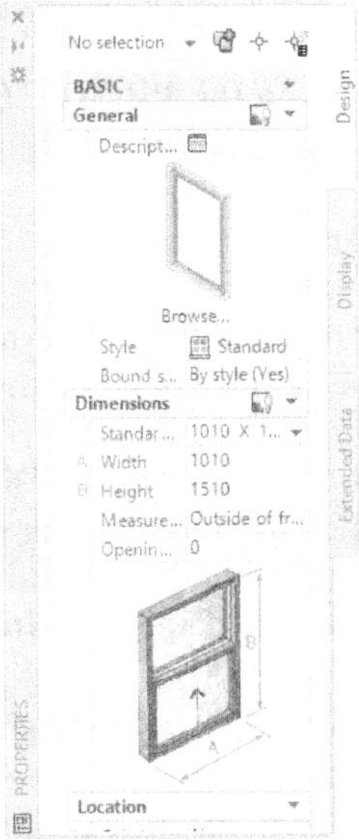

***Figure Prj1-20** The **PROPERTIES** palette on choosing the **Window** tool*

3. Click on the walls of the ground floor architectural drawing and locate the windows at the center of the wall, shown in Figure Prj1-21. Also, make sure you place the windows at the center of the walls, refer to Figure Prj1-1. After placing the windows, press ENTER to exit the tool.

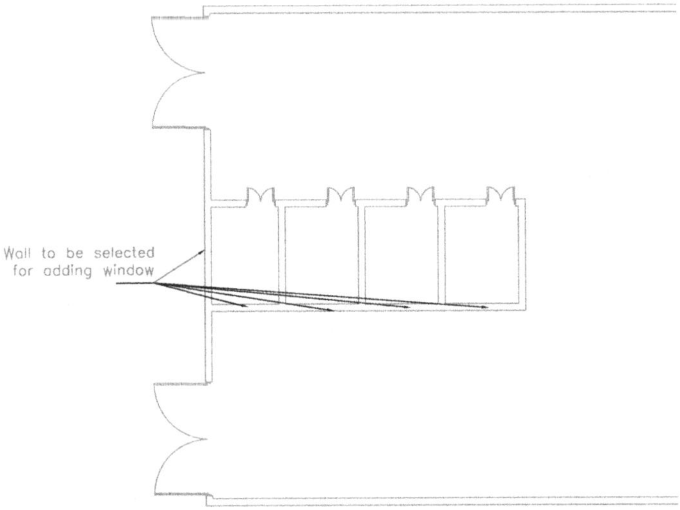

***Figure Prj1-21** The walls to be selected for adding windows*

4. Save the drawing and close it; the **Start** screen is displayed.

Creating Architectural Drawing of First Floor

1. Click on the **Forging Plant** project in the **Recent Documents** area; the **PROJECT NAVIGATOR** is displayed.

2. Select the **Architectural** category from the **PROJECT NAVIGATOR** and choose the **Add Construct** tool from the bottom; the **Add Construct** dialog box is displayed.

3. Specify the name as **First Floor Architectural** in the **Name** edit box of the dialog box.

4. Click in the **Description** field and specify the description as **This drawing is meant for architectural plan of the first floor** in the dialog box displayed. Next, choose the **OK** button.

5. Select the check box corresponding to level 2 in the **Division** column of the **Add Construct** dialog box. Also, make sure that the **Open in drawing editor** check box is selected and then choose the **OK** button to exit; the drawing is opened in AutoCAD MEP. Make sure that the **Architecture** option is chosen in the **Workspace Switching** flyout.

Creating Walls in the Architectural Drawing

1. Choose the **Wall** tool from the **Wall** drop-down in the **Build** panel of the **Home** tab in the **Ribbon**; you are prompted to specify the starting point of the wall. Also, the **PROPERTIES** palette is displayed.

2. Enter the base height of the wall as **4000**, width as **254**, and set the **Justify** option as **Right** in the **PROPERTIES** palette. Make sure the **Dynamic Input** option in the **Application Status Bar** is turned off.

3. Enter **0,0,0** at the command bar to specify the starting point of the wall and press ENTER. Press F8 to work in the ORTHOMODE and specify the vertical length of the wall as **18000** at the command prompt. Next, press ENTER.

4. Move the cursor toward right and then enter **8000** at the command prompt.

5. Move the cursor vertically downward and then enter **9000** at the command prompt.

6. Move the cursor toward right and then enter **10000** at the command prompt.

7. Move the cursor vertically downward and enter **9000** at the command bar. Enter **C** at the command prompt to create the last wall.

   The outer boundary of the first floor is created, refer to Figure Prj1-22. Now, you need to create rooms in the building.

8. Similarly, using the **Wall** tool, create the rooms, as shown in Figure Prj1-23. For dimension, refer to Figure Prj1-1.

Figure Prj1-22 Outer boundary of the first floor

Figure Prj1-23 Drawing of first floor after creating rooms

Creating Doors in the Architectural Drawing of the First Floor

1. Choose the **Door** tool from the **Door** drop-down in the **Build** panel of the **Home** tab in the **Ribbon**; you are prompted to select a wall or a grid. Also, the **PROPERTIES** palette is displayed.

2. Specify width as **1500** in the **Width** edit box and height as **3000** in the **Height** edit box of the **Dimensions** rollout in the **PROPERTIES** palette.

3. Select the **Offset/Center** option from the **Position along wall** drop-down list in the **Location** rollout of the **PROPERTIES** palette.

4. Click on a wall; the door gets attached to the cursor and can move along the walls.

5. Click on the wall again; the door is added. Similarly, add rest of the doors, refer to Figure Prj1-24. After adding all the doors, press ENTER to exit the tool.

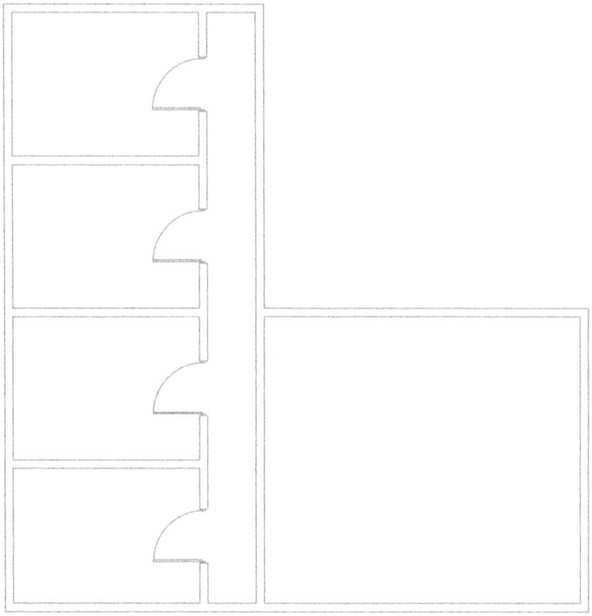

Figure Prj1-24 *Drawing of the first floor after creating doors*

Creating Windows in the Architectural Drawing of the Ground Floor

1. Choose the **Window** tool from the **Window** drop-down in the **Build** panel of the **Home** tab in the **Ribbon**; you are prompted to select a wall or a grid assembly. Also, the **PROPERTIES** palette is displayed.

2. Select the **Offset/Center** option from the **Position along wall** drop-down list of the **Location** rollout in the **PROPERTIES** palette and enter **0** in the **Automatic offset** edit box. Choose the window size **1010 X 1510** from the **Standard sizes** drop-down list in the **Dimensions** rollout. Also, select **Yes** from the **Relative to grid** drop-down list in the **Location** rollout.

3. Click on the walls, as shown in Figure Prj1-25, to add windows. After adding all the windows, press ENTER to exit the tool.

   The drawing after adding windows is displayed, as shown in Figure Prj1-26.

4. Save the drawing and close it.

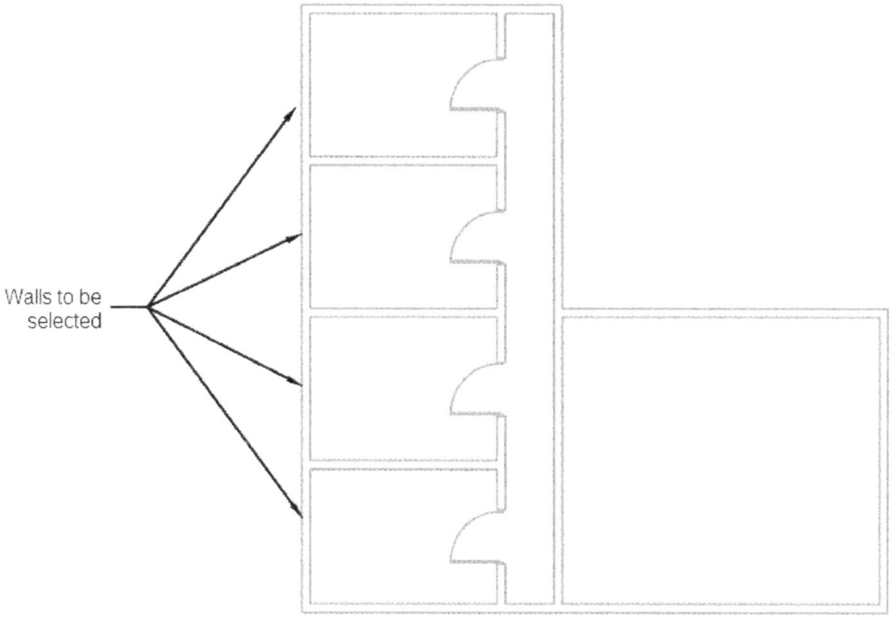

Figure Prj1-25 The walls to be selected for adding windows

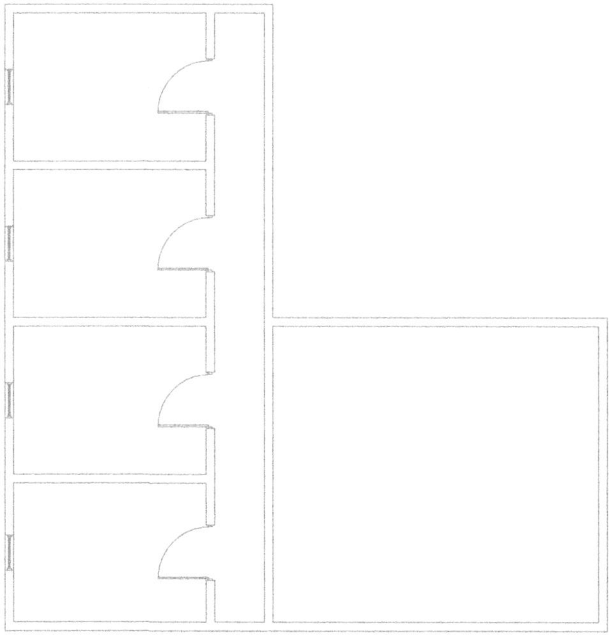

Figure Prj1-26 The drawing after adding windows

Creating HVAC Drawings

Now, you need to create HVAC drawings for the building. For creating HVAC drawings, you need to switch to the **HVAC** workspace.

Creating HVAC Drawing of the Ground Floor

1. Select the **Mechanical** category from the **PROJECT NAVIGATOR** and choose the **Add Construct** button available at the bottom; the **Add Construct** dialog box is displayed.

2. Enter the name **Ground Floor Mechanical** in the **Name** field of the dialog box.

3. Click in the **Description** field; the **Description** dialog box is displayed.

4. Enter the description as **This drawing is meant for HVAC plan of the ground floor** and then choose the **OK** button from the dialog box.

5. Select the check box corresponding to level 1 in the **Division** column and make sure that the **Open in drawing editor** check box is selected in the **Add Construct** dialog box. Next, choose the **OK** button from the dialog box; the drawing is opened. Also, the Ground Floor Mechanical drawing is displayed with a lock icon adjacent to it in the **PROJECT NAVIGATOR**.

6. Click on the **Workspace Switching** option in the **Application Status Bar** and then choose the **HVAC** option from the flyout displayed.

Importing the Architectural Drawing of the Ground Floor

Before adding any HVAC system to the project, you need to import the architectural plan of the ground floor.

1. In the **PROJECT NAVIGATOR**, click on the plus sign adjacent to the **Architectural** subcategory of the **Contructs** category in the **Constructs** tab; a list of architectural drawings is displayed.

2. Select Ground Floor Architectural drawing from the list and drag it to the current drawing; the architectural drawing is attached to the current drawing as an external reference.

Adding Diffusers to the Architectural Drawing of the Ground Floor

1. Choose the **Air Terminal** tool from the **Equipment** drop-down of the **Build** panel in the **Home** tab in the **Ribbon**; the **Add Multi-view Parts** dialog box is displayed, as shown in Figure Prj1-27.

2. Click on the + sign adjacent to the **Diffusers** and choose the **600 x 600 mm Square Faced Ceiling Diffuser** part from the **Part** tab of the dialog box; the preview of the diffuser is displayed on the right in the dialog box.

3. Select the **600 x 600 mm Square Plaque Face Ceiling Diffuser -150 mm Neck** option from the **Part Size Name** drop-down list at the bottom of the dialog box.

4. Enter the value **3200** in the **Elevation** edit box.

5. Choose the **Flow** tab; the dialog box is modified, as shown in Figure Prj1-28.

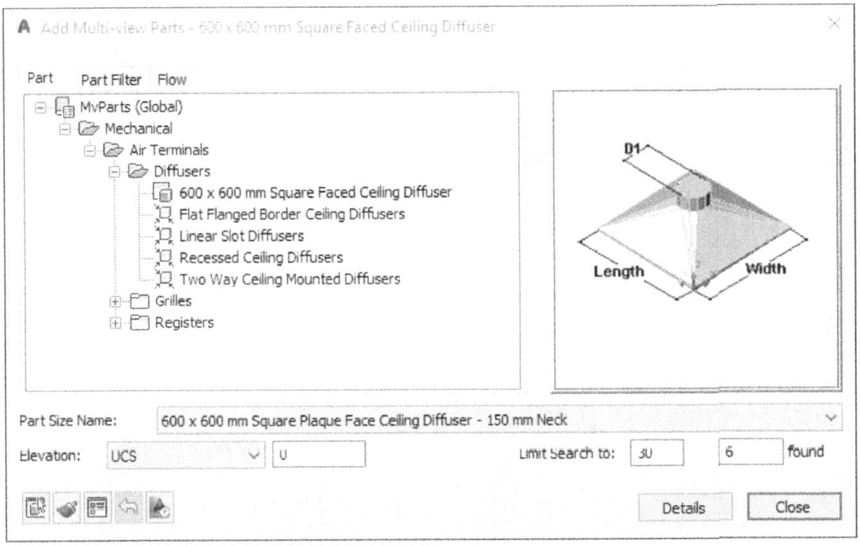

*Figure Prj1-27 The **Add Multi-view Parts** dialog box*

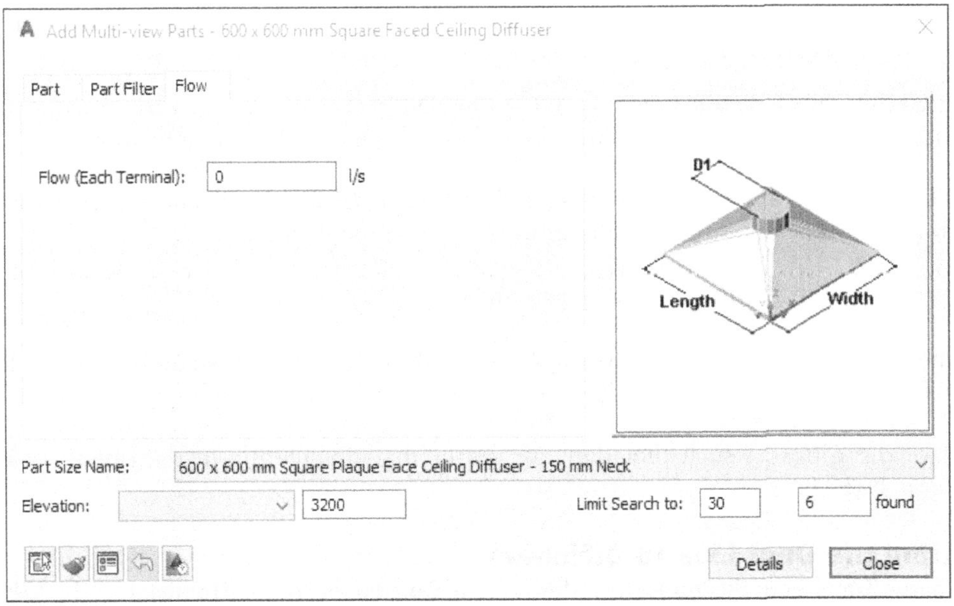

*Figure Prj1-28 The **Add Multi-view Parts** dialog box with the **Flow** tab chosen*

6. Specify **8** in the **Flow (Each Terminal)** edit box.

7. Place the diffusers centered symmetrically, as shown in Figure Prj1-29.

   Now, you need to add the air terminals to the offices having a flow rate of 2 liter per sec.

8. Choose the **Air Terminal** tool from the **Equipment** drop-down of the **Build** panel in the **Home** tab in the **Ribbon**; the **Add Multi-view Parts** dialog box is displayed.

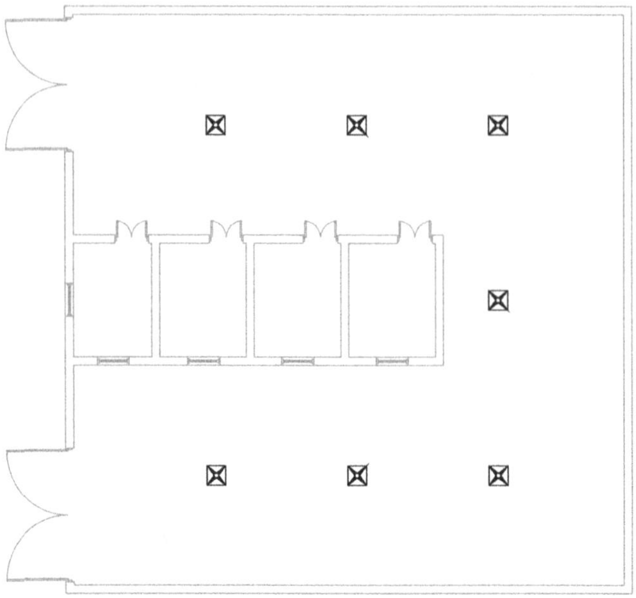

Figure Prj1-29 The drawing after adding diffusers in the outer area

9. Select the **600 x 600 mm Square Faced Ceiling Diffuser** part from the **Part** tab of the dialog box; the preview of the diffuser is displayed on the right in the dialog box.

10. Select the **600 x 600 mm Square Plaque Face Ceiling Diffuser -150 mm Neck** option from the **Part Size Name** drop-down list at the bottom in the dialog box.

11. Enter the value **3200** in the **Elevation** edit box.

12. Choose the **Flow** tab and specify the value of flow as **2** in the **Flow** edit box of the dialog box.

13. Place the diffusers such that they are centered symmetrically in the offices, refer to Figure Prj1-30.

Creating the Duct Line to Diffusers

1. Choose **Tools** from the **Tools** drop-down in the **Build** panel of the **Home** tab in the **Ribbon**; the **TOOL PALETTES** is displayed.

2. Choose the **Properties** button on the top left in the **TOOL PALETTES**; a flyout is displayed, as shown in Figure Prj1-31.

Note

*If the **TOOL PALETTES** is not displayed in the drawing area, then to display it, choose **Tools** from the **Tools** drop-down in the **Build** panel of the **Home** tab in the **Ribbon**.*

3. Choose the **HVAC** option from the flyout, if it is not already chosen; the tools related to HVAC system are displayed in the **TOOL PALETTES**, refer to Figure Prj1-32.

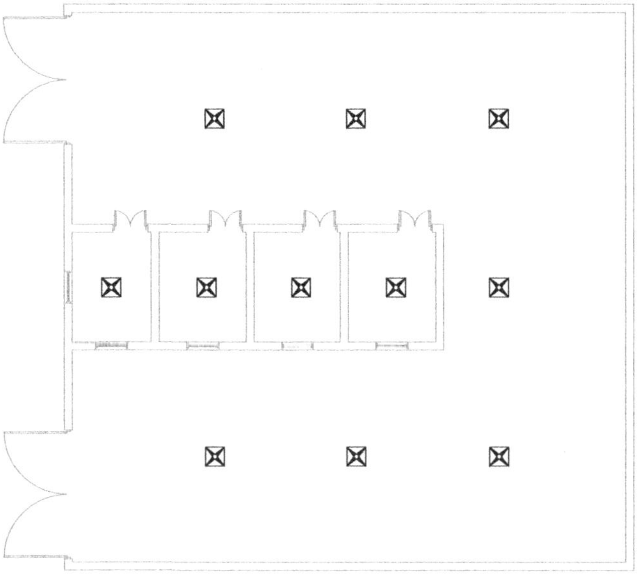

Figure Prj1-30 *The drawing after adding diffusers in the offices*

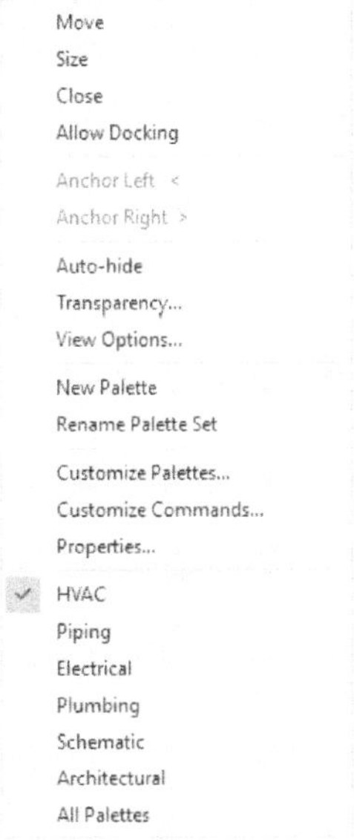

Figure Prj1-31 *The* ***Properties*** *flyout of the* ***TOOL PALETTES***

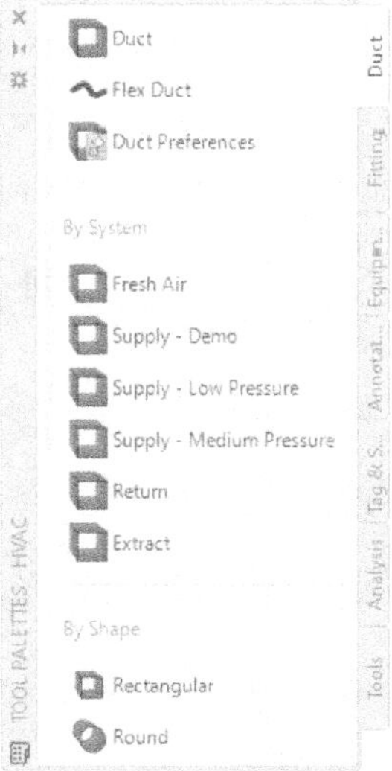

Figure Prj1-32 *The* ***TOOL PALETTES - HVAC***

4. Choose the **1-Line** tool from the **By Shape** area in the **Duct** tab of the **TOOL PALETTES**; you are prompted to specify the start point of the duct.

5. Click on the Duct End Connector of the first diffuser at the top in the outer area of the plant, refer to Figure Prj1-33.

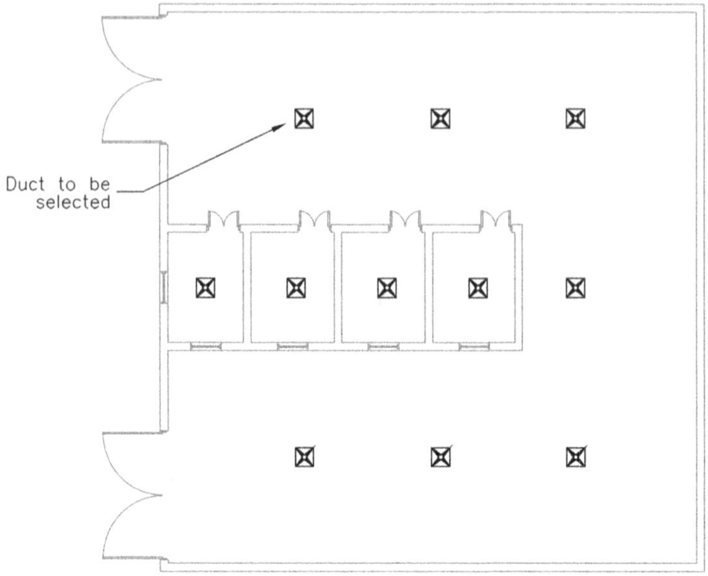

Figure Prj1-33 *The duct to be selected for adding duct line*

6. Click on the Duct End Connector of adjacent diffuser to the previous one and press ENTER to connect it to the duct line. Similarly, connect all the other ducts to the duct line, refer to Figure Prj1-34.

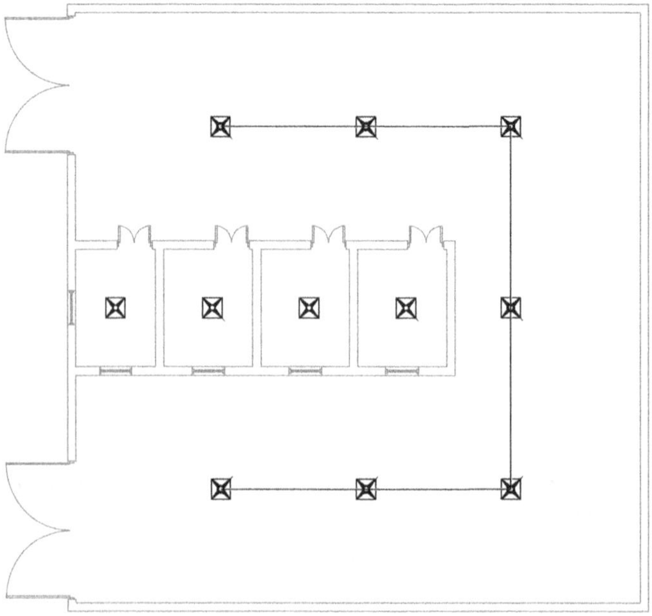

Figure Prj1-34 *The duct line created between the outer ducts*

To connect the ducts at the same elevation, you might need to switch to isometric views.

7. Connect all the ducts in the office area to the duct at the middle of the duct line using the **1-Line** tool from the **By Shape** area in the **Duct** tab of the **TOOL PALETTES**, refer to Figure Prj1-35.

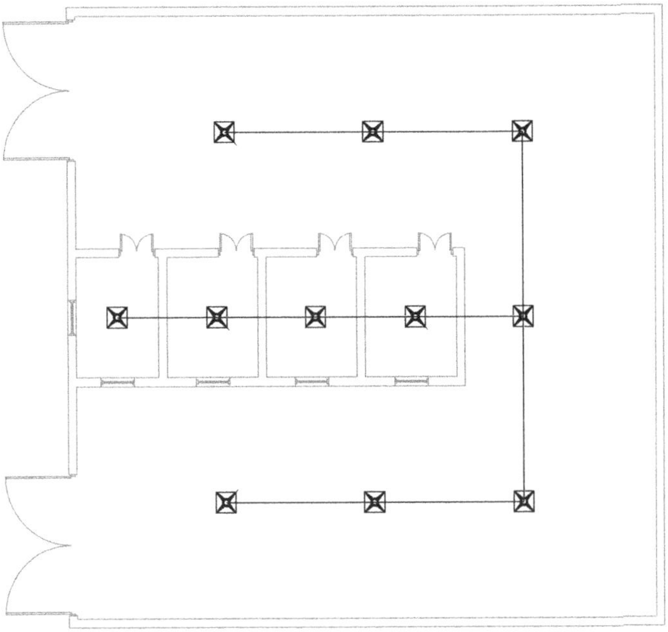

Figure Prj1-35 *Adding office ducts to the duct line*

8. Similarly, connect a duct line to the main duct line for calculating the duct size and transforming the duct line into ducts of required sizes, refer to Figure Prj1-36.

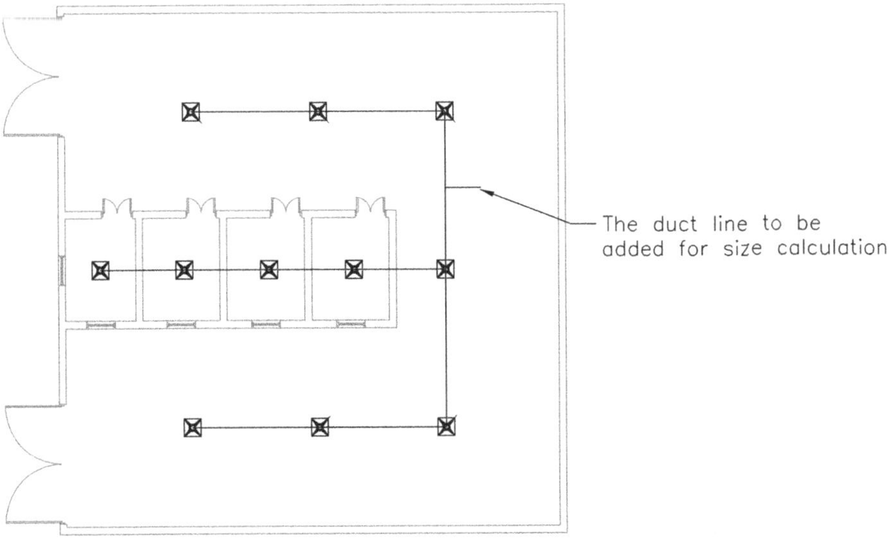

Figure Prj1-36 *Adding a duct line for size calculation*

Calculating the Duct Sizes

1. Select the duct line created for load calculations; the **Duct** contextual tab is displayed, as shown in Figure Prj1-37.

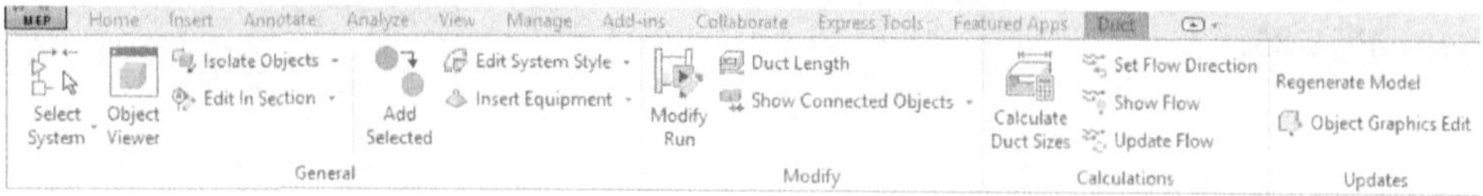

*Figure Prj1-37 The **Duct** contextual tab*

2. Choose the **Calculate Duct Sizes** tool from the **Calculations** panel of the **Duct** contextual tab in the **Ribbon**; the **Duct System Size Calculator** dialog box is displayed, as shown in Figure Prj1-38.

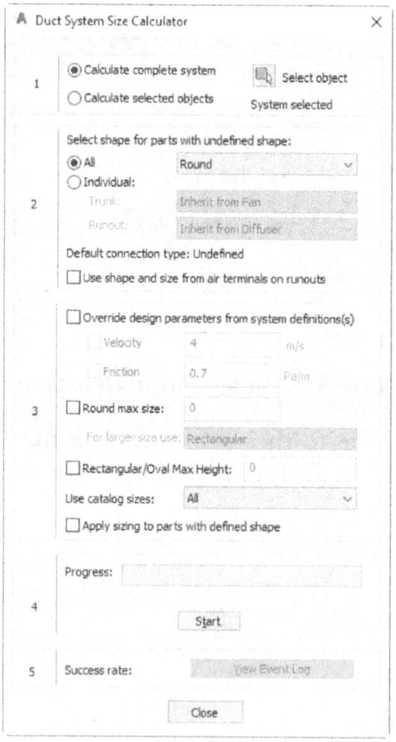

*Figure Prj1-38 The **Duct System Size Calculator** dialog box*

3. Select the **Round** option from the first drop-down list in the **2** area of the dialog box.

4. Choose the **Start** button from the **4** area of the dialog box; the **Choose a Part** dialog box is displayed, as shown in Figure Prj1-39. Also, you are prompted to select a suitable part from the part list available at the left in the dialog box.

Note

*The **Choose a Part** dialog box will be displayed during the transition only when there is an elevation or size difference between the two mating ducts.*

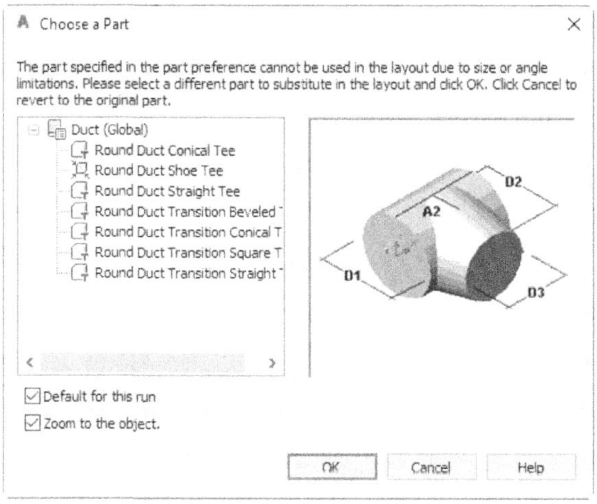

*Figure Prj1-39 The **Choose a Part** dialog box*

5. Select the desired part from the left area of the dialog box and choose the **OK** button from the dialog box; the desired part is added and the **Choose a Part** dialog box is displayed again.

6. Select the desired part from the dialog box and choose the **OK** button. Repeat the procedure till all the parts are added; the success rate of the duct size is displayed in the **5** area of the dialog box. If the success rate is not 100%, then there is an error in the fittings added to the duct line.

7. To check the problems in the duct line, choose the **View Event Log** button from the **5** area of the dialog box; the **Event Log** dialog box is displayed, refer to Figure Prj1-40. In such cases, you need to rearrange the duct system. The duct line after rearranging is shown in Figure Prj1-41.

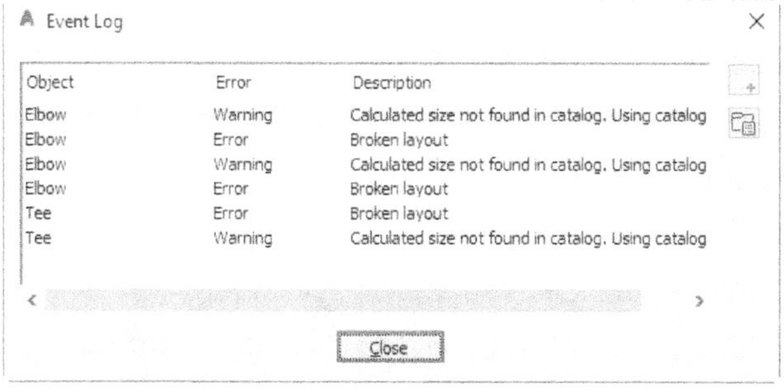

*Figure Prj1-40 The **Event Log** dialog box*

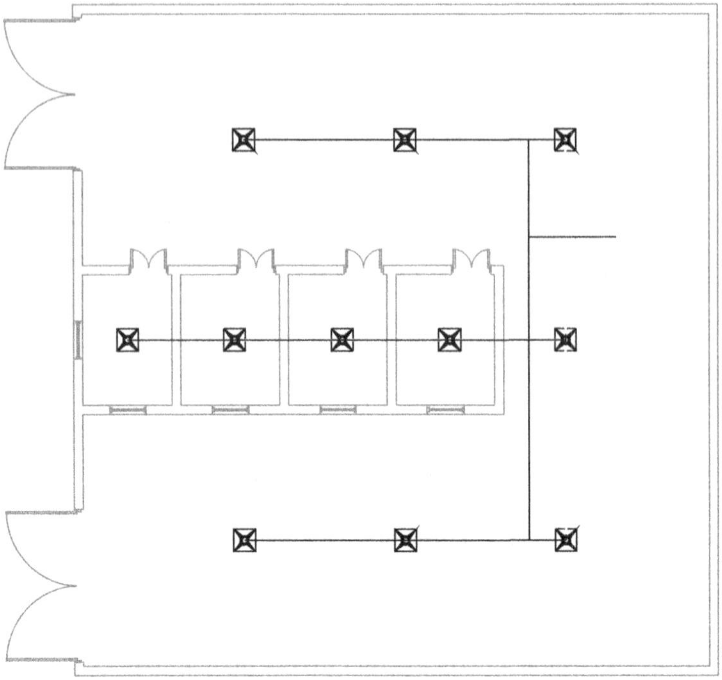

Figure Prj1-41 The duct line after rearrangement

8. Again, select the duct line created for calculating duct sizes and choose the **Calculate Duct Sizes** tool from the **Duct** contextual tab; the **Duct System Size Calculator** dialog box is displayed.

9. Choose the **Start** button from the **4** area of the dialog box and add the desired part by using the **Select a Part** dialog box; the system applies the transitions automatically and the duct system is displayed, as shown in Figure Prj1-42.

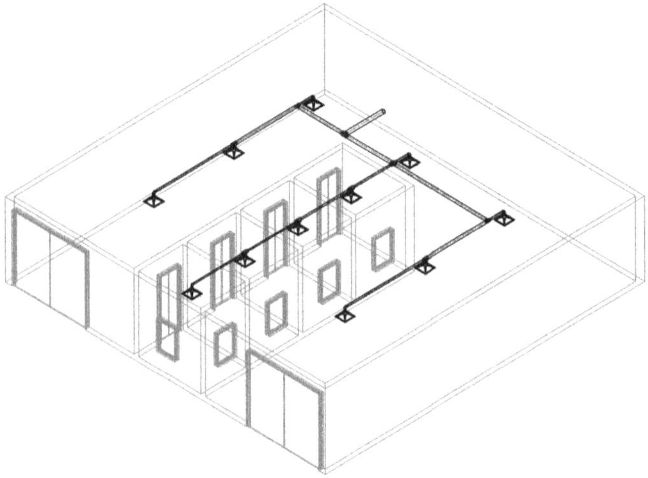

Figure Prj1-42 The Duct system after calculating duct sizes and applying transitions

10. After the ducts are connected properly, the **Event Log** dialog box is displayed, showing an error that occurs due to open end flow. This is because the main supply duct is not connected to the AHU. You can skip the error and choose the **OK** button to close the **Duct System Size Calculator** dialog box.

Creating Return Duct for the Ground Floor

1. Choose the **Air Terminal** tool from the **Equipment** drop-down in the **Build** panel of the **Home** tab in the **Ribbon**; the **Add Multi-view Parts** dialog box is displayed, as shown in Figure Prj1-43.

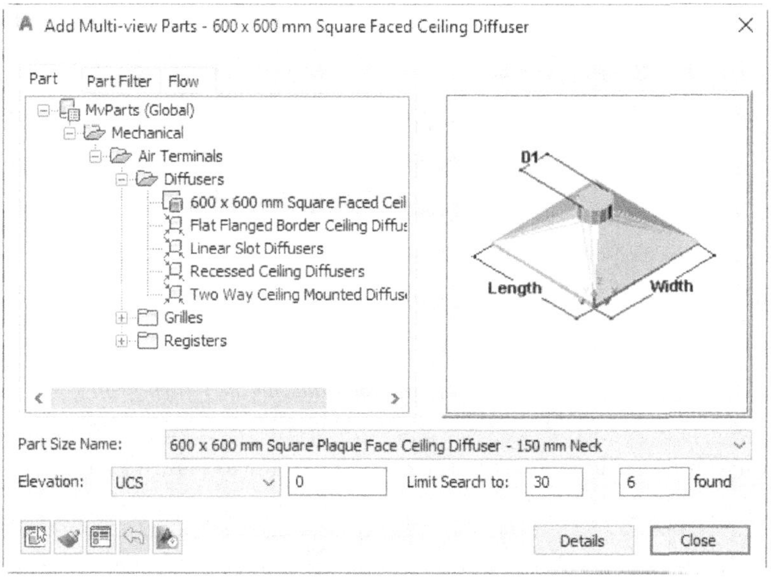

Figure Prj1-43 The ***Add Multi-view Parts*** *dialog box*

2. Click on the plus sign adjacent to **Grilles** in the **Part** tab of the dialog box; various grilles available in AutoCAD MEP are displayed.

3. Select the **Return Air Grilles** part from the part list; preview of the parts is displayed in the right of the dialog box.

4. Select the **75 X 625 mm Return Air Grille** option from the **Part Size Name** drop-down list.

5. Enter the value **3600** in the **Elevation** edit box available at the bottom.

6. Choose the **Flow** tab and specify the value **8** in the **Flow (Each Terminal)** edit box.

7. Add the return grilles, as shown in Figure Prj1-44.

Creating Return Duct Line for the Ground Floor

1. Choose the **1-Line** tool from the **By Shape** area of the **TOOL PALETTES**; you are prompted to specify the start point of the duct line.

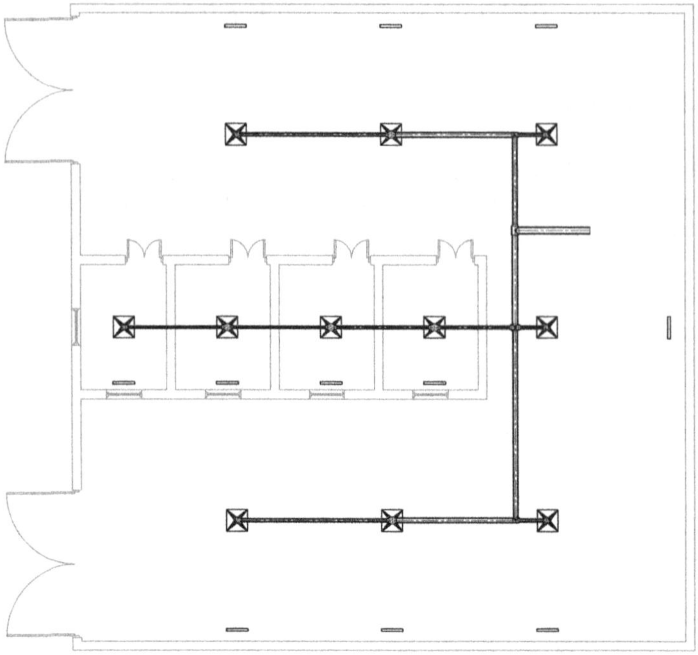

Figure Prj1-44 The drawing after adding the return grilles

2. Click on the return grille and create the duct line, refer to Figure Prj1-45.

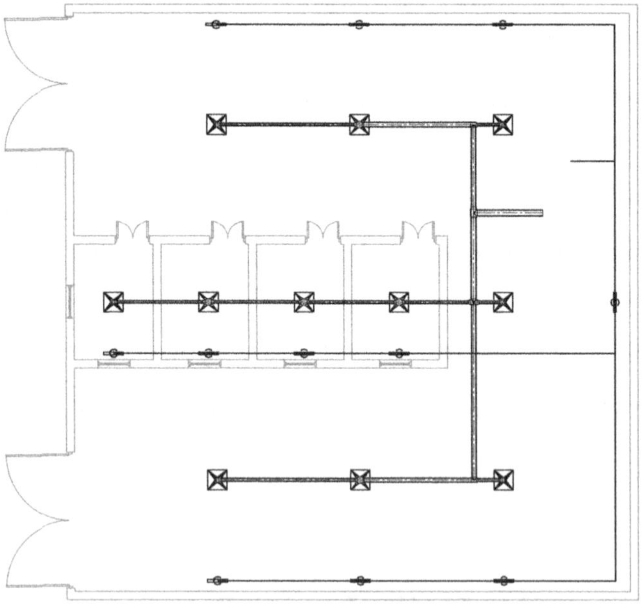

Figure Prj1-45 The drawing after connecting the return grilles with the duct line

Calculating the Duct Sizes for Return Grille System

1. Select a duct line in the return grille system; the **Duct** contextual tab is displayed.

2. Choose the **Calculate Duct Sizes** tool from the **Calculations** panel in the contextual tab; the **Duct System Size Calculator** dialog box is displayed. Make sure that **Round** is selected in the first drop-down list of the **2** area in the dialog box.

3. Choose the **Start** tool from the **4** area of the dialog box and choose the **OK** button from the successive dialog boxes; the duct sizes are calculated and transition is applied automatically.

4. Choose the **Close** button from the **Duct System Size Calculator** dialog box to exit.

5. Save the drawing and close it.

Creating Mechanical Drawing of the First Floor

1. Select the **Mechanical** category from the **PROJECT NAVIGATOR** and choose the **Add Construct** button available at the bottom; the **Add Construct** dialog box is displayed.

2. Enter the name **First Floor Mechanical** in the **Name** field of the dialog box.

3. Click in the **Description** field; the **Description** dialog box is displayed.

4. Enter the description as **This drawing is meant for mechanical plan of the first floor** and then choose the **OK** button from the dialog box.

5. Select the check box corresponding to level 2 in the **Division** column in the **Add Construct** dialog box and make sure that the **Open in drawing editor** check box is selected in the **Add Construct** dialog box. Next, choose the **OK** button from the dialog box; the drawing is opened. Also, the First Floor Mechanical drawing is displayed with a lock icon adjacent to it in the **PROJECT NAVIGATOR**.

6. Click on the **Workspace Switching** option in the **Application Status Bar** and choose the **HVAC** option from the flyout.

Importing the Architectural Drawing of the First Floor

Before adding a mechanical system to this drawing, you need to first import the architectural plan of the first floor.

1. Open the **PROJECT NAVIGATOR** and then click on the plus sign adjacent to Architectural category in the **Constructs** tab; a list of architectural drawings is displayed.

2. Select First Floor Architectural drawing from the list and drag it to the current drawing; the architectural drawing is attached to the current drawing as an external reference.

Adding Diffusers to the Architectural Drawing of the First Floor

1. Choose the **Air Terminal** tool from the **Equipment** drop-down of the **Build** panel in the **Home** tab of the **Ribbon**; the **Add Multi-view Parts** dialog box is displayed.

2. Select the **600 x 600 mm Square Faced Ceiling Diffuser** part from the **Part** tab of the dialog box; preview of the diffuser is displayed in the right of the dialog box.

3. Select the **600 x 600 mm Square Plaque Face Ceiling Diffuser -150 mm Neck** option from the **Part Size Name** drop-down list at the bottom of the dialog box.

4. Enter the value **3200** in the **Elevation** edit box.

5. Choose the **Flow** tab; the dialog box is modified, as shown in Figure Prj1-46.

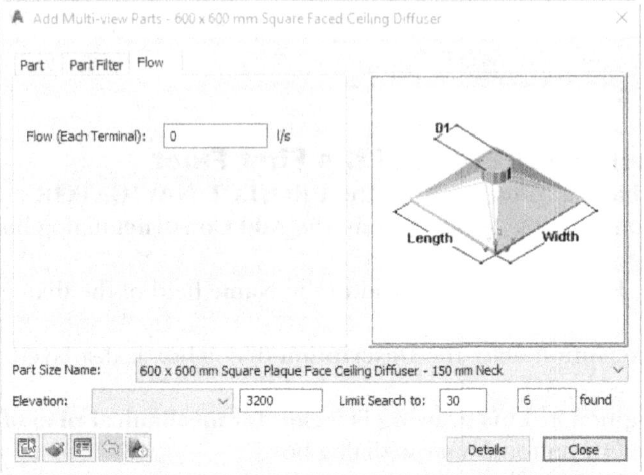

*Figure Prj1-46 The **Add Multi-view Parts** dialog box with the **Flow** tab chosen*

6. Enter the value **4** in the **Flow** edit box.

7. Place the diffusers such that they are centered symmetrically, as shown in Figure Prj1-47.

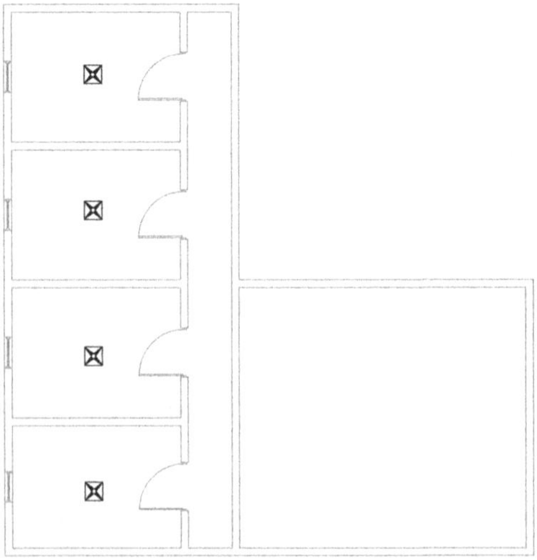

Figure Prj1-47 The drawing after adding diffusers

Note

You can also specify the Elevation value in the respective edit box of the ***BASIC > Location*** *rollout in the* ***PROPERTIES*** *palette.*

Adding Duct Line to the Diffusers

1. Choose the **1-Line** tool from the **By Shape** area of the **TOOL PALETTES**; you are prompted to specify the start point of the duct line.

2. Click on the Duct End Connectors and connect the duct line with diffuser, refer to Figure Prj1-48.

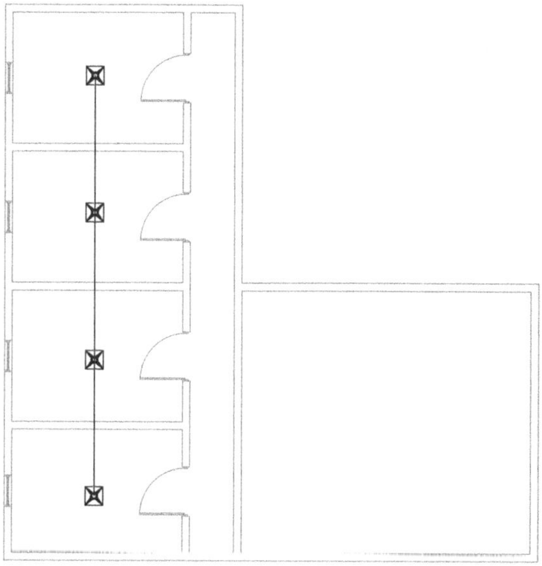

Figure Prj1-48 *The drawing after adding the duct line*

Adding Air Handling Unit

1. Choose the **Air Handler** tool from the **Equipment** drop-down in the **Build** panel of the **Home** tab in the **Ribbon**; the **Add Multi-view Parts** dialog box is displayed, as shown in Figure Prj1-49. Also, you are prompted to specify the insertion point for the air handler unit.

2. Click on the plus sign adjacent to **Packaged Air Handling Unit** in the part list; the list of air handling units is displayed.

3. Select **Air Handling Unit - Floor Mounted Front Discharge** from the list; preview of the air handling unit is displayed on the right in the dialog box.

4. Set the value of elevation as **3188** in the **Elevation** edit box available at the bottom of the dialog box and click in the drawing area; the **Air Handling Unit - Floor Mounted Front Discharge** attached to the cursor. Next, click to place the air handling unit in the drawing area, refer to Figure Prj1-50.

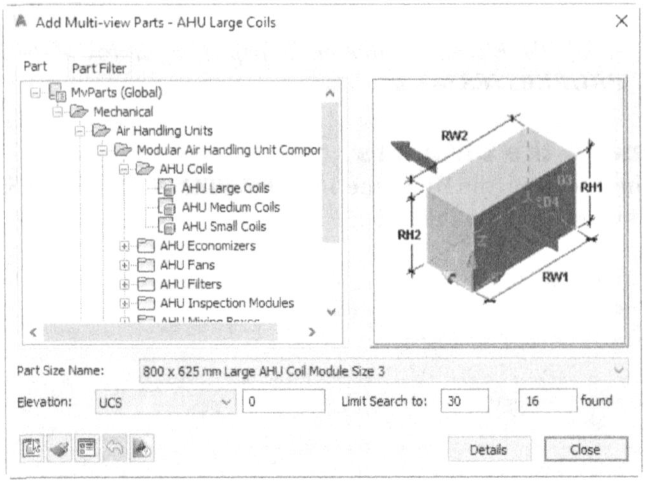

*Figure Prj1-49 The **Add Multi-view Parts** dialog box*

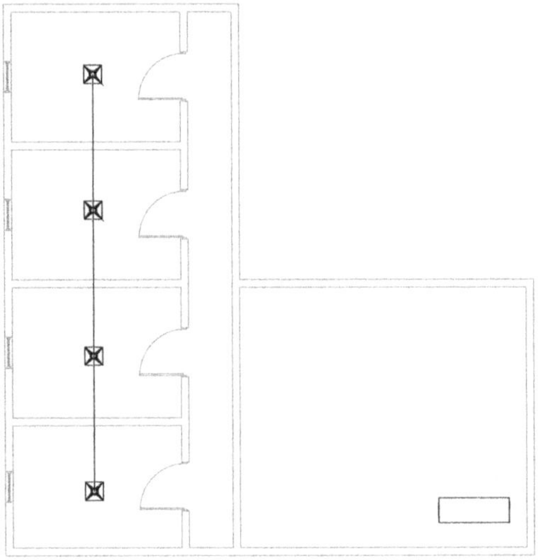

Figure Prj1-50 The drawing after placing the air handling unit

5. Connect the diffusers with the air handling unit, refer to Figure Prj1-51.

Adding Return Grilles in the Architectural Drawing of First Floor

1. Choose the **Air Terminal** tool from the **Equipment** drop-down of the **Build** panel in the **Home** tab of the **Ribbon**; the **Add Multi-view Parts** dialog box is displayed. Also, you are prompted to specify the insertion point of the air terminal.

2. Click on the plus sign adjacent to **Grilles** in the part list and then choose the **Return Air Grilles** part from the part list; the preview of the air grilles is displayed in the right of the dialog box, refer to Figure Prj1-52.

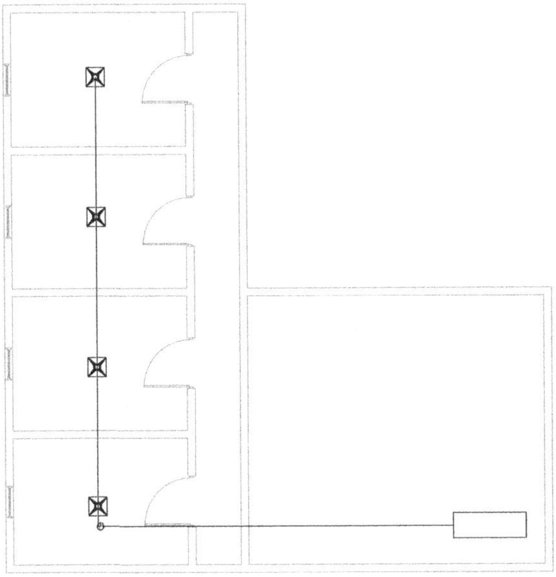

Figure Prj1-51 *The drawing after connecting the diffusers to the air handling unit*

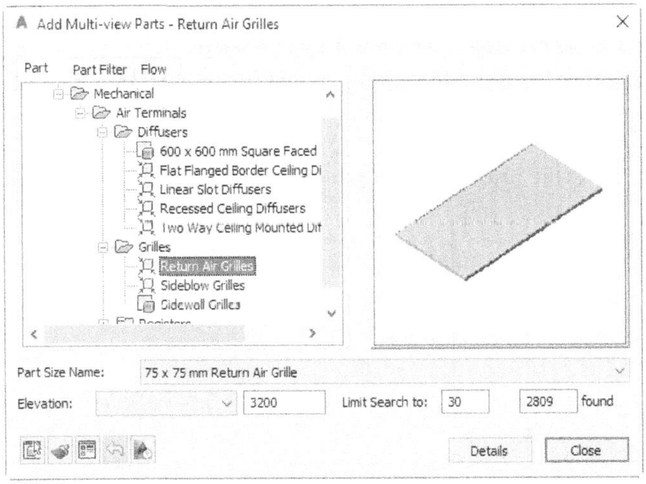

Figure Prj1-52 *The **Add Multi-view Parts** dialog box*

3. Select the **75 x 625 mm Return Air Grille** option from the **Part Size Name** drop-down list and specify the value of elevation **3600** in the **Elevation** edit box.

4. Choose the **Flow** tab and specify the value for flow as **4** in the **Flow (Each Terminal)** edit box.

5. Add the return grilles, as shown in Figure Prj1-53.

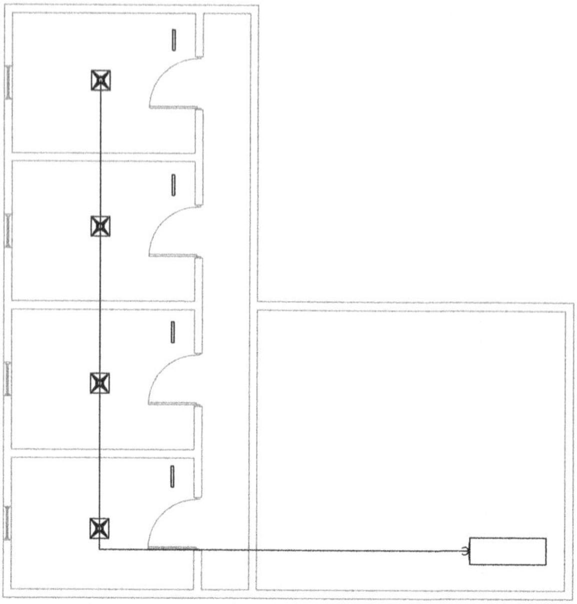

Figure Prj1-53 The drawing after adding return grilles

Creating Return Duct Line for the First Floor

1. Choose the **1-Line** tool from the **By Shape** area of the **TOOL PALETTES**; you are prompted to specify the start point of the duct line.

2. Click on the return grille and create the duct line, refer to Figure Prj1-54.

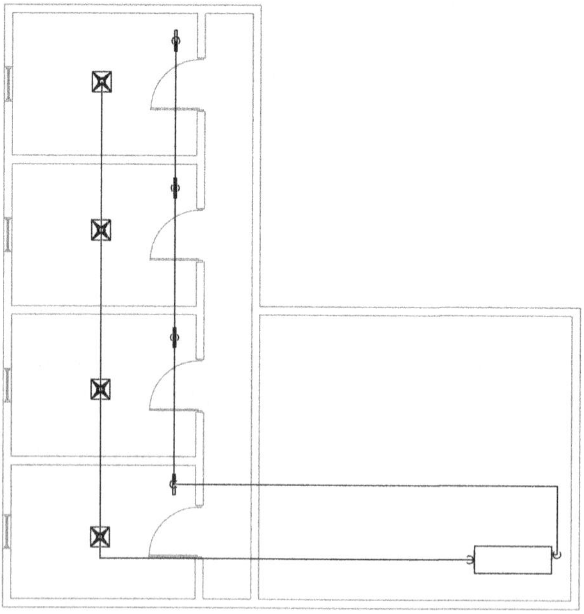

Figure Prj1-54 The drawing after adding duct line to the return grilles

Calculating the Duct Sizes

1. Select a duct line in the diffuser system; the **Duct** contextual tab is displayed.

2. Choose the **Calculate Duct Sizes** tool from the **Calculations** panel in the **Home** tab in the ribbon; the **Duct System Size Calculator** dialog box is displayed.

3. Choose the **Start** tool from the **4** area of the dialog box and choose the **OK** button from the successive dialog boxes; the duct sizes are calculated and transition is applied automatically.

4. Choose the **OK** button from the successive **Choose a Part** and **Multipart Found** dialog boxes. If the success rate is not 100%, then there is an error in the fittings added to the duct line. Remove the error, if any. Next, choose the **Close** button from the **Duct System Size Calculator** dialog box; the transitions are applied to the duct line, as shown in Figure Prj1-55.

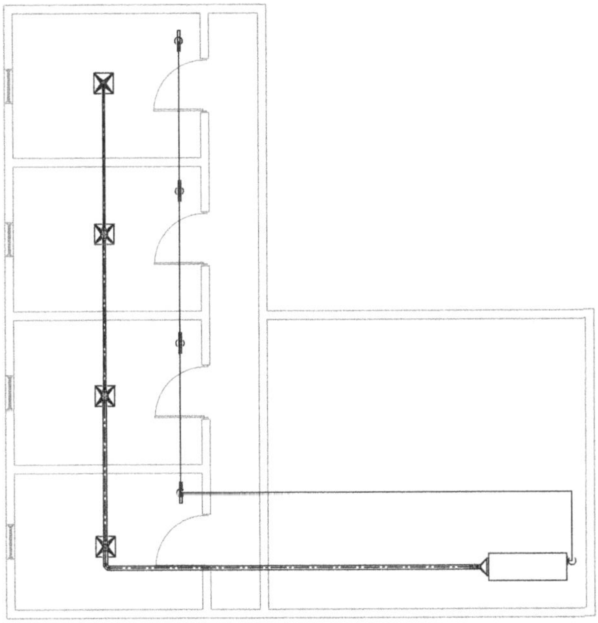

Figure Prj1-55 *The drawing after applying transitions to the diffuser duct line*

5. Similarly, calculate the duct sizes of the duct line created for return duct. On doing so, the drawing is displayed, as shown in Figure Prj1-56.

6. Save the drawing and close it.

Creating Piping Drawings

Now, you need to create piping drawings in the building. To create piping drawings, you need to switch to the **Piping** workspace.

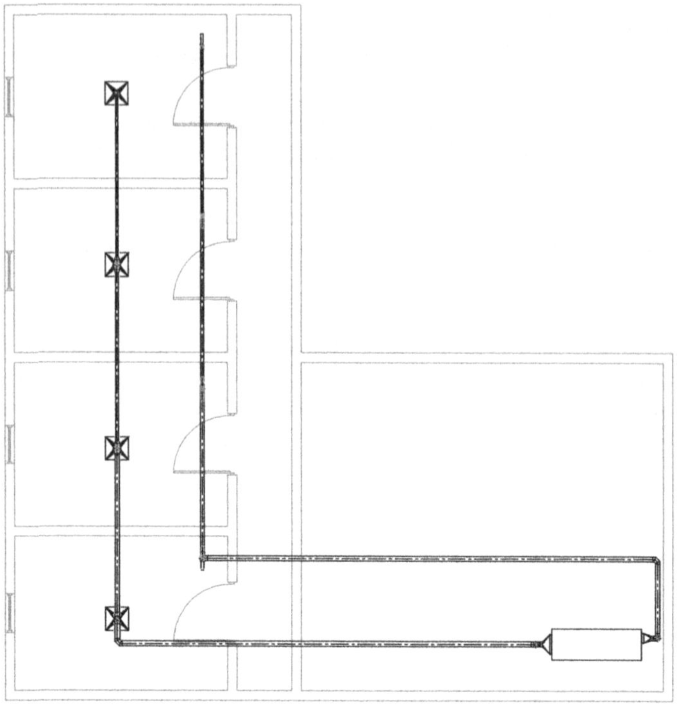

Figure Prj1-56 The drawing after applying transitions to the return grille duct line

Creating Piping Drawing of the Ground Floor

1. Select the **Piping** category from the **PROJECT NAVIGATOR** and choose the **Add Construct** button available at the bottom; the **Add Construct** dialog box is displayed.

2. Enter the name **Ground Floor Piping** in the **Name** field of the dialog box.

3. Click in the **Description** field; the **Description** dialog box is displayed.

4. Enter the description as **This drawing is meant for piping plan of the ground floor** and then choose the **OK** button from the dialog box.

5. Select the check box corresponding to level 1 in the **Division** column in the **Add Construct** dialog box and make sure that the **Open in drawing editor** check box is selected in the **Add Construct** dialog box. Next, choose the **OK** button from the dialog box; the drawing is opened. Also, the Ground Floor Piping drawing is displayed with a lock icon adjacent to it in the **PROJECT NAVIGATOR**.

6. Click on the **Workspace Switching** option in the **Application Status Bar** and choose the **Piping** option from the flyout.

Importing the Architectural Drawing of the Ground Floor

Before adding any mechanical system in the project, you need to first import the architectural plan of the ground floor.

1. Open the **PROJECT NAVIGATOR** and then click on the plus sign adjacent to **Architectural** category in the **Constructs** tab; a list of architectural drawings is displayed.

2. Select Ground Floor Architectural drawing from the list and drag it into the current drawing; the architectural drawing is attached to the current drawing as an external reference.

Adding Ball Valves in the Architectural Drawing of the Ground Floor

1. Choose the **Valve** tool from the **Equipment** drop-down of the **Build** panel in the **Home** tab in the **Ribbon**; the **Add Multi-view Parts** dialog box is displayed, as shown in Figure Prj1-57.

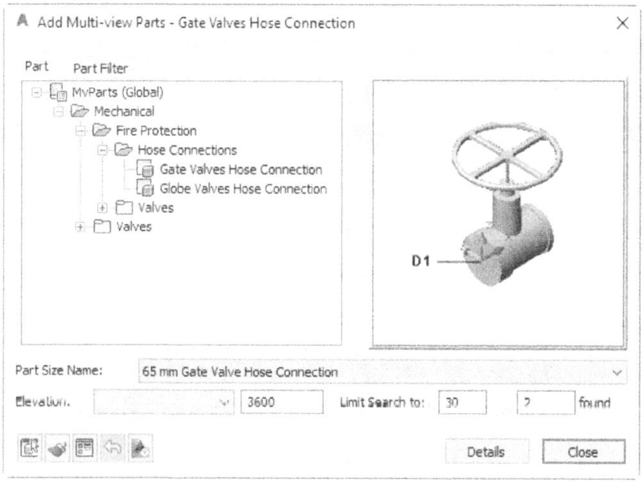

*Figure Prj1-57 The **Add Multi-view Parts** dialog box*

2. Click on the plus sign adjacent to **Valves** under the **Mechanical** node in the part list of the dialog box; various types of valves are displayed in the list.

3. Select the **Ball Valve - Threaded - Nickel plated** part from the list; the preview of the part is displayed in the right of the dialog box, refer to Figure Prj1-58.

4. Select the **40 mm Ball valve - Threaded - Nickel plated ('A' = 108 'B' = 161 'C' = 80)** option from the **Part Size Name** drop-down list.

5. Specify the elevation value as **1000** in the **Elevation** edit box.

6. Place the ball valves symmetrically, as shown in Figure Prj1-59.

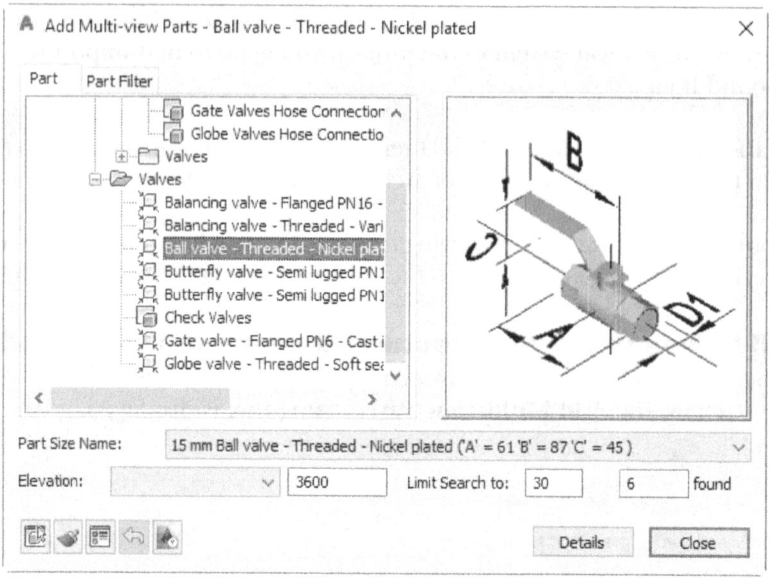

*Figure Prj1-58 The **Add Multi-view Parts** dialog box with the ball valve selected*

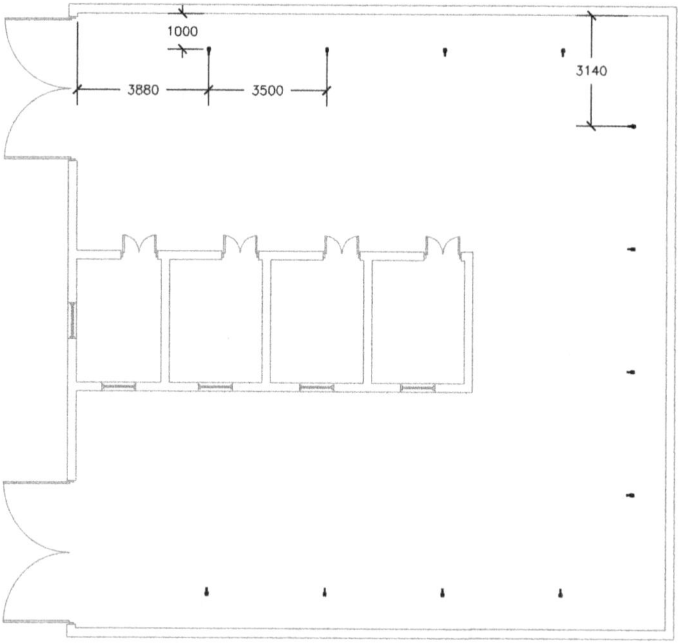

Figure Prj1-59 The drawing after adding ball valves

Adding Pipe Line in the Architectural Drawing of Ground Floor

1. Choose the **Pipe** tool from the **Pipe** drop-down in the **Build** panel of the **Home** tab in the **Ribbon**; the **PROPERTIES** palette is displayed, as shown in Figure Prj1-60. Also, you are prompted to specify the start point of the pipe.

2. Select the **40** option from the **Nominal Size** drop-down list.

3. Select the **Yes** option from the **Specify cut length** drop-down list; the **Cut length** edit box is displayed below the drop-down list.

4. Specify **6000** in the **Cut length** edit box.

5. Click in the drawing area and draw the pipe line, as shown in Figure Prj1-61.

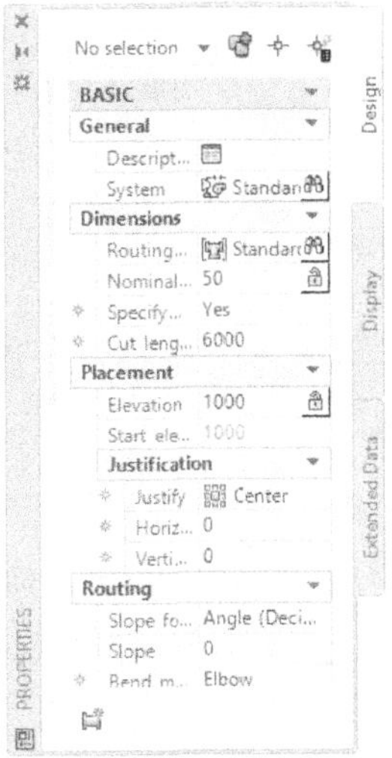

*Figure Prj1-60 The **PROPERTIES** palette displayed on choosing the **Pipe** tool*

Connecting Ball Valves with the Pipe Line

1. Click on the ball valve at the left end of the bottom row; the valve is displayed with multiple plus sign, refer to Figure Prj1-62.

2. Click on the plus sign, refer to Figure Prj1-62 and connect the ball valve with the pipe line, refer to Figure Prj1-63.

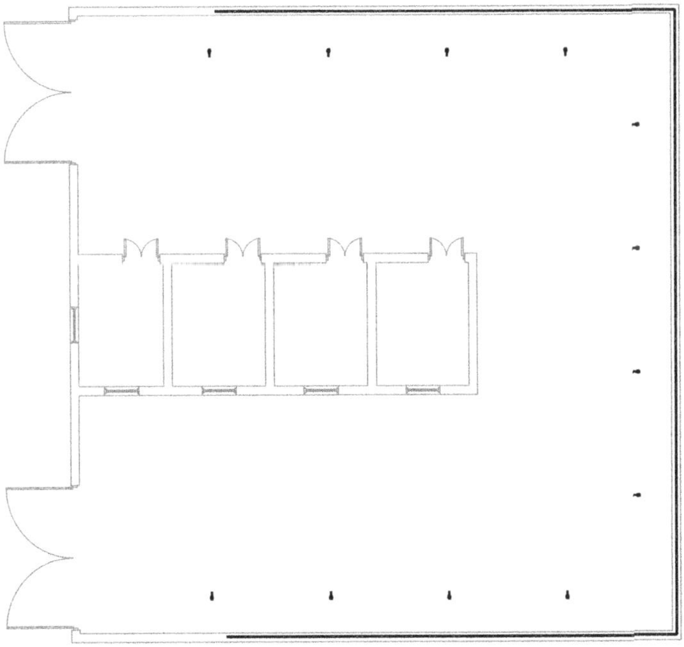

Figure Prj1-61 The drawing after drawing the pipe line

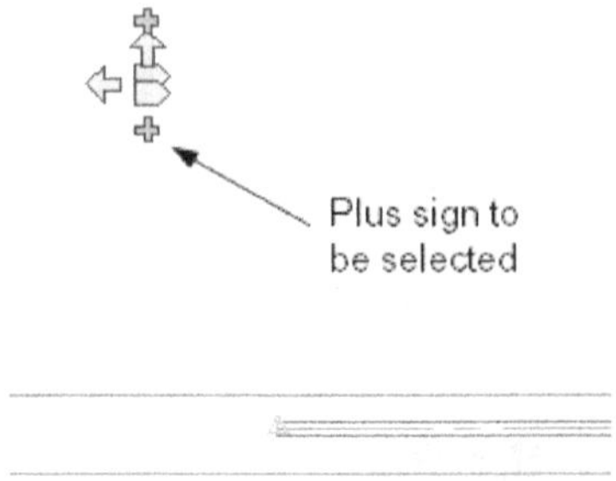

Figure Prj1-62 *The ball valve with plus signs*

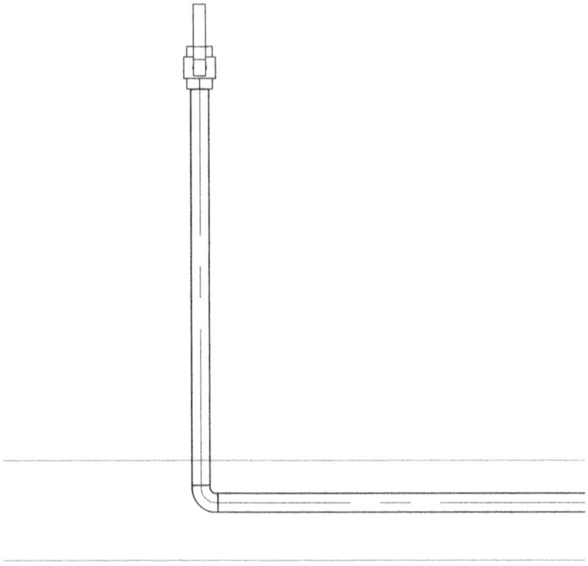

Figure Prj1-63 *The ball valve after connecting to the pipe line*

3. Similarly, connect all the ball valves to the pipe line, refer to Figure Prj1-64.

4. Select the elbow at the bottom left corner of the drawing and then click on the plus sign displayed on the elbow, as shown in Figure Prj1-65; the elbow transforms into a tee.

5. Move the cursor horizontally towards the left and specify **1000** at the command bar and press ENTER. Press ENTER again to exit the tool.

6. Save the drawing and close it.

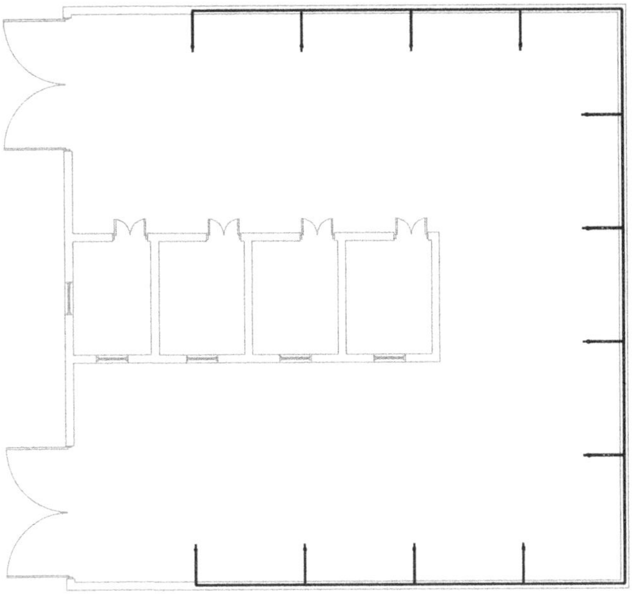

Figure Prj1-64 Piping system after connecting all the ball valves to the pipe line

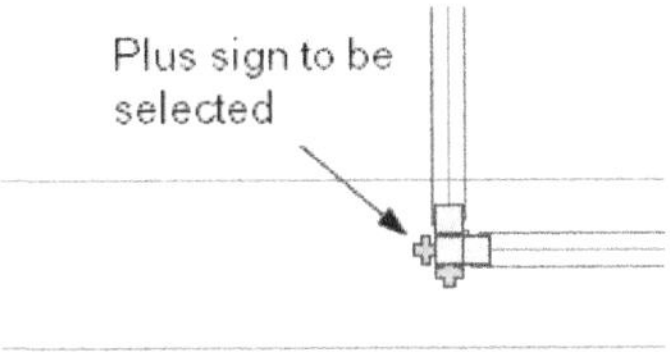

Figure Prj1-65 The plus sign to be selected

Creating Piping Drawing of the First Floor

1. Select the **Piping** category from the **PROJECT NAVIGATOR** and choose the **Add Construct** button available at the bottom; the **Add Construct** dialog box is displayed.

2. Enter **First Floor Piping** in the **Name** field of the dialog box.

3. Click in the **Description** field; the **Description** dialog box is displayed.

4. Enter the description **This drawing is meant for piping plan of the first floor** in the **Edit the Description** edit box and then choose the **OK** button from the dialog box.

5. Select the check box corresponding to level 2 in the **Division** column in the **Add Construct** dialog box and make sure that the **Open in drawing editor** check box is selected in the **Add Construct** dialog box. Next, choose the **OK** button from the dialog box; the drawing is opened. Also, the First Floor Piping drawing is displayed with a lock icon adjacent to it in the **PROJECT NAVIGATOR**.

6. Click on the **Workspace Switching** option in the **Application Status Bar** and then choose the **Piping** option from the flyout displayed; the **Piping** workspace gets activated.

Importing the Architectural Drawing of the First Floor

Before adding any piping system to the project, first you need to import the architectural plan of the first floor.

1. Open the **PROJECT NAVIGATOR** and then click on the plus sign adjacent to Architectural category in the **Constructs** tab; a list of architectural drawings is displayed.

2. Select the First Floor Architectural Drawing from the list and drag it to the current drawing; the architectural drawing is attached to the current drawing as an external reference.

Adding Tank in the First Floor

1. Choose the **Tank** tool from the **Equipment** drop-down of the **Build** panel in the **Home** tab in the **Ribbon**; the **Add Multi-view Parts** dialog box is displayed, as shown in Figure Prj1-66.

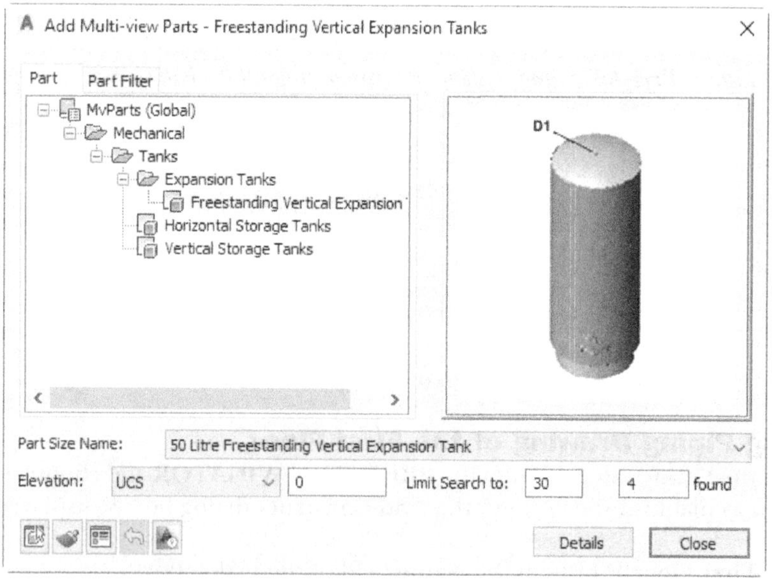

Figure Prj1-66 *The* ***Add Multi-view Parts*** *dialog box*

2. Select the **Horizontal Storage Tanks** part from the part list; the preview of the tank is displayed on the right in the dialog box.

3. Select the **1300 Liter Horizontal Storage Tank** option from the **Part Size Name** drop-down list and specify the value of elevation **0** in the **Elevation** edit box.

4. Place the tank in the drawing area, refer to Figure Prj1-67, and close the **Add Multi-view Parts** dialog box.

Adding Pumps in the First Floor

1. Choose the **Pumps** tool from the **Equipment** panel of the **Home** tab in the **Ribbon**; the **Add Multi-view Parts** dialog box is displayed.

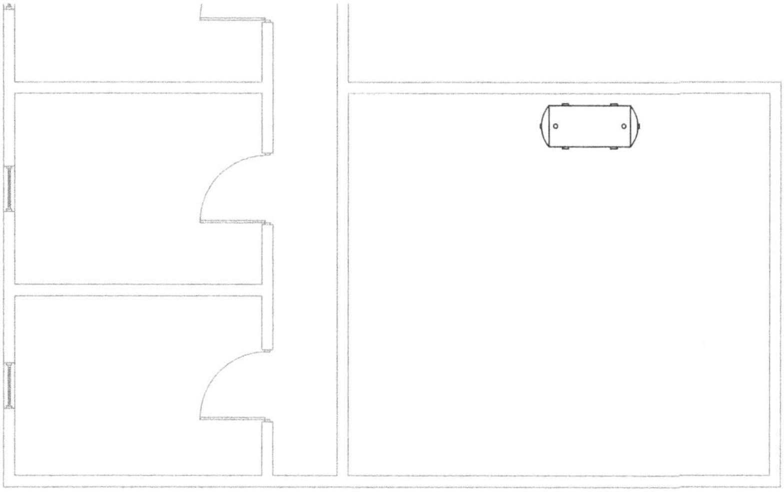

Figure Prj1-67 The drawing after adding the tank

2. Select the **Horizontal Split Case Pumps** part from the part list available at the left of the dialog box; the preview of the pump is displayed in the right of the dialog box.

3. Select the **1200 x 600 mm Horizontal Split Case** pump option from the **Part Size Name** drop-down list and specify the value of elevation as **0** in the **Elevation** edit box available at the bottom of the dialog box.

4. Place the pump in the drawing area, refer to Figure Prj1-68, and close the **Add Multi-view Parts** dialog box.

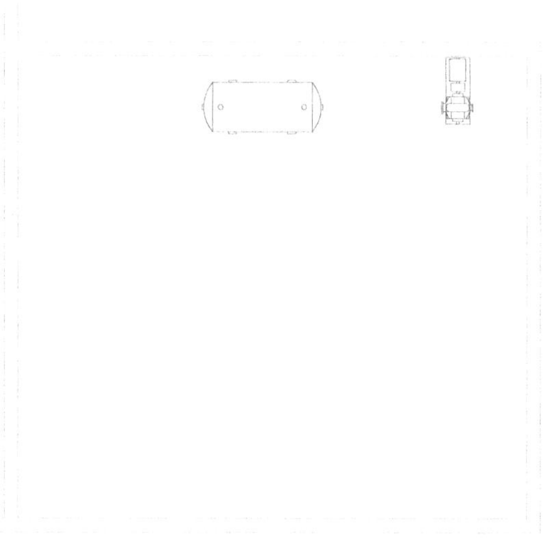

Figure Prj1-68 The drawing after adding pump

Adding Pipe Line in the First Floor

1. Select the tank in the drawing area; plus signs are displayed on the tank.

2. Click on the plus sign at the right of the tank; a rubber band pipe gets attached to the cursor, refer to Figure Prj1-69.

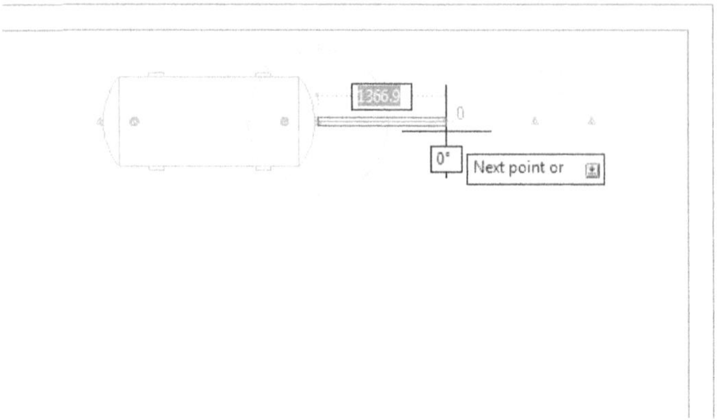

Figure Prj1-69 *The rubber band pipe attached to the cursor*

3. Click on the adjacent Pipe End Connector of the pump; the **Choose a Part** dialog box is displayed, as shown in Figure Prj1-70.

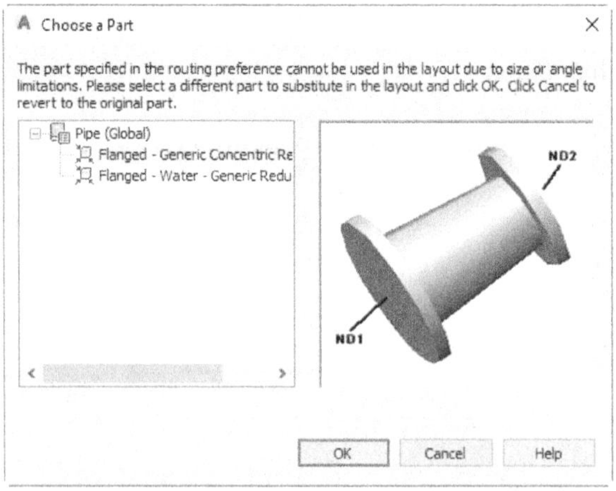

Figure Prj1-70 *The* ***Choose a Part*** *dialog box*

Note

The ***Choose a Part*** *dialog box will be displayed during the transition only when there is an elevation or size difference between the two mating ducts.*

4. Choose the **OK** button from the dialog boxes displayed successively and then press ENTER; a pipe line is created between the tank and the pump.

5. Similarly, create the pipe line on the other end connectors, as shown in Figure Prj1-71.

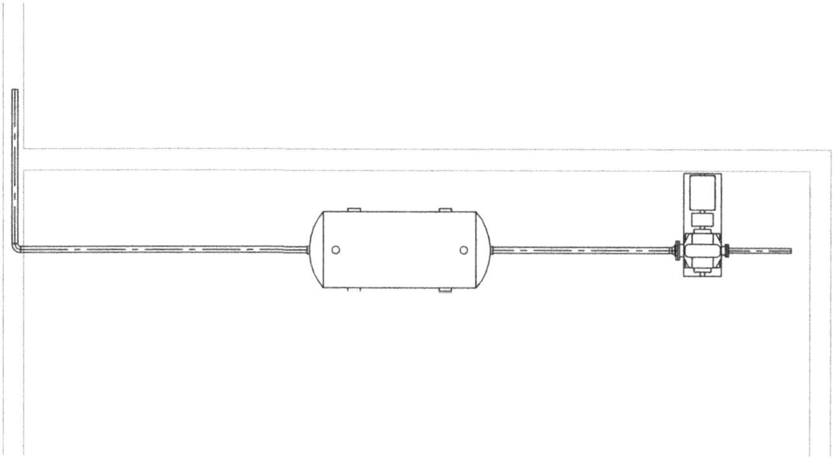

Figure Prj1-71 *The drawing after adding pipe lines*

6. Save the drawing and close it.

Creating Electrical Drawings

Now, you need to create electrical drawings of the building. To do so, switch to the **Electrical** workspace.

Creating Electrical Drawing of the Ground Floor

1. Select the **Electrical** category from the **PROJECT NAVIGATOR** and choose the **Add Construct** button available at the bottom; the **Add Construct** dialog box is displayed.

2. Enter **Ground Floor Electrical** in the **Name** field of the dialog box.

3. Click in the **Description** field; the **Description** dialog box is displayed.

4. Enter the description **This drawing is meant for electrical plan of the ground floor** in the **Edit the Description** edit box and then choose the **OK** button from the dialog box.

5. Select the check box corresponding to level 1 in the **Division** column in the **Add Construct** dialog box and make sure that the **Open in drawing editor** check box is selected in the **Add Construct** dialog box. Next, choose the **OK** button from the dialog box; the drawing is opened. Also, the Ground Floor Electrical drawing is displayed with a lock icon adjacent to it in the **PROJECT NAVIGATOR**.

6. Click on the **Workspace Switching** option in the Drawing Status Bar and select the **Electrical** option from the flyout.

Importing the Architectural Drawing of the Ground Floor

Before adding any electrical system in the project, you need to import the architectural plan of the ground floor.

1. Open the **PROJECT NAVIGATOR** and then click on the plus sign adjacent to Architectural category in the **Constructs** tab; a list of architectural drawings is displayed.

2. Select the Ground Floor Architectural drawing from the list and drag it to the current drawing; the architectural drawing is attached to the current drawing as an external reference.

Adding 300X1200 Surface Type A Lights to the Drawing

Now, you need to add lights to the drawing.

1. Choose the **Device** tool from the **Build** panel of the **Home** tab in the **Ribbon**; the **PROPERTIES** palette is modified, refer to Figure Prj1-72.

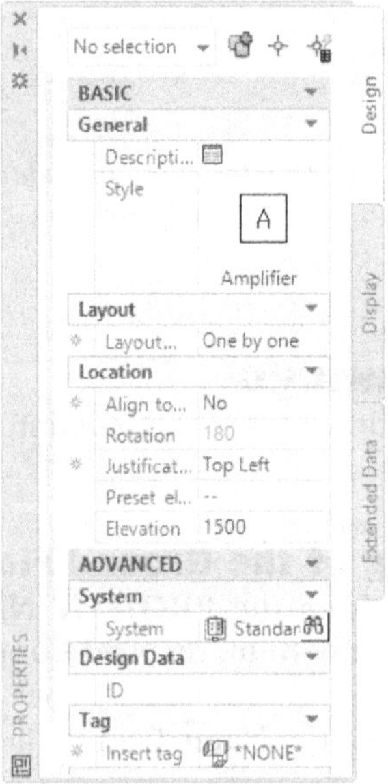

***Figure Prj1-72** The **PROPERTIES** palette displayed on choosing the **Device** tool*

2. Click in the **Style** field of the **PROPERTIES** palette; the **STYLES BROWSER** is displayed.

3. Select the **Lighting Fluorescent (Global).dwg** option from the **Drawing File** drop-down list; the light styles available in AutoCAD MEP are displayed in the gallery.

4. Double-click on the **300X1200 Surface Type A Light** option from the gallery; the light gets attached to the cursor. Specify **3700** in **Elevation** edit box in the **Location** rollout of the **PROPERTIES** palette.

5. Next, place the lights in the drawing, as shown in Figure Prj1-73.

Adding Sockets to the Drawing

Now, you need to add sockets to the drawing.

1. Choose the **Device** tool from the **Build** panel; the **PROPERTIES** palette is displayed.

2. Click in the **Style** field of the **PROPERTIES** palette; the **STYLES BROWSER** is displayed.

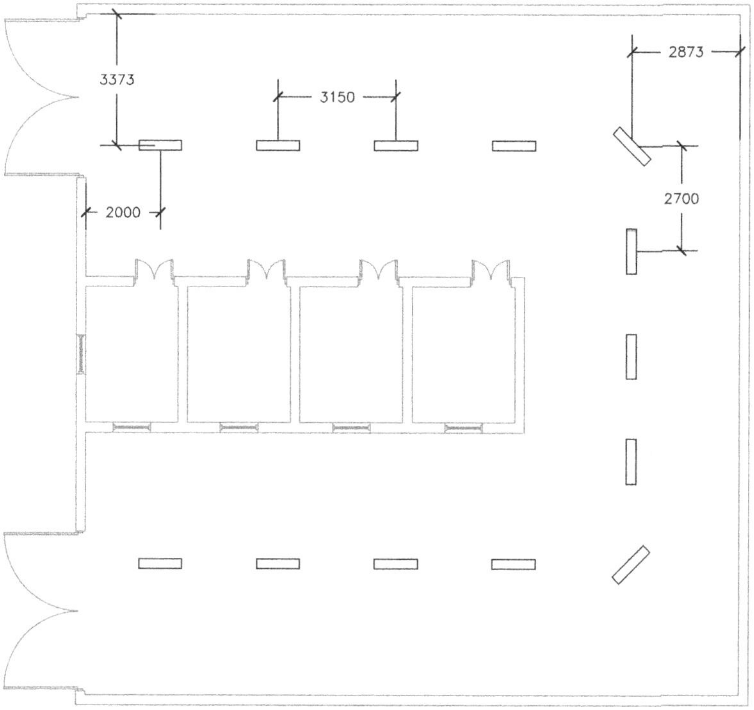

Figure Prj1-73 *The drawing after adding lights*

3. Select the **Sockets (Global).dwg** option from the **Drawing File** drop-down list; various styles of sockets available in AutoCAD MEP are displayed in the gallery.

4. Double-click on the **Single Pole Switched Outlet** socket style; the socket gets attached to the cursor. Specify **1500** in the **Elevation** edit box in the **Location** rollout of the **PROPERTIES** palette.

5. Next, place the sockets along the wall, as shown in Figure Prj1-74.

Adding 300x600 Recessed Lights to the Drawing

Now, you need to add lights to the drawing.

1. Choose the **Device** tool from the **Build** panel; the **PROPERTIES** palette is displayed.

2. Click in the **Style** field of the **PROPERTIES** palette; the **STYLES BROWSER** is displayed.

3. Select the **Lighting Fluorescent (Global).dwg** option from the **Drawing File** drop-down list; various styles of lights available in AutoCAD MEP are displayed in the gallery.

4. Double-click on the **300x600 Recessed Lights** style; the light gets attached to the cursor. Specify **3500** in the **Elevation** edit box in the **Location** rollout of the **PROPERTIES** palette.

5. Place the lights in the center of the inner area of the ground floor, refer to Figure Prj1-75.

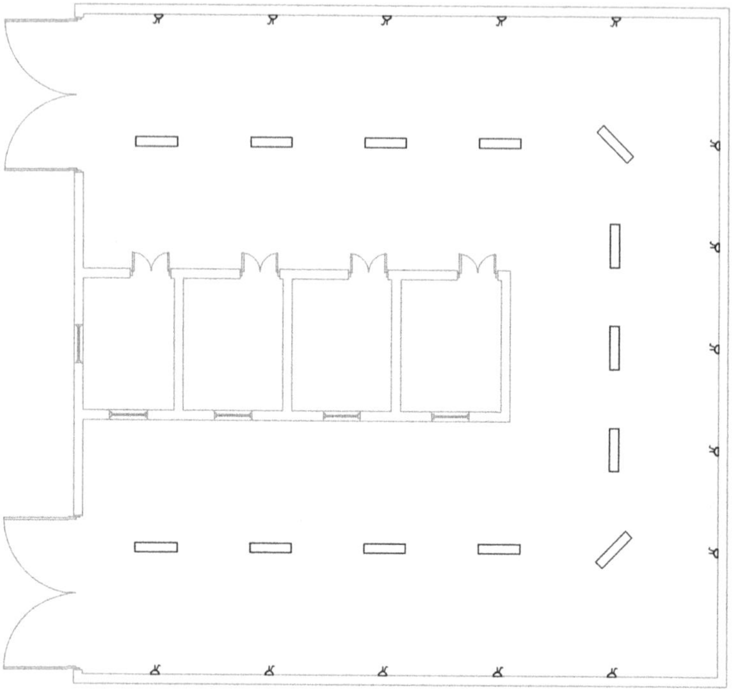

Figure Prj1-74 *The drawing after adding sockets*

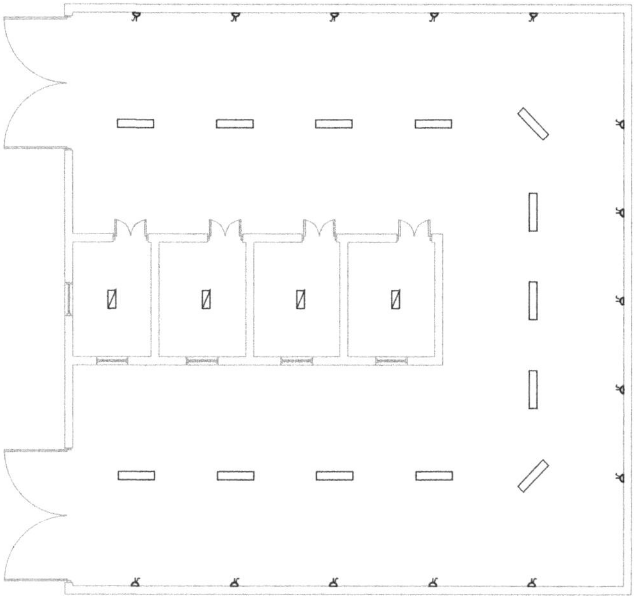

Figure Prj1-75 The drawing after adding lights in the center of the inner area

Creating Panel

All the devices are connected to circuits. These circuits are joined to a panel for electricity supply. Therefore, you need to create a panel with circuits in this section.

1. Choose the **Panel** tool from the **Build** panel in the **Home** tab of the **Ribbon**; you are prompted to specify an insertion point for the panel and the **PROPERTIES** palette is displayed, as shown in Figure Prj1-76. Select the **Surface Door 3** style from the **Style** field in the **PROPERTIES** palette.

2. Click in the **Name** edit box in the **ADVANCED > Design Data** rollout of the **PROPERTIES** palette and specify the name as **Main Panel**.

3. Specify the value **800** in the **Rating** edit box.

4. Select the **230** option from the **Voltage phase-to-neutral** drop-down list.

5. Select the **240** option from the **Voltage phase-to-phase** drop-down list.

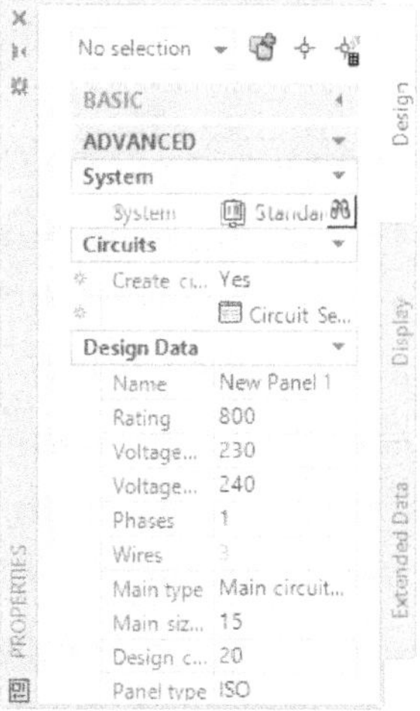

*Figure Prj1-76 The **PROPERTIES** palette displayed on choosing the **Panel** tool*

6. Specify **Main type** as **Main circuit breaker**, **Main size (amps)** as **15**, **Design capacity (amps)** as **20**, and **AIC rating** as **800** in the **PROPERTIES** palette.

Now, you need to create circuits for the panel.

7. Click in the **Circuit Settings** field under **ADVANCED > Circuits** rollout of the **PROPERTIES** palette; the **Circuit Settings** dialog box is displayed, as shown in Figure Prj1-77.

8. Set the value as **2** in the **Total number of slots** and **Number of 1-pole circuits** spinners and select the **230** option from the **Voltage** drop-down list adjacent to the spinner. Make sure that **Power and Lighting** is selected in the **System Type** drop-down list and **230V Power** is selected in the **System** drop-down list.

9. Choose the **OK** button from the dialog box to exit.

10. Select the **Yes** option from the **Create Circuit** drop-down list in the **Advanced** rollout. Click in the drawing area to place the panel, refer to Figure Prj1-78. Also, the **AutoCAD MEP - Electrical Project Database** dialog box is displayed, refer to Figure Prj1-79.

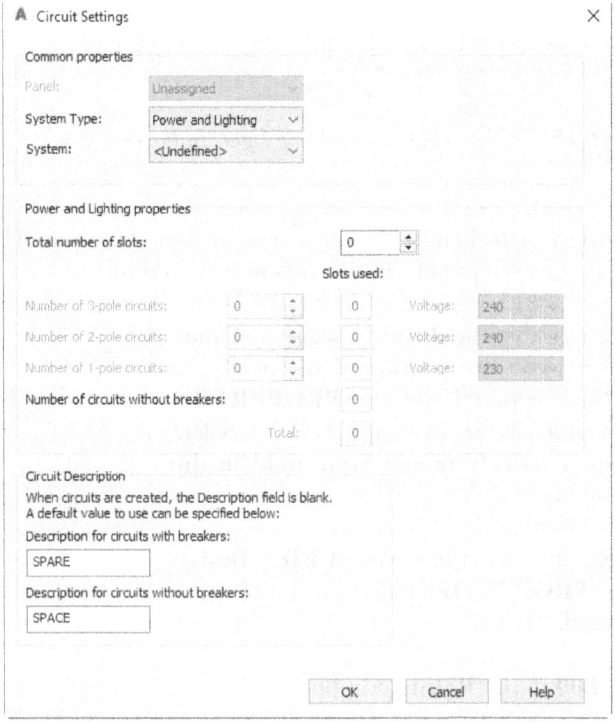

*Figure Prj1-77 The **Circuit Settings** dialog box*

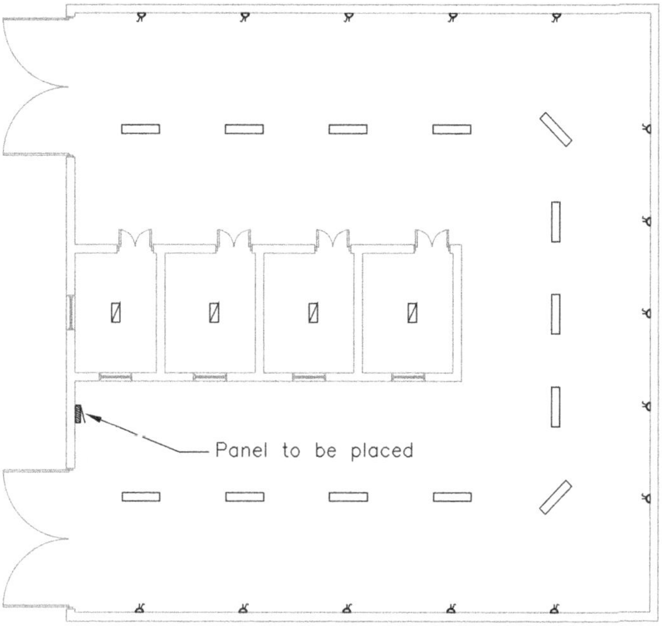

Figure Prj1-78 *The drawing with the panel placed*

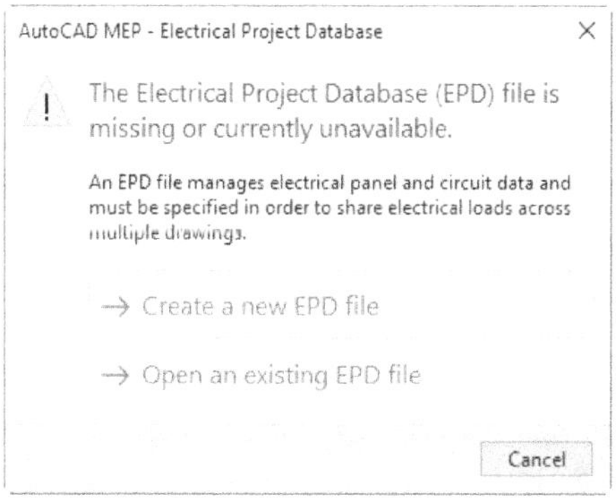

Figure Prj1-79 *The* ***AutoCAD MEP - Electrical Project Database*** *dialog box*

11. Choose the **Create a new EPD file** option from the dialog box and save the file at the desired location with the name **light_panel**; the panel is created at the specified location.

12. As explained in previous steps, place the other panel for **230V Power (230V POWER)** system and rename it as **Sockets Panel**, refer to Figure Prj1-80.

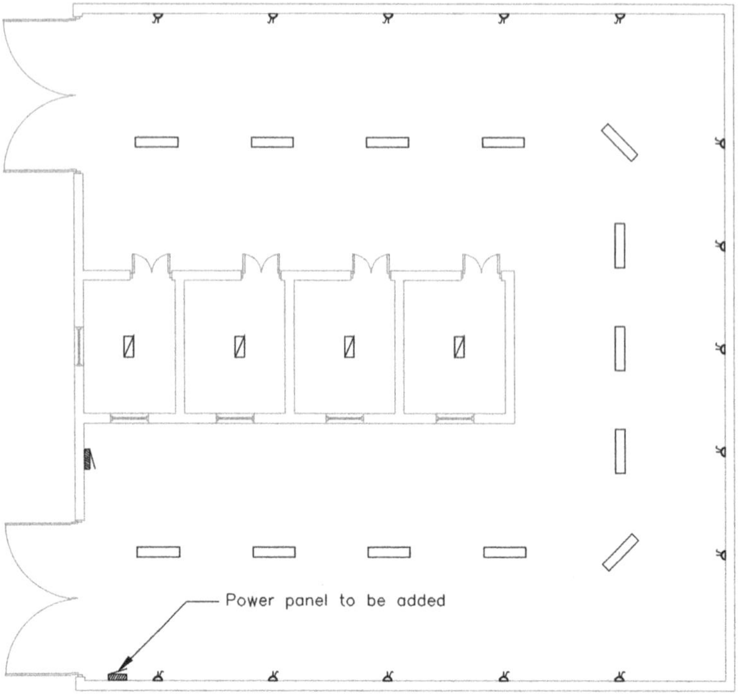

Figure Prj1-80 *The drawing with other panel for 230 V power added*

Configuring Circuits

1. Select the panel that was created first and then choose the **Circuit Manager** tool from the **Circuits** panel in the **Panel** contextual tab of the **Ribbon**; the **CIRCUIT MANAGER** is displayed, refer to Figure Prj1-81.

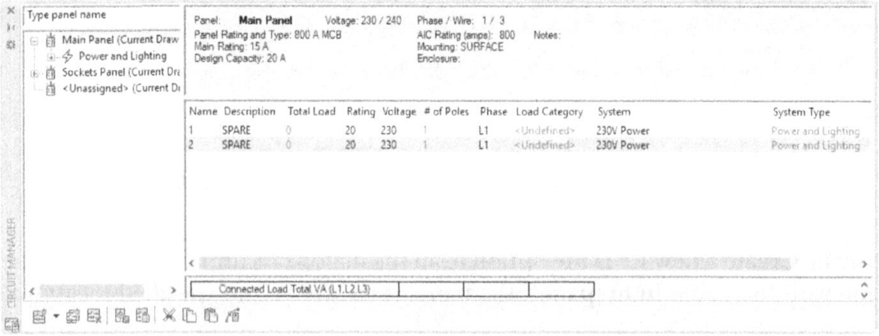

Figure Prj1-81 *The CIRCUIT MANAGER*

2. Specify the name **Outer Lights** in the field **1** of the **Name** column in the **CIRCUIT MANAGER**.

3. Specify the name **Inner Lights** in the field **2** of the **Name** column in the **CIRCUIT MANAGER**.

4. Click on the plus sign adjacent to **Sockets panel** on the left in the **CIRCUIT MANAGER**; the list of circuits available in the panel is displayed below it.

5. Select **Power and Lighting** from the left of the **CIRCUIT MANAGER**; the list of circuits is displayed on the right.

6. Double-click on **1** under the **Name** panel and specify the name as **Sockets**.

7. Double-click in the **Voltage** field for **Sockets** and select the **230** option from the drop-down list.

8. Select the **230V Power** option from the **System** drop-down list.

9. Close the **CIRCUIT MANAGER**.

Configuring Devices

1. Select a socket from the drawing area and then select the **Select Similar** option from the **Select Similar** drop-down list in the **Device** contextual tab displayed; all the sockets available in the drawing area are selected.

2. Click on the **Electrical properties** field in the **Advanced** rollout of the **PROPERTIES** palette; the **Electrical Properties** dialog box is displayed, as shown in Figure Prj1-82. Now, in this dialog box, you need to specify the parameters that are given in Table Prj1-1.

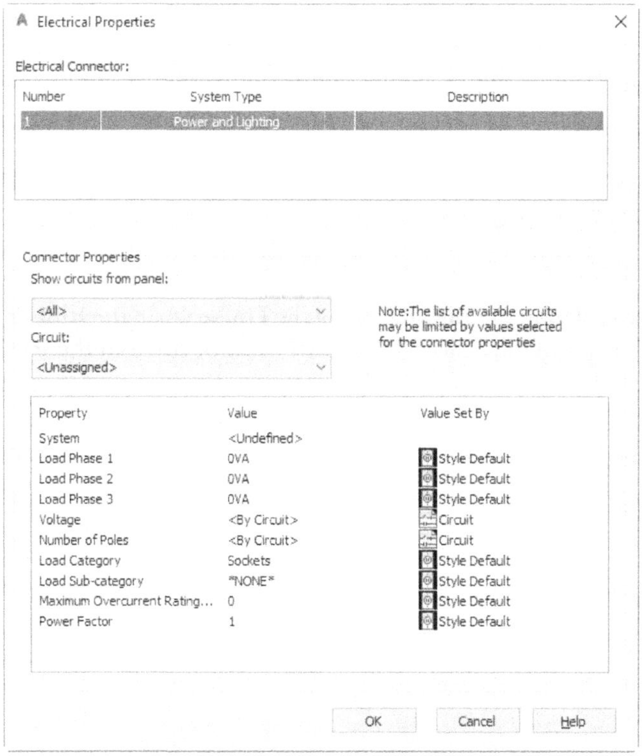

*Figure Prj1-82 The **Electrical Properties** dialog box*

3. Select the **230V Power** option from the **System** drop-down list.

4. Specify the value **300** in the **Load Phase 1** edit box, refer to Table Prj1-1.

5. Select the **230** option from the **Voltage** drop-down list.

6. Similarly, select the **1** option from the **Number of Poles** drop-down list.

7. Enter the value **10** in the **Maximum Overcurrent Rating (amps)** edit box.

8. Specify the value as **0.8** in the **Power Factor** edit box.

9. Select the **Socket Panel (Current Drawing)** option from the **Show Circuits from panel** drop-down list. Choose the **OK** button to exit the dialog box.

10. Similarly, specify the parameters for other devices in the **Electrical Properties** dialog box by using the steps discussed above. For parameters, refer to Table Prj1-1. Also, select the **Main Panel (Current Drawing)** option from the **Show circuits from panel** drop-down list for all the devices and select the **Outer Lights [Load: 0 VA]** for **300X1200 Surface Type A Light**, and **Inner Lights[Load: 0 VA]** for **300x600 Recessed Lights** from the **Circuit** drop-down list in the **Electrical Properties** dialog box.

Note

As soon as you select the ***Outer Lights [Load: 0 VA]*** *option from the* ***Circuit*** *drop-down list, it gets modified and displayed as* ***Outer Lights [Load: 2340 VA]*** *in the drop-down list. This is because the software automatically calculates the load of sockets according to number of sockets added in the drawing. Similarly,* ***Inner Lights [Load: 0 VA]*** *changes into* ***Inner Lights [Load: 400 VA]****.*

Adding Wires

1. Choose the **Wire** tool from the **Build** panel of the **Home** tab in the **Ribbon**; you are prompted to specify the start point of the wire for an electrical device and the **PROPERTIES** palette is displayed, as shown in Figure Prj1-83.

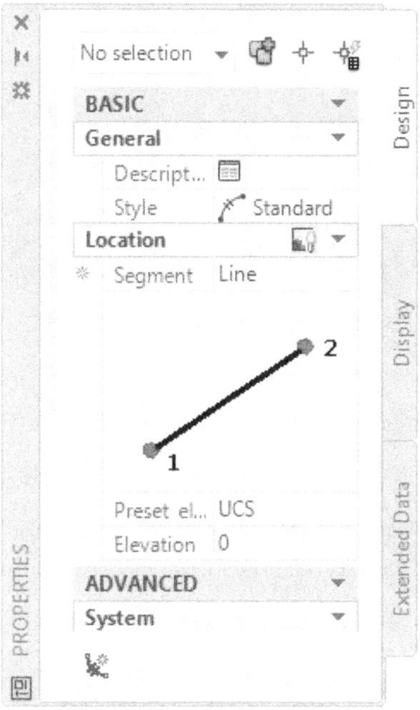

*Figure Prj1-83 The **PROPERTIES** palette displayed on choosing the **Wire** tool*

2. Select the **230V Power(230V POWER)** option from the **System** drop-down list.

3. Select the **PVC Single** option from the **Style** drop-down list under the **General** Rollout.

4. Connect all the sockets using wires, refer to Figure Prj1-84. Make sure that the **Line** option is selected in the **Segment** drop-down list.

5. Similarly, connect all the lights to the other panel using the **230V Lighting** system, refer to Figure Prj1-85. Make sure that the circuit selected for inner lights is **Inner Lights** and for outer lights is **Outer Lights**.

Calculating Load and Wire Sizes

Now, you need to calculate the total load of the electrical system and the wire size.

1. Choose the **Power Totals** tool from the **Electrical** panel in the **Analyze** tab of the **Ribbon**; you are prompted to select the devices.

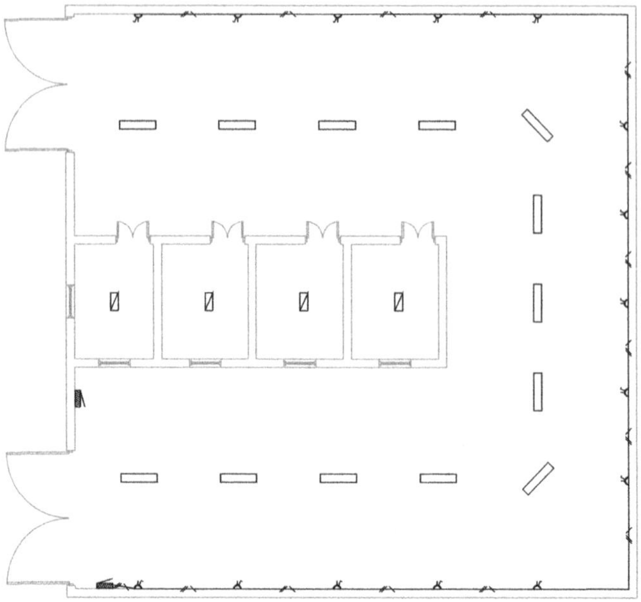

Figure Prj1-84 The drawing after connecting sockets using wires

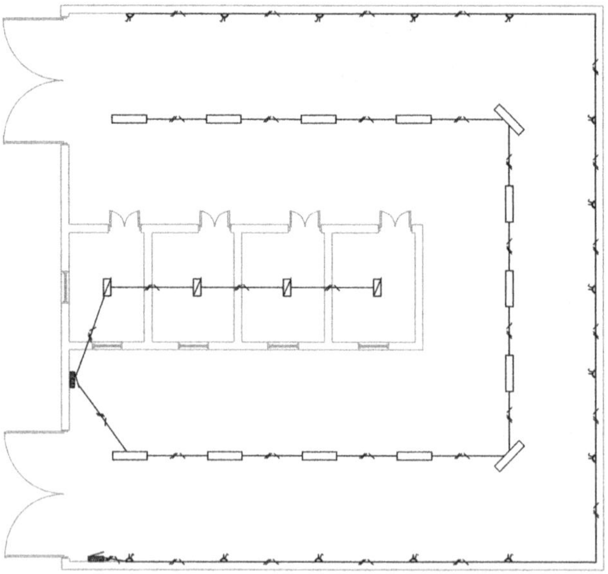

Figure Prj1-85 The drawing after adding wires to lights

2. Select all the devices available in the drawing area and press ENTER; the **Power Totals** dialog box is displayed, refer to Figure Prj1-86.

   The total load is displayed in the **Total Load** field of the dialog box. Now, you need to calculate the wire size of the circuit.

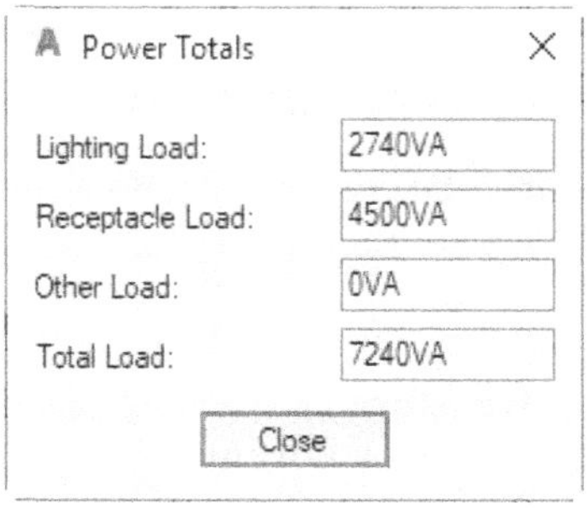

Figure Prj1-86 *The* ***Power Totals*** *dialog box*

3. To calculate wire size, select all the wires in the drawing area; the **PROPERTIES** palette is displayed.

4. Click on the **Calculate sizes for the wire** button available on the right of the **ADVANCED > Dimensions** rollout of the **PROPERTIES** palette; the wire sizes are displayed in the **Hot size**, **Neutral size**, and **Ground size** edit boxes in the **Dimensions** rollout.

Adding Transformer and Emergency Generator

After making calculations, the total load of the ground floor comes out to be approximately 7.3kVa. Assuming the same capacity for first floor and considering the peak load condition, you need to place a transformer and a generator of capacity 15 kVa in the drawing area.

1. Choose the **Equipment** tool from the **Equipment** drop-down in the **Build** panel of the **Home** tab in the **Ribbon**; the **Add Multi-view Parts** dialog box is displayed, refer to Figure Prj1-87.

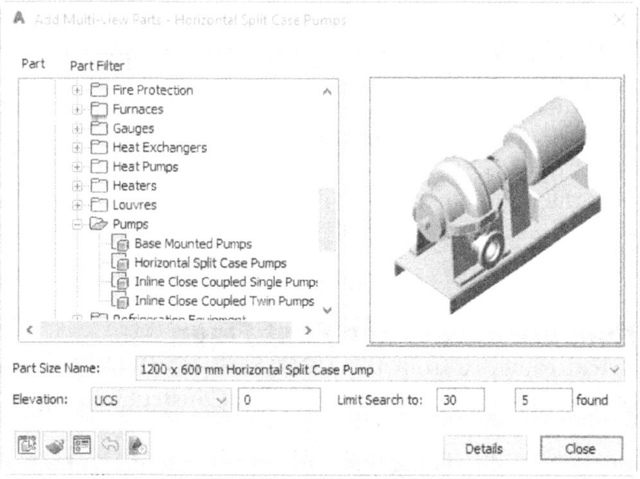

Figure Prj1-87 *The* ***Add Multi-view Parts*** *dialog box*

2. Click on the plus sign adjacent to **Electrical** in the part list available at the left of the dialog box; the electrical equipment are displayed below it.

3. Click on the plus sign adjacent to **Power Transformers** in the part list and select the **Dry Type Transformer - 3-150 kVa** part; the preview of the transformer is displayed, refer to Figure Prj1-87.

4. Select the **15 kVa Dry Type Transformer** option from the **Part Size Name** drop-down list available at the bottom in the dialog box and place the transformer at an appropriate distance from the building in the outer area with 0 Elevation, refer to Figure Prj1-88.

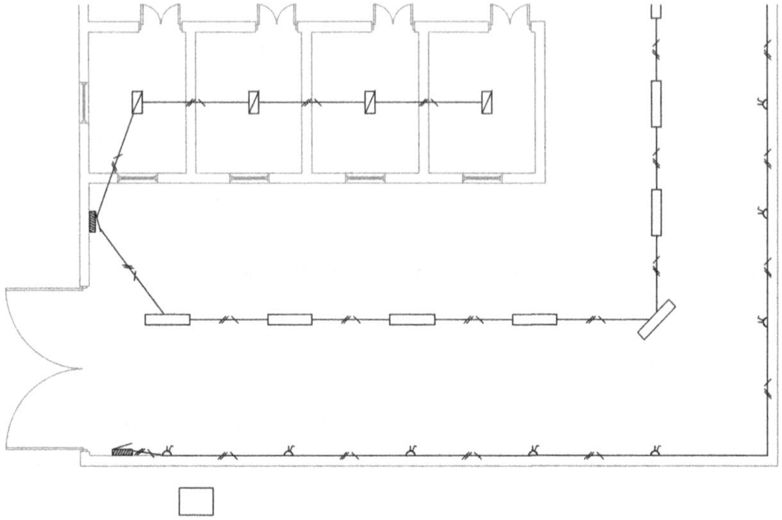

Figure Prj1-88 *The drawing after placing a transformer*

5. Similarly, place the emergency generator having the corresponding capacity with 0 elevation in the drawing adjacent to the power transformer, refer to Figure Prj1-89.

6. Connect the transformer and emergency generator with the panels, refer to Figure Prj1-89.

7. Save the drawing and close it.

Creating Electrical Drawing of the First Floor

1. Select the **Electrical** category from the **PROJECT NAVIGATOR** and choose the **Add Construct** button available at the bottom; the **Add Construct** dialog box is displayed

2. Click in the **Name** field of the dialog box and enter the name as **First Floor Electrical**.

3. Click in the **Description** field; the **Description** dialog box is displayed.

4. Enter the description **This drawing is meant for electrical plan of the first floor** and then choose the **OK** button from the dialog box.

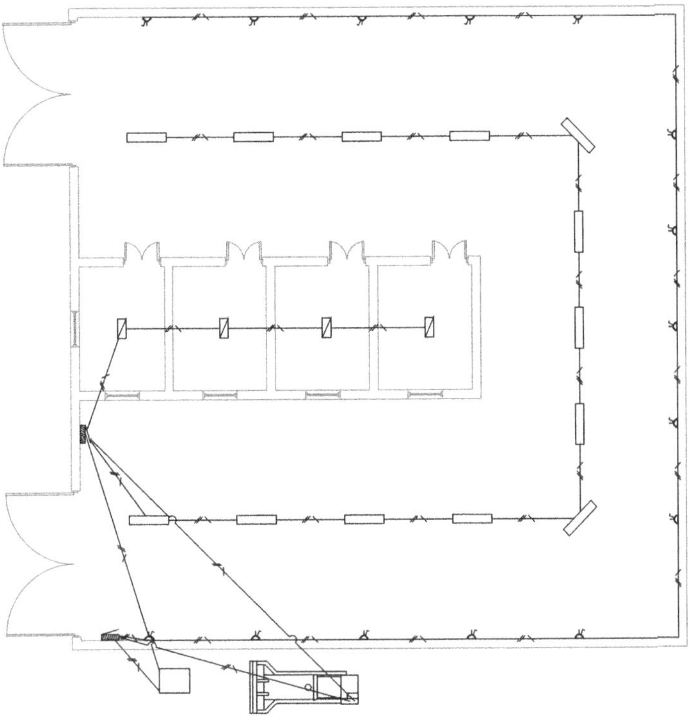

Figure Prj1-89 The drawing after connecting transformer and generator to the circuit

5. Select the check box corresponding to level 2 in the **Division** column in the **Add Construct** dialog box and make sure that the **Open in drawing editor** check box is selected in the **Add Construct** dialog box. Next, choose the **OK** button from the dialog box; the drawing is opened. Also, the Ground Floor Electrical drawing is displayed with a lock icon adjacent to it in the **PROJECT NAVIGATOR**.

6. Click on the **Workspace Switching** option of the Drawing Status Bar and choose the **Electrical** option from the flyout.

Importing the Architectural Drawing of the First Floor

Before adding any electrical system to the project, you need to first import the architectural plan of the first floor.

1. Open the **PROJECT NAVIGATOR** and then click on the plus sign adjacent to Architectural category in the **Constructs** tab; the list of architectural drawings is displayed.

2. Select First Floor Architectural drawing from the list and drag it to the current drawing; the architectural drawing is attached to the current drawing as an external reference.

Adding Lights in the Drawing

Now, you need to add lights to the drawing.

1. Choose the **Device** tool from the **Build** panel of the **Home** tab in the **Ribbon**; the **PROPERTIES** palette is displayed, refer to Figure Prj1-90.

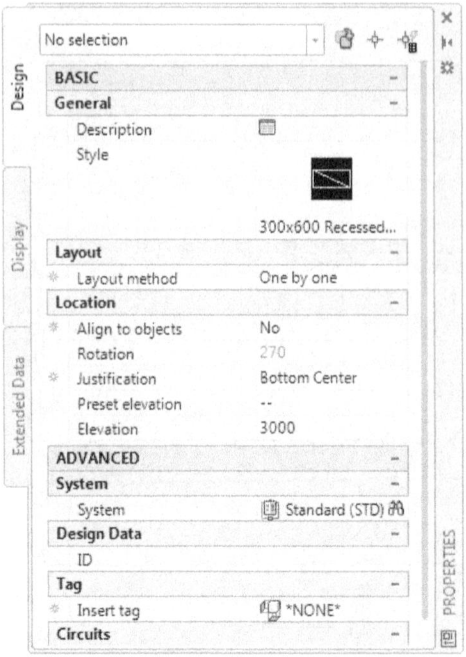

Figure Prj1-90 *The **PROPERTIES** palette displayed on choosing the **Device** tool*

2. Click in the **Style** field of the **PROPERTIES** palette; the **Select Style** dialog box is displayed.

3. Select the **Lighting Fluorescent (Global)** option from the **Drawing file** drop-down list; the light styles available in AutoCAD MEP are displayed.

4. Select the **300X600 Recessed Light** from the light styles and then choose the **OK** button from the dialog box; the light symbol gets attached to the cursor.

5. Place three equidistant lights in the middle of each room in the drawing with elevation value of **3500**, refer to Figure Prj1-91.

Adding Sockets in the Drawing

Now, you need to add sockets to the drawing.

1. Choose the **Device** tool from the **Build** panel of the **Home** tab in the **Ribbon**; the **PROPERTIES** palette is displayed.

2. Click in the **Style** field of the **PROPERTIES** palette; the **Select Style** dialog box is displayed.

3. Select the **Sockets (Global)** option from the **Drawing file** drop-down list; various styles of sockets available in AutoCAD MEP are displayed in the dialog box.

4. Select the **Single Pole Switched Outlet** socket style from the dialog box and then choose the **OK** button; the socket symbol gets attached to the cursor.

5. Place the sockets along the wall with elevation value of **700**, refer to Figure Prj1-91.

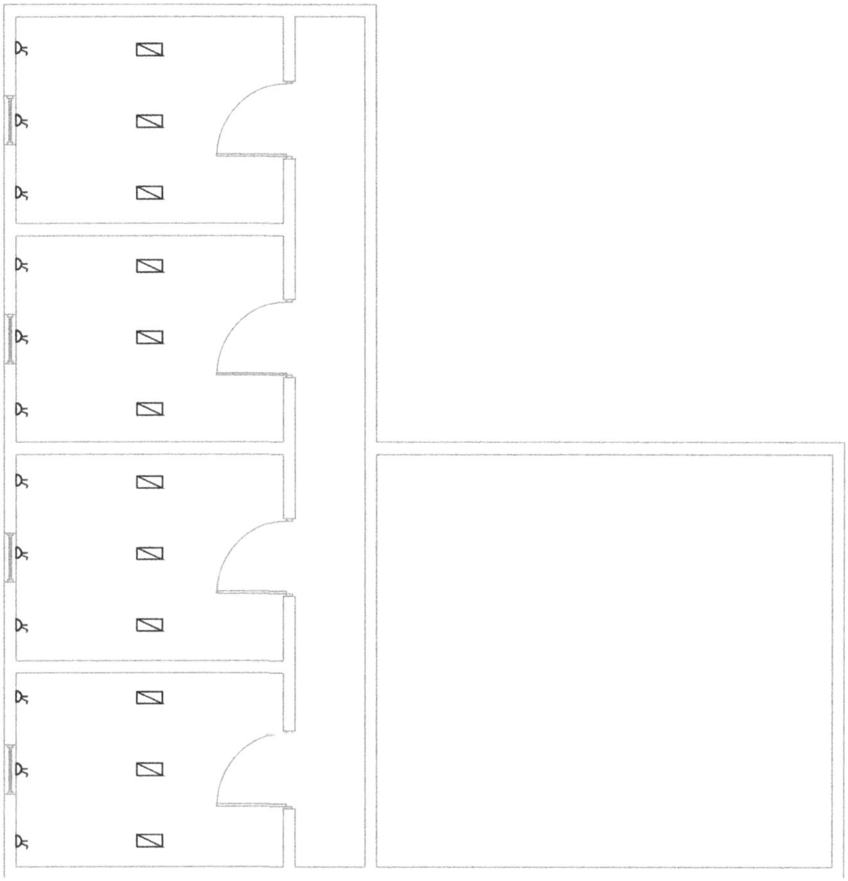

Figure Prj1-91 *The drawing after adding lights and sockets*

Creating Panel

As discussed earlier, all the devices are connected to circuits. These circuits are joined to a panel for electricity supply. So, you need to create a panel with circuits in this section.

1. Choose the **Panel** tool from the **Build** panel in the **Home** tab of the **Ribbon**; you are prompted to specify an insertion point for the panel and the **PROPERTIES** palette is displayed, as shown in Figure Prj1-92. Select the **Surface Door 3** style from the **Style** field in the **PROPERTIES** palette.

2. Click in the **Name** edit box of the **ADVANCED** > **Design Data** rollout of the **PROPERTIES** palette and specify the name as **Panel1**.

3. Specify the value **800** in the **Rating** edit box.

4. Select the **230** option from the **Voltage phase-to-neutral** drop-down list.

5. Select the **240** option from the **Voltage phase-to-phase** drop-down list.

6. Specify **Main type** as **Main circuit breaker, Main size (amps)** as **15, Design capacity (amps)** as **20**, and **AIC rating** as **800** in the **ADVANCED > Design Data** rollout in the **PROPERTIES** palette.

   Now, you need to create circuits for the panel.

7. Click in the **Circuit Settings** field in the **PROPERTIES** palette; the **Circuit Settings** dialog box is displayed, as shown in Figure Prj1-93.

8. Set the value as **2** in the **Total number of slots** and **Number of 1-pole circuits** spinners and select the **230** option from the **Voltage** drop-down list adjacent to the spinner. Make sure that **Power and Lighting** is selected in the **System Type** drop-down list and **230V Power** is selected in the **System** drop-down list.

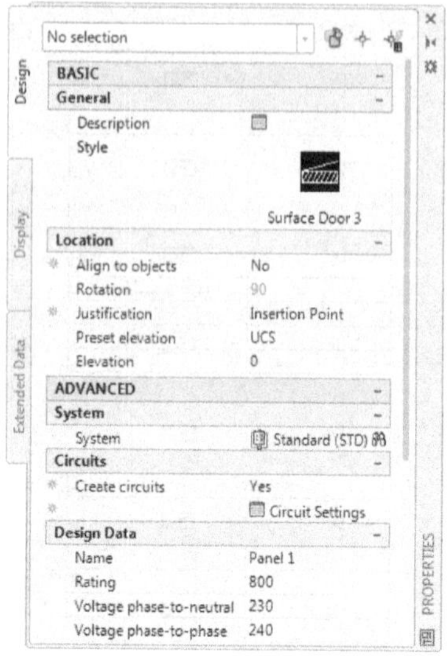

*Figure Prj1-92 The **PROPERTIES** palette*

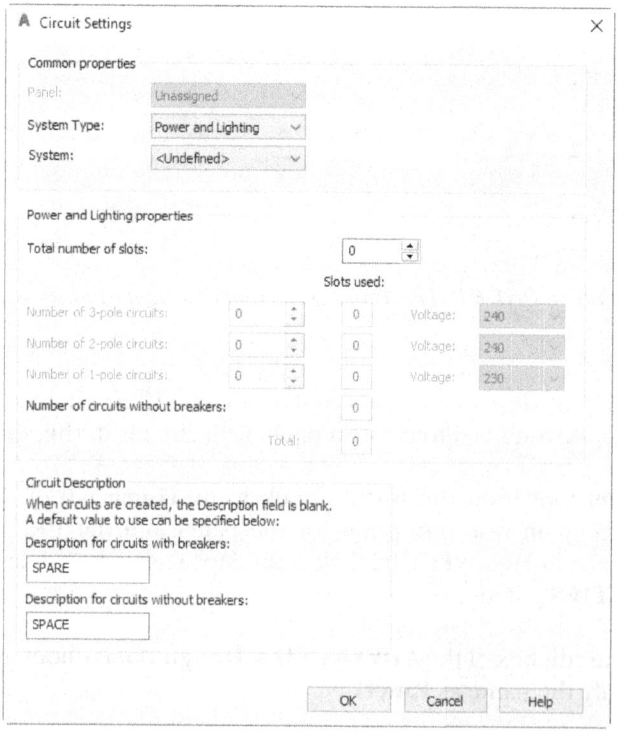

*Figure Prj1-93 The **Circuit Settings** dialog box*

9. Choose the **OK** button from the dialog box to exit. Select the **Yes** option from the **Create circuits** drop-down list in the **Circuits** rollout in the **PROPERTIES** palette.

10. Click in the drawing area to place the panel, refer to Figure Prj1-94. Also, the **AutoCAD MEP - Electrical Project Database** dialog box is displayed, refer to Figure Prj1-95.

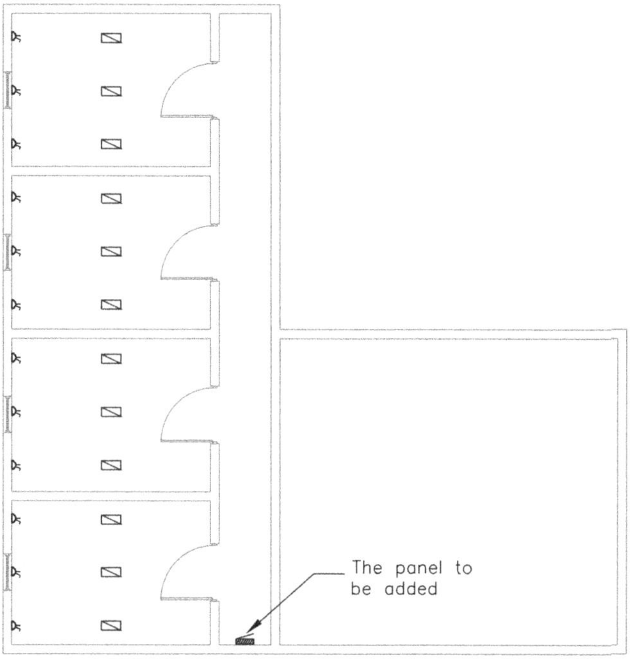

Figure Prj1-94 *The drawing with the panel to be added*

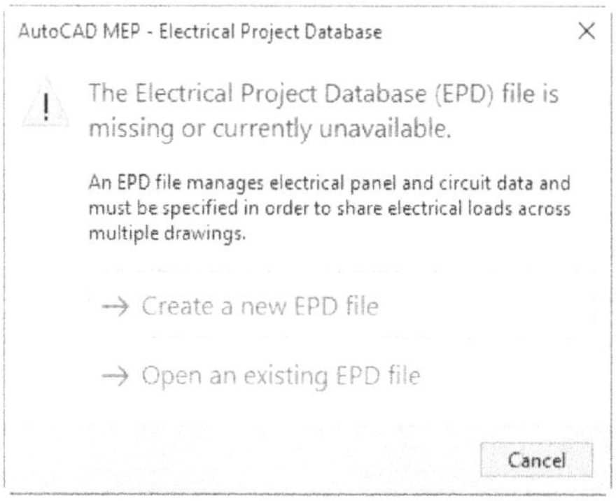

Figure Prj1-95 *The* ***AutoCAD MEP - Electrical Project Database*** *dialog box*

11. Choose the **Create a new EPD file** option from the dialog box and save the file at the desired location with the name **top_panel**; the panel is created at the specified location.

Configuring Circuits

1. Select the panel created and then choose the **Circuit Manager** tool from the **Circuits** panel in the **Panel** tab of the **Ribbon**; the **CIRCUIT MANAGER** is displayed.

2. Click in the field 1 in the **Name** column of the **CIRCUIT MANAGER** and specify the name as **Sockets**.

3. Click in the field 2 in the **Name** column of the **CIRCUIT MANAGER** and specify the name as **Lights**.

4. Double-click in the **Voltage** field for **Sockets** and select the **230** option from the drop-down list displayed.

5. Double-click in the **System** field for the circuit and select the **230V Power** option from the drop-down list displayed.

6. Double-click in the **System** field for **Lights** and select the **230V Lighting** option from the drop-down list displayed.

7. Double-click in the **Voltage** field for **Lights** and select the **230** option from the drop-down list displayed. The **CIRCUIT MANAGER** after applying the above configuration is displayed, as shown in Figure Prj1-96.

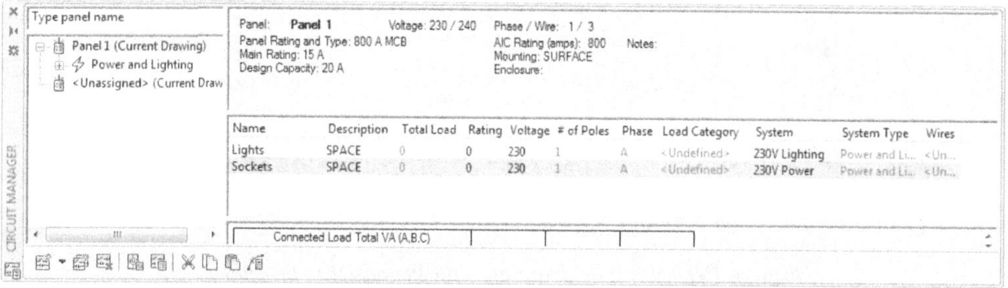

Figure Prj1-96 *The* ***CIRCUIT MANAGER*** *after applying configuration*

Configuring Devices

1. Select a socket from the drawing area and then select the **Select Similar** option from the **Select Similar** drop-down list in the **Device** contextual tab displayed; all the sockets available in the drawing area are selected.

2. Click in the **Electrical properties** field in the **Circuits** rollout of the **PROPERTIES** palette; the **Electrical Properties** dialog box is displayed, as shown in Figure Prj1-97.

   Now, you need to specify the parameters that are given in Table Prj1-1.

3. Select the **230V Power** option from the **System** drop-down list.

4. Specify the value **300** in the **Load Phase 1** edit box, refer to Table Prj1-1.

5. Select the **230** option from the **Voltage** drop-down list.

6. Similarly, select the option **1** from the **Number of Poles** drop-down list in the dialog box.

7. Specify the value **10** in the **Maximum Overcurrent Rating (amps)** edit box in the dialog box.

8. Specify the value **0.8** in the **Power Factor** edit box and then choose the **OK** button to exit the dialog box.

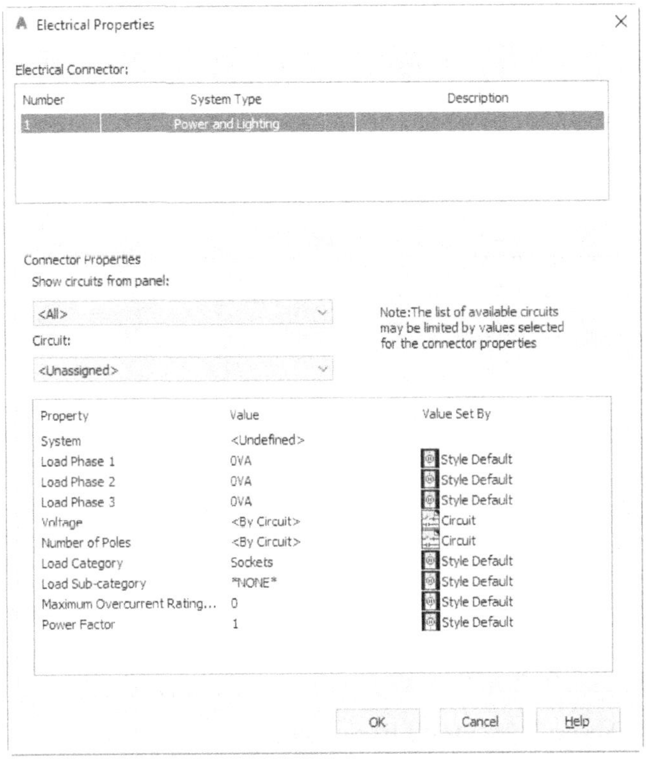

***Figure Prj1-97** The **Electrical Properties** dialog box*

9. Select the **Panel1 (Current Drawing)** option from the **Show Circuits from panel** drop-down list and also select **Sockets [Load: 0 VA]** from the **Circuit** drop-down list. Choose the **OK** button to exit the dialog box.

10. Similarly, Select all the **300x600 Recessed Light** from the drawing area. Next, click in the **Electrical properties** field in the **Circuits** rollout of the **PROPERTIES** palette; the **Electrical Properties** dialog box is displayed, refer to Figure Prj1-97.

11. Select the **230 lighting** from the **System** drop-down list in the dialog box. For other parameters, refer to Table Prj1-1. Also select the **Panel1 (Current Drawing)** option from the **Show circuits from panel** drop-down list and select the **Lights [Load: 0 VA]** for **300x600 Recessed Light from** the **Circuit** drop-down list in the **Electrical Properties** dialog box.

Adding Wires

1. Choose the **Wire** tool from the **Build** panel of the **Home** tab in the **Ribbon**; you are prompted

to specify the start point of the wire on an electrical device and the **PROPERTIES** palette is displayed, as shown in Figure Prj1-98.

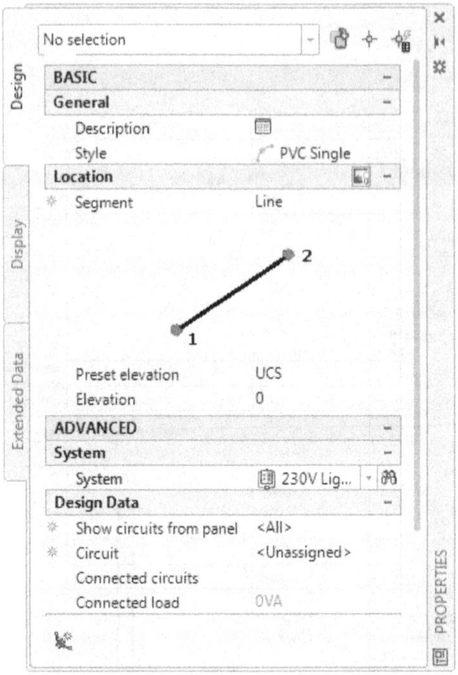

***Figure Prj1-98** The **PROPERTIES** palette displayed on choosing the **Wire** tool*

2. Select the **230V Power(230V POWER)** option from the **System** drop-down list.

3. Select the **PVC Single** option from the **Style** drop-down list.

4. Connect all the sockets to the panel using wire, refer to Figure Prj1-99. Make sure that the **Line** option is selected in the **Segment** drop-down list.

5. Similarly, connect all the lights to the panel using the 230V Lighting system, refer to Figure Prj1-100. Make sure that the circuit selected for lights is **Lights**.

Calculating Loads and Wire Sizes

1. Choose the **Power Totals** tool from the **Electrical** panel in the **Analyze** tab of the **Ribbon**; you are prompted to select the devices.

2. Select all the devices available in the drawing area and press ENTER; the **Power Totals** dialog box is displayed, refer to Figure Prj1-101.

   The total load is displayed in the **Total Load** field of the dialog box. Now, you need to calculate the wire size for the circuit.

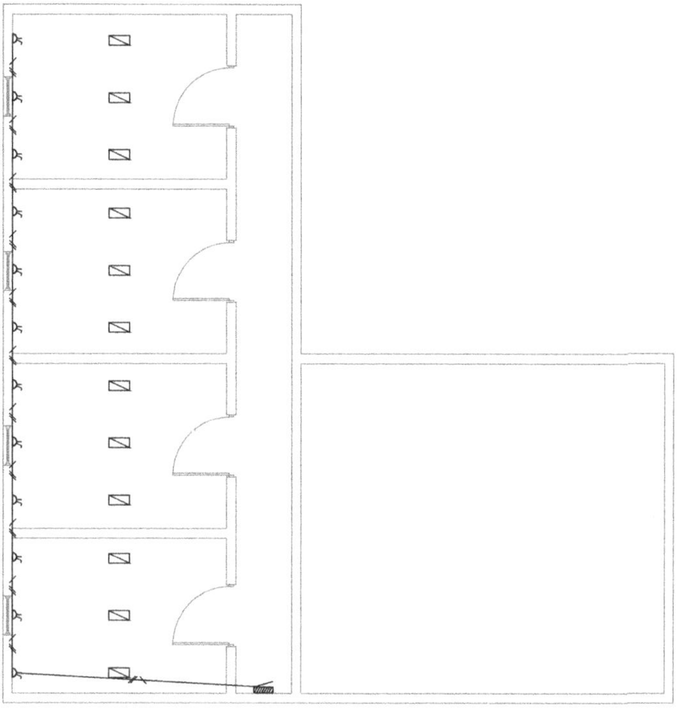

Figure Prj1-99 *The drawing after adding all the sockets with the panel*

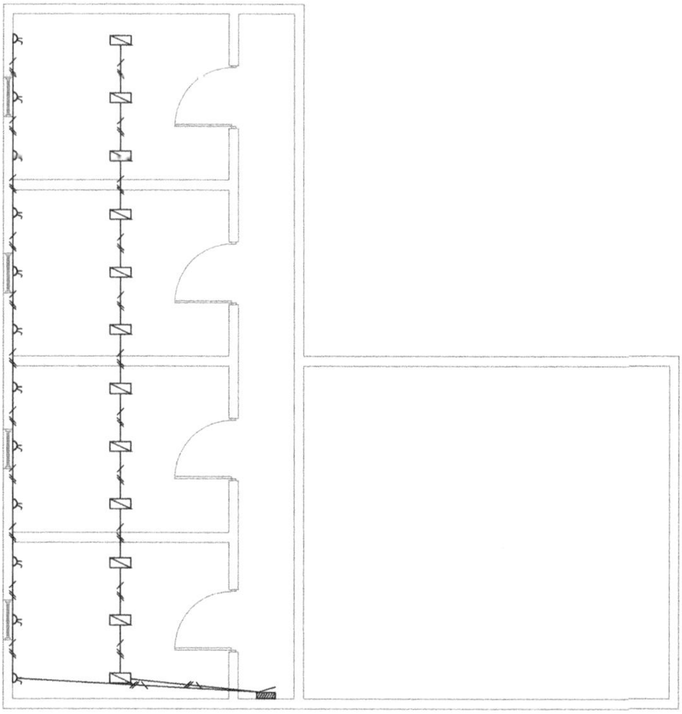

Figure Prj1-100 *The drawing after adding lights to the panel*

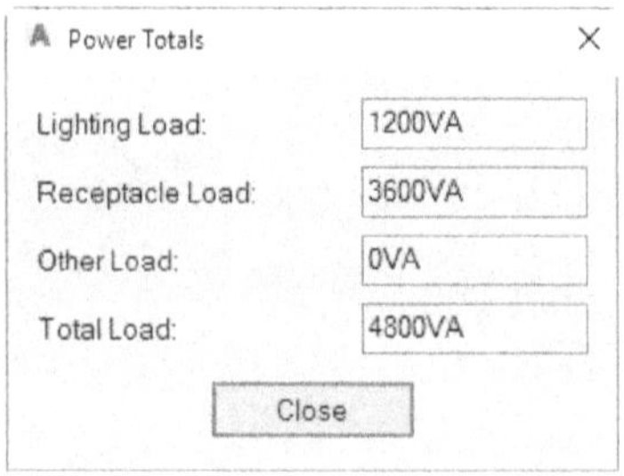

Figure Prj1-101 *The* ***Power Totals*** *dialog box*

3. In the **PROPERTIES** palette, choose the **Calculate sizes for the wire** button available on the right of **Dimensions** rollout; the wire sizes are calculated automatically and displayed in the **Hot size**, **Neutral size**, and **Ground size** edit boxes.

4. Save and close the drawing.

Project 2

Creating Complete Commercial Office Building

Project Description

In this project, you will create a complete Commercial Office Building. Figure Prj2-1 shows the architectural drawings, Figure Prj2-2 shows the HVAC drawings, Figure Prj2-3 shows the piping drawings, Figure Prj2-4 shows the electrical drawings of the office, and Figure Prj2-5 shows the plumbing drawing of the office toilet. Table Prj2-1 shows the parameters required for various electrical devices. **(Expected time: 6 hr)**

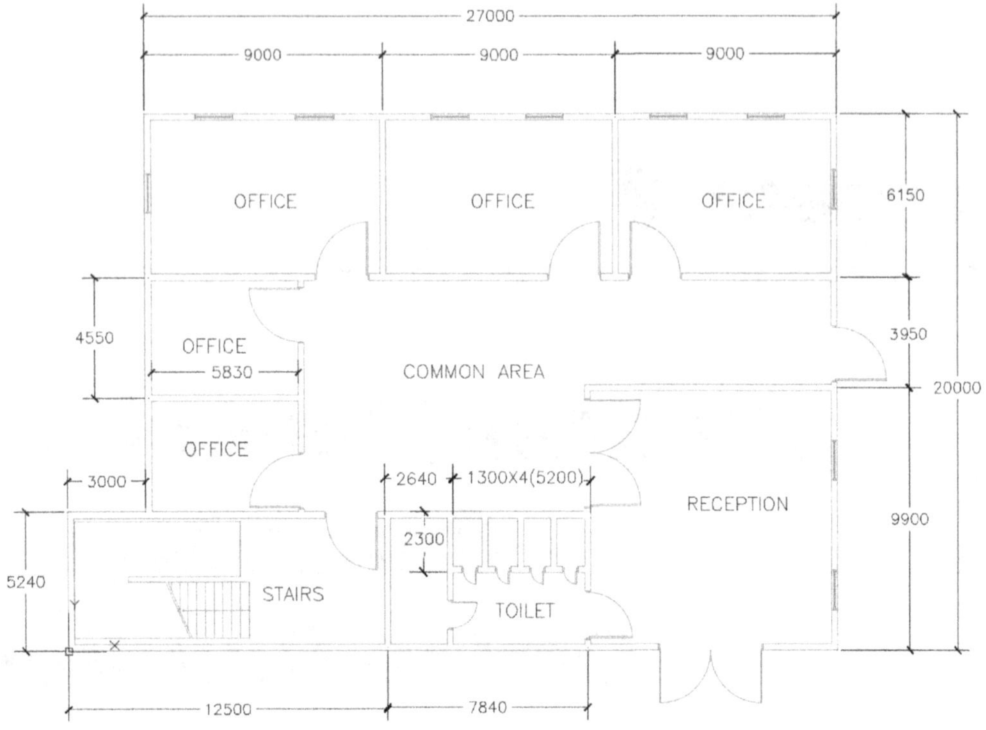

GROUND FLOOR

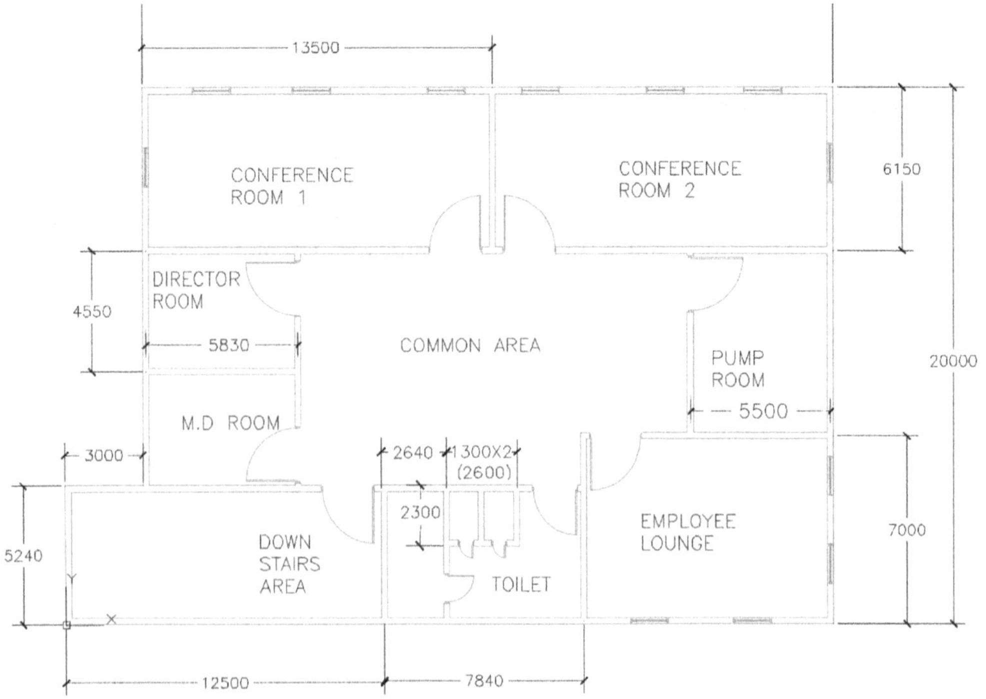

FIRST FLOOR

Figure Prj2-1 *Architectural drawings of the OFFICE*

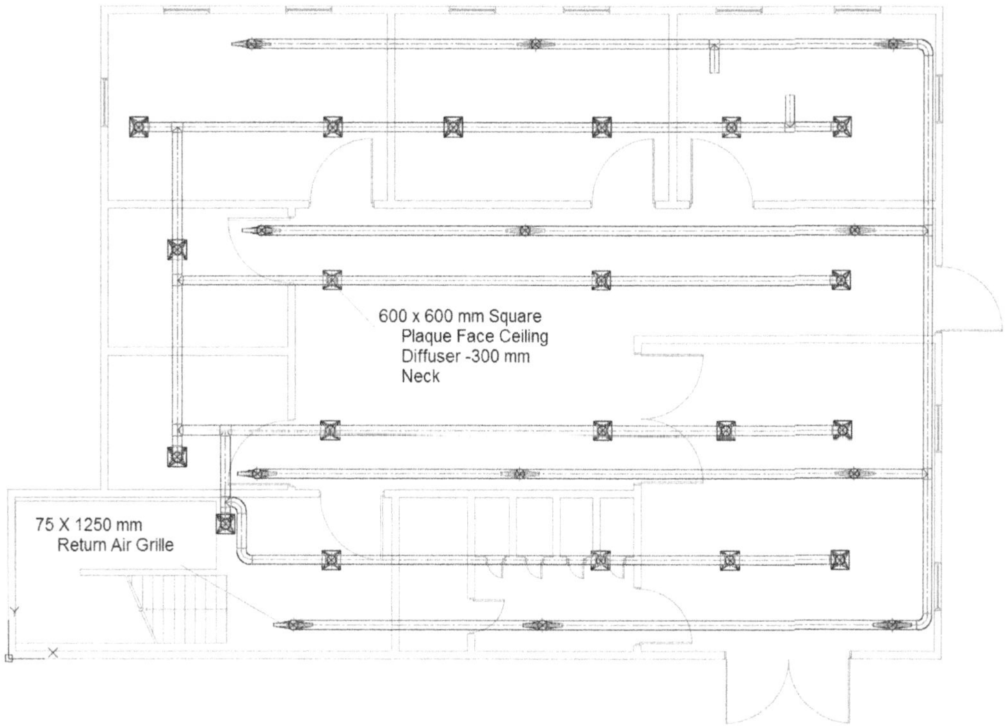

GROUND FLOOR

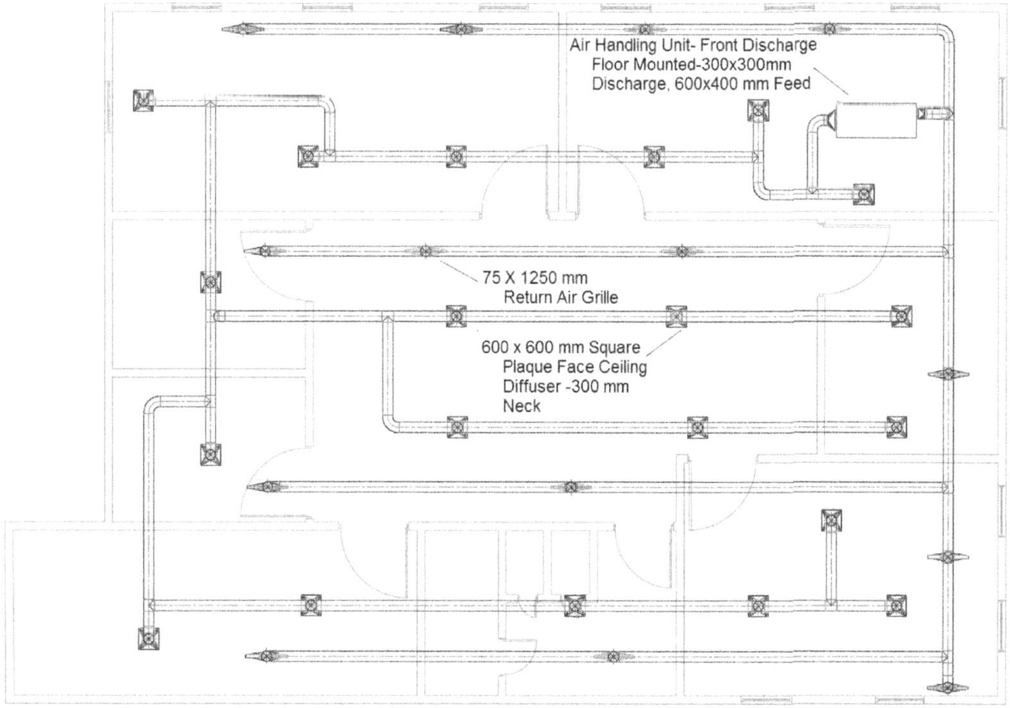

FIRST FLOOR

Figure Prj2-2 *HVAC drawings of the OFFICE*

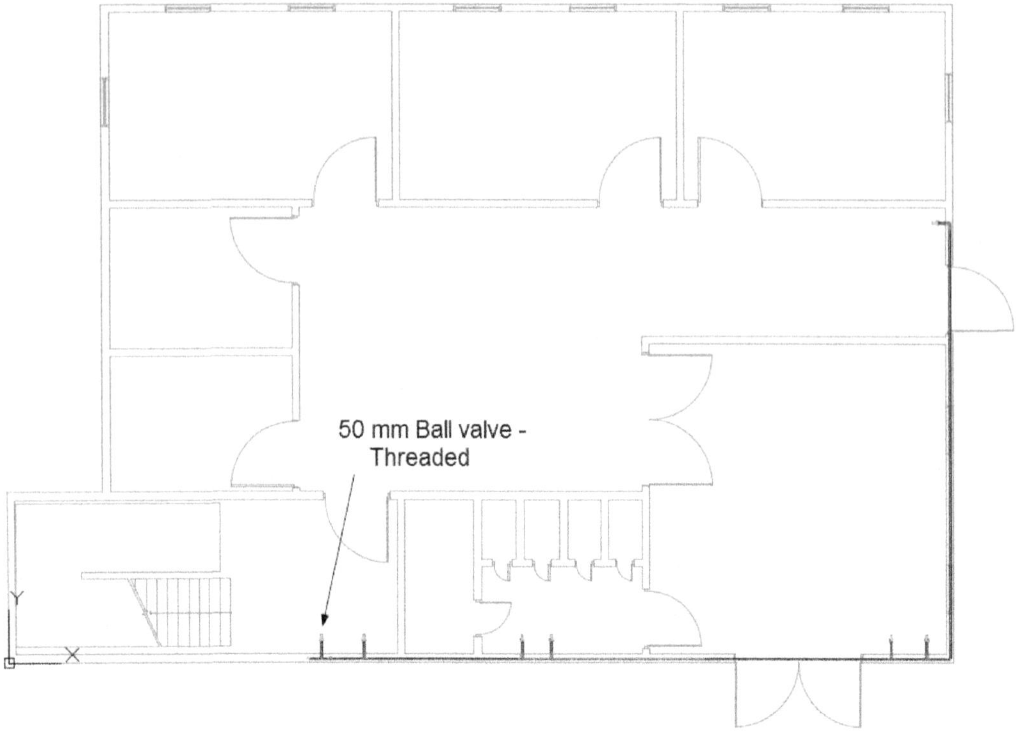

GROUND FLOOR

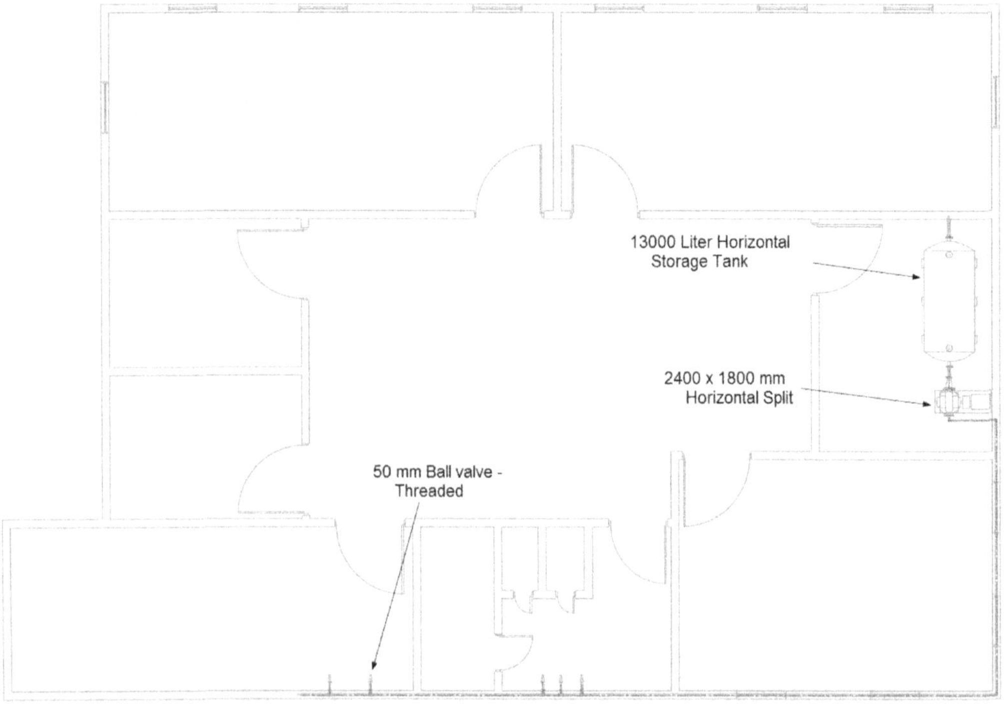

FIRST FLOOR

***Figure Prj2-3** Piping drawings of the OFFICE*

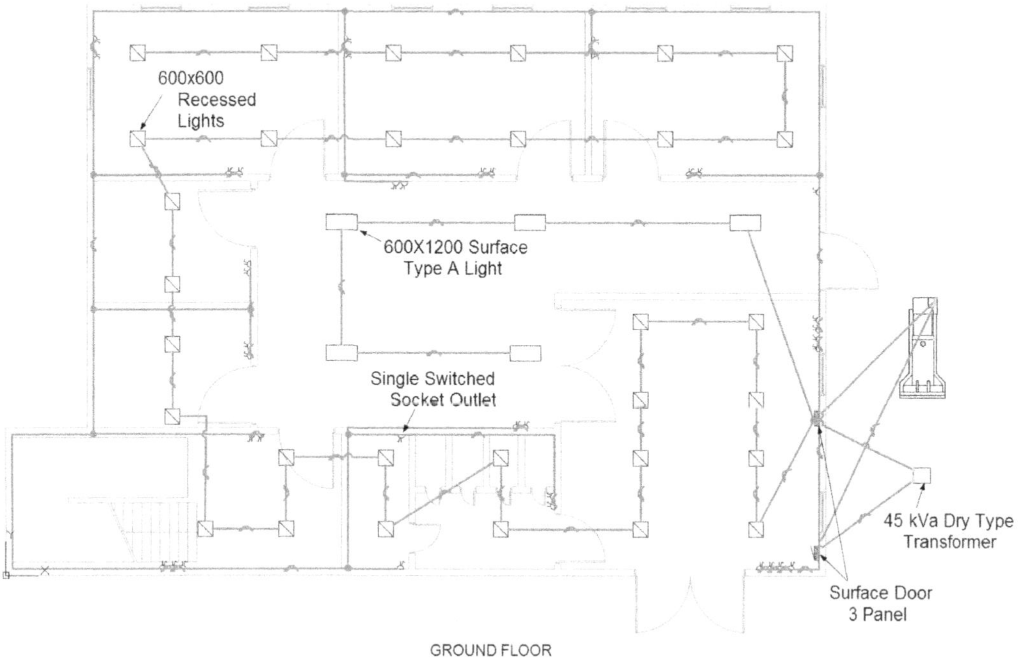

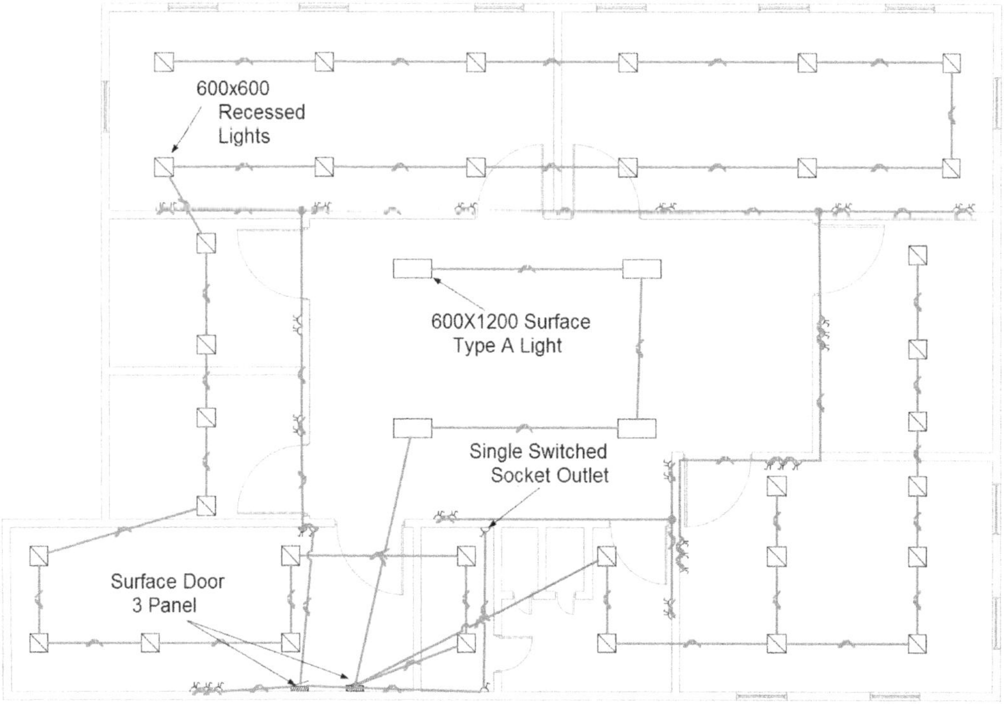

FIRST FLOOR

Figure Prj2-4 *Electrical drawings of the OFFICE*

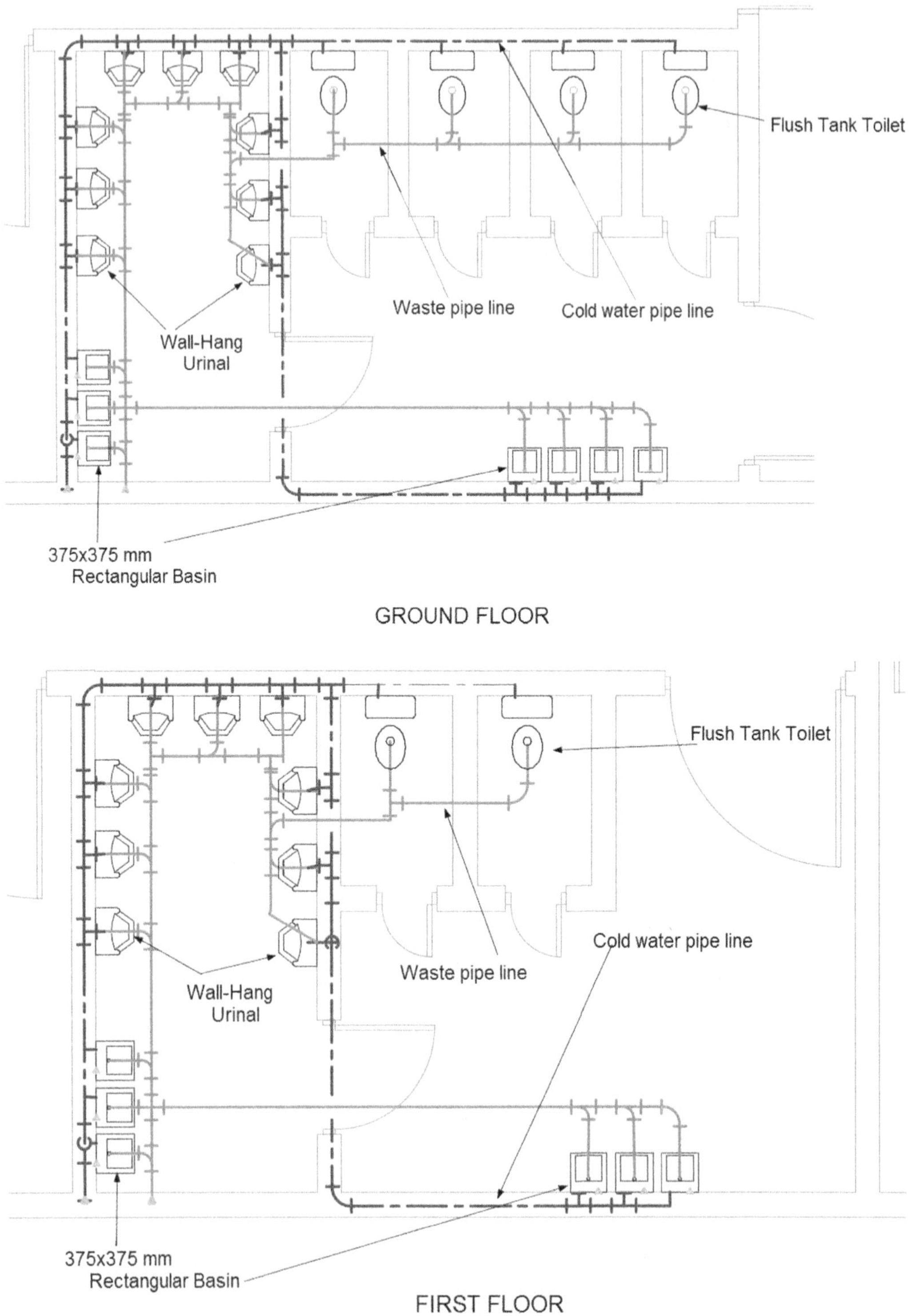

Figure Prj2-5 *Plumbing drawings of the OFFICE Toilet*

Table Prj2-1 The parameters required for various Electrical devices

Device	600X1200 Surface Type A Light	600x600 Recessed Lights	Single Switched Socket Outlet
System	230V Lighting Devices (Ceiling)	230VA Lighting Devices (Ceiling)	230VA Power
Load	220 VA	150VA	300VA
Voltage	230	230	230
Phases	1	1	1
Maximum Overcurrent rating	10	8	10
Power Factor	0.8	0.8	0.8

The following steps are required to complete this project:

1. Start a new project file
2. Create categories in the project
3. Create levels in the project
4. Create architectural drawings
   - Create architectural drawing of ground floor
   - Create walls in the architectural drawing for ground floor
   - Create doors in the architectural drawing of ground floor
   - Create windows in the architectural drawing of ground floor
   - Create stairs in the architectural drawing of ground floor
   - Create slab for roof in the architectural drawing of ground floor
   - Create cut in slab
   - Create architectural drawing of first floor
   - Create walls in the architectural drawing for first floor
   - Create doors in the architectural drawing of first floor
   - Create windows in the architectural drawing of first floor
   - Create slab for roof in the architectural drawing of first floor
5. Create HVAC drawings
   - Create HVAC drawing of ground floor
   - Import the architectural drawing of ground floor
   - Add air terminals in the architectural drawing of ground floor
   - Add duct to the diffuser
   - Calculate the duct sizes of ground floor
   - Add return air grilles
   - Create return duct line for the ground floor
   - Calculate the duct sizes of return grilles
   - Create HVAC drawing of first floor
   - Import the architectural drawing of first floor
   - Add air terminals in the architectural drawing of first floor
   - Add duct to the diffuser
   - Add air handling unit

- Add return grilles in the architectural drawing of first floor
- Create return duct for the first floor
- Calculate the duct sizes of first floor

6. Create piping drawings
   - Create piping drawing of ground floor
   - Import the architectural drawing of ground floor
   - Add ball valves in the architectural drawing of ground floor
   - Add pipe line in the architectural drawing of ground floor
   - Connect ball valves with the pipe line
   - Create piping drawing of first floor
   - Import the architectural drawing of first floor
   - Add ball valves in the architectural drawing of first floor
   - Add tank in the first floor
   - Add pumps in the first floor
   - Add pipe line in the first floor
7. Create electrical drawings
   - Create electrical drawing of ground floor
   - Import the architectural drawing of ground floor
   - Add **600x600 recessed lights** to the drawing
   - Add **600x1200 surface type lights** to the drawing
   - Add sockets to the drawing
   - Create panel of ground floor
   - Configure circuits of ground floor
   - Configure devices of ground floor
   - Add wires of ground floor
   - Calculate load and wire sizes of ground floor
   - Add transformer and emergency generator to the drawing based on total load
   - Create electrical drawing of first floor
   - Import the architectural drawing of first floor
   - Add **600x600 recessed lights** to the drawing
   - Add **600x1200 surface type lights** to the drawing
   - Add sockets in the drawing of first floor
   - Create panel of first floor
   - Configure circuits of first floor
   - Configure devices of first floor
   - Add wires of first floor
   - Calculate loads and wire sizes of first floor
8. Create plumbing drawings
   - Create plumbing drawing of ground floor
   - Import the architectural drawing of ground floor
   - Add Urinal to drawing of ground floor
   - Add rectangular basin of ground floor
   - Add water closet of ground floor
   - Create plumbing line between various equipments
   - Create plumbing drawing of first floor
   - Import the architectural drawing first floor
   - Add Urinal to drawing of ground floor
   - Add rectangular basin of ground floor

- Add water closet of ground floor
- Create plumbing line between various equipments

Starting a New Project File

1. Start AutoCAD MEP by using the *AutoCAD MEP 2022 - English (Global)* icon displayed on your desktop.

2. Choose **New > Project** from the **Application Menu**; the **Project Browser** is displayed.

3. Choose the **New Project** button available at the bottom of the **Project Browser**; the **Add Project** dialog box is displayed.

4. Enter the project name as **Commercial Office Building** in the **Project name** field, **002** in the **Project Number** field and other descriptions in their respective fields. Make sure that the **Create from template project** check box is clear.

5. Choose the **OK** button; the newly created project file name is displayed in the left pane of the **Project Browser**, refer to Figure Prj2-6.

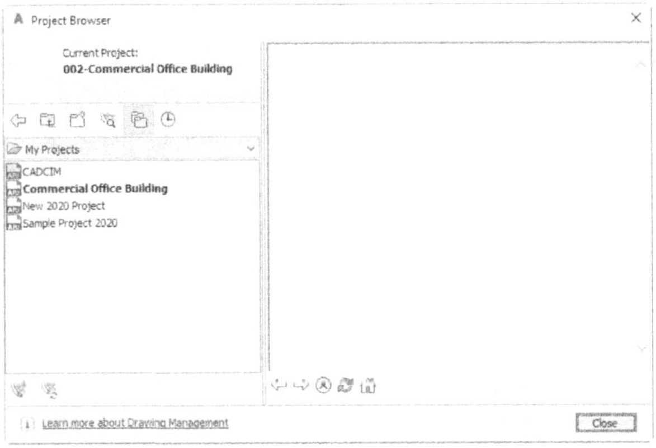

Figure Prj2-6** The **Project Browser

6. Choose the **Close** button from the **Project Browser**; the **PROJECT NAVIGATOR** is displayed in the drawing area and the new project gets activated.

Creating Categories in the Project

Now, you need to categorize the project.

1. To categorize a project, choose the **Constructs** tab and then click on the **Constructs** category in it. Choose the **Add Category** button from the bottom of the **PROJECT NAVIGATOR** in the **Constructs** tab; a new category is added to the **Constructs** node.

2. Specify the name of the category as **Architectural** and press ENTER.

3. Similarly, add other categories and name them as **Mechanical**, **Electrical**, **Piping**, and **Plumbing**.

Creating Levels in the Project

Now, you need to create levels in the project.

1. To create levels, choose the **Project** tab from the **PROJECT NAVIGATOR**; the **PROJECT NAVIGATOR** is displayed, as shown in Figure Prj2-7.

2. Choose the **Edit Levels** button from the **Levels** rollout of the **PROJECT NAVIGATOR**; the **Levels** dialog box is displayed.

3. Double-click in the edit box below the **Name** column and rename it to **1**.

4. Enter **4000** in the **Floor to Floor Height** column corresponding to **1** in the **Name** column.

5. Choose the **Add Level** button on the right in the dialog box; a new level is added with the name **2** to the list displayed in the dialog box, as shown in Figure Prj2-8.

6. Choose the **OK** button in the dialog box to exit. If you get a message box with the message that do you want AutoCAD MEP to regenerate all the views in this project, as shown in Figure Prj2-9, choose the **Yes** button from the message box.

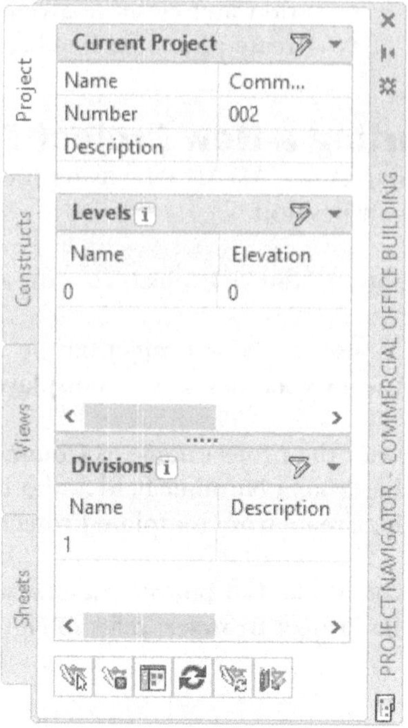

*Figure Prj2-7 The **PROJECT NAVIGATOR** with the **Project** tab chosen*

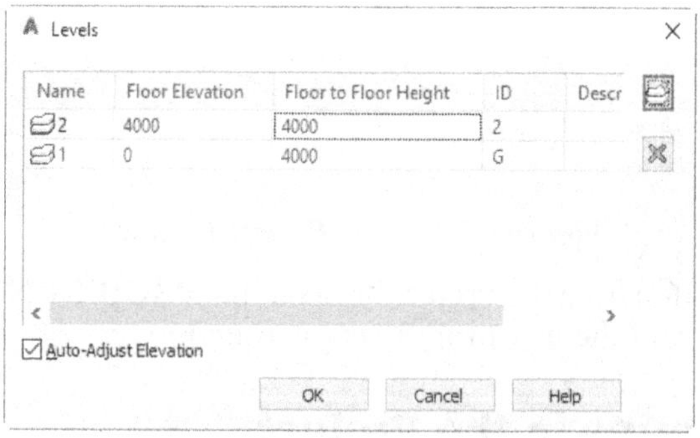

*Figure Prj2-8 The **Levels** dialog box*

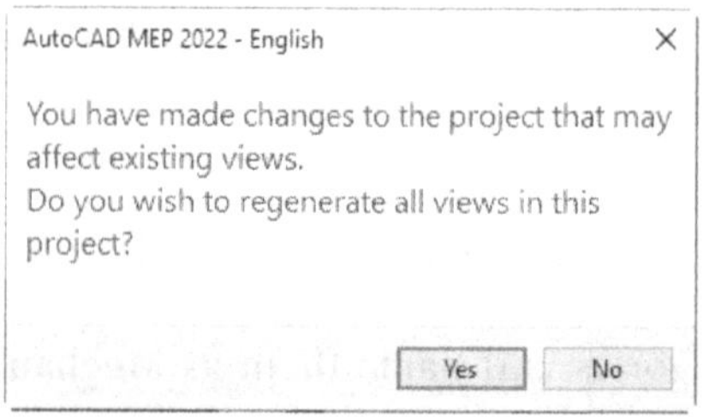

*Figure Prj2-9 The **AutoCAD MEP 2022 - English** message box*

Creating Architectural Drawings

Now, you need to create architectural drawings for the ground floor and first floor.

Creating Architectural Drawing of the Ground Floor

1. Select the **Architectural** category in the **Constructs** node from the **Constructs** tab in the **PROJECT NAVIGATOR** and then choose the **Add Construct** button available at the bottom; the **Add Construct** dialog box is displayed, refer to Figure Prj2-10.

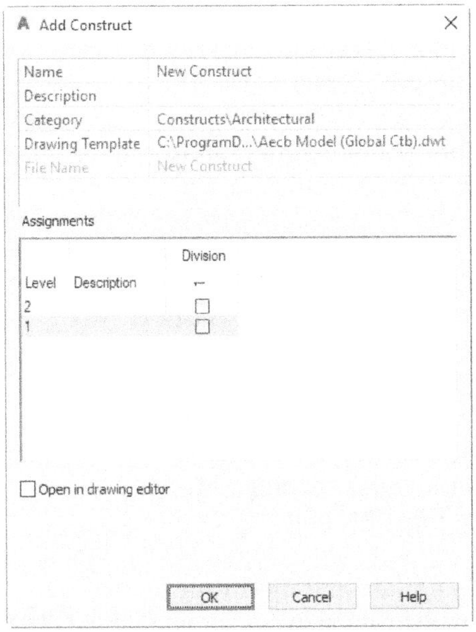

Figure Prj2-10 *The* ***Add Construct*** *dialog box*

2. Select the **Open in drawing editor** check box from the bottom of the dialog box.
3. Enter **Ground Floor Architectural** in the **Name** field of the dialog box.
4. Click in the **Description** field; the **Description** dialog box is displayed.
5. Enter the description as **This drawing is meant for architectural plan of the ground floor** in the **Edit the description** edit box and then choose the **OK** button from the dialog box.
6. Select the check box corresponding to level **1** in the **Division** column from the **Assignments** area in the **Add Construct** dialog box. Also, make sure that the **Open in drawing editor** check box is selected and then choose the **OK** button from the dialog box; the drawing is opened in AutoCAD MEP. Also, the Ground Floor Architectural drawing is displayed with a lock icon adjacent to it in the **PROJECT NAVIGATOR**.

Note

If the ***PROJECT NAVIGATOR*** *is not displayed, you can invoke it by entering the command* ***PROJECTNAVIGATOR*** *in the command prompt.*

7. Choose the **Workspace Switching** option from the **Application Status Bar** and then choose the **Architecture** option from the flyout displayed; the **Architecture** workspace is activated.

Creating Walls in the Architectural Drawing

1. Choose the **Wall** tool from the **Wall** drop-down in the **Build** panel of the **Home** tab in the **Ribbon**; you are prompted to specify the starting point of the wall. Also, the **PROPERTIES** palette is displayed, refer to Figure Prj2-11.

2. Enter the base height of the wall as **4000** and width as **254**. Select the **Right** option from the **Justify** drop-down list. Make sure the **Dynamic Input** option in the **Application Status Bar** is turned off.

3. Enter the coordinates **0,0,0** at the command prompt and press ENTER to specify the start point; a rubber band wall is displayed with its other end attached to the cursor.

4. Press F8 to work in the ORTHOMODE and specify the horizontal length of the wall as **30000** at the command prompt. Next, press ENTER.

5. Move the cursor vertically upward and specify the value **20000** at the command prompt. Next, press ENTER.

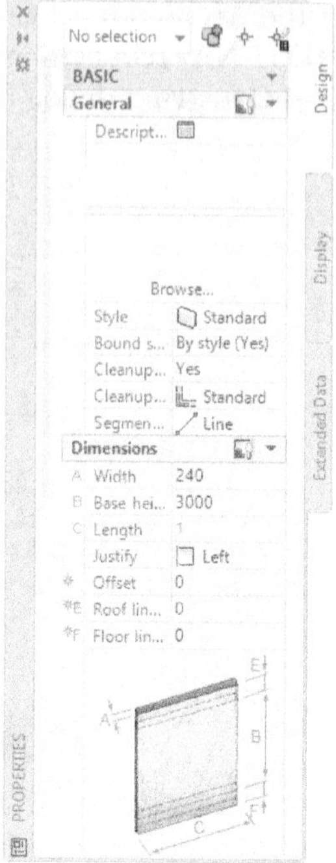

*Figure Prj2-11 The **PROPERTIES** palette*

6. Move the cursor toward the left and specify the value **27000** at the command prompt. Next, press ENTER.

7. Move the cursor vertically downward and specify the value **15000** at the command prompt. Next, press ENTER.

8. Move the cursor toward the left and specify the value **3000** at the command prompt. Next, press ENTER.

9. Enter **C** at the command prompt to create the last wall. The drawing displays the architectural outer boundary of the plant, refer to Figure Prj2-12.

Figure Prj2-12 *The architectural outer boundary of the plant*

10. Similarly, create the walls inside the building, as shown in Figure Prj2-13. For dimensions of the walls, refer to Figure Prj2-1. Note that the height of the walls inside the toilet is 3200, refer to Figure Prj2-13.

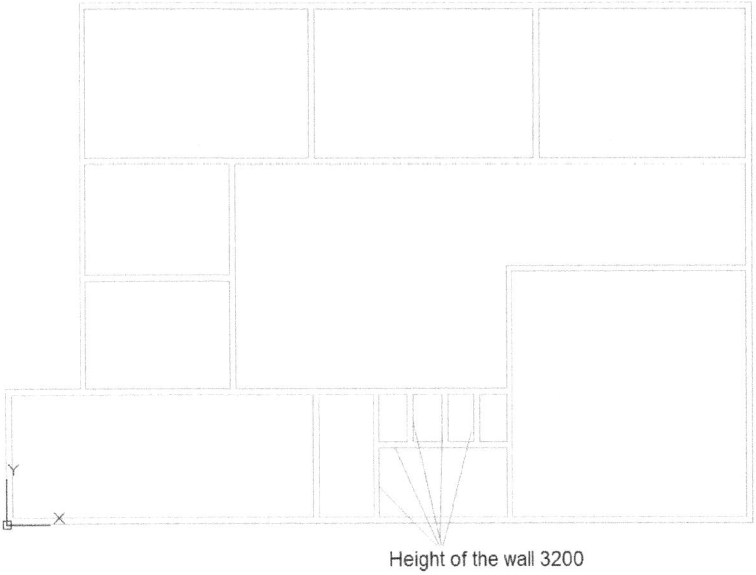

Figure Prj2-13 *The drawing after creating all walls*

Creating Doors in the Architectural Drawing of the Ground Floor

1. Choose the **Door** tool from the **Door** drop-down in the **Build** panel of the **Home** tab in the **Ribbon**; you are prompted to specify the insertion point of the door. Also, the **PROPERTIES** palette is displayed, refer to Figure Prj2-14.

2. Enter **2000** in the **Width** and **3000** in the **Height** edit box in the **Dimensions** rollout of the **PROPERTIES** palette.

3. Select the **Offset/Center** option from the **Position along wall** drop-down list in the **Location** rollout. Add all the D1 doors with the respective walls, refer to Figure Prj2-15.

4. Enter **1700** in the **Width** and **3000** in the **Height** edit box in the **Dimensions** rollout of the **PROPERTIES** palette. Add D2 doors with the respective walls, refer to Figure Prj2-15.

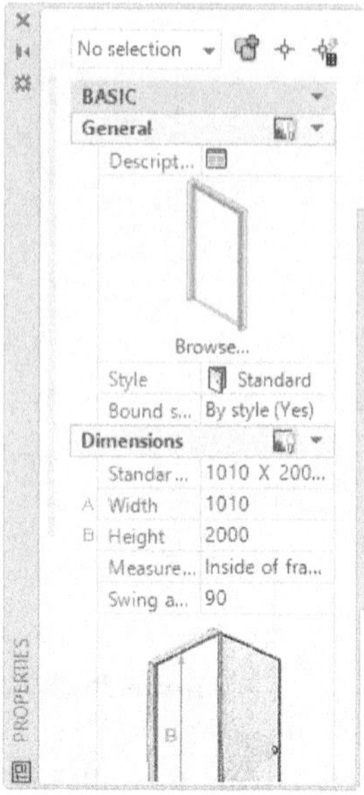

Figure Prj2-14 The ***PROPERTIES*** *palette displayed on choosing the* ***Door*** *tool*

5. Enter **1000** in the **Width** and **3000** in the **Height** edit box in the **Dimensions** rollout of the **PROPERTIES** palette. Add all the D3 doors with the respective walls, refer to Figure Prj2-15.

6. Enter **500** in the **Width** and **2000** in the **Height** edit box in the **Dimensions** rollout of the **PROPERTIES** palette. Add D4 doors with the respective walls, refer to Figure Prj2-15. Press ENTER to exit the tool.

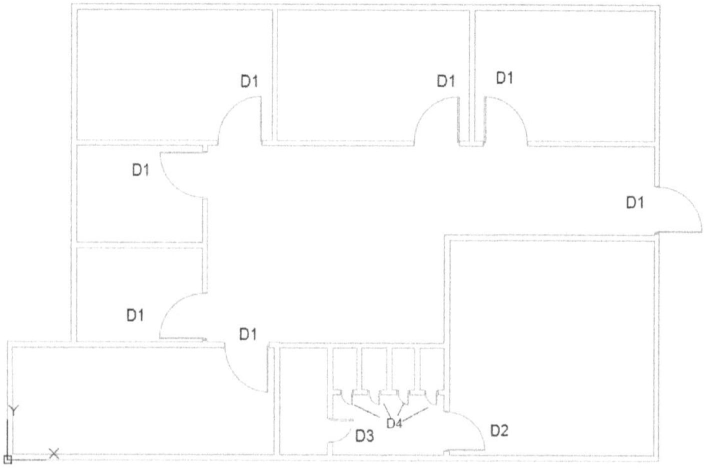

Figure Prj2-15 *The drawing after adding D1, D2, D3 and D4 doors*

7. Again, choose the **Door** tool; you are prompted to select a wall or grid. Also, the **PROPERTIES** palette is displayed. Select the Browse area in the **PROPERTIES** palette; the **STYLES BROWSER** palette will be displayed, refer to Figure Prj2-16.

8. Double click on the **Hinged - Double** door from the Preview area and close the **STYLES BROWSER** palette.

9. Enter **4000** in the **Width** and **3500** in the **Height** edit box in the **Dimensions** rollout of the **PROPERTIES** palette. Click on the walls to create main doors, refer to Figure Prj2-17.

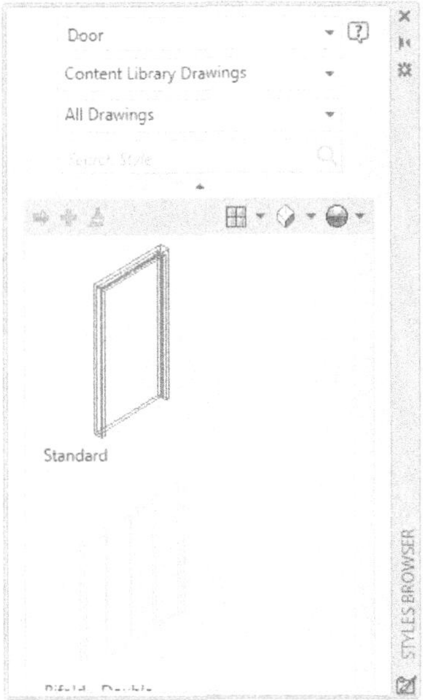

***Figure Prj2-16** The STYLE BROWSER palette*

Creating Windows in the Architectural Drawing of the Ground Floor

1. Choose the **Window** tool from the **Window** drop-down in the **Build** panel of the **Home** tab in the **Ribbon**; you are prompted to select a wall or a grid assembly. Also, the **PROPERTIES** palette is displayed, as shown in Figure Prj2-18.

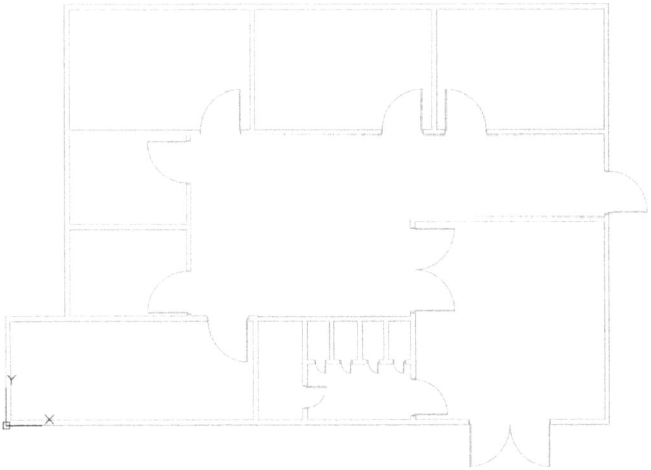

***Figure Prj2-17** The drawing after adding main and inner doors*

2. Choose the **Unconstrained** option from the **Position along wall** drop-down list in the **Location** rollout of the **PROPERTIES** palette. Enter **1500** in the **Width** and **Height** edit box in the **Dimensions** rollout. Also, select **Yes** from the **Relative to grid** drop-down list in the **Location** rollout.

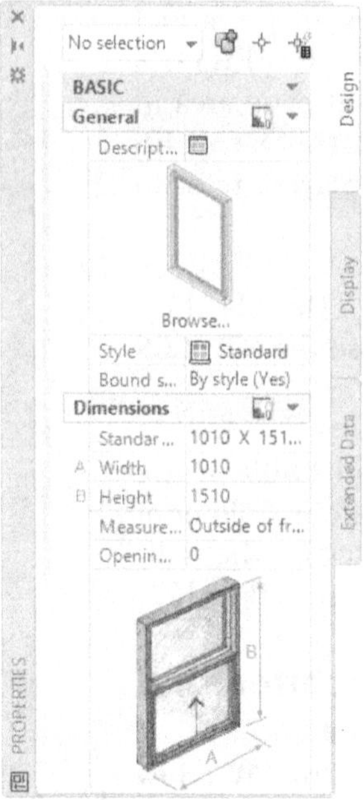

Figure Prj2-18 *The* ***PROPERTIES*** *palette on choosing the* ***Window*** *tool*

3. Click on the walls of the ground floor architectural drawing and locate the windows W as shown in Figure Prj2-19.

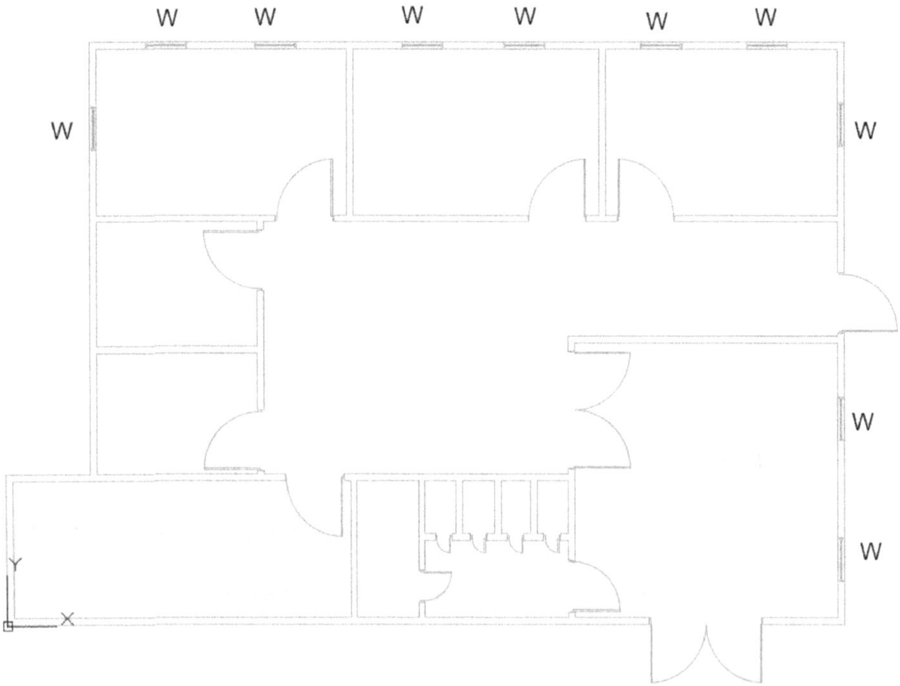

Figure Prj2-19 *The walls to be selected for adding windows*

Creating Stairs in the Architectural Drawing of the Ground Floor

1. Choose the **Stair** tool from the **Stair** drop-down in the **Build** panel of the **Home** tab in the **Ribbon**; you are prompted to select the flight start point. Also, the **PROPERTIES** palette is displayed, refer to Figure Prj2-20.

2. Select the **U-shaped** option from the **Shape** drop-down list, **1/2 landing** option from the **Turn type** drop-down list and the **Clockwise** option from the **Horizontal orientation** drop-down list in the **General** rollout of the **PROPERTIES** palette. Also, select the **Up** option from the **Vertical orientation** drop-down list.

3. Enter **2100** in the **Width** and **4000** in the **Height** edit box in the **Dimensions** rollout.

4. Select the **Tread** option from the **Calculation rules**; the **Calculation Rules** dialog box will be displayed. Click on lock button adjacent to the **Tread** edit box and the **Tread** edit box gets deactivated.

5. Next, click on button adjacent to the **Stair Length** edit box; the **Stair Length** edit box becomes active. Enter **9168** in the **Stair Length** edit box and choose the **OK** button.

6. Place the Stair, refer to Figure Prj2- 21.

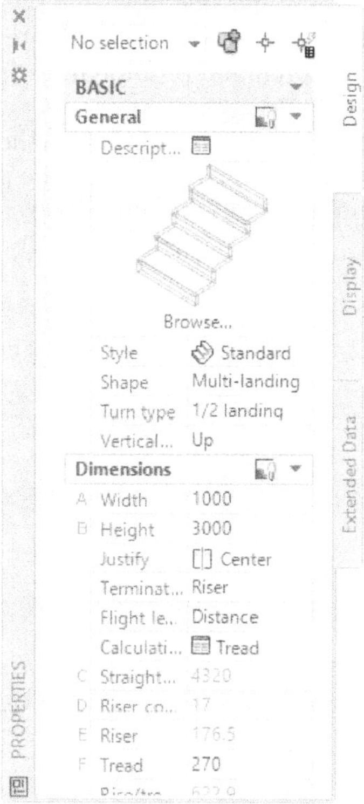

Figure Prj2-20 The ***PROPERTIES*** *palette on choosing the* ***Stair*** *tool*

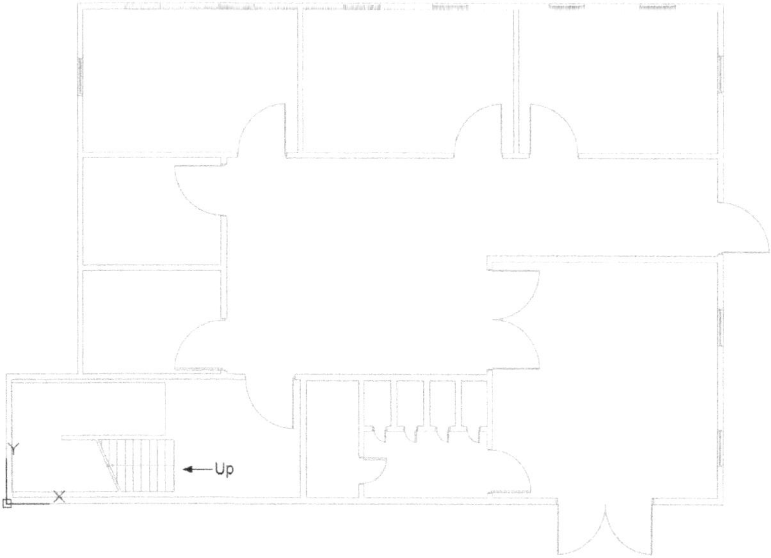

Figure Prj2-21 *The drawing after adding stair*

Creating Slab for roof in the Architectural Drawing of the Ground Floor

1. Choose the **Slab** tool from the **Roof Slab** drop-down in the **Build** panel of the **Home** tab in the **Ribbon**; you are prompted to specify the start point. Choose the **Height** option from the command prompt and specify 4000 in the command prompt and press ENTER.

2. Enter the 0,0 coordinates in the command prompt; a dotted rubber band line will be attached to the cursor. Next, select the points 1, 2, 3, 4, 5, and 6, as shown in Figure Prj2-22 and then press ENTER; a slab will be created.

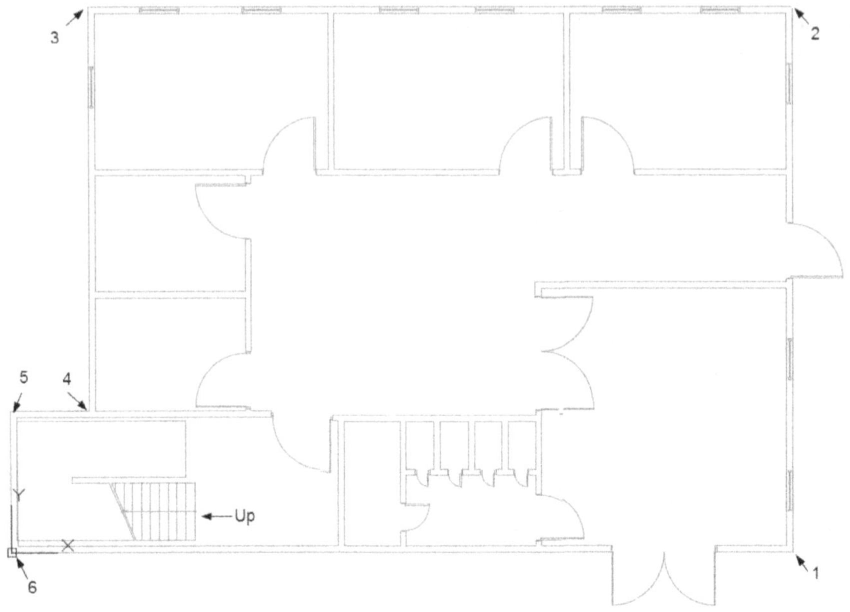

Figure Prj2-22 *Corner points for the slab*

Creating Cut in the Slab

1. Choose the **Rectangle** tool from the **Rectangle** drop-down in the **Draw** panel of the **Home** tab; you will be prompted to specify the first corner point. Specify the corner points for the rectangle, as shown in Figure Prj2-23.

2. Select the slab and choose the **Trim** tool from the **Modify** panel in the **Slab** contextual tab; you are prompted to select a trimming object like a polygon or a solid object.

3. Select the rectangle created for the cut and press ENTER; you are prompted to specify the side to be deleted.

4. Click inside the rectangle; the area covered by the rectangle is trimmed. Press ESC to exit the tool.

   Now, you need to hide the rectangle geometry created for trimming.

5. Select the rectangle and right-click; a shortcut menu is displayed. Move the cursor on the **Isolate Objects** option in the shortcut menu; a flyout is displayed. Choose the **Hide Objects** option to hide the rectangle.

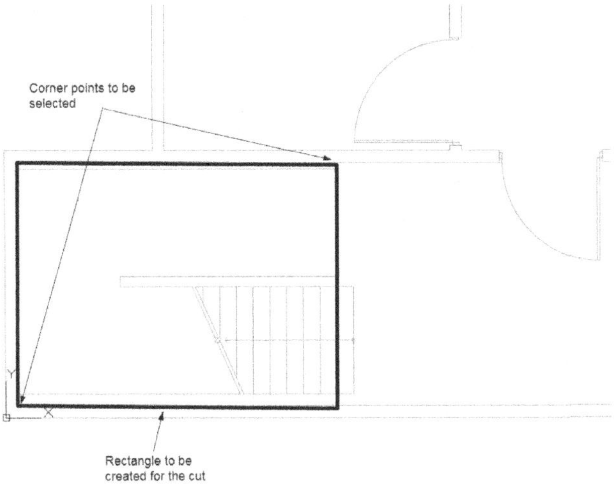

***Figure Prj2-23** Rectangle to be created for cut in the slab*

Isometric view of the drawing after creating the cut is shown in Figure Prj2-24.

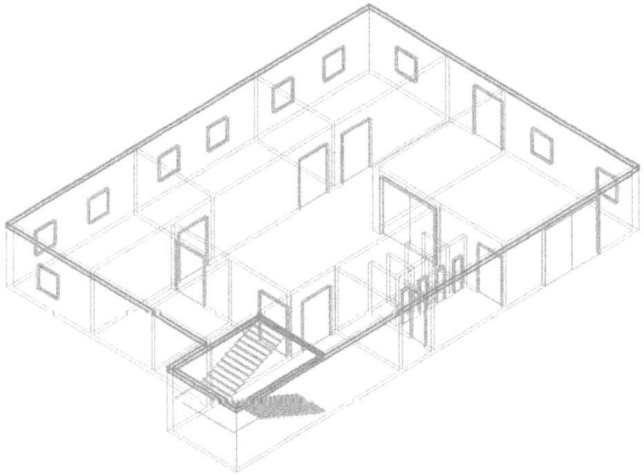

***Figure Prj2-24** Isometric view of the drawing after creating the cut in the slab*

6. Save the drawing and close it.

Creating Architectural Drawing of First Floor

1. Select the **Architectural** category from the **PROJECT NAVIGATOR** and choose the **Add Construct** tool from the bottom; the **Add Construct** dialog box is displayed.

2. Specify the name as **First Floor Architectural** in the **Name** edit box of the dialog box.

3. Click in the **Description** field and specify the description as **This drawing is meant for architectural plan of the first floor** in the dialog box displayed. Next, choose the **OK** button.

4. Select the check box corresponding to level 2 in the **Division** column in the **Assignments** area of the **Add Construct** dialog box. Also, make sure that the **Open in drawing editor** check

box is selected and then choose the **OK** button to exit; the drawing is opened in AutoCAD MEP. Make sure that the **Architecture** option is chosen in the **Workspace Switching** flyout.

Creating Walls in the Architectural Drawing

1. Choose the **Wall** tool from the **Wall** drop-down in the **Build** panel of the **Home** tab in the **Ribbon**; you are prompted to specify the starting point of the wall. Also, the **PROPERTIES** palette is displayed.

2. Enter the base height of the wall as **4000** and width as **254**. Make sure the **Dynamic Input** option in the **Application Status Bar** is turned on.

3. Enter the coordinates **0,0,0** at the command prompt and press ENTER to specify the start point; a rubber band wall is displayed with its other end attached to the cursor.

4. Press F8 to work in the ORTHOMODE and specify the horizontal length of the wall **30000** at the command prompt. Next, press ENTER.

5. Move the cursor vertically upward and specify the value **20000** at the command prompt. Next, press ENTER.

6. Move the cursor toward the left and specify the value **27000** at the command prompt. Next, press ENTER.

7. Move the cursor vertically downward and specify the value **15000** at the command prompt. Next, press ENTER.

8. Move the cursor toward the left and specify the value **3000** at the command prompt. Next, press ENTER.

9. Enter **C** at the command prompt to create the last wall. The drawing displays the architectural outer boundary of the first floor, refer to Figure Prj2-25.

Figure Prj2-25 *Outer boundary of the first floor*

10. Similarly, create the inside walls of the building, as shown in Figure Prj2-26. For dimensions of the walls, refer to Figure Prj2-1.

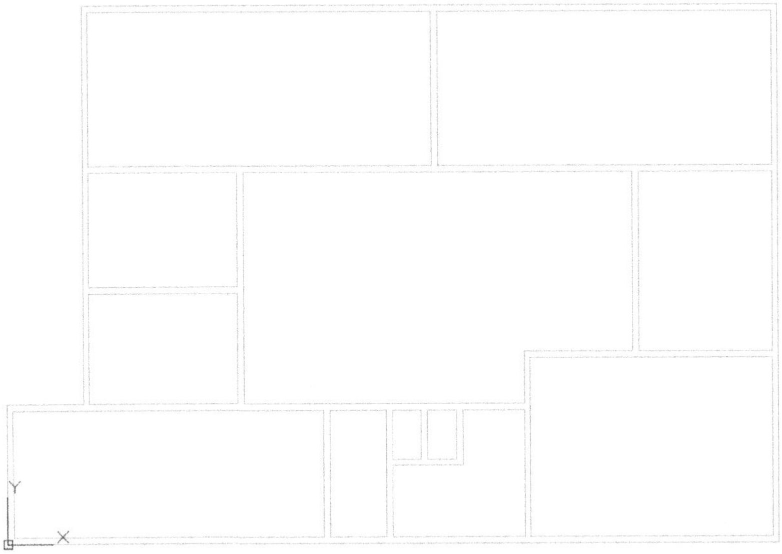

Figure Prj2-26 Drawing of first floor after creating rooms

Creating Doors in the Architectural Drawing of the First Floor

1. Choose the **Door** tool from the **Door** drop-down in the **Build** panel of the **Home** tab in the **Ribbon**; you are prompted to specify the insertion point of the door. Also, the **PROPERTIES** palette is displayed.

2. Enter **2000** in the **Width** and **3000** in the **Height** edit box in the **Dimensions** rollout of the **PROPERTIES** palette.

3. Select the **Offset/Center** option from the **Position along wall** drop-down list in the **Location** rollout. Add all the D1 doors with the respective walls, refer to Figure Prj2-27. Press ENTER to exit the tool.

4. Enter **1700** in the **Width** and **3000** in the **Height** edit box in the **Dimensions** rollout of the **PROPERTIES** palette. Add D2 doors with the respective walls, refer to Figure Prj2-27.

5. Enter **1000** in the **Width** and **3000** in the **Height** edit box in the **Dimensions** rollout of the **PROPERTIES** palette. Add all the D3 doors with the respective walls, refer to Figure Prj2-27.

6. Enter **500** in the **Width** and **2000** in the **Height** edit box in the **Dimensions** rollout of the **PROPERTIES** palette. Add all the D4 doors with the respective walls, refer to Figure Prj2-27. Press ENTER to exit the tool.

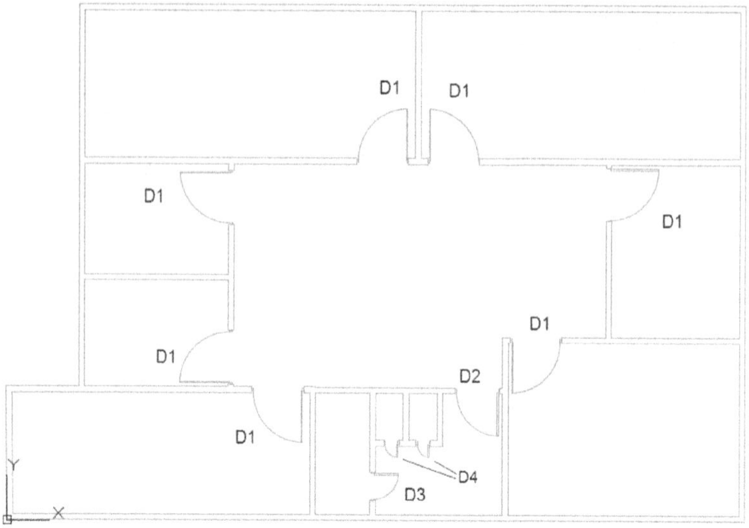

Figure Prj2-27 Drawing of the first floor after creating doors

Creating Windows in the Architectural Drawing of the First Floor

1. Choose the **Window** tool from the **Window** drop-down in the **Build** panel of the **Home** tab in the **Ribbon**; you are prompted to select a wall or a grid assembly. Also, the **PROPERTIES** palette is displayed.

2. Choose the **Unconstrained** option from the **Position along wall** drop-down list in the **Location** rollout of the **PROPERTIES** palette. Enter **1500** in the **Width** and **Height** edit box in the **Dimensions** rollout. Also, select **Yes** from the **Relative to grid** drop-down list in the **Location** rollout.

3. Click on the walls of the first floor architectural drawing and locate the windows W, as shown in Figure Prj2-28.

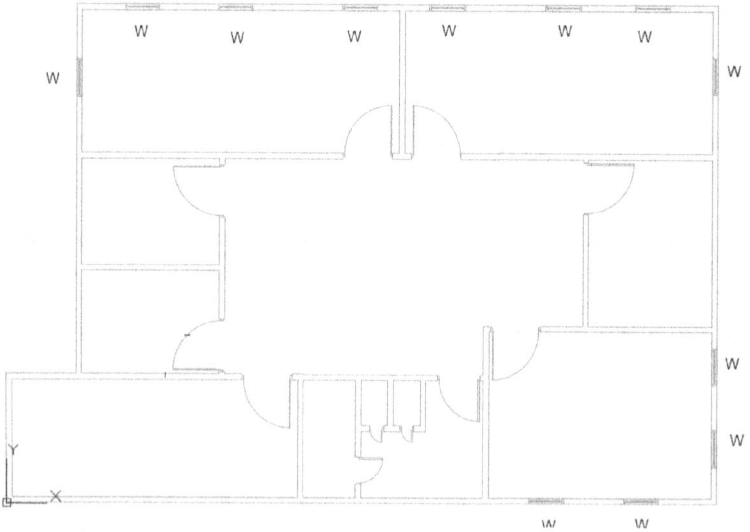

Figure Prj2-28 The drawing after adding windows

Creating Slab for Roof in the Architectural Drawing of the First Floor

1. Choose the **Slab** tool from the **Roof Slab** drop-down in the **Build** panel of the **Home** tab in the **Ribbon**; you are prompted to specify the start point. Choose the **Height** option from the command prompt and specify **4000** in the command prompt and press ENTER.

2. Enter the **0,0** coordinates in the command prompt; a dotted rubber band line will be attached to the cursor. Next, select the points 1, 2, 3, 4, 5, and 6 respectively, as shown in Figure Prj2-29, and then press ENTER; a slab will be created.

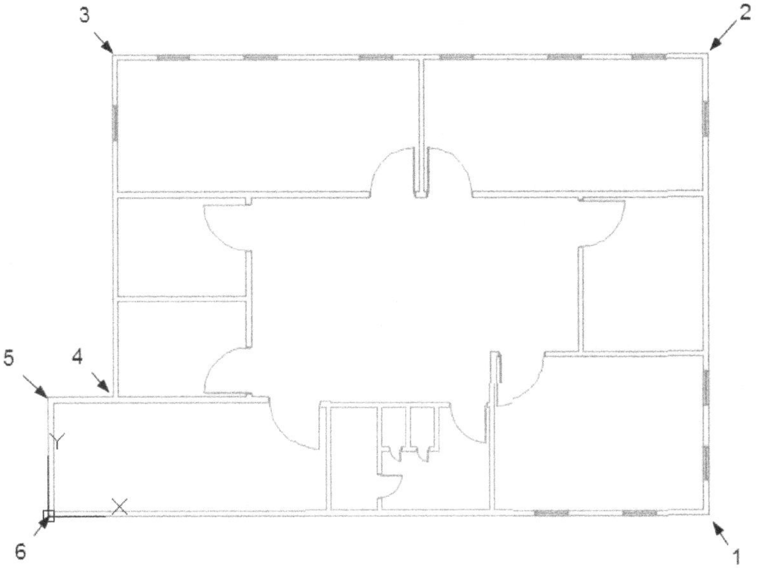

Figure Prj2-29 *Corner points for the slab*

3. Save the drawing and close it.

Creating HVAC Drawings

Now, you need to create HVAC drawings for the building. For creating HVAC drawings, you need to switch to the **HVAC** workspace.

Creating HVAC Drawing of the Ground Floor

1. Select the **Mechanical** category from the **PROJECT NAVIGATOR** and choose the **Add Construct** button available at the bottom; the **Add Construct** dialog box is displayed.

2. Enter the name **Ground Floor Mechanical** in the **Name** field of the dialog box.

3. Click in the **Description** field; the **Description** dialog box is displayed.

4. Enter the description as **This drawing is meant for HVAC plan of the ground floor** and then choose the **OK** button from the dialog box.

5. Select the check box corresponding to level 1 in the **Division** column and make sure that the **Open in drawing editor** check box is selected in the **Add Construct** dialog box. Next, choose the **OK** button from the dialog box; the drawing is opened. Also, the Ground

Floor Mechanical drawing is displayed with a lock icon adjacent to it in the **PROJECT NAVIGATOR**.

6. Click on the **Workspace Switching** option in the **Application Status Bar** and then choose the **HVAC** option from the flyout displayed.

Importing the Architectural Drawing of the Ground Floor

Before adding any HVAC system to the project, you need to import the architectural plan of the ground floor.

1. In the **PROJECT NAVIGATOR**, click on the plus sign adjacent to the **Architectural** subcategory of the **Constructs** category in the **Constructs** tab; a list of architectural drawings is displayed.

2. Select Ground Floor Architectural drawing from the list and drag it to the current drawing; the architectural drawing is attached to the current drawing as an external reference.

Adding Air Terminals to the Architectural Drawing of the Ground Floor

1. Choose the **Air Terminal** tool from the **Equipment** drop-down of the **Build** panel in the **Home** tab in the **Ribbon**; the **Add Multi-view Parts** dialog box is displayed, as shown in Figure Prj2-30.

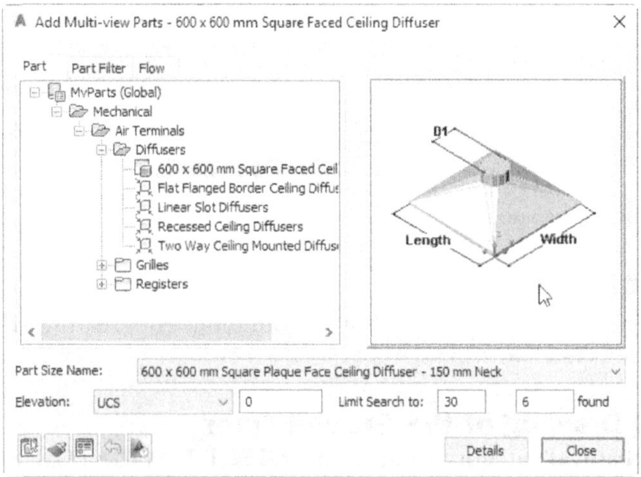

Figure Prj2-30 *The* ***Add Multi-view Parts*** *dialog box*

2. Choose the **600 x 600 mm Square Faced Ceiling Diffuser** part from the **Part** tab of the dialog box; the preview of the diffuser is displayed on the right in the dialog box.

3. Select the **600 x 600 mm Square Plaque Face Ceiling Diffuser -300 mm Neck** option from the **Part Size Name** drop-down list at the bottom of the dialog box.

4. Enter the value **3600** in the **Elevation** edit box.

5. Choose the **Flow** tab; the dialog box is modified, as shown in Figure Prj2-31.

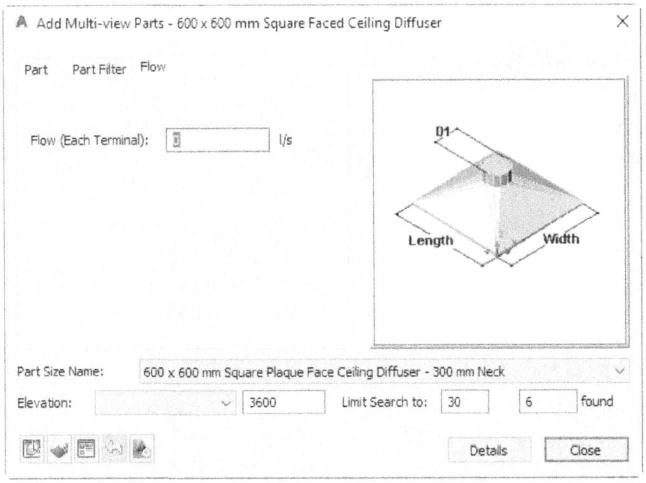

Figure Prj2-31 *The* ***Add Multi-view Parts*** *dialog box with the* ***Flow*** *tab chosen*

6. Specify **20** in the **Flow (Each Terminal)** edit box.
7. Place the diffusers, as shown in Figure Prj2-32.

Figure Prj2-32 *The drawing after adding diffusers*

Adding Duct to the Diffusers

1. Choose **Tools** from the **Tools** drop-down in the **Build** panel of the **Home** tab in the **Ribbon**; the **TOOL PALETTES** is displayed.

2. Choose the **Properties** button on the top left corner in the **TOOL PALETTES**; a flyout is displayed, as shown in Figure Prj2-33.

3. Choose the **HVAC** option from the flyout, if it is not already chosen; the tools related to HVAC system are displayed in the **TOOL PALETTES**, refer to Figure Prj2-34.

*Figure Prj2-33 The **Properties** flyout of the **TOOL PALETTES***

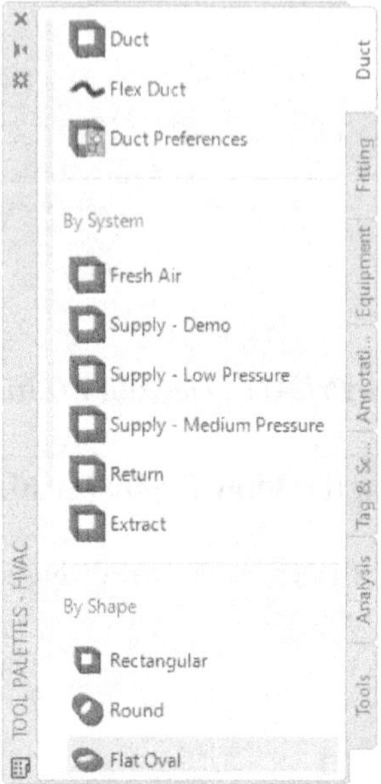

*Figure Prj2-34 The **TOOL PALETTES - HVAC***

4. Choose the **Round** tool from the **By Shape** area in the **Duct** tab of the **TOOL PALETTES**; you are prompted to specify the start point of the duct. Also, the **PROPERTIES** palette is displayed, as shown in Figure Prj2-35.

5. Specify **300** mm in the **Diameter** edit box in the **PROPERTIES** palette.

6. Click on the **Duct End Connector** of the diffuser, refer to Figure Prj2-36.

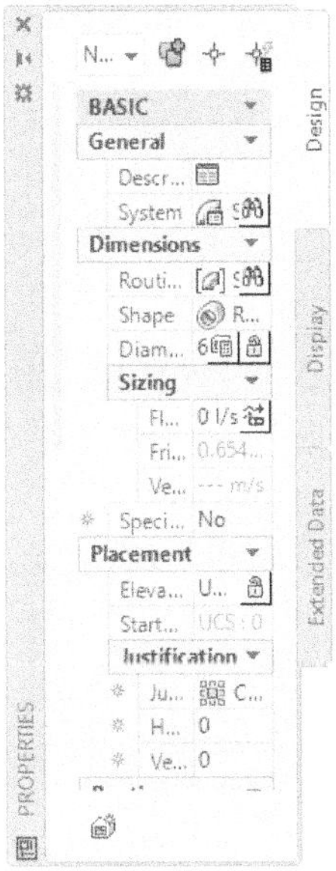

***Figure Prj2-35** The **PROPERTIES** palette on choosing the **Round** tool*

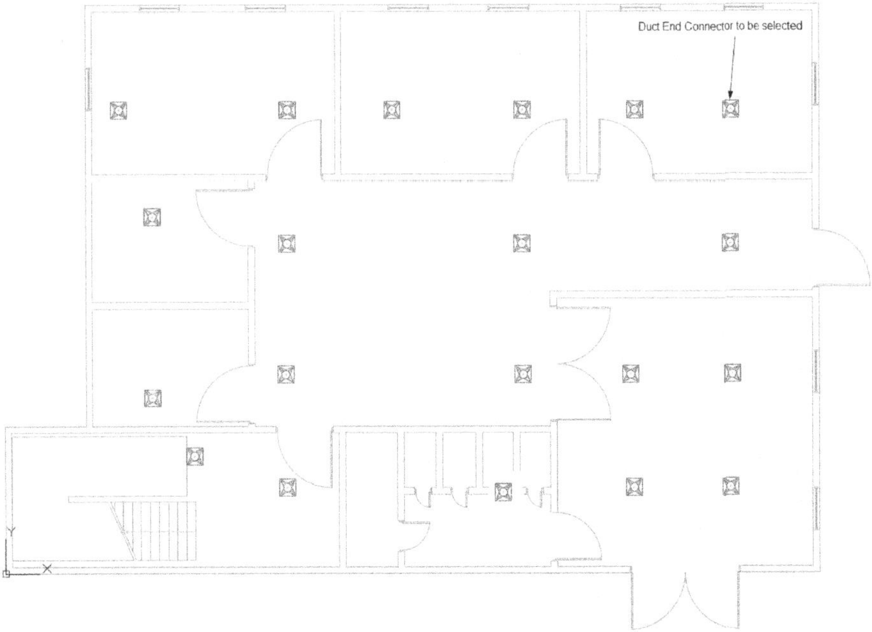

***Figure Prj2-36** The **Duct End Connector** to be selected for adding duct line*

7. Click on the air terminal adjacent to the previous one and press ENTER to connect it to the duct line. Similarly, connect all the other ducts to the air terminal, refer to Figure Prj2-37.

To connect the ducts at the same elevation, you might need to switch to isometric views.

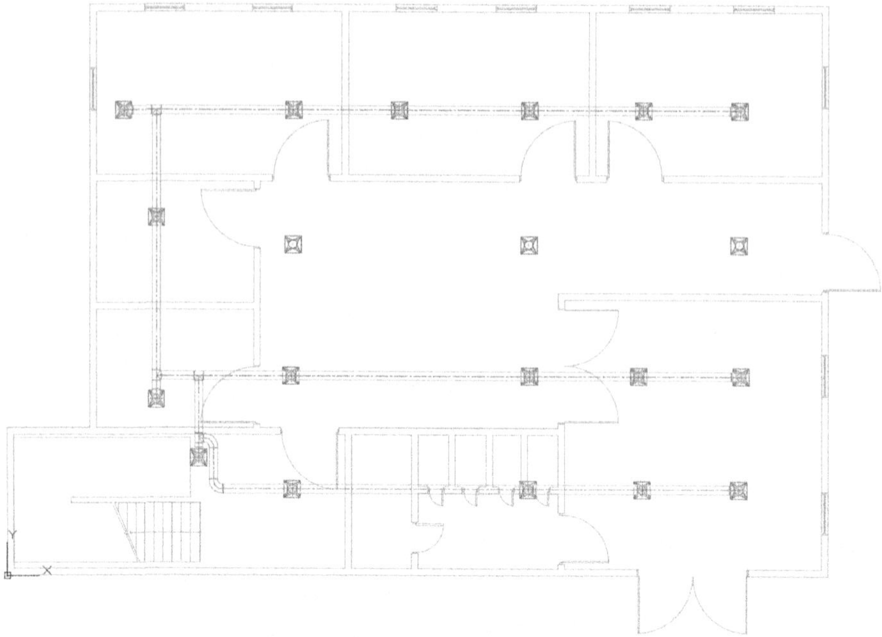

Figure Prj2-37 *The duct created between the outer ducts*

8. Connect all the ducts in the open office area to the previously connecting duct, refer to Figure Prj2-38.

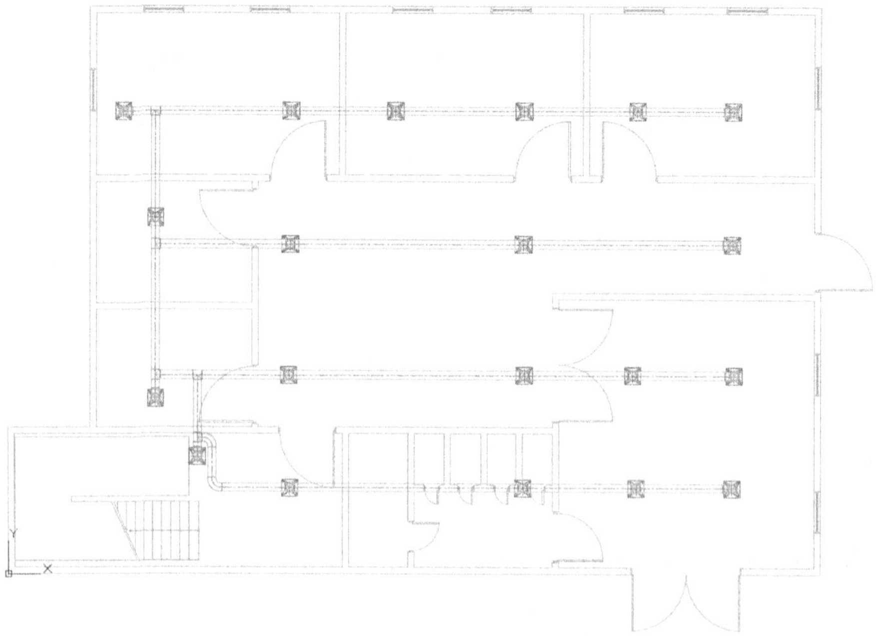

Figure Prj2-38 *Adding office ducts to the duct line*

9. Similarly, connect a duct line to the main duct line for calculating the duct size and transforming the duct line into ducts of required sizes, refer to Figure Prj2-39.

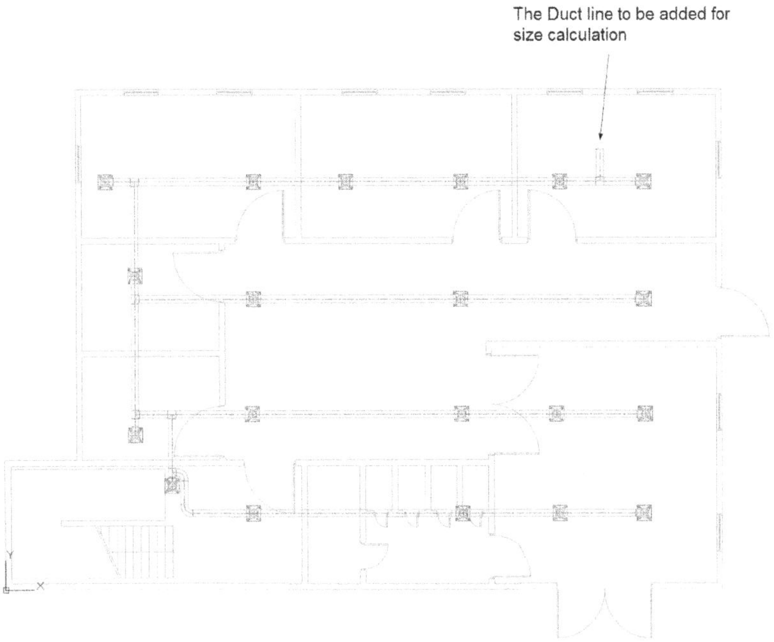

Figure Prj2-39 *Adding a duct line for size calculation*

Calculating the Duct Sizes

1. Select the duct created for size calculations; the **Duct** contextual tab is displayed, as shown in Figure Prj2-40.

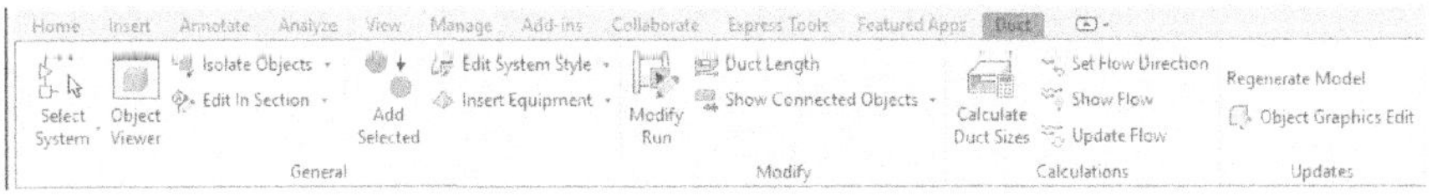

Figure Prj2-40 *The* ***Duct*** *contextual tab*

2. Choose the **Calculate Duct Sizes** tool from the **Calculations** panel of the **Duct** contextual tab in the **Ribbon**; the **Duct System Size Calculator** dialog box is displayed, as shown in Figure Prj2-41.

3. Select the **Round** option from the first drop-down list in the **2** area of the dialog box.

4. Choose the **Start** button from the **4** area of the dialog box; the **Choose a Part** dialog box is displayed, as shown in Figure Prj2-42. Also, you are prompted to select a suitable part from the part tab available at the left in the dialog box.

Note

*The **Choose a Part** dialog box will be displayed during the transition only when there is an elevation or size difference between the two mating ducts.*

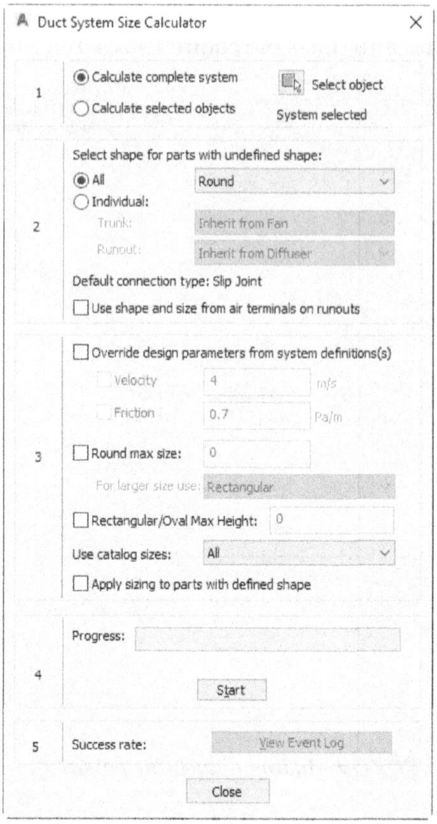

Figure Prj2-41 *The* ***Duct System Size Calculator*** *dialog box*

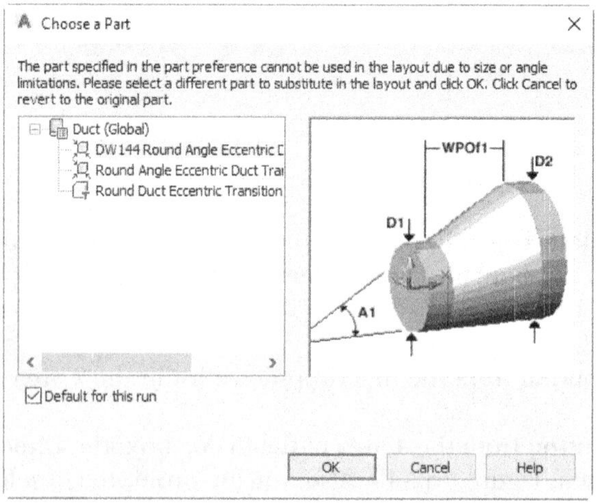

Figure Prj2-42 *The* ***Choose a Part*** *dialog box*

5. Select the desired part from the left area of the dialog box and choose the **OK** button from the dialog box; the desired part is added and the **Choose a Part** dialog box is displayed again.

6. Select the desired part from the dialog box and choose the **OK** button. Repeat the procedure till all the parts are added; the success rate of the duct size is displayed in the **5** area of the dialog box. If the success rate is not 100%, then there is an error in the fittings added to the duct line.

7. To check the problems in the duct line, choose the **View Event Log** button from the **5** area of the dialog box; the **Event Log** dialog box is displayed, refer to Figure Prj2-43. In such cases, you need to rearrange the duct system.

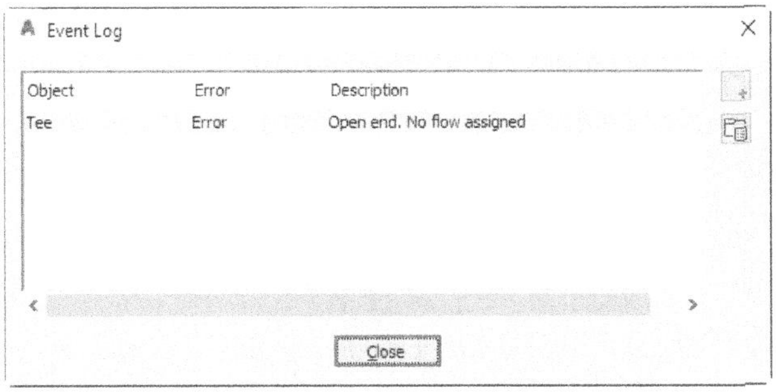

Figure Prj2-43 *The **Event Log** dialog box*

8. After rearranging, again select the duct line created for calculating duct sizes and choose the **Calculate Duct Sizes** tool from the **Duct** contextual tab; the **Duct System Size Calculator** dialog box is displayed.

9. Choose the **Start** button from the **4** area of the dialog box and add the desired part by using the **Choose a Part** dialog box; the system applies the transitions automatically and the duct system is displayed, as shown in Figure Prj2-44.

Note

If the success rate is displayed as 100% in the 6th step, then you can skip steps 7 to 9 and the duct system is displayed, as shown in Figure Prj2-44.

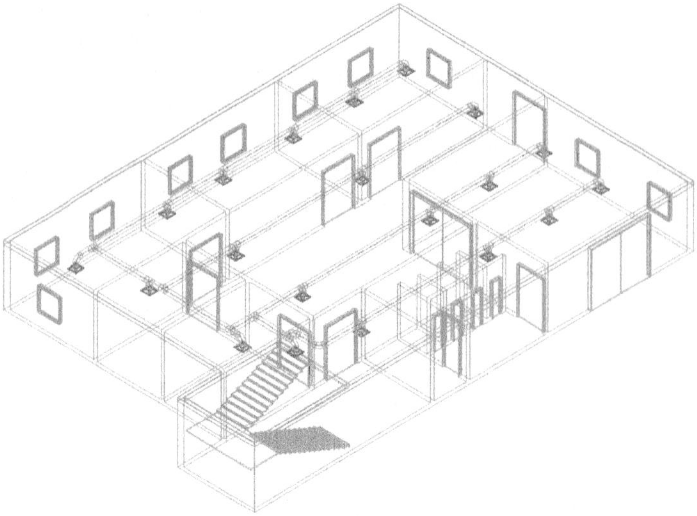

Figure Prj2-44 The Duct system after calculating duct sizes and applying transitions

Adding Return Air Grilles to the Architectural Drawing of the Ground Floor

1. Choose the **Air Terminal** tool from the **Equipment** drop-down in the **Build** panel of the **Home** tab in the **Ribbon**; the **Add Multi-view Parts** dialog box is displayed.

2. Click on the plus sign adjacent to **Grilles** in the **Part** tab of the dialog box; various grilles available in AutoCAD MEP are displayed, as shown in Figure Prj2-45.

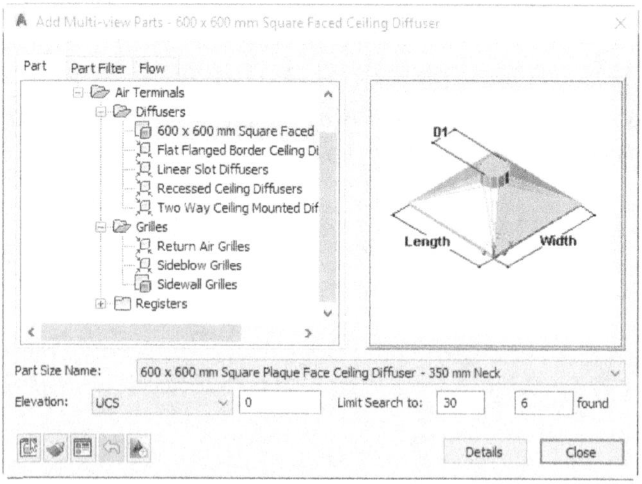

***Figure Prj2-45** The **Add Multi-view Parts** dialog box*

3. Select the **Return Air Grilles** part from the part tab; preview of the parts is displayed in the right of the dialog box.

4. Select the **75 x1250 mm Return Air Grille** option from the **Part Size Name** drop-down list.

5. Enter the value **3600** in the **Elevation** edit box available at the bottom.

6. Add the return grilles, refer to Figure Prj2-46.

   Now, you need to assign flow rate to the return grilles.

7. Select return grilles **1, 2, 3, 9, 10, 12**, as shown in Figure Prj2-46.

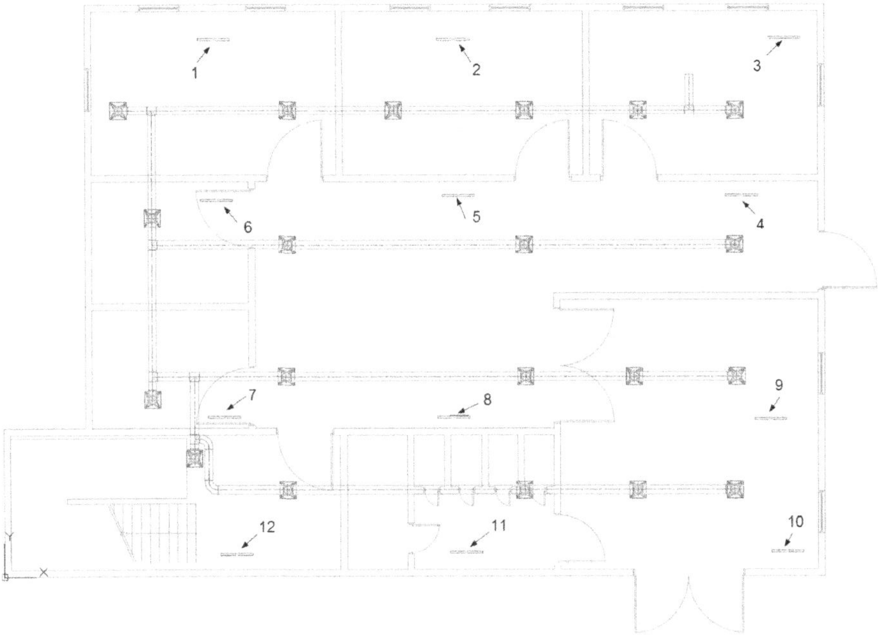

Figure Prj2-46 *The drawing after adding the return grilles*

8. Right-click and choose the **MvPart Properties** option from the shortcut menu displayed; the **Multi-view Part Properties** dialog box is displayed and choose the **Flow** tab, as shown in Figure Prj2-47. Enter the value **40 l/s** in the **Flow (Each Terminal)** edit box and close the dialog box.

9. Similarly, assign flow rate **30 l/s** to return grilles **5, 8**, refer to Figure Prj2-46.

10. Assign flow rate **20 l/s** to diffusers **4, 6, 7**, and **11**, refer to Figure Prj2-46.

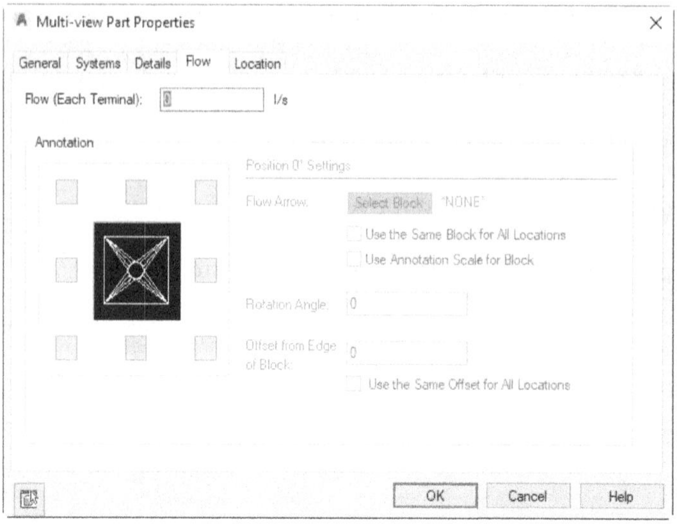

*Figure Prj2-47 The **Multi-view Part Properties** dialog box*

Creating Return Duct for the Ground Floor

1. Choose the **Round** tool from the **By Shape** area in the **Duct** tab of the **TOOL PALETTES**; you are prompted to specify the start point of the duct. Also the **PROPERTIES** palette is displayed, as shown in Figure Prj2-48.

2. Specify the **300** mm in the **Diameter** edit box in the **PROPERTIES** palette.

3. Click on the **Duct End Connector** of the return grille, refer to Figure Prj2-49; the duct will be attached to the cursor. Select the **Round** option from the **Shape** drop-down list from the **PROPERTIES** palette.

4. Click on the return grille adjacent to the previous one; the **Multiple Parts Found** dialog box will be displayed. Select the appropriate transition from the **Part Size Name** list and choose the **OK** button. Press ENTER to connect it to the return grille. Similarly, connect all the other ducts to the return grilles, refer to Figure Prj2-50.

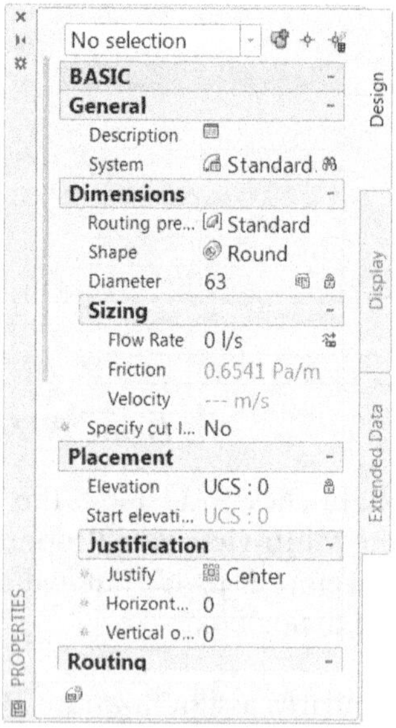

*Figure Prj2-48 The **PROPERTIES** palette on choosing the **Round** tool*

To connect the ducts at the same elevation, you might need to switch to isometric views.

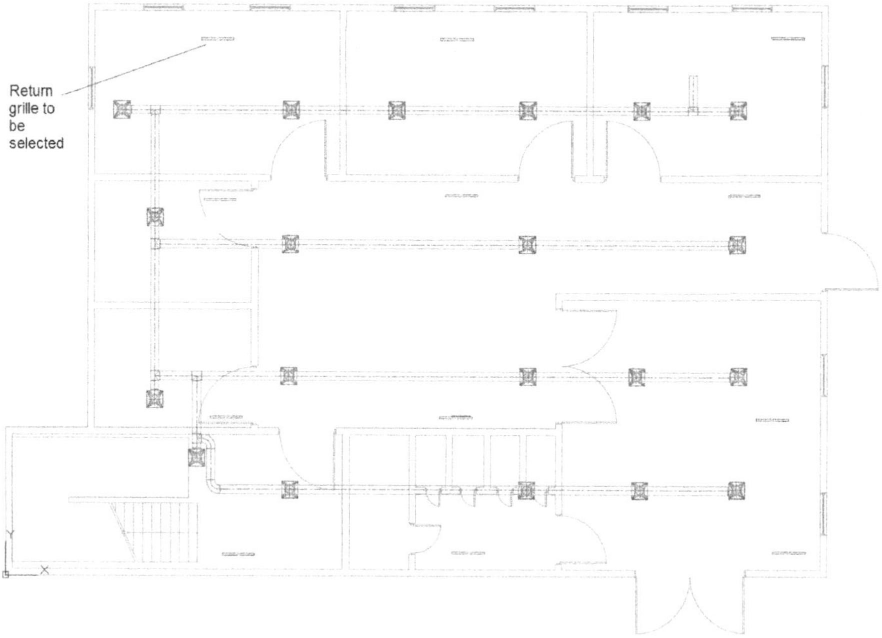

Figure Prj2-49 The return grille to be selected for adding duct

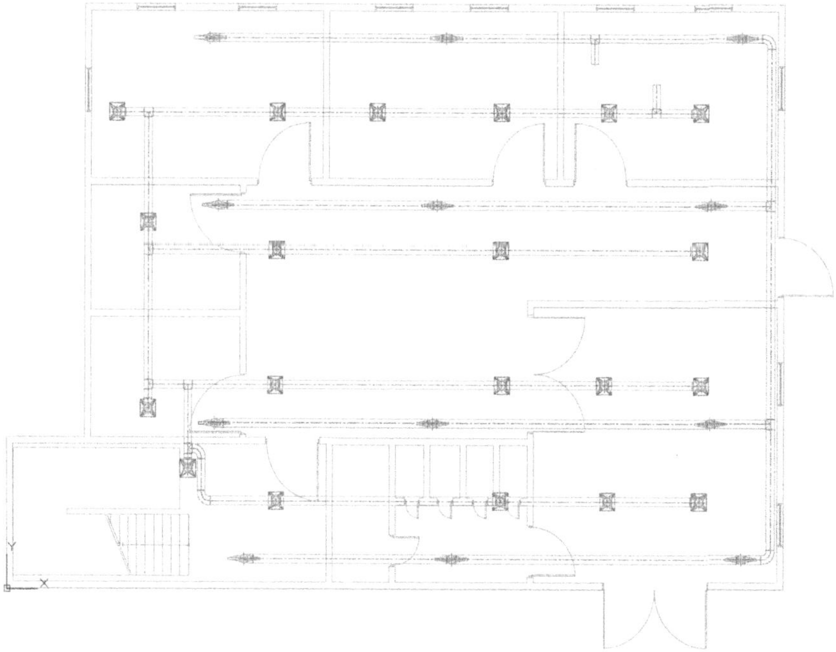

Figure Prj2-50 The drawing after connecting the return grilles with the duct line

Calculating the Duct Sizes for Return Grille System

1. Select a duct line of the return grille system; the **Duct** contextual tab is displayed.

2. Choose the **Calculate Duct Sizes** tool from the **Calculations** panel in the contextual tab; the **Duct System Size Calculator** dialog box is displayed. Make sure that **Round** is selected in the first drop-down list of the **2** area in the dialog box.

3. Choose the **Start** tool from the **4** area of the dialog box. The success rate of the duct size is displayed in the **5** area of the dialog box. If the success rate is not 100%, then there is an error in the fittings added to the duct line.

4. To check the problems in the duct line, choose the **View Event Log** button from the **5** area of the dialog box; the **Event Log** dialog box is displayed. Remove the errors and choose the **Start** button again.

5. Choose the **Close** button from the **Duct System Size Calculator** dialog box to exit; the final drawing will be displayed, as shown in Figure Prj2-51.

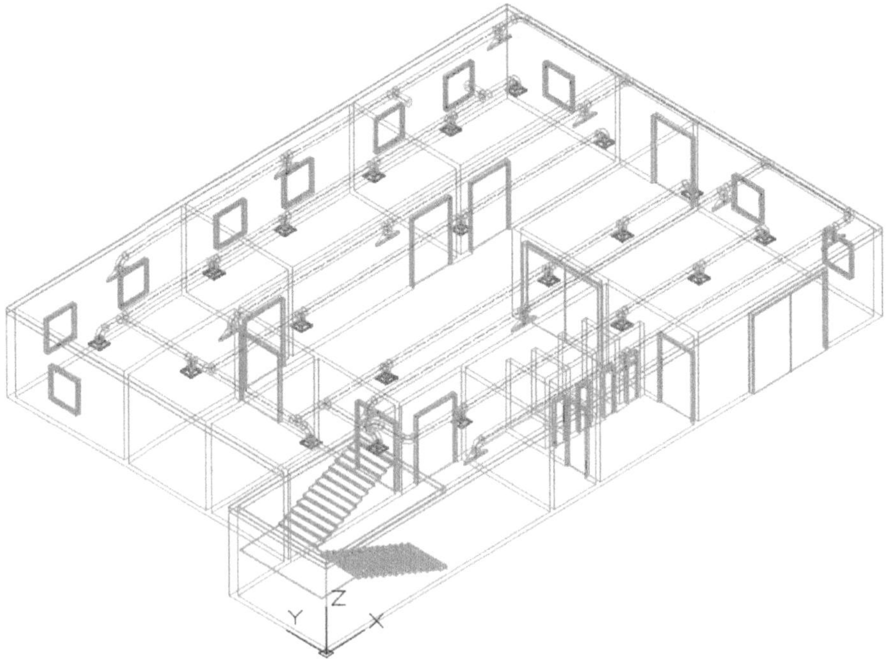

Figure Prj2-51 *The Duct system after calculating duct sizes and applying transitions*

6. Save the drawing and close it.

Creating Mechanical Drawing of the First Floor

1. Select the **Mechanical** category from the **PROJECT NAVIGATOR** and choose the **Add Construct** button available at the bottom; the **Add Construct** dialog box is displayed.

2. Enter the name **First Floor Mechanical** in the **Name** field of the dialog box.

3. Click in the **Description** field; the **Description** dialog box is displayed.

4. Enter the description as **This drawing is meant for mechanical plan of the first floor** and then choose the **OK** button from the dialog box.

5. Select the check box corresponding to level 2 in the **Division** column in the **Add Construct** dialog box. Make sure that the **Open in drawing editor** check box is selected in the **Add Construct** dialog box. Next, choose the **OK** button from the dialog box; the drawing is opened. Also, the First Floor Mechanical drawing is displayed with a lock icon adjacent to it in the **PROJECT NAVIGATOR**.

6. Click on the **Workspace Switching** option in the **Application Status Bar** and choose the **HVAC** option from the flyout.

Importing the Architectural Drawing of the First Floor

Before adding a mechanical system to this drawing, you need to first import the architectural plan of the first floor.

1. Open the **PROJECT NAVIGATOR** and then click on the plus sign adjacent to Architectural category in the **Constructs** tab; a list of architectural drawings is displayed.

2. Select First Floor Architectural drawing from the list and drag it to the current drawing; the architectural drawing is attached to the current drawing as an external reference.

Adding Air Terminals to the Architectural Drawing of the First Floor

1. Choose the **Air Terminal** tool from the **Equipment** drop-down of the **Build** panel in the **Home** tab of the **Ribbon**; the **Add Multi-view Parts** dialog box is displayed.

2. Select the **600 x 600 mm Square Faced Ceiling Diffuser** part from the **Part** tab of the dialog box; preview of the diffuser is displayed in the right of the dialog box.

3. Select the **600 x 600 mm Square Plaque Face Ceiling Diffuser -300 mm Neck** option from the **Part Size Name** drop-down list at the bottom of the dialog box.

4. Enter the value **3600** in the **Elevation** edit box.

5. Choose the **Flow** tab; the dialog box is modified, as shown in Figure Prj2-52.

6. Enter the value **20** in the **Flow** edit box.

7. Place the diffusers, as shown in Figure Prj2-53.

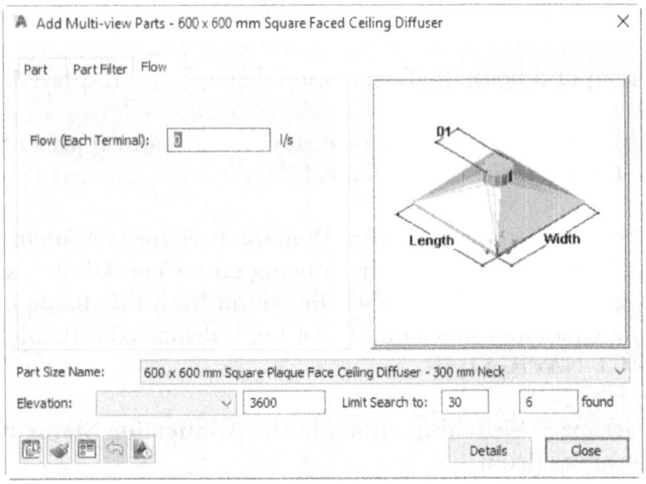

*Figure Prj2-52 The **Add Multi-view Parts** dialog box with the **Flow** tab chosen*

Figure Prj2-53 The drawing after adding diffusers

Note

*You can also specify the Elevation value in the respective edit box of the **BASIC > Location> Elevation** rollout in the **PROPERTIES** palette.*

Adding Duct to the Diffusers

1. Choose the **Round** tool from the **By Shape** area in the **Duct** tab of the **TOOL PALETTES**; you are prompted to specify the start point of the duct. Also the **PROPERTIES** palette is displayed, as shown in Figure Prj2-54.

2. Specify **300** mm in the **Diameter** edit box in the **PROPERTIES** palette.

3. Click on the Duct End Connectors of the diffuser and connect the duct with diffusers, refer to Figure Prj2-55.

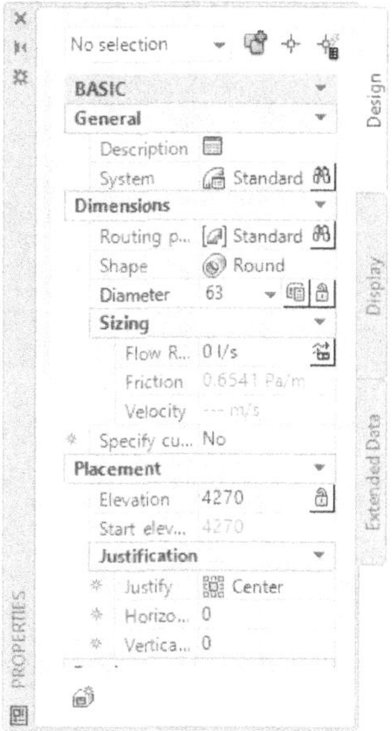

***Figure Prj2-54** The **PROPERTIES** palette on choosing the **Round** tool*

Adding Air Handling Unit

1. Choose the **Air Handler** tool from the **Equipment** drop-down in the **Build** panel of the **Home** tab in the **Ribbon**; the **Add Multi-view Parts** dialog box is displayed, as shown in Figure Prj2-56. Also, you are prompted to specify the insertion point for the air handler unit.

2. Click on the plus sign adjacent to **Packaged Air Handling Units** in the part tab; the list of air handling units is displayed.

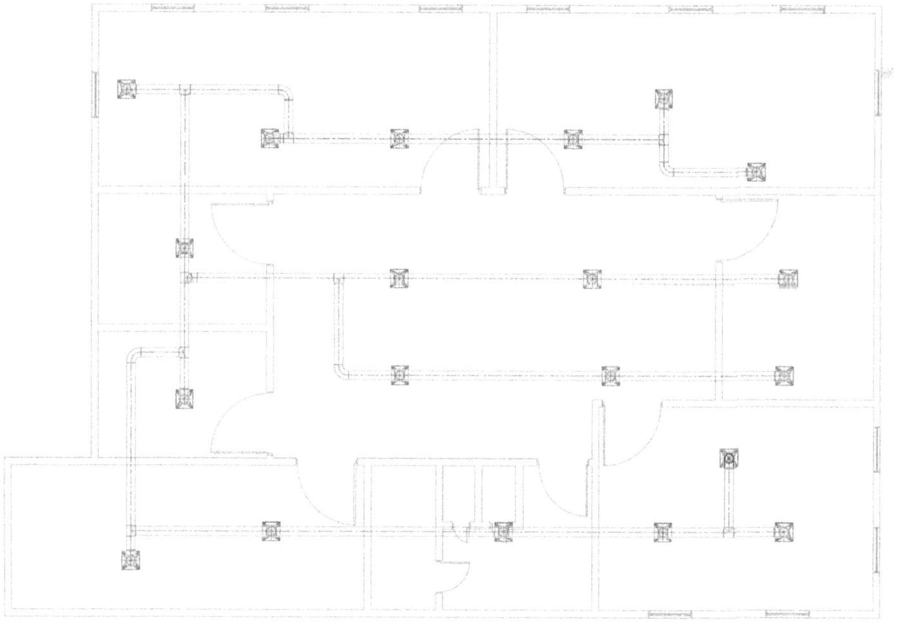

***Figure Prj2-55** The drawing after adding the duct line*

3. Select **Air Handling Units - Floor Mounted Front Discharge** from the list; preview of the air handling unit is displayed on the right in the dialog box.

4. Select the **Air Handling Unit- Front Discharge Floor Mounted-300 x 300mm Discharge, 600x400 mm Feed** option from the **Part Size Name**.

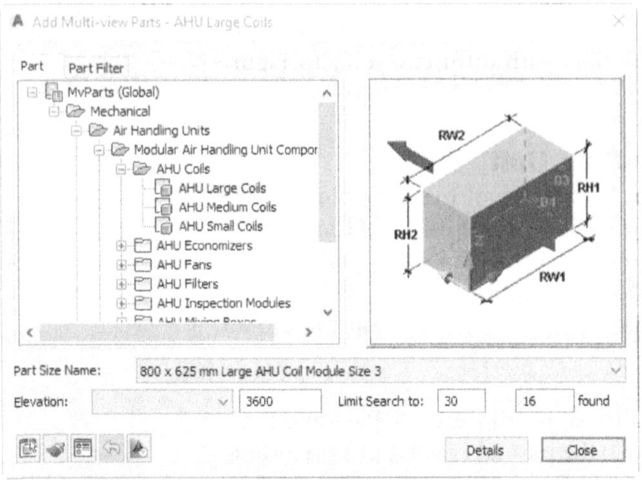

Figure Prj2-56 *The* ***Add Multi-view Parts*** *dialog box*

5. Set the value of elevation as **4000** in the **Elevation** edit box available at the bottom of the dialog box and click in the drawing area; the **Air Handling Units - Floor Mounted Front Discharge** gets attached to the cursor. Next, click to place the air handling unit in the drawing area, refer to Figure Prj2-57.

6. Connect the diffusers with the air handling unit, refer to Figure Prj2-58. Note that while connecting the diffuser with air handling unit, the **Multi Parts Found** dialog box will be displayed. Choose the **OK** button from the dialog box.

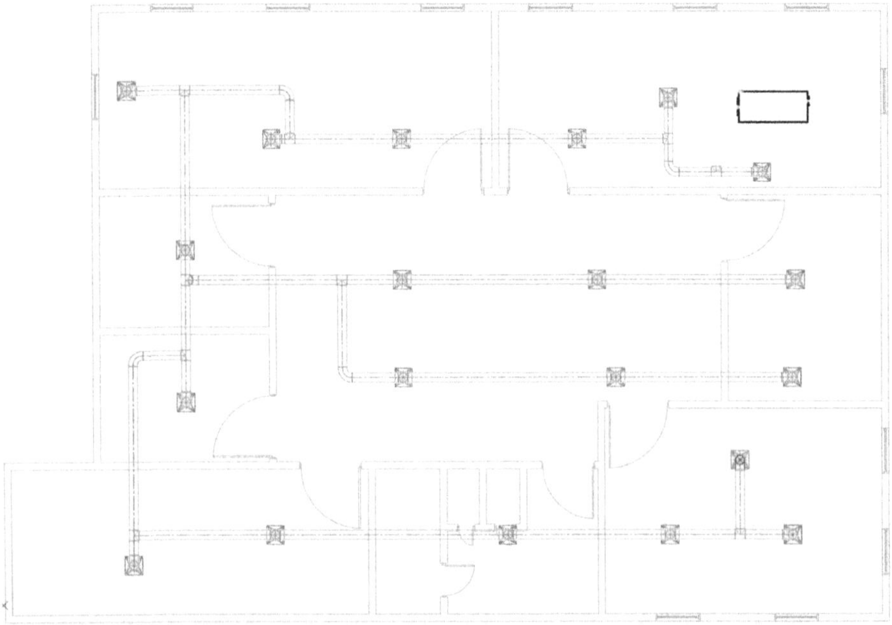

Figure Prj2-57 *The drawing after placing the air handling unit*

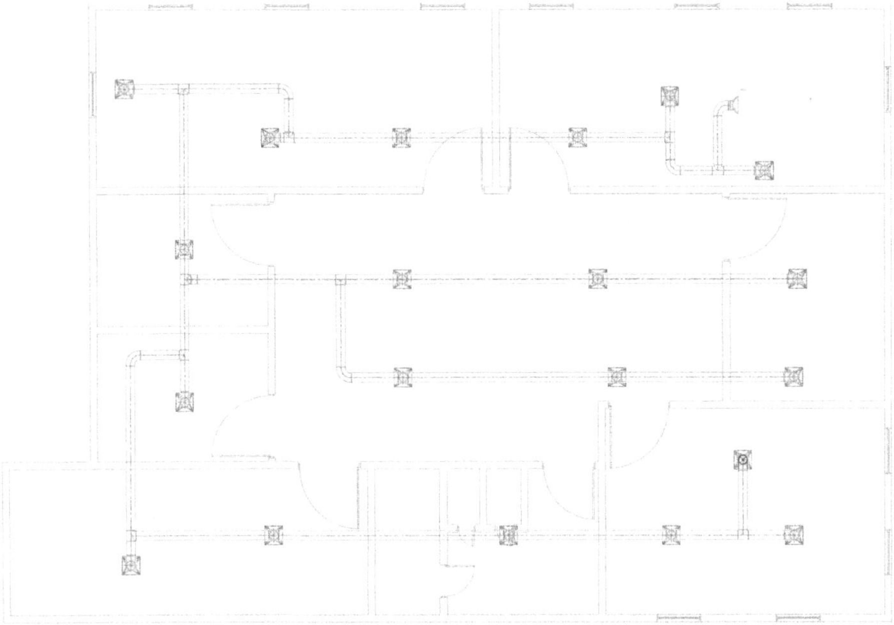

Figure Prj2-58 The drawing after connecting the diffusers to the air handling unit

Adding Return Grilles in the Architectural Drawing of First Floor

1. Choose the **Air Terminal** tool from the **Equipment** drop-down of the **Build** panel in the **Home** tab of the **Ribbon**; the **Add Multi-view Parts** dialog box is displayed.

2. Click on the plus sign adjacent to **Grilles** in the part tab and then choose the **Return Air Grilles** part from the part tab; the preview of the air grilles is displayed in the right of the dialog box, refer to Figure Prj2-59.

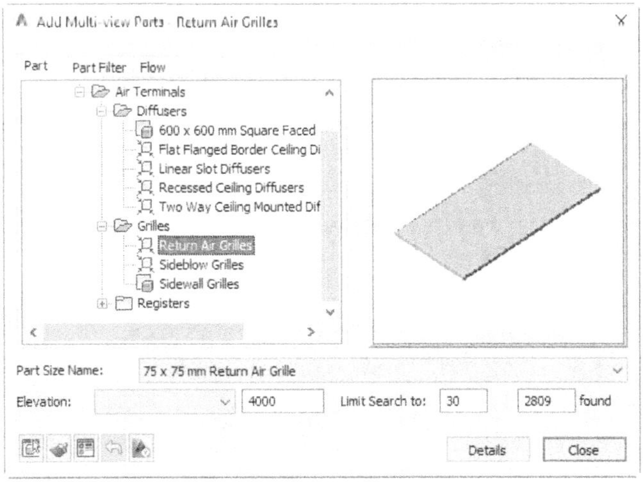

*Figure Prj2-59 The **Add Multi-view Parts** dialog box*

3. Select the **75 X 1250 mm Return Air Grille** option from the **Part Size Name** drop-down list and specify the value of elevation **3600** in the **Elevation** edit box.

4. Add the return grilles, as shown in Figure Prj2-60.

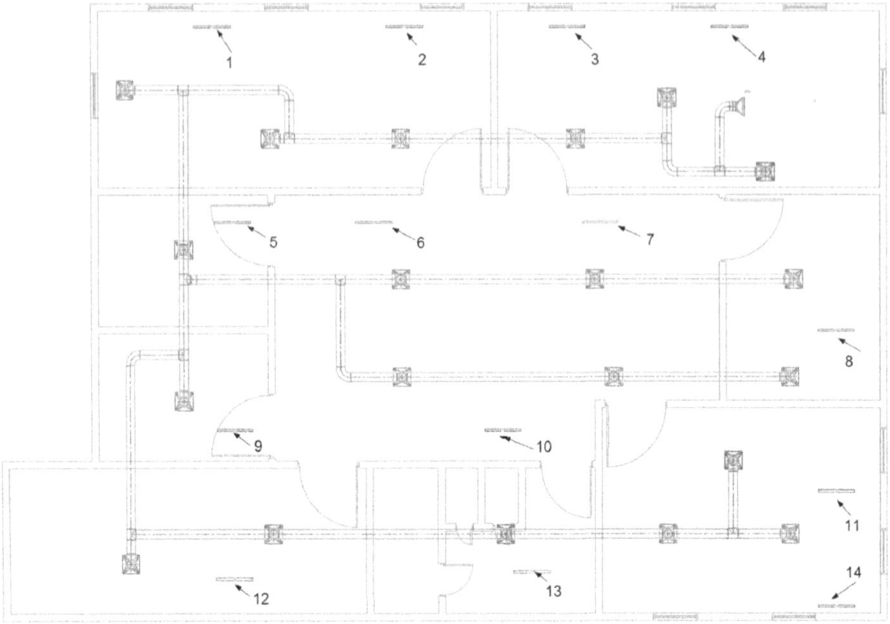

Figure Prj2-60 *The drawing after adding return grilles*

5. Select return grilles **1, 2, 3, 4, 6, 7, 11, 12,** refer to Figure Prj2-60.

6. Right-click and choose the **MvPart Properties** option from the shortcut menu displayed; the **Multi-view Part Properties** dialog box is displayed, as shown in Figure Prj2-61. Enter the value **40 l/s** in the **Flow (Each Terminal)** edit box and close the dialog box.

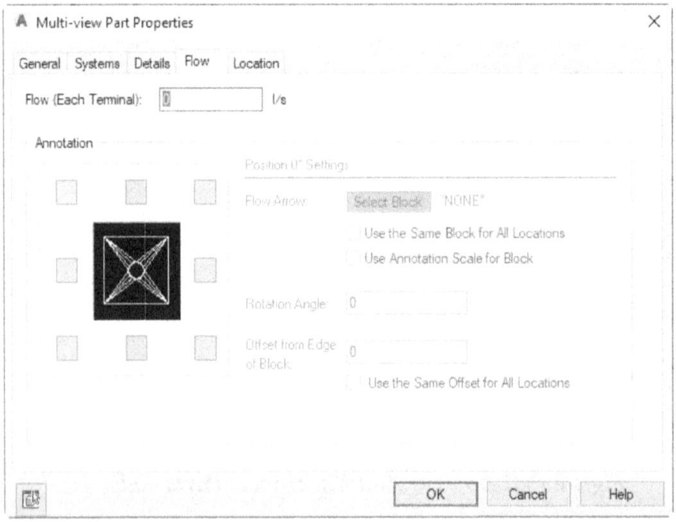

Figure Prj2-61 *The* ***Multi-view Part Properties*** *dialog box*

7. Similarly, assign flow rate **30 l/s** to return grilles **5, 8**.

8. Assign flow rate **20 l/s** to diffusers **9, 10, 13,** and **14**.

Creating Return Duct for the First Floor

1. Choose the **Round** tool from the **By Shape** area in the **Duct** tab of the **TOOL PALETTES**; you are prompted to specify the start point of the duct. Also the **PROPERTIES** palette is displayed, as shown in Figure Prj2-62.

2. Specify the **300** mm in the **Diameter** edit box in the **PROPERTIES** palette.

3. Connect the duct with return grilles, refer to Figure Prj2-63.

Calculating the Duct Sizes

1. Select a duct line in the return grille system; the **Duct** contextual tab is displayed.

2. Choose the **Calculate Duct Sizes** tool from the **Calculations** panel in the **Home** tab in the ribbon; the **Duct System Size Calculator** dialog box is displayed.

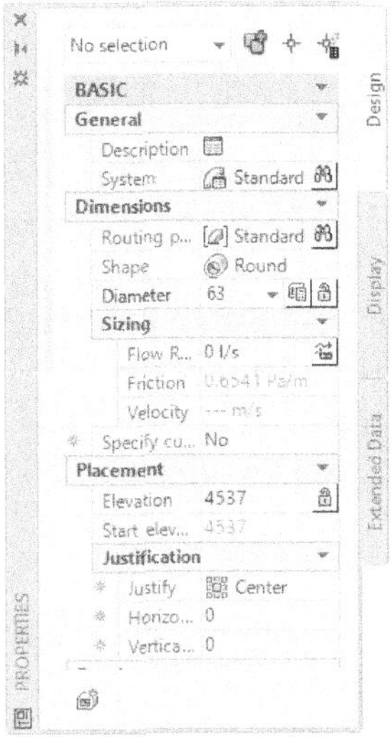

*Figure Prj2-62 The **PROPERTIES** palette on choosing the **Round** tool*

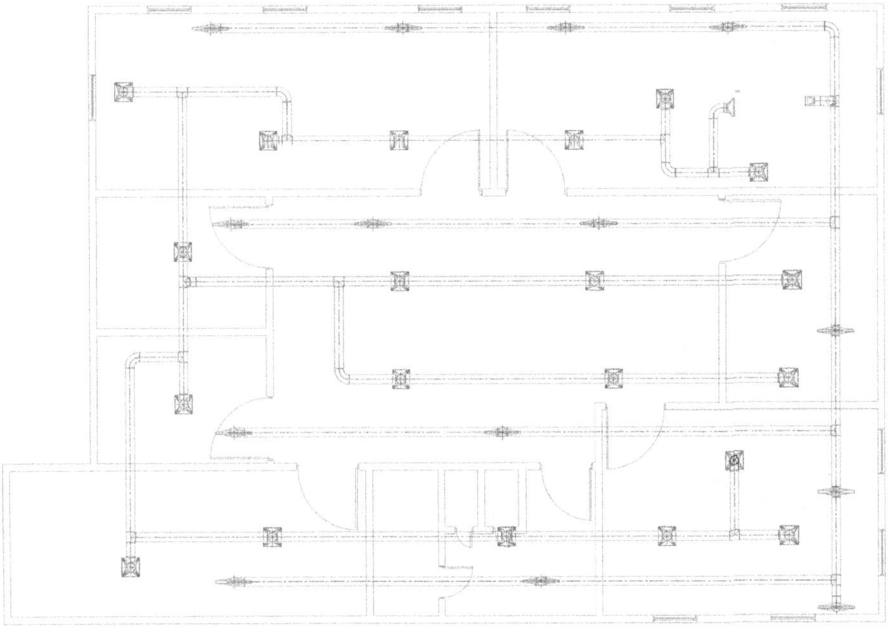

Figure Prj2-63 The drawing after adding duct to the return grilles

3. Choose the **Start** tool from the **4** area of the dialog box and choose the **OK** button from successive dialog boxes; the duct sizes are calculated and transition is applied automatically.

4. Choose the **OK** button from the successive **Choose a Part** dialog boxe. If the success rate is not 100%, then there is an error in the fittings added to the duct line. Remove the error, if any. Next, choose the **Close** button from the **Duct System Size Calculator** dialog box; the transitions are applied to the duct line.

Note

*The **Choose a Part** dialog box will be displayed during transition only when there is an elevation or size difference between the two mating ducts.*

5. The final drawing is displayed, as shown in Figure Prj2-64.

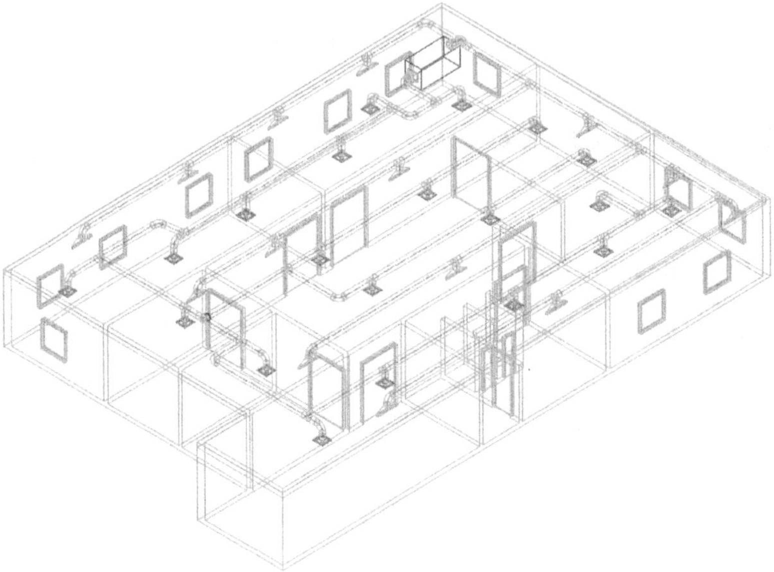

Figure Prj2-64 *The Duct system after calculating duct sizes and applying transitions*

6. Save the drawing and close it.

Creating Piping Drawings

Now, you need to create piping drawings in the building. To create piping drawings, you need to switch to the **Piping** workspace.

Creating Piping Drawing of the Ground Floor

1. Select the **Piping** category from the **PROJECT NAVIGATOR** and choose the **Add Construct** button available at the bottom; the **Add Construct** dialog box is displayed.

2. Enter the name **Ground Floor Piping** in the **Name** field of the dialog box.

3. Click in the **Description** field; the **Description** dialog box is displayed.

4. Enter the description as **This drawing is meant for piping plan of the ground floor** and then choose the **OK** button from the dialog box.

5. Select the check box corresponding to level 1 in the **Division** column in the **Add Construct** dialog box and make sure that the **Open in drawing editor** check box is selected in the **Add Construct** dialog box. Next, choose the **OK** button from the dialog box; the drawing is opened. Also, the Ground Floor Piping drawing is displayed with a lock icon adjacent to it in the **PROJECT NAVIGATOR**.

6. Click on the **Workspace Switching** option in the **Application Status Bar** and choose the **Piping** option from the flyout.

Importing the Architectural Drawing of the Ground Floor

Before adding any piping system in the project, you need to first import the architectural plan of the ground floor.

1. Open the **PROJECT NAVIGATOR** and then click on the plus sign adjacent to **Architectural** category in the **Constructs** tab; a list of architectural drawings is displayed.

2. Select Ground Floor Architectural drawing from the list and drag it into the current drawing; the architectural drawing is attached to the current drawing as an external reference.

Adding Ball Valves in the Architectural Drawing of the Ground Floor

1. Choose the **Valve** tool from the **Equipment** drop-down of the **Build** panel in the **Home** tab in the **Ribbon**; the **Add Multi-view Parts** dialog box is displayed, as shown in Figure Prj2-65.

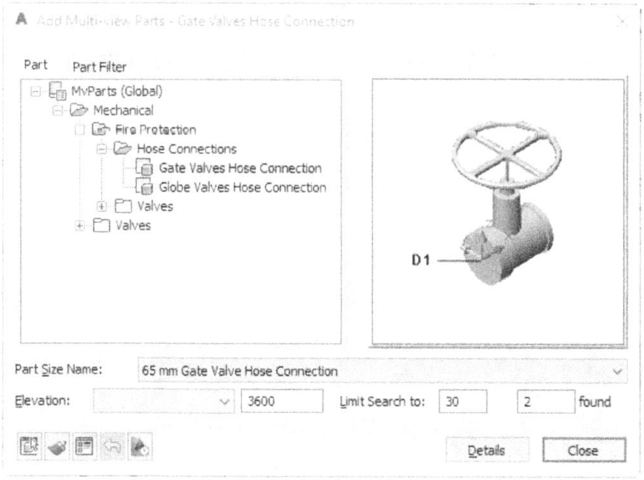

*Figure Prj2-65 The **Add Multi-view Parts** dialog box*

2. Click on the plus sign adjacent to **Valves** under the **Mechanical** node in the part tab of the dialog box; various types of valves are displayed in the list.

3. Select the **Ball Valve - Threaded - Nickel plated** part from the list; the preview of the part is displayed in the right of the dialog box, refer to Figure Prj2-66.

4. Select the **50 mm Ball valve - Threaded - Nickel plated ('A' = 128 'B' = 161 'C' = 80)** option from the **Part Size Name** drop-down list.

5. Specify the elevation value as **1000** in the **Elevation** edit box.

6. Place the ball valves symmetrically, as shown in Figure Prj2-67.

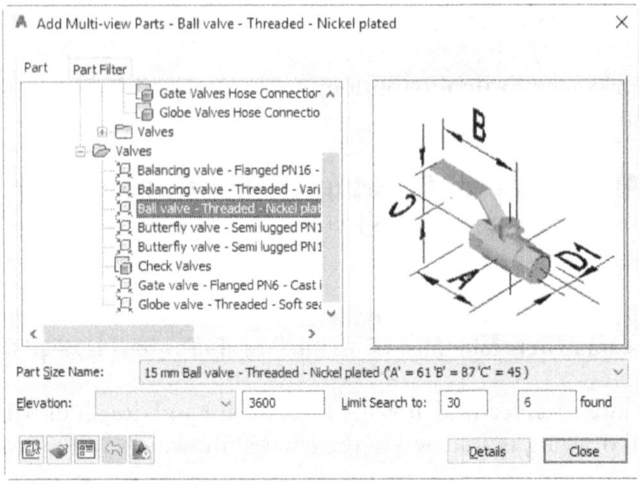

*Figure Prj2-66 The **Add Multi-view Parts** dialog box with the ball valve selected*

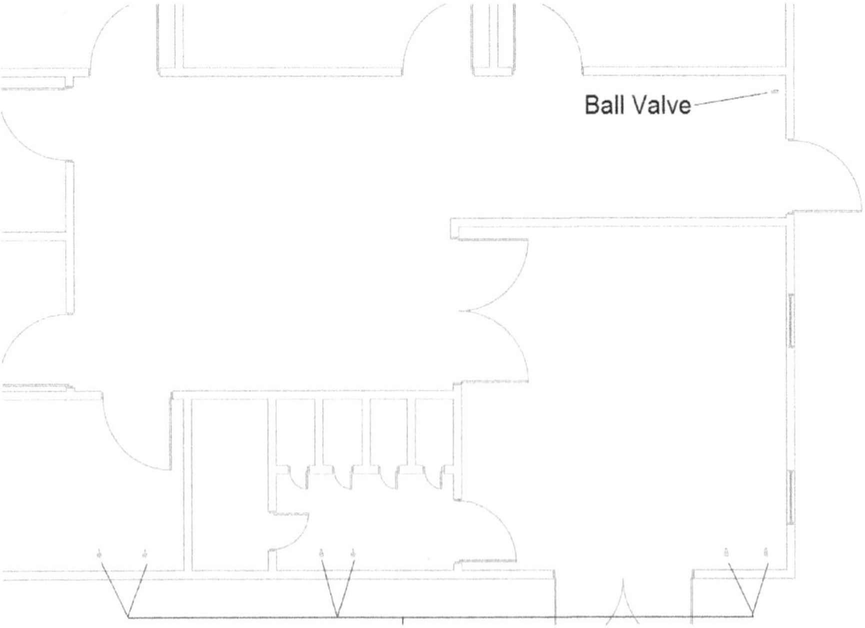

Figure Prj2-67 The drawing after adding ball valves

Adding Pipe Line in the Architectural Drawing of Ground Floor

1. Choose the **Pipe** tool from the **Pipe** drop-down in the **Build** panel of the **Home** tab in the **Ribbon**; the **PROPERTIES** palette is displayed, as shown in Figure Prj2-68. Also, you are prompted to specify the start point of the pipe.

2. Select the **50** option from the **Nominal Size** drop-down list.

3. Select the **Yes** option from the **Specify cut length** drop-down list; the **Cut length** edit box is displayed below the drop-down list.

4. Specify **6000** in the **Cut length** edit box.

5. Specify **3700** in the **Elevation** edit box.

6. Click in the drawing area and draw the pipe line, as shown in Figure Prj2-69.

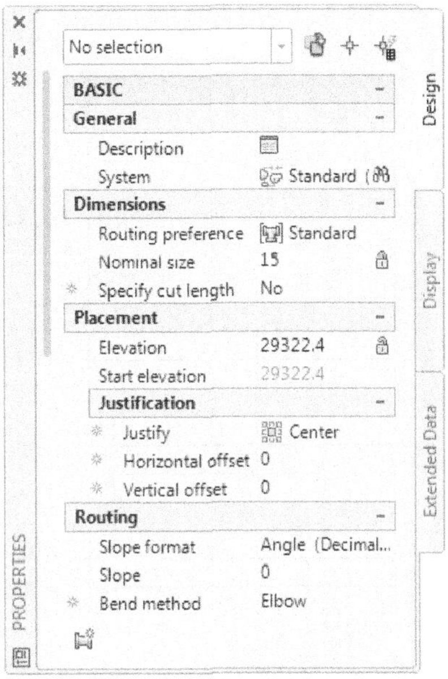

*Figure Prj2-68 The **PROPERTIES** palette displayed on choosing the **Pipe** tool*

Connecting Ball Valves with the Pipe Line

1. Click on the ball valve at the left end of the bottom row; the valve is displayed with multiple plus signs, refer to Figure Prj2-70.

2. Click on the plus sign, refer to Figure Prj2-70 and connect the ball valve with the pipe line, refer to Figure Prj2-71.

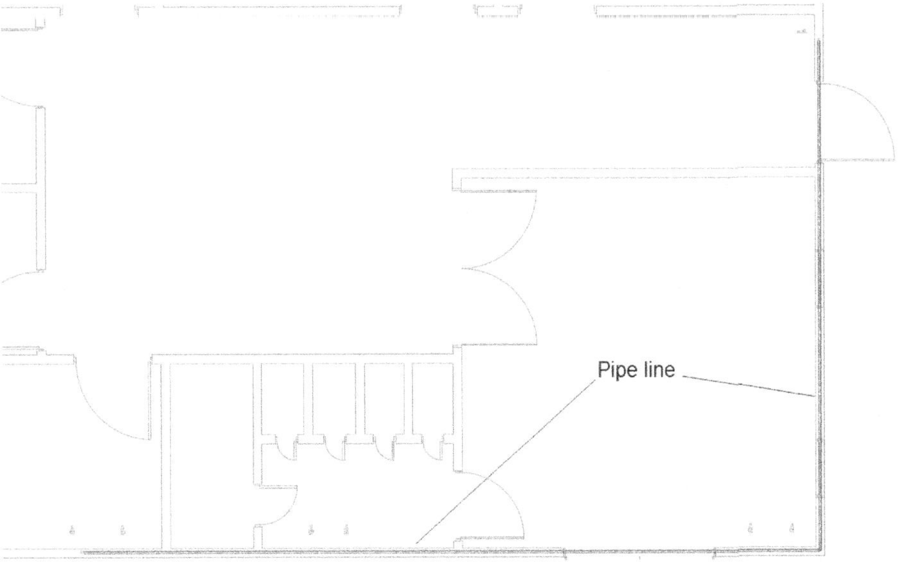

Figure Prj2-69 The drawing after drawing the pipe line

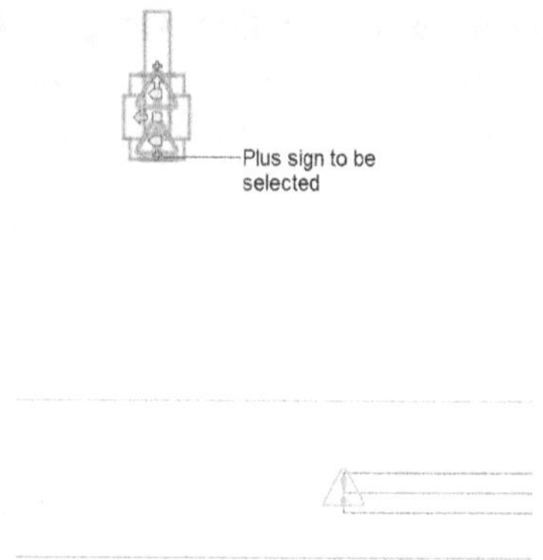

Figure Prj2-70 *The ball valve with plus signs*

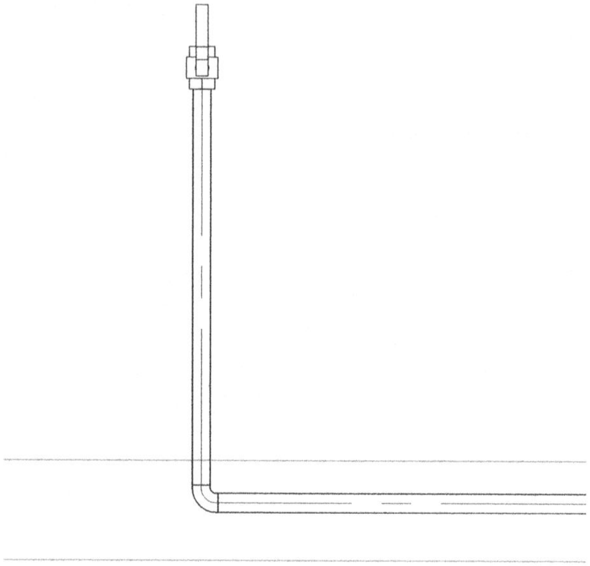

Figure Prj2-71 *The ball valve after connecting to the pipe line*

3. Similarly, connect all the ball valves to the pipe line, refer to Figure Prj2-72.

4. Select the elbow at the bottom left corner of the drawing and then click on the plus sign displayed on the elbow, as shown in Figure Prj2-73; the elbow transforms into a tee.

5. Move the cursor horizontally toward the left and specify **1000** at the command bar and press ENTER. Press ENTER again to exit the tool.

6. Save the drawing and close it.

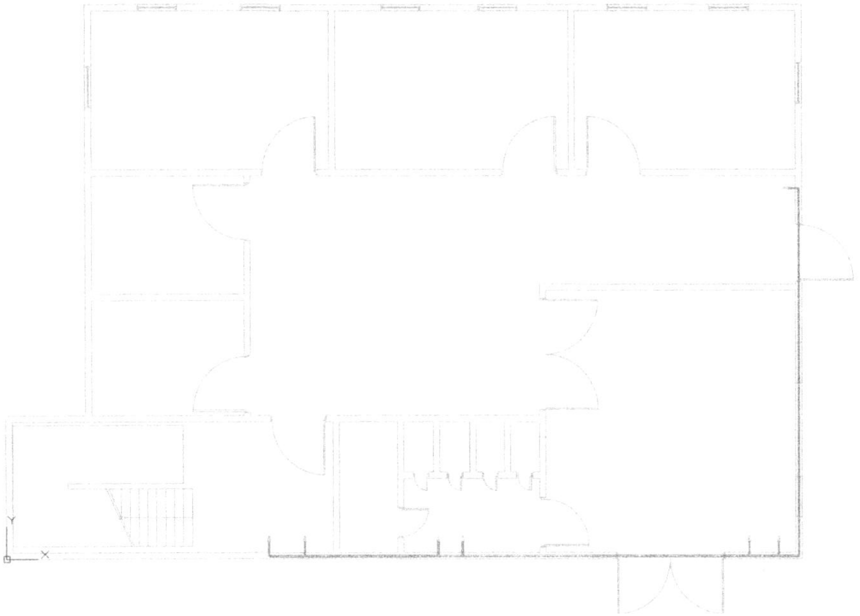

Figure Prj2-72 Piping system after connecting all the ball valves to the pipe line

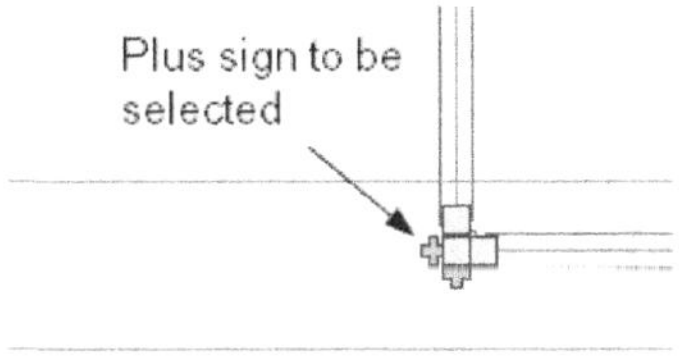

Figure Prj2-73 The plus sign to be selected

Creating Piping Drawing of the First Floor

1. Select the **Piping** category from the **PROJECT NAVIGATOR** and choose the **Add Construct** button available at the bottom; the **Add Construct** dialog box is displayed.

2. Enter **First Floor Piping** in the **Name** field of the dialog box.

3. Click in the **Description** field; the **Description** dialog box is displayed.

4. Enter the description **This drawing is meant for piping plan of the first floor** in the **Edit the description** edit box and then choose the **OK** button from the dialog box.

5. Select the check box corresponding to level 2 in the **Division** column in the **Add Construct** dialog box and make sure that the **Open in drawing editor** check box is selected in the **Add Construct** dialog box. Next, choose the **OK** button from the dialog box; the drawing is opened. Also, the First Floor Piping drawing is displayed with a lock icon adjacent to it in the **PROJECT NAVIGATOR**.

6. Click on the **Workspace Switching** option in the **Application Status Bar** and then choose the **Piping** option from the flyout displayed; the **Piping** workspace gets activated.

Importing the Architectural Drawing of the First Floor

Before adding any piping system to the project, first you need to import the architectural plan of the first floor.

1. Open the **PROJECT NAVIGATOR** and then click on the plus sign adjacent to Architectural category in the **Constructs** tab; a list of architectural drawings is displayed.

2. Select the First Floor Architectural Drawing from the list and drag it to the current drawing; the architectural drawing is attached to the current drawing as an external reference.

Adding Ball Valves in the Architectural Drawing of the First Floor

1. Choose the **Valve** tool from the **Equipment** drop-down of the **Build** panel in the **Home** tab in the **Ribbon**; the **Add Multi-view Parts** dialog box is displayed.

2. Click on the plus sign adjacent to **Valves** under the **Mechanical** node in the part tab of the dialog box; various types of valves are displayed in the list.

3. Select the **Ball Valve - Threaded - Nickel plated** part from the list; the preview of the part is displayed in the right of the dialog box.

4. Select the **50 mm Ball valve - Threaded - Nickel plated ('A' = 128 'B' = 161 'C' = 80)** option from the **Part Size Name** drop-down list.

5. Specify the elevation value as **1000** in the **Elevation** edit box.

6. Place the ball valves symmetrically, as shown in Figure Prj2-74.

Adding Tank in the First Floor

1. Choose the **Tank** tool from the **Equipment** drop-down of the **Build** panel in the **Home** tab in the **Ribbon**; the **Add Multi-view Parts** dialog box is displayed, as shown in Figure Prj2-75.

2. Select the **Horizontal Storage Tanks** part from the part tab; the preview of the tank is displayed on the right in the dialog box.

3. Select the **13000 Litre Horizontal Storage Tank** option from the **Part Size Name** drop-down list and specify the value of elevation as **0** in the **Elevation** edit box.

4. Place the tank in the drawing area, refer to Figure Prj2-76, and close the **Add Multi-view Parts** dialog box.

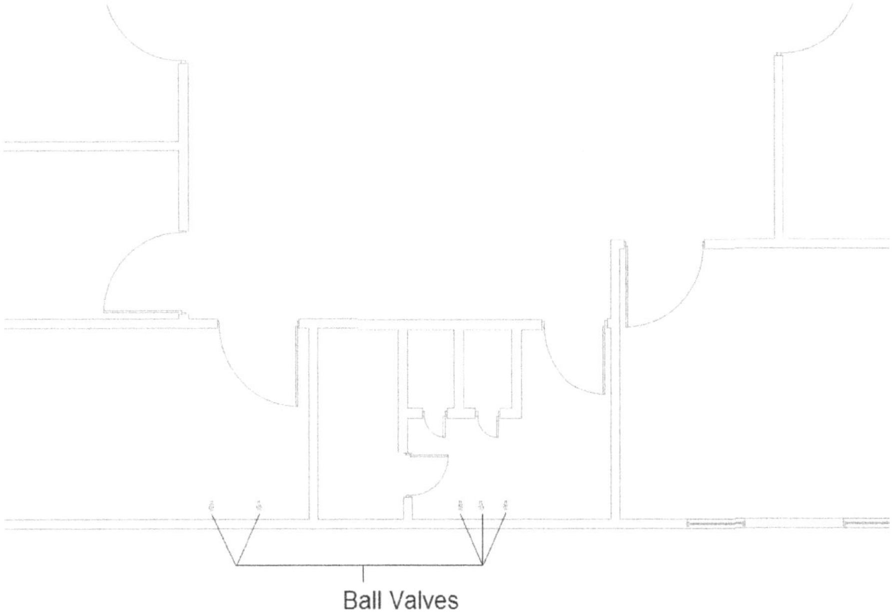

Figure Prj2-74 The drawing after adding ball valves

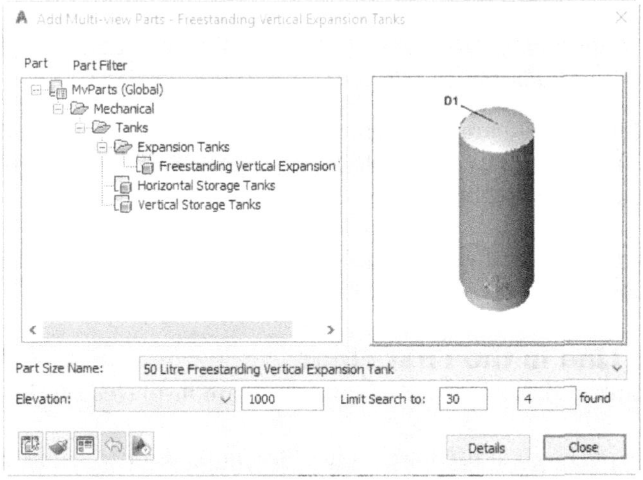

Figure Prj2-75 The ***Add Multi-view Parts*** *dialog box*

Adding Pumps in the First Floor

1. Choose the **Pump** tool from the **Equipment** drop-down list of the **Home** tab in the **Ribbon**; the **Add Multi-view Parts** dialog box is displayed.

2. Choose the **Horizontal Split Case Pumps** part from the **Part** tab available at the left of the dialog box; the preview of the pump is displayed in the right of the dialog box.

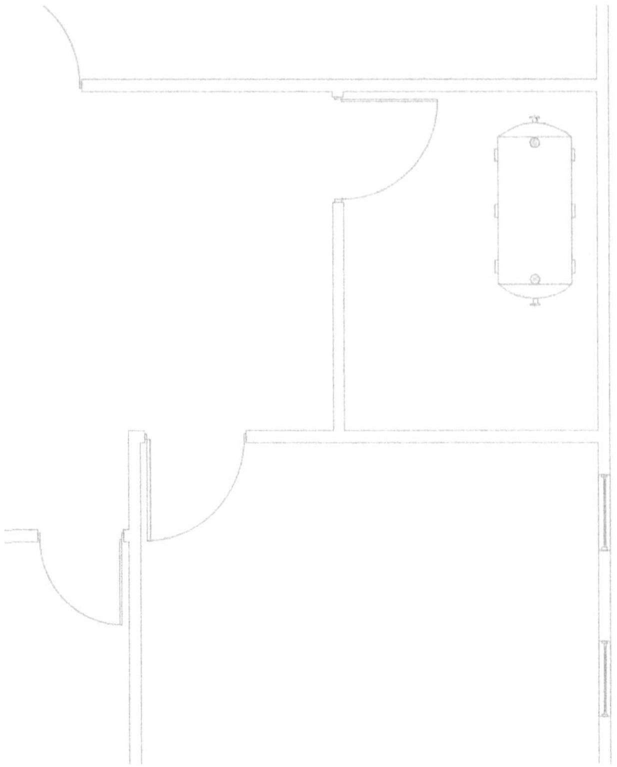

Figure Prj2-76 *The drawing after adding the tank*

3. Select the **2400 x 1800 mm Horizontal Split Case Pump** option from the **Part Size Name** drop-down list and specify the value of elevation as **0** in the **Elevation** edit box available at the bottom of the dialog box.

4. Place the pump in the drawing area, refer to Figure Prj2-77, and close the **Add Multi-view Parts** dialog box.

Adding Pipe Line in the First Floor

1. Select the tank in the drawing area; plus signs are displayed on the tank.

2. Click on the plus sign at the lower side of the tank, refer to Figure Prj2-78; a rubber band pipe gets attached to the cursor.

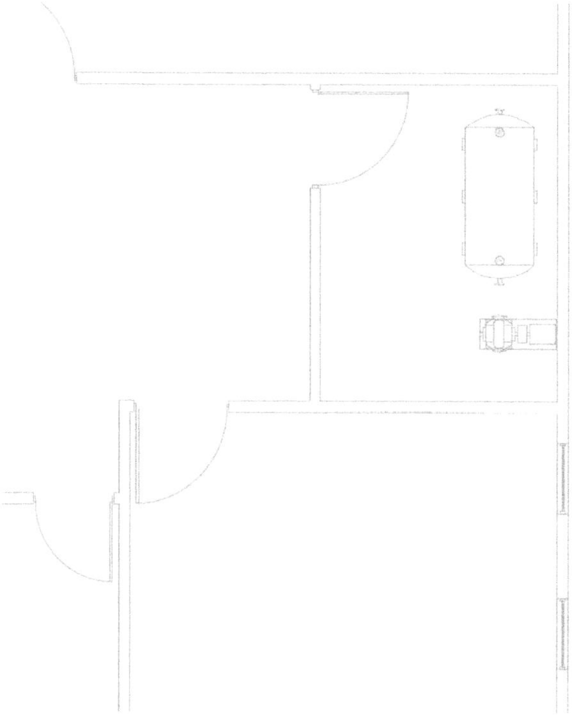

Figure Prj2-77 *The drawing after adding pump*

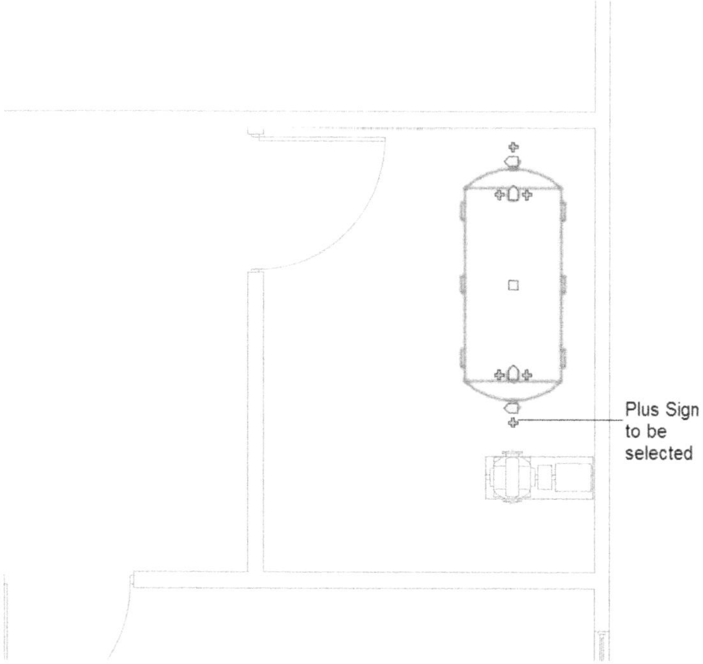

Figure Prj2-78 *The tank with plus sign*

3. Click on the adjacent Pipe End Connector of the pump; the **Choose a Part** dialog box is displayed, as shown in Figure Prj2-79.

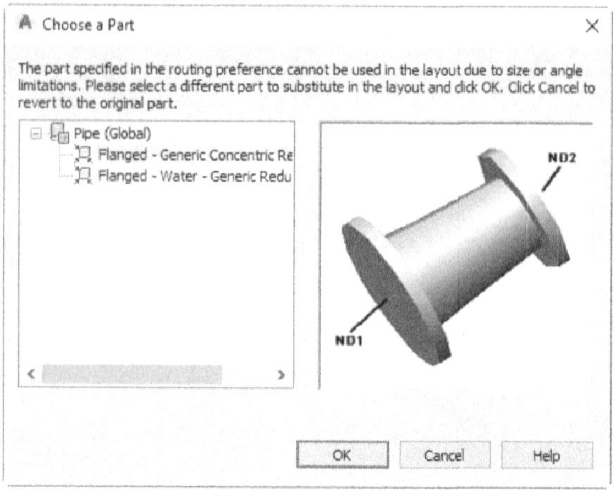

Figure Prj2-79 The ***Choose a Part*** *dialog box*

4. Choose the **OK** button from the consecutive dialog boxes displayed and then press ENTER; a pipe line is created between the tank and the pump. Also, connect the pipe with other end of tank, refer to Figure Prj2-80.

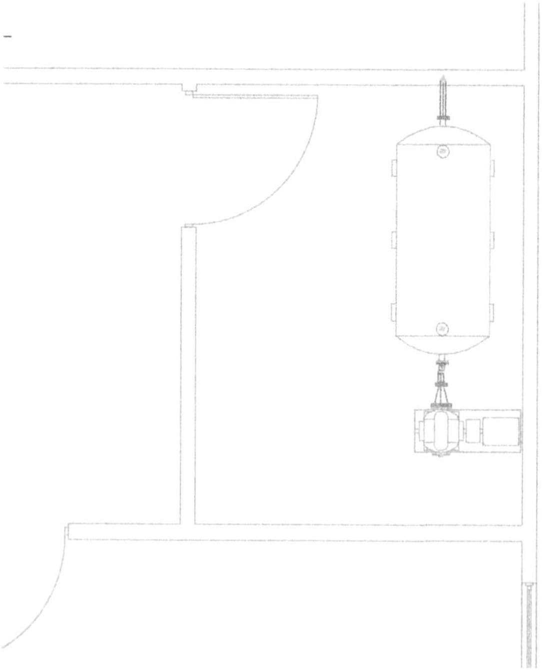

Figure Prj2-80 *The drawing after connecting the tank and pump*

5. Choose the **Pipe** tool from the **Pipe** drop-down in the **Build** panel of the **Home** tab in the **Ribbon**; the **PROPERTIES** palette is displayed, as shown in Figure Prj2-81. Also, you are prompted to specify the start point of the pipe.

6. Select the **50** option from the **Nominal Size** drop-down list.

7. Select the **Yes** option from the **Specify cut length** drop-down list; the **Cut length** edit box is displayed below the drop-down list.

8. Specify **6000** in the **Cut length** edit box.

9. Specify **2700** in the **Elevation** edit box.

10. Click in the drawing area and draw the pipe line, as shown in Figure Prj2-82.

11. Now, connect the ball valves and pump with the pipe, as shown in Figure Prj2-83.

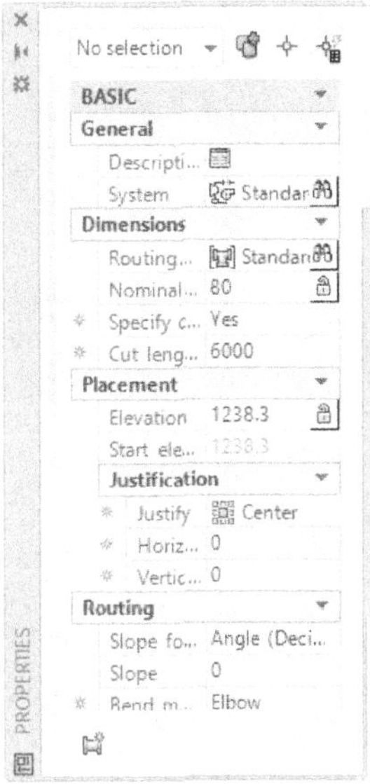

Figure Prj2-81 *The* ***PROPERTIES*** *palette displayed on choosing the* ***Pipe*** *tool*

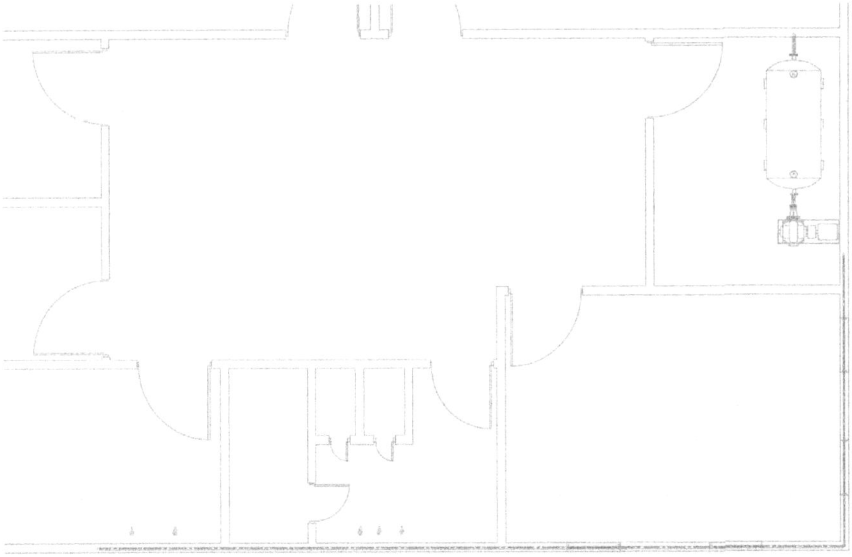

Figure Prj2-82 *The drawing after drawing the pipe line*

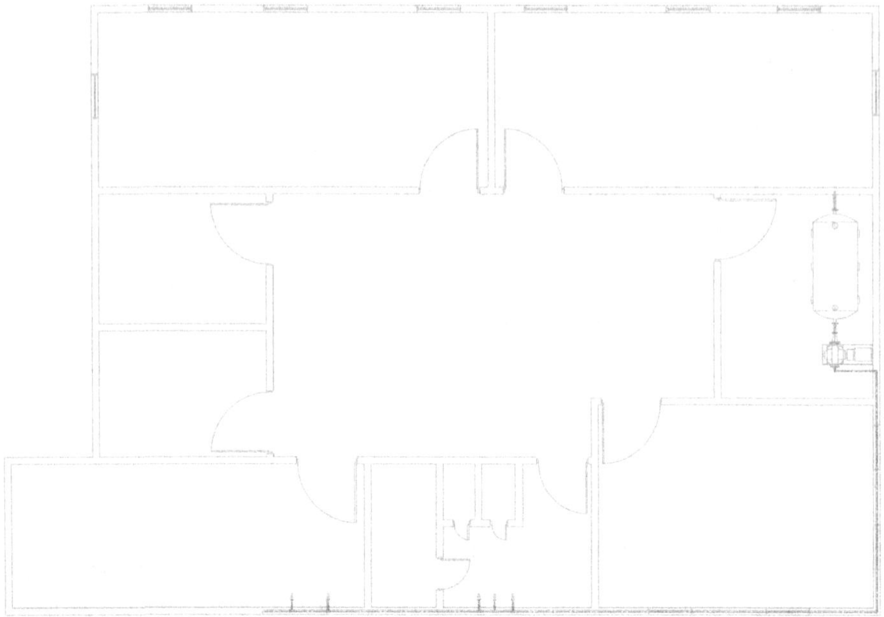

Figure Prj2-83 *Piping system after connecting all the ball valves and pump to the pipe line*

12. Save the drawing and close it.

Creating Electrical Drawings

Now, you need to create electrical drawings of the building. To do so, switch to the **Electrical** workspace.

Creating Electrical Drawing of the Ground Floor

1. Select the **Electrical** category from the **PROJECT NAVIGATOR** and choose the **Add Construct** button available at the bottom; the **Add Construct** dialog box is displayed.

2. Enter **Ground Floor Electrical** in the **Name** field of the dialog box.

3. Click in the **Description** field; the **Description** dialog box is displayed.

4. Enter the description **This drawing is meant for electrical plan of the ground floor** in the **Edit the description** edit box and then choose the **OK** button from the dialog box.

5. Select the check box corresponding to level 1 in the **Division** column in the **Add Construct** dialog box and make sure that the **Open in drawing editor** check box is selected in the **Add Construct** dialog box. Next, choose the **OK** button from the dialog box; the drawing is opened. Also, the Ground Floor Electrical drawing is displayed with a lock icon adjacent to it in the **PROJECT NAVIGATOR**.

6. Click on the **Workspace Switching** option in the **Application Status Bar** and select the **Electrical** option from the flyout.

Importing the Architectural Drawing of the Ground Floor

Before adding any electrical system in the project, you need to import the architectural plan of the ground floor.

1. Open the **PROJECT NAVIGATOR** and then click on the plus sign adjacent to Architectural category in the **Constructs** tab; a list of architectural drawings is displayed.

2. Select the Ground Floor Architectural drawing from the list and drag it to the current drawing; the architectural drawing is attached to the current drawing as an external reference.

Adding 600x600 Recessed Lights to the Drawing

Now, you need to add the recessed lights to the drawing.

1. Choose the **Device** tool from the **Build** panel of the **Home** tab in the **Ribbon**; the **PROPERTIES** palette is displayed, refer to Figure Prj2-84.

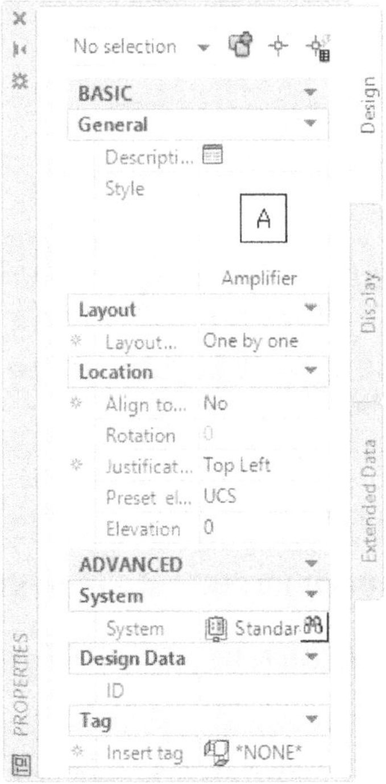

*Figure Prj2-84 The **PROPERTIES** palette displayed on choosing the **Device** tool*

2. Click in the **Style** field of the **PROPERTIES** palette; the **STYLES BROWSER** is displayed.

3. Select the **Lighting Fluorescent (Global)** option from the **Drawing file** drop-down list; various styles of lights available in AutoCAD MEP are displayed in the dialog box.

4. Double-click on the **600x600 Recessed Light** style from the **STYLES BROWSER**; the light gets attached to the cursor. Specify **3700** in the **Elevation** edit box in the **Location** rollout of the **PROPERTIES** palette.

5. Place the lights in the center of the inner area of the ground floor, refer to Figure Prj2-85.

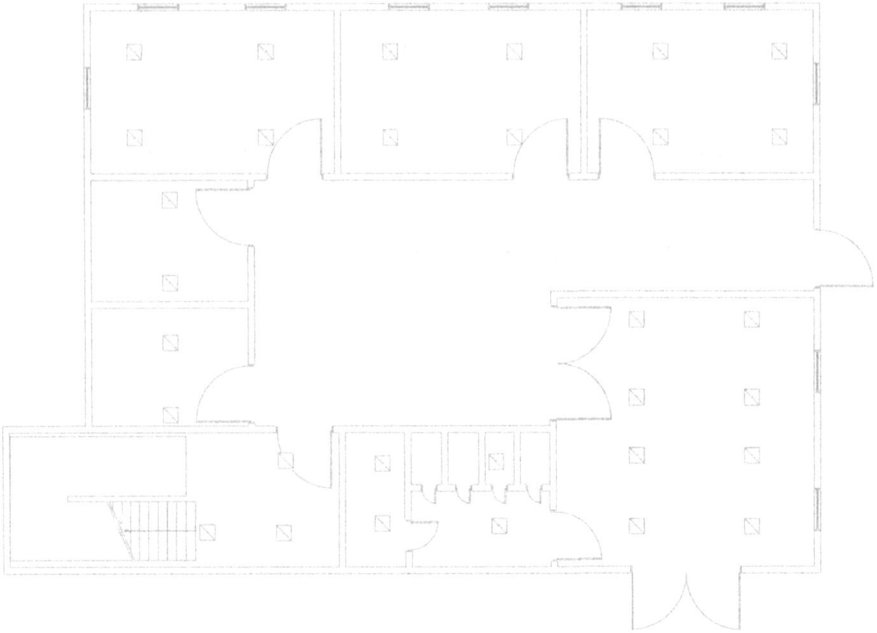

Figure Prj2-85 *The drawing after adding lights*

Adding 600X1200 Surface Type A Lights to the Drawing

Now, you need to add surface lights to the drawing.

1. Choose the **Device** tool from the **Build** panel of the **Home** tab in the **Ribbon**; the **PROPERTIES** palette is displayed.

2. Click in the **Style** field of the **PROPERTIES** palette; the **STYLES BROWSER** is displayed.

3. Select the **Lighting Fluorescent (Global)** option from the **Drawing file** drop-down list; the light styles available in AutoCAD MEP are displayed.

4. Double-click on the **600X1200 Surface Type A Light** option from the light styles; the light gets attached to the cursor. Specify **3700** in **Elevation** edit box in the **Location** rollout of the **PROPERTIES** palette.

5. Next, place the lights in the drawing, as shown in Figure Prj2-86.

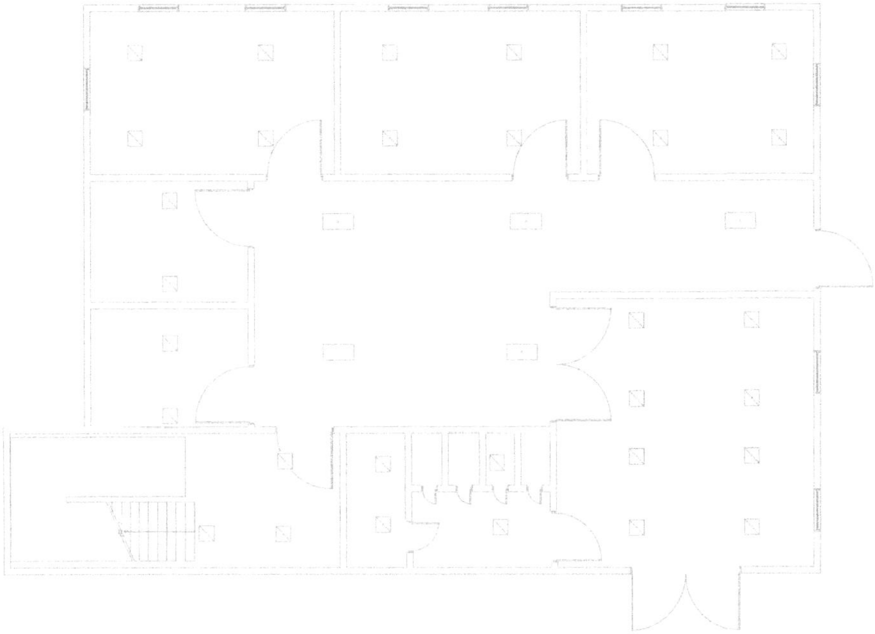

Figure Prj2-86 The drawing after adding lights in the center of the inner area

Adding Sockets to the Drawing

Now, you need to add sockets to the drawing.

1. Choose the **Device** tool from the **Build** panel; the **PROPERTIES** palette is displayed.
2. Click in the **Style** field of the **PROPERTIES** palette; the **STYLES BROWSER** is displayed.
3. Select the **Sockets (Global)** option from the **Drawing file** drop-down list; various styles of sockets available in AutoCAD MEP are displayed in the **STYLES BROWSER**.
4. Double-click on the **Single Switched Socket Outlet** socket style; the socket gets attached to the cursor. Specify **1500** in the **Elevation** edit box in the **Location** rollout of the **PROPERTIES** palette.
5. Next, place the sockets along the wall, as shown in Figure Prj2-87.

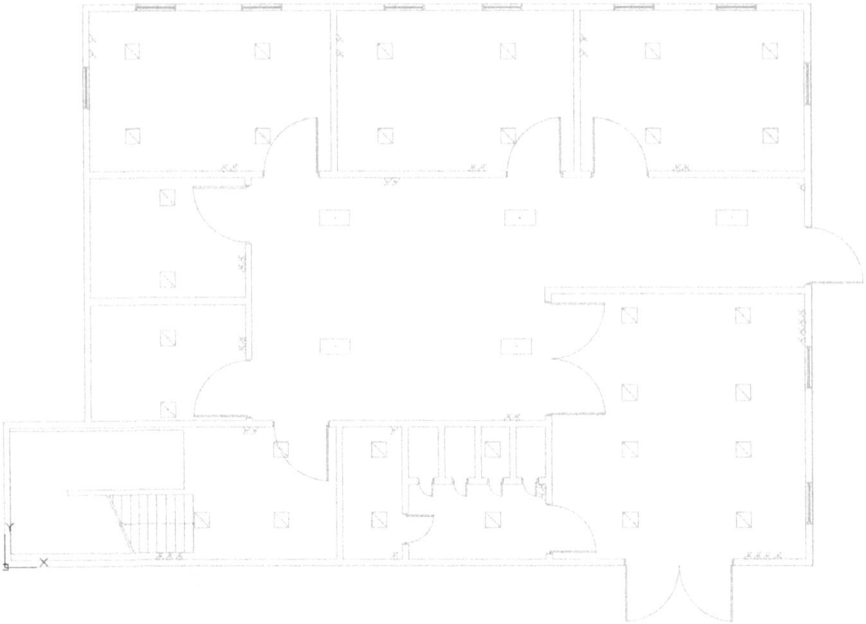

Figure Prj2-87 The drawing after adding sockets

Creating Panel

All the devices are connected to circuits. These circuits are joined to a panel for electricity supply. Therefore, you need to create a panel with circuits in this section.

1. Choose the **Panel** tool from the **Build** panel in the **Home** tab of the **Ribbon**; you are prompted to specify an insertion point for the panel and the **PROPERTIES** palette is displayed, as shown in Figure Prj2-88. Select the **Surface Door 3** style from the **Style** field in the **PROPERTIES** palette.

2. Click in the **Name** edit box in the **ADVANCED > Design Data** rollout of the **PROPERTIES** palette and specify the name as **Main Panel 1**.

3. Specify the value **800** in the **Rating** edit box.

4. Select the **230** option from the **Voltage phase-to-neutral** drop-down list.

5. Select the **240** option from the **Voltage phase-to-phase** drop-down list.

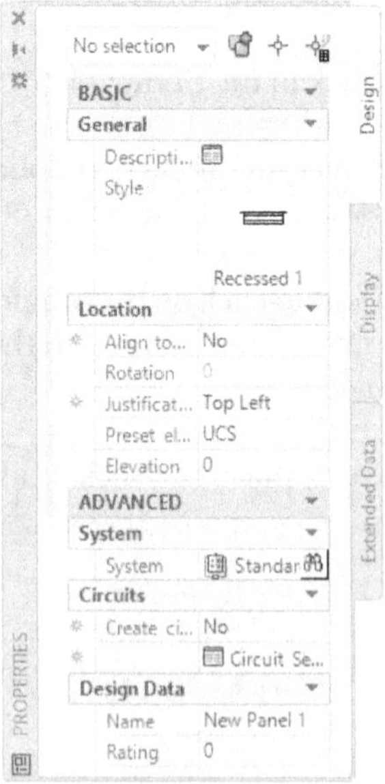

***Figure Prj2-88** The **PROPERTIES** palette displayed on choosing the **Panel** tool*

6. Specify **Main type** as **Main circuit breaker**, **Main size (amps)** as **15**, **Design capacity (amps)** as **20**, **Panel type** as **ISO** and **AIC rating** as **800** in the **PROPERTIES** palette.

   Now, you need to create circuits for the panel.

7. Click in the **Circuit Settings** field under **ADVANCED > Circuits** rollout of the **PROPERTIES** palette; the **Circuit Settings** dialog box is displayed, as shown in Figure Prj2-89.

8. Set the value as **2** in the **Total number of slots** and **Number of 1-pole circuits** spinners and select the **230** option from the **Voltage** drop-down list adjacent to the **Number of 1-pole circuits** spinner. Make sure that **Power and Lighting** is selected in the **System Type** drop-down list and **230V Lighting Devices (Ceiling)** is selected in the **System** drop-down list.

9. Choose the **OK** button from the dialog box to exit.

10. Select the **Yes** option from the **Create Circuit** drop-down list in the **Advanced** rollout. Click in the drawing area to place the panel, refer to Figure Prj2-90. As you click in the drawing area, **AutoCAD MEP - Electrical Project Database** dialog box is displayed, refer to Figure Prj2-91.

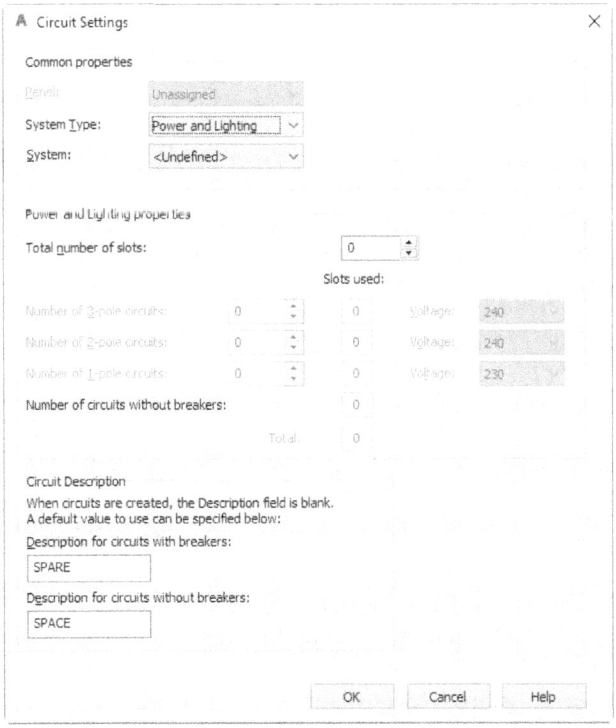

***Figure Prj2-89** The **Circuit Settings** dialog box*

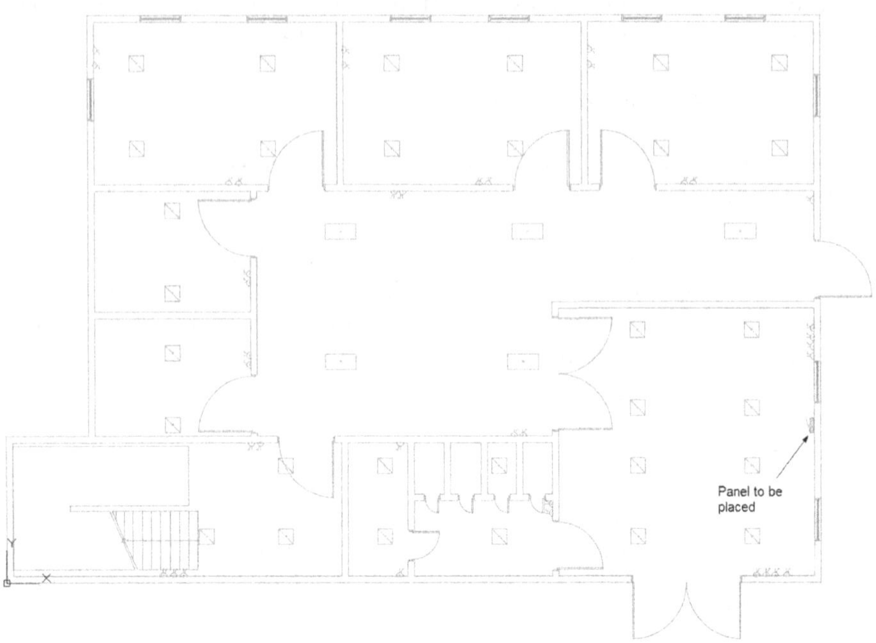

Figure Prj2-90 The drawing with the panel placed

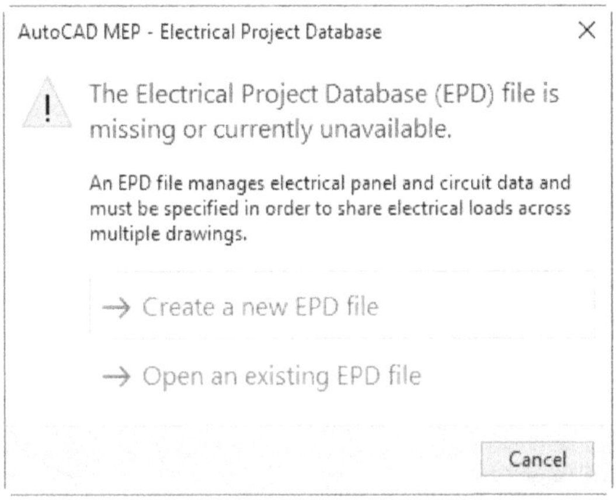

Figure Prj2-91 The ***AutoCAD MEP - Electrical Project Database*** *dialog box*

11. Choose the **Create a new EPD file** option from the dialog box and save the file at the desired location with the name **light_panel**; the panel is created at the specified location.

12. As explained in previous steps, place the other panel for **230V Power** system and rename it as **Sockets Panel**, refer to Figure Prj2-92.

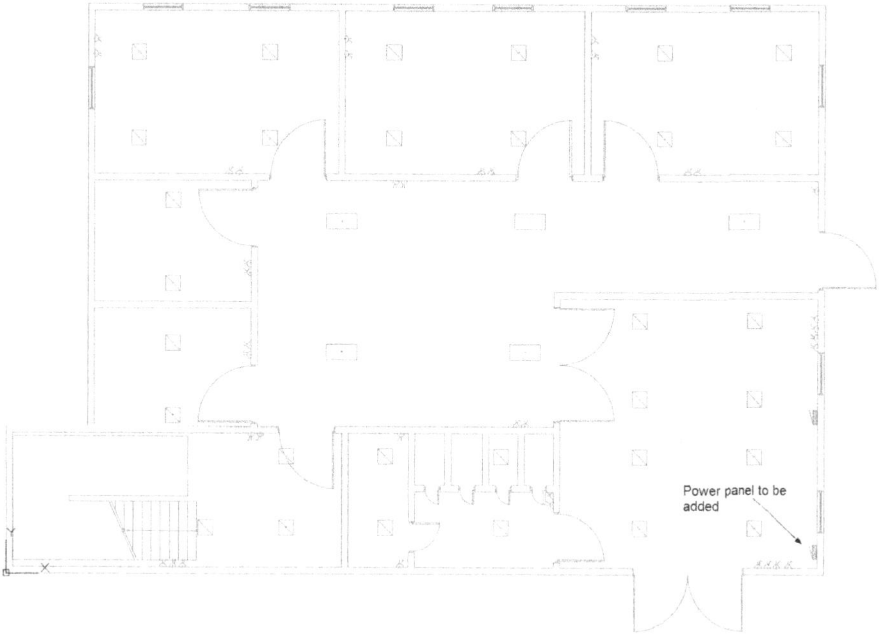

Figure Prj2-92 The drawing with other panel for 230 V power added

Configuring Circuits

1. Select the panel that was created first and then choose the **Circuit Manager** tool from the **Circuits** panel in the **Panel** contextual tab of the **Ribbon**; the **CIRCUIT MANAGER** is displayed, refer to Figure Prj2-93.

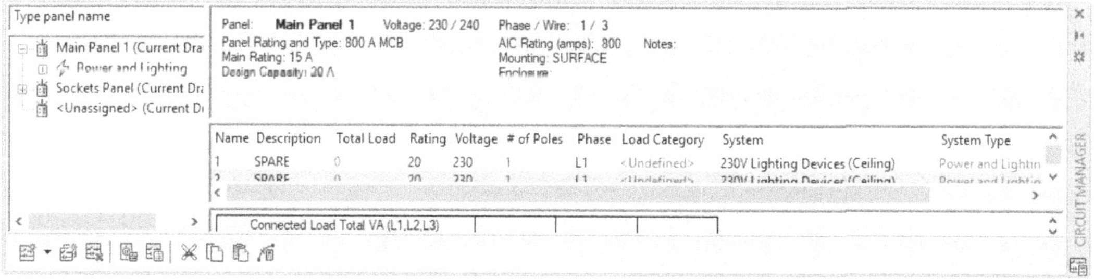

Figure Prj2-93 The CIRCUIT MANAGER

2. Specify the name **Outer Lights** in the field **1** of the **Name** column in the **CIRCUIT MANAGER**.

3. Specify the name **Inner Lights** in the field **2** of the **Name** column in the **CIRCUIT MANAGER**.

4. Click on the plus sign adjacent to **Sockets panel** on the left in the **CIRCUIT MANAGER**; the list of circuits available in the panel is displayed below it.

5. Select **Power and Lighting** from the left of the **CIRCUIT MANAGER**; the list of circuits is displayed on the right.

6. Double-click on **1** under the **Name** panel and specify the name as **Sockets**.

7. Double-click in the **Voltage** field for **Sockets** and select the **230** option from the drop-down list.

8. Select the **230V Power** option from the **System** drop-down list.

9. Close the **CIRCUIT MANAGER** dialog box.

Configuring Devices

1. Select a socket from the drawing area and then select the **Select Similar** option from the **Select Similar** drop-down list in the **Device** contextual tab displayed; all the sockets available in the drawing area are selected.

2. Click on the **Electrical properties** field in the **Circuits** rollout in the **Advanced** rollout of the **PROPERTIES** palette; the **Electrical Properties** dialog box is displayed, as shown in Figure Prj2-94. Now, in this dialog box, you need to specify the parameters that are given in Table Prj2-1.

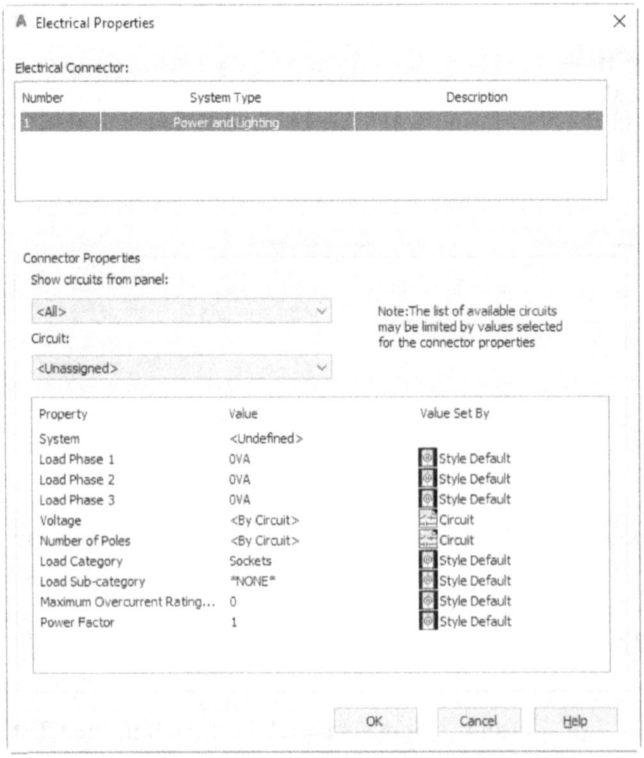

***Figure Prj2-94** The **Electrical Properties** dialog box*

3. Select the **230V Power** option from the **System** drop-down list.

4. Specify the value **300** in the **Load Phase 1** edit box, refer to Table Prj2-1.

5. Select the **230** option from the **Voltage** drop-down list.

6. Similarly, select the **1** option from the **Number of Poles** drop-down list.

7. Enter the value **10** in the **Maximum Overcurrent Rating (amps)** edit box.

8. Specify the value as **0.8** in the **Power Factor** edit box.

9. Select the **Sockets Panel (Current Drawing)** option from the **Show circuits from panel** drop-down list. Choose the **OK** button to exit the dialog box.

10. Similarly, specify the parameters for other devices in the **Electrical Properties** dialog box by using the steps discussed above. For parameters, refer to Table Prj2-1. Also, select the **Main Panel 1(Current Drawing)** option from the **Show circuits from panel** drop-down list for all the devices and select the **Outer Lights [Load: 0 VA]** for **600X1200 Surface Type A Light**, and **Inner Lights[Load: 0 VA]** for **600x600 Recessed Lights** from the **Circuit** drop-down list in the **Electrical Properties** dialog box.

Note

As soon as you select the ***Outer Lights [Load: 0 VA]*** *option from the* ***Circuit*** *drop-down list, it gets modified and displayed as* ***Outer Lights [Load: 1100 VA]*** *in the drop-down list. This is because the software automatically calculates the load of sockets according to the number of sockets added in the drawing. Similarly,* ***Inner Lights [Load: 0 VA]*** *changes into* ***Inner Lights [Load: 4650 VA]****.*

Adding Wires

1. Choose the **Wire** tool from the **Build** panel of the **Home** tab in the **Ribbon**; you are prompted to specify the start point of the wire on an electrical device and the **PROPERTIES** palette is displayed, as shown in Figure Prj2-95.

2. Select the **230V Power(230V POWER)** option from the **System** drop-down list.

3. Select the **PVC Single** option from the **Style** drop-down list under the **General** rollout.

4. Connect the sockets at the outer boundary using wire with **Sockets Panel** (2), refer to Figure Prj2-96. Make sure that the **Line** option is selected in the **Segment** drop-down list.

5. Similarly, connect the other sockets with wire line, refer to Figure Prj2-97.

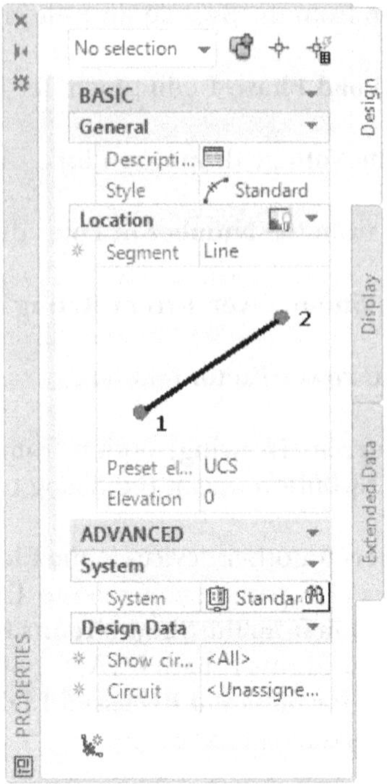

Figure Prj2-95 *The* ***PROPERTIES*** *palette displayed on choosing the* ***Wire*** *tool*

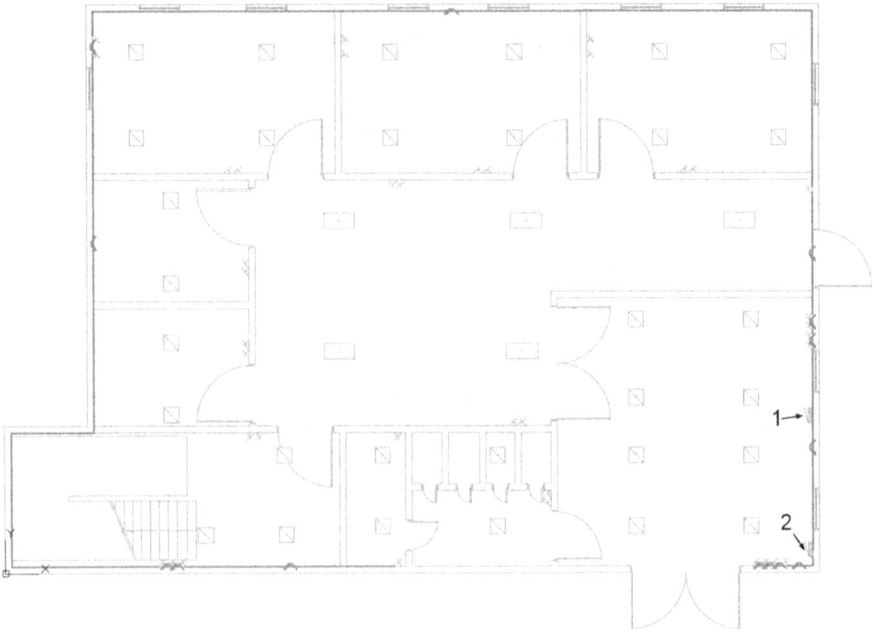

Figure Prj2-96 *The drawing after connecting sockets at the outer boundary using wires*

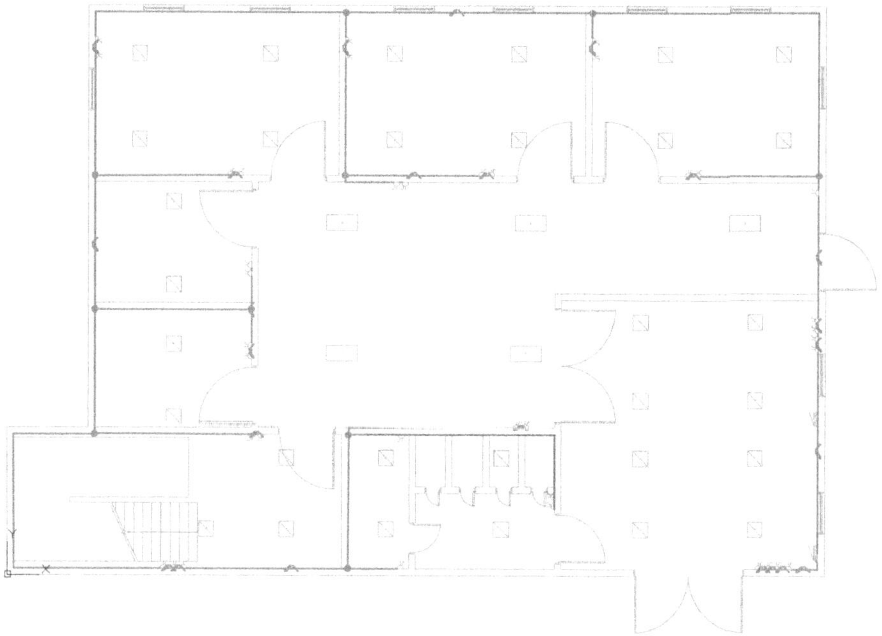

Figure Prj2-97 *The drawing after connecting all sockets using wires*

6. Similarly, connect all the lights to the panel no. 2 using the **230V Lighting** system, refer to Figure Prj2-98. Make sure that the circuit selected for inner lights is **Inner Lights** and for outer lights is **Outer Lights**.

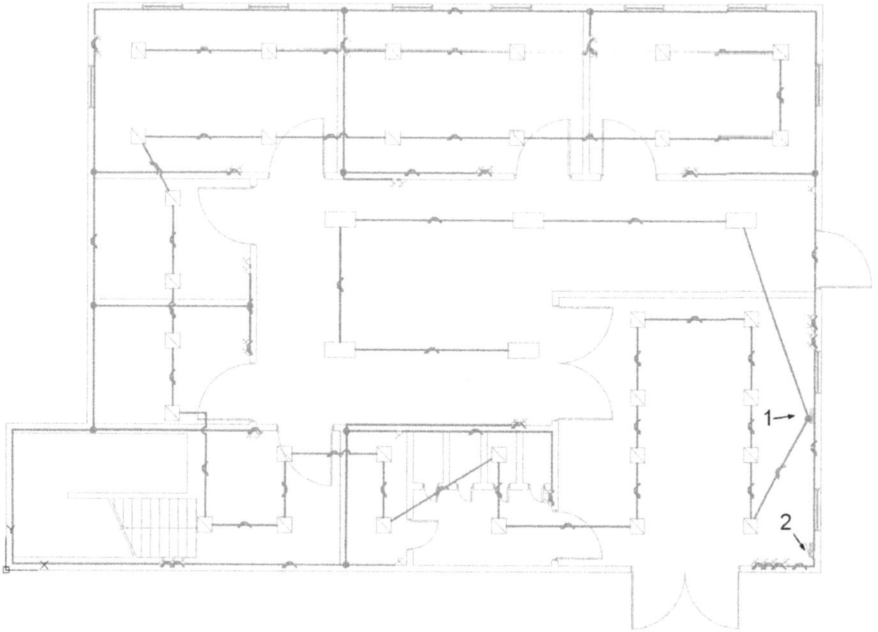

Figure Prj2-98 *The drawing after adding wires to lights*

Calculating Load and Wire Sizes

Now, you need to calculate the total load of the electrical system and the wire size.

1. Choose the **Power Totals** tool from the **Electrical** panel in the **Analyze** tab of the **Ribbon**; you are prompted to select the devices.

2. Select all the devices available in the drawing area and press ENTER; the **Power Totals** dialog box is displayed, refer to Figure Prj2-99.

   The total load is displayed in the **Total Load** field of the dialog box. Now, you need to calculate the wire size of the circuit.

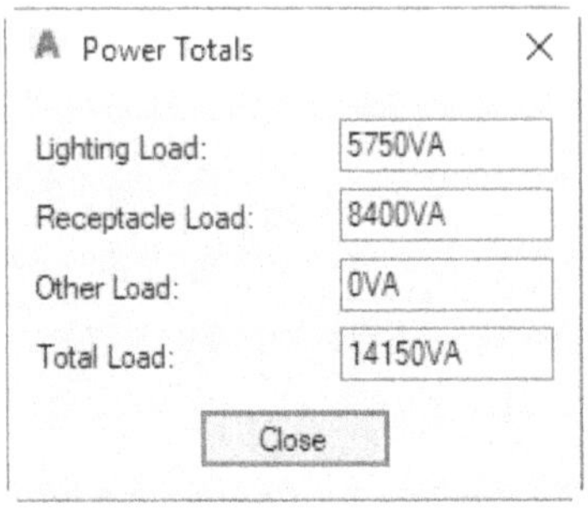

*Figure Prj2-99 The **Power Totals** dialog box*

3. To calculate wire size, select all the wires in the drawing area; the **PROPERTIES** palette is displayed.

4. Click on the **Calculate sizes for the wire** button available on the right of the **ADVANCED > Dimensions** rollout of the **PROPERTIES** palette; the wire sizes are displayed in the **Hot size, Neutral size**, and **Ground size** edit boxes in the **Dimensions** rollout.

Adding Transformer and Emergency Generator

After making calculations, the total load of the ground floor comes out to be approximately 17.2kVa. Assuming the same capacity for first floor and considering the peak load condition, you need to place a transformer and a generator of capacity 45 kVa in the drawing area.

1. Choose the **Equipment** tool from the **Equipment** drop-down in the **Build** panel of the **Home** tab in the **Ribbon**; the **Add Multi-view Parts** dialog box is displayed.

2. Click on the plus sign adjacent to **Electrical** in the part tab available at the left of the dialog box; the electrical equipment are displayed below it.

3. Click on the plus sign adjacent to **Power Transformers** in the part tab and select the **Dry Type Transformer - 3-150 kVa** part; the preview of the transformer is displayed, refer to Figure Prj2-100.

4. Select the **45 kVa Dry Type Transformer** option from the **Part Size Name** drop-down list available at the bottom in the dialog box and place the transformer at an appropriate distance from the building in the outer area with 0 Elevation, refer to Figure Prj2-101.

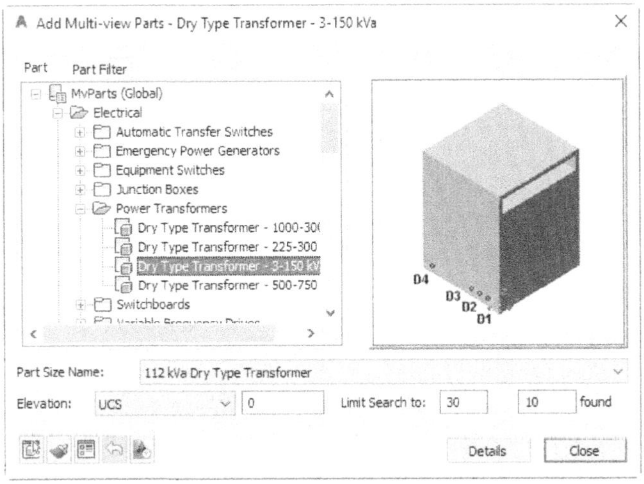

Figure Prj2-100 *The* ***Add Multi-view Parts*** *dialog box*

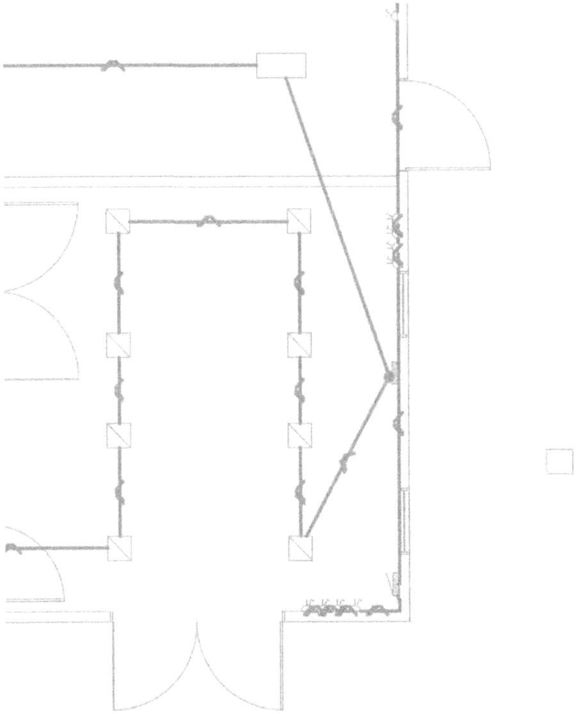

Figure Prj2-101 *The drawing after placing a transformer*

5. Similarly, place the emergency generator having the capacity of **300kw Diesel Emergency Power Generator** with 0 elevation in the drawing adjacent to the power transformer, refer to Figure Prj2-102.

6. Connect the transformer and emergency generator with the panels using **230V Power** wire, refer to Figure Prj2-102.

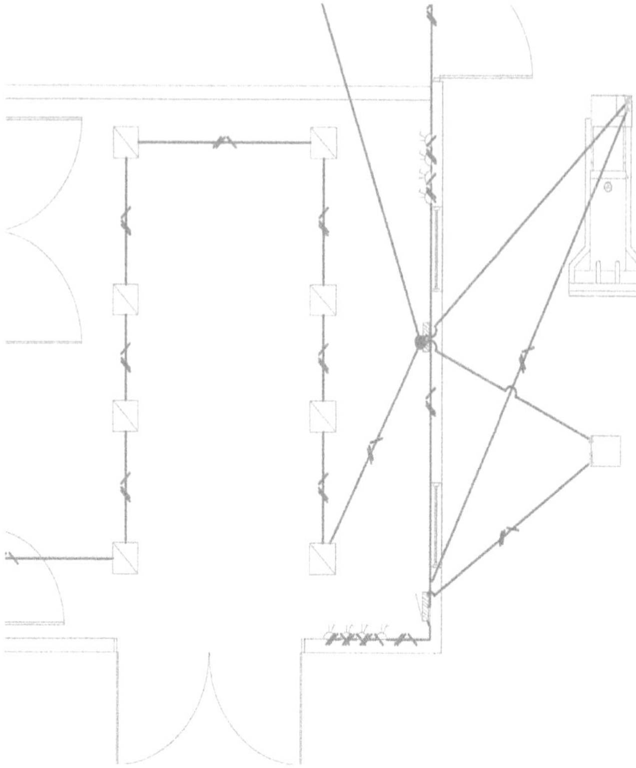

Figure Prj2-102 *The drawing after connecting transformer and generator to the circuit*

7. Save the drawing and close it.

Creating Electrical Drawing of the First Floor

1. Select the **Electrical** category from the **PROJECT NAVIGATOR** and choose the **Add Construct** button available at the bottom; the **Add Construct** dialog box is displayed

2. Click in the **Name** field of the dialog box and enter the name as **First Floor Electrical**.

3. Click in the **Description** field; the **Description** dialog box is displayed.

4. Enter the description **This drawing is meant for electrical plan of the first floor** and then choose the **OK** button from the dialog box.

5. Select the check box corresponding to level 2 in the **Division** column in the **Add Construct** dialog box and make sure that the **Open in drawing editor** check box is selected in the **Add Construct** dialog box. Next, choose the **OK** button from the dialog box; the drawing is opened. Also, the First Floor Electrical drawing is displayed with a lock icon adjacent to it in the **PROJECT NAVIGATOR**.

6. Click on the **Workspace Switching** option of the **Application Status Bar** and choose the **Electrical** option from the flyout.

Importing the Architectural Drawing of the First Floor

Before adding any electrical system to the project, you need to first import the architectural plan of the first floor.

1. Open the **PROJECT NAVIGATOR** and then click on the plus sign adjacent to Architectural category in the **Constructs** tab; the list of architectural drawings is displayed.

2. Select First Floor Architectural drawing from the list and drag it to the current drawing; the architectural drawing is attached to the current drawing as an external reference.

Adding 600x600 Recessed Lights to the Drawing

Now, you need to add lights to the drawing.

1. Choose the **Device** tool from the **Build** panel of the **Home** tab in the **Ribbon**; the **PROPERTIES** palette is displayed, refer to Figure Prj2-103.

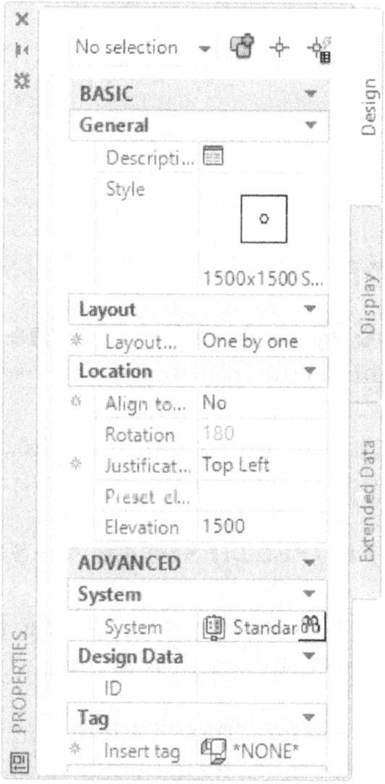

*Figure Prj2-103 The **PROPERTIES** palette displayed on choosing the **Device** tool*

2. Click in the **Style** field of the **PROPERTIES** palette; the **STYLES BROWSER** is displayed.

3. Select the **Lighting Fluorescent (Global)** option from the **Drawing file** drop-down list; the light styles available in AutoCAD MEP are displayed.

4. Double-click on the **600x600 Recessed Light** from the light styles; the light symbol gets attached to the cursor.

5. Place three equidistant lights in the middle of each room in the drawing with elevation value of **3700**, refer to Figure Prj2-104.

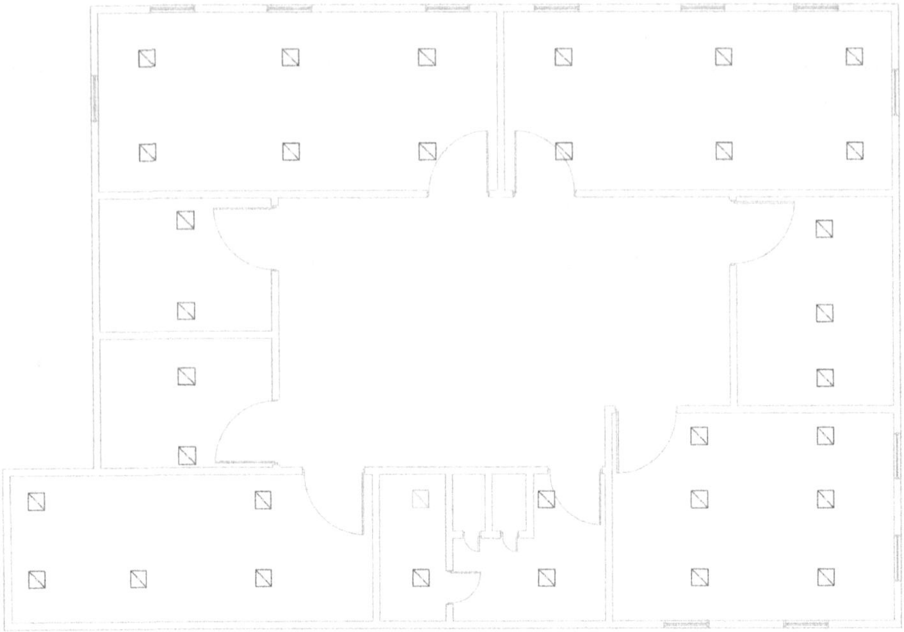

Figure Prj2-104 *The drawing after adding lights*

Adding 600X1200 Surface Type A Lights to the Drawing

Now, you need to add surface lights to the drawing.

1. Choose the **Device** tool from the **Build** panel of the **Home** tab in the **Ribbon**; the **PROPERTIES** palette is modified, refer to Figure Prj2-105.

2. Click in the **Style** field of the **PROPERTIES** palette; the **STYLES BROWSER** is displayed.

3. Select the **Lighting Fluorescent (Global)** option from the **Drawing file** drop-down list; the light styles available in AutoCAD MEP are displayed.

4. Double-click on the **600X1200 Surface Type A Light** option from the light styles; the light gets attached to the cursor. Specify the **3700** in the **Elevation** edit box in the **Location** rollout of the **PROPERTIES** palette.

5. Next, place the lights in the drawing, as shown in Figure Prj2-106.

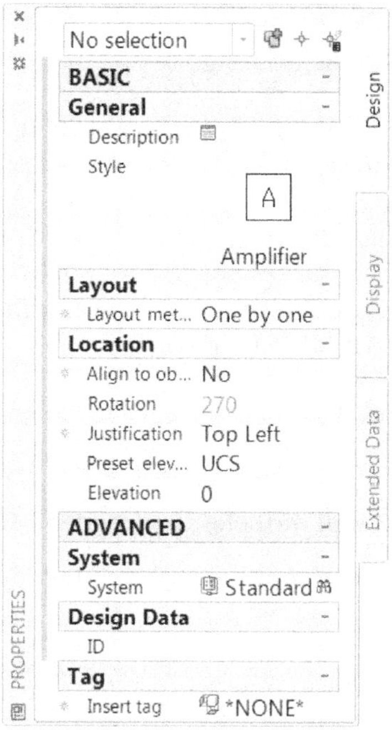

Figure Prj2-105 *The* ***PROPERTIES*** *palette displayed on choosing the* ***Device*** *tool*

Figure Prj2-106 *The drawing after adding lights in the center of the inner area*

Adding Sockets in the Drawing

Now, you need to add sockets to the drawing.

1. Choose the **Device** tool from the **Build** panel of the **Home** tab in the **Ribbon**; the **PROPERTIES** palette is displayed.

2. Click in the **Style** field of the **PROPERTIES** palette; the **STYLES BROWSER** is displayed.

3. Select the **Sockets (Global)** option from the **Drawing file** drop-down list; various styles of sockets available in AutoCAD MEP are displayed.

4. Double-click on the **Single Switched Socket Outlet** socket style; the socket symbol gets attached to the cursor.

5. Place the sockets along the wall with elevation value of **1500**, refer to Figure Prj2-107.

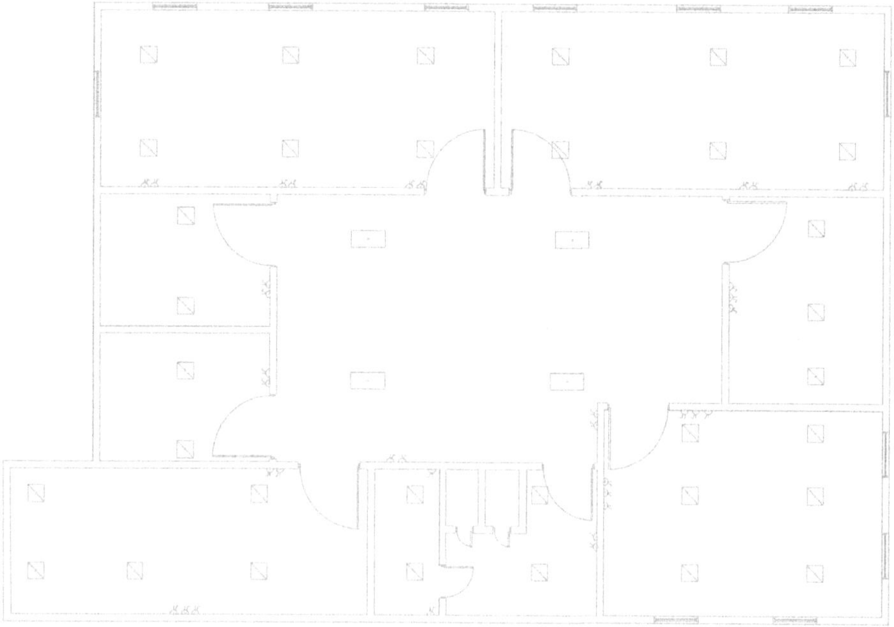

Figure Prj2-107 *The drawing after adding lights and sockets*

Creating Panel

As discussed earlier, all the devices are connected to circuits. These circuits are joined to a panel for electricity supply. So, you need to create a panel with circuits in this section.

1. Choose the **Panel** tool from the **Build** panel in the **Home** tab of the **Ribbon**; you are prompted to specify an insertion point for the panel and the **PROPERTIES** palette is displayed, as shown in Figure Prj2-108. Select the **Surface Door 3** style from the **Style** field in the **PROPERTIES** palette.

2. Click in the **Name** edit box of the **ADVANCED** > **Design Data** rollout of the **PROPERTIES** palette and specify the name as **Panel1**.

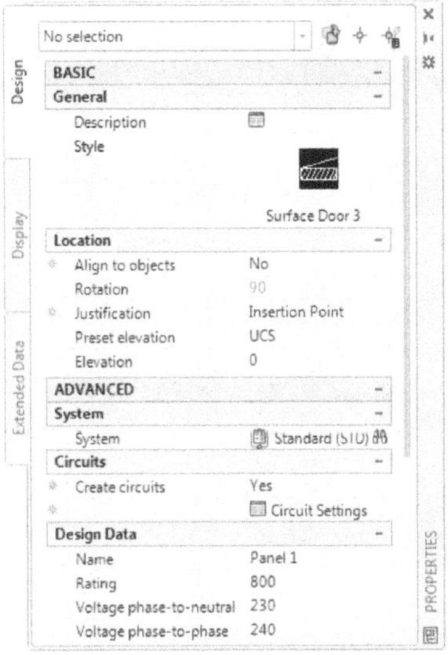

Figure Prj2-108 The ***PROPERTIES*** *palette*

3. Specify the value **800** in the **Rating** edit box.

4. Select the **230** option from the **Voltage phase-to-neutral** drop-down list.

5. Select the **240** option from the **Voltage phase-to-phase** drop-down list.

6. Specify **Main type** as **Main circuit breaker**, **Main size(amps)** as **15**, **Design capacity (amps)** as **20**, **Panel type** as **ISO** and **AIC rating** as **800** in the **ADVANCED > Design Data** rollout in the **PROPERTIES** palette.

   Now, you need to create circuits for the panel.

7. Click in the **Circuit Settings** field in the **PROPERTIES** palette; the **Circuit Settings** dialog box is displayed, as shown in Figure Prj2-109.

8. Set the value as **2** in the **Total number of slots** and **Number of 1-pole circuits** spinners and select the **230** option from the **Voltage** drop-down list adjacent to the **Number of 1-pole circuits** spinner. Make sure that **Power and Lighting** is selected in the **System Type** drop-down list and **230V Lighting Devices(Ceiling)** is selected in the **System** drop-down list.

9. Choose the **OK** button from the dialog box to exit. Select the **Yes** option from the **Create circuits** drop-down list in the **Circuits** rollout in the **PROPERTIES** palette.

10. Click in the drawing area to place the panel, refer to Figure Prj2-110. Also, the **AutoCAD MEP - Electrical Project Database** dialog box is displayed, refer to Figure Prj2-111.

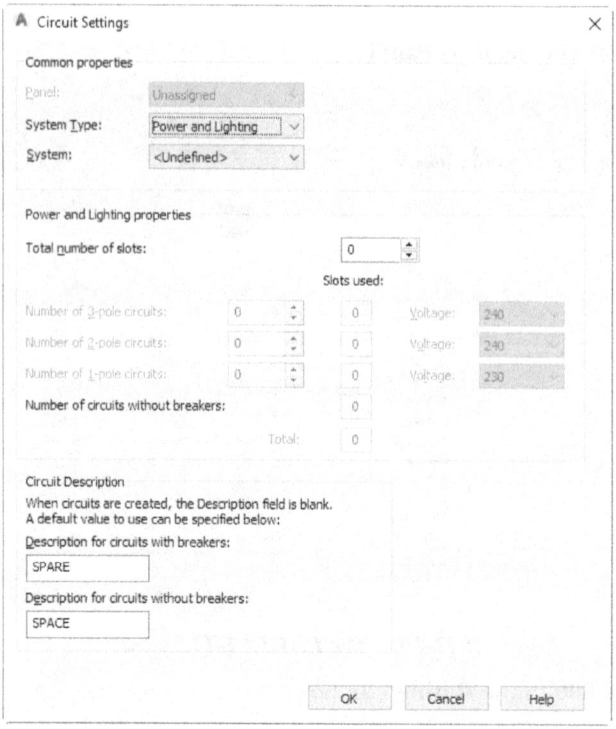

Figure Prj2-109 *The* ***Circuit Settings*** *dialog box*

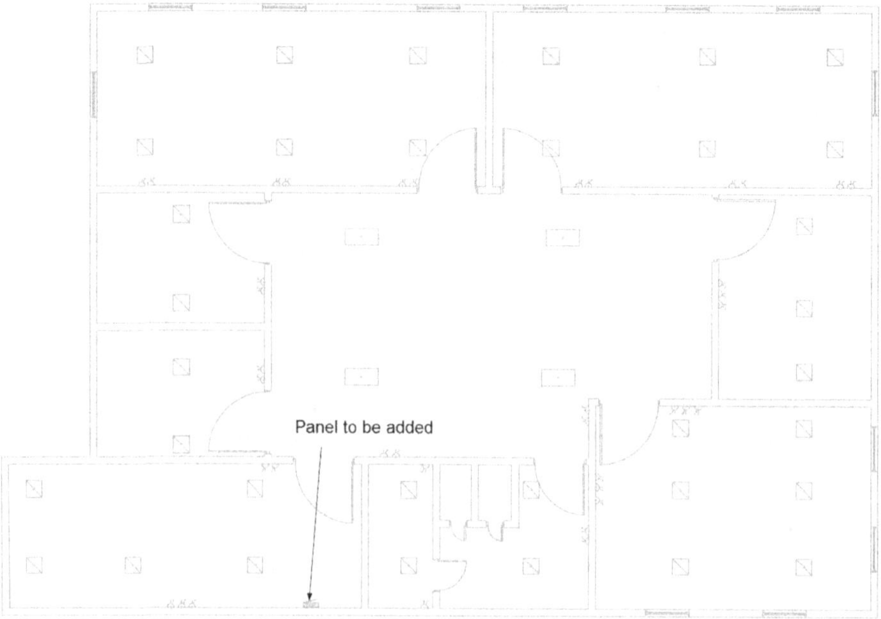

Figure Prj2-110 *The drawing with the panel to be added*

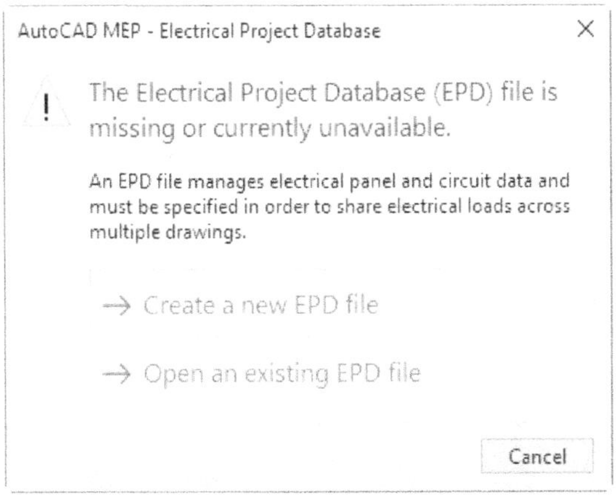

*Figure Prj2-111 The **AutoCAD MEP - Electrical Project Database** dialog box*

11. Choose the **Create a new EPD file** option from the dialog box and save the file at the desired location with the name **top_light_panel**; the panel is created at the specified location.

12. As explained in previous steps, place the other panel for **230V Power** system and rename it as **Panel 2**, refer to Figure Prj2-112.

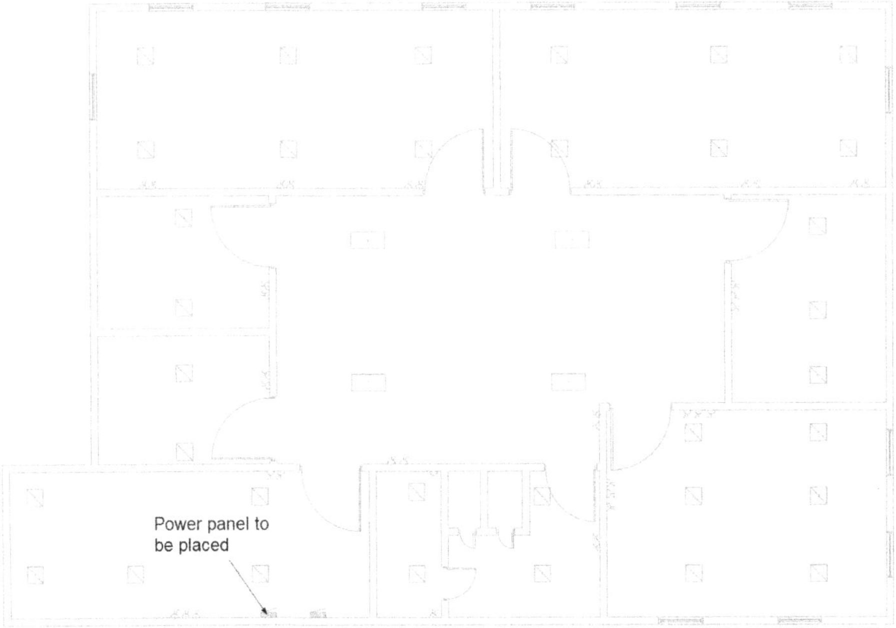

Figure Prj2-112 The drawing with other panel for 230 V power added

Configuring Circuits

1. Select the panel that was created first and then choose the **Circuit Manager** tool from the **Circuits** panel in the **Panel** contextual tab of the **Ribbon**; the **CIRCUIT MANAGER** is displayed, refer to Figure Prj2-113.

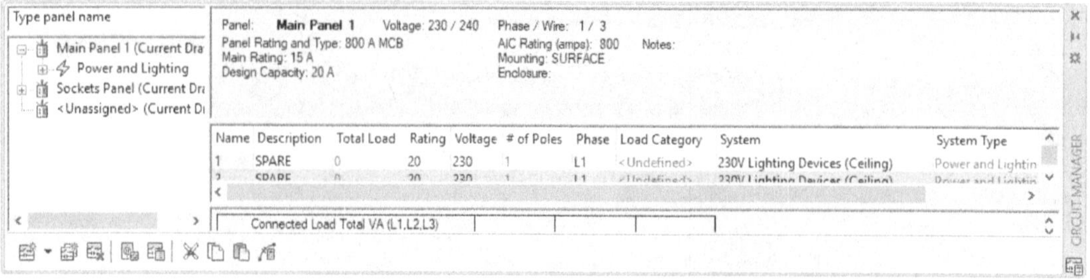

Figure Prj2-113 The CIRCUIT MANAGER

2. Specify the name **Outer Lights** in the field **1** of the **Name** column in the **CIRCUIT MANAGER**.

3. Specify the name **Inner Lights** in the field **2** of the **Name** column in the **CIRCUIT MANAGER**.

4. Click on the plus sign adjacent to **Panel 2** on the left in the **CIRCUIT MANAGER**; the list of circuits available in the panel is displayed below it.

5. Select **Power and Lighting** from the left of the **CIRCUIT MANAGER**; the list of circuits is displayed on the right.

6. Double-click on **1** under the **Name** panel and specify the name as **Sockets**.

7. Double-click in the **Voltage** field for **Sockets** and select the **230** option from the drop-down list.

8. Select the **230V Power** option from the **System** drop-down list.

9. Close the **CIRCUIT MANAGER** dialog box.

Configuring Devices

1. Select a socket from the drawing area and then select the **Select Similar** option from the **Select Similar** drop-down list in the **Device** contextual tab displayed; all the sockets available in the drawing area are selected.

2. Click on the **Electrical properties** field in the **Advanced** rollout of the **PROPERTIES** palette; the **Electrical Properties** dialog box is displayed, as shown in Figure Prj2-114. Now, in this dialog box, you need to specify the parameters that are given in Table Prj2-1.

3. Select the **230V Power** option from the **System** drop-down list.

4. Specify the value **300** in the **Load Phase 1** edit box, refer to Table Prj2-1.

5. Select the **230** option from the **Voltage** drop-down list.

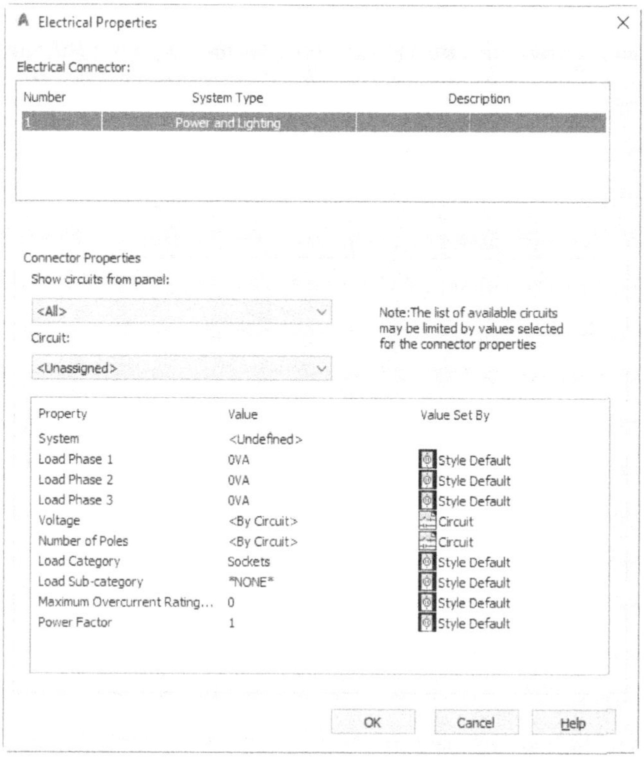

Figure Prj2-114 *The* ***Electrical Properties*** *dialog box*

6. Similarly, select the **1** option from the **Number of Poles** drop-down list.

7. Enter the value **10** in the **Maximum Overcurrent Rating (amps)** edit box.

8. Specify the value as **0.8** in the **Power Factor** edit box.

9. Select the **Panel 2 (Current Drawing)** option from the **Show Circuits from panel** drop-down list. Choose the **OK** button to exit the dialog box.

10. Similarly, specify the parameters for other devices in the **Electrical Properties** dialog box by using the steps discussed above. For parameters, refer to Table Prj2-1. Also, select the **Panel (Current Drawing)** option from the **Show circuits from panel** drop-down list for all the devices and select the **Outer Lights [Load: 0 VA]** for **600X1200 Surface Type A Light**, and **Inner Lights[Load: 0 VA]** for **600x600 Recessed Lights** from the **Circuit** drop-down list in the **Electrical Properties** dialog box.

Note

As soon as you select the ***Outer Lights [Load: 0 VA]*** *option from the* ***Circuit*** *drop-down list, it gets modified and displayed as* ***Outer Lights [Load: 880 VA]*** *in the drop-down list. This is because the software automatically calculates the load of sockets according to the number of sockets added in the drawing. Similarly,* ***Inner Lights [Load: 0 VA]*** *changes into* ***Inner Lights [Load: 5100 VA]****.*

Adding Wires

1. Choose the **Wire** tool from the **Build** panel of the **Home** tab in the **Ribbon**; you are prompted to specify the start point of the wire on an electrical device and the **PROPERTIES** palette is displayed, as shown in Figure Prj2-115.

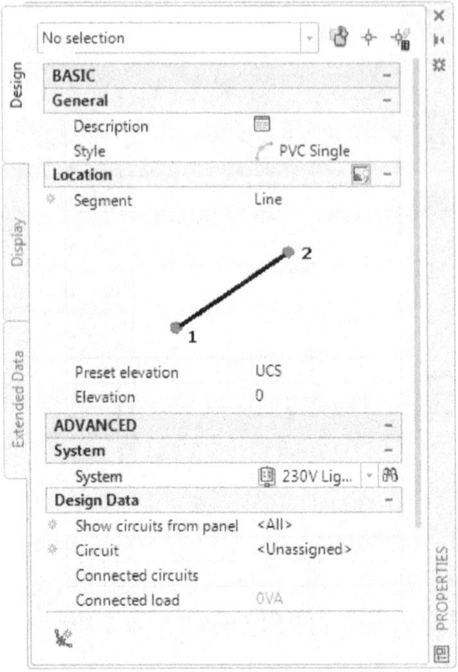

*Figure Prj2-115 The **PROPERTIES** palette displayed on choosing the **Wire** tool*

2. Select the **230V Power(230V POWER)** option from the **System** drop-down list.

3. Select the **PVC Single** option from the **Style** drop-down list.

4. Connect all the sockets to the panel using wire, refer to Figure Prj2-116. Make sure that the **Line** option is selected in the **Segment** drop-down list.

5. Similarly, connect all the lights to the panel using the 230V Lighting system, refer to Figure Prj2-117. Make sure that the circuit selected for inner lights is **Inner Lights** and for outer lights is **Outer Lights** in the **PROPERTIES** Palette.

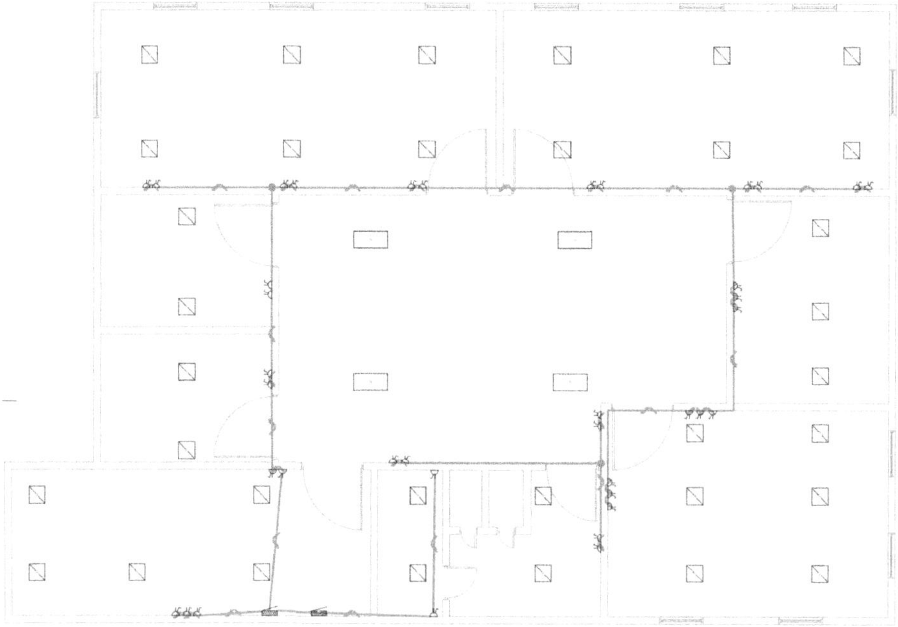

Figure Prj2-116 The drawing after adding all the sockets with the panel

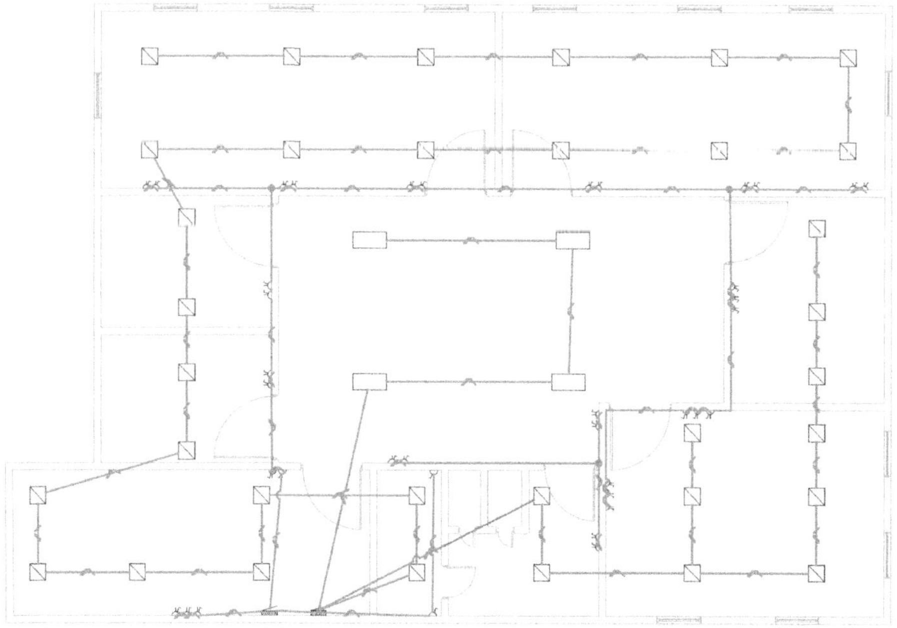

Figure Prj2-117 The drawing after adding lights to the panel

Calculating Loads and Wire Sizes

1. Choose the **Power Totals** tool from the **Electrical** panel in the **Analyze** tab of the **Ribbon**; you are prompted to select the devices.

2. Select all the devices available in the drawing area and press ENTER; the **Power Totals** dialog box is displayed, refer to Figure Prj2-118.

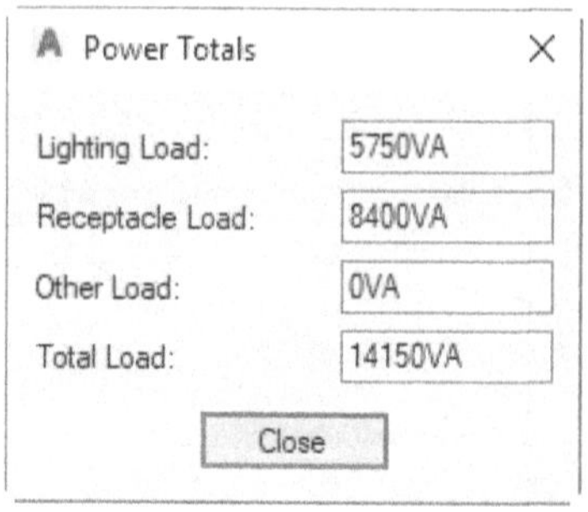

Figure Prj2-118 *The* ***Power Totals*** *dialog box*

The total load is displayed in the **Total Load** field of the dialog box. Now, you need to calculate the wire size for the circuit.

3. To calculate wire size, select all the wires in the drawing area; the **PROPERTIES** palette is displayed.

4. In the **PROPERTIES** palette, choose the **Calculate sizes for the wire** button available on the right of **Dimensions** rollout; the wire sizes are calculated automatically and displayed in the **Hot size**, **Neutral size**, and **Ground size** edit boxes.

5. Save and close the drawing.

Creating Plumbing Drawing of the Ground Floor

1. Select the **Plumbing** category from the **PROJECT NAVIGATOR** and choose the **Add Construct** button available at the bottom; the **Add Construct** dialog box is displayed.

2. Enter **Ground Floor Plumbing** in the **Name** field of the dialog box.

3. Click in the **Description** field; the **Description** dialog box is displayed.

4. Enter the description **This drawing is meant for plumbing plan of the ground floor** in the **Edit the description** edit box and then choose the **OK** button from the dialog box.

5. Select the check box corresponding to level 1 in the **Division** column in the **Add Construct** dialog box and make sure that the **Open in drawing editor** check box is selected in the **Add Construct** dialog box. Next, choose the **OK** button from the dialog box; the drawing is opened. Also, the Ground Floor Plumbing drawing is displayed with a lock icon adjacent to it in the **PROJECT NAVIGATOR**.

6. Click on the **Workspace Switching** option in the **Application Status Bar** and select the **Plumbing** option from the flyout.

Importing the Architectural Drawing of the Ground Floor

Before adding any plumbing system in the project, you need to import the architectural plan of the ground floor.

1. Open the **PROJECT NAVIGATOR** and then click on the plus sign adjacent to Architectural category in the **Constructs** tab; a list of architectural drawings is displayed.

2. Select the Ground Floor Architectural drawing from the list and drag it to the current drawing; the architectural drawing is attached to the current drawing as an external reference.

Adding Urinal to the Drawing

Now, you need to add Urinal to the drawing.

1. Choose the **Urinal** tool from the **Equipment** drop-down available in the **Build** panel of the **Home** tab in the **Ribbon**; the **Add Multi-view Parts** dialog box is displayed, as shown in Figure Prj2- 119. Also, the urinal stall is displayed attached to the cursor.

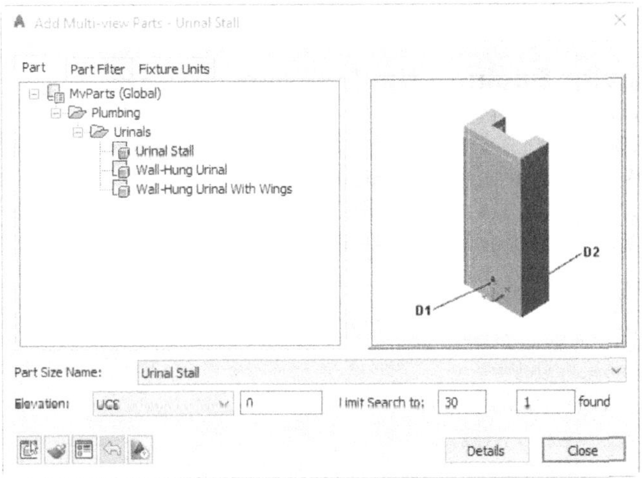

*Figure Prj2-119 The **Add Multi-view Parts** dialog box*

2. Choose the **Wall-Hang Urinal** from the dialog box; the wall-hang urinal is attached with cursor. Specify **500** in the **Elevation** edit box and place the wall-hang urinal in toilet area, as shown in Figure Prj2-120.

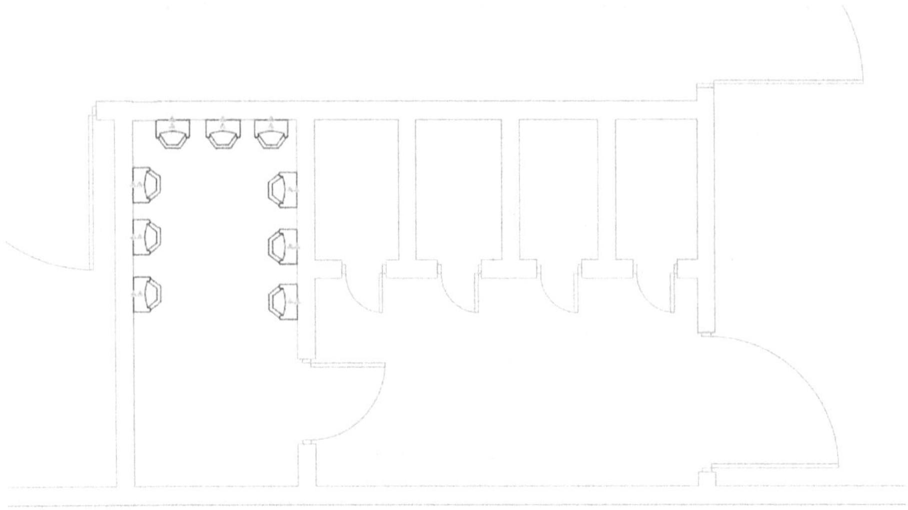

Figure Prj2-120 The drawing after placing the wall-hang urinal

Adding Rectangular Basin to the Drawing

Now, you need to add Sink to the drawing.

1. Choose the **Sink** tool from the **Equipment** drop-down available in the **Build** panel of the **Home** tab in the **Ribbon**; the **Add Multi-view Parts** dialog box is displayed, as shown in Figure Prj2- 121. Also, the sink is displayed attached to the cursor.

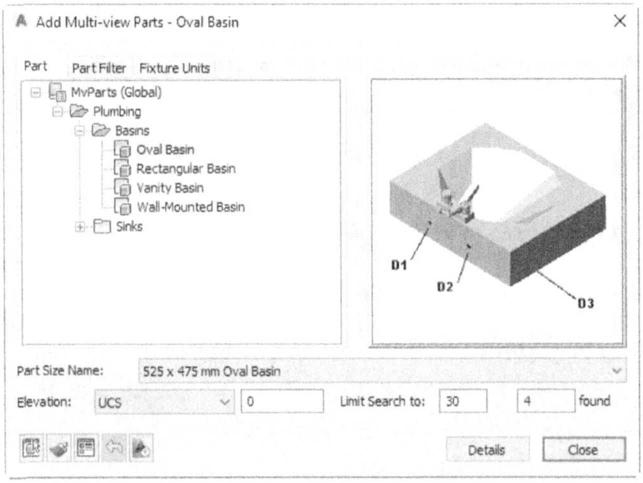

*Figure Prj2-121 The **Add Multi-view Parts** dialog box*

2. Choose the **Rectangular Basin** from the dialog box; the rectangular basin is attached with cursor. Select the **375x375 mm Rectangular Basin** option from the **Part Size Name** drop-down list.

3. Specify **800** in the **Elevation** edit box and place the rectangular basin in toilet area, as shown in Figure Prj2-122.

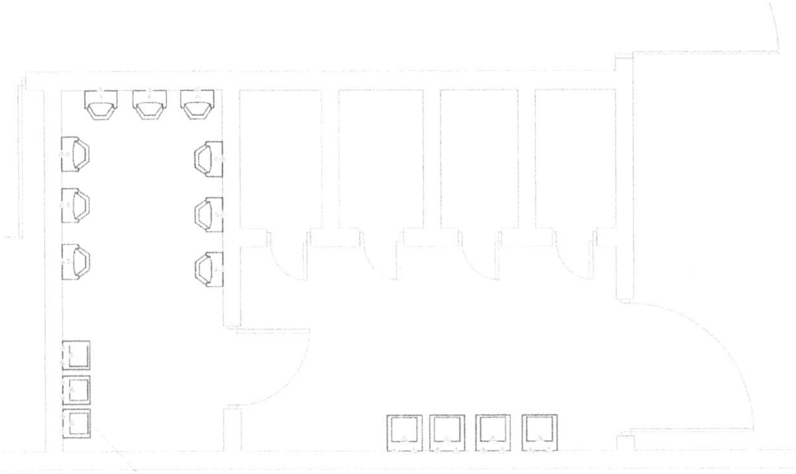

Figure Prj2-122 *The drawing after placing the wall-hang urinal and rectangular basin*

Adding Water Closet to the Drawing

Now, you need to add Water closet to the drawing.

1. Choose the **Water Closet** tool from the **Equipment** drop-down available in the **Build** panel of the **Home** tab in the **Ribbon**; the **Add Multi-view Parts** dialog box is displayed, as shown in Figure Prj2-123. Also, the bidet is displayed attached to the cursor.

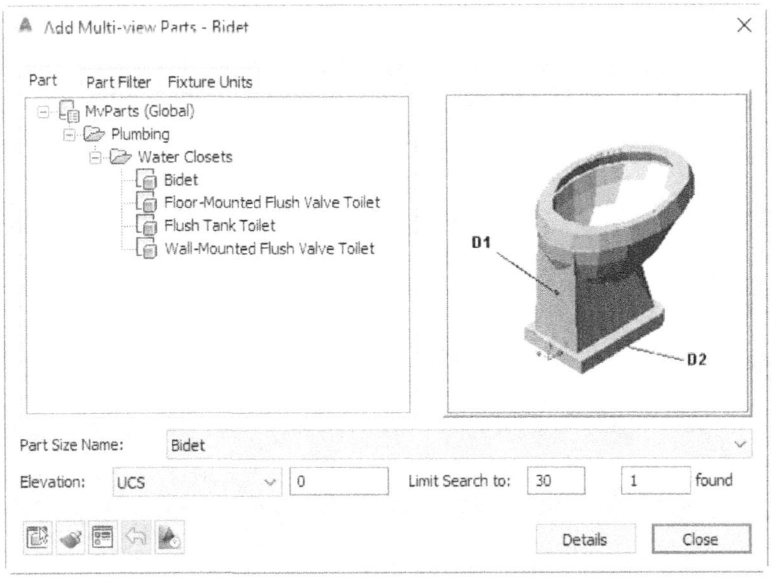

Figure Prj2-123 *The **Add Multi-view Parts** dialog box*

2. Choose the **Flush Tank Toilet** from the dialog box; the flush tank toilet is attached with the cursor.

3. Specify **0** in the **Elevation** edit box and place the flush tank toilet in toilet area, as shown in Figure Prj2-124.

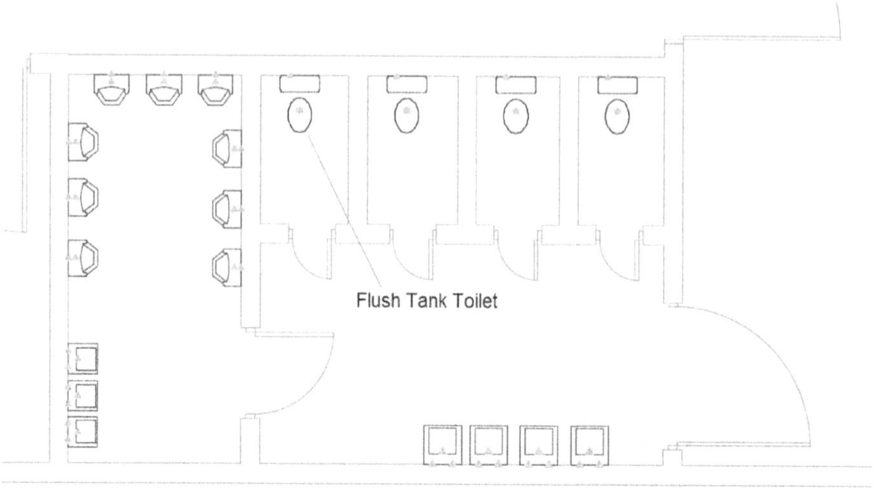

Figure Prj2-124 *The drawing after placing the wall-hang urinal, rectangular basin and flush tank toilet*

Creating Plumbing Line between Various Equipment

There are two plumbing lines to be added to the system: Waste (WP) and Domestic Cold Water.

1. Choose the **Waste (WP)** tool from the **TOOL PALETTES - PLUMBING** displayed, refer to Figure Prj2-125; you are prompted to select the starting point for Waste plumbing line.

2. Select the Waste Pipe End Connector of the extreme right flush tank toilet; the other end of the waste plumbing line gets attached to the cursor and you are prompted to specify the next end point.

3. Select the Waste Pipe End Connector of adjacent flush tank toilet; the **Select Connector** dialog box is displayed, as shown in Figure Prj2-126.

4. Select the **Connector 2: Waste** option from the dialog box and flush tank toilet is connected with each other. Similarly, connect all the flush tank toilet as displayed in drawing, refer to Figure Prj2-127.

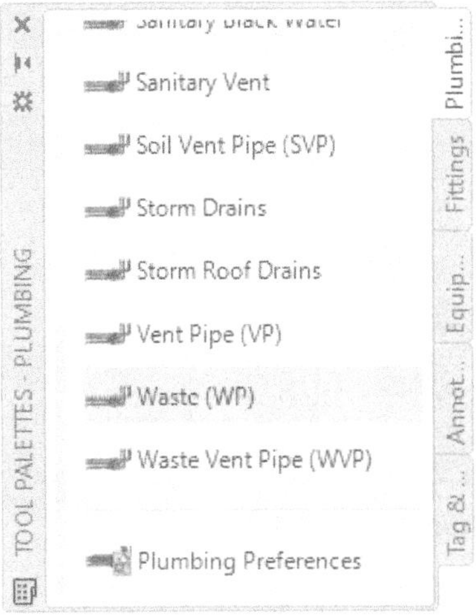

*Figure Prj2-125 The **TOOL PALETTES - PLUMBING***

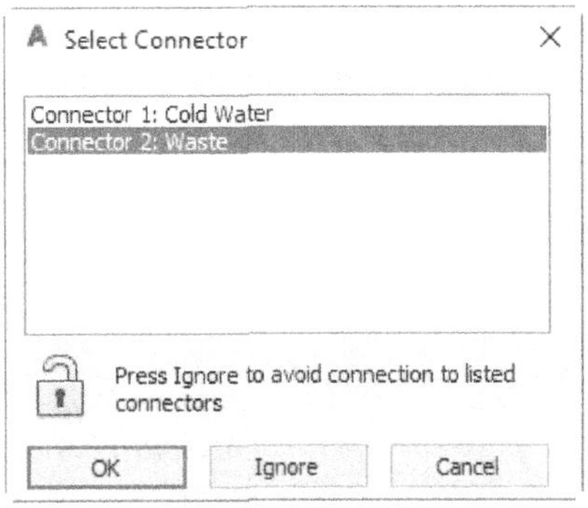

*Figure Prj2-126 The **Select Connector** dialog box*

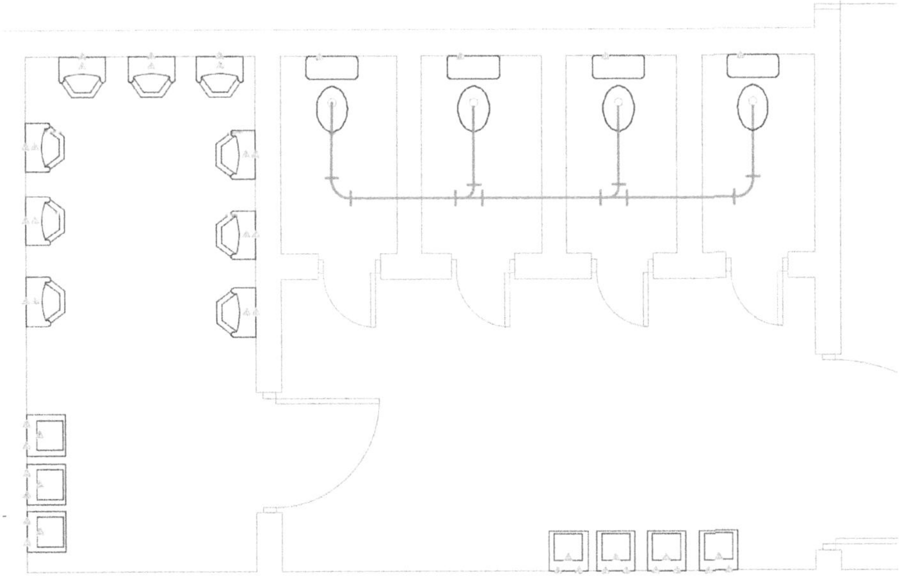

Figure Prj2-127 The drawing after connecting all the flush tank toilet with waste pipe line

Note that while connecting the equipments with piping line, the **Plumbing Line- Elevation Mismatch** dialog box is displayed, as shown in Figure Prj2-128. This dialog box is displayed because of the elevation difference between the equipments.

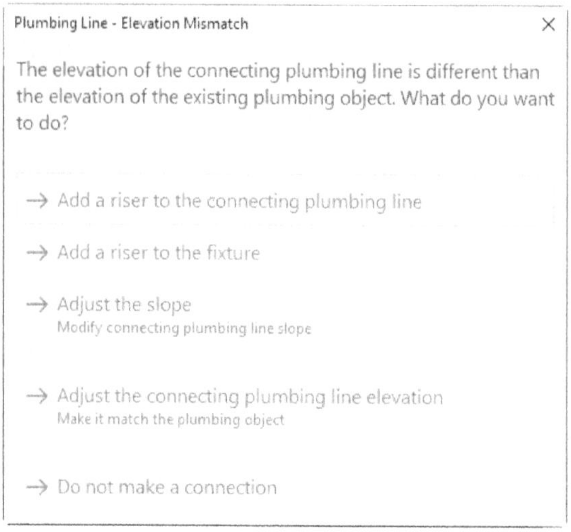

***Figure Prj2-128** The **Plumbing Line - Elevation Mismatch** dialog box*

5. So, choose the **Adjust the slope** option from it whenever it is displayed and press ENTER. The drawing after connecting the basin and urinal is shown in Figure Prj2-129.

6. Now, choose the **Waste (WP)** tool from the **TOOL PALETTES - PLUMBING** and connect the Waste Pipe End Connector of the rectangular basin and urinal.

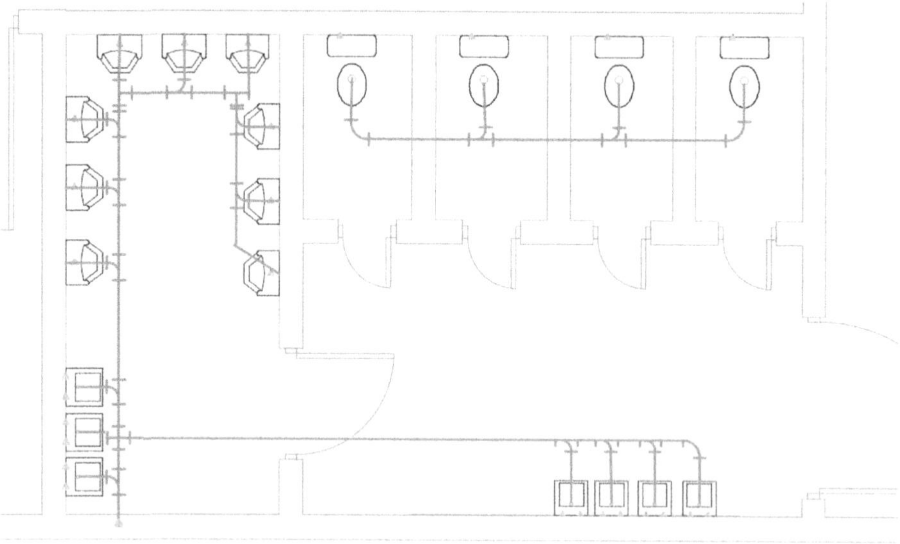

***Figure Prj2-129** The drawing after connecting basin and urinal with waste pipe line*

7. Next, connect the waste pipe line of flush tank toilet with urinal line as displayed in drawing, refer to Figure Prj2-130.

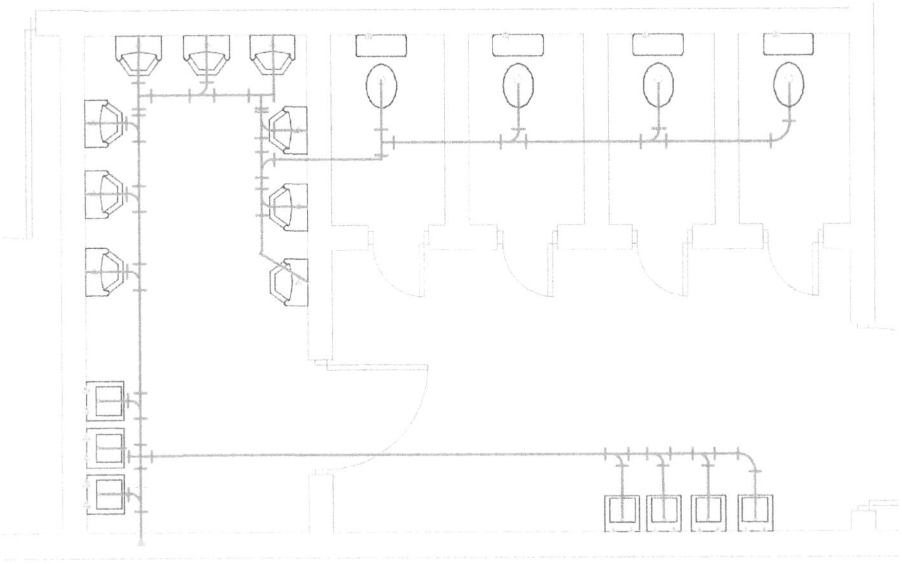

Figure Prj2-130 *The drawing after connecting waste pipe line with the equipments*

8. Choose the **Domestic Cold Water** tool from the **TOOL PALETTES - PLUMBING** and add the cold water plumbing line, as shown in Figure Prj2-131.

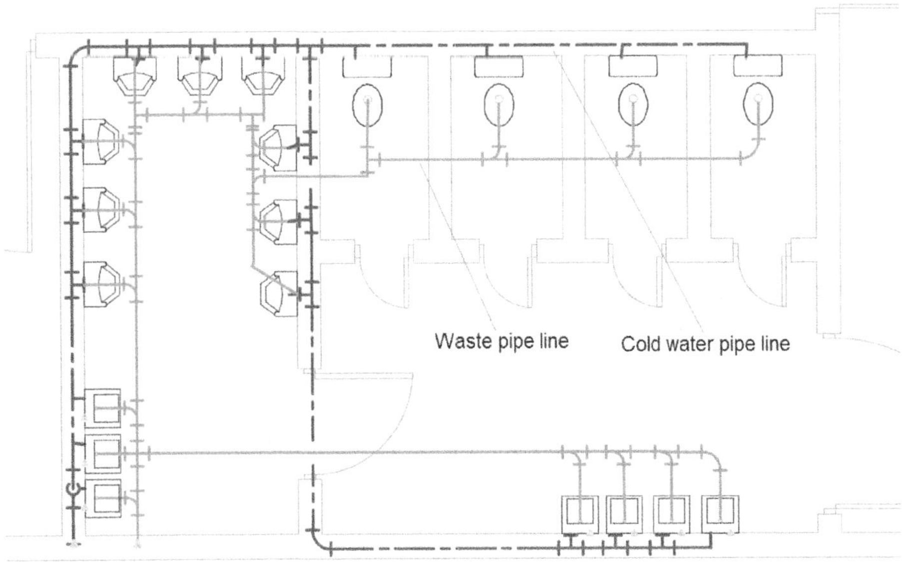

Figure Prj2-131 *The drawing after connecting waste pipe line and cold water pipe line with the equipments*

Note

Choose the ***Connector1: Cold Water*** *from the* ***Select Connector*** *dialog box when it is displayed while connecting the cold water plumbing line.*

9. Save the drawing and close it.

Creating Plumbing Drawing of the First Floor

1. Select the **Plumbing** category from the **PROJECT NAVIGATOR** and choose the **Add Construct** button available at the bottom; the **Add Construct** dialog box is displayed.

2. Enter **First Floor Plumbing** in the **Name** field of the dialog box.

3. Click in the **Description** field; the **Description** dialog box is displayed.

4. Enter the description **This drawing is meant for plumbing plan of the first floor** in the **Edit the description** edit box and then choose the **OK** button from the dialog box.

5. Select the check box corresponding to level 2 in the **Division** column in the **Add Construct** dialog box and make sure that the **Open in drawing editor** check box is selected in the **Add Construct** dialog box. Next, choose the **OK** button from the dialog box; the drawing is opened. Also, the First Floor plumbing drawing is displayed with a lock icon adjacent to it in the **PROJECT NAVIGATOR**.

6. Click on the **Workspace Switching** option in the **Application Status Bar** and select the **Plumbing** option from the flyout.

Importing the Architectural Drawing of the First Floor

Before adding any plumbing system in the project, you need to import the architectural plan of the first floor.

1. Open the **PROJECT NAVIGATOR** and then click on the plus sign adjacent to Architectural category in the **Constructs** tab; a list of architectural drawings is displayed.

2. Select the First Floor Architectural drawing from the list and drag it to the current drawing; the architectural drawing is attached to the current drawing as an external reference.

Adding Urinal to the Drawing

Now, you need to add Urinal to the drawing.

1. Choose the **Urinal** tool from the **Equipment** drop-down available in the **Build** panel of the **Home** tab in the **Ribbon**; the **Add Multi-view Parts** dialog box is displayed, as shown in Figure Prj2-132. Also, the urinal stall displayed gets attached to the cursor.

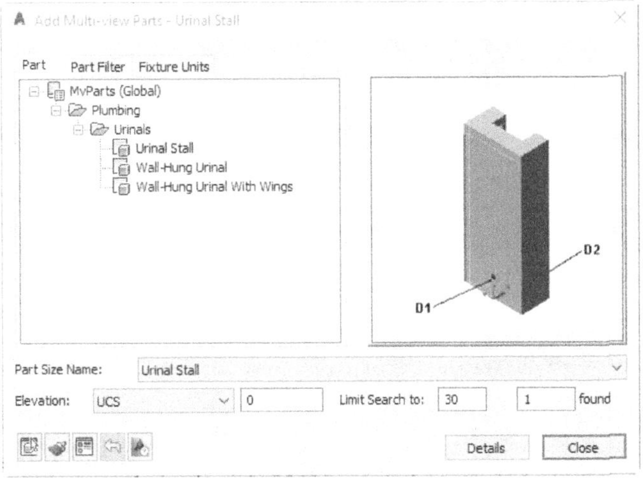

Figure Prj2-132 The ***Add Multi-view Parts*** *dialog box*

2. Choose the **Wall-Hung Urinal** from the dialog box; the wall-hang urinal is attached with the cursor. Specify **500** in the **Elevation** edit box and place the wall-hang urinal in toilet area, as shown in Figure Prj2-133.

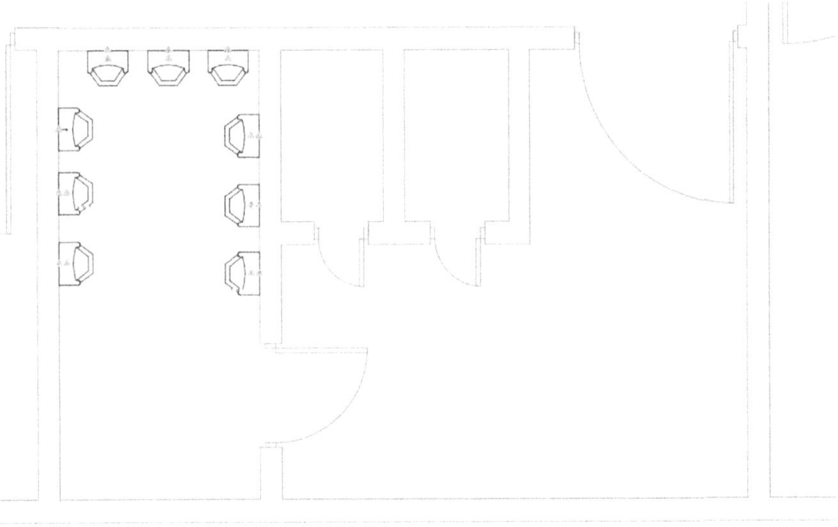

Figure Prj2-133 The drawing after placing the wall-hang urinal

Adding Rectangular Basin to the Drawing

Now, you need to add Sink to the drawing.

1. Choose the **Sink** tool from the **Equipment** drop-down available in the **Build** panel of the **Home** tab in the **Ribbon**; the **Add Multi-view Parts** dialog box is displayed, refer to Figure Prj2-134. Also, the sink displayed gets attached to the cursor.

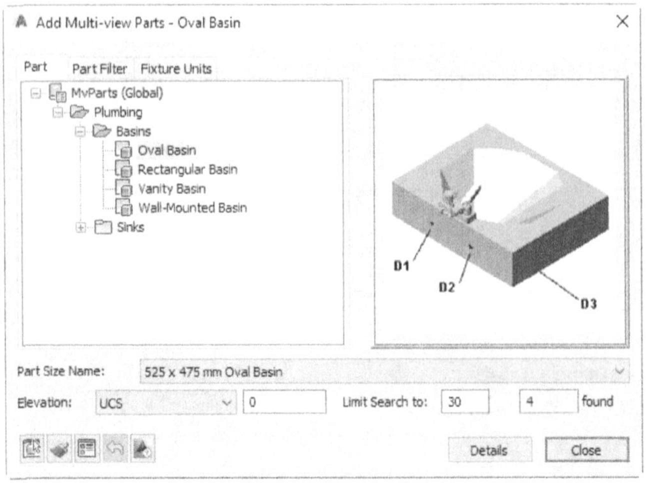

*Figure Prj2-134 The **Add Multi-view Parts** dialog box*

2. Choose the **Rectangular Basin** from the dialog box; the rectangular basin is attached with the cursor. Select the **375x375 mm Rectangular Basin** option from the **Part Size Name** drop-down list.

3. Specify the **800** in the **Elevation** edit box and place the rectangular basin in toilet area, as shown in Figure Prj2-135.

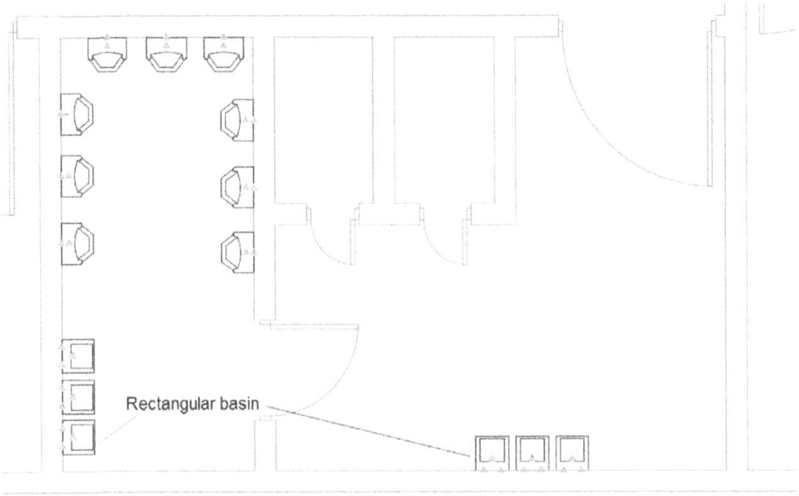

Figure Prj2-135 The drawing after placing the wall-hang urinal and rectangular basin

Adding Water Closet to the Drawing

Now, you need to add Water closet to the drawing.

1. Choose the **Water Closet** tool from the **Equipment** drop-down available in the **Build** panel of the **Home** tab in the **Ribbon**; the **Add Multi-view Parts** dialog box is displayed, as shown in Figure Prj2-136. Also, the bidet displayed gets attached to the cursor.

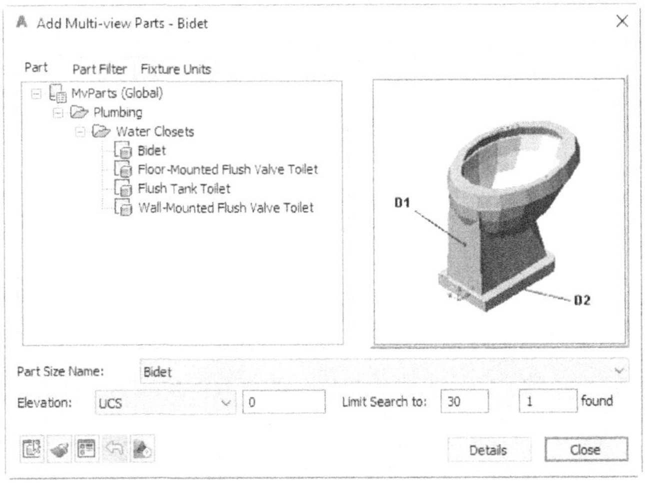

Figure Prj2-136 *The **Add Multi-view Parts** dialog box*

2. Choose the **Flush Tank Toilet** from the dialog box; the flush tank toilet is attached with the cursor.

3. Specify **0** in the **Elevation** edit box and place the flush tank toilet in toilet area, as shown in Figure Prj2-137.

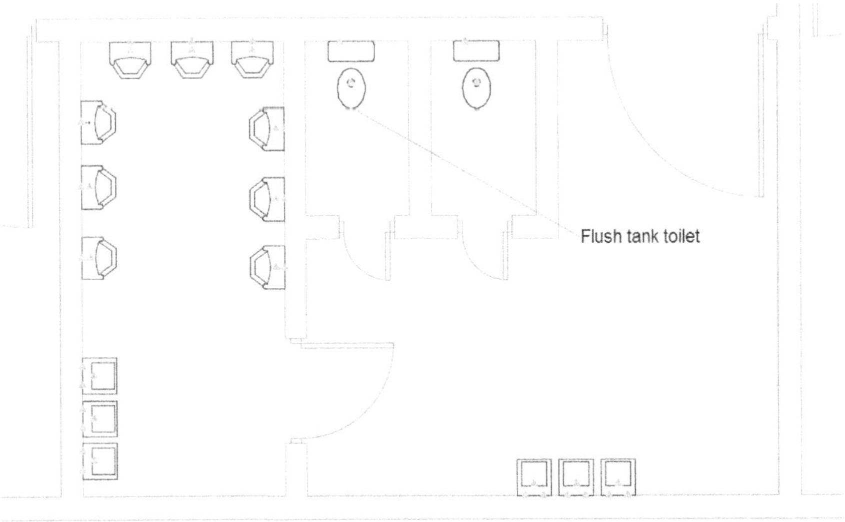

Figure Prj2-137 *The drawing after placing the wall-hang urinal, rectangular basin and flush tank toilet*

Creating Plumbing Line between Various Equipment

There are two plumbing lines to be added to the system: Waste (WP) and Domestic Cold Water.

1. Choose the **Waste (WP)** tool from the **TOOL PALETTES - PLUMBING** displayed at the right in the AutoCAD MEP window, refer to Figure Prj2-138; you are prompted to select the starting point for Waste plumbing line.

2. Select the Waste Pipe End Connector of the extreme right flush tank toilet; the other end of the waste plumbing line gets attached to the cursor and you are prompted to specify the next end point.

3. Select the Waste Pipe End Connector of adjacent flush tank toilet; the **Select Connector** dialog box will be displayed, as shown in Figure Prj2-139.

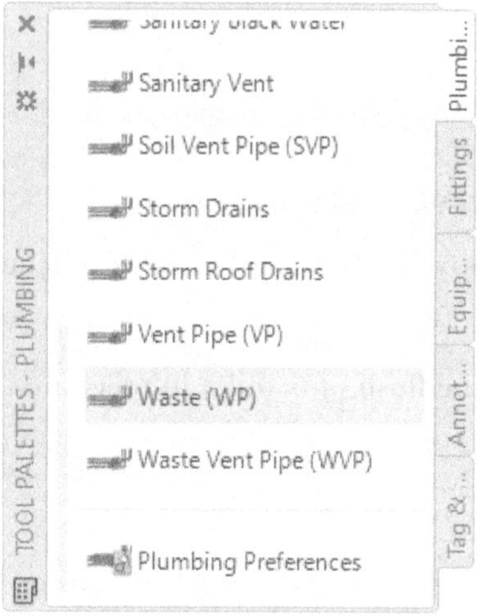

Figure Prj2-138 The ***TOOL PALETTES - PLUMBING***

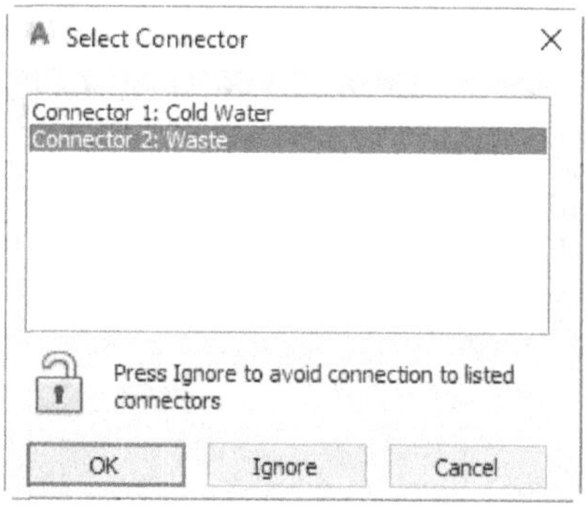

Figure Prj2-139 The ***Select Connector*** *dialog box*

4. Select the **Connector 2: Waste** option from the dialog box and flush tank toilets get connected with each other. Similarly, connect all the flush tank toilets as displayed in drawing, refer to Figure Prj2-140.

   Note that while connecting the equipments with piping line, the **Plumbing Line- Elevation Mismatch** dialog box is displayed, as shown in Figure Prj2-141. This dialog box is displayed because of the elevation difference between the equipments.

5. So, choose the **Adjust the slope** option from it whenever it is displayed and press ENTER. The drawing after connecting the basin and urinal is shown in Figure Prj2-142.

6. Now, choose the **Waste (WP)** tool from the **TOOL PALETTES - PLUMBING** and connect Waste Pipe End Connector of the rectangular basin and urinal.

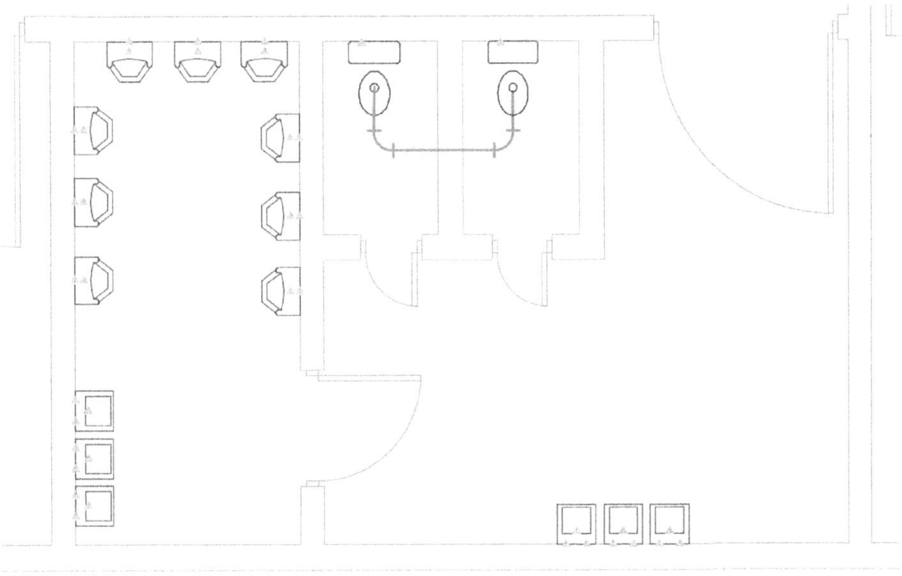

Figure Prj2-140 The drawing after connecting the flush tank toilets with waste pipe line

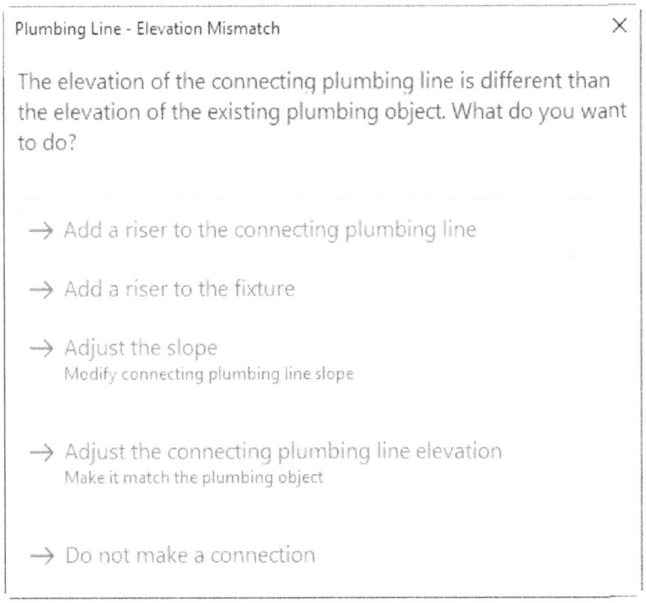

Figure Prj2-141 The ***Plumbing Line - Elevation Mismatch*** *dialog box*

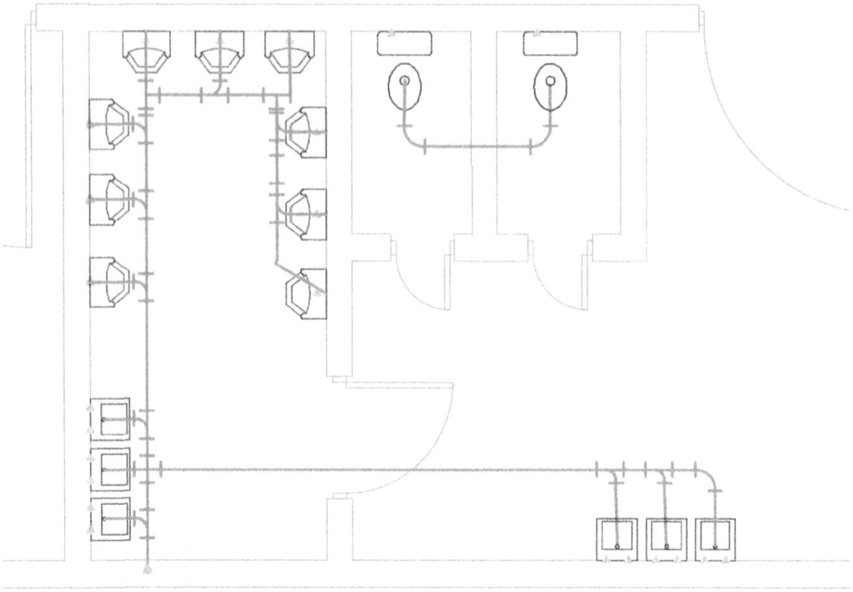

Figure Prj2-142 The drawing after connecting basin and urinal with waste pipe line

7. Next, connect the waste pipe line of flush tank toilet with urinal line, as shown in Figure Prj2-143.

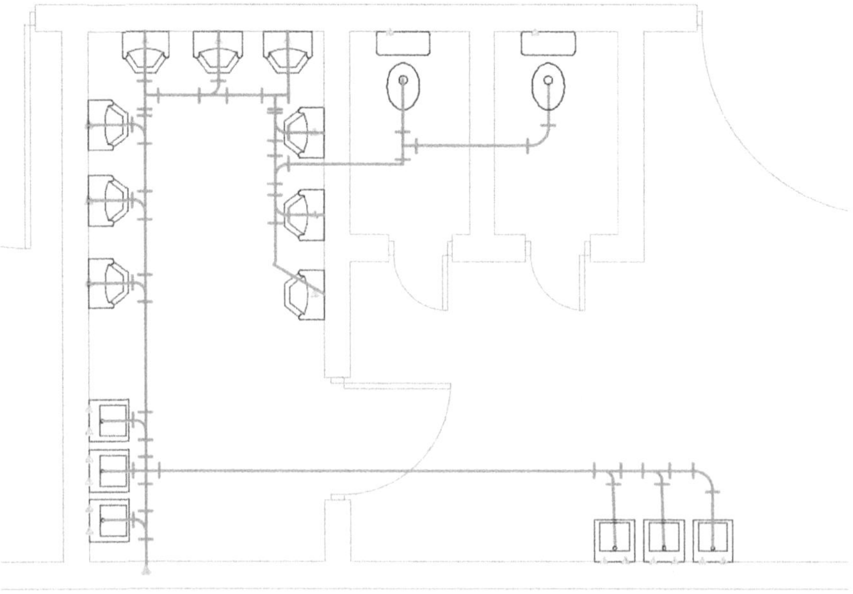

Figure Prj2-143 The drawing after connecting waste pipe line with the eqipments

8. Choose the **Domestic Cold Water** tool from the **TOOL PALETTES - PLUMBING** and add the cold water plumbing line, as shown in Figure Prj2-144.

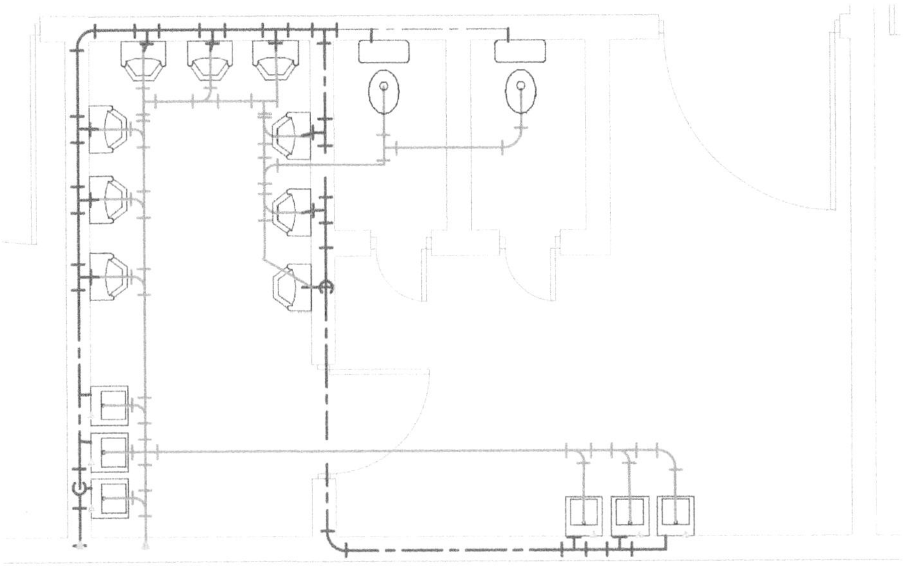

Figure Prj2-144 *The drawing after connecting waste pipe line and cold water pipe line with the equipments*

9. Save the drawing and close it.

This page is intentionally left blank

Index

Symbols

This page is intentionally left blank

Other Publications by CADCIM Technologies

The following is the list of some of the publications by CADCIM Technologies. Please visit *www.cadcim.com* for the complete listing.

AutoCAD Textbooks

- AutoCAD 2022: A Problem-Solving Approach, Basic and Intermediate, 28th Edition
- AutoCAD 2021: A Problem-Solving Approach, Basic and Intermediate, 27th Edition
- AutoCAD 2020: A Problem-Solving Approach, Basic and Intermediate, 26th Edition
- AutoCAD 2019: A Problem-Solving Approach, Basic and Intermediate, 25th Edition
- AutoCAD 2018: A Problem-Solving Approach, Basic and Intermediate, 24th Edition
- Advanced AutoCAD 2021: A Problem-Solving Approach (3D and Advanced), 25th Edition
- Advanced AutoCAD 2018: A Problem-Solving Approach, 3D and Advanced, 24th Edition

Autodesk Inventor Textbooks

- Autodesk Inventor Professional 2022 for Designers, 22nd Edition
- Autodesk Inventor Professional 2021 for Designers, 21st Edition
- Autodesk Inventor Professional 2020 for Designers, 20th Edition
- Autodesk Inventor Professional 2019 for Designers, 19th Edition

AutoCAD MEP Textbooks

- AutoCAD MEP 2020 for Designers, 5th Edition
- AutoCAD MEP 2018 for Designers, 4th Edition
- AutoCAD MEP 2016 for Designers, 3rd Edition

AutoCAD Plant 3D Textbooks

- AutoCAD Plant 3D 2021 for Designers, 6th Edition
- AutoCAD Plant 3D 2020 for Designers, 5th Edition

Autodesk Fusion 360 Textbook

- Autodesk Fusion 360: A Tutorial Approach, 2nd Edition

Solid Edge Textbooks

- Solid Edge 2021 for Designers, 18th Edition
- Solid Edge 2020 for Designers, 17th Edition
- Solid Edge 2019 for Designers, 16th Edition

NX Textbooks

- Siemens NX 2021 for Designers, 14th Edition
- Siemens NX 2020 for Designers, 13th Edition
- Siemens NX 2019 for Designers, 12th Edition

NX Mold Textbook

- Mold Design Using NX 11.0: A Tutorial Approach

NX Nastran Textbook
- NX Nastran 9.0 for Designers

SOLIDWORKS Textbooks
- SOLIDWORKS 2021 for Designers, 19th Edition
- SOLIDWORKS 2020 for Designers, 18th Edition
- SOLIDWORKS 2019 for Designers, 17th Edition
- Learning SOLIDWORKS 2019: A Project Based Approach

SOLIDWORKS Simulation Textbooks
- SOLIDWORKS Simulation 2018: A Tutorial Approach
- SOLIDWORKS Simulation 2016: A Tutorial Approach

CATIA Textbooks
- CATIA V5-6R2020 for Designers, 18th Edition
- CATIA V5-6R2019 for Designers, 17th Edition
- CATIA V5-6R2018 for Designers, 16th Edition

Creo Parametric Textbooks
- Creo Parametric 7.0 for Designers, 7th Edition
- Creo Parametric 6.0 for Designers, 6th Edition

ANSYS Textbooks
- ANSYS Workbench 2019 R2: A Tutorial Approach
- ANSYS Workbench 14.0: A Tutorial Approach

Creo Direct Textbook
- Creo Direct 2.0 and Beyond for Designers

Autodesk Alias Textbooks
- Learning Autodesk Alias Design 2016, 5th Edition
- Learning Autodesk Alias Design 2015, 4th Edition

AutoCAD LT Textbooks
- AutoCAD LT 2022 for Designers, 14th Edition
- AutoCAD LT 2020 for Designers, 13th Edition

EdgeCAM Textbooks
- EdgeCAM 11.0 for Manufacturers
- EdgeCAM 10.0 for Manufacturers

Autodesk Revit MEP Textbooks
- Exploring Autodesk Revit 2021 for MEP, 7th Edition
- Exploring Autodesk Revit 2019 for MEP, 6th Edition
- Exploring Autodesk Revit 2018 for MEP, 5th Edition

AutoCAD Civil 3D Textbooks
- Exploring AutoCAD Civil 3D 2020, 10th Edition
- Exploring AutoCAD Civil 3D 2019, 9th Edition
- Exploring AutoCAD Civil 3D 2018, 8th Edition

AutoCAD Map 3D Textbooks
- Exploring AutoCAD Map 3D 2018, 8th Edition
- Exploring AutoCAD Map 3D 2017, 7th Edition

RISA-3D Textbook
- Exploring RISA-3D 14.0

Autodesk Navisworks Textbooks
- Exploring Autodesk Navisworks 2021, 8th Edition
- Exploring Autodesk Navisworks 2020, 7th Edition
- Exploring Autodesk Navisworks 2019, 5th Edition

AutoCAD Raster Design Textbooks
- Exploring AutoCAD Raster Design 2017
- Exploring AutoCAD Raster Design 2016

Bentley STAAD.Pro Textbooks
- Exploring Bentley STAAD.Pro CONNECT Edition, 4th Edition
- Exploring Bentley STAAD.Pro (CONNECT) Edition
- Exploring Bentley STAAD.Pro V8i (SELECTseries 6)

Autodesk 3ds Max Design Textbooks
- Autodesk 3ds Max Design 2015: A Tutorial Approach, 15th Edition
- Autodesk 3ds Max Design 2014: A Tutorial Approach

Autodesk 3ds Max Textbooks
- Autodesk 3ds Max 2021: A Comprehensive Guide, 21st Edition
- Autodesk 3ds Max 2020: A Comprehensive Guide, 20th Edition
- Autodesk 3ds Max 2019: A Comprehensive Guide, 19th Edition

Autodesk Maya Textbooks
- Autodesk Maya 2020: A Comprehensive Guide, 12th Edition
- Autodesk Maya 2019: A Comprehensive Guide, 11th Edition

Pixologic ZBrush Textbooks
- Pixologic ZBrush 2021: A Comprehensive Guide, 7th Edition
- Pixologic ZBrush 2020: A Comprehensive Guide, 6th Edition
- Pixologic ZBrush 2018: A Comprehensive Guide, 5th Edition

Fusion Textbooks
- Blackmagic Design Fusion 7 Studio: A Tutorial Approach, 3rd Edition
- The eyeon Fusion 6.3: A Tutorial Approach

Flash Textbooks
- Adobe Flash Professional CC 2015: A Tutorial Approach, 3rd Edition
- Adobe Flash Professional CC: A Tutorial Approach

Computer Programming Textbooks
- Introducing PHP 7/MySQL
- Introduction to C++ programming, 2nd Edition
- Learning Oracle 12c - A PL/SQL Approach
- Learning ASP.NET AJAX
- Introduction to Java Programming, 2nd Edition
- Learning Visual Basic.NET 2008

MAXON CINEMA 4D Textbooks
- MAXON CINEMA 4D R20 Studio: A Tutorial Approach, 7th Edition
- MAXON CINEMA 4D R19 Studio: A Tutorial Approach, 6th Edition
- MAXON CINEMA 4D R18 Studio: A Tutorial Approach, 5th Edition

Oracle Primavera Textbooks
- Exploring Oracle Primavera P6 Professional 18, 3rd Edition
- Exploring Oracle Primavera P6 v8.4

AutoCAD Textbooks Authored by Prof. Sham Tickoo and Published by Autodesk Press
- AutoCAD: A Problem-Solving Approach: 2013 and Beyond
- AutoCAD 2012: A Problem-Solving Approach
- AutoCAD 2011: A Problem-Solving Approach
- AutoCAD 2010: A Problem-Solving Approach
- Customizing AutoCAD 2010

Coming Soon from CADCIM Technologies
- Flow Simulation Using SOLIDWORKS 2021

Online Training Program Offered by CADCIM Technologies
CADCIM Technologies provides effective and affordable virtual online training on animation, architecture, and GIS softwares, computer programming languages, and Computer Aided Design, Manufacturing, and Engineering (CAD/CAM/CAE) software packages. The training will be delivered 'live' via Internet at any time, any place, and at any pace to individuals, students of colleges, universities, and CAD/CAM/CAE training centers. For more information, please visit the following link: ***https://www.cadcim.com.***

Made in United States
North Haven, CT
10 November 2026

22106113R00304